GW00808325

WORLD
TRAVEL
ATLAS

IN ASSOCIATION WITH
THE ROYAL GEOGRAPHICAL SOCIETY
WITH THE INSTITUTE OF BRITISH GEOGRAPHERS

COVER PHOTOGRAPHS COURTESY OF:
Still Pictures /François Pierrel (top left); ImageState (bottom left); © Corbis /Stephen Frink (top right), /Steve Prezant (bottom right).

Published in Great Britain in 2006 by Philip's,
a division of Octopus Publishing Group Limited,
2–4 Heron Quays, London E14 4JP

Copyright © 2006 Philip's

Cartography by Philip's

CITY PLANS
Page 14, Dublin: The town plan of Dublin is based on
Ordnance Survey Ireland by permission of the Government
Permit Number 8097. © Ordnance Survey Ireland and
Government of Ireland.

 Ordnance Survey® Page 16, London: This product
includes mapping data licensed
from Ordnance Survey® with the permission of
the Controller of Her Majesty's Stationery Office.
© Crown copyright 2006. All rights reserved.
Licence number 100011710.

Vector data: Courtesy of Gräfe and Unser Verlag GmbH,
München, Germany (city-centre maps of Bangkok,
Cape Town, Mexico City, Singapore, Sydney and Tokyo).

ISBN-13 978–0–540–08893–5
ISBN-10 0–540–08893–5

A CIP catalogue record for this book is available from the
British Library.

Printed in Hong Kong

Details of other Philip's titles and services can be found
on our website at: www.philips-maps.co.uk

Philip's World Atlases are published in association
with The Royal Geographical Society (with The
Institute of British Geographers).
The Society was founded in 1830 and given a
Royal Charter in 1859 for 'the advancement of
geographical science'. Today it is a leading world
centre for geographical learning – supporting
education, teaching, research and expeditions, and
promoting public understanding of the subject.
Further information about the Society and how
to join may be found on its website at: www.rgs.org

CONTENTS

WORLD STATISTICS

4   World Time Zones and
       Distance Table
5   World Climate and
       Flight Paths

CITY PLANS

6   City plans – legend
7   Amsterdam
8   Athens
9   Bangkok
10   Berlin
11   Brussels
12   Cape Town
13   Chicago
14   Dublin
15   Hong Kong
16   London
17   Madrid
18   Mexico City
19   Moscow
20   New York
21   Paris
22   Prague
23   Rio de Janeiro
24   Rome
25   San Francisco
26   Singapore
27   Sydney
28   Tokyo
29   Toronto
30   Vienna

GAZETTEER OF NATIONS

31   Gazetteer of Nations –
          contents
32–56   Country-by-country profiles

NOTE:
For reasons of safety or politics, there may be times
when it is not advisable, or desirable, to visit one
or more of the countries described in the Gazetteer
of Nations section. If in doubt, please check with the
Foreign Office (www.fco.gov.uk).

WORLD MAPS
I   World Maps – general reference
2–3   The Land Hemisphere 1:100M
4–5   The Water Hemisphere 1:100M

EUROPE
6–7   Europe 1:20M
8–9   Scandinavia and the Baltic Lands 1:10M
10–11   British Isles 1:5M
12–13   France 1:5M
14–15   Germany and Benelux 1:5M
16–17   Central Europe 1:5M
18–19   Spain and Portugal 1:5M
20–21   Italy and the Adriatic 1:5M
22–23   Greece and the Balkans 1:5M
24–25   Eastern Europe 1:10M

ASIA
26–27   Asia 1:50M
28–29   Western Russia and Central Asia 1:20M
30–31   Eastern Siberia 1:20M
32–33   Japan 1:6.4M
34–35   China 1:20M
36–37   Philippines and Eastern Indonesia 1:12.5M
38–39   South-east Asia 1:12.5M
40–41   Eastern India, Bangladesh and Burma 1:10M
42–43   Western India, Pakistan and Sri Lanka 1:10M
44–45   Persian Gulf, Iran and Afghanistan 1:10M
46–47   The Middle East and Turkey 1:10M
48–49   Arabia and the Horn of Africa 1:15M

AFRICA
50–51   Africa 1:42M
52–53   North-west Africa 1:15M
54–55   North-east Africa 1:15M
56–57   Central Africa 1:15M
58–59   Southern Africa 1:15M

AUSTRALASIA
60–61   Australia 1:20M
62–63   South-east Australia 1:8M
64–65   New Zealand 1:6M
        Central and South-west Pacific 1:55M

NORTH AMERICA
66–67   North America 1:35M
68–69   Western Canada 1:15M
        Alaska 1:30M
70–71   Eastern Canada 1:15M
72–73   North-west USA 1:6M
74–75   North-central USA 1:6M
76–77   North-east USA 1:6M
78–79   South-west USA 1:6M
80–81   Southern USA 1:6M
82–83   South-east USA 1:6M
84–85   Mexico 1:15M
86–87   Caribbean and Central America 1:15M

SOUTH AMERICA
88–89   South America 1:35M
90–91   South America – North-west 1:16M
92–93   South America – North-east 1:16M
94–95   South America – South 1:16M

POLAR REGIONS
96   Antarctica 1:35M

INDEX
97–160   Index to World Maps

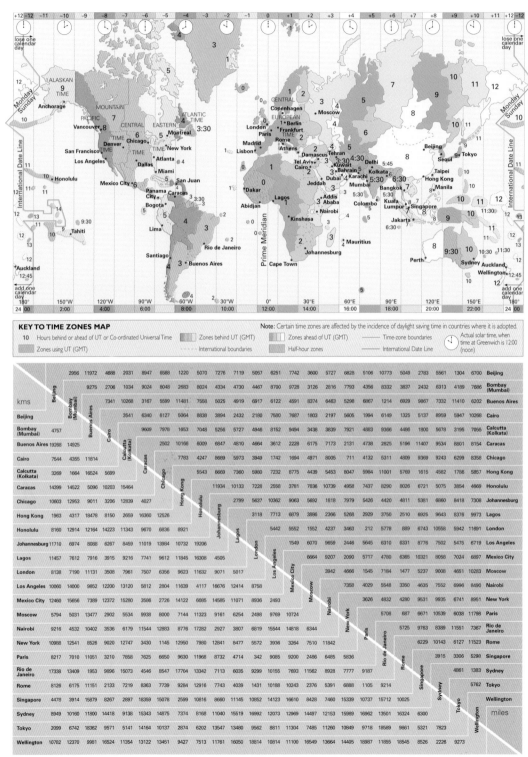

The table above shows air distances in miles and kilometres between 30 major cities. Known as 'great circle' distances, these measure the shortest routes between the cities.

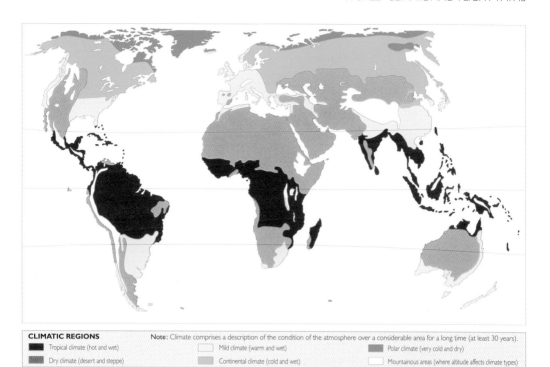

CLIMATIC REGIONS

Note: Climate comprises a description of the condition of the atmosphere over a considerable area for a long time (at least 30 years).

- Tropical climate (hot and wet)
- Dry climate (desert and steppe)
- Mild climate (warm and wet)
- Continental climate (cold and wet)
- Polar climate (very cold and dry)
- Mountainous areas (where altitude affects climate types)

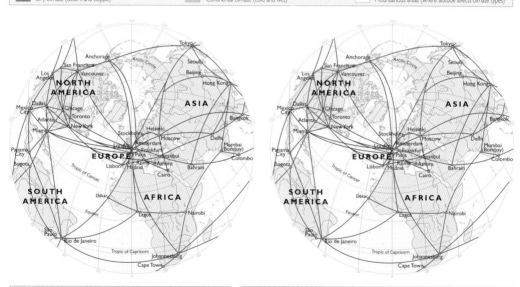

WORLD'S BUSIEST AIRPORTS TOTAL NUMBER OF PASSENGERS IN MILLIONS (2004)	
ATLANTA HARTSFIELD INTL. (ATL)	83.6
CHICAGO O'HARE INTL. (ORD)	75.4
LONDON HEATHROW (LHR)	67.3
TOKYO HANEDA (HND)	62.3
LOS ANGELES INTL. (LAX)	60.7
DALLAS/FORT WORTH INTL. (DFW)	59.4
FRANKFURT INTL. (FRA)	51.1
PARIS CHARLES DE GAULLE (CDG)	50.9
AMSTERDAM SCHIPHOL (AMS)	42.5

FLIGHT TIMES FROM LONDON		FLIGHT TIMES FROM NEW YORK	
ATHENS	4hrs 05mins	FRANKFURT	8hrs 35mins
AUCKLAND	24hrs 20mins	JOHANNESBURG	17hrs 45mins
BANGKOK	14hrs 30mins	MEXICO CITY	5hrs 45mins
BUENOS AIRES.	14hrs 20mins	PARIS	8hrs 15mins
HONG KONG.	14hrs 10mins	ROME	9hrs 35mins
LOS ANGELES	12hrs 00mins	SANTIAGO	12hrs 55mins
MOSCOW	3hrs 50mins	SINGAPORE.	23hrs 10mins
MUMBAI (BOMBAY)	11hrs 15mins	TOKYO	14hrs 35mins
NEW YORK	6hrs 50mins	VANCOUVER	7hrs 25mins

CITY PLANS

7 Amsterdam

8 Athens

9 Bangkok

10 Berlin

11 Brussels

12 Cape Town

13 Chicago

14 Dublin

15 Hong Kong

16 London

17 Madrid

18 Mexico City

19 Moscow

20 New York

21 Paris

22 Prague

23 Rio de Janeiro

24 Rome

25 San Francisco

26 Singapore

27 Sydney

28 Tokyo

29 Toronto

30 Vienna

LEGEND TO CITY PLANS

Motorway		✝	Abbey/cathedral
Through route		†	Church of interest
Secondary road		⊞	Hospital
Other road		☽	Mosque
Limited access / pedestrian road		▲	Shrine
Railway		✡	Synagogue
Tramway/monorail		卍	Temple
Rail/bus station		*i*	Tourist information centre
Underground/Metro station	⊖ ⊜ Ⓤ Ⓜ Ⓢ		Public building
Ferry route/destination	MANLY	Museum	Place of interest

0   km   2

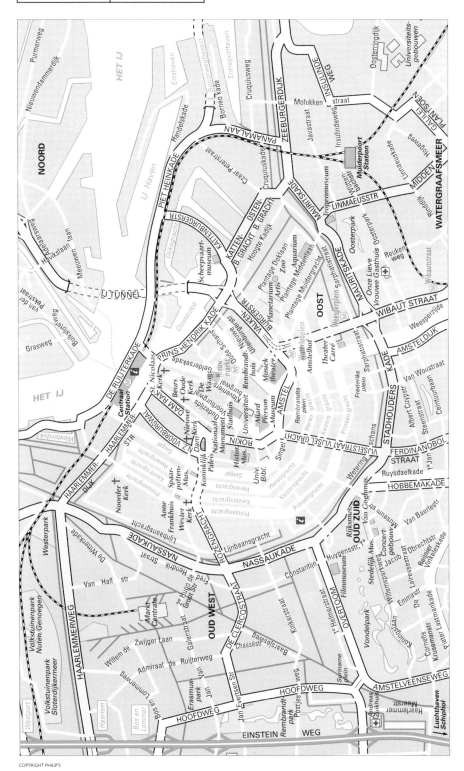

0   km   1

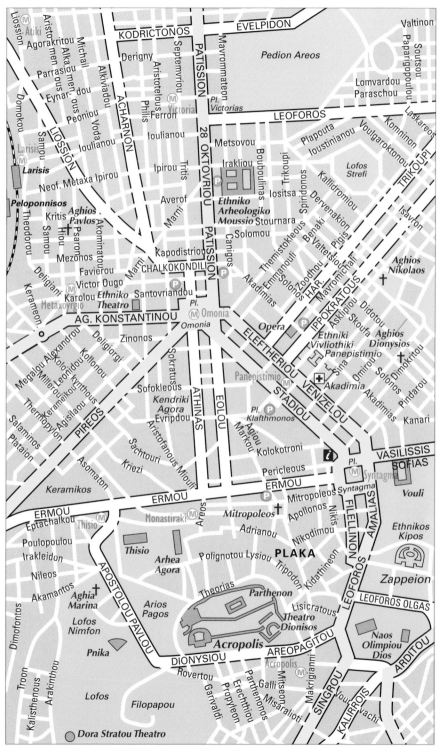

0   km   2

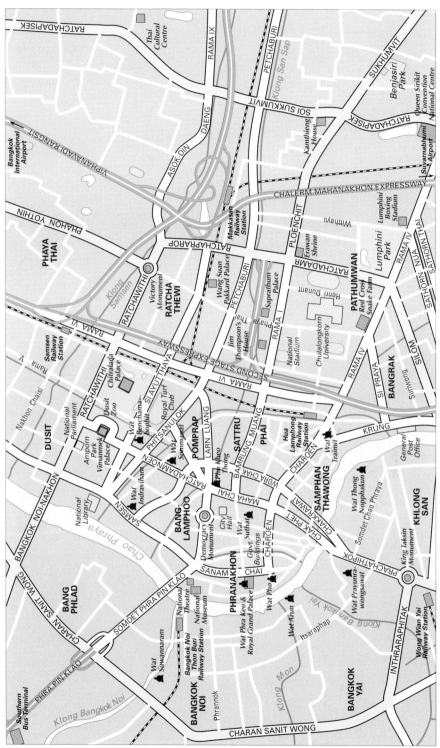

0   km   1

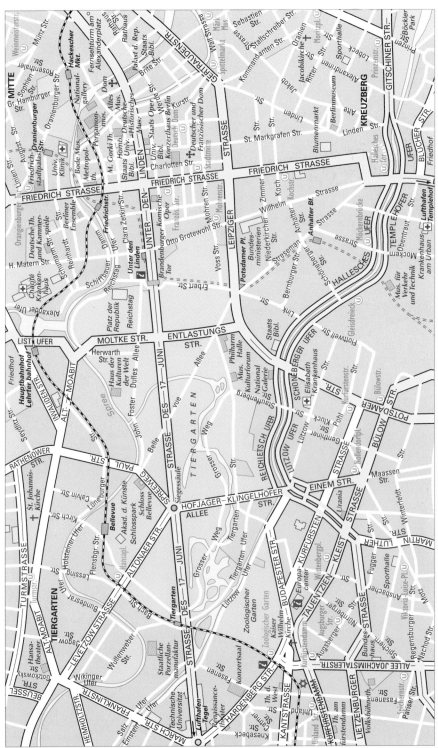

0   km   1

CITY PLANS **BRUSSELS**

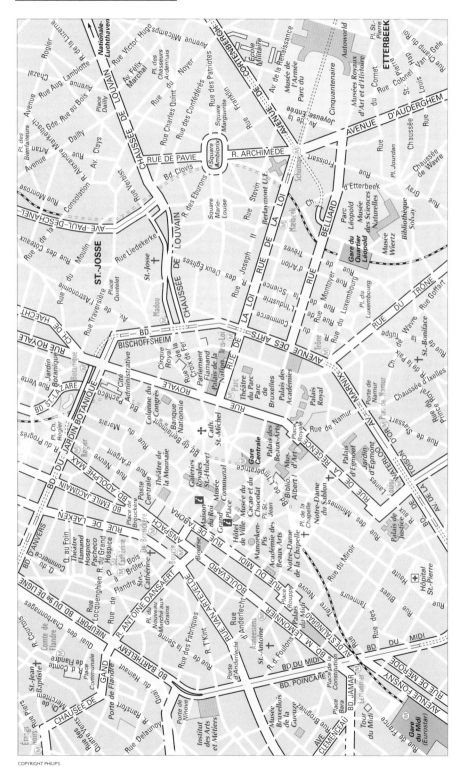

0   km   1

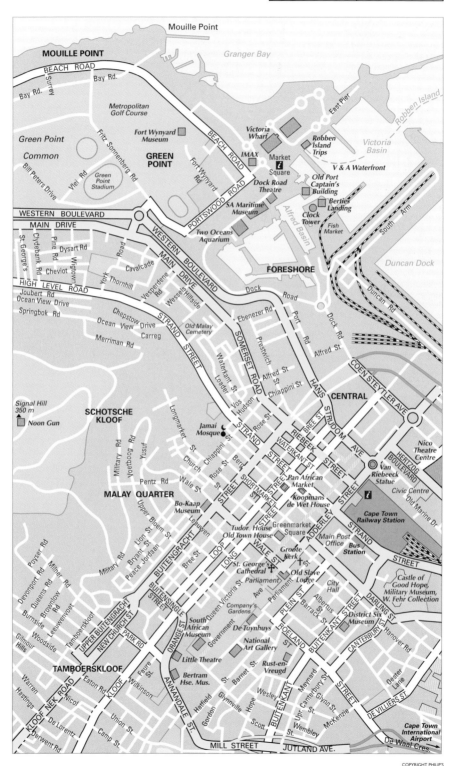

Mouille Point

Granger Bay

MOUILLE POINT

BEACH ROAD

Bay Rd.

Surrey Bay Rd.

Bay Rd.

Metropolitan Golf Course

Fort Wynyard Museum

Green Point

Common

Fritz Sonnenberg Rd

BEACH ROAD

GREEN POINT

Green Point Stadium

Vlei Rd

Fort Wynyard Rd

PORTSWOOD ROAD

Victoria Wharf

IMAX

Market Square

Robben Island Trips

V & A Waterfront

Victoria Basin

Robben Island

East Pier

Dock Road Theatre

Old Port Captain's Building

SA Maritime Museum

Berties Landing

WESTERN BOULEVARD

MAIN DRIVE

Bill Peters Drive

WESTERN BOULEVARD

Clock Tower

Fish Market

Alfred Basin

South Arm

Two Oceans Aquarium

St George's

Clydebank Rd

Pine Rd

Dysart Rd

Cheviot

Cavalcade

Road

MAIN DRIVE

FORESHORE

Duncan Dock

Duncan Rd

Wigtown

York

Thornhill

HIGH LEVEL ROAD

Joubert Rd

Ocean View Drive

Springbok Rd

Vesperdene Rd

Wessels Hillside

STRAND STREET

Dock

Road

Ebenezer Rd

Port Rd

Dock Rd

COEN STEYTLER AVE

Chepstow Drive

Ocean View Drive

Carreg

Merriman Rd

Old Malay Cemetery

Prestwich

SOMERSET ROAD

Alfred St

Alfred St

Chiappini St

HANS STRIJDOM AVE

Alfred St

CENTRAL

Signal Hill 350 m

Noon Gun

SCHOTSCHE KLOOF

Longmarket

St

Military Rd

Voetboog Rd

Yusuf

Waterkant St

Loader

Vos

Hudson

Rose St

STRAND

BREE STREET

WATERKANT ST

BUITENGRACHT

Berg

Rose St

Chiappini

Church

Wale St

Jamai Mosque

Pentz Rd

MALAY QUARTER

Bo-Kaap Museum

Upper Bloem St

Lion St

Leeuwen

SHORTMARKET STREET

LONG

STREET

LOOP STREET

Pan African Market

Koopmans de Wet House

BREE STREET

STRIJDOM

STREET

Van Riebeeck Statue

Nico Theatre Centre

HERTZOG BOULEVARD

Oswald Pirow

Civic Centre

Cape Town Railway Station

Poyser Rd

Milner Rd

Bryant St

Peace Jordaan

Military Rd

Bree St

Tudor House

Old Town House

Greenmarket Square

WALE ST

STRAND STREET

ADDERLEY STREET

Devonport Rd

Queens Rd

Brownlow Rd

Burnside

Leeuwenvoet

Tamboerskloof

UPPER BUITENGRACHT

PARK RD

NEW CHURCH ST

BUITENSINGLE STREET

BUITENGRACHT

ORANGE ST

Bree St

LONG STREET

St. George's Cathedral

Parliament Ave

Groote Kerk

Old Slave Lodge

Main Post Office

Bus Station

City Hall

STRAND STREET

Castle of Good Hope, Military Museum, W. Fehr Collection

Gilmour Hills

Warren

Hastings

KLOOF NEK ROAD

Nicol

Eaton Rd

Wilkinson

Woodside

ANNANDALE ST

KLOOF

Faure St

Queen Victoria St

Company's Gardens

South African Museum

Government

De Tuynhuys

Parliament

PLEIN ST

BUITENKANT STREET

Albertus St

Barrack St

ROELAND ST

District Six Museum

CANTERBURY STREET

Hanover Rd

Oester Lane

De Lorentz

Camp St

Derwent Rd

Union St

Little Theatre

Bertram Hse. Mus.

Barnet

Rust-en-Vreugd

National Art Gallery

St.

St.

Hatfield

Gordon

Glynnville

Wesley

Hope

Maynard St

Upr. Canterbury St

Glynn St

McKenzie

Wembley

Scott

BUITENKANT

DE VILLIERS ST

TAMBOERSKLOOF

MILL STREET

JUTLAND AVE.

Cape Town International Airport

Da Waal Cres.

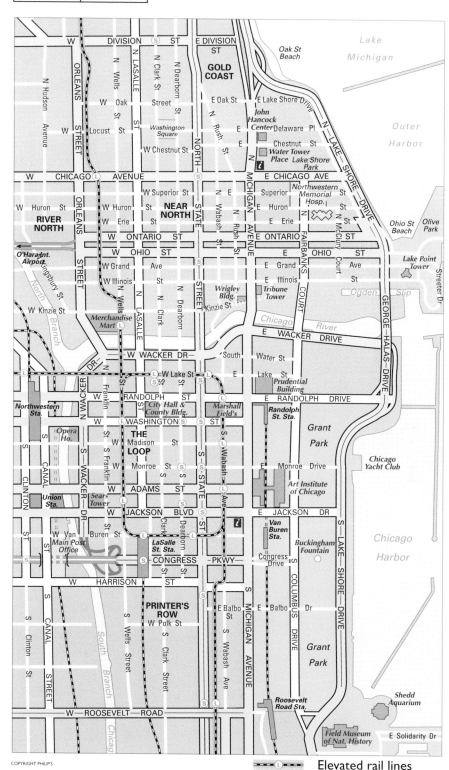

0 km 0.5

Elevated rail lines

0   km   0.5

—— Light Rail (LUAS)

COPYRIGHT PHILIP'S

0   km   1

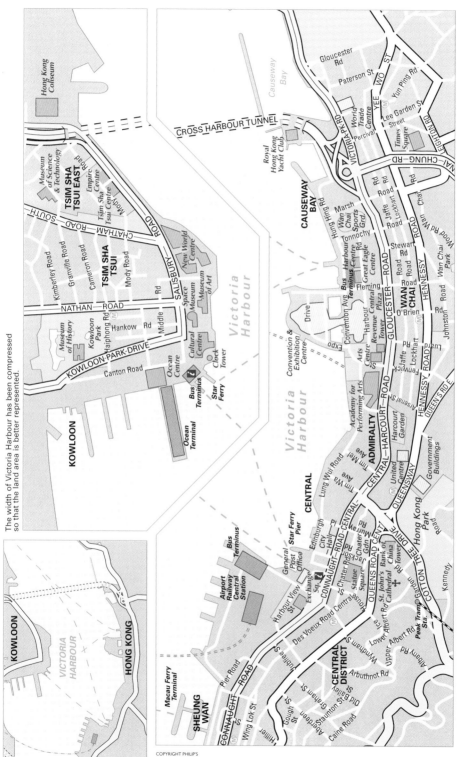

The width of Victoria Harbour has been compressed so that the land area is better represented.

Hong Kong Coliseum

Museum of Science & Technology

TSIM SHA TSUI EAST

Empire Centre

Tsim Sha Tsui Centre

Mody Road

New World Centre

Kimberley Road

Granville Road

Cameron Road

CHATHAM ROAD SOUTH

TSIM SHA TSUI

SALISBURY ROAD

Mody Road

Space Museum

Museum of Art

NATHAN ROAD

Museum of History

Haiphong Rd

Kowloon Park

Hankow Rd

Middle Rd

Rd

Cultural Centre

KOWLOON-PARK-DRIVE

Canton Road

Ocean Centre

Clock Tower

Bus Terminus

Star Ferry

KOWLOON

Ocean Terminal

CROSS HARBOUR TUNNEL

Gloucester Rd

Paterson St

Causeway Bay

YEE WO ST

Yun Ping Rd

World Trade Centre

Lee Garden St

Street

Percival

Times Square

VICTORIA PK RD

CHUNG RD

NAI EIGHTON RD

Royal Hong Kong Yacht Club

CAUSEWAY BAY

Hung Hing Rd

Marsh Rd

Wan Chai Sports Grd

Rd

Tonnochy Rd

Jaffe Road

Lockhart Rd

Stewart Rd

Road

Rd

Wan Chai Park

Wood Rd

Victoria Harbour

Great Eagle Centre

Fleming

Bus Terminus

Harbour Centre

WAN CHAI

Road

Johnston Rd

HENNESSY

Road

Convention Ave

Harbour Centre

Central Plaza

Revenue Tower

GLOUCESTER ROAD

O'Brien Rd

Jaffe Rd

Lockhart Rd

Luard Rd

HENNESSY ROAD

QUEEN'S RD E.

Drive

Arts Centre

Convention & Exhibition Centre

Fenwick St

Victoria Harbour

Academy for Performing Arts

Harcourt Garden

ADMIRALTY

CENTRAL-HARCOURT-ROAD

Tim Wa Ave

United Centre

Harcourt

QUEENSWAY

Government Buildings

CENTRAL

Lung Wui Road

Tim Mei Ave

Hong Kong Park

COTTON TREE DRIVE

Kennedy Road

Bus Terminus

Star Ferry Pier

General Post Office

Edinburgh Pl

City Hall

Chater Rd

Statue Square

Chater Gdn

Rd

Bank of China Tower

Airport Railway Central Station

Harbour View St

Exchange Sq

CONNAUGHT-ROAD-CENTRAL

QUEENS ROAD CENTRAL

St. John's Cathedral

Ice Ho St

Lower Albert Rd

Garden Rd

Peak Tram Sta.

Des Voeux Road Central

Pedder St

Upper Albert Rd

Albany Rd

Macau Ferry Terminal

Pier Road

CONNAUGHT ROAD

Jubilee St

Wyndham St

CENTRAL DISTRICT

Old Bailey St

SHEUNG WAN

Wing Lok St

Hillier St

Gough St

Aberdeen St

Graham St

Staunton St

Arbuthnot Rd

Caine Road

COPYRIGHT PHILIP'S

KOWLOON

VICTORIA HARBOUR

HONG KONG

0   km   2

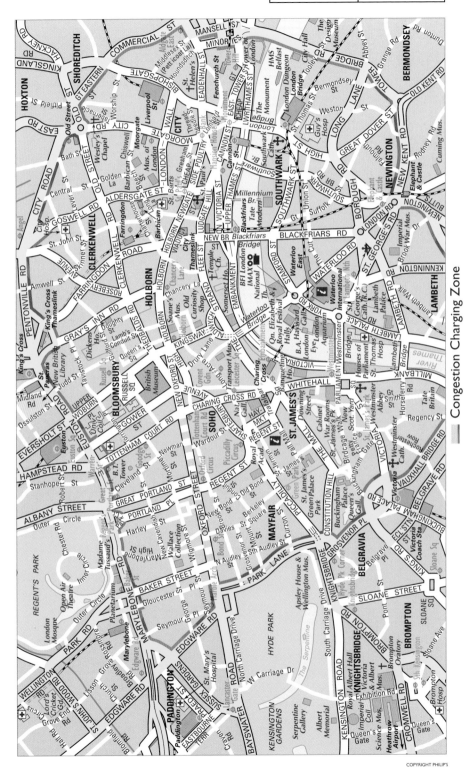

▬ Congestion Charging Zone

COPYRIGHT PHILIP'S

0   km   1

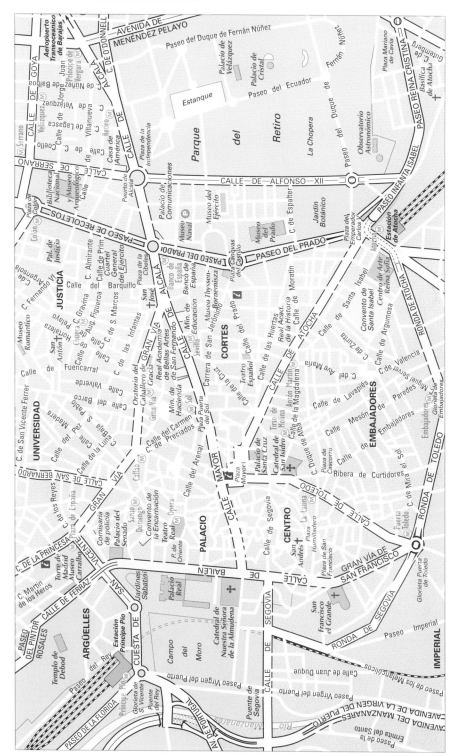

0   km   1

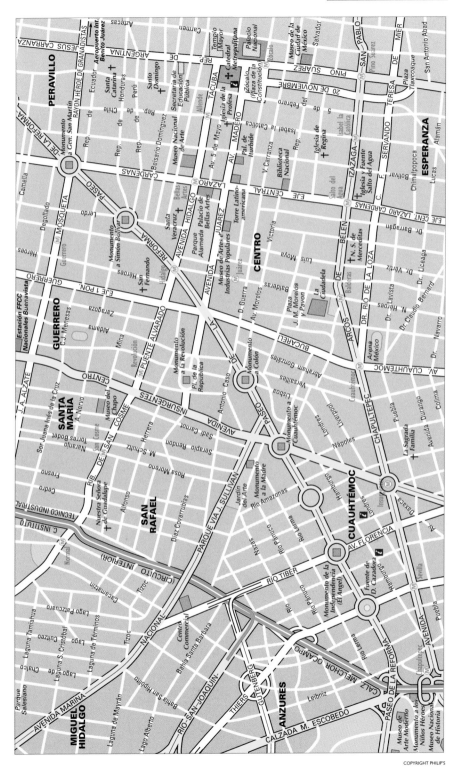

0 ___ km ___ 1

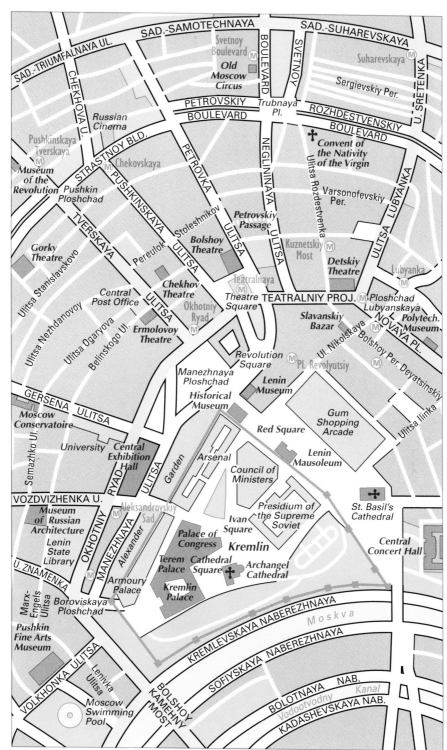

SAD.-SAMOTECHNAYA
SAD.-SUHAREVSKAYA
SAD.-TRIUMFALNAYA UL.
Svetnoy Boulevard
Suharevskaya Ⓜ
Sergievskiy Per.
U. SRETENKA
CHEKHOVA U.
Old Moscow Circus
BOULEVARD
SVETNOY
PETROVSKIY
Trubnaya Pl.
ROZHDESTVENSKIY
Russian Cinema
BOULEVARD
PUSHKINSKAYA
PETROVSKIY
BOULEVARD
NEGLININAYA
✝ *Convent of the Nativity of the Virgin*
Pushkinskaya Tverskaya Ⓜ
STRASTNOY BLD.
Chekovskaya Ⓜ
PETROVKA
Ulitsa Rozhdestvenka
Museum of the Revolution
Pushkin Ploshchad
ULITSA
Varsonofevskiy Per.
ULITSA LUBYANKA
TVERSKAYA
PUSHKINSKAYA
Stoleshnikov
Petrovskiy Passage
Gorky Theatre
Pereulok
ULITSA
Bolshoy Theatre
ULITSA
NEGLININAYA
Kuznetskiy Most Ⓜ
ULITSA
Detskiy Theatre
Lubyanka
Ulitsa Stanislavskovo
Central Post Office
Chekhov Theatre
ULITSA
Okhotniy Ryad Ⓜ
Teatralnaya Ⓜ
Theatre Square
TEATRALNIY PROJ. Ⓜ
Ploshchad Lubyanskaya
Ulitsa Nezhdanovoy
Ermolovoy Theatre
Slavanskiy Bazar
NOVAYA PL.
Polytech. Museum
Ulitsa Ogaryova
Belinskogo Ul.
Ul. Nikolskaya Ⓜ
Bolshoy Per. Deyatsinskiy
Revolution Square Ⓜ
Pl. Revolyutsiy Ⓜ
GERSENA ULITSA
Manezhnaya Ploshchad
Lenin Museum
Semazhko Ul.
Moscow Conservatoire
Historical Museum
Gum Shopping Arcade
Ulitsa Ilinka
University
Central Exhibition Hall
RYAD
ULITSA
Garden
Arsenal
Red Square
Lenin Mausoleum
Ulitsa Ilinka
VOZDVIZHENKA U.
Aleksandrovskiy Sad
Council of Ministers
Museum of Russian Architecture
OKHOTNIY
MANEZHNAYA
Alexander
Ivan Square
Presidium of the Supreme Soviet
St. Basil's Cathedral ✚
Lenin State Library
U. ZNAMENKA
Palace of Congress
Kremlin
Central Concert Hall
Marx-Engels Ulitsa
Ⓜ
Terem Palace
Cathedral Square ✝
Archangel Cathedral
Boroviskaya Ploshchad
Armoury Palace
Kremlin Palace
Pushkin Fine Arts Museum
VOLKHONKA ULITSA
Lenivka Ulitsa
KREMLEVSKAYA NABEREZHNAYA
M o s k v a
SOFIYSKAYA NABEREZHNAYA
BOLSHOY KAMEHNY MOST
Moscow Swimming Pool
BOLOTNAYA NAB.
Kanal
Vodootvodny
KADASHEVSKAYA NAB.

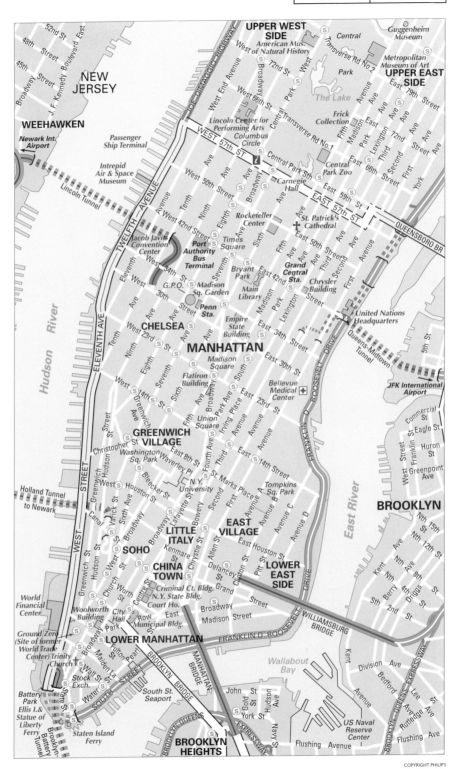

0   km   2

NEW
JERSEY

WEEHAWKEN

Newark Int.
Airport

Passenger
Ship Terminal

Intrepid
Air & Space
Museum

Lincoln Tunnel

Holland Tunnel
to Newark

Hudson River

WEST STREET

ELEVENTH AVE

TWELFTH AVENUE

JOE DIMAGGIO HIGHWAY

West End Avenue

West 72nd St

West 66th St

West 57th ST

West 50th Street

West 42nd Street

Jacob Javits
Convention
Center

Port
Authority
Bus
Terminal

G.P.O.

Tenth
Ninth
Eighth
Seventh
Sixth

West 34th St

West 30th Street

CHELSEA

West 23rd St

MANHATTAN

West 14th St

GREENWICH
VILLAGE

Washington
Sq. Park

Waverley Pl

N.Y.
University

Bleecker St

Christopher St

Houston St

Greenwich
Hudson
Varick St
Sixth Ave
Broadway

Canal St

Church St

Hudson St

SOHO

LITTLE
ITALY

CHINA
TOWN

Kenmare
St

Chrystie
St

Delancey
St

Grand St

Criminal Ct. Bldg.
N.Y. State Bldg.
Court Ho.

Broadway

Clinton St

Allen St

Bowery

Lafayette St

St Marks Place

EAST
VILLAGE

East Houston St

LOWER
EAST
SIDE

Tompkins
Sq. Park

Avenue A
Avenue B
Avenue C
Avenue D

FRANKLIN D. ROOSEVELT DRIVE

East River

BROOKLYN

UPPER WEST
SIDE

American Mus.
of Natural History

72nd St
West
Park

Broadway
Columbus Ave
Amsterdam Ave

Central
Park

The Lake

Lincoln Center for
Performing Arts
Columbus
Circle

Carnegie
Hall

Times
Square

Rockefeller
Center

St. Patrick's
Cathedral

Bryant
Park

Madison
Sq. Garden

Penn
Sta.

Empire
State
Building

Madison
Square

Flatiron
Building

Union
Square

East 8th St

Fourth Ave
Third Ave
Second

Transverse Rd No 2
Transverse Rd No.1

Central Park South

Central Park Fifth

Central
Park Zoo

EAST 57th ST

East 59th St

East 50th Street

East 42nd
Grand
Central
Sta.

Main
Library

Chrysler
Building

East 34th Street

East 30th St

Bellevue
Medical
Center

East 23rd
St

Irving Place

East 14th Street

Fifth
Madison
Park
Lexington
Third
Second
First

Broadway

Sixth
Seventh
Eighth
Ninth
Tenth

Frick
Collection

Guggenheim
Museum

Metropolitan
Museum of Art

UPPER EAST
SIDE

East 79th Street

East 72nd
Street

East 66th
Street

Fifth
Madison
Park
Lexington
Third
Second
First
York

QUEENSBORO BR

United Nations
Headquarters

Queens-Midtown
Tunnel

JFK International
Airport

5th St

Commercial
St
Eagle St
Franklin
Huron
St
Greenpoint
Ave

Nth 15th
Nth 12th St

Nth 8th
St

Nth

Kent
Berry

Driggs

4th St

5th
2nd
St

BROOKLYN-
QUEENS EXPRESSWAY

Division Ave
Bedford
Lee
Rutledge
Flushing Ave

World
Financial
Center

Ground Zero
(Site of former
World Trade
Center)

Trinity
Church

Woolworth
Building

City
Hall

City
Hall
Park

Row
East
Municipal Bldg.

Stock
Exch.

Wall St

Battery
Park

Ellis I. &
Statue of
Liberty
Ferry

Staten Island
Ferry

Brooklyn-
Battery
Tunnel

Greenwich
West
Church

Broadway
Fulton
Maiden La
Pearl

Water St

SOUTH STREET

South St
Seaport

LOWER MANHATTAN

BROOKLYN BRIDGE

MANHATTAN BRIDGE

Madison Street

Street

FRANKLIN D. ROOSEVELT

John
St
Gold
Hudson
York St

WILLIAMSBURG
BRIDGE

Wallabout
Bay

Navy

US Naval
Reserve
Center

Flushing Avenue

Kent
Avenue

BROOKLYN-QUEENS
EXPRESSWAY

BROOKLYN
HEIGHTS

20

0 km 1

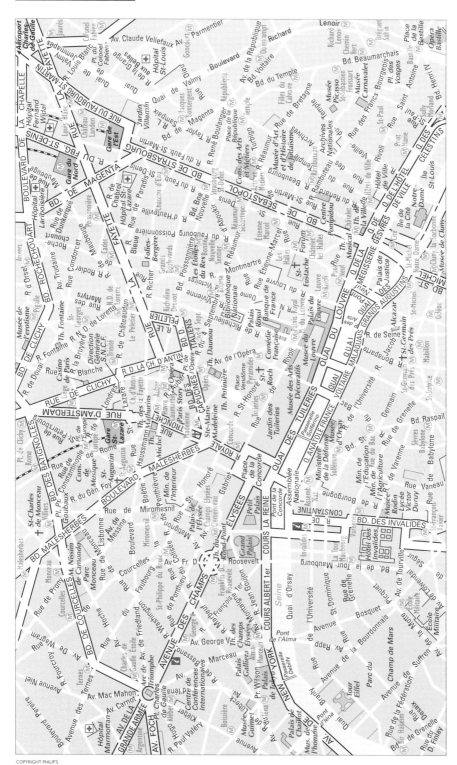

21

0　　　km　　　0.5

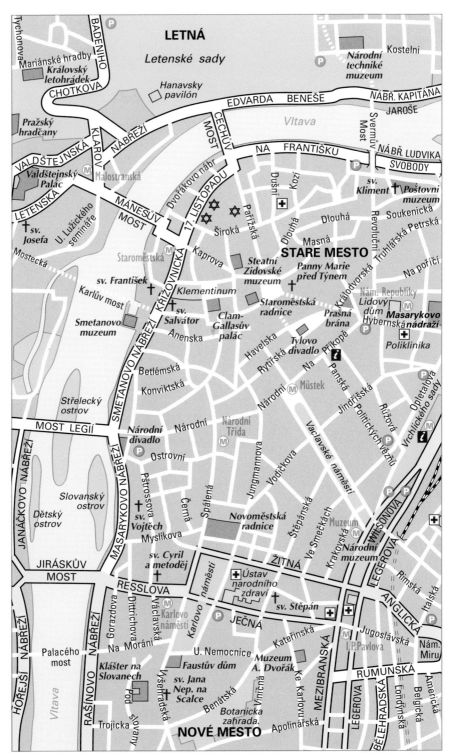

LETNÁ

Letenské sady

Tychonova
Marionova
BADENIHO

Mariánské hradby
Královský
letohrádek
CHOTKOVA

Kostelni

Národní
technické
muzeum

Hanavsky
pavilón

EDVARDA BENEŠE

NÁBŘ. KAPITÁNA
JAROŠE

Pražský
hradčany

KLAROV

NÁBŘEŽI

MOST

ČECHŮV

Vltava

Svermův
Most

NÁBŘ. LUDVIKA
SVOBODY

VALDŠTEJNSKÁ

Valdštejnský
Palác

Malostranská

Dvořákovo nábr

NA FRANTIŠKU

Dušní

Kozí

sv.
Kliment **Poštovní**
muzeum

Soukenická

LETENSKÁ

sv.
Josefa

U. Lužického
semináře

MÁNESŮV
MOST

17. LISTOPADU

Široká

Pařížská

Dlouhá

Dlouhá

Masná

Revoluční

Truhlářská Petrská

Mostecká

Staroměstská

Kaprova

Steatní
Zidovské
muzeum

STARE MESTO

Na poříčí

sv. František

Karlův most

Smetanovo
muzeum

KŘIŽOVNICKÁ

SMETANOVO NÁBŘEŽI

Klementinum

sv.
Salvátor

Clam-
Gallasův
palác

Anenska

Betlémská

Konviktská

Staroměstská
radnice

Panny Marie
před Týnem

Královdvorská

Nám. Republiky

Lidový
dům

Hybernská

Masarykovo
nádraží

Prašná
brána

Havelska

Tylovo
divadlo

Rytířská

Na

Příkopě

Panská

Jindřišská

Politických vězňů

Poliklinika

Müstek

Národní

Opletalova

Vrchlického sady

Střelecký
ostrov

MOST LEGIÍ

Národní
divadlo

Národní

Ostrovní

Národní
Třída

Václavské náměstí

Ružová

JANÁČKOVO NÁBŘEŽI

MASARYKOVO NÁBŘEŽI

Pštrossova

Slovanský
ostrov

Dětský
ostrov

sv.
Vojtěch

Myslíkova

Černá

Spálená

Jungmannova

Novoměstská
radnice

Vodičkova

Štěpánská

Ve Smečkách

Krakovská

Muzeum

Národní
muzeum

WILSONOVA

LEGEROVA

Rimská

JIRÁSKŮV
MOST

RESSLOVA

sv. Cyril
a metoděj

Gorazdova

Dittrichova

Václavská

Karlovo
náměstí

Karlovo
náměstí

ŽITNÁ

JEČNÁ

Ústav
narodního
zdraví

sv. Štěpán

Kateřinská

Jugoslávská

I.P.Pavlova

ANGLICKÁ

Italská

Nám.
Miru

HOŘEJŠÍ NÁBŘEŽI

RAŠINOVO NÁBŘEŽI

Na Moráni

Palacého
most

Kláster na
Slovanech

Vyšehradská

sv. Jana
Nep. na
Scalce

U. Nemocnice

Faustův dům

Muzeum
A. Dvořák

Benátská

Ke Karlovu

MEZIBRANSKÁ

LEGEROVA

BĚLEHRADSKÁ

RUMUNSKÁ

Americká

Belgická

Londýnská

Vltava

Trojicka

slovany

Viničná

Botanicka
zahrada.

Apolinářská

NOVÉ MESTO

COPYRIGHT PHILIP'S

0 km 0.5

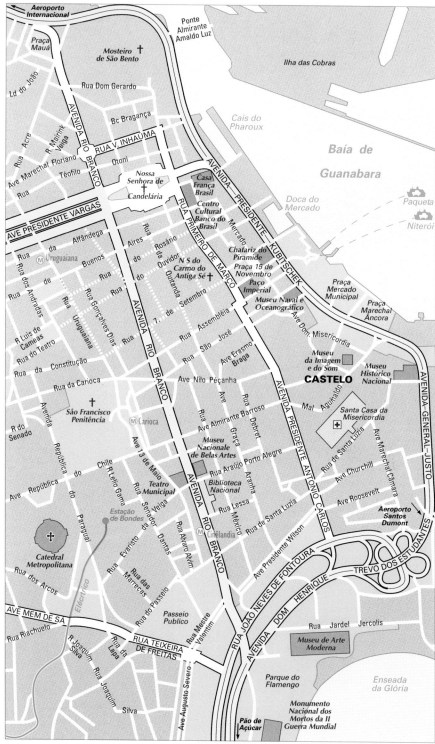

Aeroporto Internacional

Praça Mauá

Ld do João

Mosteiro de São Bento †

Rua Dom Gerardo

Bc Bragança

AVENIDA RIO BRANCO

RUA V. INHAUMA

Rua Acre
R. Marrink Veiga
Ave Marechal Floriano
Téofilo
Otoni

Nossa Senhora de † Candelária

Casa França Brasil

Centro Cultural Banco do Brasil

RUA PRIMEIRO DE MARÇO

AVENIDA PRESIDENTE KUBITSCHEK

Ponte Almirante Arnaldo Luz

Ilha das Cobras

Cais do Pharoux

Baía de Guanabara

Doca do Mercado

Paqueta

Niterói

AVE PRESIDENTE VARGAS

Rua da Alfândega
Ⓜ Uruguaiana
Rua dos Andradas
Buenos
Rua de
Rua Gonçalves Dias
Rua Uruguaiana
Rua Aires do
Rua Rosário do
Ouvidor
Quitanda
N S do Carmo do Antiga Sé †
Rua 7. de Setembro

Mercado
Chafariz do Piramide
Praça 15 de Novembro
Paço Imperial
Museu Naval e Oceanográfico

Praça Mercado Municipal
Praça Marechal Âncora

R Luis de Cameas
Rua do Teatro
Rua da Constituição

AVENIDA RIO BRANCO

Rua Assembléia
Rua São José
Ave Erasmo Braga

Ave Dom. Misericordia

Museu da Imagem e do Som

CASTELO

Museu Histórico Nacional

AVENIDA GENERAL JUSTO

Rua da Carioca

São Francisco Penitência †

Ⓜ Carioca

Ave Nilo Peçanha

Ave
Rua Debret
Mal Aguinaldo

Santa Casa da Misericordia ✚

AVENIDA PRESIDENTE ANTONIO CARLOS

R do Senado
Avenida
República do
Ave República do
Chile

Ave Almirante Barroso

Museu Nacionale de Belas Artes

Rua Graça
Rua Araújo Porto Alegre
Rua Aranha

Rua de Santa Luzia
Ave Churchill
Ave Marechal Camara

Ave 13 de Maio
R Lélio Gama
Rua
Senador
Veiga

Teatro Municipal

Biblioteca Nacional

Rua Lessa
Rua México
Rua de Santa Luzia

Ave Roosevelt

Aeroporto Santos Dumont

AVENIDA RIO BRANCO

Estação de Bondes

Ⓜ Cinelândia

Elêctrico

Paraguai
Rua Evaristo da
Senador Dantas
Rua Alvaro Alvim

Catedral Metropolitana †
Rua dos Arcos

AVE MEM DE SA

Rua das Marrecas
Rua do Passeio
Rua Mestre Valentim

Rua Riachuelo
R Joaquim Silva
Rua da Lapa
Rua Joaquim

RUA TEIXEIRA DE FREITAS

Passeio Publico

Ave Augusto Severo

Ave Presidente Wilson

RUA JOAO NEVES DE FONTOURA

AVENIDA DOM HENRIQUE

TREVO DOS ESTUDANTES

Rua Jardel Jercolis

Museu de Arte Moderna

Parque do Flamengo

Enseada da Glória

Silva

Pão de Açúcar

Monumento Nacional dos Mortos da II Guerra Mundial

0   km   1

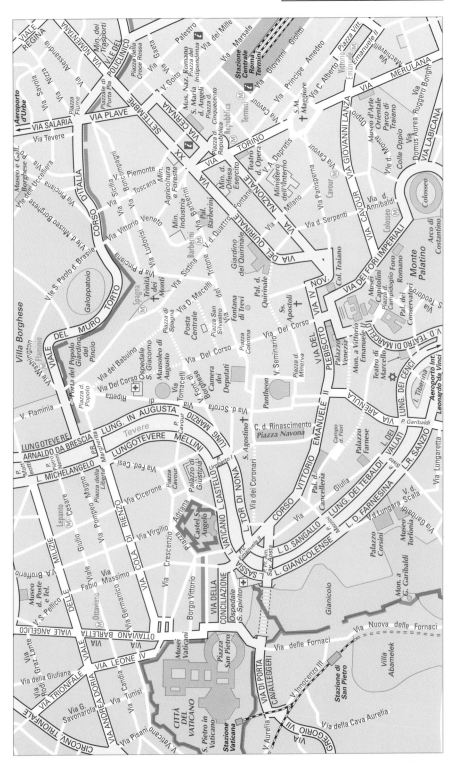

0   km   0.5

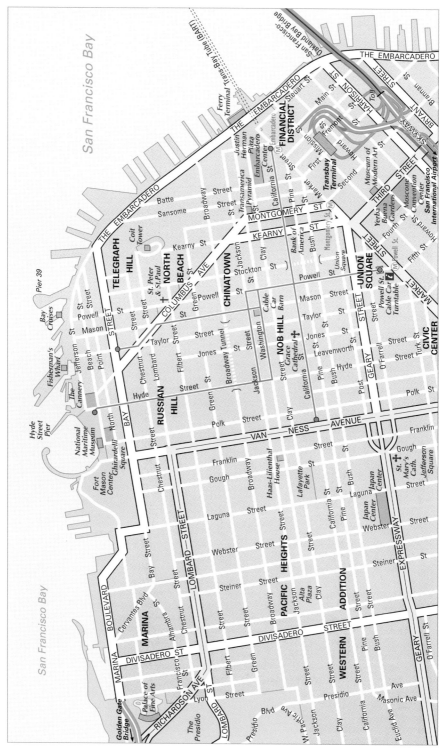

San Francisco Bay

THE EMBARCADERO

San Francisco–Oakland Bay Bridge

Terminal Trans-Bay Tube (BART)

Ferry Terminal

THE EMBARCADERO

Justin Herman Plaza

Transamerica Pyramid

Embarcadero Center

Steuart St
Main St
Steuart St

FINANCIAL DISTRICT

California St

Pine
Market St
Mission St
Howard St

Fremont St
First St
Second St

Transbay Terminal

Museum of Modern Art

THIRD STREET

Yerba Buena Gardens

Moscone Convention Center

San Francisco International Airport

Batte
Sansome
Broadway Street
Street St

Montgomery St

KEARNY ST

Bank of America

Bush St

Howard St

Fourth St
Fifth St

SKYWAY

HARRISON ST

BRYANT
Bryant St

TELEGRAPH HILL

Coit Tower

NORTH BEACH

St Peter & St Paul

Kearny St
AVE
Green St
Powell St

CHINATOWN

Jackson St
Clay St
Stockton St

Washington

Powell St

Mason Street
Taylor
Jones St
Leavenworth

Union Square

STREET

Powell St Cable Car Turntable

Montgomery St

Pier 39

Bay Cruises

Fisherman's Wharf

The Cannery

Mason St
Powell St
Taylor Street
Jefferson
Beach
Point

COLUMBUS AVE
STREET
Street
Chestnut
Lombard
Filbert Street
Green
Street
Jones St

Cable Car Barn

Broadway Tunnel

NOB HILL

Grace Cathedral

California St
Pine St
Bush St
Hyde

Post St
Pine St

STREET GEARY

O'Farrell
Turk St
Street St

CIVIC CENTER

MARKET

Hyde Street Pier

National Maritime Museum

Fort Mason Center

Ghirardelli Square

North Point St

BAY

RUSSIAN HILL

Polk Street
Clay St

VAN   NESS   AVENUE

Polk St

Franklin

Chestnut
Gough

Franklin St
Gough

Broadway
Street

Haas-Lilienthal House

Lafayette Park

Bush St
Laguna

Japan Center

St Mary's Cath.

Jefferson Square

Gough St

BOULEVARD

MARINA

DIVISADERO ST

Chestnut

Laguna Street

Webster Street

Steiner Street

PACIFIC HEIGHTS

Jackson
Broadway
Alta Plaza
Clay

Webster Street

WESTERN ADDITION

California St
Pine St

Laguna St
Webster

Steiner

EXPRESSWAY

O'Farrell St
Street St

LOMBARD STREET

Cervantes Blvd
Alhambra St
Chestnut St
Filbert St
Green St

Bay Street

Street

DIVISADERO   STREET

California
Clay

Pine St
Bush St

GEARY

Ave
O'Farrell St

Palace of Fine Arts

Golden Gate Bridge

The Presidio

RICHARDSON AVE

Lyon St
Francisco St

LOMBARD

Presidio Ave

W. Pacific Ave
Jackson
Blvd
Clay

Presidio Ave
Masonic Ave
Euclid Ave

San Francisco Bay

25

0   km   1

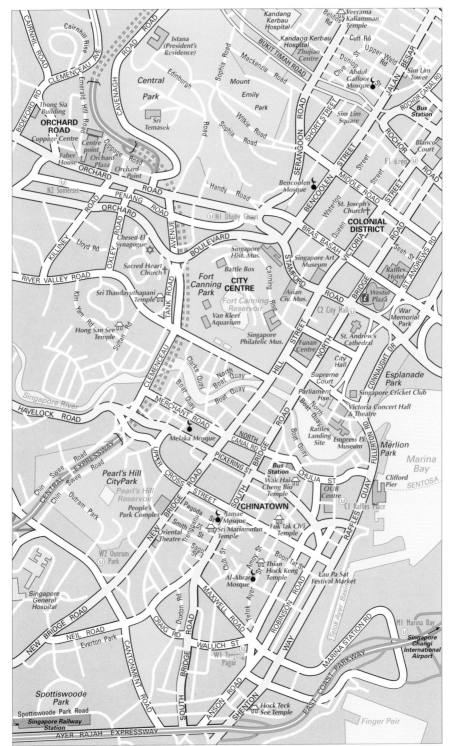

COPYRIGHT PHILIP'S

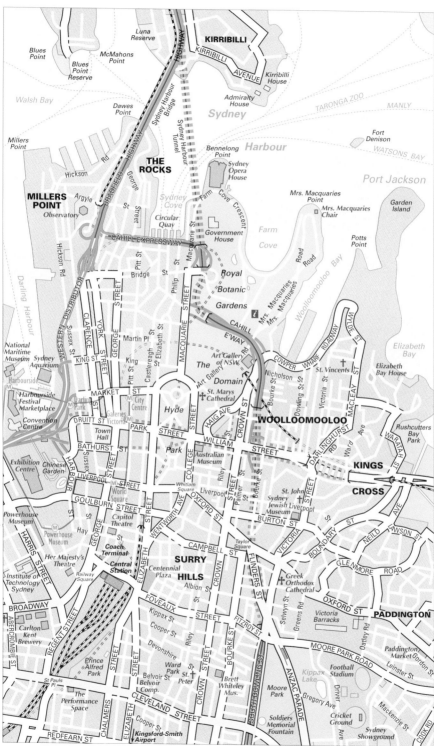

0   km   2

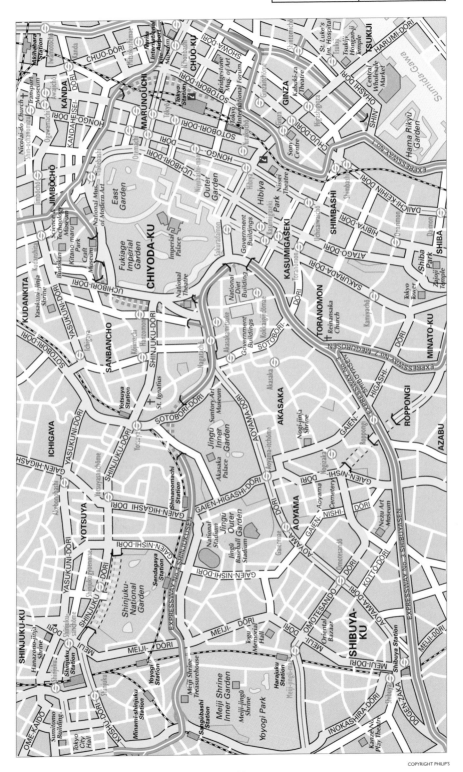

0   km   1

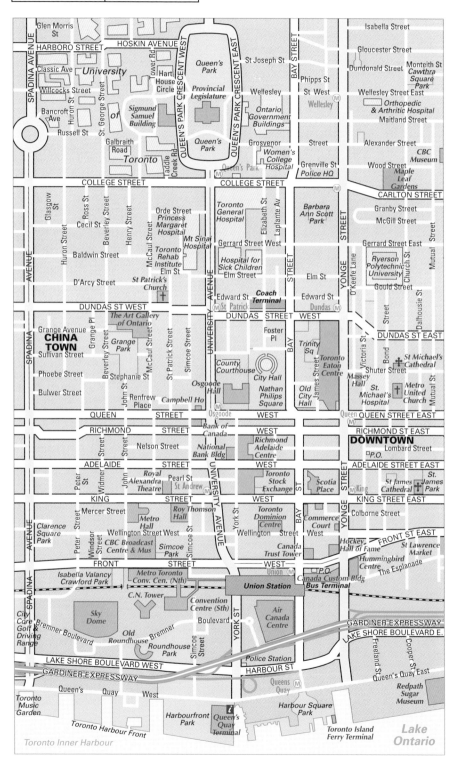

Glen Morris St
HARBORO STREET
HOSKIN AVENUE
Isabella Street
Gloucester Street
Classic Ave
University
Monteith St
Dundonald Street
Cawthra Square Park
Willcocks Street
Tower Rd
Hart House Circle
Queen's Park
St Joseph St
Phipps St
Wellesley Street East
Bancroft Ave
Huron St
St. George Street
of
Sigmund Samuel Building
Provincial Legislature
Wellesley
St West
Orthopedic & Arthritic Hospital
Maitland Street
Russell St
Toronto
Galbraith Road
Queen's Park
Ontario Government Buildings
Street
Alexander Street
CBC Museum
Queen's Park
Grosvenor
Women's College Hospital
Wood Street
Maple Leaf Gardens
COLLEGE STREET
COLLEGE STREET
Grenville St
Police HQ
CARLTON STREET
Glasgow St
Ross St
Cecil St
Beverley Street
Henry Street
McCaul Street
Orde Street
Princess Margaret Hospital
Toronto General Hospital
Elizabeth St
Laplante Av
Barbara Ann Scott Park
Granby Street
McGill Street
Huron Street
Baldwin Street
Mt Sinai Hospital
Gerrard Street West
STREET
Gerrard Street East
Mutual Street
Toronto Rehab Institute
Hospital for Sick Children
Elm Street
Ryerson Polytechnic University
Church St
O'Keefe Lane
D'Arcy Street
Elm St
St Patrick's Church
Elm St
Edward Street
Coach Terminal
Elm St
Edward Street
Gould Street
YONGE STREET
Street
Dalhousie St
DUNDAS ST WEST
St Patrick
DUNDAS STREET WEST
Dundas
CHINA TOWN
The Art Gallery of Ontario
Grange Avenue
Grange Pl
Beverley Street
McCaul Street
St Patrick Street
Simcoe Street
DUNDAS ST EAST
Victoria St
Bond
St Michael's Cathedral
Mutual St
Sullivan Street
Grange Park
Foster Pl
Trinity Sq
Toronto Eaton Centre
James Street
Massey Hall
Shuter Street
Phoebe Street
Stephanie St
County Courthouse
City Hall
Metro United Church
Bulwer Street
John St
Renfrew Place
Campbell Ho
Osgoode Hall
Nathan Philips Square
Old City Hall
St. Michael's Hospital
QUEEN STREET
WEST
Osgoode
Queen
QUEEN STREET EAST
RICHMOND STREET
Bank of Canada
WEST
RICHMOND ST EAST
DOWNTOWN
Street
Street
Nelson Street
National Bank Bldg
Richmond Adelaide Centre
Lombard Street
P.O.
ADELAIDE STREET
WEST
ADELAIDE STREET EAST
Peter St
Widmer St
John St
Royal Alexandra Theatre
Pearl St
St Andrew
UNIVERSITY AVENUE
Toronto Stock Exchange
ST
Scotia Place
King
St James Cathedral
St. James Park
KING STREET
WEST
KING STREET EAST
Mercer Street
Metro Hall
Roy Thomson Hall
York St
Toronto Dominion Centre
YONGE STREET
Colborne Street
Clarence Square Park
Windsor Street
Peter Street
Wellington Street West
Simcoe Park
Simcoe St
Wellington
Commerce Court West
Street
FRONT ST EAST
Hockey Hall of Fame
St Lawrence Market
CBC Broadcast Centre & Mus
Canada Trust Tower
Hummingbird Centre
The Esplanade
FRONT
STREET
WEST
Union
P.O.
Canada Custom Bldg
Bus Terminal
Isabella Valancy Crawford Park
Metro Toronto Conv. Cen. (Nth)
Union Station
SPADINA
C.N. Tower
Convention Centre (Sth)
Air Canada Centre
GARDINER EXPRESSWAY
LAKE SHORE BOULEVARD E.
City Care Golf & Driving Range
Bremner Boulevard
Sky Dome
Old Roundhouse
Bremner
Boulevard
York St
Simcoe Street
Freeland St
Cooper St
Queen's Quay East
Roundhouse Park
LAKE SHORE BOULEVARD WEST
Police Station
Redpath Sugar Museum
GARDINER EXPRESSWAY
HARBOUR ST
Queen's
Queens Quay
Toronto Music Garden
Queen's
Quay
West
Harbour Square Park
Toronto Harbour Front
Harbourfront Park
Queen's Quay Terminal
Toronto Island Ferry Terminal
Lake Ontario
Toronto Inner Harbour

0   km   1

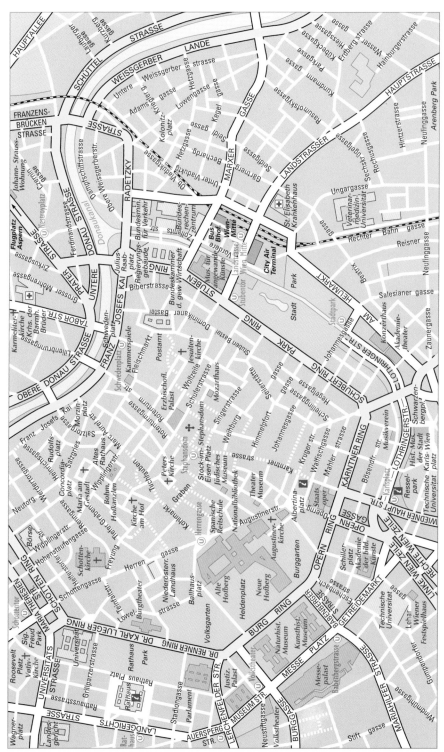

GAZETTEER OF NATIONS

32 Afghanistan
 Albania
 Algeria
 American Samoa
 Andorra
 Angola

33 Anguilla
 Antigua & Barbuda
 Argentina
 Armenia
 Aruba
 Australia

34 Austria
 Azerbaijan
 Azores
 Bahamas
 Bahrain
 Bangladesh

35 Barbados
 Belarus
 Belgium
 Belize
 Benin
 Bermuda

36 Bolivia
 Bosnia-Herzegovina
 Botswana
 Brazil
 Bulgaria
 Burma (= Myanmar)

37 Cambodia
 Canada
 Canary Islands
 Cape Verde
 Cayman Islands
 Chad

38 Chile
 China
 Colombia

 Comoros
 Costa Rica
 Croatia

39 Cuba
 Cyprus
 Czech Republic
 Denmark
 Dominica
 Dominican Republic

40 Ecuador
 Egypt
 El Salvador
 Estonia
 Ethiopia
 Fiji Islands

41 Finland
 France
 French Polynesia
 Gambia, The
 Georgia
 Germany

42 Gibraltar
 Greece
 Grenada
 Guadeloupe
 Hong Kong
 Hungary

43 Iceland
 India
 Indonesia
 Iran
 Ireland
 Israel

44 Italy
 Jamaica
 Japan
 Jordan
 Kenya
 Korea, South

45 Kuwait
 Latvia
 Lebanon
 Libya
 Liechtenstein
 Lithuania

46 Luxembourg
 Madagascar
 Malawi
 Malaysia
 Maldives
 Malta

47 Martinique
 Mauritius
 Mexico
 Monaco
 Mongolia
 Morocco

48 Namibia
 Nepal
 Netherlands
 Netherlands
  Antilles
 New Zealand
 Nigeria

49 Norway
 Oman
 Pakistan
 Paraguay
 Peru
 Philippines

50 Poland
 Portugal
 Puerto Rico
 Qatar
 Réunion
 Romania

51 Russia
 St Kitts & Nevis

 St Lucia
 St Vincent & the
  Grenadines
 Samoa
 Saudi Arabia

52 Serbia &
  Montenegro
 Seychelles
 Singapore
 Slovak Republic
 Slovenia
 South Africa

53 Spain
 Sri Lanka
 Sweden
 Switzerland
 Syria
 Taiwan

54 Tanzania
 Thailand
 Trinidad &
  Tobago
 Tunisia
 Turkey
 Uganda

55 Ukraine
 United Arab
  Emirates
 United Kingdom
 United States
  of America
 Uruguay
 Venezuela

56 Vietnam
 Virgin Islands,
  British
 Virgin Islands, US
 Yemen
 Zambia
 Zimbabwe

AFGHANISTAN

GOVERNMENT Transitional
LANGUAGES Pashtu, Dari/Persian, Uzbek
CURRENCY Afghani = 100 puls
MEDICAL Visitors should protect against yellow fever, polio, typhoid and malaria
TRAVEL Most governments currently advise against all travel to Afghanistan. The security situation remains serious, with danger away from main roads from mines and unexploded ordnance
WEATHER Jun to Aug very hot; Dec to Mar very cold; Jun to Sep scanty rainfall; mild at other times
BANKING 0800–1200 and 1300–1630 Sat to Wed; 0830–1330 Thu. However, at the time of writing, many banks are closed
EMERGENCY Unavailable
TIME ZONE GMT +4.30
INTERNATIONAL DIALLING CODE Unavailable

ALBANIA

GOVERNMENT Multiparty republic
LANGUAGES Albanian (official)
CURRENCY Lek = 100 qindars
MEDICAL Water is untreated and not safe to drink. Medical facilities in the country are poor
TRAVEL Crime is high throughout the country and visitors should remain vigilant at all times. It is advisable to dress down and avoid carrying expensive items. Street demonstrations against the government are common
WEATHER Jun to Sep warm and dry; Oct to May cool and wet
BANKING 0700–1500 Mon to Fri
EMERGENCY Police 24445; Fire 23333; Ambulance 22235
TIME ZONE GMT +1
INTERNATIONAL DIALLING CODE 355

ALGERIA

GOVERNMENT Socialist republic
LANGUAGES Arabic and Berber (both official), French
CURRENCY Algerian dinar = 100 centimes
MEDICAL There is a risk of yellow fever, malaria, hepatitis A, typhoid and polio
TRAVEL Most governments currently advise against all tourist and non-essential travel to Algeria. Travel by public transport should be avoided and only secure accommodation used
WEATHER Jun to Sep in the north is usually hot with high humidity along the coast; Oct to Feb wet and mild
BANKING 0900–1630 Sun to Thu
EMERGENCY Unavailable
TIME ZONE GMT +1
INTERNATIONAL DIALLING CODE 213

AMERICAN SAMOA

GOVERNMENT US overseas territory
LANGUAGES Samoan, English
CURRENCY US dollar = 100 cents
MEDICAL Water is untreated and is unsafe to drink. Vaccination against polio and typhoid is recommended
TRAVEL Most visits to American Samoa are trouble-free and crime is low. Tourists should respect local culture and take usual precautions, especially in the towns
WEATHER Hot, tropical climate with heavy rainfall from Dec to Apr. The most comfortable time to visit is May to Sep
BANKING 0900–1500 Mon to Fri
EMERGENCY All services 911
TIME ZONE GMT –11
INTERNATIONAL DIALLING CODE 1 684

ANDORRA

GOVERNMENT Parliamentary co-princedom
LANGUAGES Catalan, Spanish, French
CURRENCY Euro = 100 cents
MEDICAL There are no specific health risks
TRAVEL In Andorra, visitors will find some of the most stunning scenery and the best skiing in the Pyrenees. Shopping around, prices may often be up to 30% below those in France and Spain
WEATHER Jun to Sep warm and pleasant; Dec to Apr sunny but cold with abundant snow; rain falls throughout the year; snow often remains on the peaks of mountains until July
BANKING 0900–1300 and 1500–1700 Mon to Fri; 0900–1200 Sat
EMERGENCY Police 110; Fire/Ambulance 118
TIME ZONE GMT +1
INTERNATIONAL DIALLING CODE 376

ANGOLA

GOVERNMENT Multiparty republic
LANGUAGES Portuguese (official), many others
CURRENCY Kwanza = 100 lwei
MEDICAL There is a risk of yellow fever, hepatitis A, polio, typhoid and malaria
TRAVEL Most governments currently advise against tourist and non-essential travel to Angola due to the aftermath of civil war. Visitors should remain vigilant, particularly after dark. Crime levels are high and land mines are widely distributed and unmarked
WEATHER Warm to hot all year; Nov to Apr wet; cooler and wetter climate in the south
BANKING 0845–1600 Mon to Fri
EMERGENCY Unavailable
TIME ZONE GMT +1
INTERNATIONAL DIALLING CODE 244

ANGUILLA

GOVERNMENT UK overseas territory
LANGUAGES English (official)
CURRENCY East Caribbean dollar = 100 cents
MEDICAL There are no specific health risks, but medical facilities are limited on the island
TRAVEL Most visits are trouble-free, but beachwear should be confined to resort areas. Travellers should take normal precautions, such as locking doors and securing valuables
WEATHER Tropical climate. Hurricane risk from Jun to Nov; Oct to Dec is the rainy season. Optimum diving conditions in summer months
BANKING 0800–1500 Mon to Thu; 0800–1700 Fri
EMERGENCY All services 911
TIME ZONE GMT –4
INTERNATIONAL DIALLING CODE 1 264

ANTIGUA & BARBUDA

GOVERNMENT Constitutional monarchy
LANGUAGES English (official), English patois
CURRENCY East Caribbean dollar = 100 cents
MEDICAL Visitors should take normal precautions against mosquito bites. Vaccinations recommended against polio and typhoid
TRAVEL Generally trouble-free, but visitors should avoid isolated areas, including beaches, after dark
WEATHER Tropical with little variation between the seasons; rainfall is minimal. The islands are at risk from hurricanes from Jun to Nov
BANKING 0800–1400 Mon to Thu; 0800–1700 Fri
EMERGENCY All services 999/911
TIME ZONE GMT –4
INTERNATIONAL DIALLING CODE 1 268

ARGENTINA

GOVERNMENT Federal republic
LANGUAGES Spanish (official)
CURRENCY Argentine peso = 10,000 australs
MEDICAL Cholera is a risk in the subtropical northern region
TRAVEL Occasional outbreaks of social unrest. It is inadvisable to walk in isolated, poorly-lit areas. Visitors should avoid carrying too much cash or wearing jewellery. Avoid military areas, which usually allow no stopping
WEATHER Jun to Aug cool in Buenos Aires area; Dec to Feb hot and humid; rain falls all year round
BANKING 1000–1500 Mon to Fri
EMERGENCY Police 101/107
TIME ZONE GMT –3
INTERNATIONAL DIALLING CODE 54

ARMENIA

GOVERNMENT Multiparty republic
LANGUAGES Armenian (official)
CURRENCY Dram = 100 couma
MEDICAL Visitors should protect against hepatitis and bacterial infection
TRAVEL The border areas with Azerbaijan should be avoided at all times. Crime remains relatively low in Armenia, but occasional thefts from cars and pickpocketing may occur. The local standard of driving is poor, but most visits are generally trouble-free
WEATHER Apr to Oct hot and sunny; Jul to Sep little rainfall; Dec to Feb cold with heavy snow
BANKING 0930–1730 Mon to Fri
EMERGENCY Unavailable
TIME ZONE GMT +4
INTERNATIONAL DIALLING CODE 374

ARUBA

GOVERNMENT Parliamentary democracy
LANGUAGES Dutch, English, Spanish, Papiamento
CURRENCY Aruba florin = 100 cents
MEDICAL Water is purified and should be safe; normal precautions should be taken with food
TRAVEL Beachwear should be confined to the beach. Travellers should take normal precautions, such as avoiding isolated areas after dark
WEATHER Tropical marine climate, warm and dry with average temperatures of 28°C [82°F]. Nov and Dec experience short showers
BANKING 0800–1200 and 1300–1600 Mon to Fri
EMERGENCY Police 11 000; Ambulance 74 300; Fire 115
TIME ZONE GMT –4
INTERNATIONAL DIALLING CODE 297

AUSTRALIA

GOVERNMENT Federal constitutional monarchy
LANGUAGES English (official)
CURRENCY Australian dollar = 100 cents
MEDICAL No vaccinations required. There are few health hazards, but visitors should protect against sunburn, spider and snake bites
TRAVEL Visitors should exercise caution in major urban areas, particularly after dark
WEATHER Tropical to temperate; Nov to Mar warm or hot in all areas; Jun to Aug mild in south-eastern region; Sep to May warm to hot; rain falls all year round and is heaviest Mar to Jul
BANKING 0930–1600 Mon to Thu; 0930–1700 Fri, but hours vary throughout the country
EMERGENCY Emergency Services 000
TIME ZONE East GMT +10; Cen. +9.30; West +8
INTERNATIONAL DIALLING CODE 61

AUSTRIA

GOVERNMENT Federal republic
LANGUAGES German (official)
CURRENCY Euro = 100 cents
MEDICAL There are no specific health risks in Austria
TRAVEL Visitors to the Alps should contact the Austrian Tourist Agency for advice on safety. Austria benefits all year round by providing summer sightseeing and winter sports
WEATHER Jun to Aug warm and pleasant; Oct to Apr cold; Mar to Aug higher rainfall
BANKING 0800–1230 and 1330–1500 Mon, Tue, Wed and Fri; Thu 0800–1230 and 1330–1730
EMERGENCY Emergency Services 112; Police 133; Ambulance 144
TIME ZONE GMT +1
INTERNATIONAL DIALLING CODE 43

AZERBAIJAN

GOVERNMENT Federal multiparty republic
LANGUAGES Azerbaijani (official), Russian
CURRENCY Azerbaijani manat = 100 gopik
MEDICAL Visitors should protect against malaria, yellow fever, diptheria, tick-borne encephalitis, hepatitis, rabies and typhoid fever
TRAVEL Travel to the western region of Nagorno-Karabakh and surrounding occupied area should be avoided. Passport photocopies should be carried at all times. Do not enter or leave the country via the land borders with Russia
WEATHER May to Sep sunny, warm and dry; Oct to Apr mild with some rain
BANKING 0930–1730 Mon to Fri
EMERGENCY Unavailable
TIME ZONE GMT +4
INTERNATIONAL DIALLING CODE 994

AZORES

GOVERNMENT Portuguese autonomous region
LANGUAGES Portuguese
CURRENCY Euro = 100 cents
MEDICAL There are no specific health risks in the Azores
TRAVEL Most visits to the Azores are trouble-free. The nine large islands and numerous small ones are situated in the middle of the Atlantic Ocean and offer the traveller a wealth of stunning scenery
WEATHER Mild throughout the year; Jun to Sep sunny and warm; Jan to Apr changeable; Oct to Mar wet
BANKING Visitors should check at their hotel
EMERGENCY Unavailable
TIME ZONE GMT –1
INTERNATIONAL DIALLING CODE Unavailable

BAHAMAS

GOVERNMENT Constitutional parliamentary democracy
LANGUAGES English (official), Creole
CURRENCY Bahamian dollar = 100 cents
MEDICAL Visitors should protect against dehydration, sunburn, tetanus and jellyfish
TRAVEL Most visits are trouble-free, but crime exists in the cities of Nassau and Freeport. Keep valuables hidden and avoid walking alone
WEATHER Mild throughout the year; May to Oct warm and wet; Dec to Mar cooler and drier; Jun to Nov hurricanes occur
BANKING 0930–1500 Mon to Thu; 0930–1700 Fri, but hours on each island vary
EMERGENCY All Services 911
TIME ZONE GMT –5
INTERNATIONAL DIALLING CODE 1 242

BAHRAIN

GOVERNMENT Monarchy (emirate) with a cabinet appointed by the Emir
LANGUAGES Arabic (official), English, Farsi, Urdu
CURRENCY Bahrain dinar = 1,000 fils
MEDICAL There are no specific health risks
TRAVEL Generally calm, but any increase in regional tension may affect travel advice. Visitors should avoid village areas, particularly after dark. Keep cash and valuables out of sight at all times
WEATHER Jun to Sep very hot; Nov to Mar milder and pleasant
BANKING 0800–1200 and 1600–1800 Sat to Wed; 0800–1100 Thu
EMERGENCY All Services 999
TIME ZONE GMT +3
INTERNATIONAL DIALLING CODE 973

BANGLADESH

GOVERNMENT Multiparty republic
LANGUAGES Bengali (official), English
CURRENCY Taka = 100 paisas
MEDICAL Visitors should protect against cholera, dysentery, hepatitis, malaria and meningitis
TRAVEL Avoid political gatherings. Driving conditions are very poor. Visitors should keep valuables hidden and avoid travel after dark
WEATHER Jun to Sep monsoon with heavy rain and very high humidity; Nov to Feb sunny and cool; Mar to Jun hot with thunderstorms
BANKING 0830–1430 Sun to Wed; 0830–1300 Thu. Closed Fri and Sat
EMERGENCY Police Dhaka 866 551–3; Fire and Ambulance Service Dhaka 9 555 555
TIME ZONE GMT +6
INTERNATIONAL DIALLING CODE 880

BARBADOS

GOVERNMENT Parliamentary democracy
LANGUAGES English (local Bajan dialect also spoken)
CURRENCY Barbados dollar = 100 cents
MEDICAL The sun is intense and visitors should wear strong sunscreen at all times. Other health risks include dengue fever
TRAVEL Travel is generally risk-free, but visitors should avoid deserted beaches at night
WEATHER Warm all year round; Jun to Dec wet season; Feb to May cooler and drier
BANKING 0800–1500 Mon to Thu; 0800–1300 and 1500–1700 Fri
EMERGENCY Police 112; Ambulance 115; All Services 119
TIME ZONE GMT −4
INTERNATIONAL DIALLING CODE 1 246

BELARUS

GOVERNMENT Multiparty republic
LANGUAGES Belarusian and Russian (both official)
CURRENCY Belarusian rouble = 100 kopecks
MEDICAL Visitors should avoid eating dairy produce, mushrooms and fruits of the forests which can carry high levels of radiation. Other health risks include hepatitis A and B, and typhoid
TRAVEL Pickpocketing and theft from vehicles or hotel rooms is common. Visitors should avoid demonstrations and rallies, and remain vigilant at all times
WEATHER May to Aug mild; Oct to Apr cold; Jan to Mar snow cover; rain falls all year round
BANKING 0900–1730 Mon to Fri
EMERGENCY Police 02; Ambulance 03
TIME ZONE GMT +2
INTERNATIONAL DIALLING CODE 375

BELGIUM

GOVERNMENT Federal constitutional monarchy
LANGUAGES Dutch, French, German (all official)
CURRENCY Euro = 100 cents
MEDICAL There are no specific health risks, but medical care is expensive
TRAVEL Most visits are trouble-free, but visitors should take sensible precautions to avoid the increasing threat of mugging, bag-snatching and pickpocketing, particularly in Brussels
WEATHER May to Sep mild; Nov to Mar cold; rain falls all year round, often as snow in winter
BANKING 0900–1200 and 1400–1600 Mon to Fri. Some banks open 0900–1200 Sat
EMERGENCY Police 101; Emergency Services 112 Fire/Ambulance 100 (112 from a mobile phone)
TIME ZONE GMT +1
INTERNATIONAL DIALLING CODE 32

BELIZE

GOVERNMENT Constitutional monarchy
LANGUAGES English (official), Spanish, Creole
CURRENCY Belizean dollar = 100 cents
MEDICAL Precautions should be taken against polio, typhoid and cholera. Malaria is present throughout the year, excluding urban areas
TRAVEL Nov to May is the best time to visit, but this is the busy tourist season when prices rise and hotels fill up. Belize has one of the longest barrier reefs in the world
WEATHER Hot and humid climate. Monsoon and hurricane season runs from Jun to Sep
BANKING 0800–1300 Mon to Thu; 0800–1200 and 1500–1800 Fri
EMERGENCY All services 911
TIME ZONE GMT −6
INTERNATIONAL DIALLING CODE 501

BENIN

GOVERNMENT Multiparty republic
LANGUAGES French (official), Fon, Adja, Yoruba
CURRENCY CFA franc = 100 centimes
MEDICAL Visitors should protect against cholera and malaria. Yellow fever vaccination certificates are required for entry. Water is unsafe to drink
TRAVEL Travel is generally safe, but driving out of towns at night should be avoided due to poor street lighting. Occasional incidents of mugging and armed robberies occur in Cotonou
WEATHER Warm to hot all year round; Mar to Jul and Sep to Oct are rainy seasons in the south
BANKING 0800–1100 and 1500–1600 Mon to Fri
EMERGENCY Consult foreign embassy
TIME ZONE GMT +1
INTERNATIONAL DIALLING CODE 229

BERMUDA

GOVERNMENT Self-governing British dependency
LANGUAGES English (some Portuguese is also spoken)
CURRENCY Bermuda dollar = 100 cents
MEDICAL There are no specific health risks
TRAVEL Most visits to Bermuda are trouble-free. Accommodation can be up to 40% cheaper between Nov and Mar, but events and entertainment are less plentiful at this time
WEATHER Jun to Sep very warm; Nov to Apr mild; rainfall is abundant and evenly distributed all year round
BANKING 0930–1500 Mon to Thu; 0930–1500 and 1630–1730 Fri
EMERGENCY All Services 911
TIME ZONE GMT −4
INTERNATIONAL DIALLING CODE 1 441

BOLIVIA

GOVERNMENT Multiparty republic
LANGUAGES Spanish, Aymara, Quechua (official)
CURRENCY Boliviano = 100 centavos
MEDICAL Altitude sickness is common. Visitors should drink plenty of water and protect against cholera, hepatitis, malaria, polio and tetanus
TRAVEL Pickpocketing is common and visitors are advised to remain vigilant at all times. The country is going through a period of unrest
WEATHER Average max. daily temperature of 17–19°C [62–66°F] all year round; low annual rainfall, most falling Dec to Mar
BANKING 0930–1500 Mon to Thu; 0930–1500 and 1630–1730 Fri
EMERGENCY All Services 911
TIME ZONE GMT –4
INTERNATIONAL DIALLING CODE 591

BOSNIA-HERZEGOVINA

GOVERNMENT Federal republic
LANGUAGES Bosnian, Serbian, Croatian
CURRENCY Convertible marka = 100 convertible pfenniga
MEDICAL Medical facilities are limited. There is a risk of hepatitis and typhoid fever
TRAVEL Crime level is generally low, but isolated incidents of violence can flare up. Unexploded land mines and other ordnance still remain in certain areas
WEATHER Jun to Sep warm; Dec to Feb cold; spring and autumn mild; rain falls all year round
BANKING 0730–1530 Mon to Fri
EMERGENCY Consult foreign office in country of residence before departure
TIME ZONE GMT +1
INTERNATIONAL DIALLING CODE 387

BOTSWANA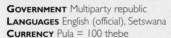

GOVERNMENT Multiparty republic
LANGUAGES English (official), Setswana
CURRENCY Pula = 100 thebe
MEDICAL There are no specific health risks, but visitors should protect against malaria
TRAVEL Most visits are trouble-free, but there is an increasing incidence of crime. Prolonged rainfall may cause flooding and block roads from Dec to Apr
WEATHER In the east, May to Sep mild with little rainfall; Nov to Mar warm, rainy season but nights can be cold
BANKING 0900–1430 Mon, Tue, Thu and Fri; 0815–1200 Wed; 0815–1045 Sat
EMERGENCY Police 351161
TIME ZONE GMT +2
INTERNATIONAL DIALLING CODE 267

BRAZIL

GOVERNMENT Federal republic
LANGUAGES Portuguese (official)
CURRENCY Real = 100 centavos
MEDICAL Visitors should take precautions against AIDS, malaria, meningitis and yellow fever
TRAVEL High crime rate in major cities of Rio de Janeiro and São Paulo. Dress down and avoid wearing jewellery
WEATHER Jun to Sep pleasant in south-east; Dec to Mar hot and humid with high rainfall
BANKING 1000–1630 Mon to Fri
EMERGENCY All Services 0
TIME ZONE Eastern GMT –3; North East and East Pará –3; Western –4; Amapa and West Para –4; Acre State –5; Fernando de Noronha Archipelago –2
INTERNATIONAL DIALLING CODE 55

BULGARIA

GOVERNMENT Multiparty republic
LANGUAGES Bulgarian (official), Turkish
CURRENCY Lev = 100 stotinki
MEDICAL There are no specific health risks
TRAVEL Most visits to Bulgaria are trouble-free, but there is a risk of robbery. Pickpockets operate in downtown Sofia and in the Black Sea resorts. Car theft is commonplace
WEATHER May to Sep warm with some rainfall; Nov to Mar cold with snow; rain falls frequently during spring and autumn
BANKING 0800–1130 and 1400–1800 Mon to Fri; 0830–1130 Sat
EMERGENCY Police 166; Fire 160; Ambulance 150
TIME ZONE GMT +2
INTERNATIONAL DIALLING CODE 359

BURMA (= MYANMAR)

GOVERNMENT Military regime
LANGUAGES Burmese (official); minority ethnic groups have their own languages
CURRENCY Kyat = 100 pyas
MEDICAL Visitors should protect against cholera, dysentery, hepatitis, malaria, rabies and typhoid
TRAVEL Politically unsettled. Visitors should avoid large crowds and should not visit Aung San Suu Kyi without prior arrangement. Terrorist attacks have been reported in some areas
WEATHER Monsoon climate; Feb to May hot with very little rain; May to Oct wet; Nov to Feb cooler and drier
BANKING 1000–1400 Mon to Fri
EMERGENCY Unavailable
TIME ZONE GMT +6.30
INTERNATIONAL DIALLING CODE 95

CAMBODIA

GOVERNMENT Constitutional monarchy
LANGUAGES Khmer (official), French, English
CURRENCY Riel = 100 sen
MEDICAL Visitors should protect against cholera, hepatitis, malaria, typhoid and rabies
TRAVEL Visitors should seek advice before travelling. The greatest risks are from traffic accidents and armed robbery after dark. Land mines exist in certain rural areas
WEATHER Tropical monsoon climate; May to Oct monsoon; Dec to Jan lower humidity and little rainfall; Feb to Apr hot; temperatures are constant throughout the country
BANKING 0800–1500 Mon to Fri
EMERGENCY Unavailable
TIME ZONE GMT +7
INTERNATIONAL DIALLING CODE 855

CANADA

GOVERNMENT Federal multiparty constitutional monarchy
LANGUAGES English and French (both official)
CURRENCY Canadian dollar = 100 cents
MEDICAL Medical treatment is expensive and it is essential that visitors have travel insurance. Blackfly and mosquitoes can cause problems in areas near water
TRAVEL Most visits to Canada are trouble-free
WEATHER Varies considerably; Jul to Aug tend to be warm all round the country; Nov to Mar very cold everywhere except west coast
BANKING 1000–1500 Mon to Fri
EMERGENCY Emergency Services 911 or 0
TIME ZONE Six zones exist from GMT −3.30 in Newfoundland to −8 on the Pacific coast
INTERNATIONAL DIALLING CODE 1

CANARY ISLANDS

GOVERNMENT Spanish autonomous region
LANGUAGES Spanish
CURRENCY Euro = 100 cents
MEDICAL The Canary Islands are part of Spain and there are no specific health risks
TRAVEL The islands are volcanic and the landscape is varied. Many resorts suffer the effects of mass tourism, but beyond these areas there are stunning, peaceful regions to be enjoyed
WEATHER Subtropical climate; generally hot and sunny all year round, but Dec to Feb slightly cooler than rest of year
BANKING Visitors should enquire at hotel
EMERGENCY Unavailable
TIME ZONE GMT
INTERNATIONAL DIALLING CODE 34

CAPE VERDE

GOVERNMENT Multiparty republic
LANGUAGES Portuguese, Creole
CURRENCY Cape Verde escudo = 100 centavos
MEDICAL Water is untreated and unsafe to drink. Avoid dairy products as they are unpasteurized. Polio and typhoid vaccinations are recommended; there is a risk of cholera and malaria
TRAVEL Most visits to Cape Verde are trouble-free. Visitors should avoid carrying valuables in public and remain vigilant at all times
WEATHER Warm and temperate climate with a dry summer. The islands suffer periodically from drought
BANKING 0800–1400 Mon to Fri
EMERGENCY All services 87
TIME ZONE GMT −1
INTERNATIONAL DIALLING CODE 238

CAYMAN ISLANDS

GOVERNMENT British crown colony
LANGUAGES English (local dialects also spoken)
CURRENCY Cayman Islands dollar = 100 cents
MEDICAL There is a risk of sunburn and poisonous plants are present
TRAVEL Most visits to the Cayman Islands are trouble-free. Car hire is a good way to move around the islands
WEATHER Warm tropical climate all year round; May to Oct wet season with usually brief showers
BANKING 0900–1600 Mon to Thu; 0900–1630 Fri
EMERGENCY Police 911; Ambulance 555; All Services 911
TIME ZONE GMT −5
INTERNATIONAL DIALLING CODE 1 345

CHAD

GOVERNMENT Multiparty republic
LANGUAGES French and Arabic (both official)
CURRENCY CFA franc = 100 centimes
MEDICAL Visitors should be vaccinated against yellow fever, tetanus, cholera and hepatitis A
TRAVEL Visitors to Chad should remain vigilant at all times especially in the south-west region along the border with Cameroon. Areas to avoid include the Aozou Strip and the Tibesti area on the border with Libya, where minefields exist
WEATHER Hot tropical climate; Mar to May very hot; May to Oct wet in south; Jun to Sep wet in central areas; little rain in northern regions
BANKING 0900–1400 Mon to Fri
EMERGENCY Unavailable
TIME ZONE GMT +1
INTERNATIONAL DIALLING CODE 235

CHILE

GOVERNMENT Multiparty republic
LANGUAGES Spanish (official)
CURRENCY Chilean peso = 100 centavos
MEDICAL Visitors should protect themselves against cholera
TRAVEL Most visits are trouble-free, but visitors are advised to keep in groups and avoid walking alone, particularly after dark. Pickpockets and muggers are active in cities. Passport photocopies should be carried at all times
WEATHER Variable climate; Sep to Nov and Feb to Apr pleasant temperatures; Dec to Mar hotter; skiing is popular from Jun to Aug
BANKING 0900–1400 Mon to Fri
EMERGENCY Police 133; Fire 132
TIME ZONE GMT –4; Easter Island –6
INTERNATIONAL DIALLING CODE 56

CHINA

GOVERNMENT Single-party Communist republic
LANGUAGES Mandarin Chinese (official)
CURRENCY Renminbi yuan = 10 jiao = 100 fen
MEDICAL Rabies is widespread. A virulent strain of viral pneumonia has emerged in the south-east and malaria is common in southern areas
TRAVEL Violent crimes are rare. Crime occurs in cities, and extra care should be taken around street markets and popular bar areas at night
WEATHER Climate varies; Apr to Sep humid and hot; Jan to Mar very cold; rainfall high in central areas; Jul to Sep typhoon season in the south
BANKING 0930–1200 and 1400–1700 Mon to Fri; 0900–1700 Sat
EMERGENCY Police 110; Fire 119
TIME ZONE GMT +8
INTERNATIONAL DIALLING CODE 86

COLOMBIA

GOVERNMENT Multiparty republic
LANGUAGES Spanish (official)
CURRENCY Colombian peso = 100 centavos
MEDICAL Visitors should protect against altitude sickness, cholera, hepatitis A, B and D, and malaria
TRAVEL Guerrilla and criminal attacks close to Bogota are increasing. Violence and kidnapping are serious problems in Colombia. The border area with Panama and the Uraba region of Antioquia are particularly dangerous
WEATHER Hot and humid; May to Nov rainy season; cooler in upland areas
BANKING 0900–1500 Mon to Fri
EMERGENCY All Services 112 (01 in smaller towns and rural areas)
TIME ZONE GMT –5
INTERNATIONAL DIALLING CODE 57

COMOROS

GOVERNMENT Multiparty republic
LANGUAGES Arabic and French (both official)
CURRENCY CFA franc = 100 centimes
MEDICAL Strict food hygiene precautions are essential. Cholera and malaria are prevalant and medical facilities are basic and limited
TRAVEL Generally crime-free, but be aware of pickpockets. Visitors should not walk around town centres unaccompanied at night
WEATHER Tropical climate with average temperatures of 25°C [77°F]. Cyclone risk between Jan and Apr
BANKING 0730–1300 Mon to Thu; 0730–1100 Fri
EMERGENCY Unavailable
TIME ZONE GMT +3
INTERNATIONAL DIALLING CODE 269

COSTA RICA

GOVERNMENT Multiparty republic
LANGUAGES Spanish (official), English
CURRENCY Costa Rican colón = 100 céntimos
MEDICAL Cases of dengue fever have been confirmed. Visitors should protect themselves against malaria, cholera and hepatitis
TRAVEL Daylight muggings can occur. Do not wear jewellery or carry large amounts of cash. Riptides are very common on all beaches
WEATHER Coastal areas warmer than inland low-lying regions; Dec to Apr warm and dry; May to Nov rainy season; landslides can occur
BANKING 0900–1500 Mon to Fri
EMERGENCY Police 104; Fire 103; Ambulance 225/1436 and 228/2187
TIME ZONE GMT –7
INTERNATIONAL DIALLING CODE 506

CROATIA

GOVERNMENT Multiparty republic
LANGUAGES Croatian
CURRENCY Kuna = 100 lipas
MEDICAL No specific health risks, although the health system is severely stretched at present
TRAVEL Exercise caution in the areas bordering Bosnia-Herzegovina and Serbia and Montenegro. There continue to be incidents of violence and many unexploded land mines remain undetected. It is inadvisable to use the Debelli Brijeg crossing-points into Montenegro
WEATHER Continental climate in the north and Mediterranean on the Adriatic Coast
BANKING 0700–1500 Mon to Fri
EMERGENCY Police 92; Fire 93; Ambulance 94
TIME ZONE GMT +1
INTERNATIONAL DIALLING CODE 385

CUBA

GOVERNMENT Socialist republic
LANGUAGES Spanish (official)
CURRENCY Cuban peso = 100 centavos
MEDICAL Tap water is unsafe to drink, with a risk of contracting hepatitis A
TRAVEL Street theft occurs, especially in Old Havana and major tourist sites. Do not carry large amounts of cash or jewellery. Do not travel with anyone other than your recognized tour operator. Avoid military zones
WEATHER May to Oct hot rainy season; Aug to Nov hurricane season; Dec to Apr cooler
BANKING 0830–1200 and 1330–1500 Mon to Fri; 0830–1030 Sat
EMERGENCY All Services 26811
TIME ZONE GMT –4
INTERNATIONAL DIALLING CODE 53

CYPRUS

GOVERNMENT Multiparty republic
LANGUAGES Greek and Turkish (both official)
CURRENCY Cypriot pound = 100 cents
MEDICAL There are no specific health risks, but visitors should be protected against hepatitis
TRAVEL Travel is generally trouble-free, but attempts to pass overland from the northern Turkish sector into the southern Greek region are not recommended
WEATHER Apr to May and Sep to Oct cool and pleasant; Jun to Aug hot and dry; Nov to Mar rainfall is heavier, but temperatures remain warm
BANKING 0815–1230 in tourist areas; 1530–1730 in winter; 1630–1830 in summer
EMERGENCY All Services 199
TIME ZONE GMT +2
INTERNATIONAL DIALLING CODE 357

CZECH REPUBLIC

GOVERNMENT Multiparty republic
LANGUAGES Czech (official)
CURRENCY Czech koruna = 100 haler
MEDICAL Visitors to forested areas should seek advice about immunization against tick-borne encephalitis and lyme disease
TRAVEL Most visits are trouble-free, but petty theft is a growing problem, particularly in Prague. Pickpocketing is very common at tourist attractions
WEATHER May to Sep mild; Apr and Oct much cooler
BANKING 0800–1800 Mon to Fri
EMERGENCY Police 158; Fire 150; Ambulance 155
TIME ZONE GMT +1
INTERNATIONAL DIALLING CODE 42

DENMARK

GOVERNMENT Parliamentary monarchy
LANGUAGES Danish (official), English
CURRENCY Danish krone = 100 øre
MEDICAL There are no specific health risks in Denmark
TRAVEL Visits to Denmark are generally trouble-free. Visitors will enjoy relatively low prices compared to other European countries
WEATHER Jun to Aug warm summer season; Oct to Mar cold and wet with chance of frost; spring and autumn are usually mild and pleasant
BANKING 0930–1700 Mon, Tue, Wed and Fri; 0930–1800 Thu. Some foreign exchange bureaux remain open until midnight
EMERGENCY Emergency Services 112
TIME ZONE GMT +1
INTERNATIONAL DIALLING CODE 45

DOMINICA

GOVERNMENT Parliamentary democracy
LANGUAGES English (official), Creole, French
CURRENCY East Caribbean dollar = 100 cents
MEDICAL Dengue fever is prevalent and visitors should guard against mosquito bites
TRAVEL Most visits are trouble-free. Visitors are advised to take sensible precautions and be vigilant at all times
WEATHER Tropical climate with heavy rainfall, particularly in Jun to Oct, which is also the hottest period. Tropical storms and hurricanes can occur between Jun and Nov
BANKING 0800–1500 Mon to Thu; 0800–1700 Fri
EMERGENCY All services 999
TIME ZONE GMT –4
INTERNATIONAL DIALLING CODE 1 767

DOMINICAN REPUBLIC

GOVERNMENT Multiparty republic
LANGUAGES Spanish (official)
CURRENCY Dominican peso = 100 centavos
MEDICAL Tourists should protect against polio and typhoid. There are occasional outbreaks of malaria and dengue fever; anti-mosquito skin repellants are recommended
TRAVEL Border areas should be avoided while the political unrest in neighbouring Haiti continues. Avoid any excursions that are not recommended by tour operators
WEATHER Hot tropical climate; Jun to Nov rainy season with the risk of hurricanes
BANKING 0800–1600 Mon to Fri
EMERGENCY Emergency Services 711
TIME ZONE GMT –4
INTERNATIONAL DIALLING CODE 1 809

ECUADOR

GOVERNMENT Multiparty republic
LANGUAGES Spanish (official), Quechua
CURRENCY US dollar = 100 cents
MEDICAL There is a risk of dengue fever,
hepatitis, malaria, typhoid, diptheria and rabies
TRAVEL Street crimes such as muggings and
pickpocketing are common in the cities. Visitors
should avoid travel to the provinces bordering
Colombia due to incidents of kidnapping
WEATHER Jan to Apr warm and rainy on
mainland and Galapagos; Jun to Aug cold; Jun to
Aug dry in Highlands; Aug to Feb dry in Oriente
BANKING 0900–1330 and 1430–1830 Mon
to Fri
EMERGENCY Police 101; Ambulance 131
TIME ZONE GMT –5; Galapagos Islands –6
INTERNATIONAL DIALLING CODE 593

EGYPT

GOVERNMENT Republic
LANGUAGES Arabic (official), French, English
CURRENCY Egyptian pound = 100 piastres
MEDICAL There are no specific health risks
in Egypt
TRAVEL Due to continuing tensions, visitors
should keep in touch with developments in the
Middle East and remain vigilant at all times.
Particular care should be taken when travelling
in Luxor and beyond in the Nile Valley
WEATHER Jun to Aug very hot and dry; Sep to
May dry and cooler; spring and autumn months
are pleasant; dusty Saharan winds during Apr
BANKING 0830–1400 Sun to Thu
EMERGENCY Unavailable
TIME ZONE GMT +2
INTERNATIONAL DIALLING CODE 20

EL SALVADOR

GOVERNMENT Republic
LANGUAGES Spanish (official)
CURRENCY US dollar = 100 cents
MEDICAL Tourists should protect against
cholera, hepatitis, malaria, rabies and typhoid
TRAVEL El Salvador is more politically stable
than ever, but has high levels of violent crime.
Visitors travelling alone should be vigilant at
all times
WEATHER Hot subtropical climate; Nov to Apr
dry season; May to Oct rainy season with cooler
evenings
BANKING 0900–1300 and 1345–1600 Mon
to Fri
EMERGENCY All Services 123/121
TIME ZONE GMT –6
INTERNATIONAL DIALLING CODE 503

ESTONIA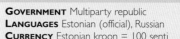

GOVERNMENT Multiparty republic
LANGUAGES Estonian (official), Russian
CURRENCY Estonian kroon = 100 senti
MEDICAL There are no specific health risks
TRAVEL Most visits are trouble-free. Despite
independence in 1991, much tradition exists in
Estonia. Skiing, skating and ice fishing are popular
during the winter months
WEATHER Large temperature variations;
Apr to May warm and pleasant; Jun to Sep hot.;
Dec to Mar very cold with heavy snowfall; rain
falls all year round
BANKING 0930–1630 Mon to Fri
EMERGENCY Police 02; Fire 01; Ambulance 03
(dial an extra 0 first if in Tallinn)
TIME ZONE GMT +2
INTERNATIONAL DIALLING CODE 372

ETHIOPIA

GOVERNMENT Federation of nine provinces
LANGUAGES Amharic (official), many others
CURRENCY Birr = 100 cents
MEDICAL Water-borne diseases and malaria
are prevalent. Medical facilities outside the capital
are extremely poor
TRAVEL Most governments advise against travel
to the Gambella region and the Eritrean border.
There is currently a high risk of terrorism
throughout the country
WEATHER Lowlands are hot and humid, it is
warm in the hills and cool in the upland areas
BANKING 0800–1200 and 1300–1700 Mon to
Thu; 0830–1100 and 1300–1700 Fri
EMERGENCY Not available
TIME ZONE GMT +3
INTERNATIONAL DIALLING CODE 251

FIJI ISLANDS

GOVERNMENT Transitional
LANGUAGES English (official), various Fijian
dialects
CURRENCY Fijian dollar = 100 cents
MEDICAL Visitors should protect against dengue
fever and should avoid mosquito bites
TRAVEL There has been an increase in petty
crime due to the unsettled economic and
political situations
WEATHER Tropical climate; Dec to Apr humid,
rainy season with a risk of tropical cyclones;
May to Oct cooler, dry season
BANKING 0930–1500 Mon to Thu;
0930–1600 Fri
EMERGENCY All Services 000
TIME ZONE GMT +12
INTERNATIONAL DIALLING CODE 679

FINLAND

GOVERNMENT Multiparty republic
LANGUAGES Finnish and Swedish (both official)
CURRENCY Euro = 100 cents
MEDICAL There are no specific health risks, but if mushroom-picking/eating, seek advice on safety
TRAVEL Visits to Finland are generally trouble-free
WEATHER Temperate climate; May to Sep warm with midnight sun; Oct to Mar very cold; Nov to May snow cover in the north; skiing starts in Feb, the coldest month, and continues until Jun in Lapland
BANKING 0915–1615 Mon to Fri
EMERGENCY Police 002; Fire/Ambulance 000; Emergency Services 112; Doctor 008
TIME ZONE GMT +2
INTERNATIONAL DIALLING CODE 358

FRANCE

GOVERNMENT Multiparty republic
LANGUAGES French (official)
CURRENCY Euro = 100 cents
MEDICAL There are no specific health risks
TRAVEL Most visits to France are trouble-free. There have been sporadic bomb attacks on the island of Corsica and care should be exercised
WEATHER Temperate climate in the north; rain falls all year round; Mediterranean climate in the south; mild in the west; May to Sep hot and sunny; Oct to Nov pleasant temperatures
BANKING 0900–1200 and 1400–1600 Mon to Fri. Some banks close on Mondays
EMERGENCY Police 17; Fire 18; Ambulance 15; Emergency Services 112
TIME ZONE GMT +1
INTERNATIONAL DIALLING CODE 33

FRENCH POLYNESIA

GOVERNMENT French overseas territory
LANGUAGES French and Polynesian (both official)
CURRENCY French Pacific franc = 100 cents
MEDICAL Water is untreated and dairy foods are unpasteurized. Vaccinations against polio and typhoid are recommended
TRAVEL Most visits are trouble-free, but visitors should remain vigilant at al times. French Polynesia is made up of 130 islands, Tahiti being the most popular
WEATHER Tropical but moderate climate with occasional cyclonic storms in Jan. Cool and dry Mar to Nov
BANKING 0745–1530 Mon to Fri
EMERGENCY Dial operator
TIME ZONE GMT –9 to GMT –10
INTERNATIONAL DIALLING CODE 689

GAMBIA, THE

GOVERNMENT Military regime
LANGUAGES English (official), Mandinka, Wolof
CURRENCY Dalasi = 100 butut
MEDICAL Water-borne diseases and malaria are common. Other health risks include yellow fever, hepatitis, rabies and typhoid
TRAVEL Exercise caution when walking at night. Do not travel with valuables and dress modestly
WEATHER Nov to Mar dry and cool with winds from the Sahara; Jun to Oct rainy season; inland the cool season is shorter and temperatures are hot from Mar to Jun
BANKING 0800–1330 Mon to Thu; 0800–1100 Fri
EMERGENCY Consult foreign embassy
TIME ZONE GMT
INTERNATIONAL DIALLING CODE 220

GEORGIA

GOVERNMENT Multiparty republic
LANGUAGES Georgian (official), Russian
CURRENCY Lari = 100 tetri
MEDICAL Diptheria and rabies cases have been reported. Tap water is unsafe to drink. Anthrax has been reported in the east. Medical care is poor and visitors should carry their own syringes
TRAVEL The regions of Abkhazia and South Ossetia should be avoided. Do not attempt access across the land borders with Russia
WEATHER Jul to Sep hot; Dec to Mar mild, especially in the south-west; low temperatures in alpine areas; rainfall heavy in south-west
BANKING 0930–1730 Mon to Fri
EMERGENCY Police 02; Fire 01; Ambulance 03
TIME ZONE GMT +4
INTERNATIONAL DIALLING CODE 995

GERMANY

GOVERNMENT Federal multiparty republic
LANGUAGES German (official)
CURRENCY Euro = 100 cents
MEDICAL There are no specific health risks, but medical care is expensive
TRAVEL Visits to Germany are generally trouble-free. Travellers are able to enjoy a wealth of arts and culture, plus stunning natural scenery
WEATHER Very variable, temperate climate throughout the country; May to Oct warm; Nov to Apr cold; rain falls all year round
BANKING 0830–1300 and 1400/30–1600 Mon to Fri
EMERGENCY Police 110; Fire 112; Emergency Services 112
TIME ZONE GMT +1
INTERNATIONAL DIALLING CODE 49

GIBRALTAR

GOVERNMENT UK overseas territory
LANGUAGES English and Spanish
CURRENCY Gibraltar pound = 100 pence
MEDICAL There are no specific health risks in Gibraltar
TRAVEL Most visits to Gibraltar are trouble-free. The country was recognized as a British possession in 1713, and despite Spanish claims, its population has consistently voted to retain its contacts with Britain
WEATHER Warm all year round; Jun to Sep hot and can be humid; Nov to Mar mild
BANKING 0900–1530 and 1630–1800 Mon to Fri
EMERGENCY All Services 999
TIME ZONE GMT +1
INTERNATIONAL DIALLING CODE 350

GREECE

GOVERNMENT Multiparty republic
LANGUAGES Greek (official)
CURRENCY Euro = 100 cents
MEDICAL There is a risk of sunburn
TRAVEL Visitors should exercise normal precautions regarding safety and security. Tourists are strongly advised not to hire motorcycles, scooters or mopeds
WEATHER Mediterranean climate; Aug to Nov pleasant temperatures; Nov to Mar heavy rainfall; Apr to Jun hot
BANKING 0800–1400 Mon to Fri
EMERGENCY Police 100; Fire 199; Ambulance 166; Emergency Services 112
TIME ZONE GMT +2
INTERNATIONAL DIALLING CODE 30 + 1 for Athens; 31 Thessaloniki; 81 Heraklion; 661 Corfu

GRENADA

GOVERNMENT Constitutional monarchy
LANGUAGES English (official)
CURRENCY East Caribbean dollar = 100 cents
MEDICAL Tourists should protect against polio and typhoid. Anti-mosquito repellants are recommended
TRAVEL Trips are mostly trouble-free; however, tourists should remain vigilant at all times
WEATHER Tropical climate, rainy season is Jun to Sep when tropical storms and hurricanes occur. Jan to May is drier and less humid
BANKING 0800–1400 Mon to Thu; 0800–1300 and 1400–1700 Fri
EMERGENCY Police 112; Ambulance 434; Emergency services 911
TIME ZONE GMT –4
INTERNATIONAL DIALLING CODE 1 473

GUADELOUPE

GOVERNMENT French overseas territory
LANGUAGES French (official), Creole
CURRENCY Euro = 100 cents
MEDICAL Polio and typhoid vaccinations are recommended. Water is untreated and unsafe to drink
TRAVEL Visits to Guadeloupe are generally trouble-free, and the French culture and influence is clearly evident. Soufriere de Guadeloupe is an active volcano
WEATHER Warm, humid weather all year round. Rainy season from Jun to Oct, when there is a risk of hurricanes
BANKING 0800–1600 Mon to Fri
EMERGENCY Police 17; Fire and Ambulance 18
TIME ZONE GMT –4
INTERNATIONAL DIALLING CODE 590

HONG KONG

GOVERNMENT Special administrative region of China
LANGUAGES Chinese and English; Cantonese is most widely spoken
CURRENCY Hong Kong dollar = 100 cents
MEDICAL Visitors should protect against polio and typhoid. Slight risk of malaria in rural areas
TRAVEL Most visits are trouble-free
WEATHER Nov to Dec warm with pleasant breeze; Jan to Feb much cooler; Mar to Apr warmer; May to Sep very humid and uncomfortable, with a risk of cyclones in Sep
BANKING 0900–1630 Mon to Fri; 0900–1330 Sat
EMERGENCY All Services 999
TIME ZONE GMT +8
INTERNATIONAL DIALLING CODE 852

HUNGARY

GOVERNMENT Multiparty republic
LANGUAGES Hungarian (official)
CURRENCY Forint = 100 fillér
MEDICAL There are no specific health risks in Hungary
TRAVEL Street theft is common in tourist areas, particularly in Budapest. It is illegal to drive having consumed alcohol. Passports to be carried at all times. Do not take photographs of anything connected with the military
WEATHER Jun to Aug very warm and sunny; spring and autumn mild and pleasant; Jan to Mar very cold
BANKING 0900–1400 Mon to Fri
EMERGENCY Police 107; Fire/Ambulance 104
TIME ZONE GMT +1
INTERNATIONAL DIALLING CODE 36

ICELAND

GOVERNMENT Multiparty republic
LANGUAGES Icelandic (official)
CURRENCY Icelandic króna = 100 aurar
MEDICAL There is a risk of hypothermia if trekking during the winter months
TRAVEL Visitors planning to travel off-road do so at their own risk and must contact the local authorities (Vegagerdin) prior to departure. Interior roads are closed in winter
WEATHER Weather is highly changeable all year round; May to Aug is mild with nearly 24 hours of daylight in Reykjavik; Sep to Apr is cold
BANKING 0915–1600 Mon to Fri
EMERGENCY Unavailable
TIME ZONE GMT
INTERNATIONAL DIALLING CODE 354

INDIA

GOVERNMENT Multiparty federal republic
LANGUAGES Hindi, English, Telugu, Bengali, Marathi, Tamil, Urdu, Gujarati, Malayalam, Kannada, Oriya, Punjabi, Assamese, Kashmiri, Sindhi and Sanskrit (all official)
CURRENCY Indian rupee = 100 paisa
MEDICAL There is a risk of malaria, AIDS and intestinal problems. Precautions should be taken
TRAVEL Visitors are advised to avoid the Pakistan border areas, as well as Jammu and Kashmir
WEATHER Hot tropical climate that varies from region to region; Apr to Sep very hot with monsoon rains
BANKING 1000–1400 Mon to Fri
EMERGENCY Unavailable
TIME ZONE GMT +5.30
INTERNATIONAL DIALLING CODE 91

INDONESIA

GOVERNMENT Multiparty republic
LANGUAGES Bahasa Indonesian (official)
CURRENCY Indonesian rupiah = 100 sen
MEDICAL There is a risk of polio, typhoid, hepatitis B, yellow fever and TB. Unpasteurized dairy produce should be avoided
TRAVEL Non-essential travel to Indonesia is not recommended due to the risk of terrorism against Western interests
WEATHER Tropical, varying climate; May to Oct dry weather from eastern monsoon; Nov to Apr rains from western monsoon. In northern Sumatra this pattern is reversed
BANKING 0800–1500 Mon to Fri
EMERGENCY Police 110; Ambulance 118
TIME ZONE West GMT +7; Central +8; East +9
INTERNATIONAL DIALLING CODE 62

IRAN

GOVERNMENT Islamic republic
LANGUAGES Persian, Turkic, Kurdish
CURRENCY Iranian rial = 100 dinars
MEDICAL There is a risk of polio, typhoid, malaria and cholera
TRAVEL Visitors should monitor media reports before travelling. Any increase in regional tension will affect travel advice. Visitors should exercise caution and avoid carrying large sums of money since robbery and bag-snatching are common
WEATHER Dec to Mar very cold; Apr to Jun and Sep to Nov warm; Jun to Sep extremely hot
BANKING 0900–1600 Sat to Wed; 0900–1200 Thu. Closed on Fri
EMERGENCY Unavailable
TIME ZONE GMT +3.30
INTERNATIONAL DIALLING CODE 98

IRELAND

GOVERNMENT Multiparty republic
LANGUAGES Irish (Gaelic) and English (both official)
CURRENCY Euro = 100 cents
MEDICAL There are no specific health risks
TRAVEL The Irish usually have close community bonds. Visitors should find people very friendly. Strong economic growth continues
WEATHER Rain falls all year round; Jul to Sep warm; Nov to Mar wet and cold; spring and autumn mild
BANKING 1000–1600 Mon to Fri. Banks may open later in Dublin
EMERGENCY Emergency Services 112; All Services 999
TIME ZONE GMT
INTERNATIONAL DIALLING CODE 353

ISRAEL

GOVERNMENT Multiparty republic
LANGUAGES Hebrew and Arabic (both official)
CURRENCY New Israeli shekel = 100 agorot
MEDICAL There are no specific health risks
TRAVEL Most governments currently strongly advise against travel to the West Bank, Gaza and Jerusalem, or near their border areas with Israel. Visitors should keep car doors locked when travelling and avoid carrying large sums of cash
WEATHER Jul to Sep hot and windy; Dec to Mar cool in the north; spring and autumn are warm and pleasant
BANKING 0830–1230 and 1600–1730 Mon, Tue and Thu; 0830–1230 Wed; 0830–1200 Fri
EMERGENCY Police/Fire 100; Ambulance 101
TIME ZONE GMT +2
INTERNATIONAL DIALLING CODE 972

ITALY

GOVERNMENT Multiparty republic
LANGUAGES Italian (official), German, French, Slovene
CURRENCY Euro = 100 cents
MEDICAL There are no specific health risks
TRAVEL Crime is rare, but visitors in tourist areas and city centres should remain vigilant after dark
WEATHER Apr to May and Oct to Nov warm and pleasant; Jun to Sep hot; Dec to Mar colder temperatures with heavy snow in mountain areas; warmer in the south
BANKING Generally 0830–1330 and 1530–1930 Mon to Fri
EMERGENCY Police 112; Fire 115; Ambulance 113; Emergency Services 112
TIME ZONE GMT +1
INTERNATIONAL DIALLING CODE 39

JAMAICA

GOVERNMENT Constitutional monarchy
LANGUAGES English (official), patois English
CURRENCY Jamaican dollar = 100 cents
MEDICAL There are no specific health risks
TRAVEL Most visits are trouble-free, but violent crime does exist, mainly in Kingston. Visitors should avoid walking alone in isolated areas, and be particularly alert after dark and using public transport
WEATHER Tropical climate; temperatures remain high all year round; May to Oct rainy season, but showers can occur at any time
BANKING 0900–1400 Mon to Thu; 0900–1500 Fri
EMERGENCY Police 119; Fire/Ambulance 110
TIME ZONE GMT –5
INTERNATIONAL DIALLING CODE 1 876

JAPAN

GOVERNMENT Constitutional monarchy
LANGUAGES Japanese (official)
CURRENCY Yen = 100 sen
MEDICAL Health and hygiene standards are high and visitors are not required to have vaccinations
TRAVEL Most visits remain trouble-free. There is a high risk of earthquakes and typhoons which often hit the country
WEATHER Sep to Nov typhoons and rain; Jun to Sep warm/very hot with rain in Jun; Mar to May pleasant; Dec to Feb cold winds and snow in western areas, but dry and clear on Pacific coast
BANKING 0900–1500 Mon to Fri
EMERGENCY Tokyo English Life Line 3403 7106; Japan Helpline 0120 461 997
TIME ZONE GMT +9
INTERNATIONAL DIALLING CODE 81

JORDAN

GOVERNMENT Constitutional monarchy
LANGUAGES Arabic (official)
CURRENCY Jordan dinar = 1,000 fils
MEDICAL There are no specific health risks, but visitors should consider vaccination against hepatitis, polio, tetanus, typhoid and diptheria
TRAVEL Before travelling, visitors should monitor media reports for any increase in regional tension. Crime is low, but visitors should dress modestly and respect local customs
WEATHER Jun to Sep hot and dry with cool evenings; Nov to Mar cooler with rainfall
BANKING 0830–1230 and 1530–1730 Sat to Thu; 0830–1000 during Ramadan
EMERGENCY Police 192; Fire/Ambulance 193
TIME ZONE GMT +2
INTERNATIONAL DIALLING CODE 962

KENYA

GOVERNMENT Multiparty republic
LANGUAGES Kiswahili and English (both official)
CURRENCY Kenyan shilling = 100 cents
MEDICAL Malaria is endemic and AIDS is widespread. Water is unsafe to drink
TRAVEL Be alert at all times, particularly in Nairobi and Mombasa. Avoid travelling after dark and in isolated areas
WEATHER Complex and changeable; Jan to Feb hot and dry; Mar to May hot and wet; Jun to Oct warm and dry; Nov to Dec warm and wet; Cooler with rain at any time at higher altitudes
BANKING 0900–1500 Mon to Fri; 0900–1100 on first and last Sat of each month
EMERGENCY All Services 336886/501280
TIME ZONE GMT +3
INTERNATIONAL DIALLING CODE 254

KOREA, SOUTH

GOVERNMENT Multiparty republic
LANGUAGES Korean (official)
CURRENCY South Korean won = 100 chon
MEDICAL There are no specific health risks, but medical and dental treatment can be expensive
TRAVEL Travel to South Korea is generally trouble-free, but some form of identification should be carried at all times
WEATHER Jul to Aug hot with heavy rainfall and a chance of typhoons; Sep to Nov and Apr to May mild and dry; Dec to Mar cold but dry, with good skiing
BANKING 0930–1630 Mon to Fri; 0930–1330 Sat
EMERGENCY Unavailable
TIME ZONE GMT +9
INTERNATIONAL DIALLING CODE 82

KUWAIT

GOVERNMENT Constitutional monarchy
LANGUAGES Arabic (official), English
CURRENCY Kuwaiti dinar = 1,000 fils
MEDICAL Vaccinations against polio, typhoid and cholera are recommended
TRAVEL Visitors should monitor media reports before travelling. Any increase in regional tension will affect travel advice. There is a danger from unexploded bombs and land mines on beaches and in rural areas. All Islamic laws should be respected. Photography permits are required
WEATHER Apr to Oct hot, humid with little rain; Nov to Mar cool and dry
BANKING 0800–1200 Sun to Thu
EMERGENCY Unavailable
TIME ZONE GMT +3
INTERNATIONAL DIALLING CODE 965

LATVIA

GOVERNMENT Multiparty republic
LANGUAGES Latvian (official), Lithuanian, Russian
CURRENCY Latvian lat = 10 santimi
MEDICAL Visitors should protect themselves against tick-borne encephalitis, particularly if visiting forested areas
TRAVEL Most visits are trouble-free, but tourists should exercise caution since muggings and pickpocketing have increased recently. Use guarded car parks and keep valuables hidden
WEATHER Temperate climate; Apr to Sep warm and clear; Nov to Mar extremely cold; spring and autumn mild
BANKING 1000–1800 Mon to Fri
EMERGENCY Police 02; Fire 01; Ambulance 03
TIME ZONE GMT +2
INTERNATIONAL DIALLING CODE 371

LEBANON

GOVERNMENT Multiparty republic
LANGUAGES Arabic (official), French, English
CURRENCY Lebanese pound = 100 piastres
MEDICAL Protection against polio and typhoid is recommended
TRAVEL Visitors should remain alert to international developments in the Middle East. Most governments currently advise against travel to areas within the Israeli Occupied Zone
WEATHER Jun to Sep hot and dry, but humid along the coast; Dec to May high rainfall with snow in mountains; spring and autumn pleasant
BANKING 0830–1200 Mon to Sat
EMERGENCY Police 386 440 425; Fire 310 105; Ambulance 386 675
TIME ZONE GMT +2
INTERNATIONAL DIALLING CODE 961

LIBYA

GOVERNMENT Single-party socialist state
LANGUAGES Arabic (official), Berber
CURRENCY Libyan dinar = 1,000 dirhams
MEDICAL There is a slight risk of malaria, cholera and hepatitis
TRAVEL Most visits to Libya are trouble-free, but any increase in regional tension will affect travel advice
WEATHER Warm all year round; Nov to Mar occasional rainfall; Apr to Sep can be very hot; May to Jun severe sandstorms from the south
BANKING 0800–1200 Sat to Wed (during winter); 0800–1200 Sat to Thu; 1600–1700 Sat and Wed (during summer)
EMERGENCY Unavailable
TIME ZONE GMT +1
INTERNATIONAL DIALLING CODE 218

LIECHTENSTEIN

GOVERNMENT Hereditary constitutional monarchy
LANGUAGES German (official)
CURRENCY Swiss franc = 100 centimes
MEDICAL There is a risk of altitude sickness, sunburn and hypothermia in the Alps
TRAVEL Most visits to Liechtenstein are trouble-free. The country is culturally and economically extremely similar to Switzerland. Winter sports are very popular in the Alps from Nov to Apr
WEATHER Temperate climate; Nov to Apr cool or cold; Jun to Sep warm with high rainfall
BANKING 0800–1630 Mon to Fri
EMERGENCY Police 117; Ambulance 144
TIME ZONE GMT +1
INTERNATIONAL DIALLING CODE 41 75

LITHUANIA

GOVERNMENT Multiparty republic
LANGUAGES Lithuanian (official), Russian, Polish
CURRENCY Litas = 100 centai
MEDICAL Travellers to forested areas should seek advice about protection against rabies and tick-borne encephalitis
TRAVEL There is a risk of pickpocketing, mugging and bag-snatching, particularly on public transport. Be alert at all times and avoid quiet areas after dark
WEATHER Temperate climate; May to Sep warm; Oct to Nov mild; Nov to Mar can be very cold with snowfall common
BANKING 0900–1700 Mon to Fri
EMERGENCY Police 02; Fire 01; Ambulance 03
TIME ZONE GMT +2
INTERNATIONAL DIALLING CODE 370

LUXEMBOURG

GOVERNMENT Constitutional monarchy (Grand Duchy)
LANGUAGES Luxembourgish (official), French, German
CURRENCY Euro = 100 cents
MEDICAL There are no specific health risks
TRAVEL Most travel to Luxembourg is trouble-free. The country is prosperous with a very high quality of life. Visitors may find it expensive compared to other European countries
WEATHER May to Sep warm with rainfall; Oct to Apr cold with snow
BANKING Varies greatly but generally 0900–1200 and 1330–1630 Mon to Fri
EMERGENCY Police 113; Fire/Ambulance 112
TIME ZONE GMT +1
INTERNATIONAL DIALLING CODE 352

MADAGASCAR

GOVERNMENT Republic
LANGUAGES Malagasy and French (both official)
CURRENCY Malagasy franc = 100 centimes
MEDICAL There is a risk of polio, typhoid, bilharzia, cholera, rabies and hepatitis. Precautions should be taken. Water is unsafe to drink and unpasteurized dairy products should be avoided
TRAVEL Locals are very welcoming and have a relaxed attitude towards time. Local culture should be respected
WEATHER Generally hot and subtropical with varying temperatures. Inland is more temperate, and the south is dry and arid
BANKING 0800–1300 Mon to Fri
EMERGENCY Unavailable
TIME ZONE GMT +3
INTERNATIONAL DIALLING CODE 261

MALAWI

GOVERNMENT Multiparty republic
LANGUAGES Chichewa and English (both official)
CURRENCY Malawian kwacha = 100 tambala
MEDICAL AIDS and malaria are very common. Outbreaks of cholera do occur, particularly during the rainy season
TRAVEL Be alert at all times, particularly after dark. Avoid travel out of town at night since the condition of roads is poor. Cases of muggings and bag-snatching are increasing. Do not resist demands since attacks can be very violent
WEATHER Apr to Oct hot and dry; May to Jul cool and cold at night; Nov to Apr rainy season
BANKING 0800–1300 Mon to Fri
EMERGENCY Unavailable
TIME ZONE GMT +2
INTERNATIONAL DIALLING CODE 265

MALAYSIA

GOVERNMENT Federal constitutional monarchy
LANGUAGES Malay (official), Chinese, English
CURRENCY Ringgit (Malaysian dollar) = 100 cents
MEDICAL No vaccinations required, but visitors should be up-to-date with typhoid, tetanus and hepatitis B. Also check malarial status of region
TRAVEL The penalty for all drug offences is harsh. There has been a recent increase in street crime in Kuala Lumpur
WEATHER Nov to Feb heavy rains in eastern areas; Apr to May and Oct thunderstorms in western areas; showers can occur all year round
BANKING 1000–1500 Mon to Fri
EMERGENCY All Services 999
TIME ZONE GMT +8
INTERNATIONAL DIALLING CODE 60

MALDIVES

GOVERNMENT Republic
LANGUAGES Maldivian Dhivehi, English
CURRENCY Rufiyaa = 100 laari
MEDICAL There is a high risk of sunburn all year round
TRAVEL Travel to the Maldives is generally trouble-free, but visitors should be aware that there are very harsh penalties for drug offences. Visitors should respect the Islamic religion and act accordingly
WEATHER Hot, tropical climate; May to Oct warm, but humid and wet from the south-west monsoon; Nov to Apr hot and dry
EMERGENCY Police 119; Fire 118; Ambulance 102
TIME ZONE GMT +5
INTERNATIONAL DIALLING CODE 960

MALTA

GOVERNMENT Multiparty republic
LANGUAGES Maltese and English (both official)
CURRENCY Maltese lira = 100 cents
MEDICAL There are no specific health risks
TRAVEL Most visits are trouble-free and crime is rare. However, bag-snatching and pickpocketing can occur. Caution should be exercised when travelling by car since many roads are poorly maintained. Visitors should dress modestly when visiting churches
WEATHER Jul to Sep hot with cool breezes; Feb to Jun mild; occasional sudden bursts of rain
BANKING 0800–1200 Mon to Thu; 0800–1200 and 1430–1600 Fri; 0800–1130 Sat
EMERGENCY Police 191; Ambulance 196
TIME ZONE GMT +1
INTERNATIONAL DIALLING CODE 356

MARTINIQUE

GOVERNMENT Overseas department of France
LANGUAGES French, French Creole patois, English
CURRENCY Euro = 100 cents
MEDICAL There is a risk of sunburn and intestinal parasites. Bilharzia (schistosomiasis) may be present in fresh water
TRAVEL Travel to Martinique is generally trouble-free
WEATHER Warm all year round; Sep can be very humid; Feb to May cooler and dry; Oct to Dec higher rainfall; upland areas are cooler than lowlands
BANKING 0800–1600 Mon to Fri
EMERGENCY Police 17; Fire/Ambulance 18
TIME ZONE GMT –4
INTERNATIONAL DIALLING CODE 596

MAURITIUS

GOVERNMENT Multiparty democracy
LANGUAGES French (official), Creole, English
CURRENCY Mauritian rupee = 100 cents
MEDICAL Malaria exists in the northern rural areas and there is a risk of bilharzia
TRAVEL Visitors should always respect local customs and traditions. Most visits are trouble-free, crime levels are low, but sensible precautions should be taken
WEATHER The weather is warm with a year-round sea breeze. Jan to May are the best months to visit. Tropical storms are likely to occur from Dec to Mar
BANKING 0930–1430 Mon to Fri; 0930–1130 Sat
EMERGENCY Unavailable
TIME ZONE GMT +4
INTERNATIONAL DIALLING CODE 230

MEXICO

GOVERNMENT Federal republic
LANGUAGES Spanish (official)
CURRENCY Mexican peso = 100 centavos
MEDICAL Visitors should protect themselves against polio, tetanus, typhoid and hepatitis A
TRAVEL Most visits are trouble-free, but visitors should remain aware of incidents of armed robbery in urban areas, particularly Mexico City, and should dress down accordingly
WEATHER May to Oct humid, rainy season; Oct to May warm and dry; lowland areas are warmer and upland areas are cooler all year round
BANKING 0900–1330 Mon to Fri
EMERGENCY All Services 08
TIME ZONE Spans three time zones from GMT –6 to –8
INTERNATIONAL DIALLING CODE 52

MONACO

GOVERNMENT Constitutional monarchy
LANGUAGES French, English, Italian, Monegasque
CURRENCY Euro = 100 cents
MEDICAL There are no specific health risks, but visitors should protect against hepatitis
TRAVEL Most visits to Monaco are trouble-free. This is the country where Europe's wealthiest are to be found living a rich, glamorous lifestyle
WEATHER Mild climate throughout the country; Jun to Aug can be very hot; Jan to Feb cool with low rainfall; Apr to May and Sep to Oct warm and dry
BANKING 0900–1200 and 1400–1630 Mon to Fri
EMERGENCY Police 17; Fire/Ambulance 18
TIME ZONE GMT +1
INTERNATIONAL DIALLING CODE 377

MONGOLIA

GOVERNMENT Multiparty republic
LANGUAGES Khalkha Mongolian (official), Turkic, Russian
CURRENCY Tugrik = 100 möngös
MEDICAL Visitors should protect against brucellosis, cholera and meningitis
TRAVEL Petty street crime is increasing. Visitors should avoid travelling alone after dark. In rural areas always carry a GPS and satellite phone
WEATHER May to Oct dry and mild; Nov to Apr bitterly cold. Note that between Oct and May sudden snowstorms can block roads and bring transport systems to a standstill
BANKING 1000–1500 Mon to Fri
EMERGENCY Unavailable
TIME ZONE GMT +9
INTERNATIONAL DIALLING CODE 976

MOROCCO

GOVERNMENT Constitutional monarchy
LANGUAGES Arabic (official), Berber, French
CURRENCY Moroccan dirham = 100 centimes
MEDICAL There are no specific health risks, but malaria is present in northern coastal areas
TRAVEL Visits are usually trouble-free, but visitors should only use authorized guides. Theft is increasing in major cities and valuables should be hidden at all times
WEATHER Winter cool and wet in north; Oct to Apr warm to hot in lowlands; Dec to Mar very cold in upland areas
BANKING 0830–1130 and 1430–1700 Mon to Fri (winter); 0800–1530 Mon to Fri (summer)
EMERGENCY Police 19; Fire/Ambulance 15
TIME ZONE GMT
INTERNATIONAL DIALLING CODE 212

NAMIBIA

GOVERNMENT Multiparty republic
LANGUAGES English (official), Afrikaans, German
CURRENCY Namibian dollar = 100 cents
MEDICAL Malaria and bilharzia are endemic in the north and east respectively
TRAVEL Most visits are trouble-free. The Angola border should be avoided because of land mines left undetected after the civil war. Visitors should seek advice before travelling to townships
WEATHER Oct to Apr rain inland; May to Oct hot and dry; the coast is cool and relatively free of rain all year round
BANKING 0900–1530 Mon to Fri
EMERGENCY Police 1011; Fire 2032270; Ambulance 2032276
TIME ZONE GMT +2
INTERNATIONAL DIALLING CODE 264

NEPAL

GOVERNMENT Constitutional monarchy
LANGUAGES Nepali (official), local languages
CURRENCY Nepalese rupee = 100 paisa
MEDICAL There is a risk of altitude sickness, hepatitis A, malaria (in lowland areas) and typhoid
TRAVEL There is now a cease-fire between the government and the Communist party. Trekkers should not venture out without a professional guide and should obtain up-to-date advice regarding the safety of their chosen route
WEATHER Oct to Nov clear and dry, and not too cold at higher altitudes; Dec to Jan cool; Feb to Apr warm; Jun to Sep monsoon season
BANKING 1000–1450 Sun to Thu; 1000–1230 Fri
EMERGENCY Unavailable
TIME ZONE GMT +5.45
INTERNATIONAL DIALLING CODE 977

NETHERLANDS

GOVERNMENT Constitutional monarchy
LANGUAGES Dutch (official), Frisian
CURRENCY Euro = 100 cents
MEDICAL There are no specific health risks in the Netherlands
TRAVEL Most visits to the Netherlands are trouble-free. Attitudes here are very liberal. Locals are extremely welcoming and speak very good English
WEATHER Jun to Sep usually warm but changeable; Nov to Mar can be bitterly cold with some snow; rain falls all year round; Apr is best for daffodils and May is best for tulips
BANKING 0900–1600 Mon to Fri
EMERGENCY Emergency Services 112
TIME ZONE GMT +1
INTERNATIONAL DIALLING CODE 31

NETHERLANDS ANTILLES

GOVERNMENT Parliamentary democracy
LANGUAGES Dutch (official), French, English, Spanish, many others
CURRENCY Netherlands Antillean gilder = 100 cents
MEDICAL Polio and typhoid vaccinations are recommended. Water is considered drinkable and normal precautions should be taken with food
TRAVEL Most visits to the Netherlands Antilles are trouble-free
WEATHER Hot and tropical climate with cool sea breezes
BANKING 0830–1530 Mon to Fri
EMERGENCY Police 599/5/22222; Ambulance 599/5/22111
TIME ZONE GMT –4
INTERNATIONAL DIALLING CODE 599

NEW ZEALAND

GOVERNMENT Constitutional monarchy
LANGUAGES English and Maori (both official)
CURRENCY New Zealand dollar = 100 cents
MEDICAL There are no specific health risks
TRAVEL Most visits are trouble-free, but visitors should take precautions against street crime in urban areas after dark. Travel within the country is relatively cheap and efficient, and accommodation is varied and affordable
WEATHER Subtropical climate in North Island; no extremes of heat or cold, but Nov to Apr warmer; temperate in South Island with cool temperatures; rainfall occurs all year round
BANKING 0900–1630 Mon to Fri
EMERGENCY All Services 111
TIME ZONE GMT +12
INTERNATIONAL DIALLING CODE 64

NIGERIA

GOVERNMENT Federal multiparty republic
LANGUAGES English (official), Hausa, Yoruba, Ibo
CURRENCY Naira = 100 kobo
MEDICAL Visitors must have a yellow fever vaccination and protect against cerebral malaria
TRAVEL Incidences of kidnapping are increasing. Violent street crime, armed robberies and car theft are common throughout the country. Visitors should avoid using public transport and travelling after dark outside tourist areas
WEATHER Mar to Nov hot, humid and wet; Apr to Sep wet; Dec to Mar dusty winds, but cooler
BANKING 0800–1500 Mon; 0800–1330 Tue to Fri
EMERGENCY Unavailable
TIME ZONE GMT +1
INTERNATIONAL DIALLING CODE 234

NORWAY

GOVERNMENT Constitutional monarchy
LANGUAGES Norwegian (official)
CURRENCY Norwegian krone = 100 ore
MEDICAL There are no specific health risks in Norway
TRAVEL Most visits to Norway remain trouble-free. The country offers beautiful mountain scenery and year-round skiing
WEATHER May to Sep sunny and warm with long daylight hours; Dec to Mar very cold and dark; midnight sun occurs from 13 May to 29 Jul, and from 28 May to 14 Jul in the Lofoten Islands
BANKING 0900–1700 Mon to Thu; 0900–1530 Fri
EMERGENCY Police (Oslo) 002; Ambulance 003
TIME ZONE GMT +1
INTERNATIONAL DIALLING CODE 47

OMAN

GOVERNMENT Monarchy with consultative council
LANGUAGES Arabic (official), Baluchi, English
CURRENCY Omani rial = 100 baizas
MEDICAL Visitors should protect against malaria
TRAVEL Most visits to Oman are trouble-free, but visitors should remain informed of developments in the Middle East. There are harsh penalties, including the death penalty, for drug offences. Driving conditions are hazardous
WEATHER Jun to Sep very hot; Oct to Mar pleasant; the rest of the year is cooler
BANKING 0800–1200 Sat to Wed; 0800–1130 Thu
EMERGENCY All Services 999
TIME ZONE GMT +4
INTERNATIONAL DIALLING CODE 698

PAKISTAN

GOVERNMENT Military regime
LANGUAGES Urdu (official), many others
CURRENCY Pakistan rupee = 100 paisa
MEDICAL Visitors should protect against dengue fever, hepatitis A and malaria. There is also a risk of encephalitis in rural regions
TRAVEL Due to the threat from terrorism, most Western governments advise against all travel to Pakistan, except for their nationals of Pakistan origin
WEATHER Nov to Apr warm; Apr to Jul hot; Jul to Sep monsoon with high rainfall in upland areas
BANKING 0900–1300 and 1500–2000 Sun to Thu; closed on Fri. Some banks open on Sat
EMERGENCY Unavailable
TIME ZONE GMT +5
INTERNATIONAL DIALLING CODE 92

PARAGUAY

GOVERNMENT Multiparty republic
LANGUAGES Spanish and Guaraní (both official)
CURRENCY Guaraní = 100 céntimos
MEDICAL There is a risk of cholera, hepatitis, hookworm, typhoid, malaria and tuberculosis
TRAVEL Most visits to Paraguay are trouble-free, but there is economic recession and some political instability. Attractions include several national parks, including the Chaco – South America's great wilderness
WEATHER Subtropical climate; Dec to Mar is the hottest and wettest season, but rain falls all year round
BANKING 0845–1215 Mon to Fri
EMERGENCY All Services 00
TIME ZONE GMT +5
INTERNATIONAL DIALLING CODE 595

PERU

GOVERNMENT Transitional republic
LANGUAGES Spanish and Quechua (both official), Aymara
CURRENCY New sol = 100 centavos
MEDICAL Visitors should protect against altitude sickness, cholera, typhoid, hepatitis and malaria
TRAVEL Tourist areas are generally safe, but visitors should exercise caution, particularly in Lima and Cuzco, where crime has become a serious problem for foreign visitors
WEATHER Oct to Apr hot and dry in coastal areas, but much rainfall in highlands; May to Sep is dry and the best time to visit the highlands
BANKING 0930–1600 Mon to Fri
EMERGENCY All Services 011/5114
TIME ZONE GMT –5
INTERNATIONAL DIALLING CODE 51

PHILIPPINES

GOVERNMENT Multiparty republic
LANGUAGES Filipino (Tagalog) and English (both official), Spanish, many others
CURRENCY Philippine peso = 100 centavos
MEDICAL Visitors should protect against cholera, malaria, rabies and hepatitis
TRAVEL Visitors should check developments before travelling. Bomb explosions and kidnapping by organized gangs or terrorists have occurred in Manila and Mindanao
WEATHER Tropical climate with sea breeze; Jun to Sep wet; Oct to Feb cool and dry; Mar to May hot and dry; Jun to Sep typhoons occur
BANKING 0900–1600 Mon to Fri
EMERGENCY Unavailable
TIME ZONE GMT +8
INTERNATIONAL DIALLING CODE 63

POLAND

GOVERNMENT Multiparty republic
LANGUAGES Polish (official)
CURRENCY Zloty = 100 groszy
MEDICAL Medical care is generally poor,
particularly in rural regions
TRAVEL Most visits to Poland are trouble-free,
but there is a serious risk of robbery when using
public transport. Locals are very hospitable and
welcoming
WEATHER Temperate climate; May to Sep
warm; Nov to Mar cold and dark; spring and
autumn are warm and pleasant; rain falls all
year round
BANKING 0800–1800 Mon to Fri
EMERGENCY Police 997; Ambulance 999
TIME ZONE GMT +1
INTERNATIONAL DIALLING CODE 48

PORTUGAL

GOVERNMENT Multiparty republic
LANGUAGES Portuguese (official)
CURRENCY Euro = 100 cents
MEDICAL Sunburn is a risk during summer
TRAVEL Most visits are trouble-free. Children
under 18 years travelling to Portugal should be
accompanied by parents/guardians, or someone
in the country should be authorized to have
responsibility for them
WEATHER Apr to Oct hot and sunny; Nov to
Mar wetter, particularly in the north; summers
are hotter and winters are longer in the north
BANKING 0830–1500 Mon to Fri
EMERGENCY Emergency Services 112;
All Services 115
TIME ZONE GMT
INTERNATIONAL DIALLING CODE 351

PUERTO RICO

GOVERNMENT Commonwealth of the
United States
LANGUAGES Spanish and English (both official)
CURRENCY US dollar = 100 cents
MEDICAL There is a risk of sunburn and a slight
risk of hepatitis and bilharzia
TRAVEL Most visits to Puerto Rico are
trouble-free
WEATHER Tropical climate with little variation
in temperature all year round; May to Nov
hurricane season; cooler in upland regions
BANKING 0900–1430 Mon to Thu; 0900–1430
and 1530–1700 Fri
EMERGENCY Police 787 343 2020; Fire 787 343
2330; All Services 911
TIME ZONE GMT –4
INTERNATIONAL DIALLING CODE 1 787

QATAR

GOVERNMENT Constitutional absolute monarchy
LANGUAGES Arabic (official), English,
CURRENCY Qatari riyal = 100 dirhams
MEDICAL There are no specific health risks
TRAVEL Visitors should keep informed of
international developments before travelling.
It is prohibited to bring drugs, alcohol, religious
material or pork products into the country;
videos may be censored. Visitors should dress
modestly and respect local customs
WEATHER Jun to Sep very hot and dry; Apr
to May and Dec to Feb frequent sandstorms;
Nov and Feb to Mar warm with little wind
BANKING 0730–1130 Sat to Thu
EMERGENCY All Services 999
TIME ZONE GMT +3
INTERNATIONAL DIALLING CODE 974

RÉUNION

GOVERNMENT Overseas department of France
LANGUAGES French (official), Creole
CURRENCY Euro = 100 cents
MEDICAL Precautions should be taken against
typhoid and rabies. Water is unsafe to drink and
dairy products should be avoided as they are
unpasteurized
TRAVEL Most trips to Réunion are trouble-free.
Its society and culture are similar to Western
Europe. Usual precautions should be taken
WEATHER Hot and tropical with cooler
temperatures in the hills. Cool and dry from
May to Nov; hot and wet from Dec to Apr
BANKING 0800–1600 Mon to Fri
EMERGENCY Police 17; Fire 18; Ambulance 15
TIME ZONE GMT +4
INTERNATIONAL DIALLING CODE 262

ROMANIA

GOVERNMENT Multiparty republic
LANGUAGES Romanian (official), Hungarian
CURRENCY Leu = 100 bani
MEDICAL Visitors should protect against rabies,
typhoid and encephalitis
TRAVEL Petty theft is common in urban areas.
It is illegal to exchange money on the street.
Corruption is widespread. Roads are poorly
maintained
WEATHER May to Oct warm, but coastal areas
are cooled by sea breezes; Nov to Apr harsh
winter with snow, but milder along the coast
BANKING 0900–1200 Mon to Fri; 1300–1500
Mon to Fri (currency exchange only)
EMERGENCY Police 955; Fire 981; Ambulance 961
TIME ZONE GMT +2
INTERNATIONAL DIALLING CODE 40

RUSSIA

GOVERNMENT Federal multiparty republic
LANGUAGES Russian (official), many others
CURRENCY Russian ruble = 100 kopeks
MEDICAL Visitors should protect against diptheria, hepatitis A, typhoid and encephalitis
TRAVEL Travel to the Chechen Republic and northern Caucasus is inadvisable. Visitors should keep all valuables out of sight
WEATHER Variable climate in north and central regions; Jul to Aug warm and wet; May to Jun and Sep to Oct dry; Nov to Apr very cold with snow
BANKING 0930–1730 Mon to Fri
EMERGENCY Police 02; Fire 01; Ambulance 03
TIME ZONE GMT +3 in Moscow and St Petersburg. Other areas vary
INTERNATIONAL DIALLING CODE 7

ST KITTS & NEVIS

GOVERNMENT Constitutional monarchy
LANGUAGES English
CURRENCY East Caribbean dollar = 100 cents
MEDICAL Visitors should protect against mosquito bites as dengue fever is present. Water is untreated and is unsafe to drink
TRAVEL Most visits are trouble-free. The islands are now commercialized and tourists are welcomed. Usual precautions should be taken
WEATHER Hot and tropical with cooling sea breezes. There is little seasonal temperature variation. Hurricane season is Aug to Oct
BANKING 0800–1500 Mon to Thu; 0800-1500/1700 Fri; 0830–1100 Sat
EMERGENCY All Services 911
TIME ZONE GMT –4
INTERNATIONAL DIALLING CODE 1 869

ST LUCIA

GOVERNMENT Parliamentary democracy
LANGUAGES English (official), French patois
CURRENCY East Caribbean dollar = 100 cents
MEDICAL Dengue fever is present; precautions should be taken against mosquito bites. Polio and typhoid vaccinations are recommended
TRAVEL Most trips to St Lucia are trouble-free, but sensible precautions should be taken. Beachwear should not be worn in towns
WEATHER Tropical climate moderated by trade winds. Temperatures are uniform at about 26°C [79°F]. St Lucia lies in the hurricane belt
BANKING 0800–1500 Mon to Thu; 0800–1700 Fri; 0800–1200 Sat
EMERGENCY All Services 999
TIME ZONE GMT –4
INTERNATIONAL DIALLING CODE 1 758

ST VINCENT & THE GRENADINES

GOVERNMENT Parliamentary democracy
LANGUAGES English
CURRENCY East Caribbean dollar = 100 cents
MEDICAL Protection from polio, typhoid and mosquito bites are recommended
TRAVEL Sensible precautions should be taken. There is a relaxed society and most visits are trouble-free. Excellent West Indian cuisine can be found on St Vincent
WEATHER Tropical climate with cooling trade winds. Hottest months are Jun and Jul. Tropical storms may occur from Jun to Nov
BANKING 0800–1500 Mon to Thu; 0800–1700 Fri
EMERGENCY All Services 999
TIME ZONE GMT –4
INTERNATIONAL DIALLING CODE 1 809

SAMOA

GOVERNMENT Mix of parliamentary democracy and constitutional monarchy
LANGUAGES Samoan (Polynesian), English
CURRENCY Samoan dollar = 100 sene
MEDICAL Vaccination against polio and typhoid are recommended. Water is untreated and is unsafe to drink
TRAVEL Most visits are trouble-free, but traditional moral and religious codes are very important. Beachwear should not be worn outside resorts
WEATHER Tropical climate with cooler temperatures in the evenings. The rainy season is from Dec to Apr
BANKING 0900–1500 Mon to Fri; 0830–1130 Sat
EMERGENCY All services 999
TIME ZONE GMT –11
INTERNATIONAL DIALLING CODE 685

SAUDI ARABIA

GOVERNMENT Absolute monarchy with consultative assembly
LANGUAGES Arabic (official)
CURRENCY Saudi riyal = 100 halalas
MEDICAL Cases of cerebral malaria have been reported in Jizan, south-west Saudi Arabia
TRAVEL Visitors should seek advice on recent developments. Islamic customs must be followed. Bombings have occurred in Riyadh and visitors should remain extremely vigilant
WEATHER Desert climate; extremely dry; May to Oct very hot; Nov to Feb mild
BANKING 0830–1200 and 1700–1900 Sat to Wed; 0830–1200 Thu
EMERGENCY Unavailable
TIME ZONE GMT +3
INTERNATIONAL DIALLING CODE 966

SERBIA & MONTENEGRO

GOVERNMENT Federal republic
LANGUAGES Serbian (official), Albanian
CURRENCY New dinar = 100 paras
MEDICAL Visitors should protect themselves against hepatitis
TRAVEL The situation in Serbia and Montenegro is calm at present, though visitors should seek advice on developments before travelling. Travel to Kosovo is still inadvisable
WEATHER Serbia has a continental climate; Nov to Mar very cold; Jun to Sep warm; Montenegro is similar with colder conditions in mountain regions
BANKING 0900–1400 Mon to Fri
EMERGENCY Police 107; Fire/Ambulance 104
TIME ZONE GMT +1
INTERNATIONAL DIALLING CODE 36

SEYCHELLES

GOVERNMENT Democratic republic
LANGUAGES English, French, French Creole
CURRENCY Seychelles rupee = 100 cents
MEDICAL There are no specific health risks
TRAVEL Crime is relatively rare, but incidents of theft do occur in tourist areas. Visitors, particularly women, should remain vigilant and avoid walking in quiet areas after dark. Roads often have sheer drops and no barriers
WEATHER Nov to Feb hot, humid monsoon; very warm temperatures all year round; May and Oct breezy at the start and finish of the trade winds
BANKING 0830–1430 Mon to Fri
EMERGENCY Unavailable
TIME ZONE GMT +4
INTERNATIONAL DIALLING CODE 248

SINGAPORE

GOVERNMENT Multiparty republic
LANGUAGES Chinese, Malay, Tamil and English (all official)
CURRENCY Singapore dollar = 100 cents
MEDICAL There are no specific health risks
TRAVEL The crime rate is very low in Singapore and most visits remain trouble-free. There are harsh penalties, including the death penalty, for all drug offences. Smoking is illegal in public places
WEATHER Hot and humid all year round; Nov to Jan cool with most rainfall
BANKING 1000–1500 Mon to Fri; 1100–1600 Sat
EMERGENCY All Services 999
TIME ZONE GMT +8
INTERNATIONAL DIALLING CODE 65

SLOVAK REPUBLIC

GOVERNMENT Multiparty republic
LANGUAGES Slovak (official), Hungarian
CURRENCY Slovak koruna = 100 halierov
MEDICAL There is risk from rabies and tick-borne encephalitis in forested areas during summer months
TRAVEL Pickpockets operate around the main tourist areas, and foreigners are easily identified and targeted. Sensible precautions should be taken
WEATHER A temperate climate with cold winters and mild summers
BANKING 0800–1700 Mon to Fri
EMERGENCY Fire 150; Ambulance 155; Police 158
TIME ZONE GMT +1 in winter; GMT +2 in summer
INTERNATIONAL DIALLING CODE 42

SLOVENIA

GOVERNMENT Multiparty republic
LANGUAGES Slovene (official), Serbo-Croatian
CURRENCY Tolar = 100 stotin
MEDICAL Summer visitors to forested areas should seek advice about protection against tick-borne encephalitis
TRAVEL Harsh fines are given for traffic offences and jaywalking. Passports and international driving licences should be carried at all times
WEATHER Continental climate inland; Jun to Sep warm; Nov to Mar cold; Mediterranean climate in coastal areas; Sep is the best time for hiking and climbing
BANKING 0800–1800 Mon to Fri
EMERGENCY Police 92; Fire 93; Ambulance 94
TIME ZONE GMT +1
INTERNATIONAL DIALLING CODE 386

SOUTH AFRICA

GOVERNMENT Multiparty republic
LANGUAGES Afrikaans, English, Ndebele, Pedi, Sotho, Swazi, Tsonga, Tswana, Venda, Xhosa and Zulu (all official)
CURRENCY Rand = 100 cents
MEDICAL There is a high incidence of HIV/AIDS. Malaria is a risk in certain areas. Hygiene and water standards are high in tourist areas
TRAVEL Violent crime is high in the townships. There is a risk of car-jacking and armed robbery. Visitors should hide valuables and seek advice about which areas to avoid
WEATHER Generally warm and sunny all year
BANKING 0830–1530 Mon to Fri
EMERGENCY Police 1011; Ambulance 10222
TIME ZONE GMT +2
INTERNATIONAL DIALLING CODE 27

SPAIN

GOVERNMENT Constitutional monarchy
LANGUAGES Castilian Spanish (official), Catalan, Galician, Basque
CURRENCY Euro = 100 cents
MEDICAL There are no specific health risks in Spain
TRAVEL Most visits to Spain are trouble-free. The country is rich in arts and culture
WEATHER Temperate in north; Apr to Oct hot and dry, particularly in the south; central plateau can by very cold during winter
BANKING 0900–1400 Mon to Fri; 0900–1300 Sat (but not during summer)
EMERGENCY Police 091; Fire/Ambulance 085; Emergency Services 112
TIME ZONE GMT +1
INTERNATIONAL DIALLING CODE 34

SRI LANKA

GOVERNMENT Multiparty republic
LANGUAGES Sinhala and Tamil (both official)
CURRENCY Sri Lankan rupee = 100 cents
MEDICAL There is a risk of cholera and malaria. Rabies is widespread
TRAVEL The northern region and the eastern coast remain heavily mined. A cease-fire between the Tamil Tigers and the government was signed in February 2002
WEATHER Tropical climate; May to Jul and Dec to Jan monsoon seasons; coastal regions are cool due to sea breezes
BANKING 0900–1300 Mon to Sat; 0900–1500 Tue to Fri
EMERGENCY All Services 1 691095/699935
TIME ZONE GMT +5.30
INTERNATIONAL DIALLING CODE 94

SWEDEN

GOVERNMENT Constitutional monarchy
LANGUAGES Swedish (official), Finnish, Sami
CURRENCY Swedish krona = 100 öre
MEDICAL There are no specific health risks
TRAVEL Most visits to Sweden are generally trouble-free. Since devaluation of the Swedish currency, the country has become considerably more affordable
WEATHER May to Jul hot and dry, but Aug can be wet; the midnight sun can be seen from May to Jun above the Arctic Circle; Nov to Apr extremely cold, particularly in the north
BANKING 0930–1500 Mon to Fri
EMERGENCY Emergency Services 112; All Services 90 000/112
TIME ZONE GMT +1
INTERNATIONAL DIALLING CODE 46

SWITZERLAND

GOVERNMENT Federal republic
LANGUAGES French, German, Italian and Romansch (all official)
CURRENCY Swiss franc = 100 centimes
MEDICAL There is a risk of altitude sickness, sunburn and hypothermia in the Alps
TRAVEL Most visits to Switzerland remain trouble-free
WEATHER Climate varies from region to region; Alpine regions have lower temperatures; Jun to Sep warm and sunny; Nov to Apr cold with snow which starts to melt in Apr
BANKING 0830–1630 Mon to Fri
EMERGENCY Police 117; Fire 118; Ambulance 144
TIME ZONE GMT +1
INTERNATIONAL DIALLING CODE 41

SYRIA

GOVERNMENT Multiparty republic
LANGUAGES Arabic (official), Kurdish, Armenian
CURRENCY Syrian pound = 100 piastres
MEDICAL Visitors should vaccinate against polio, hepatitis A and B, and tetanus
TRAVEL Visitors should keep informed of developments in the Middle East. They should dress modestly and avoid driving out of main cities at night. Harsh penalties exist for drug offences
WEATHER Apr to Jun mild and dry; Jun to Sep hot; Dec to Mar very cold, particularly in coastal and upland regions
BANKING 0800–1400 Sat and Thu
EMERGENCY Contact hotel operator
TIME ZONE GMT +2
INTERNATIONAL DIALLING CODE 963

TAIWAN

GOVERNMENT Unitary multiparty republic
LANGUAGES Mandarin Chinese (official)
CURRENCY New Taiwan dollar = 100 cents
MEDICAL There are no specific health risks, but visitors should be vaccinated against hepatitis
TRAVEL Most visits to Taiwan are trouble-free. Petty crime exists, but is not common. Some roads in central and southern areas may still be blocked by landslides following the 1999 earthquake
WEATHER Subtropical climate with moderate temperatures in the north; Jun to Sep very hot and humid; Jun to Oct typhoon season
BANKING 0900–1530 Mon to Fri; 0900–1230 Sat
EMERGENCY Police 110
TIME ZONE GMT +8
INTERNATIONAL DIALLING CODE 886

TANZANIA

GOVERNMENT Multiparty republic
LANGUAGES Swahili and English (both official)
CURRENCY Tanzanian shilling = 100 cents
MEDICAL There is a risk of yellow fever, malaria, cholera and hepatitis. AIDS is widespread
TRAVEL Most visits are trouble-free, but crime does occur, particularly on public transport and in tourist areas. There are increased risks in Zanzibar where bomb explosions have occurred
WEATHER Tropical climate; Mar to May rainy season in coastal areas; Jan to Feb hot and dry; Nov to Dec and Feb to May rainy season in highland areas
BANKING 0830–1600 Mon to Fri
EMERGENCY Unavailable
TIME ZONE GMT +3
INTERNATIONAL DIALLING CODE 255

THAILAND

GOVERNMENT Constitutional monarchy
LANGUAGES Thai (official), English, local dialects
CURRENCY Baht = 100 satang
MEDICAL Visitors should protect against malaria, dengue fever, AIDS and cholera
TRAVEL Harsh penalties exist for drug offences. Tourists should use licensed taxis with yellow number plates. Visitors should seek advice before travelling to border areas with Burma or Cambodia. Riptides occur off the coast of Phuket
WEATHER Jun to Oct hot and rainy monsoon; Nov to Feb dry and pleasant; Mar to May hot; temperatures are more consistent in the south
BANKING 0830–1530 Mon to Fri
EMERGENCY Unavailable
TIME ZONE GMT +7
INTERNATIONAL DIALLING CODE 66

TRINIDAD & TOBAGO

GOVERNMENT Parliamentary democracy
LANGUAGES English (official), Spanish
CURRENCY Trinidad & Tobago dollar = 100 cents
MEDICAL Dengue fever has become a problem in recent years. Medical facilities are basic and limited
TRAVEL While most visits are trouble-free, attacks on travellers are on the increase. Visitors should remain vigilant and alert at all times, and take sensible precautions
WEATHER Tropical climate with cooling trade winds. Hottest and wettest time is Jun to Nov
BANKING 0900–1400 Mon to Thu; 0900–1200 and 1500–1700 Fri
EMERGENCY Police 999; Ambulance/Fire 990
TIME ZONE GMT –4
INTERNATIONAL DIALLING CODE 1 868

TUNISIA

GOVERNMENT Multiparty republic
LANGUAGES Arabic (official), French
CURRENCY Tunisian dinar = 1,000 millimes
MEDICAL There is a risk of yellow fever and malaria
TRAVEL Travel to Tunisia is generally trouble-free, but visitors to southern desert areas and to areas close to the Algerian border should exercise caution. Tunisian laws and customs should be respected. Drug offences carry harsh penalties
WEATHER Jun to Aug hot and humid; Jan to Feb. cooler; hotter inland; higher rainfall in winter
BANKING 0830–1200 and 1300–1700 Mon to Fri
EMERGENCY Unavailable
TIME ZONE GMT +1
INTERNATIONAL DIALLING CODE 216

TURKEY

GOVERNMENT Multiparty republic
LANGUAGES Turkish (official), Kurdish, Arabic
CURRENCY New Turkish lira = 100 kurus
MEDICAL Contagious diseases are increasing and visitors should keep inoculations up-to-date
TRAVEL Most visits are trouble-free, but visitors should exercise caution, particularly in the tourist areas of Istanbul where street robbery is common, and seek recent advice before travelling
WEATHER Mediterranean climate; summers are hot and winters are mild
BANKING 0830–1200 and 1300–1700 Mon to Fri
EMERGENCY Police 155; Fire 111; Ambulance 112
TIME ZONE GMT +2
INTERNATIONAL DIALLING CODE 90

UGANDA

GOVERNMENT Republic in transition
LANGUAGES English and Swahili (both official)
CURRENCY Ugandan shilling = 100 cents
MEDICAL There is a risk of AIDS, yellow fever and malaria
TRAVEL Most visits to Uganda are trouble-free, but visitors should seek recent advice before travelling. It is inadvisable to travel to areas bordering the Democratic Republic of the Congo or Sudan, and visitors should remain cautious if travelling to areas bordering Rwanda
WEATHER Dec to Feb and Jun to Aug hot and dry; Mar to May and Oct to Nov heavy rain
BANKING 0830–1400 Mon to Fri
EMERGENCY Unavailable
TIME ZONE GMT +3
INTERNATIONAL DIALLING CODE 256

UKRAINE

GOVERNMENT Multiparty republic
LANGUAGES Ukrainian (official), Russian
CURRENCY Hryvnia = 100 kopiykas
MEDICAL There is a risk of diptheria in western Ukraine. Tick-borne encephalitis is common in forested areas. Do not drink tap water without first boiling it
TRAVEL Crime in the Ukraine remains low, but visitors should remain vigilant and keep valuables out of sight, particularly in crowded areas where pickpocketing and bag-snatching can occur
WEATHER Jun to Aug warm; Oct to Nov sunny but cold; Dec to Mar cold with snowfall
BANKING 0900–1600 Mon to Fri
EMERGENCY Unavailable
TIME ZONE GMT +2
INTERNATIONAL DIALLING CODE 380

UNITED ARAB EMIRATES

GOVERNMENT Federation of seven emirates, each with its own government
LANGUAGES Arabic (official), English
CURRENCY Dirham = 100 fils
MEDICAL There is a risk of hepatitis A and B
TRAVEL Visitors should remain informed of recent international developments before travelling. They should dress modestly and respect local customs. Penalties for all drug offences are harsh and can include the death penalty
WEATHER Jun to Sep very hot and dry; Oct to May cooler and is the best time to visit
BANKING 0800–1200 Sat to Wed and 0800–1100 Thu
EMERGENCY All Services 344 663
TIME ZONE GMT +4
INTERNATIONAL DIALLING CODE 971

UNITED KINGDOM

GOVERNMENT Constitutional monarchy
LANGUAGES English (official), Welsh, Gaelic
CURRENCY Pound sterling = 100 pence
MEDICAL No vaccinations are required in the UK and citizens of all EU countries are entitled to free medical treatment at National Health Service hospitals
TRAVEL Most visits are trouble-free, but visitors should exercise caution in urban areas after dark
WEATHER May to Aug warm and wet; Sep to Apr mild and wet
BANKING 0900–1730 Mon to Fri. Some bank branches open on Saturday mornings
EMERGENCY Police/Fire/Ambulance 999; Emergency Services 112
TIME ZONE GMT
INTERNATIONAL DIALLING CODE 44

UNITED STATES OF AMERICA

GOVERNMENT Federal republic
LANGUAGES English (official), Spanish, more than 30 others
CURRENCY US dollar = 100 cents
MEDICAL There are no specific health risks, but medical treatment is expensive
TRAVEL Most visits to the USA are trouble-free, but visitors should remain vigilant and avoid wearing valuable jewellery or walking through isolated urban areas after dark
WEATHER Varies considerably; check climate before travelling
BANKING 0900–1500 Mon to Fri
EMERGENCY Emergency Services 911
TIME ZONE USA has six time zones from GMT −5 on East coast to −10 in Hawai'i
INTERNATIONAL DIALLING CODE 1

URUGUAY

GOVERNMENT Multiparty republic
LANGUAGES Spanish (official)
CURRENCY Uruguayan peso = 100 centésimos
MEDICAL There are no specific health risks, but medical treatment can be expensive
TRAVEL Most visits to Uruguay are trouble-free, but street crime exists in urban areas, including Montevideo. It is, however, less common than in other Latin American countries
WEATHER Dec to Mar hot, but nights can be cool; Apr to Nov mild
BANKING 1330–1730 Mon to Fri (summer); 1300–1700 Mon to Fri (winter)
EMERGENCY Police 109; Fire 104; Ambulance 105; All Services 999
TIME ZONE GMT −3
INTERNATIONAL DIALLING CODE 598

VENEZUELA

GOVERNMENT Federal republic
LANGUAGES Spanish (official), local dialects
CURRENCY Bolívar = 100 céntimos
MEDICAL There is a risk of yellow fever, cholera, dengue fever and hepatitis
TRAVEL The incidence of violent crime is high and the political situation is volatile. Visitors should take precautions. Terrorist and narcotic gangs are active in areas bordering Colombia, where there is the risk of kidnapping
WEATHER May to Dec rainy season; Jan to Apr pleasant temperatures
BANKING 0830–1130 and 1400–1630 Mon to Fri
EMERGENCY Doctor 02 483 7021; Ambulance 02 545 4545
TIME ZONE GMT −4
INTERNATIONAL DIALLING CODE 58

VIETNAM

GOVERNMENT Socialist republic
LANGUAGES Vietnamese (official), English, Chinese
CURRENCY Dong = 10 hao = 100 xu
MEDICAL Malaria, dengue fever and encephalitis are common throughout the country. Visitors should avoid mosquito bites. Typhoid is common in the Mekong Delta
TRAVEL Take care if travelling in border areas. Unexploded mines and bombs still exist in certain areas. Drug smuggling carries the death penalty. Serious flooding can occur in central areas
WEATHER May to Oct tropical monsoons; Nov to Apr hot and dry
BANKING 0800–1630 Mon to Fri
EMERGENCY Police 13; Fire 14; Ambulance 15
TIME ZONE GMT +7
INTERNATIONAL DIALLING CODE 84

VIRGIN ISLANDS, BRITISH

GOVERNMENT UK overseas territory
LANGUAGES English (official)
CURRENCY US dollar = 100 cents
MEDICAL Medical facilities are limited. Precautions should be taken against polio, typhoid and dengue fever
TRAVEL There is a low crime rate, but sensible precautions should be taken. Backpacking is discouraged throughout the 60 islands
WEATHER Subtropical and humid climate moderated by trade winds. Hurricanes are a risk from Jul to Oct
BANKING 0900–1500 Mon to Thu; 0900–1700 Fri
EMERGENCY Police 114; Ambulance 112
TIME ZONE GMT –4
INTERNATIONAL DIALLING CODE 1 284

VIRGIN ISLANDS, US

GOVERNMENT US overseas territory
LANGUAGES English, Spanish, French, Creole
CURRENCY US dollar = 100 cents
MEDICAL Visitors should protect against typhoid and polio. Water is generally considered drinkable
TRAVEL Most visit are trouble-free and normal precautions should be taken. There is a large selection of hotel accommodation available
WEATHER Hot climate with cool winds. Low humidity with little seasonal temperature variation. The rainy season is Sep to Nov
BANKING 0900–1430 Mon to Thu; 0900–1400 and 1530–1700 Fri
EMERGENCY All services 911
TIME ZONE GMT –4
INTERNATIONAL DIALLING CODE 1 340

YEMEN

GOVERNMENT Multiparty republic
LANGUAGES Arabic (official)
CURRENCY Yemeni rial = 100 fils
MEDICAL Visitors should protect against hepatitis A and B
TRAVEL Most governments currently strongly advise against travel to Yemen. Random armed kidnapping is common, and foreigners remain targets for crime and terrorism
WEATHER Varies with altitude; Oct to Mar nights can be very cold in upland regions; Apr to Sep very hot; Oct to Apr cool, dry and dusty
BANKING 0800–1200 Sat to Wed; 0800–1100 Thu. Closed on Fridays
EMERGENCY Unavailable
TIME ZONE GMT +3
INTERNATIONAL DIALLING CODE 967

ZAMBIA

GOVERNMENT Multiparty republic
LANGUAGES English (official), Bemba, Nyanja
CURRENCY Zambian kwacha = 100 ngwee
MEDICAL Outbreaks of cholera and dysentery are common. Malaria is endemic, and cases of AIDS and tuberculosis are very high
TRAVEL Visitors should avoid travelling to areas bordering Angola and the Democratic Republic of the Congo. Armed robbery, bag-snatching and mugging are increasing, particularly in downtown areas. Keep valuables out of sight
WEATHER May to Sep very cool and dry; Oct to Nov hot and dry; Dec to Apr hot and wet
BANKING 0815–1430 Mon to Fri
EMERGENCY All Services 1 2 25067/254798
TIME ZONE GMT +2
INTERNATIONAL DIALLING CODE 260

ZIMBABWE

GOVERNMENT Multiparty republic
LANGUAGES English (official), Shona, Ndebele
CURRENCY Zimbabwean dollar = 100 cents
MEDICAL There is a risk of bilharzia, cholera, malaria, yellow fever and rabies. Incidences of HIV/AIDS are very high
TRAVEL There is currently political and social unrest throughout the country, in both rural and urban areas. Visitors should exercise caution and avoid large crowds and demonstrations
WEATHER May to Oct warm and dry, but cold at night; Nov to Apr wet and hot
BANKING 0800–1500 Mon, Tue, Thu and Fri. 0800–1300 Wed and 0800–1130 Sat
EMERGENCY Police 995; Ambulance 994
TIME ZONE GMT +2
INTERNATIONAL DIALLING CODE 263

WORLD MAPS — GENERAL REFERENCE

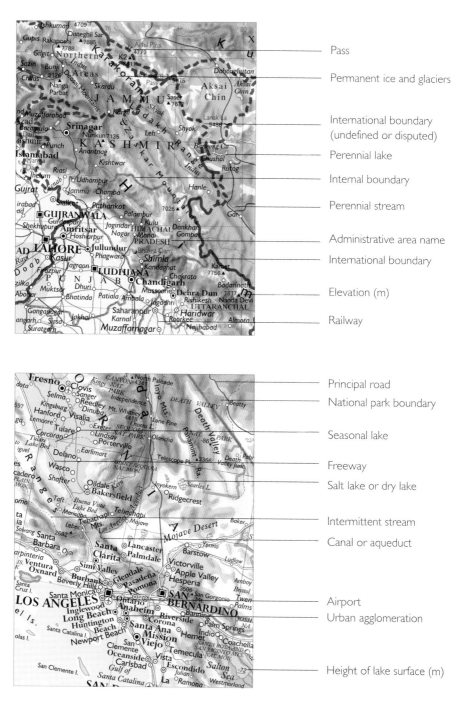

Pass

Permanent ice and glaciers

International boundary
(undefined or disputed)

Perennial lake

Internal boundary

Perennial stream

Administrative area name

International boundary

Elevation (m)

Railway

Principal road

National park boundary

Seasonal lake

Freeway

Salt lake or dry lake

Intermittent stream

Canal or aqueduct

Airport

Urban agglomeration

Height of lake surface (m)

Settlements

Capital cities have red infills

Settlement symbols and type styles vary
according to the scale of each map and
indicate the importance of towns rather
than specific population figures.

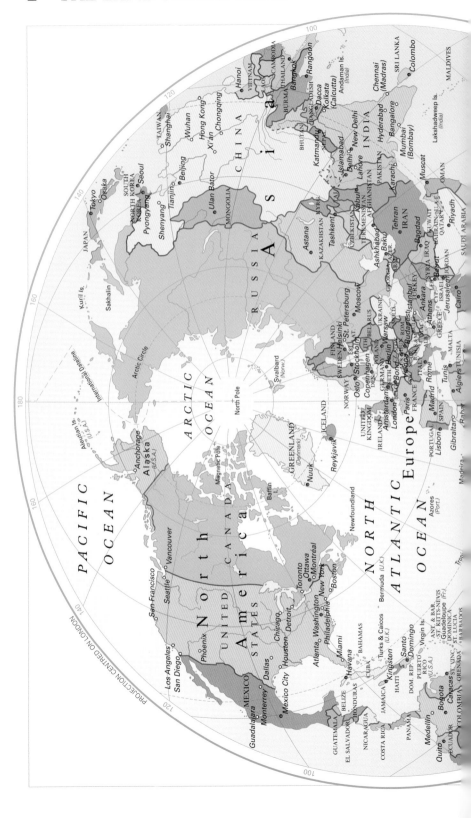

3

A T L A N T I C   O C E A N

Chagos Arch.
(U.K.)

SEYCHELLES

MAURITIUS

Réunion
(Fr.)

Antananarivo

MADAGASCAR

Mayotte
(Fr.)

COMOROS

Dar es Salaam

Dodoma

TANZANIA

MOZAMBIQUE

Maputo

Pretoria

Johannesburg

Durban

SWAZILAND

LESOTHO

SOUTH AFRICA

Cape Town

Windhoek

NAMIBIA

BOTSWANA

Gaborone

ZIMBABWE

Harare

Lilongwe

MALAWI

ZAMBIA

Lusaka

ANGOLA

Luanda

Brazzaville

CONGO
(DEM. REP.
OF THE)

Kinshasa

Libreville

GABON

EQUAT.
GUINEA

SÃO TOMÉ & P.

St. Helena
(U.K.)

Ascension
(U.K.)

Tropic of Capricorn

Maranhão

SOMALIA

Mogadishu

DJIBOUTI

Asmera

ETHIOPIA

Addis Ababa

Khartoum

SUDAN

KENYA

Nairobi

UGANDA

Kampala

RWANDA

BURUNDI

CENTRAL
AFRICA

Bangui

CHAD

Ndjaména

CAMEROON

Yaoundé

Yamoussoukro

Accra

GHANA

TOGO

BENIN

NIGERIA

Abuja

Lagos

NIGER

Niamey

MALI

Bamako

MAURITANIA

Nouakchott

Dakar

SENEGAL

GAMBIA

Banjul

GUINEA BISSAU

GUINEA

Conakry

SIERRA LEONE

Freetown

LIBERIA

Monrovia

IVORY
COAST

BURKINA
FASO

CAPE VERDE
IS.

Equator

S o u t h   A m e r i c a

SURINAME   FRENCH GUIANA

Manaus

Belém

Fortaleza

Recife

Salvador

BRAZIL

Brasília

Belo Horizonte

São Paulo

Rio de Janeiro

BOLIVIA

S O U T H

A T L A N T I C

O C E A N

60

40

20

West from Greenwich

0   East from Greenwich

20

40

60

Capital cities have red infills

The maps have been constructed on an Oblique Azimuthal Equidistant projection, on which all distances measured through the centre point are true to scale. The green lines are drawn at 5,000, 10,000 and 15,000 km from the central city.

PROJECTION CENTRED ON TOKYO

Buenos
Aires

Rio de
Janeiro

Caracas

Mexico City

Los Angeles

Honolulu

New
York

Toronto
Chicago

Reykjavik

London

Copenhagen

Lisbon

Paris

Rome

Berlin

Moscow

Tokyo

Beijing

Hong
Kong

Darwin

Sydney

Wellington

Cairo

Bahrain

Mumbai
(Bombay)

Kolkata
(Calcutta)

Singapore

Nairobi

Lagos

Johannesburg

COPYRIGHT PHILIP'S

Projection: Oblique Azimuthal Equidistant

PROJECTION CENTRED ON MEXICO CITY

Nairobi

Mumbai
(Bombay)

Bahrain

Moscow

Copenhagen

Berlin
Rome

London
Paris

Reykjavik

Lisbon

Cairo

Lagos

Rio de
Janeiro

Caracas

Buenos
Aires

**Mexico
City**

New
York

Toronto

Chicago

Los
Angeles

Honolulu

Kolkata
(Calcutta)

Beijing

Hong
Kong

Tokyo

Singapore

Darwin

Sydney

Wellington

Johannesburg

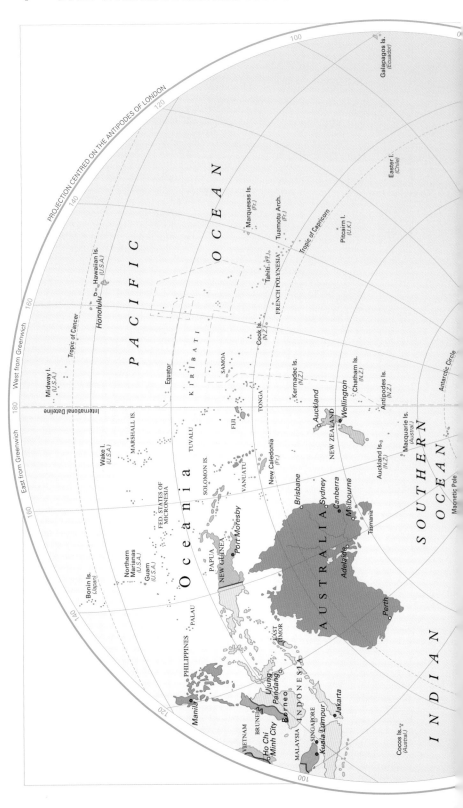

5

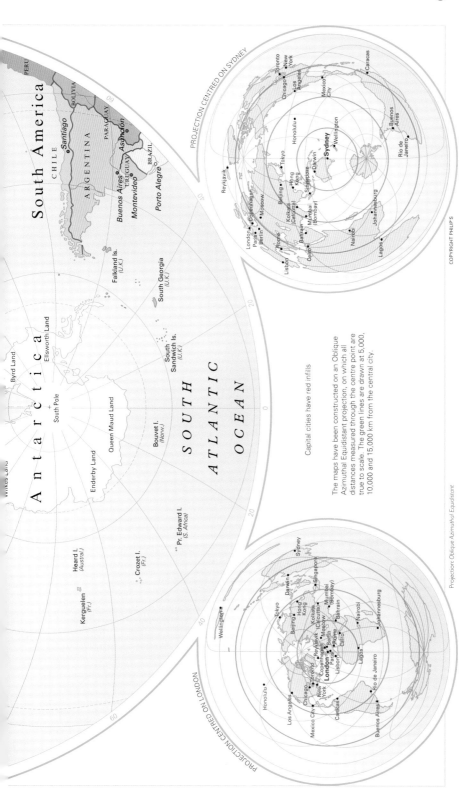

South America

PERU
BOLIVIA
PARAGUAY
CHILE
Santiago
ARGENTINA
Asunción
URUGUAY
Buenos Aires
Montevideo
BRAZIL
Porto Alegre

Falkland Is.
(U.K.)

South Georgia
(U.K.)

South
Sandwich Is.
(U.K.)

Antarctica

Byrd Land
Ellsworth Land
South Pole
Queen Maud Land
Enderby Land
Wilkes Land

Bouvet I.
(Norw.)

** Pr. Edward I.
(S. Africa)

S O U T H

A T L A N T I C

O C E A N

Heard I.
(Austral.)

Crozet I.
(Fr.)

Kerguelen
(Fr.)

PROJECTION CENTRED ON SYDNEY

Reykjavik
London
Paris
Berlin
Lisbon
Rome
Copenhagen
Moscow
Beijing
Tokyo
Hong Kong
Singapore
Kolkata
(Calcutta)
Bahrain
Mumbai
(Bombay)
Cairo
Nairobi
Johannesburg
Lagos
Honolulu
Darwin
Sydney
Wellington
Chicago
Toronto
New York
Los Angeles
Mexico City
Caracas
Buenos Aires
Rio de Janeiro

Capital cities have red infills

The maps have been constructed on an Oblique Azimuthal Equidistant projection, on which all distances measured through the centre point are true to scale. The green lines are drawn at 5,000, 10,000 and 15,000 km from the central city.

PROJECTION CENTRED ON LONDON

Wellington
Sydney
Darwin
Tokyo
Beijing
Hong Kong
Singapore
Kolkata
(Calcutta)
Mumbai
(Bombay)
Reykjavik
Moscow
Berlin
Bahrain
Cairo
Nairobi
Johannesburg
Toronto
Copenhagen
London
Paris
Rome
Lisbon
Lagos
Honolulu
Chicago
New York
Los Angeles
Mexico City
Caracas
Rio de Janeiro
Buenos Aires

Scale bars:
100 0 100 200 300 400 500 600 700 800 km
100 0 100 200 300 400 500 miles

Hammerfest
Murmansk
Luleå
White Sea
Arkhangelsk
KOMI
Ob
KARELIA
N. Dvina
Kotlas
Nizhniy Tagil
FINLAND
Vaasa
Kotlas
Perm
Yekaterinburg
Chelyabinsk
L. Onega
Vyborg
L. Ladoga
Kirov
Turku
Helsinki
ST. PETERSBURG
Vologda
UDMURTIA
Ufa
BASHKORTOSTAN
Tallinn
Rybinsk Res.
Kostroma
Kazan
Magnitogorsk
ESTONIA
L. Chudskoye
Yaroslavl
Ivanovo
Nizhniy Novgorod
MARI EL
TATARSTAN
Riga
R U S S I A
CHUVASIA
LATVIA
MOSCOW
Simbirsk
Samara
Orenburg
Vilnius
MORDVINIA
Penza
Volga
Uralsk
LITHUANIA
W. Dvina
Vitebsk
Smolensk
Tula
Tambov
Saratov
KAZAKHSTAN
Kaliningrad
Minsk
Orel
Voronezh
Ural
Atyraū
Białystok
BELARUS
Gomel
Kursk
Volgograd
Brest
Pripet
Chernihiv
Warsaw
Lublin
Kiev
Dnieper
Kharkov
Astrakhan
Caspian Sea
Lvov
Zhytomyr
U K R A I N E
Don
Kraków
Dniester
Dnepropetrovsk
Donetsk
Taganrog
KALMYKIA
Bug
Krivoy Rog
Zaporozhye
Rostov
Kolc
Debrecen
MOLDOVA
Nikolayev
Kherson
Stavropol
Makhachkala
Cluj-Napoca
Kishinev
Odessa
NORTH OSSETIA
CHECHENIA
DAGESTAN
ROMANIA
CRIMEA
Krasnodar
ADYGEA
INGUSHETIA
Timișoara
Galați
Sevastopol
KARACHAY-CHERKESSIA
KABARDINO-BALKARIA
GEORGIA
Tbilisi
Baku
Brașov
Ploiești
Black Sea
ARMENIA
AZERBAIJAN
Belgrade
Bucharest
Constanța
Yerevan
SERBIA & MONTENEGRO
Danube
Varna
Bosporus
Aras
Niš
Sofia
Samsun
Erzerum
Tabrīz
BULGARIA
Plovdiv
İSTANBUL
Ankara
T U R K E Y
IRAN
Skopje
MACEDONIA
Thessaloníka
Bursa
Kayseri
Diyarbakir
A s i a
GREECE
İzmir
Konya
Adana
Euphrates
Tigris
IRAQ
Patra
Aegean Sea
Antalya
Aleppo
Baghdad
Athens
SYRIA
Rhodes
CYPRUS
Nicosia
Crete

COPYRIGHT PHILIP'S

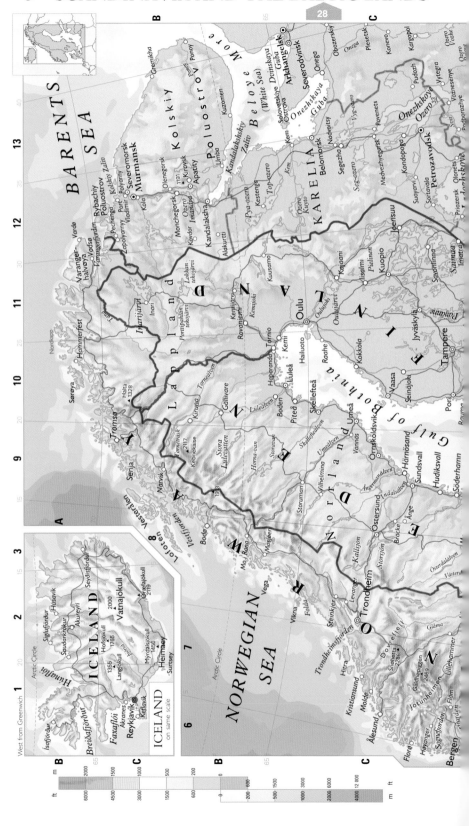

24

50 0 100 200 300 400 km

50 0 50 100 150 200 250 miles

COPYRIGHT PHILIP'S

12

17

11

10

16

9

8

7

Projection: Conical with two standard parallels

20 East from Greenwich

R U S S I A

Cherepovets

Rybinsk Res.

Tikhvin
Borovichi
Bologoye

Tver
Vyshniy Volochek

Staritsa
Rzhev

Vyazma

Zelenograd
MOSKVA
(Moscow)
Odintsovo

Kaluga
Beley
Oka

Orel

Okhtyrka
Poltava

Sumy

Konotop

Nizhyn
Pryluky
Pereyaslav-
Khmelnytskyy

Cherkasy

Kotka
Helsinki
Espoo
Hanko

Gulf of Finland

Tallinn

ESTONIA

Hiiumaa
(Dago)
Saaremaa
(Ösel)

L A T V I A

Ventspils

Liepāja

Klaipėda

K A L I N I N G R A D

L I T H U A N I A

Šiauliai
Panevėžys
Kaunas
Vilnius
Jelgava

Riga

Gulf of
Riga

Pärnu
Tartu
Valga
Rēzekne

Pskov
Gdov
Ozero
Chudskoye

Narva
Kingisepp
Kohtla-
Järve

Kronshtadt
SANKT-
PETERBURG
(St. Petersburg)

Luga
Novgorod
Dno
Staraya
Russa

Ozero
Ilmen

Kholm
Velikiye
Luki

Nevel
Polatsk
Vitsyebsk

Daugavpils
Daugava

Orsha
Mahilyow

Smolensk
Roslavl

Chernihiv
Chornobyl

Mazyr

Homyel
Zhlobin

Babruysk
Bryansk

Seym

Novhorod-
Siverskyy

U K R A I N E

KYIV
(Kiev)
Berdychiv
Zhytomyr

Bila Tserkva

Korosten
Rivne
Chervonohrad

Lutsk
Kovel

B E L A R U S

MINSK
Barysaw
Slutsk

Baranavichy

Pinsk

Brest
Hrodna

Polesye

Pripyat

Nyoman

Sovetsk
Elbląg
(Russia)

Gdynia
Gdańsk

Suwałki
Białystok

Olsztyn

Łomża
Byd
Toruń

Bydgoszcz

Płock

WARSZAWA
(Warsaw)

Radom

Lublin

Rzeszów
Przemyśl

Lviv

P O L A N D

Wisła
Poznań
Warta
Kalisz
Łódź

Częstochowa
Katowice
Kraków

Kielce

Tarnów
Tychy
Chorzów

Wrocław
Opole
Legnica

Wałbrzych
Śnieżka

Žilina

Ostrava
Cieszyn

CZECH REP.

Hradec
Králové

PRAHA
(Prague)
Plzeň
Drážďany
Görlitz

G E R M A N Y

BERLIN
Potsdam
Magdeburg
Braunschweig
Hannover

Leipzig
Halle
Chemnitz
Erfurt

Dresden

Zittau

Frankfurt
Oder

Szczecin
Świnoujście
Koszalin
Rügen
Stralsund
Rostock

Sassnitz

Bornholm

Odra
Spree

Saale
Elbe

Plauen
Thüringer Wald
Fulda

Kassel
Göttingen

Würzburg
Nürnberg

Frankfurt
Darmstadt
Heidelberg
Main

Osnabrück
Münster
Dortmund

Bremen
HAMBURG
Lübeck
Kiel
Flensburg

Emden
Helgoland
Weser
Ems

DENMARK
København
(Copenhagen)
Odense
Sjælland
Fyn
Randers
Århus
Aalborg
Esbjerg
Holstebro
Frederikshavn
Skagen

Lund
Malmö
Helsingborg
Halmstad
Varberg

Göteborg
(Gothenburg)
Borås
Trollhättan
Jönköping
Skien

Kattegat
Skagerrak
Lille Bælt
Store Bælt

Kristiansand
Mandal
Lindesnes
Arendal
Larvik
Drammen
Haugesund
Stavanger

Oslofjord

Vänern

Göta kanal

S W E D E N

Götaland

Gotland
Visby

Öland
Kalmar
Karlskrona

Karlstad
Örebro
Västerås
Uppsala
STOCKHOLM
Södertälje
Eskilstuna
Norrköping
Linköping
Motala

Svealand
Sala
Avesta
Fredrikstad
Fagersta
Hofors

Vättern

Bornholm

B A L T I C   S E A

Gulf of
Finland

Gotland

Åland
(Ahvenanmaa)

Volga
Volkhov
Lovat'

Dvina

Dnyapro

Dnyapro

Desna

Dniester

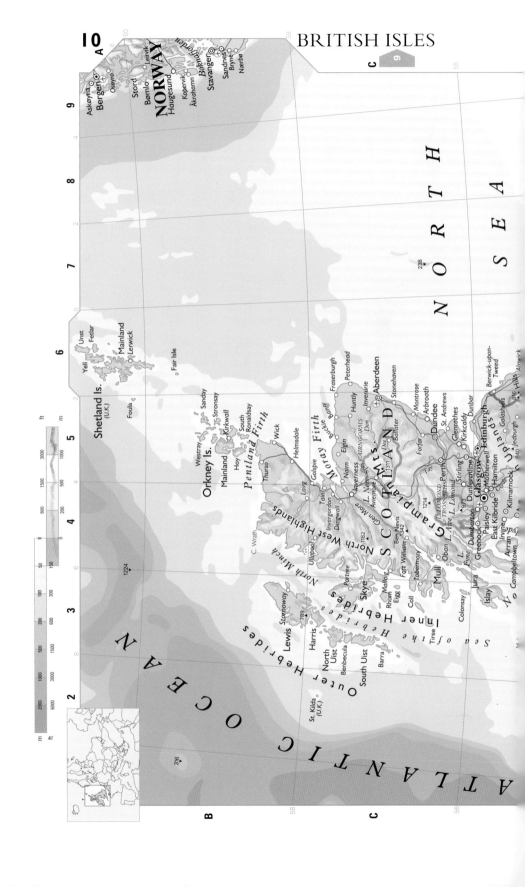

NORWAY

Askøyna
Bergen
Osøyro
Stord
Bømlo
Haugesund
Kopervik
Åkrahamn
Stavanger
Bryne
Sandnes
Nærbø
Leirvik
Boknlo
Sjøfjorden
Upplen

NORTH SEA

Shetland Is.
(U.K.)
Yell
Unst
Fetlar
Mainland
Lerwick
Foula

Fair Isle

238

Orkney Is.
Westray
Sanday
Stronsay
Mainland
Kirkwall
Hoy
South
Ronaldsay

Pentland Firth
Thurso
Wick
Helmsdale
Golspie
Lairg

Moray Firth
Tain
Dingwall
Invergordon
Nairn
Elgin
Buckie
Banff
Fraserburgh
Peterhead
Huntly
Inverurie
Aberdeen
Stonehaven
Montrose
Arbroath
Dundee
St. Andrews
Forfar
Ballater
Glenrothes
Kirkcaldy
Dunbar
Edinburgh
Galashiels
Jedburgh
Hawick
Berwick-upon-Tweed
Cheviot Hills
Alnwick

C. Wrath

North West Highlands
Ullapool
Inverness
Aviemore
CAIRNGORMS
Dee
Don
Spey

SCOTLAND
Grampian Mts.
Ben Nevis
1344
Fort William
Glen More
L. Ness
1182
Tay
1214
Perth
Stirling
Dunfermline
Glasgow
Motherwell
Hamilton
973
L. LOMOND
THE TROSSACHS
L. Awe
L. Lomond
Dumbarton
Paisley
East Kilbride
Kilmarnock
Greenock
Oban
Irvine
Southern Uplands
840

N. Minch

Stornoway
Lewis
Harris
789
North Uist
Benbecula
South Uist
Barra
Outer Hebrides

Skye
Portree
Mallaig
Rhum
Eigg
Coll
Tiree
Mull
Tobermory
Colonsay
Islay
Jura
Arran
Campbeltown

Sea of the Hebrides
Inner Hebrides

St. Kilda
(U.K.)

1224

316

ATLANTIC OCEAN

m   ft
3000
1500   1000
600   500
200
50
0   0
150
600   200
1500   500
3000   1000
6000   2000
m   ft

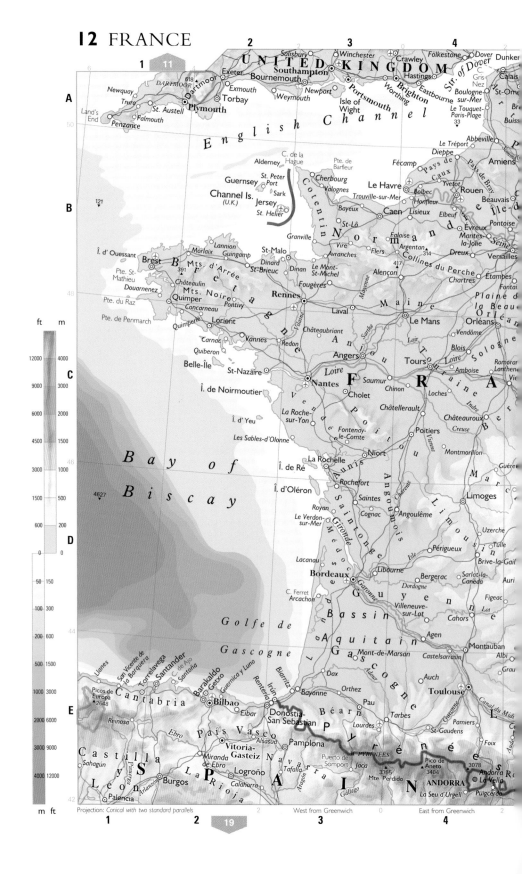

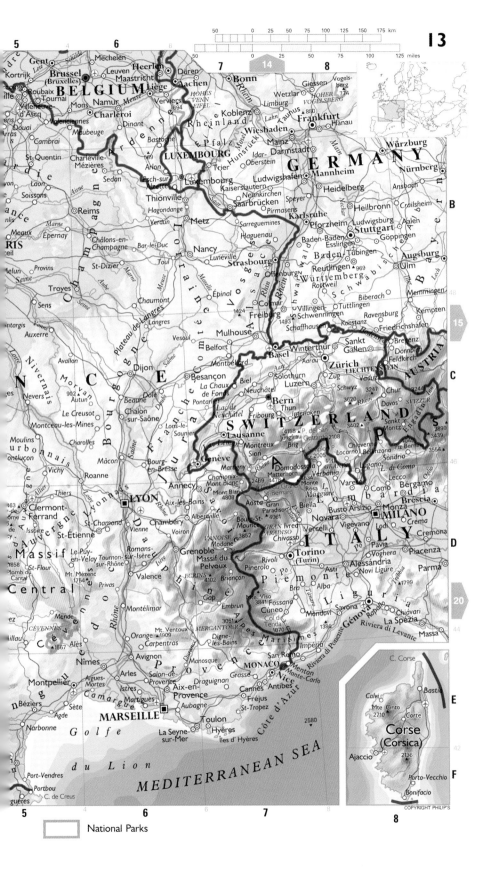

National Parks

NORTH SEA

UNITED KINGDOM

Cromer
Norwich
THE BROADS
Great Yarmouth
Lowestoft
Ipswich
Felixstowe
Harwich
Margate
Dover

NETHERLANDS
's-Gravenhage (Den Haag)
Hoek van Holland
Leiden
Gouda
ROTTERDAM
Dordrecht
AMSTERDAM
Hilversum
Utrecht
Arnhem
Nijmegen
's-Hertogenbosch

Sylt
Westerland
Föhr
Flensburg
Nordfriesische Inseln
Helgoland
Ost-friesische Inseln
Norderney
Wangerooge
Borkum
Cuxhaven

Abenrå
Sø
Schleswig
Rendsburg
Holstein
Kiel-Kanal
Itzehoe
Elmshorn
Stade
Buxtehude
Lüneburg

Texel
Den Helder
Alkmaar
Haarlem
Hoorn
Kampen
Zwolle
Almelo
Deventer
Apeldoorn
Enschede
Münster

Leeuwarden
Sneek
Groningen
Assen
Emmen
Meppel
Lingen
Rheine
Osnabrück

Wilhelmshaven
Emden
Aurich
Leer
Oldenburg
Delmenhorst

Bremerhaven
Bremen
Verden
Nienburg

Zeebrugge
Oostende
Vlissingen
Breda
Tilburg
Antwerpen
Brugge
Gent
Turnhout
Eindhoven
Krefeld
Mönchengladbach
Heerlen
Maastricht

BELGIUM
Brussel (Bruxelles)
Mechelen
Leuven
Namur
Liège
Aachen
Verviers
Charleroi
Dinant

Calais
Dunkerque
Kortrijk
St-Omer
Tourcoing
Roubaix
Lille
Tournai
Mons
Béthune
Bruay-la-Buissière
Lens
Arras
Douai
Valenciennes
Maubeuge
Cambrai

LUXEMBOURG
Arlon
Esch-sur-Alzette
Luxembourg
Trier
Idar-Oberstein
Thionville
Hagondange
Metz
Saarbrücken

Duisburg
Essen
Bochum
Dortmund
Hagen
Wuppertal
Düsseldorf
Solingen
Köln (Cologne)
Düren
Bonn

FRANCE
Amiens
Beauvais
Noyon
Laon
St-Quentin
Compiègne
Soissons
Reims
St-Denis
PARIS
Créteil
Meaux
Épernay
Melun
Évry
Fontainebleau
Provins
Troyes
Sens
Auxerre
Chaumont
Chālons-en-Champagne
Bar-le-Duc
Verdun
Nancy
Lunéville
Toul
Sedan
Charleville-Mézières
Bastogne

Karlsruhe
Pforzheim
Baden-Baden
Strasbourg
Offenburg
Freiburg
Colmar
Mulhouse
Belfort
Montbéliard
Besançon

Frankfurt
Hanau
Offenbach
Aschaffenburg
Darmstadt
Ludwigshafen
Mannheim
Heidelberg
Worms
Speyer
Neunkirchen
Pirmasens
Kaiserslautern
Sarreguemines
Haguenau
Heilbronn
Ludwigsburg
Stuttgart
Esslingen
Göppingen
Aalen
Reutlingen
Tübingen
Rottweil
Ulm

Würzburg

SWITZERLAND
Basel
Winterthur
Zürich
Sankt Gallen
Bern
Thun
Interlaken
Fribourg
Neuchâtel
Luzern
Zug
Schwyz
Chur
Davos
Lausanne
Genève
Montreux
Sion
Brig
Martigny
Chamonix-Mont Blanc
Mont Blanc
Matterhorn
Monte Rosa
Aosta
Gran Paradiso

LIECHTENSTEIN
Vaduz
Feldkirch
Bregenz
Dornbirn
Landeck

LYON
St-Chamond
St-Étienne
Vichy
Roanne
Thiers
Mâcon
Bourg-en-Bresse
Annecy
Aix-les-Bains
Chambéry
Albertville
Voiron
Vienne

Domodossola
Verbania
Varese
Busto Arsizio
Como
Lecco
Bérgamo
Lago di Garda

3 18 **4** **8** 20 **5** 22

1 RÜGEN **2**

A

SŁOWIŃSKI
Zatoka
Baltiysk
Kaliningrad (Russia)
Gvardeysk Chernyakhovsk
Bagrationovsk
Wejherowo Rumia *Gdańska*
Darłowo Słupsk Lębork Sopot Gdynia
Gdańsk Zalew Braniewo
Kołobrzeg Koszalin Bytów 329 Tczew Wiślany Elbląg
Usedom
Wolin Białogard Starogard Malbork Kętrzyn Giżycko
Świnoujście *WOLIŃSKI* Szczecinek Gdański Kwidzyn Olsztyn Szczytno
Stettiner Police Goleniów Chojnice Iława Ostróda
Haff Szczecin Stargard *Pojezierze Pomorskie* Świecie Grudziądz Pojezierze Mazursk
Neubrandenburg Szczeciński Wałcz Chełmno Brodnica Działdowo Ostrołęka
MÜRITZ Choszczno Piła Bydgoszcz Mława Ciechanów Narew
B Schwedt *DRAWIEŃSKI* Toruń Rypin *W'kra* Mo

Eberswalde- Gorzów Noteć Inowrocław Włocławek Pułtusk Bug Soł
Finow Wielkopolski Płock Legionowo
Kostrzyn Gniezno WARSZAWA Mazowiecki
BERLIN Międzychód Poznań Września (Warsaw) Otwock
Fürstenwalde *Warta* *WIELKOPOLSKI* Koło Kutno Łowicz Pruszków
Frankfurt Nowy Tomyśl Śrem Konin Łęczyca Skierniewice Żyrardów
Spree Zielona Leszno Kościan *Prosna* Turek Kalisz Grójec *Pilica*
GERMANY Góra POLAND Zduńska Łódź
Forst Kościan Sieradz Wola Pabianice Radom
Cottbus Nowa Sól Żagań *Odra* Krotoszyn Ostrów Piotrków Końskie Skarżysko-
Lauchhammer Żary *Bóbr* Głogów Wielkopolski Wieluń Trybunalski Tomaszów Kamienna
Hoyerswerda Bolesławiec Lubin Mazowiecki Starachowi
Bautzen Legnica Oleśnica Kluczbork Radomsko Kielce 612
C Dresden Görlitz Zgorzelec Wrocław Częstochowa Ostrowiec-
Elbe Jelenia Góra Świdnica Oława Świętokrzyski
Chemnitz Děčín Liberec Wałbrzych Dzierżoniów Opole Tarnowskie Myszków Jędrzejów *Wisła* Tarnob
Erzgebirge Teplice Ústí nad 1602 *KRKONOŠE* Kłodzko Góry Zawiercie Pińczów
Most Labem Jablonec Śněžka Nysa Bytom Sosnowiec
Chomutov nad Nisou Mladá Trutnov Racibórz Zabrze Gliwice Katowice Tarnów Mie
1244 Litoměřice Boleslav Hradec Opava Chorzów Oświęcim Kraków Bochnia Dęb
Karlovy Vary Kladno Králové Pardubice 1428 1492 Ostrava Havířov Tychy *Wisła*
Cheb PRAHA Kolín Šumperk Frýdek- Cieszyn Bielsko-Biała Jasło
Beroun (Prague) Olomouc Místek Karviná Żywiec 1725 *GORCZAŃSKI* Nowy
Plzeň Příbram *Vltava* Tábor *Českomoravská* 836 Prostějov Přerov 1324 Zakopane Sącz *MAGU*
CZECH REP. *Vrchovina* Havlíčkův Brod Zlín *Považská* Západné Nowy *BRANSKÝ* Bardejov
1042 Klatovy Jihlava Vyškov Bystrica Žilina Beskydy Targ *TRANSKÝ* Poprad 1157
Pisek Třebíč Brno Bielé Karpaty Martin 2655 Prešov
SUMAVA *Grosse* České Jindřichův Znojmo Trenčín Nízke *Tatry* 2043 *SLOVENSKÝ RAJ*
Arber Budějovice Hradec *PODYJI* Hodonín Prievidza Banská Bystrica
1456 Plöckenstein Gmünd 768 Kos
Böhmerwald 1378 Horn *Morava* *Male* Topol'čany *Slovenské Rudohorie* 1458 *AGGTELEKI*
D Passau *Danube* Zwettl Krems Stockerau Trnava Zvolen Nitra Lučenec *Bodva* Sátoraljaújhel
1042 (Donau) Freistadt Melk Sankt Levice Nové Ózd *Sajó* Kos
Ried Linz Pölten WIEN Bratislava Zámky Salgótarján Miskolc
Wels Amstetten (Vienna) Bruck an Komárno Vác *BÜKKI* Eger
Steyr Baden der Leitha Mosonmagyaróvár Dunakeszi Gyöngyös Mezőkövesd
Gmunden *SÖLKTÄLER* Wiener Sopron Győr Esztergom Jászberény Hajdú-
2514 Neustadt 985 Tatabánya Pápa 709 Érd BUDAPEST Debrece
2995 Mürzzuschlag Semmering P. Tisza *HORTO*
AUSTRIA Eisenerz Kapfenberg Győr Székesfehérvár Cegléd Karcag
2449 Bruck an der Mur Szombathely Ajka Veszprém Szolnok Mezőtúr
Leoben *POLLAUER TAL* Nagykőrös
E Graz Zalaegerszeg *BALATON FELVIDÉKI* HUNGARY Kecskemét
2441 *NOCKBERGE* Wolfsberg *Mur* Balaton *KISKUNSÁGI* Csongrád Békéscsaba
Klagenfurt Nagykanizsa Dunaújváros Siófok Kalocsa Kiskőrös Szentes Gyula
Drava Maribor Kaposvár Szekszárd Kiskunhalas Oroshaza
Triglav *KARAWANKEN* Kranj Celje Varaždin 681 Mako Hódmezővásár
2558 Koprivnica Szeged Arad
E 2863 *TRIGLAVSKI* Sava Bjelovar Pécs *DUNA DRAVA* Baja Subotica
Ljubljana Kalce 1035 Virovitica Mohács Sännicolau
SLOVENIA ZAGREB *Drava* Sombor Senta Mare
F Trieste Postojna Sisak 984 Osijek SERB. & M. Kikinda
1796 CROATIA Vukovar *Vojvodina* Timişo
Rijeka Karlovac Novi Sad Zrenjanin

ft m 48
6000 2000
3000 1000
1500 500
600 200
0 0
50
100 300
m ft

Projection: *Conical with two standard parallels*

20 **2** 16 **3** 18 **4** 20 **5**

National Parks

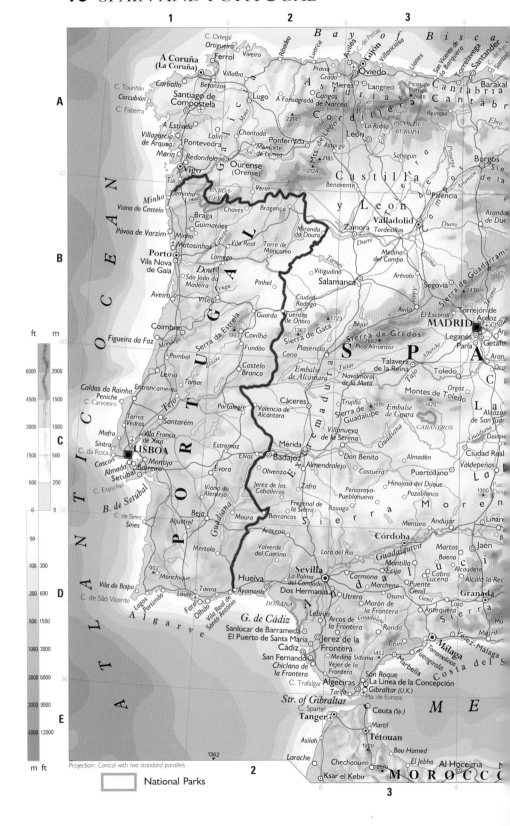

Projection: Conical with two standard parallels

National Parks

ft	m
6000	2000
4500	1500
3000	1000
1500	500
600	200
0	0
50	
100	300
200	600
500	1500
1000	3000
2000	6000
3000	9000
4000	12000

m ft

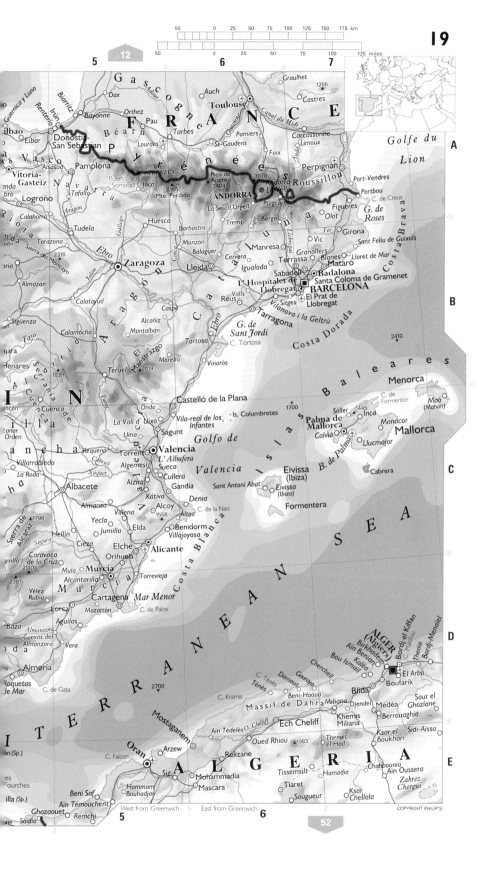

50   0   25   50   75   100   125   150   175 km
50   0   25   50   75   100   125 miles

Graulhet
1266
Auch
Gascogne   Dax   Orthez   Toulouse
Béarn   Pau   Tarbes   Castres
Biarritz   Bayonne   Pamiers   Carcassonne
Guernica y Luno   Irún   Lourdes   St-Gaudens   Foix   Limoux   Perpignan
Bilbao   Eibar   Donostia-San Sebastián   Canal du Midi   Port-Vendres
as Vasco   Alsásua   Pamplona   Pyrénées   Pico de   3078   Roussillon   Portbou
Vitoria-Gasteiz   Navarra   Puerto de   Aneto   Andorra la Vella   C. de Creus
bro   Tafalla   Jaca   3355   3404   ANDORRA   Figueres   G. de
Logroño   Aragón   Mte. Perdido   La Seu d'Urgell   Puigcerdà   Roses
Rioja   Calahorra   Huesca   Tremp   Berga   Olot   Girona
Tudela   Barbastro   Segre   Ter   Vic   Sant Feliu de Guixols
nda   Monzón   Manresa   Granollers   Blanes   Lloret de Mar
ión   Sierra del Moncayo   2316   Balaguer   Cervera   Terrassa   Mataró   Costa
Tarazona   Zaragoza   Lleida   Igualada   Sabadell   Badalona   Brava
Almazán   Catalunya   L'Hospitalet de   Santa Coloma de Gramenet
Calatayud   Caspe   Llobregat   BARCELONA
Sigüenza   Calamocha   1839   Alcañiz   Ebro   Valls   Reus   El Prat de   Vilanova i la Geltrú
ijara   Montalbán   Vinaròs   Tarragona   Llobregat   Sitges
Tajo   Teruel   Morella   G. de   Costa Dorada   2410
Henares   El   Sant Jordi
I   Cuenca   Maestrazgo   2019   Tortosa   C. Tortosa
N   Serranía   Castelló de la Plana   Baleares
lla   Cuenca   1700   Menorca
anar   Onda   Vila-real de los   Ils. Columbretes   C. de
Orden   La Vall d' Uixó   Infantes   Formentor   Maó
La Roda   Requena   Lliria   Sagunt   Sóller   1445   Inca   (Mahón)
Villarrobledo   Cabriel   Torrent   Valencia   Golfo de   Palma de   Calvià   Manacor   Mallorca
cha   Albacete   Algemesí   L'Albufera   Valencia   Mallorca   Llucmajor
a   Almansa   Alzira   Sueca   B. de Palma
Yecla   Cullera   Cabrera
Villena   Xàtiva   Gandía   Eivissa
Hellín   1558   Alcoy   Denia   Sant Antoni Abat   (Ibiza)
Jumilla   Elda   Altea   C. de la Nao   Eivissa
Cieza   Benidorm   (Ibiza)
Caravaca   Elche   Villajoyosa   Formentera
de la Cruz   2001   Orihuela   Alicante
2381   Mula   Murcia   Islas
Vélez Rubio   Alcantarilla   Torrevieja
Lorca   Cartagena   Mar Menor
Aguilas   Mazarrón   C. de Palos   MEDITERRANEAN   SEA
Almanzora
Cuevas del   2700
Almanzora   Vera
Almería   ALGER   Bordj el Kiffan
Roquetas   C. de Gata   (Algiers)   Birkhadem   C. Matifou
le Mar   Ain Benian   Kolea   Bordj-Menaïel
C. Ténès   Cherchell   Bou Ismaïl   El Arba
011   Damous   Boufarik
Oran   C. Kramis   Gouraya   Blida
Arzew   Ténès   Beni-Haoua   Djendel   Médéa   Sour el
n (Sp.)   Massif de Dahra   Miliana   Berrouaghia   Ghozlane
C. Falcon   Relizane   Khemis   Ksar el   Sidi-Aissa
ourches   Sig   Mostaganem   Ech Cheliff   Miliana   Boukhari
lla (Sp.)   Mohammadia   Aïn Tédelès   O. Chéliff   1983
Ghazaouet   Mascara   Oued Rhiou   Theniet   Chahbounia   Aïn Oussera
Saïdia   Remchi   ALGERIA   el Had   Hamadia   Zahrez
Beni Saf   Hammam   Tissemsilt   Chergui
Aïn Témouchent   Bouhadjar   Tiaret   Ksar
Sougueur   Chellala

A
Golfe du
Lion
42
B
40
C
38
D
36
E

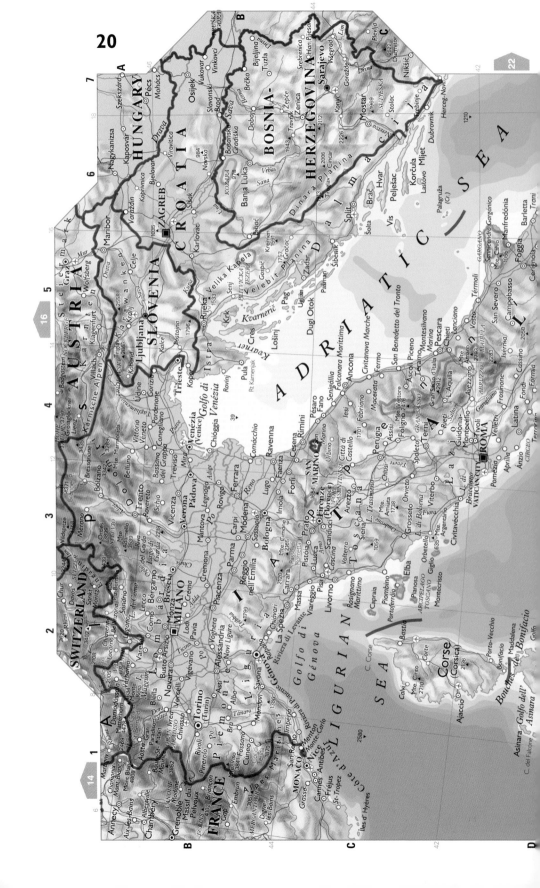

50   0   25   50   75   100 125 150 175 km
50   0   25   50   75   100 125 miles

IONIAN SEA

TYRRHENIAN SEA

MEDITERRANEAN SEA

National Parks

East from Greenwich

COPYRIGHT PHILIP'S

Projection: Conical with two standard parallels

Sardegna (Sardinia)

TUNISIA

ALGERIA

MALTA

m ft
4000 12000
3000 9000
2000 6000
1500 4500
1000 3000
600 1800
300 900
150 450
0 0

4000 12000
3000 9000
2000 6000
1000 3000
500 1500
200 600
0 0

Lecce
Brindisi
Francavilla
Fontana
Ostuni
Fasano
Otranto
Gallipoli
Nardo
Galatina
Taranto
Golfo di Táranto
Martina
Fuggiano
Altamura
Matera
Potenza
2248
Sala Consilina
Sele
CILENTO
Salerno
Napoli
Ischia
Torre del Greco
Castellammare di Stabia
Capri
Ventotene
C. Rizzuto
Crotone
Catanzaro
Rossano
Corigliano Cálabro
1928
Cosenza
Nicastro
Sambiase
L'ASPROMONTE
1423
Taurianova
Palmi
Reggio di Calábria
C. Spartivento
Messina
Str. di Messina
Vibo Valéntia
Scilla
POLLINO
2248
Cetraro
Craro
Lauria
Catania
Siracusa
Augusta
Avola
Noto
C. Passero
Ispica
Módica
Ragusa
Vittória
Giarre
Acireale
Etna 3323
Adrano
Paternò
Lentini
986
Caltagirone
Gela
Licata
Canicatti
Caltanissetta
Enna 986
Salso
Barcellona Pozze di Gotto
Milazzo
Isole Eólie
Strómboli
Salina
Lipari
Vulcano
Patti
Monti Nébrodi
1847
Términi Imerese
Bagheria
Palermo
Portúno
Alcamo 1613
Partinico
Castelvetrano
Sciacca
Salso
Porto Empédocle
Agrigento
Favara
SEGESTA
Érice
Trápani
Favignana
Isole Égadi
Marsala
Mazara del Vallo
Ustica (Italy)
Pantelleria (Italy)
Lampione
Linosa
Lampedusa
Isole Pelagie (Italy)
Gozo
Valletta
Rabat
MALTA
Ra's at Tib (C. Bon)
Kelibia
Ra's Muştafá
Menzel-Temime
Korba
Nabeul
Hammamet
Golfe de Hammamet
Sousse
Monastir
Mahdia
Mokmine
M'Saken
Zaghouan
Ben Arous
Soliman
Manouba
Bardo
TUNIS
Golfe de Tunis
L'Ariana
La Marsa
C. Blanc
Bizerte
Menzel-Bourguiba
Mateur
Béja
Tébourba
Téboursouk
El Fahs
Zaghouan
Kairouan
Kalaâ-Kebira
Sobkhat Sidi el Hani
C. Serrat
Tabarka
Is. de la Galite (Tunisie)
Rosa
C. di Monte Santu
C. Comino
Sardegna (Sardinia)
Nuoro
Gennargentu
Mt. di Gennargentu 1834
Arbatax
Lanusei
Quartu Sant' Elena
Cágliari
G. di Cágliari
C. Carbonara
C. Spartivento
Sorgono
Oristano
G. di Oristano
Bosa 1200
Iglésias
Portoscuso
Carbónia
1236
San Pietro
Sant' Antíoco
G. di Pálmas
Tirso
Terralba
C. di Monte Santu
Souk-Ahras
Annaba
Guelma
Sedrata
Ouenza
Aïn Beïda
Tébessa
Kasserine
Hadjeb el Aïoun
Thala
1378
Makthar
Kalaâ-Kebira
El Kef
Ghardimaou
Jendouba
Bou Salem
Mokhtar
Thala
El Kala
Souk-Ahras
Kasserine
3580
2500

5   4   3

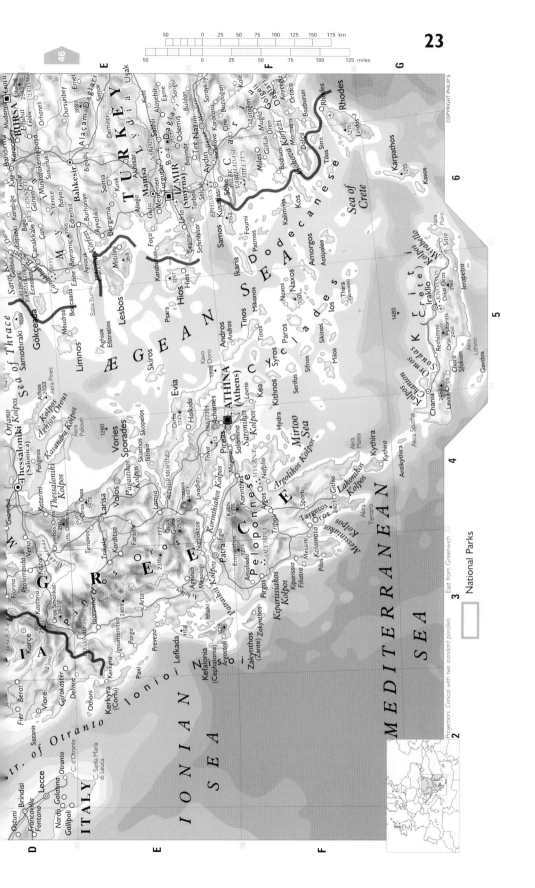

46

50 0 25 50 75 100 125 150 175 km
50 0 25 50 75 100 125 miles

COPYRIGHT PHILIP'S

E · D · G

National Parks

Projection: Conical with two standard parallels
East from Greenwich

TURKEY

BURSA
Balıkesir
İZMİR (Smyrna)
Manisa
Aydın
EPHESUS
MILETUS
Muğla
Rhodes
Lindos

Sea of Thrace
Gökçeada
Samothraki
Limnos
Lesbos
Hios
Psara

ÆGEAN SEA

Skiros
Evia
Andros
Tinos
Mikonos
Naxos
Paros
Ios
Amorgos
Astipalea
Kos
Dodecanese
Karpathos
Kasos

Sporades
Vories
Skopelos
Skiathos

Thessaloniki (Salonica)
Thessaliki Kolpos
Kassandha Kolpos
Aghiou Orous

Larisa
Volos
Trikala
Kardica

GREECE

ATHINA (Athens)
Pireas
Salamina
Korinthos
MYCENAE
OLYMPIA
Peloponnese
Patra
Tripoli
Kalamata
Sparti

Mirtoo Sea
Hydra
Kythira

Kriti (Crete)
Iraklio
KNOSSOS
Chania
Rethimno
Ierapetra

Sea of Crete

IONIAN SEA

ITALY
Brindisi
Lecce
Otranto
Gallipoli

ALBANIA
Gjirokastër
Vlorë
Korçë

Kerkyra (Corfu)
Levkada
Kefallonia (Cephalonia)
Zakynthos (Zante)

MEDITERRANEAN SEA

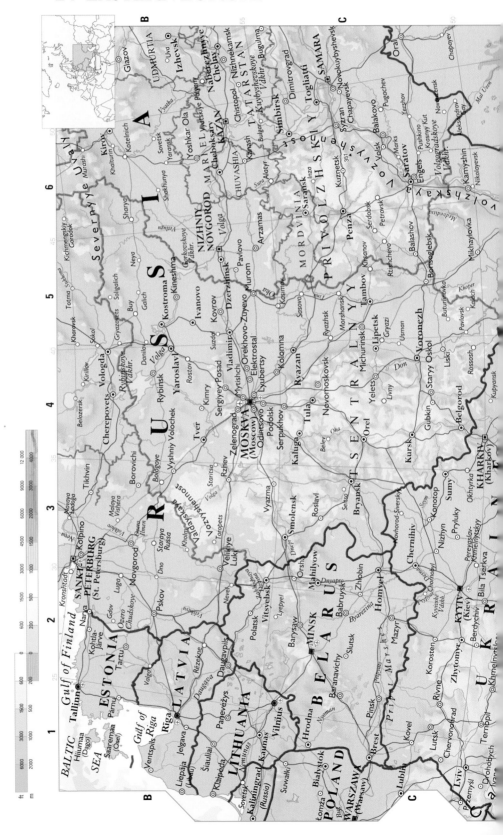

CASPIAN SEA

BLACK SEA

Sea of Azov

Scale

50 0 100 200 300 400 km
50 0 50 100 150 200 250 miles

Projection: Conical with two standard parallels

East from Greenwich

Countries and regions

ROMANIA
MOLDOVA
BULGARIA
TURKEY
GEORGIA
ARMENIA
AZERBAIJAN
IRAN
DAGESTAN
CHECHENIA
KABARDINO-BALKARIA
KARACHEVO-CHERKESSIA
NORTH OSSETIA
INGUSHETIA
ADYGEYA
ABKHAZIA
AJARIA
KALMYKIA
VOLGOGRAD
VOZYSHENNOST
YUZHNYY

Physical features

Caucasus Mountains
Kuzey Anadolu Dağları
Anadolu
Besarabia
Crimea
Caspian Depression
Prikaspiyskaya

Cities and towns

Astrakhan
Elista
Makhachkala
Derbent
Groznyy
Nalchik
Mozdok
Vladikavkaz
Stavropol
Nevinnomyssk
Cherkessk
Pyatigorsk
Kislovodsk
Nazran
Budennovsk
Blagodarnyy
Neftekumsk
Kizlyar
Baku (Bakı)
Sumqayıt
Ağdam
Xaçmaz
Quba
Qusar
Şäki
Ganca
Mingäçevir
Yevlax
Rustavi
Tbilisi
Telavi
Gyumri
Vanadzor
Kars
Yerevan
Ağrı
Van
Malazgirt
Muş
Bitlis
Erzurum
Erzincan
Kızıltepe
Tabrīz
Marand
Khvoy
Kapan
Ordubad
Naxçıvan
Ardabīl
Astara
Lānkārān
Neftçala
Salyan
Älät
Poti
Batumi
Sokhumi
Kutaisi
Sochi
Tuapse
Novorossiysk
Gelendzhik
Krasnodar
Maykop
Labinsk
Armavir
Kropotkin
Tikhoretsk
Pavlovskaya
Salsk
Rostov
Novocherkassk
Shakhty
Volgodonsk
Kotelnikovo
Krasnyy
Krasnyy Luch
Lysychansk
Luhansk
Stakhanov
Alchevsk
Horlivka
Makiyivka
Donetsk
Artemovsk
Kramatorsk
Sloviansk
Pavlohrad
Dniprodzerzhynsk
Dnipropetrovsk
Kryvyy Rih
Nikopol
Zaporizhzhya
Mariupol
Berdyansk
Melitopol
Kakhovka
Kherson
Mykolaiv
Odesa
Simferopol
Sevastopol
Yalta
Feodosiya
Kerch
Dzhankoy
Yevpatoriya
Balaklava
Voznesensk
Pervomaysk
Uman
Chişinău
Tiraspol
Tighina
Izmayil
Bălţi
Chernivtsi
Botoşani
Iaşi
Bacău
Focşani
Galaţi
Brăila
Buzău
Ploieşti
Bucureşti (Bucharest)
Piteşti
Braşov
Constanţa
Silistra
Dobrich
Ruse
Varna
Veliko Tŭrnovo
Burgas
Sliven
Khaskovo
Edirne
Tekirdağ
İstanbul
Çanakkale
Bandırma
Balıkesir
Bursa
Kocaeli (İzmit)
İzmir (Smyrna)
Manisa
Akhisar
Turgutlu
Uşak
Afyon
Kütahya
Eskişehir
Bilecik
Adapazarı
Sakarya
Ereğli
Zonguldak
Bolu
Bolvadin
Akşehir
Aksaray
Kırşehir
Ankara
Kırıkkale
Çankırı
Kastamonu
Sinop
Samsun
Bafra
Çarşamba
Ordu
Giresun
Trabzon
Rize
Artvin
Bayburt
Gümüşhane
Sivas
Tokat
Amasya
Çorum
Yozgat
Kayseri
Malatya
Elazığ
Keban Barajı

Water bodies

Volga
Don
Terek
Kuma
Manych
Tsimlyanskoye Vdkhr.
Ozero Manych-Gudilo
Dnipro
Dniester
Prut
Siret
Danube (Dunărea)
Tuz Gölü
Van Gölü
Marmara Denizi
Karkinitska Zatoka
Sea of Azov

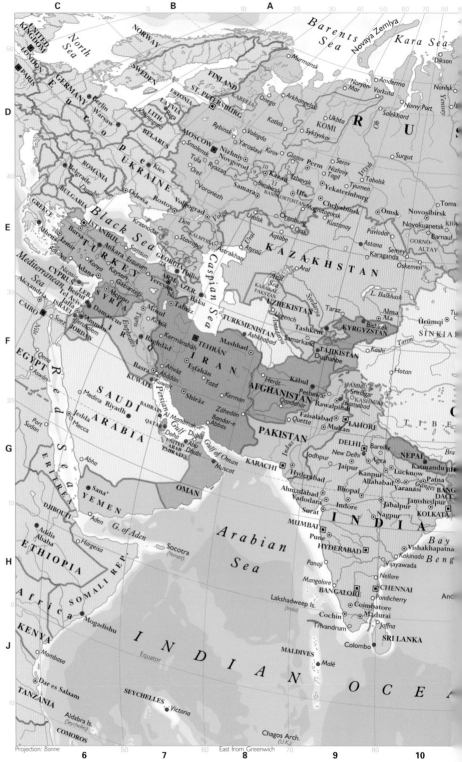

100 0 200 400 600 800 1000 1200 1400 km

100 0   200   400   600   800   1000 miles

C   B   A

Barents Sea   Novaya Zemlya   **Kara Sea**

UNITED KINGDOM
North Sea
NORWAY
Murmansk   Amderma
Dikson
LONDON
PARIS
SWEDEN
FINLAND
ST. PETERSBURG
Naryan-Mar
Vorkuta
Norilsk
Novvy Port
Yenisey

D

GERMANY
Berlin
Warsaw
ESTONIA
LATVIA
Riga
LITH.
Königsberg
BELARUS
Kiev
MOSCOW
Nizhniy
Smolensk
Novgorod
Tula
Ryazan
Orel
Voronezh
Samara
Rybinsk
Vologda
Yaroslavl Kirov
KOMI
Ukhta
Syktyvkar
R
U
Ob
Salekhard
Surgut
Toms

UKRAINE
Belgrade
ROMANIA
Danube
BULGARIA
Odessa
Rostov
Volgograd
Volga
Kazan
Simbirsk
BASHKORTOSTAN
Ufa
Izhevsk
Perm
Glazov
Serov
Nizhniy Tagil
Yekaterinburg
Chelyabinsk
Magnitogorsk
Kustanay
Tyumen
Tobolsk
Omsk
Novosibirsk
Novokuznetsk
GORNO-ALTAY
Barnaul

E

GREECE
Athens
Izmir
Bursa
ISTANBUL
TURKEY
Ankara
Samsun
Erzurum
GEORGIA
Tbilisi
Krasnodar
Don
Stavropol
Astrakhan
KALMYKIA
Ural
Uralsk
Orenburg
Orsk
Aqtöbe
Aral
Aqtau
Atyraū
KAZAKHSTAN
Pavlodar
Astana
Semey
Öskemen
Karaganda

Aral Sea

MEDITERRANEAN Sea
CYPRUS
Nicosia
Adana
Konya
Kayseri
Gaziantep
Aleppo
ARM. AZER.
Yerevan
Baku
Tabriz
Mosul
Tehrān
TURKMENISTAN
Ashkhabad
UZBEKISTAN
Urgench
Amudarya
Syrdarya
Tashkent
Samarkand
Taraz
L. Balkhash
Alma Ata
Bishkek
KYRGYZSTAN
SINKIAN
Ürümqi
Kashi
Tarim

F

EGYPT
Alexandria
CAIRO
Suez
Qena
Aswān
Red Sea
LEB.
Beirut
Damascus
SYRIA
Jerusalem
Amman
JORDAN
ISRAEL
Tel Aviv
Jaffa
IRAQ
Baghdād
Tigris
Euphrates
Kirkuk
Kermānshāh
Mashhad
Esfahān
IRAN
Yazd
Kerman
Zāhedān
AFGHANISTAN
Herāt
Qandahār
Kābul
Peshawar
Rawalpindi
Islamabad
JAMMU
Srinagar
KASHMIR
PAKISTAN
Faisalabad
Quetta
LAHORE
Multan
TIBET
C

SAUDI ARABIA
Medina
Jedda
Mecca
Riyadh
BAHRAIN
KUWAIT
Kuwait
Al Manamah
QATAR
Doha
Persian Gulf
UNITED ARAB EMIRATES
Abu Dhabi
Dubai
Gulf of Oman
Muscat
Basra
Abādān
Ahvāz
Shirāz
Bandar-e Abbas
KARACHI
Hyderabad
Jodhpur
New Delhi
DELHI
Jaipur
Bareilly
Agra
Kanpur
Lucknow
Allahabad
NEPAL
Katmandu
BHUTAN
Patna
Varanasi
Ganges
Bra

G

ERITREA
Port Sudan
Abha
YEMEN
Sana'
Aden
DJIBOUTI
G. of Aden
Socotra (Yemen)
OMAN
Arabian Sea
Ahmadābād
Vadodara
Surat
Bhopal
Indore
MUMBAI
Pune
HYDERABAD
Jabalpur
Nagpur
Jamshedpur
KOLKATA
DACC
BANG
I N D I A
Panaji
Vishakhapatna
Kakinada
Vijayawada
Bay
of Beng

H

ETHIOPIA
Addis Ababa
Hargeisa
SOMALI REP.
Mogadishu
Mangalore
BANGALORE
Lakshadweep Is. (India)
Nellore
CHENNAI
Pondicherry
Coimbatore
Cochin
Madurai
Trivandrum
Jaffna
SRI LANKA
Colombo
And

KENYA
Mombasa
I N D I A N
Equator
MALDIVES
Malé

J

TANZANIA
Dar es Salaam
SEYCHELLES
Aldabra Is. (Seychelles)
Victoria
O C E A
O C E

COMOROS
Chagos Arch. (U.K.)

Projection: Bonne   East from Greenwich

m ft

0
200   600
1000 3000
2000 6000
4000 12000
6000 18000
8000 24000

6   7   8   9   10

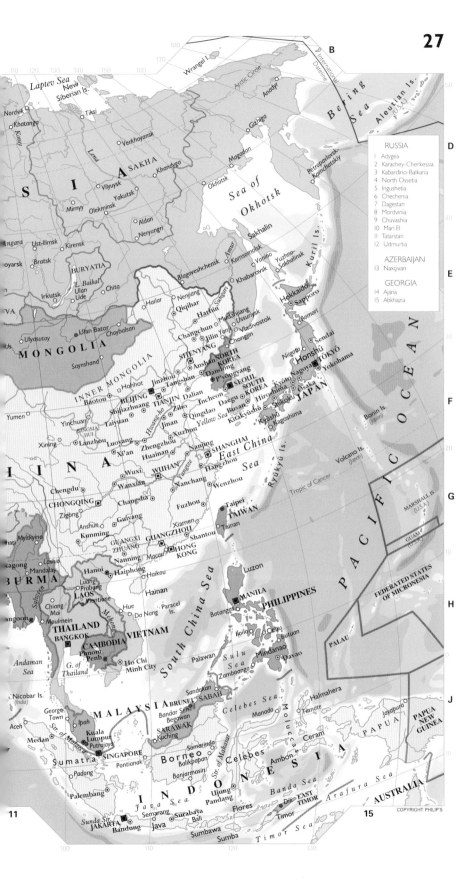

B

Wrangel I.

Laptev Sea
New
Siberian Is.
Tiksi
Nordvik
Khatanga
Kotuy

Bering Sea
Arctic Circle
Anadyr
Gizhiga
Aleutian Is.
(U.S.A.)

Verkhoyansk
Magadan
Petropavlovsk-
Kamchatskiy

S   I   A
SAKHA

Lena
Vilyuysk
Yakutsk
Khandyga
Okhotsk
Mirnyy
Olekminsk
Aldan
Neryungri

Ust-Ilimsk
Kirensk

Angara
oyarsk
Bratsk
BURYATIA
L. Baikal
Irkutsk   Ulan
Ude
Chita
VA
Ulan Bator
Choybalsan
Ulyasutay

Sea of Okhotsk

Komsomolsk
Blagoveshchensk
Amur
Khabarovsk
Vanino
Sungari
Hailar
Nenjiang
Qiqihar
Harbin
Changchun
Jilin Yenji
Sakhalin
Yuzhno-
Sakhalinsk

Kuril Is.

Mudanjiang
Ussuriysk
Vladivostok
Chongjin

Hokkaido
Sapporo

MONGOLIA
Saynshand

Aomori

INNER MONGOLIA
Hohhot
Baotou
BEIJING
Jinzhou
Tangshan
TIANJIN
Shijiazhuang
Zibo
Dalian

SHENYANG
Anshan
Dandong
NORTH
KOREA
P'yongyang

Niigata
Sendai
Honshū
TŌKYŌ
Yokohama

Yumen
Yinchuan
Taiyuan
Hoang-ho
Jinan
Qingdao
Incheon
Daegu
SEOUL
SOUTH
KOREA
Busan
Hiroshima
Ōsaka
Kyōto
Nagoya
JAPAN
Shikoku
Kyūshū
Kagoshima
Kitakyūshū

SINGSIA
HUI
Xining
Lanzhou
Luoyang
Xi'an
Zhengzhou
Huainan
Xuzhou
Nanjing
Yellow Sea

I   I   N   A

Wuxi
SHANGHAI
*East China
Sea*
WUHAN
Yangtze
Hangzhou

Chengdu
Wanxian
Nanchang
Wenzhou
Ryūkyū Is.

Chongqing
Changsha
Fuzhou

Zigong
Anshun
Guiyang
Xiamen
Taipei
TAIWAN
Tainan

Kunming
GUANGXI
ZHUANG
GUANGZHOU
Shantou
Nanning
Macau
HONG
KONG

Tropic of Cancer

Volcano Is.
(Japan)

Bonin Is.
(Japan)

PACIFIC

MARSHALL IS.
(U.S.A.)

GUAM
(U.S.A.)

OCEAN

FEDERATED STATES
OF MICRONESIA

PALAU

Myitkyina
hati
Lashio
tagong
Mandalay
BURMA
Hanoi
Haiphong
Haikou
Hainan
Luzon
MANILA
PHILIPPINES

Luang
Prabang
LAOS
Vientiane
Chiang
Mai
Moulmein
ngoon
THAILAND
BANGKOK
Hue
Da Nang
Paracel
Is.
Batangas
Iloilo
Cebu
Butuan
Davao
Mindanao

CAMBODIA
VIETNAM
Phnom
Penh
Ho Chi
Minh City
Palawan
South China Sea
Sulu
Sea
Zamboanga

*Andaman
Sea*
G. of
Thailand

*Nicobar Is.
(India)*

George
Town
Ipoh
MALAYSIA
BRUNEI
SABAH
Sandakan
Celebes Sea
Manado
Ternate
Halmahera
Jayapura
PAPUA
NEW
GUINEA

Aceh
Medan
Kuala
Lumpur
Putrajaya
Bandar Seri
Begawan
SARAWAK
Kuching
Samarinda
PAPUA

Str. of Malacca
SINGAPORE
Pontianak
Borneo
Balikpapan
Str. of Macassar
Celebes
Ambon
Ceram
Moluccas

Padang
Banjarmasin
Sumatra
INDONESIA

Palembang
Ujung
Pandang
Banda Sea
Arafura Sea
AUSTRALIA

Java Sea
Semarang
Surabaya
Dili
EAST
TIMOR
Timor

Sunda Str.
JAKARTA
Bandung
Java
Bali
Sumbawa
Flores
Sumba
Timor Sea

D

E

F

G

H

J

11

15

COPYRIGHT PHILIP'S

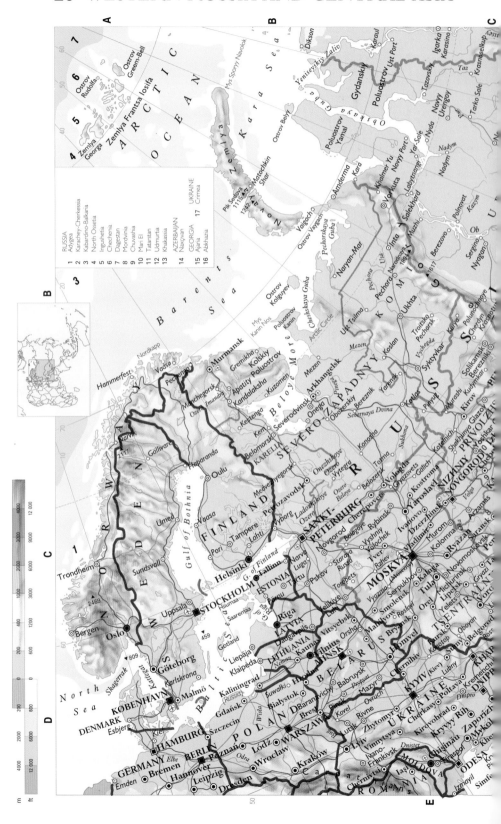

RUSSIA
1 Adygea
2 Karachey-Cherkessia
3 Kabardino-Balkaria
4 North Ossetia
5 Ingushetia
6 Chechenia
7 Dagestan
8 Mordvinia
9 Chuvashia
10 Mari El
11 Tatarstan
12 Udmurtia
13 Khakassia
14 Naxçvan

AZERBAIJAN
14 Naxçvan

GEORGIA
15 Ajaria
16 Abkhazia

UKRAINE
17 Crimea

100 0 100 200 300 400 500 600 700 800 km
100 0 100 200 300 400 500 miles

COPYRIGHT PHILIP'S

Projection: Conical Orthomorphic with two standard parallels

East from Greenwich

S   I   B   I   R   S   K   I   Y

Sym
Nizhnevartovsk
Strezhevoy
Yugan
Kolpashevo
Kozhasok
Molchanovo
Belyy Yar
Bogotol
Chulym
Asino
Leninsk-Kuznetsky
Kemerovo
Kuznetsk
Novo-
Kuznetsk
Belovo
Prokopyevsk
Novoaltaysk
Temirtau
Barnaul
Biysk
Gorno-Altaysk
Gorno-Altaysk
Belukha
4506
Abaza
Gorn-Altaysk
Belokha
Kut
Ob
Asino
Tomsk
Anzhero-Sudzhensk
Cherepanovo
Berdsk
NOVOSIBIRSK
Kuybyshev
Ob
Kolyvan
Kamen
Slavgorod
Aleysk
Rubtsovsk
Zmeinogorsk
Leninogorsk
Oskemen
Ziryan
Zaysan
Zaysan
Köli

OMSK
Tyukalinsk
Kalachinsk
Pavlodar
Ekibastuz
Semiyarka
Semey
Georgieyka
Ayagöz

Tyumen
Ishim
Petropavl
Kochny
Boyaraul
Bayanaul
Qaraghandy
Balqash
Köli
1565
Saryshagan
Sha
Balqash

YEKATERINBURG
Kurgan
Shadrinsk
Kostanay
Qobstany
Atbasar
Astana
Temirtaü
Qaraghandy
Moyynty
Gulshad

CHELYABINSK
Troitsk
Rudnyy
Zhetiqara
Arqalyq
Amangeldi
Zhezqazghan
Qarazhal
Shu

K   A   Z   A   K   H   S   T   A   N

Qyzylorda
Shieli
Taraz
Qarataü
KYRGYZSTAN

Aral
Baykonyr
Zhangaqazaly
Syrdarya
Türkistan
Shymkent
Chirchiq
Shu
Bishkek

Magnitogorsk
Orsk
Qarabutaq
Qarasköl
Karsakpay
Ulutau

VOLGOGRAD
Astrakhan
Atyraü
Maqat
Kulsary
Beyneü
Aqtaü
QORAQALPOGHISTON
Nukus
Qünghirot
Muynak
Chimbay
UZBEKISTAN
TOSHKENT
Nawoiy
Samarqand
TAJIKISTAN
Dushanbe

Fort Shevchenko
Aqtaü
Garabogazköl Aylagy
Türkmenbashi
TURKMENISTAN
Ashgabat
Daşoguz
Khiwa
Urganch
Amudarya
Bukhoro
Qarshi
Termiz
AFGHANISTAN

BAKI (Baku)
Hazar
Esenguly
Gorgan
MASHHAD
Herat

ROSTOV
Krasnodar
Stavropol
Elista
KALMYKIA
Makhachkala
Derbent

GEORGIA
TBILISI
ARMENIA
YEREVAN
AZERBAIJAN
Gäncä
Ardabil
Rasht
TABRIZ
Qazvin
TEHRAN
Qom
ESFAHAN

TURKEY
Erzurum
Erzincan
Trabzon
Samsun
Sinop

Black Sea

AL MAWSIL (Mosul)
BAGHDAD
I   R   A   Q

I   R   A   N
Hamadan
Arāk
Kühhā-ye Zagros
Ahvāz
Abādān
SHIRAZ
Yazd
Dasht-e Kavir

C   H   I   N   A
ÜRÜMQI
Turpan
Bosten Hu
Korla
Tarim He
Aksu
Kashi
Yining

Junggar Pendi
Altay
Karamay
Bole
Tacheng
 Usu

100 0 100 200 300 400 500 600 700 800 km

0 100 200 300 400 500 miles

C

Mys Dezhneva
(East C.)

B

16

14

15

170

Uelen

Chukchi Sea

60

St. Lawrence I.
(U.S.A.)

Ostrov Gerntyety
Ostrov
Znamnety
Ostrova Deonga
Ostrov Zhokhova

Vankarem

Ostrova
meta
Ostrova Deonga

Ostrov
Faddeyevskiy

Ostrov
Novaya Sibir

Pevek
Chukotskoye Nagorye

1843

Ust Chaun

Egvekinot
Provideniya
Anadyrskiy Zaliv

Beringovskiy

Ostrov Malyy
Lyakhovskiy

Ostrov Bolshoy
Lyakhovskiy

Ostrova
Medvezhi

Ayon

1853

Bilibino

Ambarchik

Cherskiy

Anadyr

D

Proliv Dmitriya Laptev

Nizhne Kolymsk

1752

Yerepol

Markovo

Penzhino

Koryakskoye Nagorye

2652

Khatyrka

Kovacha

Bering
Sea

Buorkhaya

Oloy

Anadyr

Kamenskoye

Tilichiki

Ossora
Ostrov
Karaginskiy

Kazachye

Ust Kuyga

Srednekolymsk

Indigirka

Bolshoy Anyuy

Poren

Grizhiga

Penzhinskaya Guba

Komandorskiye
Ostrova

Deputatskiy

Druzhina

Zyryanka

Kolyma

Gishiginskaya

Palana

Uka

Yana

Khonuu

Pobeda
3147

Kolymskoye Nagorye

Zaliv
Shelikhova

Tigil

Sredinny

DALNEVOSTOCHNYY

Gora Chen
2682

Ust-Nera

Taskan

Omsukchon

Oroukan

Evensk
Noyakhar

Palana

Poluostrov

Gora
3621
Ust-Kamchatsk

Verkhoyansk

Batagai

Khrebet Cherskogo

Susuman

Yagodnoye

Aka

Palatka

Ust-Khayryuzovo

Klyuchevskaya
Nikolskoye

Ostrova

2389

Oymyakon

2959

Ust-Omchug

Magadan

4750

Kamchatka

3466

Petropavlovsk-
Kamchatskiy

KH
OYANSKIY Khrebet

Khandyga

Okhotsk

Kirovsky

Khrebet

Sangar

Batamay

Okhotskiy
Perevoz

Ulya

Sea

Severo-

Kuril'sk

Lena

Borogontsy

of

Ust-Bolsheretsk

Namtsy

Yyk-Kyuyel

Okhotsk

Ostrov
Paramushir

Pokrovsk

Yakutsk

Mayya

Amga

Arka

1780

Ostrov
Onekotan

Sinsk

Ust-Mil

Aimu

Maya

Nelkan

Okhotsk

50

Olekminsk

Chagda

Khrebet Dzhugdzur

Ayan

Kurilskiye Ostrova

Ostrov
Simushir

Tommot

Uchur

2246

Ostrov Bolshoy
Shantar

Ostrov
Urup

Aldan

Okha

Sakhalinskiy
Zaliv

Nikolayevsk-
na-Amure

Ostrov Iturup

2246

Neryungri

Chumikan

Tugur

Sakhalin

Kuril'sk

Nagornyy

Stanovoy Khrebet

Zeya

Uda

Aleksandrovsk-
Sakhalinskiy
1609 Gora Lopatina

Tatarskiy
Proliv

Ostrov
Kunashir

Tynda

Skovorodino

Zeya

Selemdzha

Amgun

Poronaysk

Uglegorsk

Yuzhno-Sakhalinsk

Wakkanai

2290

Khrebet

Mogocha

Dzhalinda

Ushumun

Norsk

Komsomolsk

Korsakov

Kholmsk

La Perouse Str.

Rebun

Gulian

Shimanovsk

Belogorsk

Chegdomyn

2640

Amursk

Vanino

Rumoi

Kushiro

Chara

Nyukzha

Svobodnyy

Zavitinsk

Obluchye

Birobidzhan

2078

Khrebet

Otaru

SAPPORO

Sretensk

1054

Blagoveshchensk

Poyarkovo

Roychikhinsk

Smidovich

Khabarovsk

Sikhote Alin

Hokkaido

Hakodate

Nerchinsk

Da Hinggan Ling

Amur

Bikin

Amgu

Terney

3669

Aomori

Hachinohe

Oloyyannaya

Shilka

Argun

Zabaykalsk

Gulian

Amur

Nenjiang

Beian

Hegang

Tyozemskaya

Lesozavodsk

Dalnegorsk

Olga

Manzhouli

Hailar

CHINA

QIQIHAR

Yichun

Jiamusi

Spassk

Dalniy

Hulun Nur

Baicheng

DAQING

Songhua Jiang

Jixi

Samka

Ussuriysk

Artem

Vladivostok

Nakhodka

JAPAN

HARBIN

Mudanjiang

Kraskino

Nen Jiang

East from Greenwich

120

9

Yanji

10

11

COPYRIGHT PHILIP'S

E

40

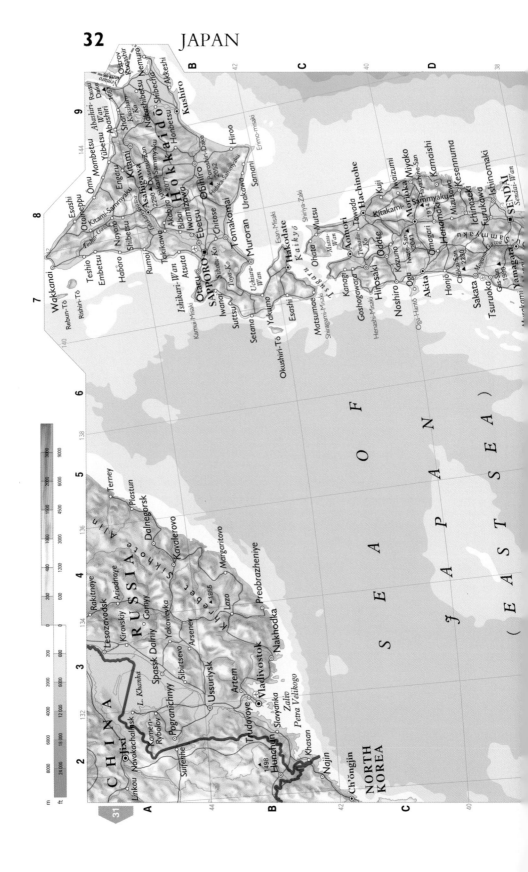

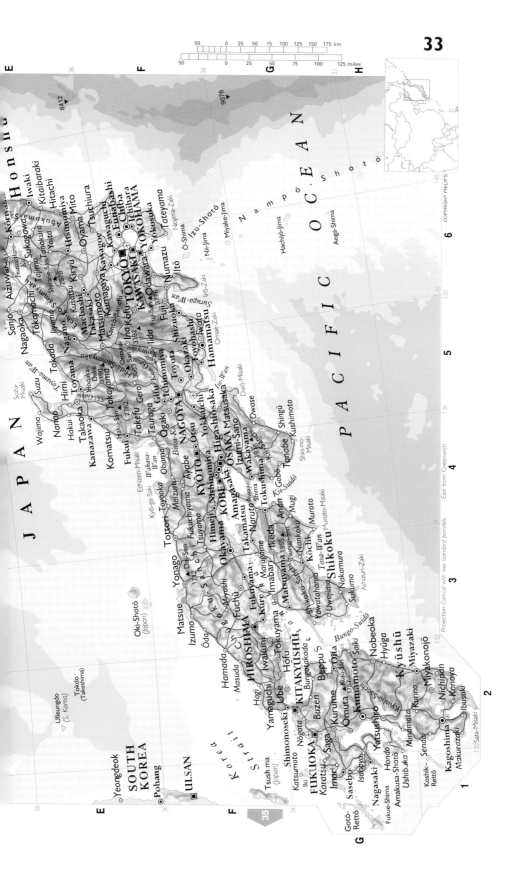

50 0 25 50 75 100 125 150 175 km
50 0 25 50 75 100 125 miles

E F G H

JAPAN

Honsu

8412 9076

SOUTH KOREA

Yeongdeok
Pohang
ULSAN

Ulleungdo (S. Korea)

Tokdo (Takeshima)

Oki-Shotō (Japan)

Tsushima (Japan)

Yonago
Matsue
Izumo
Ōda
Hamada
Masuda
Hagi
Yamaguchi
Ube
Shimonoseki
Nōgata
KITAKYŪSHŪ
FUKUOKA
Saga
Karatsu
Imari
Sasebo
Nagasaki
Fukue-Shima
Gotō-Rettō
Isahaya
Hondo
Amakusa-Shotō
Ushib ıka
Katsumoto
Iki
Bungo-takada
Buzen
Beppu
Ōita
Kurume
Ōmuta
Kumamoto
Minamata
Kurino
Yatsushiro
Sata-Misaki
Makurazaki
Ibusuki
Kagoshima
Sendai
Koshik- Rettō
Kanoya
Nichinan
Miyakonojō
Kyūshū
Kyūshū-Sanchi
Miyazaki
Hyūga
Nobeoka
Saiki
Kuju-San
Bungo-Suidō

Tottori
Toyooka
Maizuru
Fukuchiyama
KYOTO
Ōtsu
Ōsaka
KOBE
Himeji
Okayama
Nishinomiya
Amagasaki
Izumi-Sano
Wakayama
HIROSHIMA
Fuchū
Fukuyama
Kure
Iwakuni
Hōfu
Marugame
Takamatsu
Imabari
Matsuyama
Kōchi
Ikeda
Nankoku
Kawanohama
Tosa-Wan
Sukumo
Nakamura
Ashizuri-Zaki
Shikoku
Shikoku-Sanchi
Uwajima
Shimanto
Shikoku
Tokushima
Naruto
Awaji
Anan
Mugi
Muroto
Muroto-Misaki
Shio-no-Misaki
Tanabe
Shingū
Kushimoto
Gobō
Owase
Daiō-Misaki

JAPAN

Sanjō
Nagaoka
Aizuwakamatsu
Kōriyama
Iwaki
Kitaibaraki
Hitachi
Mito
Utsunomiya
Tsuchiura
Funabashi
Chiba
TOKYO
YOKOHAMA
KAWASAKI
Kawaguchi
Yokosuka
Tateyama
Nojima-Zaki
Odawara
Numazu
Itō
Ō-Shima
Izu-Shotō
Niī-Jima
Miyake-Jima
Hachijō-Jima
Aoga-Shima

Niigata
Takada
Toyama
Himi
Takaoka
Kanazawa
Komatsu
Fukui
Nandao
Hokui
Wajima
Suzu
Suzu-Misaki
Toyama-Wan
Noto-Hantō
Echizen-Misaki
Kyō-ga-Saki
Wakasa-Wan
Obama
Tsuruga
Gifu
Ōgaki
NAGOYA
Ichinomiya
Toyota
Okazaki
Toyohashi
Iwata
Hamamatsu
Shizuoka
Fuji
Fujisan 3776
Suruga-Wan
Irō-Zaki
Ōmae-Zaki

Takada
Nagano
Matsumoto
Ōyama
Ōmiya
Kasukabe
Kumagaya
Kawagoe
Kiryū
Takasaki
Machi
Iida
Ichinomiya
Tajimi
Gero
Takefu
Nara
Tsu
Matsusaka
Higashiōsaka
Kōchi
Yokkaichi
Ayabe
Kii-Suidō

Zampo-Shotō

PACIFIC OCEAN

Projection: Conical with two standard parallels

East from Greenwich

COPYRIGHT PHILIP'S

35

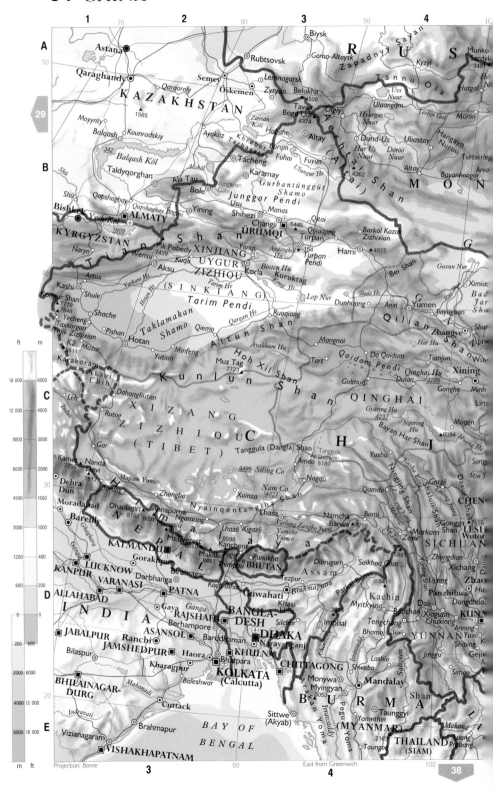

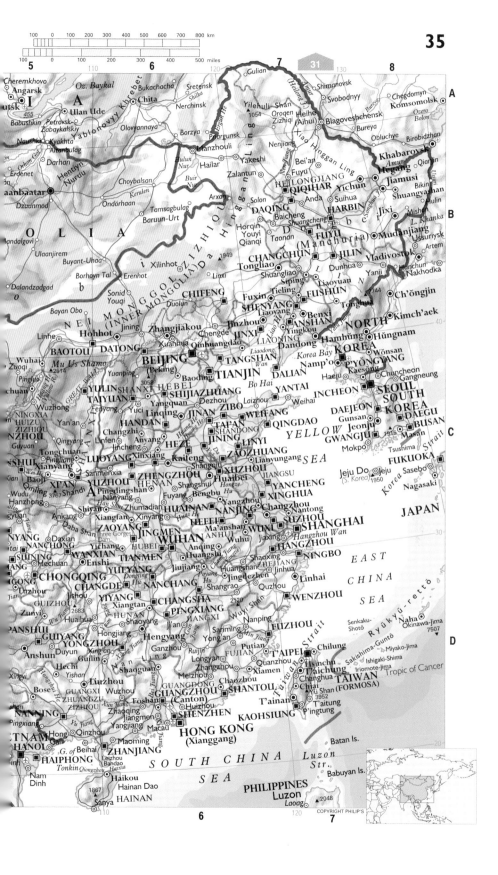

31

100	0	100	200	300	400	500	600	700	800 km	
100		0	100	200	300	400	500 miles			

A

B

C

D

Cheremkhovo
Angarsk
utsk
455
Babushkin Petrovsk-
Zabaykalskiy
Naushki Kyakhta
Orhon Gol
Darhan
Erdenet
aanbaatar
Dzuunmod
Ulaanjirem
andalgovi
Dalandzadgad

I A
Oz. Baykal
Ulan Ude
Buil Nur
Olovyannaya
Choybalsan
Baruun-Urt
Tamsagbulag
Borhoyn Tal
Bayan Obo
Sonid
Youqi
Duolun

O L I A

Bukachacha
Chita
Sretensk
Nerchinsk
Shilka
Borzya
Priargunsk
Manzhouli
Hailar
Yakeshi
Zalantun
Solon
Horqin
Youyi
Qianqi
Taonan
Xilinhot
Erenhot
Linxi

Gulian
Yilehuli Shan
Orogen Zizhiqi
Nenjiang
Bei'an
Fuyu
Anda
Baicheng
Shuangcheng
Tongliao
Shuangliao
Siping
Tieling

Shimanovsk
Svobodnyy
Heihe
Aihui Blagoveshchensk
Bureya
Obluchye Birobidzhan
Khabarovsk
Hegang Qianjin
Jiamusi
Shuangyashan
Jixi
Mishan
Mudanjiang
Ussuriysk Artem
Vladivostok
Yanji
Hunchun
Nakhodka

NEI MONGGOL ZIZHIQU
(INNER MONGOLIA)

HEILONGJIANG
QIQIHAR
DAQING
HARBIN
FUYU
JILIN
CHANGCHUN
Dunhua

Chegdomyn
Komsomolsk
Ozero Bolon
L. Khanka

Ch'ŏngjin
Kimch'aek
Hŭngnam

Linhe
Hohhot
Zhangjiakou
Chengde
Xuanhua
CHIFENG
Fuxin
SHENYANG
Benxi
ANSHAN
Yingkou
Jinzhou
JINXI
LIAONING
Qinhuangdao
Dandong

NORTH
KOREA
PYONGYANG
Namp'o
Haeju Kaesŏng

BAOTOU DATONG
BEIJING (Peking)
TANGSHAN
TIANJIN
DALIAN
Baoding
YULIN
TAIYUAN
SHIJIAZHUANG
YANTAI
Yangquan
HANDAN
JINAN
ZIBO
WEIFANG
QINGDAO
Weihai

Korea Bay
Bo Hai

INCHEON
SEOUL
DAEJEON
SOUTH
KOREA
Gunsan
Jeonju
GWANGJU
Mokpo

DAEGU
BUSAN
Masan
Jeju Do
(S. Korea)
Jeju

FUKUOKA
Sasebo
Nagasaki

JAPAN

Y E L L O W   S E A

K o r e a   S t r a i t

Tsushima

Wuhai
Zuoqi
Pingluo
chuan
Yuanping
SHANXI HEBEI
Fenyang
Yuci
Linqing
Dezhou
Laizhou
TAIAN
SHANDONG
JINING
LINYI
ZAOZHUANG
Lianyungang

Changzhi
Xinxiang
HEZE
Kaifeng
Shangqiu
XUZHOU
JIANGSU

LUOYANG
ZHENGZHOU
HENAN
Shangshui
Huaibei
YANCHENG
XINGHUA

XI'AN
Sanmenxia
YUZHOU
Pingdingshan
Nanyang
Zhumadian
Xinyang
Fuyang
Bengbu
HUAIAN
Yangzhou
Changzhou
NANJING
SUZHOU
WUXI
SHANGHAI
Nantong

Baoji
Shandi
Hanzhong
Shiyan
Xiangfan
ZAOYANG
JINGMEN
HEFEI
ANHUI
Ma'anshan
Wuhu
Jiaxing
HANGZHOU
Hangzhou Wan
NINGBO

NANCHONG
SUINING
WANXIAN
TIANMEN
WUHAN
Huangshi
HUBEI
Anqing
Shaoxing
ZHEJIANG
Jinhua
Linhai

CHONGQING
CHANGDE
YUEYANG
NANCHANG
Jingdezhen
Quzhou

YIYANG
CHANGSHA
PINGXIANG
JIANGXI
Shangrao

WENZHOU

E A S T
C H I N A
S E A

GUIYANG
YONGZHOU
Hengyang
Shaoyang
HUNAN
Ji'an
Nanping
Sanming
FUJIAN
FUZHOU

GUILIN
Liuzhou
Shaoguan
Meizhou
Zhangzhou
Xiamen
Changhua
Chilung
T'AIPEI
T'aichung
Hsinchu

Ryūkyū-rettō
Naha
Okinawa-jima
Sakishima-Guntō
Miyako-Jima
Ishigaki-Shima
Iriomote-Jima

Tropic of Cancer

NANNING
GUANGXI
ZHUANGZU
ZIZHIQU
Wuzhou
GUANGDONG
(Canton)
GUANGZHOU
SHANTOU
Chaozhou
Foshan
SHENZHEN
Macau
HONG KONG
(Xianggang)
KAOHSIUNG
T'ainan
TAIWAN
(FORMOSA)
P'ingtung
T'aitung

Batan Is.

Pingxiang
ETNAM
HANOI
HAIPHONG
Tonkin
ZHANJIANG
Leizhou
Bandao
Qiongzhou

S O U T H   C H I N A
S E A

Luzon
Str.
Babuyan Is.
Luzon

Nam
Dinh
Haikou
Hainan Dao
Sanya HAINAN
PHILIPPINES
Luzon
Laoag

COPYRIGHT PHILIP'S

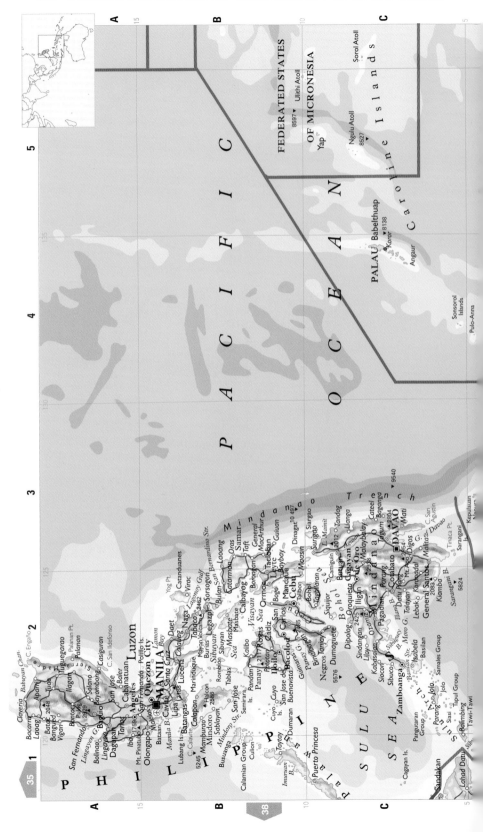

PACIFIC OCEAN

FEDERATED STATES OF MICRONESIA

8597▾ Ulithi Atoll

Soral Atoll

Ngulu Atoll
8527▾

Yap°

Caroline Islands

PALAU Babelthuap
▾8138
Koror°
A11
Angaur

Sonsorol Islands

Pulo-Anna

Mindanao Trench

▾9540

10 497

PHILIPPINE SEA

SULU SEA

MANILA
Luzon
Quezon City

Mindanao
DAVAO

CELEBES SEA

Sandakan

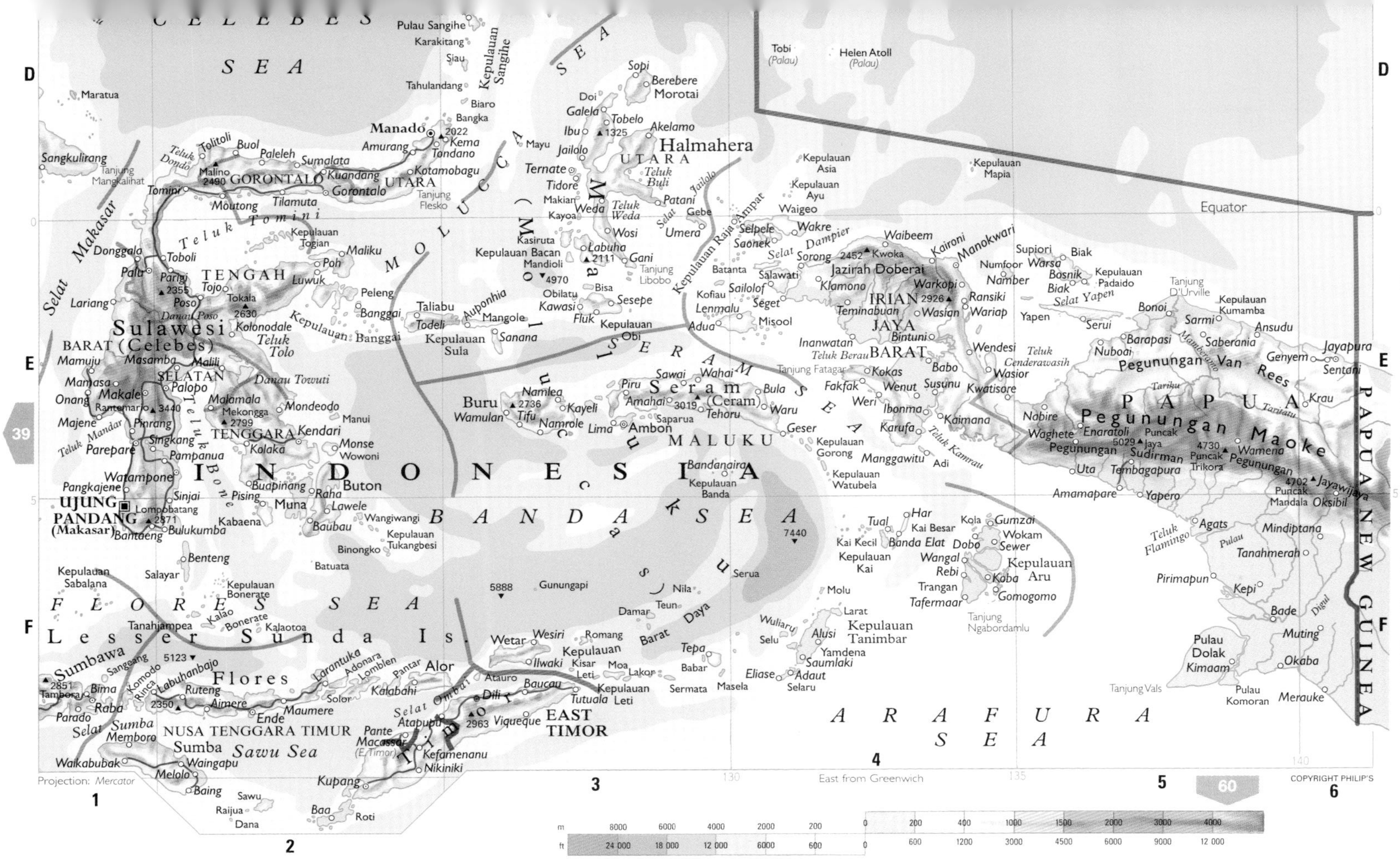

100 0 100 200 300 400 500 km
100 0 50 100 150 200 250 300 350 miles

COPYRIGHT PHILIP'S

PAPUA NEW GUINEA

P A P U A

Pegunungan Van Rees

Pegunungan Maoke

Pegunungan Jayawijaya

I R I A N   J A Y A   B A R A T

Jayapura · Sentani · Kau

Jazirah Doberai

Biak · Yapen · Serui · Nabire

Teluk Cenderawasih

A R A F U R A   S E A

Kepulauan Aru

Kepulauan Tanimbar

C E R A M   S E A

S e r a m (Ceram)

M A L U K U

Halmahera

UTARA

Ternate · Tidore

M a l u k u

Buru · Ambon

B A N D A   S E A

C E L E B E S   S E A

Manado

GORONTALO · UTARA

Sulawesi (Celebes)

TENGAH

BARAT · SELATAN · TENGGARA

UJUNG PANDANG (Makasar)

I N D O N E S I A

Selat Makasar

F L O R E S   S E A

Flores · Sumbawa · Sumba

NUSA TENGGARA TIMUR

Flores Sea · Sawu Sea

EAST TIMOR · Baucau · Dili

Lesser Sunda Is.

Kupang · Roti

Equator

East from Greenwich

Projection: Mercator

39

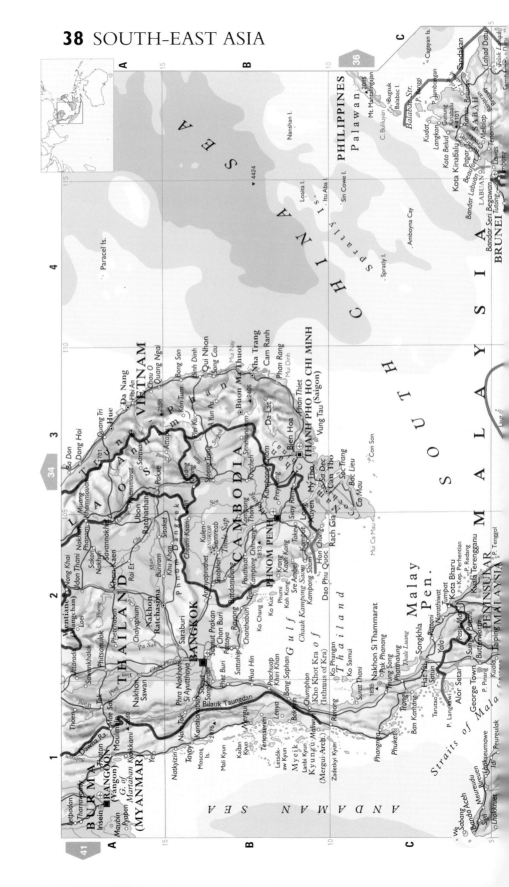

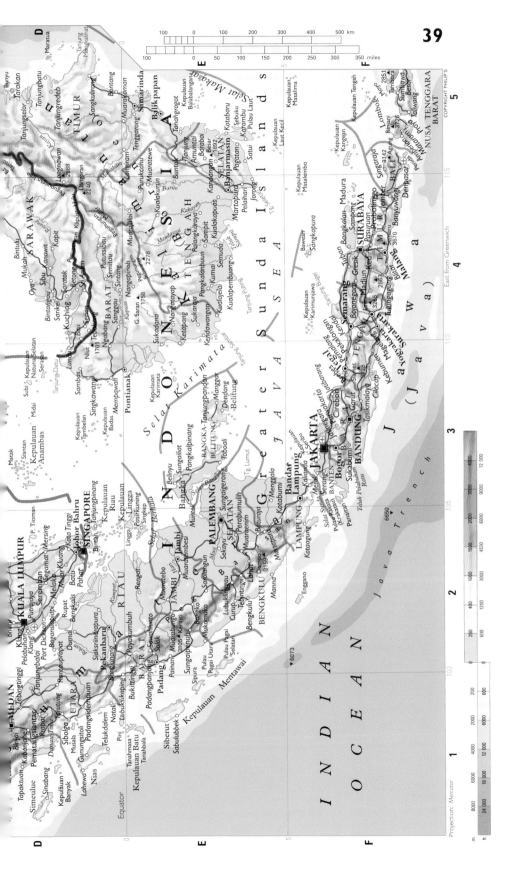

100   0   100   200   300   400   500 km
100   0   50   100   150   200   250   300   350 miles

COPYRIGHT PHILIP'S

East from Greenwich

Projection: Mercator

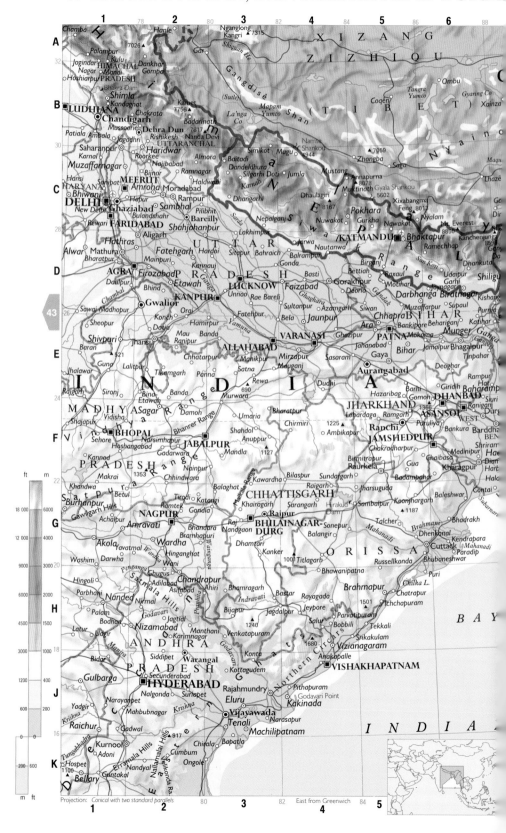

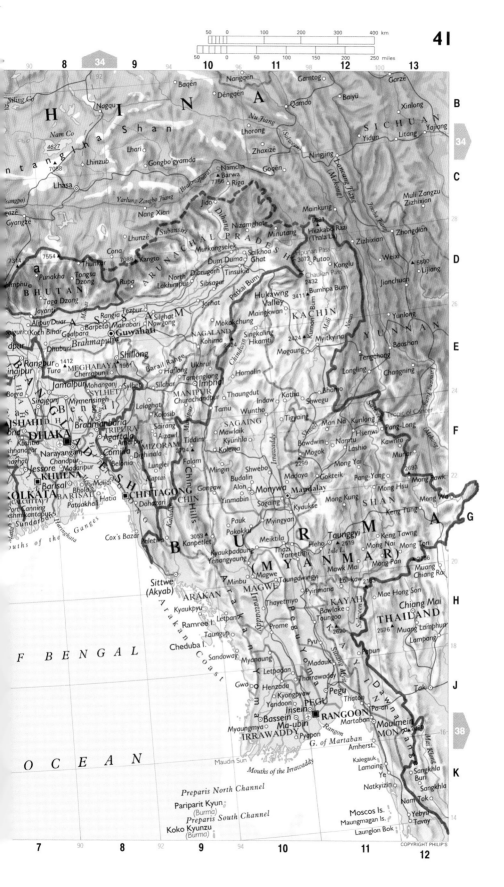

50 0   100   200   300   400 km
50   0   50   100   150   200   250 miles

90   **8**   **34**   **9**   94   96   **10**   96   **11**   98   **12**   100   **13**

B

C H I N A

Nanggen   Gamtog   Garzê

Baqên   Dêngqên   Qamdo   Baiyü   Xinlong

Nagqu   Lhorong   Litang   Yajiang
Shing Co   S I C H U A N
Nam Co   Zhaxizê   Ningjing   Yidun   Litang
4627   Yajiang   **34**
Lhari   Lhinzub   Goqên
Gongbo'gyamda   Namcha
7088   Barwa   Riga   **C**
Lhasa   7756
Yarlung Zangbo Jiang   Jido   Nizamghat   Mainkung   Muli Zangzu
Nang Xian   Suhansiri   Minutang   Hkakabo Razi   Zizhixian
Gyangzê   Lhunzê   Murkongselek   (Thala La)   Zizhixian   Zhongdian
7314   Cona   7089 Kangto   Saikhoa Ghat   Jpunan Pass   Weixi   **28**   **D**
7554   Thunkar   Dum Duma   3072 Putao   Konglu   5500
Punakha   Tongsa   Rupa   North   Dibrugarh   Tinsukia   Chaukan Pass   Jianchuan   Lijiang
a   Taga Dzong   Dzong   Lakhimpur   Sibsagar   2432   Bumpha Bum
B H U T A N   A S S A M   Patkai Bum   Hukawng   3411
Jayanti   Rangia   Tezpur   Jorhat   Valley   K A C H I N   Yunlong   **26**
Alipur Duar   Barpeta Mairabari   Nowgong   Maingkwan   Y U N N A N
eiguri   Koch Bihar   Galpara   Silghat   Mokokchung   Singkaling   2424   Myitkyina   Baoshan   **E**
dpur   Dhubri   Brahmaputra   Guwahati   N A G A L A N D   Hkamti   Kunon Bum
Rangpur   1412   Shillong   Kohima   3824   Mogaung   Tengchong
najpur   Tura   M E G H A L A Y A   1961   Barail Range   Ukhrul   Homalin   Longling   Changning
Jamalpur   Mohanganj   Cherrapunji   Haflong   Tamenglong   Bhamo   Tropic of Cancer   **24**   **F**
Bogra   Sirajganj   SYLHET   Silchar   Imphal   M A N I P U R   Thaungdut   Indaw   Katha   Shwegu
I Rajshahi   Mymensingh   Sylhet   Churachandpur   Tamu   Wuntho   Tigyaing   Man Na   Kunlong   Hsenwi   Pang-Long
bnd   DHAKA   Lalaghat   Kolosib   S A G A I N G   Mawlaik   Bawdwin   Namtu   Lashio   Kawnro
Kushtia   Narayanganj   Brahmanbaria   Sairang   Tiddim   Kyunhla   Mogok   Mong Yai   Munar   2693
shnanagar   Chandpur   Agartala   Aizawl   Kalewa   2299   Gokteik   Pang-Yang   Mong Pawk   **22**   **G**
ghat   TRIPURA   Amarpur   2704   Falam   Mingin   Madaya   Mandalay   Mong Kung   S H A N   Mong Wa
Jessore   KHULNA   Comilla   Belonia   Lunglei   Shwebo   Budalin   Alon   Monywa   Keng Tung   Mong Hsu
OLKATA   Barisal   M I Z O R A M   Dinhinala   Gangaw   Yinmabin   Sagaing   Kyaukse
(CALCUTTA)   BARISAL   Bhola   Chaptai   C H I N   Pauk   Myingyan   Mong Nai   Keng Tawng
Port Canning   Patuakhali   Hatia   CHITTAGONG   Hills   3053   Pakokku   Meiktila   Heho   Taunggyi   Mong Ton
shmikantapur   Dohazari   Kanpetlet   Kyaukpadaung   2519   Mawk Mai   Mong Pan
Sundarbans   Cox's Bazar   Paletwa   B   U   R   M   A   Thazi   Yamethin   Loi-kaw   2786   **20**   **H**
Mouths of the Ganges   Kyaukpadaung   Magwe   (M   Y   A   N   M   A   R   )   2163   Muang
Hooghly   Yenangyaung   Taungdwingyi   Pyinmana   Mae Hong Son   Chiang Rai
    Sittwe   A R A K A N   Minbu   M A G W E   K A Y A H   Chiang Mai
    (Akyab)   Kyaukpyu   Letpan   Thayetmyo   Bawlake   Toungoo   2576   2620   Muang Lamphun   **18**
    Ramree I.   Letpan   Prome   Toungoo   T H A I L A N D   Lampang
    Taungup   Pyu   Papun
    Cheduba I.   Sandoway   Myanaung   Madauk   K   Y   A   I   D   A   W   N   A   Tak   **J**
F   B E N G A L   Arakan Coast   Letpadan   Tharrawaddy   Maudin   A   Y   A   H
Gwa   Henzada   Pegu   Thaton
Kyongpyaw   Yandoon   PEGU   N   A   **16**   **38**
Myaungmya   Bassein   Insein   RANGOON   Martaban   Moulmein
Ma-ubin   Pyapon   Rangon   M   O   N   2098
I R R A W A D D Y   G. of Martaban   Amherst
Mouths of the Irrawaddy   Kalegauk   Mai Klong
Maudin Sun   Lamaing   Sangkhla
O   C   E   A   N   Ye   Buri   **14**   **K**
Preparis North Channel   Natkyizin   Sangkhla
Pariparit Kyun   Nam Tok
(Burma)   Moscos Is.   Yebyu
Preparis South Channel   Maungmagan Is.   Tavoy
Koko Kyunzu   Launglon Bok
(Burma)   COPYRIGHT PHILIP'S

7   90   **8**   92   **9**   94   **10**   **11**   **12**

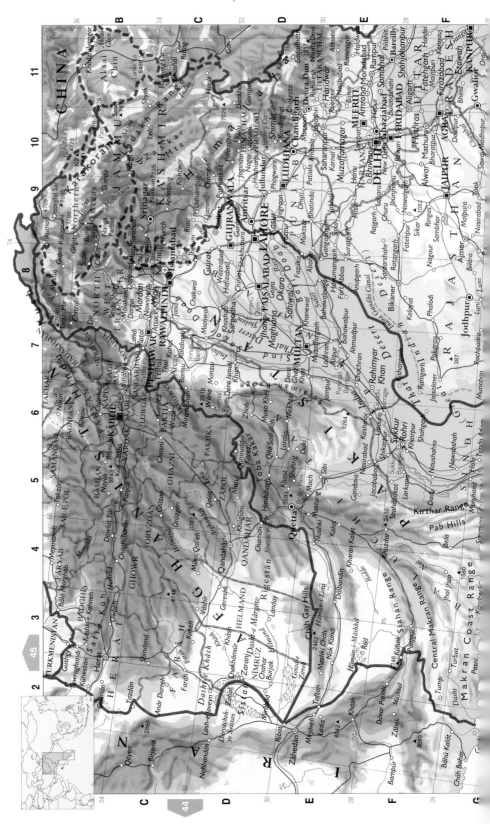

50 0 100 200 300 400 km
50 0 50 100 150 200 250 miles

G **H** 22 **J** 20 **K** 18 **L** **M**

Chhatarpur
Chhindwara
Panna
Tikamgarh
Lalitpur
Bina
Etawah
Bander
Damoh
Bhamer Range
Nasirabad
Waingang
Pranhita
Chikhli
16

Ranthar
Gund
1321
Saugor
Ratanpur
MADHYA
Sehore
BHOPAL JABALPUR
PRADESH
Hoshangabad
Betul
NAGPUR
Wardha
Bhandara
Balaghat
Nizampur
Chanda
Sironj
Vidisha
Nagpur
Amravati
Akola
Chandrapur
Ongole
11

INDORE
Ujjain
Dewas
Makrai
1353
Satpura Range
Burhanpur Hills
Akola
Achalpur
Yavatmal
Wardha
Wani
Bhainsa
Adilabad
Manthani
Warangal
HYDERABAD
Secunderabad
Nalgonda
Mahbubnagar
Cumbum
Velikonda Ra
Kurnool

INDIA
Kota
Bhinmal
Mandsaur
Neemuch
Ratlam
Dhar
Mhow
Khargon
Khandwa
Shegaon
Chalisgaon
Jalna
Aurangabad
Ahmadnagar
Osmanabad
Sholapur
Gulbarga
Raichur
Adoni
Guntakal
10

Chittaurgarh
Gandhi Sagar
Banswara
Bhopal
Narmada
Indore
Amalner
Dhule
Manmad
Yeola
Deolali
Kharda
796
Barsi
Madha
Bijapur
Bagalkot
Dharwad
Gadag
Kotturu
Bellary
Hospet

Udaipur
Nagda
Sirohi
1722
Kaned Brahma
Dahod
Godhra
Godhra
Ratlam
Jhabua
Rajpipla
Tapti
Nandurbar
Malegaon
NASIK
699
Kalyan
Ulhasnagar
Thane
PUNE (Poona)
Satara
Karad
Kolhapur
Sangli
Miraj
Belgaum
Hubli
Gadag
Karwar
Ranibennur

Palanpur
Mahesana
Patan
Nadiad
AHMADABAD
Godhra
VADODARA (Baroda)
1325
Bharuch
SURAT
Navsari
Valsad
Daman
DADRA AND
NAGAR HAVELI
Bhiwandi
MUMBAI
(BOMBAY)
Mahabaleshwar
1438

Disa
Khedaa
1117
Viramgam
Petlad
Khambhat
Bhavnagar
Palitana
Amreli
Junagadh
Gulf of Khambhat
Diu
Victor
Mahuva
Veraval

Kachchh
Little
A Rann
Rajkot
Gondal
Gadhada
Dhari
Kathiawar
Gulf of Khambhat

Nagar Parkar
Bhachau
Halvad
Morvi
Wankaner
Jamnagar
Gop
Porbandar

Radhanpur
Tharad
Kandla
Mandvi
Bhuj
Gulf of Kachchh
Okha
Dwarka

Khavda
Khdir
Lakhpat
Rann of Kachchh

Badin
Nagar
Nari
Khara
Nan
Mouths of the Indus
Indus (Sind)
68

ARABIAN
SEA

ARABIAN
SEA

Nallamalai Hills
Cumbum
Kavali
Nellore
CHENNAI (Madras)
Pulicat L.
Kanchipuram
Mahabalipuram
12

Ongole
Chidru
Gudur
Chittoor
Tirupati
Arcot
Vellore
Cuddalore
Chidambaram
Nagappattinam
SRI LANKA
Trincomalee
Batticaloa

Kurnool
Adoni
Guntakal
Gooty
Anantapur
Proddatur
Cuddapah
Velikonda Range
1151
Tiruvannamalai
Villupuram
Pondicherry
Karaikal
Point Pedro
Mullaittivu
Jaffna
Kankesanturai
Kandy
Kalmunai
Badulla
Pottuvil

Raichur
Hindupur
1255
Kolar
Gold Fields
Dharmapuri
Salem
1628
Tiruchchirappalli
Karaikkudi
Adam's Bridge
Mannar
Palk Strait
Anuradhapura
Negombo
Kegalla
2225
Adam's Peak
Hambantota

Hubli
Davangere
Shimoga
Chikmagalur
1923
Hassan
Mysore
1745
BANGALORE
KARNATAKA
Channapatna
Melkote
Hills
Erode
Perambalur
Pudukkottai
Devakottai
Ramanathapuram
Pamban
Gulf of
Mannar
Puttalam
Chilaw
Kurunegala
Matale
COLOMBO
Moratuwa
Kalutara
Dondra Head

Dandeli
GOA
Karwar
Kumta
Udupi
Mangalore
Kasaragod
Cannanore
Tellicherry
Calicut (Kozhikode)
Badagara
Ponnani
Trichur (Kochi)
COCHIN
Ernakulam
Mattancheri
Alleppey (Alappuzha)
Quilon (Kollam)
TAMIL
MADURAI
Virudunagar
Rajapalaiyam
Tuticorin
Tirunelveli
Palayankottai
Kulasekarappattinam
Kanniyakumari
NADU
Coimbatore
Udagamandalam
2637
Palghat
Pollachi
2695
Palani Hills
Dindigul
1654
Chinganacheri
Palai
Kottayam
TRIVANDRUM (Thiruvananthapuram)
Nagercoil
C. Comorin

KERALA
Malabar Coast

INDIAN
OCEAN

N 14 P 12 Q 10 R 8

H 76 62 64 **M** 66 68 **N** 70 72 74 **P** 76 78 **Q** 80 82 **R**

East from Greenwich

m ft
6000 18 000
4000 12 000
3000 9000
2000 6000
1500 4500
1000 3000
400 1200
200 600
0 0
200 600

Continuation Southwards
on same scale

Projection: Conical with two standard parallels

Projection: Conical Orthomorphic with two standard parallels   East from Greenwich

C. M. va B.= CHAHĀR MAḤĀLL VA BAKHTĪARĪ
K. va B. A. = KOHKĪLŪYEH VA BŪYER AḤMADI

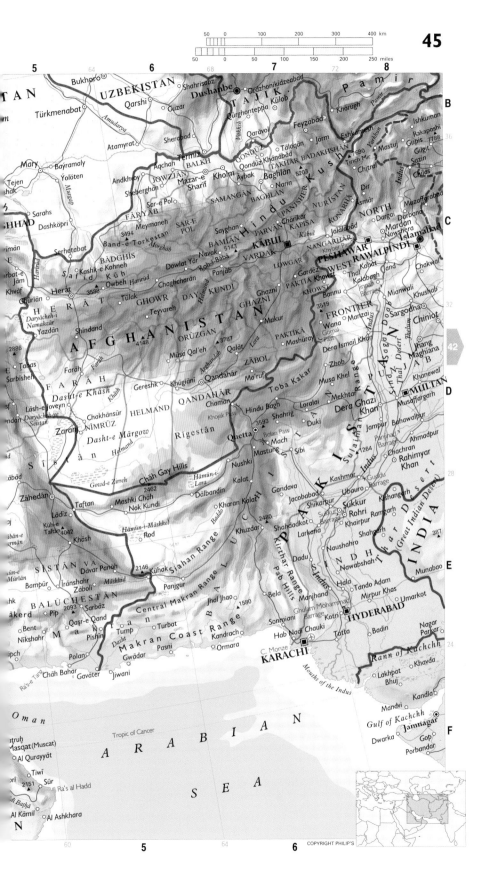

50 0 100 200 300 400 km
50 0 50 100 150 200 250 miles

5   64   6   68   7   72   8

UZBEKISTAN

Bukhoro
Shahrisabz
Qarshi
Guzar
Dushanbe
Ordzhonikidzeabad
TAJIK
Kŭlob
Qŭrghonteppa
Pamir
Khorugh

Türkmenabat
Amudarya
Aqchah
Termiz
Feyzābād
Eshkāmesh
Ishkuman
Rakaposhi 7788
Gupis
Gilgit
Chilas

Atamyrat
Sherabad
BALKH
Qonduz
Khānābād
TAKHĀR BADAKHSHĀN
Tirich Mir 7690
Mastuj
Sazin
Indus
Muzaffarabad

Mary
Bayramaly
Yōlöten
Murgap
Andkhvoy
JOWZJĀN
Mazar-e
Sharif
Kholm
Aybak
Baghlān 5203
Narin
PANJSHER
NURISTAN
Dir
Asmar
NORTH
Dargai
Darband

Tejen
Sarahs
Dashköpri
Sar-e Pol
Meymaneh
SAR-E
POL
Sayghan
BAMIĀN
Charīkar
PARVĀN
KAPISA
Konarha
Jalālābād
NANGARHĀR
Khyber Pass
PESHAWAR
Mardan
Nowshera
Islamabad
RAWALPINDI

Sarhetabat
BĀDGHIS
Band-e Torkestan
Morghāb
Dowlat Yār Navak
VARDAK
KĀBUL
Kābul
LOWGAR
Gardēz
WEST
Kohat
Jinnah Barrage
Chakwal

Herāt
3588
Tūlak
Chaghcharān
Panjāb
DAY
KUNDI
Ghazni
PAKTIĀ
Khōwst
FRONTIER
Bannu
Mianwali
Khushab
Sargodha
Chiniot

HERĀT
GHŌWR
ORŪZGĀN
4787
GHAZNĪ
3519
KHŌWST
Wana
Manzai
INDUS
Jhang
Maghiana

Shindand
Owbeh Hariūd
4148
Mūsā Qal'eh
Arghandāb
Qalāt
PAKTĪKĀ
Mashūray
Zhob
Musa Khel
KHAN
Khanewal

Daryācheh-i
Namakzār
Yazdān
2886
Tabas
Sarbisheh
FARĀH
Farah
ZĀBOL
Ma'ruf
Toba Kakar
Dera Ismail Khan
Loralai
Mekhtar
Dera Ghazi
Khan
Muzaffargarh
MULTAN
Ahmadpur

Lāsh-e Joveyn
Chakhānsūr
NIMRŪZ
HELMAND
QANDAHĀR
Khūgiāni
QANDAHĀR
Chaman
Hindu Bagh
3593
Shahrig
Duki
Sulaiman Range
Bahawalpur
Panjnad Barrage
Rahimyar
Khan

Daryācheh-ye
Seistan
Zaranj
Dasht-e Mārgow
Rīgestān
Khojak Pass
Bolan Pass
Quetta
Sibi
1264
Guddu
Barrage
Chachran

Zāhedān
Gowd-e Zirreh
Chāh Gay Hills
2462
Hāmūn-i-Lora
Nushki
Mastung
Mach
Kashmor
Ubauro
Kandhkot
Kashangarh

Taftan
Mashki Chāh
Nok Kundi
Dālbandin
Kalat
Gandava
Jacobabad
Shikarpur
Sūkkur
Rohri
Ramzani
Khairpur

Lādīz
Kāh-e Taftan
4042
Khāsh
Hāmūn-i-Māshkel
Rod
Kharan Kalat
Khuzdar
2480
Shahdadkot
Larkana
Sukkur
Barrage
Shahgarh
387

SISTĀN VA
Dāvar Panah
2146
Kūhak
Siahan Range
Bela
Dadu
INDH
Nawabshah
INDIA
Munabao

Bampūr
Īrānshahr
Zābol
Māshkid
Panjgur
Central Makran Range
Jhal Jhao
1580
Pab Hills
Kirthar Range
Hala
Tando Adam
Mirpur Khas
Umarkot

BALŪCHESTĀN
2093
Sarbāz
Tump
Turbat
Kandrach
Ormara
Sonmiani
Ghulam Mohammad Barrage
Kotri
HYDERABAD
Nagar Parkar

Bent
Nikshahr
Qasr-e Qand
Pishin
Dasht
Pasni
Hab Nagr Chauki
KARACHI
C. Monze
Tatta
Badin
Khavda

Polan
Gavater
Gwādar
Jiwani
Makran Coast Range
Mouths of the Indus
Rann of Kachchh
Lakhpat
Bhuj
Kandla

Ra's-e Tang
Chāh Bahar

O m a n
A R A B I A N
Tropic of Cancer
Gulf of Kachchh
Dwarka
Jamnagar
Gop
Porbandar

Masqat (Muscat)
Al Qurayyāt
S E A

Tiwī
2151
Sūr
Ra's al Hadd
Baṭḥā
Al Kāmil
Al Ashkhara

B
C
42
D
E
F
N

60   5   64   6

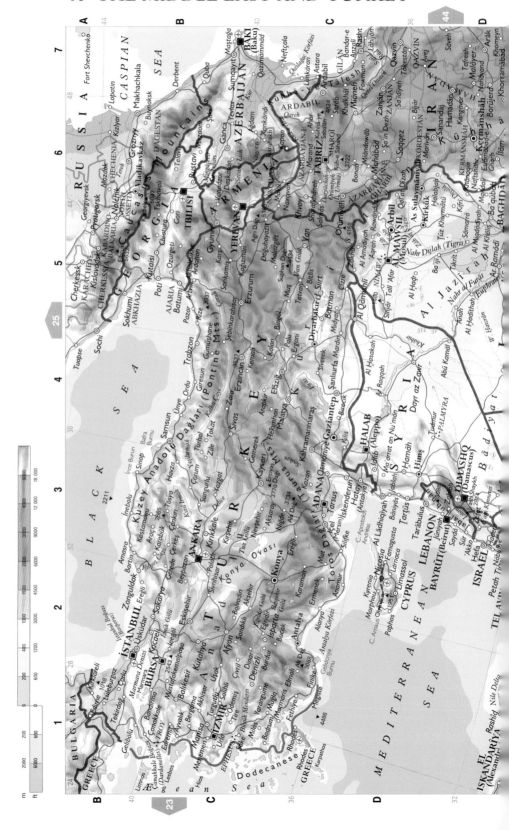

50 0   100   200   300   400 km
50 0   50   100   150   200   250 miles

44

48

54

54

East from Greenwich

Projection: Conical Orthomorphic with two standard parallels

PERSIAN GULF

Kūh-e Zard 4548▲
Dezfūl
Masjed-e Soleymān
Shūshtar
Naft-e Safīd
Safīd Gel Haft Gel
KHOZESTAN
Ahvāz
Bandar-e Māh shur
Bandar-e Deylam
Behbehān
Bushehr

Al Fāw Khorramshahr
Ābādān
Jazīrat Abū Zubar Shatt al 'Arab
Ra's al Mish'āb
Mīnā Su'ud
Al Kuwayt (Kuwait)
KUWAIT
Mīnā al Ahmadi
Al Jahrah
Wafrah
Burgān

Az Zubair
AL BASRAH
An Nāṣirīyah
Ur
Al Qurnah
Al Khidr
Al 'Amārah
Al Kūt
Ar Rifā'ī
Ash Shatrah
Ad Dīwānīyah
Ḥillah
BABYLON
Al Ḥillah
An Najaf
Karbalā'
Ash Shanāfiyah
As Samāwah
As Salmān
Niṣāb
Hafar al Bāṭin
Ash Shu'bah
Turabah
Rafḥā
Ar Rifā'ī

SAUDI ARABIA

Abū 'Alī
Abū Jubayl
Al Qaṭīf
Ad Dammām
Al Mubarraz
Al Hufūf
Uqayr
Al Jāfūrah
Al Ḥaraḍ
Al Khunn
Wadi al Sahba
Harad
Al Khārsānīyah
Al Faqlī
As Saffānīyah
Manīfah

Ad Dahnā'
An Nu'ayrīyah

AR RIYĀD (Riyadh)
Rumāḥ
Jubaylah
Al 'Aramah
Ath Thādiq
Al Majma'ah
Az Zilfī
Marāt
Al 'Uwaynid
Ad Dawādimi
Shaqrā'
'Afīf
Ar Ruwaydah
As Sulaymānīyah
Ad Dilam
Al Ḥillah
Al Ḥulwah
Al Ḥariq
Ghaīyl
Layla
Al Badī
Al Ḥamar
Al Ḥaddar

'Uyūn
Burayḍah
Al 'Uyūn
Al Midhnab
Ar Rass
Al Qā'īyah
Uqlat aṣ Ṣuqūr
Al Qaṣīm
Fayd
Ṭabah
Ḥā'il
Hulayfā'
Wadi ar Rimah
Al Ḥanākīyah
Mahd adh Dhahab
Al Dafīnah
Urūq Subay'
Ḥarrat Nawāsif
Harrat al Kishb

An Nafūd
Jabal Shammar
Ṣafājah
Ḥarrat Khaybar
Al Madīnah (Medina)
Al Ḥamrā'
Tayma'
Madā in Ṣāliḥ
Al 'Ulā
Hanak
Umm Lajj
Yanbu' 'al Baḥr
Ra's Bāridī
Rābigh
Usfān
Zaymah
Mastūrah
Al Qaḍīmah
MAKKAH (Mecca) 2565▲
Ushayqir
Aṭ Ṭā'if

Sakākah
Al Jalāmīd
Badanah
Hamad
Ṭurayf
Al 'Īsāwīyah
Al Jawf
Kāf
Wadi Fajr
Qārat al Akhḍar
Ḥarrat al 'Uwairiḍ 1147
Jabal

Aṭ Tubayq
Ma'ān
Aṭ Ṭafīlah
Dead Sea -411
Al 'Aqabah
Ḥaql
Ra's Fartak
Ḍuba'
Al Muwaylih
Dhabbagh 2350▲
Ash Sharmah 2578▲
Maqnā
Al Wajh
Mashābih
Shaybārā
Ra's Abū Madd
Jazā'ir Qur'ān
1814

PETRA
Elath
El 'Arīsh
El Qanṭara
Es Suweis (Suez)
Abū Suweis
Ismā'īlīya
Zagazig
Banhā
EL QAHIRA (Cairo)
El Gîza
PYRAMIDS
Helwân

Gebel Mûsa 2637▲
Gebel Katherîna 2285▲
El Ṭûr
Sharm el Sheikh
Ra's Muhammad
Hurghada
El Tûr
Es Sina'
Sheikh
Khalîg el Suweis
Nakhl
Gebel Shayib el Banat 2187▲
Gebel Hamâta 1977▲
Esh Sharqîya
Bûr Safâga

EGYPT
Beni Suef
El Fayyûm
Birket Qârûn
El Wâsta
Maghâgha
Beni Mazâr
El Minyâ
Mallawi
Deirût
Manfalût
Asyûṭ
Abû Tîg
Ṭahta
Sohâg
Akhmîm
Girga
Nag Hammâdi
THEBES
Qena
Qûs
El Uqṣur
Kôm Ombo
Aswân
Idfu
Sadd el 'Aâli (Aswan High Dam)
El Khârga
Bâris

Kôm Behîra
Simnûd
El Wâdi ul Gedîd
Nahr en Nîl (Nile)

RED SEA
Gebel el Sibâ'i 1464▲
Ra's Banâs
Umm el Kḍef
Ḥalaib 2216
HALAIB TRIANGLE
Ras Hadarba
Muhammad Qol
Gebel 1464
Gebjt

SUDAN
Es Sahrâ' en Nûbîya
Wadi Halfa
Dungula
Buheirat en Naser (Lake Nasser)
Tropic of Cancer

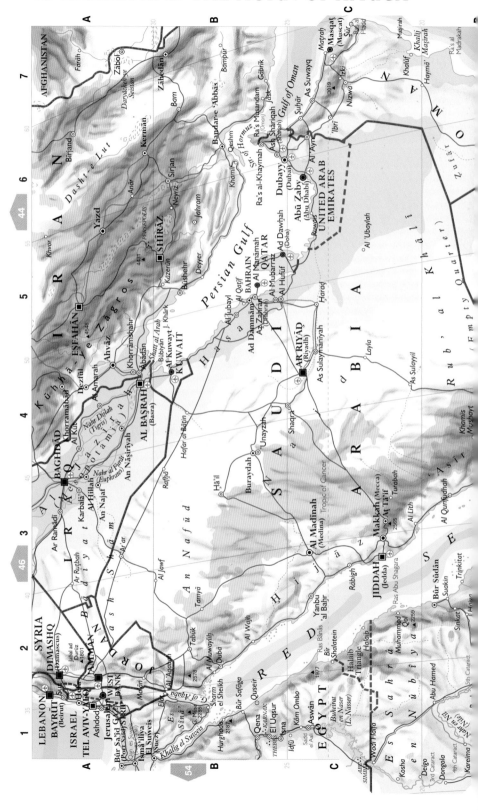

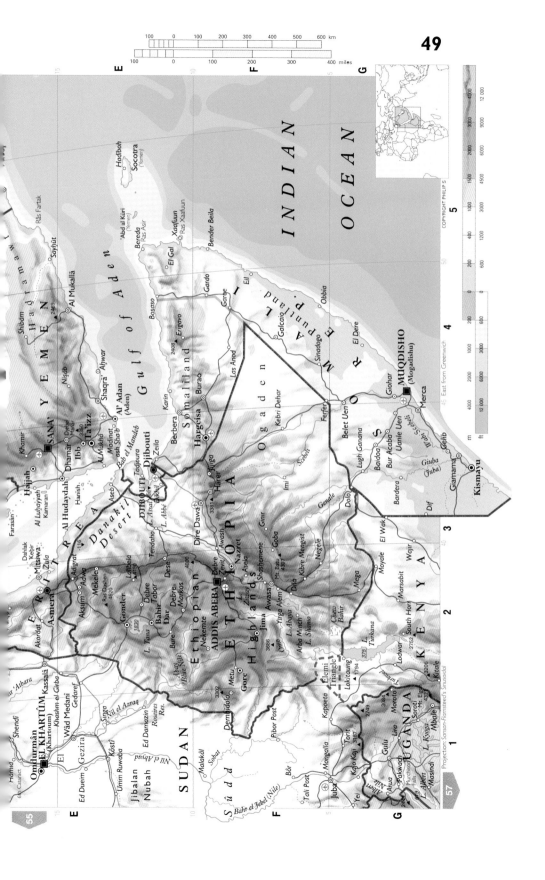

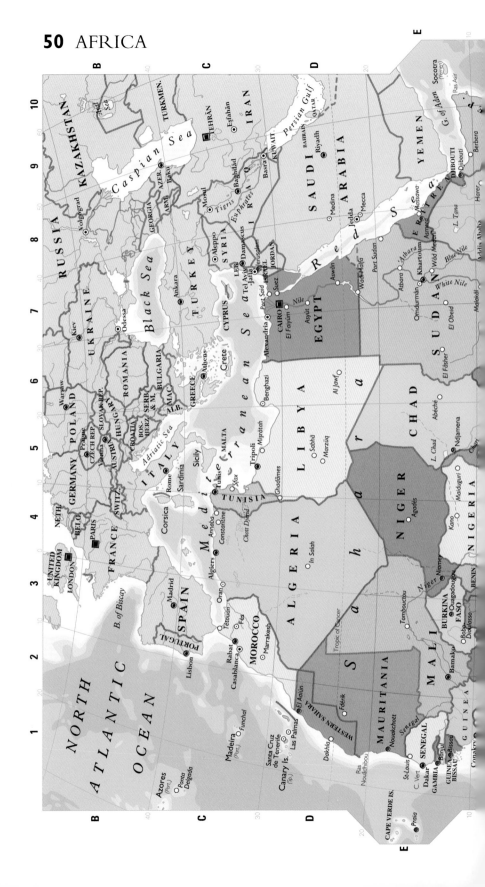

NORTH
ATLANTIC
OCEAN

Azores
(Port.)
Ponta
Delgada

Madeira
(Port.)
Funchal

Santa Cruz
de Tenerife
Canary Is.
(Sp.)
Las Palmas

Dakhla

Rás
Nouâdhibou

CAPE VERDE IS.
Praia

C. Vert
Dakar
St-Louis
SENEGAL
GAMBIA Banjul
GUINEA-
BISSAU Bissau
Conakry
GUINEA

Nouakchott
MAURITANIA
Senegal
WESTERN SAHARA
El Aaiún
Fdérik

Tombouctou
MALI
Bamako
Bobo-
Dioulasso
BURKINA
FASO
Ouagadougou
Niamey
Niger
BENIN
NIGERIA
Kano
Maiduguri
Agadès
NIGER
Abéché
CHAD
Ndjamena
L. Chad
Chari

SPAIN
Madrid
Lisbon
PORTUGAL
B. of Biscay

PARIS
UNITED
KINGDOM
LONDON
NETH.
BELG.
FRANCE
SWITZ.
GERMANY
POLAND
Warsaw
Prague
Vienna
CZECH REP.
SLOVAK REP.
AUSTRIA
HUNGARY
CROATIA
BOS.-
HERZ.
SERB.
& M.
ROMANIA
BULGARIA
MAC.
ALB.
GREECE
Athens
ITALY
Rome
Corsica
Sardinia
Sicily
MALTA
Adriatic Sea
Tetouan
Fès
Rabat
Casablanca
Marrakesh
MOROCCO
Tunis
Sfax
TUNISIA
Annaba
Constantine
Chott Djerid
Ghadāmes
Algiers
Oran
In Salah
ALGERIA
Sahara
Tropic of Cancer

Mediterranean Sea
Crete
Tripoli
Mişrātah
Sabhā
Marzūq
LIBYA
Benghazi
Al Jawf
Sahara

Alexandria
CAIRO
El Faiyûm
Asyût
EGYPT
Nile
Aswân
Wadi Halfa

RUSSIA
Volgograd
Aral
Sea
KAZAKHSTAN
Caspian Sea
Kiev
UKRAINE
Odessa
Black Sea
Ankara
TURKEY
GEORGIA
ARM.
AZER.
Baku
TURKMEN.
Mosul
Tigris
Euphrates
IRAQ
Baghdad
Basra
IRAN
TEHRÁN
Eşfahān
KUWAIT
Persian Gulf
BAHRAIN
QATAR
Riyadh
SAUDI
ARABIA
Medina
Jedda
Mecca
Aleppo
Damascus
SYRIA
LEB.
Tel Aviv
Jerusalem
Jaffa
ISRAEL
JORDAN
CYPRUS
Port Said
Suez

Red Sea
Port Sudan
Atbara
Atbara
Omdurmân
Khartoum
Wad Medani
El Obeid
El Fâsher
SUDAN
White Nile
Blue Nile
Malakâl
L. Tana
ERITREA
Massawa
Asmera
Harer
Addis Ababa
DJIBOUTI
Djibouti
Berbera
G. of Aden
YEMEN
Socotra
(Yemen)
Rás Asir

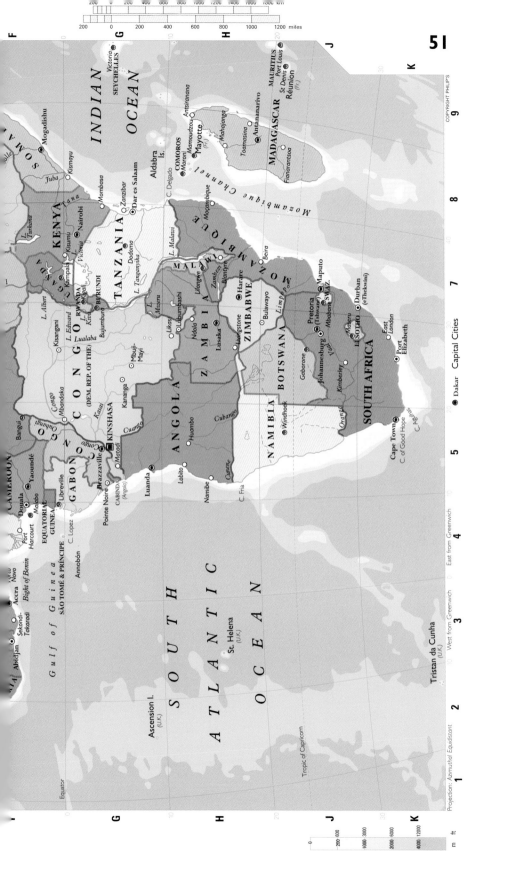

200 400 600 800 1000 1400 1600 1800 km

200 0 200 400 600 800 1000 1200 miles

INDIAN

OCEAN

Victoria
SEYCHELLES

MAURITIUS
Port Louis
St Denis Réunion
(Fr.)

Antsiranana

Mamoudzou
Mayotte
COMOROS
Moroni

Mahajanga

Toamasina

Antananarivo

MADAGASCAR

Fianarantsoa

Aldabra
Is.

Mozambique Channel

C. Delgado

Mogadishu

Kismayu

Juba

Mombasa

Zanzibar

Dar es Salaam

KENYA

Nairobi

Kisumu

L. Turkana

Tana

Kampala

UGANDA

Dodoma

TANZANIA

L. Victoria

L. Albert

L. Edward

RWANDA

Kigali

BURUNDI

Bujumbura

L. Tanganyika

Kisangani

Lualaba

CONGO

(DEM. REP. OF THE)

Mbuji-
Mayi

Kananga

L. Mweru

Lubumbashi

L. Malawi

Lilongwe

MALAWI

Blantyre

Zambezi

Beira

MOZAMBIQUE

Mozambique

Likasi

Ndola

ZAMBIA

Lusaka

Livingstone

Harare

ZIMBABWE

Bulawayo

Limpopo

Maputo

Pretoria
(Tshwane)
Mbabane SWAZ.

Johannesburg

Vaal

Maseru

LESOTHO

Durban
(eThekwini)

East
London

SOUTH AFRICA

Port
Elizabeth

Cape Town

C. of Good Hope

Kimberley

Gaborone

BOTSWANA

Orange

C. Agulhas

Windhoek

NAMIBIA

Cubango

Cunene

Namibe

C. Fria

Lobito

Huambo

ANGOLA

Cuanza

Luanda

KINSHASA

Matadi

CABINDA
(Angola)

Pointe Noire

Brazzaville

CONGO

Congo

Kasai

GABON

Libreville

C. Lopez

EQUATORIAL
GUINEA

Malabo

CAMEROON

Douala

Yaoundé

Bangui

Ogooué

Ubangi

Mbandaka

Congo

SÃO TOMÉ & PRÍNCIPE

Annobón

Gulf of Guinea

Bight of Benin

Porto
Novo

Accra

Sekondi-
Takoradi

Abidjan

Port
Harcourt

Ascension I.
(U.K.)

St. Helena
(U.K.)

SOUTH

ATLANTIC

OCEAN

Tristan da Cunha
(U.K.)

Tropic of Capricorn

Equator

Projection: Azimuthal Equidistant

West from Greenwich

East from Greenwich

● Dakar   Capital Cities

m ft

0

200 600

1000 3000

2000 6000

4000 12000

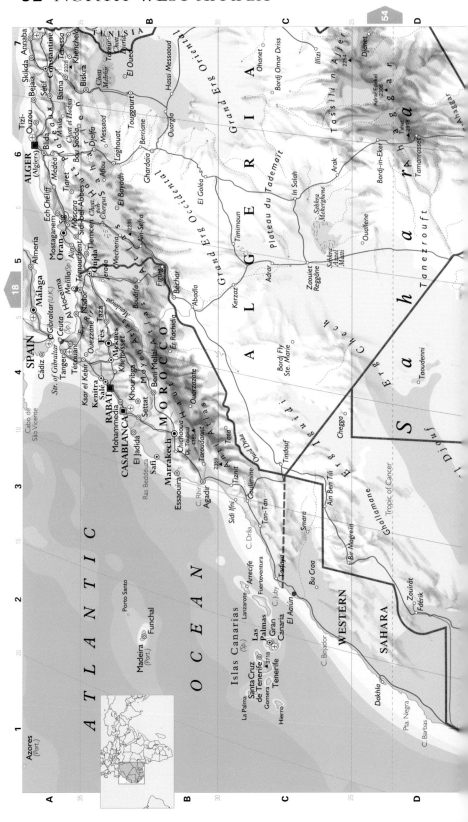

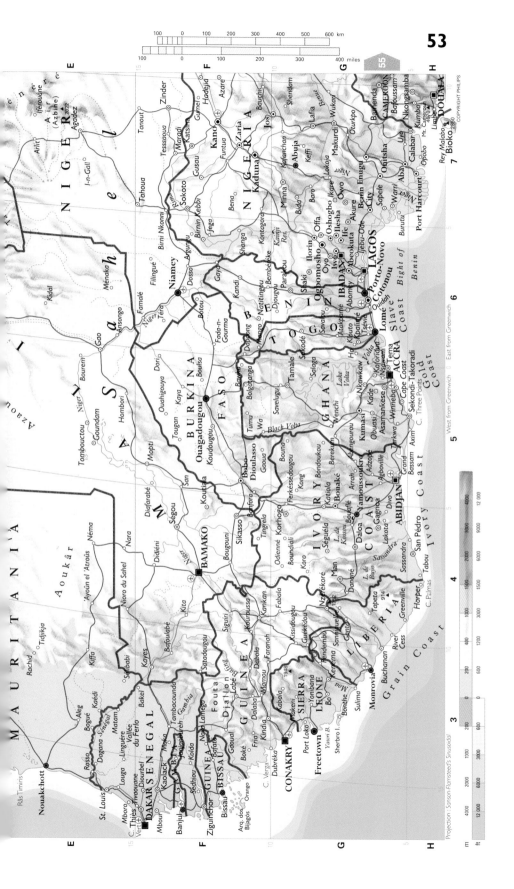

55

100 0 100 200 300 400 500 600 km

100 0 100 200 300 400 miles

COPYRIGHT PHILIPS

E · F · G · H

MAURITANIA

NIGER

Aïr (Azbine) 2022

I-n-Gall

Agadez

Arlit

Iférouâne

Tiféfrouâne

Zinder

Hadejia

Azare

Gumel

Katsina

Maradi

Tessaoua

Tanout

Tahoua

Kano

Funtua

Zaria

Bauchi

Shendam

Lafia

Gombe

Jos

Kaduna

Abuja

Keffi

Makurdi

Wukari

Otukpo

Benue

Birni Nkonni

Sokoto

Gusau

Gawa

Kainji Res.

Safwanchan

Yola

Numan

Garoua

CAMEROON

Barenda

Bafoussam

Nkongsamba

DOUALA

Kumba

Mt. Cameroon 4070

Bafoussam

Limbe

Rey Malabo

BIOKO 3000

NIGERIA

Minna

Bida

Lokoja

Idah

Owo

Akure

Benin City

Sapele

Warri

Buruta

Onitsha

Enugu

Aba

Calabar

Oron

Opobo

Port Harcourt

Niger

Niger

Rima

Argungu

Jega

Birnin Kebbi

Bena

Kontagora

Baro

Offa

Ilorin

Ilesha

Ile

Oshogbo

Iwo

Ede

Ogbomosho

Oyo

IBADAN

Abeokuta

LAGOS

Porto-Novo

Cotonou

Ouidah

Abomey

Sakété

Pobe

Shaki

Niamey

Dosso

Filingué

Ménaka

Famalé

Tera

Botou

Goya

Fada-n-Gourma

Kandi

Natitingou

Djougou

Parakou

Bembéréke

Nikki

Kainji

Djila

Mali

SAHEL

SAHARA

NIGER

Bourem

Gao

Ansongo

Gourma

Hombori

Dori

Boulsa

Ouahigouya

Kaya

BURKINA FASO

Koudougou

OUAGADOUGOU

Tenkodogo

Bawku

Tougan

Dédougou

Bobo-Dioulasso

Gaoua

Batié

BENIN

Savalou

Savé

Atakpamé

Badou

Tchetti

Kpalimé

Kpandu

Sokodé

Kete-Krachi

Kara

Dapango

Mango

TOGO

GHANA

Ho

Kpandu

Hohoe

LOMÉ

ACCRA

Tema

Nsawam

Koforidua

Kade

Nkawkaw

Mpraeso

Kpong

Akosombo

Lake Volta

Salaga

Tamale

Bolgatanga

Wa

Tumu

Bawku

Navrongo

Yendi

Damongo

Black Volta

White Volta

Kintampo

Wenchi

Techiman

Sunyani

Berekum

Kumasi

Obuasi

Bibiani

Dunkwa

Oda

Winneba

Cape Coast

Sekondi-Takoradi

C. Three Points

Slave Coast

Gold Coast

Bight of Benin

Tombouctou

Goundam

Mopti

San

Djenné

Diafarabé

Ségou

Koutiala

Sikasso

BAMAKO

Bougouni

Koro

Tengréla

Odienné

Katiola

Seguéla

Bouaké

Dimbokro

Bondoukou

Bouna

Ferkessédougou

Korhogo

Bobo

Banfora

Boundiali

Man

Danané

Gagnoa

Daloa

Divo

YAMOUSSOUKRO

Toumodi

Agboville

Adzopé

Abengourou

Grand Bassam

ABIDJAN

Axim

Arrah

Aboisso

Sassandra

San Pédro

Tabou

IVORY COAST

Grain Coast

Ivory Coast

L. de Buyo

L. de Kossou

C. Palmas

Harper

Greenville

River Cess

Buchanan

Monrovia

Tapeta

914

Sanniquellie

Ganta

Gbarnga

Zwedru

LIBERIA

Bafing

SIERRA LEONE

Freetown

Makeni

Port Loko

Bo

Kenema

Bonthe

Sulima

Sherbro I.

Yawri B.

Tombali

Sefadu

Kabala

GUINEA

CONAKRY

Kindia

Fria

Dalaba

Dabola

Mamou

Kissidougou

Guékédou

Macenta

Nzérékoré

Kankan

Siguiri

Kouroussa

Dinguiraye

Kérouané

Beyla

Faranah

Fabala

Kurussa

Boké

Dubréka

C. Verga

Arq. dos Bijagós

Bubaque

Orango

GUINEA-BISSAU

BISSAU

Bissorã

Bafatá

Gabú

Ziguinchor

THE GAMBIA

BANJUL

Brikama

Basse

Tambacounda

Kolda

Velingara

Kaolack

SENEGAL

DAKAR

Thiès

Mbour

Diourbel

Kaffrine

Kayes

Bakel

Matam

Linguère

Louga

Mboro

St. Louis

Vallée du Ferlo

FOUTA DJALLON

Labé

Gaoual

Koundara

Kédougou

Saraya

Kita

Nara

Nioro du Sahel

Néma

Ayoûn el 'Atroûs

Kiffa

Aleg

Boghé

Kaédi

Rosso

Dagana

Richard-Toll

C. Vert

Rufisque

Nouakchott

Râs Timirist

Tidjikja

Rachid

Aoukâr

Néma

Azaouad

Sénégal

Niger

Projection: Sanson-Flamsteed's Sinusoidal

5 · West from Greenwich · East from Greenwich · 6

7

6

5

4

3

m   ft
4000 12 000
3000 9000
2000 6000
1500 4500
1000 3000
400   1200
200   600
0   0
200   600
1300 3000
2000 6000
4000 12 000

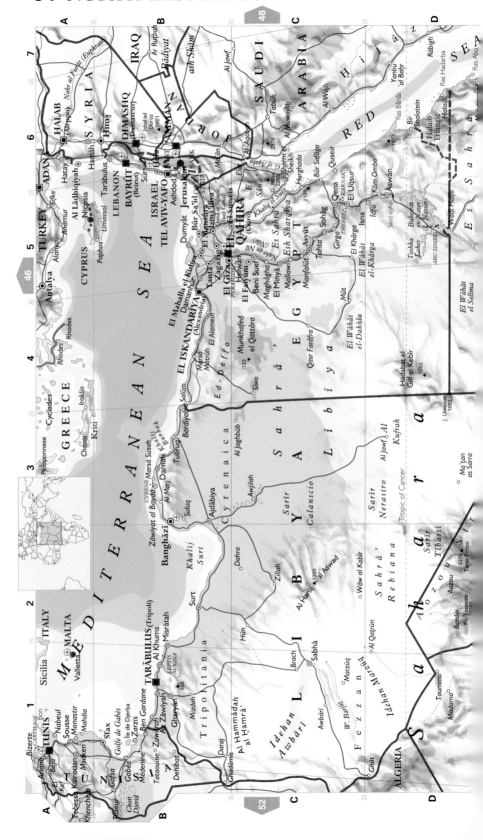

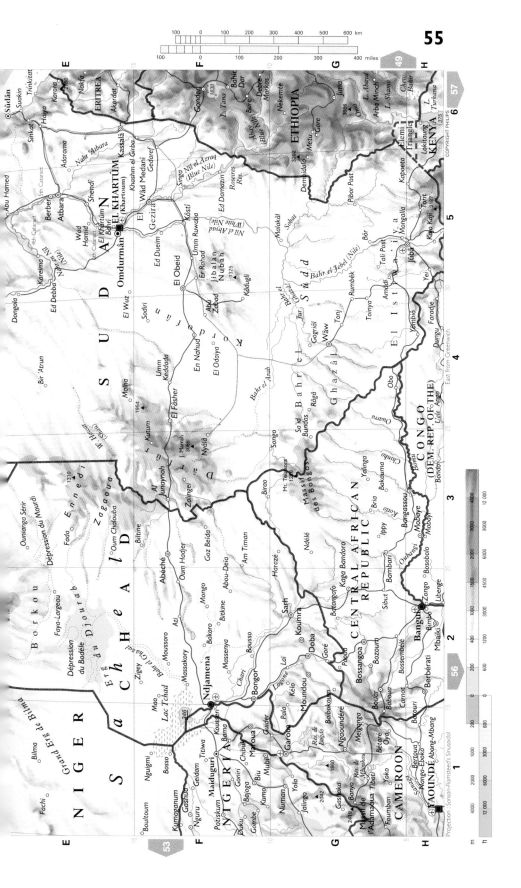

100   0   100   200   300   400   500   600 km
100   0   100   200   300   400 miles

E   F   G   H

6   5   4   3   2   1

COPYRIGHT PHILIPS

East from Greenwich

Projection: Sanson-Flamsteed's Sinusoidal

ERITREA
Trinkitat
Suakin
Sudan
Nakfa
Karora
Akordat
ETHIOPIA
Bahir Dar
L. Tana
Gonder
Debre Markos
Nekemte
Jima
L. Abaya
Arba Minch
L. Stamo
Chew Bahir
KENYA
Turkana
Elemi Triangle
Lokichokio
Kapoeta
Torit
Tali Post
Kajo Kaji
Yei
Jūba
Mongalla
Bōr
Pibor Post
Rumbēk
Malakāl
Sobat
Amādī
Dungu
Faradje
Obo
Yambio
Tonj
Wāw
Gogriāl
Wād Medanī
Gedaref
Kassalā
Khashm el Girba
EL KHARTŪM (Khartoum)
El Khartūm Bahrī
Omdurmān
Atbara
Berber
Shendī
Wad Hāmid
5th Cataract
4th Cataract
6th Cataract
Kareima
Ed Debba
Dongola
Abu Hamed
Sudān
Sinkat
Haya
Adarama
Nahr Atbara
Singa
Ed Damazin
Roseires Res.
Nīl el Azraq (Blue Nile)
Kōstī
Umm Ruwāba
Er Rahad
El Obeid
Ed Dueim
Nīl el Abyad (White Nile)
Jibalan Nūbah
Kādugli
Kordofan
En Nahud
El Odaiya
Abu Zabad
Umm Keddada
El Fāsher
Kutum
J. Marrah
Nyālā
Al Junaynah
Zalingei
Geneina
Songo
Birao
Raga
Sa'id Bundas
Mt. Toukhora
Massif des Bongo
Ndele
Bria
Kotto
Bambari
Ippy
Kaga Bandoro
Batangafo
Bangui
Zongo
Bimbo
Mbaiki
Libenge
Bossangoa
Bozoum
Bossembélé
Berbérati
Carnot
Bokaga
Bouar
Baboua
Bocaranga
Baibokoum
Bétaré Oya
Ngaoundéré
Meiganga
Garoua
Maroua
Bogo
Guider
Yola
Numan
Jalingo
Gashaka
Banyo
Foumban
Yoko
Abong-Mbang
YAOUNDÉ
CAMEROON
Bertoua
Mango-Eboko
Massif de l'Adamaoua (Tibati)
Réserve de Bouba
Pala
Kélo
Moundou
Doba
Goré
Bongor
Lai
Bousso
Sarh
Kyabé
Kouma
Doba
Am Timan
Harazé
Abou-Deïa
Goz Beida
Mongo
Birkine
Ati
Bokoro
Massenya
Ndjamena
Lac Tchad
Massakory
Moussoro
Mao
Bol
Bahr el Ghazal
Chari
Logone
CENTRAL AFRICAN REPUBLIC
CONGO (DEM. REP. OF THE)
Uele
Ouarra
Chinko
Bomu
Mobaye
Bangassou
Obangi
Bosobolo
Bondo
SUDAN
KORDOFAN
DARFUR
Bahr el Arab
Bahr el Ghazāl
Bahr el Jebel (Nile)
El Istiwa'iya
ENNEDI
Fada
Biltine
Abéché
Oum Hadjer
TCHAD
Borkou
Ounianga Sérir
Dépression du Mourdi
Bir 'Atrun
Malha
Faya-Largeau
Dépression du Bodélé
Erg du Djourab
Zigey
Bahr el Ghazal
Ergueni du Ténéré
NIGER
Grand Erg de Bilma
Bilma
Fachi
Boultoum
Nguigmi
Bosso
N'guru
Gashua
Maiduguri
Damaturu
NIGERIA
Potiskum
Kumagunam
Gombe
Bajoga
Biu
Kumo
Mubi
Gwoza
Gombi
Bama
Kousséri
Goniri
Chibok
Titiwa

m   ft
4000   12 000
3000   9000
2000   6000
1500   4500
1000   3000
400   1200
280   600
0   0
200   600
1000   3000
2000   6000
4000   12 000

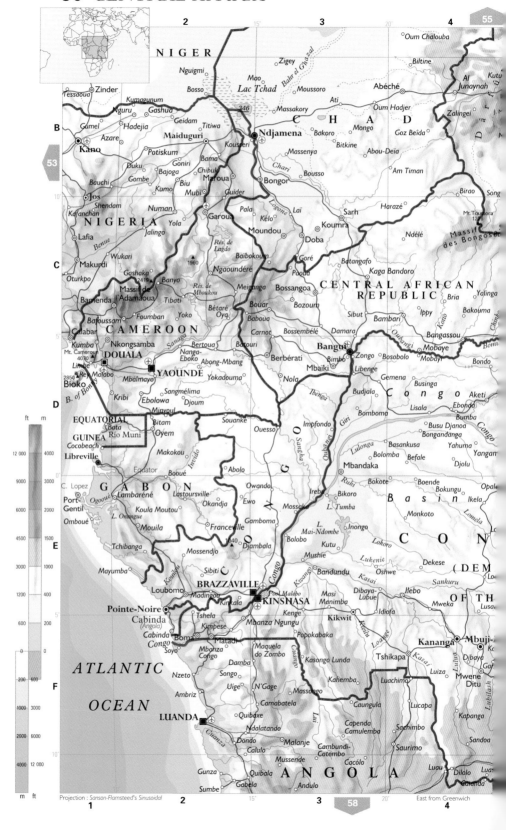

2   15°   3   20°   4

NIGER

Oum Chalouba
Biltine
Zigey
Al Junaynah
Kutu

Nguigmi
Mao   Bahr el Ghazal
Moussoro   Abéché   Zalingei
Bosso   *Lac Tchad*   Ati
346   Massakory   Oum Hadjer   C H A D   *Darfur*
Kumagunum
Nguru   Gashua   Geidam   Titiwa   Ndjamena   Bokoro   Mongo   Goz Beïda
B   Gumel   Hadejia   **Maiduguri**   Kousseri   Massenya   Bitkine   Abou-Deïa
Azare   Potiskum   Bama   *Chari*   Bongor   Bousso   Am Timan
Kano   Duku   Goniri   Chibuk   **Maroua**   Birao   Song
Bauchi   Bajoga   Biu   Kumo   Mubi   Guider   *Logone*   Sarh   Harazé   Mt. Toussoro   *Massif des Bongos*
Jos   Gombe   Numan   Garoua   Pala   Laï   Koumra
Shendam   Kafanchan   Yola   Jalingo   Moundou   Doba   Ndélé
NIGERIA   *Rés. de Lagdo*   Goré   Batangafo   Kaga Bandoro
Lafia   Wukari   Baibokoum   Pooua   Yalinga
Makurdi   1960   Ngaoundéré   Bossangoa   **CENTRAL AFRICAN**   Bria   Bakouma
C   Oturkpo   Gashaka   Banyo   Meiganga   Bozoum   **REPUBLIC**   Ippy   Kotto
2419   *Rés. de Mbonkou*   Bouar   Sibut   Bambari   Bangassou
Massif de   Bouali   Bozoum   Damara   Bimbo
Bamenda   **l'Adamaoua**   Tibati   Bétaré Oya   Baboua   Carnot   Bossembélé   Mobaye   Bomu
Bafoussam   Foumban   Yoko   Bangui   Zongo   Bosobolo   Mobayi
Benue   **Bangui**
C   Calabar   **CAMEROON**   Sanaga   Bertoua   Batouri   Berbérati   Zongo   Libenge   Gemena   Businga   Aketi
Kumba   Nkongsamba   Nanga-   Abong-Mbang   Mbaïki   C o n g o   Ebondo
Mt. Cameroun   Eboko   Nola   Budjala   Lisala   Bumba
4070   **DOUALA**   **YAOUNDE**   Yokadouma   Bomboma   Busu Djanoa
Limbe   Mbalmayo   Ibenga   Giri   Bongandanga   Yahuma
Bioko   2850   Rey   Mofabo   Sangmélima   Budjala   Basankusa   Yangam
2850   Kribi   Ebolowa   Djoum   Souanké   Impfondo   Bolomba   Befale   Djolu
D   B. of Bonny   Minvoul   C   Bokote   Boende   Bokungu   Opal
EQUATORIAL   Bitam   Oyem   Ouesso   O   Mbandaka   B a s i n   Ikela
Bata   Rio Muni   Sangha   N   L. Tumba   Monkoto   Lomela   Lo
GUINEA   Cocobeach   Makokou   Ivindo   G   Owando   Bikoro   Inongo   C O N
Libreville   Abolo   O   L. Mai-Ndombe   Lokoro   Dekese   (DEM
Equator   Boué   Ogooué   Lastoursville   Owando   Ewo   Mossaka   Lukenie   Oshwe   Lo
E   C. Lopez   **GABON**   Lambaréné   Okandja   Gamboma   Bolobo   Kutu   Mushie   Sankuru
Port-Gentil   Koula Moutou   Franceville   Djambala   1040   Bandundu   Kasai   Ilebo   Mweka   Lusa
Omboué   Mouila   Mossendjo   Sibiti   **BRAZZAVILLE**   Kwango   Dibaya-Lubue   **OF TH**
Tchibanga   Kouilou   **KINSHASA**   Masi-Manimba   Idiofa
Mayumba   Loubomo   Madingou   Pool Malebo   Kenge   Kikwit   Kenge   **Kananga**   **Mbuji-**
F   **Pointe-Noire**   Kinkala   Mbanza Ngungu   Popokabaka   Kwilu   Tshikapa   Dibaya   Ko
Cabinda   Tshela   Kimpese   Mbanza Ngungu   Kasongo Lunda   Luiza   Mwene Ditu
(Angola)   Boma   Matadi   Maquela   Kahemba   Luachimo
Cabinda   Mbanza   do Zombo   Damba   Caungula   Lucapa   Kapanga
ATLANTIC   *Congo*   Soyo   Songo   Massango   Sachimbo   Sandoa
Nzeto   Uíge   N'Gage   Camabatela   Capenda   Saurimo
OCEAN   Ambriz   Quibaxe   Camulemba   Luau   Dilolo   Luas
LUANDA   Ndalatando   Cuanza   Cacólo   Calanda
Gunza   Dondo   Malanje   Cambundi-   **ANGOLA**
Quibala   Calulo   Mussende   Catembo   Andulo
Sumbe   Gabela   Gunza

ft   m
12 000   4000
9000   3000
6000   2000
4500   1500
3000   1000
1200   400
600   200
0   0
200   600
1000   3000
2000   6000
4000   12 000
m   ft

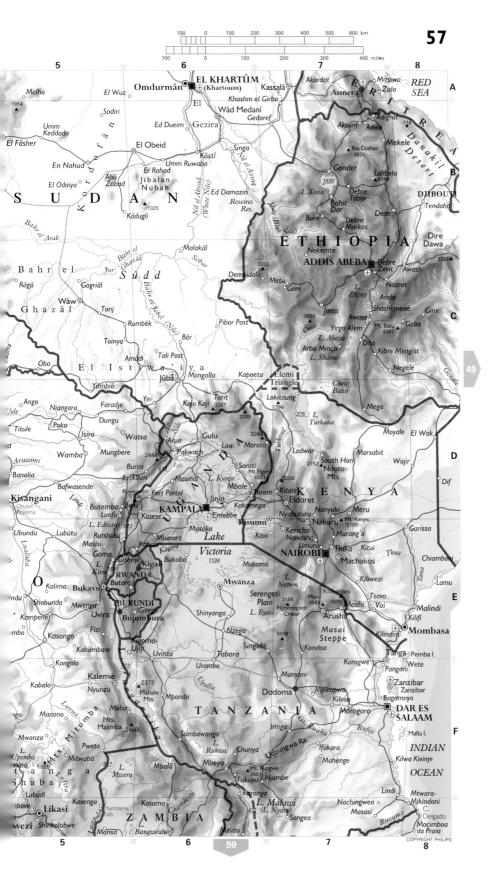

100 0 100 200 300 400 500 600 km
100 0 100 200 300 400 miles

5   6   7   8

A

Malha
1954
Umm
Keddada
El Fâsher
En Nahud
El Odaiya
Sodiri
El Wuz
Abû
Zabad
Jibalan
Nubah
1325
Kâdugli
El Obeid
Er Rahad
Umm Ruwaba
Kôstî
Singa

EL KHARTÎM
(Khartoum)
Omdurmân
El
Gezira
Wâd Medanî
Gedaref
Khashm el Girba
Kassalâ

Akordat
Mitsiwa
Zula
Asmera

RED
SEA

Adigrat
Aksum
Adwa
Mekele
Ras Dashen
4620
Gonder
1830
Lalibela
4190
DJIBOUTI
Tendaho

B

S U D A N
K o r d o f â n
Nubah
Ed Damazin
Roseires
Res.

L. Tana
Debre
Tabor
Bahir
Dar
Bure
Dese
Debre
Markos

Dire
Dawa

C

Bahr el Arab
Bahr el Sudd
Râga
Gogriâl
Wâw
Tonj
G h a z â l
Rumbêk
Bôr
Toinya
Amâdi
Tali Post
Jûba
Mongalla
Pibor Post
Malakâl
Sobat

E T H I O P I A
Nekemte
ADDIS ABEBA
Debre
Zeyit
Awash
Nazret
3381

Dempidolo
Metu
Gore
L.
Ziway
Asela
Jima
Awasa
Shashemene
Ginir
Omo
3686
Yirga Alem
Mt. Batu
4307
Goba
Arba Minch
L. Abaya
Dîla
L. Shamo
Kibre Mengist
Negele
Genale
3202

D

El Istwa'iya
Yambiô
Yei
Kojo Kaji
Torit
3187
Elemi
Triangle
Lokitaung
1794
Chew
Bahir
Mega

Ango
Niangara
Faradje
2749
Turkwel
Lodwar
376
L.
Turkana
Moyale
El Wak

Titule
Poko
Dungu
Gulu
3084
Moroto
South Horn
2752
Ndoto
Marsabit
Wajir
Dif

Isiro
Watsa
Arua
Lira
Soroti
Mt. Elgon
4321
9206
Kitale
Eldoret
Garissa

Banalia
Mungbere
Bunia
2444
610
Pakwach
Murchison
Falls
Masindi
L. Kyoga
Mbale
Tororo
K E N Y A
Meru

E

Kisangani
Bafwasende
Lindi
Boyoma
Butembo
Beni
Luofu
Fort Portal
Kasese
Jinja
Kakamega
Nyahururu
Nanyuki
Mt. Kenya
5199
Kitui
Chiamboni

U G A N D A
KAMPALA
Entebbe
Kisumu
Kericho
Naivasha
NAIROBI
Thika
Machakos
Lamu

Ubundu
L. Edward 913
Masaka
Kisii
Limuru
Thua
Tana

O
Kalima
Rutshuru
Goma
Gisenyi
Kigali
Butare
Kahale
Kabale
Masisi
L.
Kivu
1460
Lake
Victoria
1134
Musoma
L.
Natron
Kibwezi
Tsavo
Malindi

Shabunda
Bukavu
Mwenga
Uvira
RWANDA
BURUNDI
Gitega
Bujumbura
Mbarara
Bukoba
Mwanza
Serengeti
Plain
L. Eyasi
Kilimanjaro
Meru
4565
5895
Moshi
Voi
Kilifi

Kampene
Fizi
Shinyanga
Nzega
Ngorongoro
Crater
3188
Arusha
Kilindini
Mombasa

Kasongo
Kongolo
Kigoma-
Ujiji
Uvinza
Tabora
3418
Masai
Steppe
Korogwe
Tanga
Pemba I.
Wete

F

Kabambare
Kalemie
Nyunzu
273
Urambo
Singida
Kondoa
Pangani

Kabalo
Moba
Mahale
Mts.
2373
Mpanda
Dodoma
Mpwapwa
Kilosa
Zanzibar
Bagamoyo

Marioni
Mts.
Malimba
2460
Manyoni
Morogoro
DAR ES
SALAAM

Mwanza
T A N Z A N I A
Uralla
Iringa
Udzungwa Ra.
Rufiji
Mafia I.

Upemba
1889
Pweto
Mitwaba
Sumbawanga
L.
Rukwa
Chunya
Ifakara
Mahenge
Kilwa Kivinje
INDIAN

Lubudi
Kasenga
Mambilima
Falls
L.
Mweru
Mbala
Mbeya
Mt. Rungwe
2961
Njombe
Karonga
Lindi
Mtwara-
Mikindani
OCEAN

Shaba
Likasi
Shinkolobwe
wezi
ZAMBIA
Mansa
Bangweulu
Kasama
Chambeshi
Tukuyu
472
L. Malawi
L. Nyasa
Songea
Nachingwea
Masasi
Ruvuma
C.
Delgado
Mocimboa
da Praia

49

59

COPYRIGHT PHILIPS

5   6   7   8

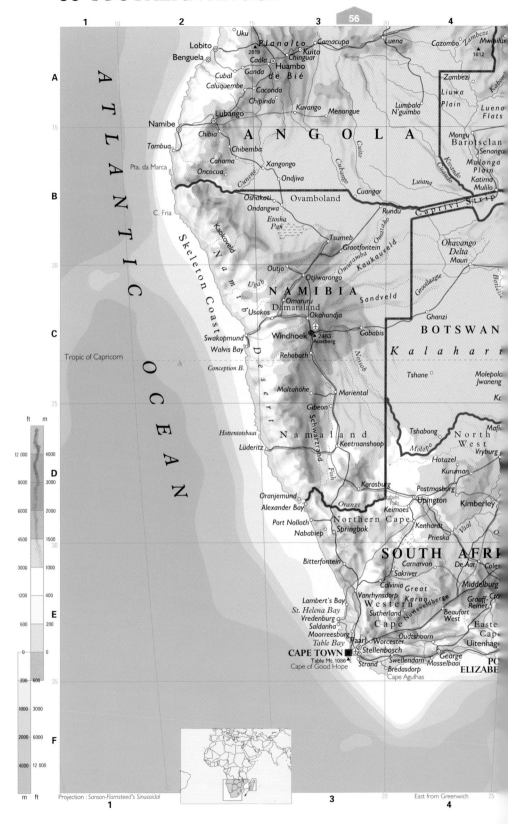

1   10   2   15   3   20   4

A T L A N T I C   O C E A N

Lobito
Benguela
Uku
Planalto
Camacupa
Luena
Cazombo
Zambeze
Mwinilu
2619
Cadla
Kuito
Chinguar
Ganda
Huambo
de Bié
Cubal
Caluquembe
Caconda
Chipindo
Kuyango
Menongue
Lumbala
N'guimbo
Liuwa
Plain
1612
Zambezi
Kabon
Luena
Flats
Namibe
Lubango
Chibia
Tombua
Chibemba
Cahama
Xangongo
Oncócua
Ondjiva
Cunene
Cubango
Cuito
Luiana
Cuando
Kavango
Mongu
Barotselan
Senanga
Mulonga
Plain
Katima
Mulilo

A N G O L A

Pta. da Marca

C. Fria

Skeleton Coast

Oshakati
Ondangwa
Ovamboland
Etosha
Pan
Rundu
Cuangar
Caprivi Strip
Tsumeb
Grootfontein
Okavango
Delta
Maun

Outjo
Otjiwarongo
Omaruru
Damaraland
Okahandja
Usakos
Sandveld
Ghanzi

B O T S W A N

N A M I B I A

Kaokoveld
Namib
Ugab
Kaukauveld
Omuramba
Omatako
Groolaagte
Botlet

Swakopmund
Walvis Bay
Windhoek
2483
Auasberg
Gobabis
K a l a h a r i

Tropic of Capricorn

Conception B.
Rehoboth
Nossob

Maltahöhe
Mariental
Tshane
Molepol
Jwaneng
Ko

Gibeon
Hottentotsbaai
Lüderitz
N a m a l a n d
Keetmanshoop
Schwarzrand
Fish
Tshabong
Molopo
N o r t h
W e s t
Mafi
Vryburg

Karasburg
Hotazel
Kuruman
Postmasburg
Upington
Kimberley

Oranjemund
Alexander Bay
Orange
Augrabies Falls
Keimoes
Kenhardt
Vaal
O

Port Nolloth
Nababiep
Springbok
N o r t h e r n   C a p e
Prieska

Bitterfontein
Carnarvon
De Aar
Coles

Sakriver
S O U T H   A F R I
Middelburg

Calvinia
Great
Vanrhynsdorp
Karoo
Nuweveldberge
Graaff-
Reinet
Cla

Lambert's Bay
W e s t e r n
Sutherland
Beaufort
West
Easte
Cap

St. Helena Bay
Vredenburg
Saldanha
Moorreesburg
C a p e
Oudtshoorn
Uitenhage

Table Bay
Paarl
Worcester
Stellenbosch
George
Mosselbaai
PO
ELIZABE

CAPE TOWN
Table Mt. 1086
Cape of Good Hope
Strand
Swellendam
Bredasdorp
Cape Agulhas

East from Greenwich

ft	m
12 000	4000
9000	3000
6000	2000
4500	1500
3000	1000
1200	400
600	200
0	0
200	600
1000	3000
2000	6000
4000	12 000
m	ft

Projection : Sanson-Flamsteed's Sinusoidal

1   3   20   4   25

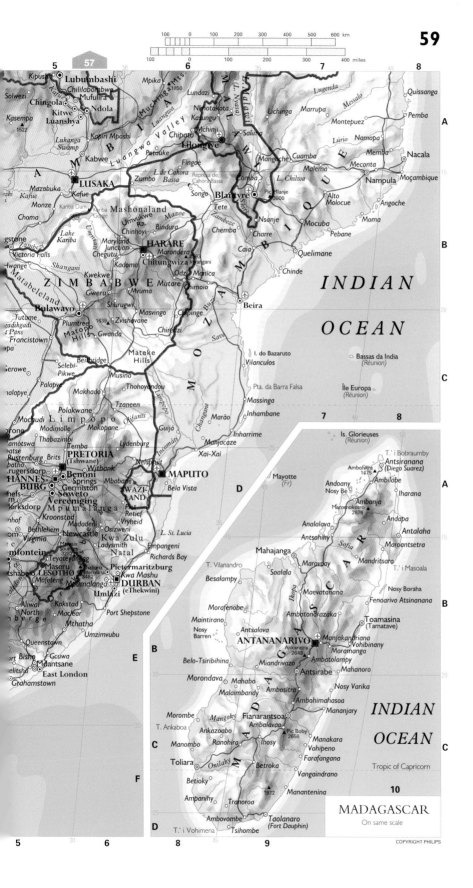

100 0 100 200 300 400 500 600 km
100   0   100   200   300   400 miles

Kipushi Lubumbashi Mpika Mchinga Mts 1850 Lundazi Lugenda Messalo Quissanga
Solwezi Chililabombwe Mufulira MUCHINGA Nkhotakota Lichinga Marrupa Messalo Pemba
Chingola Kitwe Ndola Kasungu Mchinji Salima Montepuez Namapa Nacala
Kasempa Luanshya 1522 Kabin Mpashi Chipata Petauke Fingoe Mangoche Cuamba Malema Memba Moçambique
Kabwe Luangwa Valley Lilongwe L. de Cahora Zomba L. Chilwa Alto Nampula
Mazabuka Kafue Zumbo Bassa Represa de Pic Mlanje Molocue Angoche
LUSAKA Monze Kariba Dam Songo Cahora Bassa Blantyre 3000 Moma
Choma Mashonaland Tete Nsanje Mocuba Pebane
Lake Umvukwe Ra. Bindura Zambeze Charre Chemba Caia Quelimane
Victoria Falls Kariba Maryland Chinhoyi HARARE Mazoe Chinde
Hwange Shangani Junction Marondera 2593 INDIAN
Matabeleland Chegutu Chitungwiza Inyangani Manica
ZIMBABWE Kadoma Odzi Chimoio OCEAN
Bulawayo Gweru Mvuma Mutare
Tutume Kwekwe Masvingo Chipinge Beira
Makgadikgadi 1639 Zvishavane Chiredzi
Pans Matopo Gwanda Mateke I. do Bazaruto Bassas da India
Francistown Hills Hills Vilanculos (Réunion)
Serowe Selebi- Beitbridge Musina Île Europa
Palapye Pikwe (Réunion)
Nalapye Makhado Thohoyandou Massinga
Mochudi Limpopo Tzaneen Marão Inhambane
Modimolle Mokopane Guijá Inharrime
Thabazimbi Temba Lydenburg Manjacaze
PRETORIA Witbank Nelspruit Xai-Xai
(Tshwane) MAPUTO
Rustenburg Brits Mbabane Bela Vista

INDIAN OCEAN

MADAGASCAR
On same scale

COPYRIGHT PHILIPS

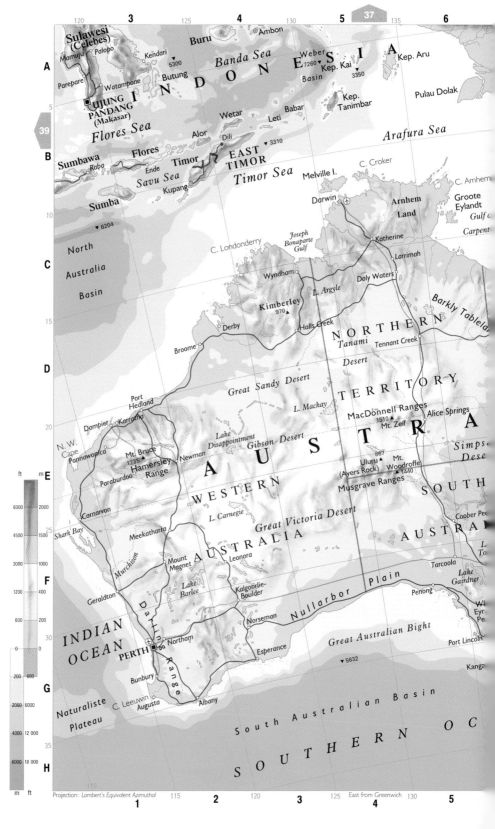

Projection: Lambert's Equivalent Azimuthal   East from Greenwich

100 0 100 200 300 400 500 600 700 800 km
100 0 100 200 300 400 500 miles

7 145 **8** 150 **9** 155 **10** 160 **11**

New
Guinea

Mount Hagen 4508 ▲ Mt. Wilhelm Lae New
PAPUA⊙NEW GUINEA Britain New Britain *Trench* 2743▲ Bougainville
Fly *Owen Stanley Range* Mt. Balbi SOLOMON
Gulf of Solomon 9140 ▼ Shortland Choiseul ISLANDS
Papua Port Sea Is. Santa Isabel
Moresby Vella Lavella B
New Vanguru
Torres Strait D'Entrecasteaux Georgia Is. Russell Is. Florida Malaita
Badu I. Moa I. Islands Is. ▲ 2439
Prince C. York Honiara⊙ 10
of Wales I. Louisiade Pocklington Guadalcanal
Weipa Cape Archipelago Reef Bellona San Cristóbal
York Rennell (Makira)
Peninsula Coral Sea C

ellesley Cooktown Basin 64
s. Queensland C o r a l   S e a 15
Mitchell Plateau P A C I F I C
Normanton Cairns CORAL Îles D'Entrecasteaux D
Forsayth 1611▲ SEA
ISLANDS Îles Chesterfield
Townsville Reef TERRITORY 20
Flinders Charters Towers Whitsunday Is. O C E A N
Isa Hughenden L. Mackay Chain
Cloncurry Dalrymple Tropic of Capricorn E
QUEENSLAND Emerald Rockhampton Lord Howe Seamount 25
Longreach Gladstone
Winton I A 1312▲ Bundaberg
Yaraka Maryborough
Diamantina Charleville Gympie Sunshine F
216▲ Roma Coast
rt Quilpie BRISBANE
ny Toowoomba Ipswich
ert Thargomindah Dirranbandi Gold
Creek Cunnamulla Coast
Eyre Moree Lismore
rree Bourke Walgett Grafton
Tamworth 1615▲ 30
NEW SOUTH Round Port
Flinders Ranges Broken Hill Cobar Mt. Macquarie
WALES Dubbo Taree Lord Howe I.
ort Pirie Orange Bathurst (Austral.) G
Murray Griffith Newcastle⊙ ▼ 734
Mildura Hay SYDNEY 35
ADELAIDE Wagga Wagga Goulburn Wollongong
Swan Hill Murray Canberra T a s m a n   S e a
Shepparton Albury- Mt. A.C.T.
Bendigo Wodonga Kosciuszko Snowy Mts.
Horsham 2230▲ Bombala
VICTORIA Sale C. Howe H
Ballarat MELBOURNE
Mount Gambier Geelong Tasman Abyssal Plain
N Warrnambool
Bass Strait Flinders I.
King I. Furneaux ▼ 5267
Group
Burnie
1617▲ Launceston
Mt. Ossa
TASMANIA Hobart
6 7 **8** S.E.Cape 150 **9** 155 **10**

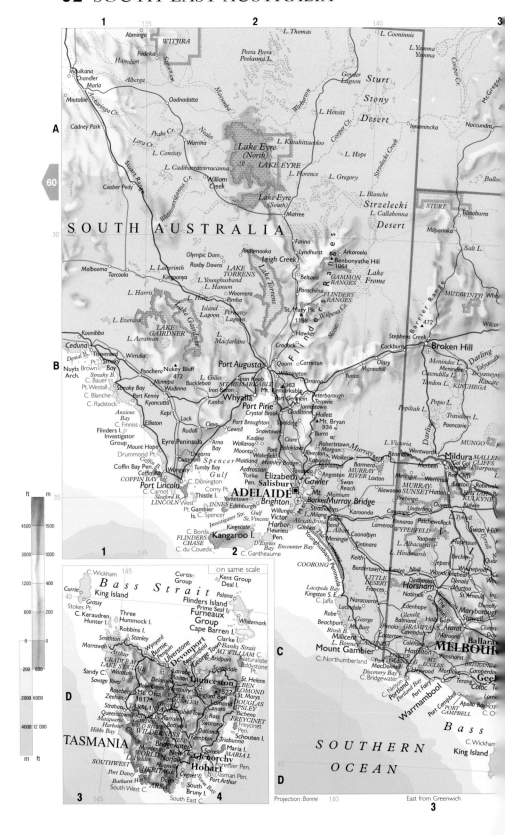

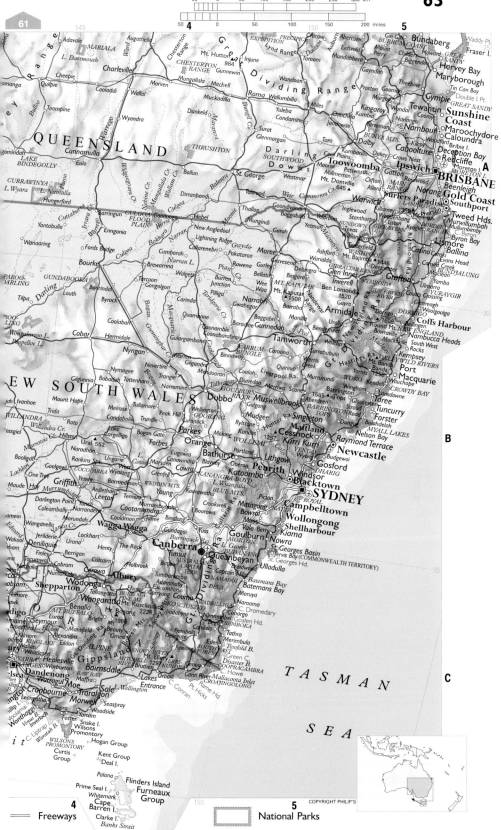

50   0   50   100   150   200   250   300 km
50   0   50   100   150   200 miles

QUEENSLAND

N EW SOUTH WALES

SYDNEY

BRISBANE

Gold Coast

Sunshine Coast

Toowoomba

Ipswich

Newcastle

Canberra

Wollongong

Albury

T A S M A N

S E A

WILSONS
PROMONTORY

Flinders Island
Furneaux
Group

Cape
Barren I.

Clarke I.

Banks Strait

═══ Freeways

☐ National Parks

4   5

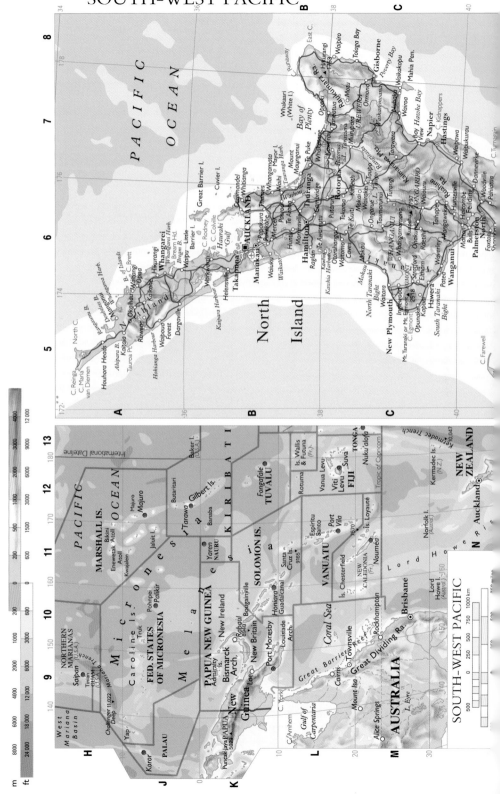

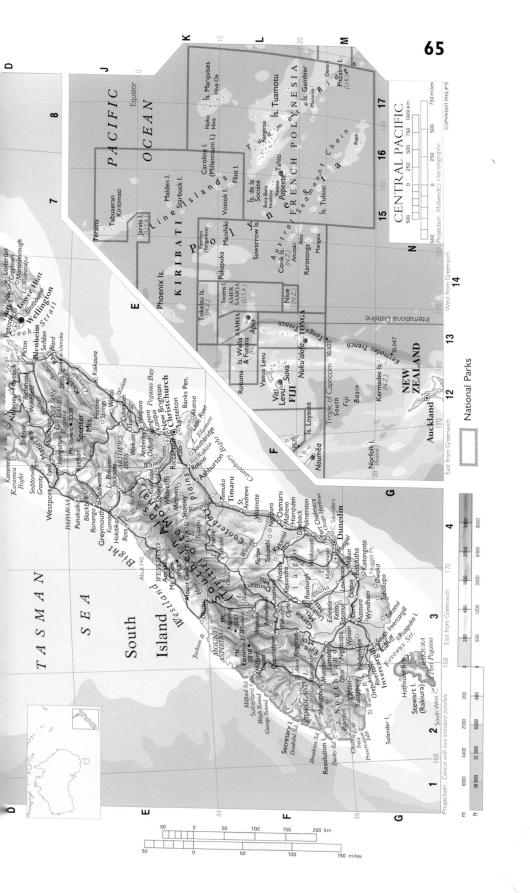

65

PACIFIC OCEAN

Equator

CENTRAL PACIFIC

Projection: Mollweide's Homolographic

500   0   250   500   750   1000 km

0   250   500   750 miles

COPYRIGHT PHILIPS

TUAMOTU

Is. Marquises
Nuku Hiva
Hiva Oa

Caroline I. (Millennium I.)
Flint I.

FRENCH POLYNESIA

Rangiroa
Tahiti
Papeete
Is. de la Société
Bora Bora
Huahine
Raiatea
Moorea
Is. Gambier
Mururoa
R. Omo
Pitcairn I. (U.K.)

Rapa

Is. Tubuai

Austral Is.
Anutaki
Abu
Mangaia

Line Islands
Tabuaeran
Kiritimati
Teraina
Jarvis I. (U.S.A.)
Starbuck I.
Malden I.
Vostok I.

KIRIBATI

Penrhyn (Tongareva)
Manihiki
Pukapuka
Suwarrow Is.
Cook Is. (N.Z.)
Rarotonga

Phoenix Is.

Tokelau Is. (N.Z.)
Swains I.
AMER. SAMOA (U.S.A.)
SAMOA
Apia
Niue (N.Z.)

Is. Wallis & Futuna (Fr.)
Rotuma
Vanua Levu
Viti Levu
FIJI
Suva
Is. Loyauté
Nouméa

TONGA
Nuku'alofa
Tonga Trench
10,822

Kermadec Trench
10,047

Tropic of Capricorn
South Fiji Basin
Norfolk I. (Austral.)

7520

Kermadec Is. (N.Z.)

NEW ZEALAND
Auckland

West from Greenwich

International Dateline

National Parks

TASMAN SEA

South Island

Karamea Bight
Karamea
Seddonville
Granity
Westport
Cape Foulwind
Punakaiki
Big Hd.
Blackball
Runanga
Greymouth
Hokitika
Ross

PAPAROA

WESTLAND

NELSON LAKES
Tadmor
Wakefield
Motueka
Nelson
Richmond
Mt Travers 3338
Spenser Mts
Reefton
Murchison
L. Rotoroa
Owen
Upper Buller Gorge
L. Brunner
Jacksons
Stillwater

ARTHUR'S PASS

Mt Cook 3753
Westland
Aoraki
MOUNT COOK
L. Tekapo
L. Pukaki

L. Ohau
MOUNT ASPIRING
3027
Mt Aspiring
Makarora
L. Hawea
L. Wanaka
Wanaka
Hawea
Cromwell
Arrowtown
Queenstown
L. Wakatipu
Kingston
Glenorchy

Milford Sd.
Sutherland Falls
Bligh Sound
George Sound
Milford
Te Anau
FIORDLAND
L. Te Anau
L. Manapouri
Manapouri
Secretary I.
Doubtful Sd.
Breaksea Sd.
Dusky Sd.
Resolution I.
Preservation Inlet
Chalky Inlet
Puysegur Pt.
Solander I.

Southern Alps
The Remarkables
Eyre Mts
Garvie Mts
Hokonui Hills
Mataura

South Island

Stewart I. (Rakiura)
RAKIURA
Halfmoon Bay
Ruapuke I.
Foveaux Str.
Port Pegasus

Te Waewae Bay
Orepuki
Riverton
Otautau
Winton
Invercargill
Bluff
Nightcaps
Mossburn
Lumsden
Athol
Ohai
Edendale
Wyndham
Gore
Clinton
Balclutha
Owaka
Nugget Pt.
Kaitangata
Lawrence
Roxburgh
Alexandra
Clyde
Millers Flat
Kelso
Tapanui
Heriot
Waikaia
Riversdale

Tasman Mts
Abel Tasman
D'Urville I.
Stephens I.
Takaka
Collingwood
Golden Bay
Farewell Spit

Nelson
Blenheim
Seddon
Picton
Havelock
Kaikoura
Cape Campbell
Clarence
Ward
Cloudy Bay
Cook Strait

Lower Hutt
Wellington
Porirua
Upper Hutt
Paraparaumu
Otaki
Levin
Greytown
Martinborough
Masterton
Carterton
Wairarapa

Cheviot
Waiau
Hanmer Springs
Culverden
Waipara
Amberley
Rangiora
Oxford
Kaiapoi
Christchurch
New Brighton
Lyttelton
Banks Pen.
Akaroa
Little River
Rakaia
Methven
Whitecliffs
Springfield
Darfield
Southbridge
Ellesmere
Ashburton

Canterbury Plains
Canterbury Bight
Rakaia River
Rangitata
Geraldine
Temuka
Timaru
St. Andrews
Waimate
Fairlie
Albury
Pleasant Point

Oamaru
Ngapara
Moeraki
Hampden
Palmerston
Dunback
Port Chalmers
Otago Harbour
C. Saunders
Dunedin
Mosgiel
Taieri
Outram
Waikouaiti

Kurow
Omarama
Tarras
Lindis Pass
St. Bathans
Naseby
Ranfurly
Middlemarch
Waipiata
Patearoa

Otago

Central Otago
Tokanui
Tokomairiro

South West C.

Auckland

East from Greenwich

South West C.

National Parks

Projection : Conical with two standard parallels   East from Greenwich

m   6000   4000   2000   1000   600   400   200   0
ft   18 000   12 000   6000   3000   2000   1200   600   0

m   3000   2000   1000   400   200   0
ft   9000   6000   3000   1200   600   0

50   0   50   100   150   200 km
50   0   50   100   150 miles

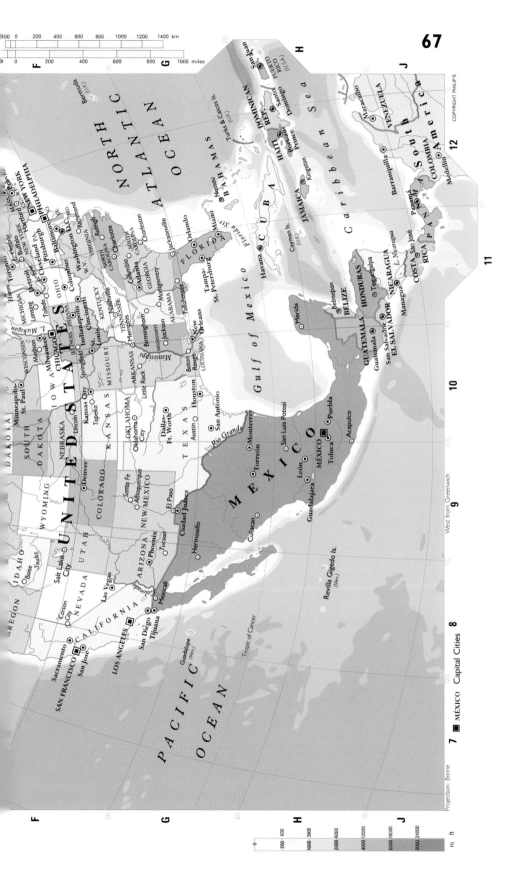

100 0   200   400   600   800   1000   1200   1400 km
0   200   400   600   800   1000 miles

F   G   H

J

12

11

10

West from Greenwich

9

8

7 ■ MÉXICO   Capital Cities

Projection: Bonne

COPYRIGHT PHILIP'S

PACIFIC OCEAN

NORTH ATLANTIC OCEAN

UNITED STATES

MEXICO

Gulf of Mexico

Caribbean Sea

BAHAMAS

CUBA

JAMAICA

HAITI

DOMINICAN REP.

PUERTO RICO (U.S.A.)

GUATEMALA

BELIZE

HONDURAS

EL SALVADOR

NICARAGUA

COSTA RICA

PANAMA

COLOMBIA

VENEZUELA

South America

Tropic of Cancer

m ft
0
-200 -600
1000 3000
2000 6000
4000 12000
6000 18000
8000 24000

Peel Sd.
Somerset Island
Prince of Wales I.
Boothia Peninsula 573▲
King William I.
Taloyoak
Gjoa Haven
Adelaide Pen.
Kent Pen.
Franklin Str.
Viscount Melville Sound
M'Clintock Channel
Victoria Island
Cambridge Bay
Queen Maud Gulf
Chantrey Inlet
Arctic Circle
Chesterfield Inlet
Rankin Inlet
Whale Cove
Baker Lake L.
Baker L.
Arviat
Yathkyed L.
Nueltin L.
Sulb.
C. Churchill
Hudson Bay
Banks Island 747▲
Prince Albert Pen.
Holman
Dolphin and Union Str.
E. Bering
Prince Albert Sd.
Wollaston Pen.
Coronation Gulf
Bathurst Inlet
Coppermine
Contwoyto L.
MacAlpine L.
Garry L.
Aberdeen L.
Back
Clinton Colden L.
Kasba L.
Wholdaia L.
Thelon
Dubawnt L.
Dubawnt
Fond-du-Lac
Lake Athabasca
Uranium City
Fort Chipewyan
N U N A V U T
N O R T H W E S T
T E R R I T O R I E S
C. Bathurst
Franklin B.
Tuktoyaktuk
Inuvik
Aklavik
Fort McPherson
Tsiigehtchic
Mackenzie
Fort Good Hope
Norman Wells
Amundsen Gulf
Kugluktuk
Great Bear L.
Echo Bay
Déline
Tulita
Great Bear L.
1462
Franklin Mts.
Wrigley
Fort Simpson
South Nahanni
Mackenzie Mountains
Fort Providence
Hay River
Yellowknife 156
Wha Ti
Rae
Great Slave L.
Resolution
Pine Point
Fort Smith
Fort Liard
Liard
Fort Nelson
Kutsoki
Slave
Caribou Mts. 1036▲
High Level
Manning
Rainbow Lake
Peace
Peace River
Wabasca
Dawson Creek
Chetwynd
Fort McMurray
Alaska Hwy.
N140
Mt. Sanford 3959
Wrangell Mts. 4228
Mt. Lucania 5226
Mt. Logan 5959
Mt. St. Elias 5489
St. Elias Mts.
Mt. Fairweather 4663
Fairbanks
Eagle
Tanana
Tok
Delta Junction
Glennallen
Valdez
Cordova
Yakutat
Anchorage
Wasilla
Palmer
Kenai
Soldotna
Homer
Seward
Cook Inlet
A L A S K A
Y U K O N   T E R R I T O R Y
Old Crow
Dawson
Pelly
Stewart
Mayo
Carmacks
Pelly River
Ross River
Faro
Whitehorse
Teslin
Watson Lake
Selwyn Mts.
2961
Mt. St. James 4562
MacBrien
Cassiar Mountains
Atlin
Dease Lake
Telegraph Creek
Stikine
Skagway
Carcross
Haines Junction
Beaver Creek
Snag
Kluane L.
Juneau
Admiralty I.
Chichagof I.
Baranof I.
Sitka
Petersburg
Wrangell
Ketchikan
Metlakatla
Prince of Wales I.
Dixon Entrance
Prince Rupert
Alexander Archipelago
Cross Sound
Graham I.
Queen Charlotte Is.
Moresby I.
Hecate Str.
R o c k y
2743
Finlay
Williston L.
Mackenzie
Fort St. John
Fort Nelson
Great Snow Mts. 2350
Stewart
Smithers
Terrace
Kitimat
Babine L.
Stuart L.
Vanderhoof
Prince George
B R I T I S H   C O
Queen
3959
P A C I F I C

70 · 70 · 69

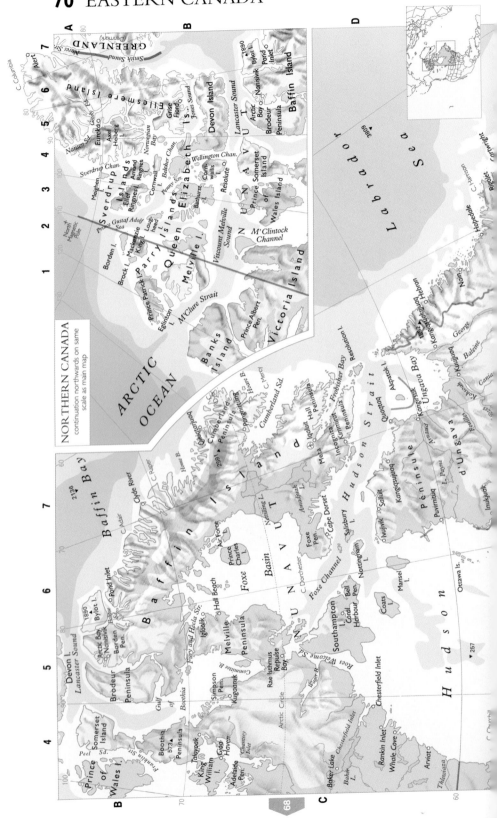

NORTHERN CANADA
continuation northwards on same
scale as main map

GREENLAND
(Denmark)

A 80 7

C. Columbia

Alert

Nares Str.

Smith Sound

Ellesmere Island

Greely Fd.

Nansen Sd.

Eureka

Axel Heiberg I.

Sverdrup Chan.

Meighen I.

Prince Gustaf Adolf Sea

Mackenzie King I.

Sverdrup Islands

Borden I.

Brock I.

Ellef Ringnes I.

Amund Ringnes I.

Cornwall I.

Loughheed I.

Prince Patrick I.

Eglinton I.

M'Clure Strait

Parry Islands

Banks Island

Prince Albert Pen.

Bathurst I.

Queen Elizabeth

Cornwall I.

Penny Str.

Baker Chan.

Norwegian Bay

Grise Fiord

Devon Island

B

1990

Bylot I.

Narsivik

Pond Inlet

Arctic Bay

Brodeur Peninsula

Baffin Island

Jones Sound

Lancaster Sound

Wellington Chan.

Cornwallis I.

Resolute

Somerset Island

Prince of Wales Island

M'Clintock Channel

Viscount Melville Sound

Melville I.

North Magnetic Pole

Victoria Island

ARCTIC OCEAN

D

Labrador

Sea

3869

Rigolet

C. Harrison

Hopedale

Nain

George

Balance

Kobuk

Canio

Revillon

Kangiqsualujjuaq

Hebron

Saglek

Kangirsuk

Kuujjuaq

Péninsule d'Ungava

Inukjuak

R. Payne

Puvirnituq

Kangiqsujuaq

Ivujivik

Salluit

Quaqtaq

Kangirsuk

Aupaluk

Ungava Bay

Arnaud

Hudson Strait

Baffin Bay

2136

C. Adair

Clyde River

C. Raper

Howe B.

Qikiqtarjuaq

C. Hooti

Home B.

Cumberland Sd.

Cumberland Peninsula

Pangnirtung

2591

Iqaluit

Meta

Hall Peninsula

Frobisher Bay

Incognita Pen.

Kimmirut

Resolution I.

B

60

Baffin Island

Pond Inlet

Bylot I.

Narsivik

1890

Arctic Bay

Borden Pen.

Brodeur Peninsula

Devon I.

Lancaster Sound

Somerset Island

Prince of Wales I.

Peel Sd.

Boothia

573

Boothia Peninsula

Taloyoak

Gjoa Haven

King William I.

Adelaide Pen.

Franklin Str.

Chantrey Inlet

100

Simpson Pen.

Kugaaruk

Committee B.

Rae Isthmus

Repulse Bay

Melville Peninsula

Fury and Hecla Str.

Igloolik

Hall Beach

Prince Charles I.

Air Force I.

Foxe Basin

Foxe Pen.

Nettilling L.

Amadjuak L.

Foxe Channel

C. Dorchester

Cape Dorset

Nottingham I.

Salisbury I.

Mansel I.

Coats I.

Southampton I.

Coral Harbour

Bell Pen.

Roes Welcome Sd.

Wager B.

NUNAVUT

Arctic Circle

Baker Lake

Baker L.

Chesterfield Inlet

Chesterfield Inlet

Whale Cove

Rankin Inlet

Arviat

Thelon

Hudson Bay

257

Ottawa Is.

60

C. Churchill

70

90

C

68

71

1 2 3 120 4 118 5

VANCOUVER
Nanaimo
Ladysmith
VANCOUVER
Island Duncan
PACIFIC RIM NAT. PARK
Port Renfrew
Juan de Fuca Strait
C. Flattery
Neah Bay
C. Alava
Coquitlam
Surrey New Westminster
Chilliwack
Blaine Lynden
Ferndale
Mt. Baker
5285
Ross L.
NORTH CASCADES NAT. PARK
Grand Forks
Rossland
Trail
Greston
BRITISH CO

Victoria
Esquimalt
Port Angeles
Port Townsend
Anacortes
Oak Hbr
Sedro-Woolley
Concrete
Oliver
Osoyoos
Oroville
Tonasket
Republic
Kettle Falls
Northport
Metaline Falls
Bonners Ferry
Priest L.

La Push
Olympic Mts.
Mt. Olympus
2428
OLYMPIC NAT. PARK
Forks
Port Angeles
Sequim
Port Townsend
Burlington
Mount Vernon
Arlington
Darrington
Winthrop
Okanogan
Omak
Brewster
Franklin D. Roosevelt L.
Colville
Chewelah
Newport
Sandpoint
Coeur d'Alene
Pend Oreille L.

Moclips
Neilton
Hoodsport
Shelton
Poulsbo
Edmonds
Bremerton
SEATTLE
Bellevue
Skykomish
Glacier Peak
3213
Chelan
Leavenworth
Waterville
Grand Coulee
Coulee City
Grand Coulee Dam
Deer Park
Spokane
Opportunity
Post Falls
Coeur d'Alene

Hoquiam
Aberdeen
Grays Harbor
Westport
Raymond
Willapa B.
Ocean Park
Long Beach
Olympia
Lacey
Tumwater
Tacoma
Kent
Renton
Kenumclaw
Puyallup
Ellensburg
WASHINGTON
Wenatchee
Ephrata
Quincy
Moses Lake
Columbia
Odessa
Sprague
Ritzville
Cheney
Davenport
Rosalia
Tekoa
Oakesdale
St. Maries

46
Montesano
Centralia
Chehalis
Morton
Naches
Yakima
Wapato
Toppenish
Sunnyside
Richland
Basin
Othello
Connell
Lind
Garfield
Colfax
Pullman
Moscow
Bovill

Warrenton
Astoria
Seaside
Cathlamet
Longview
Kelso
Kalama
Battle Ground
Vancouver
PORTLAND
MOUNT ST. HELENS NAT. VOLC. MON.
Mt. St. Helens 2550
Mt. Adams 3751
HANFORD REACH NAT. REC. AREA
Union Gap
Grandview
Prosser
Kennewick
Pasco
Wallula
Waitsburg
Pomeroy
Dayton
Clarkston
Lewiston
Orofino

C. Meares
Tillamook
Wheeler
St. Helens
Hillsboro
Beaverton
Newberg
Gresham
Milwaukie
Oregon City
Hood River
The Dalles
Goldendale
Columbia
Wasco
Arlington
Umatilla
Hermiston
Pendleton
Milton-Freewater
Walla Walla
Elgin
Winchester
Nezperce
Grange

Lincoln City
McMinnville
Dallas
Monmouth
Salem
Keizer
Woodburn
Canby
Mt. Hood 3427
Maupin
Grass Valley
Condon
Heppner
Pilot Rock
HELLS CANYON NAT. REC. AREA
Wallowa
Enterprise
White Bird
Salmon

Newport
Toledo
Waldport
Corvallis
Albany
Lebanon
Philomath
Stayton
Mt. Jefferson 3200
JOHN DAY FOSSIL BEDS NAT. MON.
John Day
Spray
Mitchell
Blue Mountains
North Powder
Haines
Wallowa Mts.
Baker City
Riggins
New Meadows
McCall

44
Florence
OREGON DUNES NAT. REC. AREA
Reedsport
Mapleton
Junction City
Brownsville
Sweet Home
McKenzie
Three Sisters 3156
Sisters
Crooked River
Redmond
Prineville
John Day
Dayville
Prairie City
Brogan
Council
Cascade Res.
Cascade

North Bend
Coos Bay
Eugene
Springfield
Cottage Grove
Oakridge
OREGON
Bend
NEWBERRY NAT. VOLCANIC MON.
Huntington
Weiser
Payette
New Plymouth
Ontario

Coquille
Myrtle Point
C. Blanco
Port Orford
Gold Beach
Camas Valley
Green
Roseburg
Myrtle Creek
Canyonville
Sutherlin
Drain
La Pine
Brothers
Silver L.
Harney Basin
Harney L.
Crane
Burns
Riley
Burns Junction
Malheur
Juntura
Nyssa
Parma
Caldwell
Nampa
Meridian
Boise
Eagle
Garden City
Homedale
Murphy
Jordan Valley

42
Brookings
SMITH RIVER NAT. REC. AREA
Crescent City
REDWOOD NAT. PARK
Rogue
Grants Pass
Central Point
Medford
Gold Hill
White City
Mt. McLoughlin 2894
Upper Klamath
Klamath Falls
Altamont
Talent
Ashland
Merrill
CRATER LAKE NAT. PARK
Fort Klamath
Chemult
Silver Lake
Paisley
Summer L.
Bly
Valley Falls
Lakeview
Abert L.
Steens Mountain 2962
Alvord Desert
Owyhee
Murphy
Jordan Valley
Bruneau
HAGERMAN FOSSIL BEDS NAT. MON.
Mountain Ho

Happy Camp
Hornbrook
Yreka
Dorris
Clear Lake Res.
Goose L.
Upper Alkali L.
McDermitt
Owyhee
Mountain City

F
Klamath
CALIFORNIA
Mts.
Weed
Mount Shasta
Mt. Shasta 4317
Dunsmuir
McCloud
WHISKEYTOWN-SHASTA-TRINITY NAT. REC. AREA
Burney
Canby
Alturas
Warner Mts.
Middle Alkali L.
Lower Alkali L.
Santa Rosa Range
Paradise Valley
Little Humboldt
Independence Mts.
Mountain City
Co

McKinleyville
Arcata
Eureka
Fortuna
Thompson Pk. 2724
Shasta L.
Bieber
LASSEN VOLCANIC NAT. PARK & WILDERNESS
Eagle L.
Winnemucca
Golconda
Humboldt
Carlin
Elko
Spring Creek
Ruby Mts.
Franklin
Ruby L.

Scotia
Weott
Garberville
Redding
Anderson
Red Bluff
Lassen Peak 3187
Chester
Susanville
Westwood
Greenville
Honey L.
Gerlach
Rye Patch Res.
Imlay
Battle Mountain
Dunphy
Diamond Mts.
Eureka
McGill

Cape Mendocino
Laytonville
Ft. Bragg
Willits
Mendocino
Corning
Orland
Willows
Quincy
Paradise
Sierra
Chico
Pyramid L.
Winnemucca L.
G
Lovelock
Wadsworth
Fernley
NEVADA
Austin
Toiyabe Ra.
Ely

124
Ukiah
Lakeport
Hopland
Cloverdale
Clear
Upper Lake
Colusa
Gridley
Oroville
Palermo
Marysville
Yuba City
Grass Valley
Nevada City
Truckee
Reno
Sparks
Carson Sink
Fallon
Stillwater Ra.
Shoshone Mountains
Diamond Mts.
Currant

Pt. Arena
Healdsburg
Windsor
Santa Rosa
Petaluma
Napa
Calistoga
St. Helena
Davis
Woodland
Olivehurst
Auburn
Roseville
Arden
Placerville
Camino
Incline Village
Virginia City
Carson City
South Tahoe
Minden
Gardnerville
Yerington
Schurz
Walker L.
Hot Creek Ra.
Round Mountain 3599

38
POINT REYES NAT. SEASHORE
San Rafael
Berkeley
Richmond
Golden Gate
Vallejo
Fairfield
Vacaville
Elk Grove
SACRAMENTO
Lodi
Ione
San Andreas
Mt. Grant 3426
Hawthorne
Luning
Mt. Jefferson 3599

Projection: Albers' Equal Area with two standard parallels

2 120 3 4 118 78 5 116 6

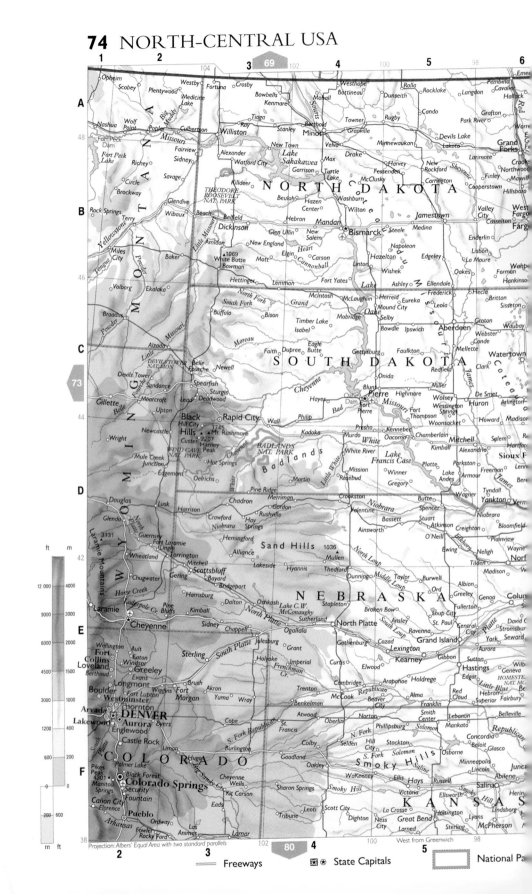

—— Freeways   ⊞ ⊛ State Capitals   National Pa

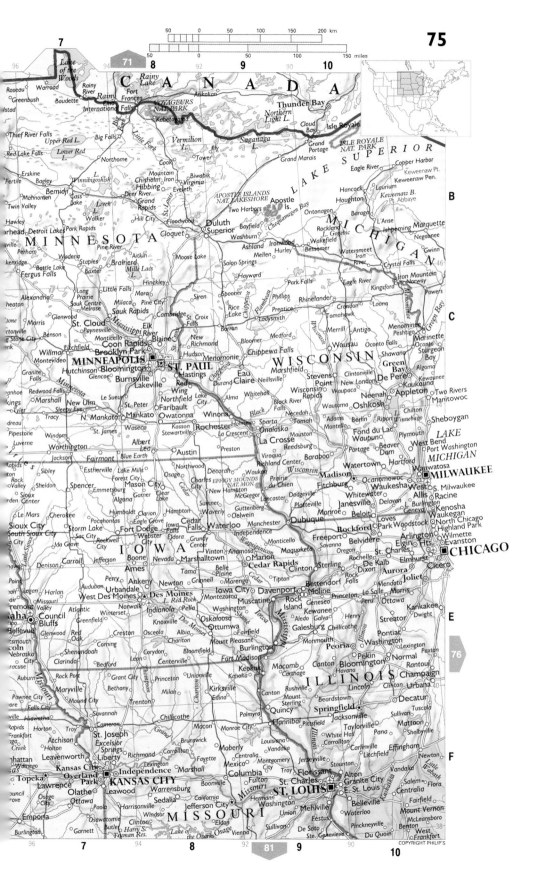

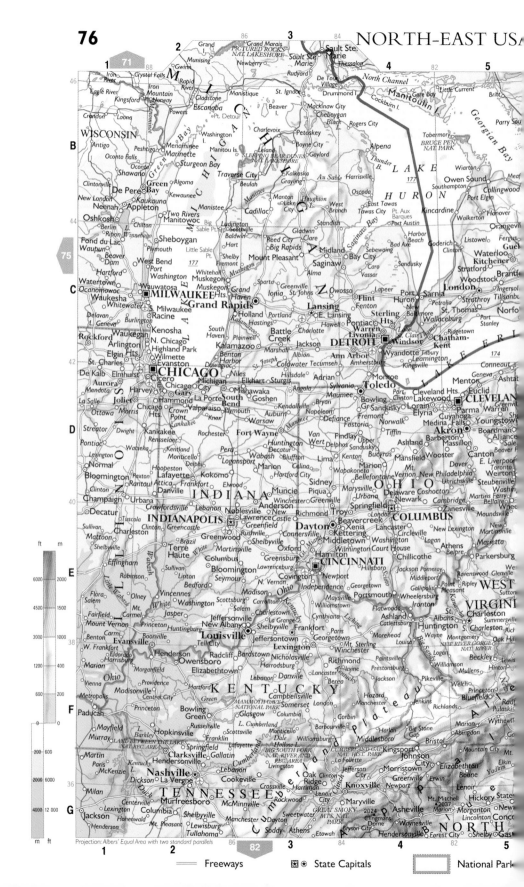

West from Greenwich

continuation
eastwards
on same scale

COPYRIGHT PHILIP'S

1 122 **2** 120 **3** 118 **4** 72 116 **5**

NEVADA

SAN FRANCISCO
Oakland
Stockton
Angels Camp
Bridgeport
Grant Ra.
Sonora
YOSEMITE NAT. PARK
Mono Lake
Warm Springs
Tonopah
Hayward
Tracy
Manteca
Modesto
San Mateo
Fremont
Redwood City
Patterson
Turlock
White Mountain Pk. 4341
Goldfield
Sunnyvale
Gustine
Atwater
Pioche
SAN JOSE
San Joaquin
Merced
Bishop
Panaca
Santa Cruz
Gilroy
Mariposa
Big Pine
Caliente
Watsonville
Los Banos
Chowchilla
Hiko
Salinas
Hollister
Madera
Alamo
Pinos Pt.
Gonzales
Mendota
Fresno
North Palisade 4341
Beatty
Seaside
Sanger
Clovis
KINGS CANYON NAT. PARK
Kings
Independence
DEATH VALLEY
Indian Springs
Monterey
Soledad
Selma
Reedley
Lone Pine
Mesquite
Pt. Sur
36
King City
Kingsburg
Visalia
Dinuba
Mt. Whitney 4418
Owens L.
D. NAT.
Spring Mts. 3633
North Las Vegas
Cambria
Hanford
Lemoore
Exeter
Tulare
SEQUOIA NAT. PARK
Olancha
-86
Death Valley Junc.
Pahrump
LAS VEGAS
Morro Bay
Paso Robles
Corcoran
Lindsay
Porterville
GIANT SEQUOIA NAT. MON.
Telescope Pk. 4366
Sunrise Manc
San Luis Obispo
Atascadero
CARRIZO PLAIN NAT. MON.
Wasco
Delano
Earlimart
Henderson
Paradise
Arroyo Grande
Shafter
Oildale
Kern
Inyokern
Searles L.
Jean
Boulder City
LAKE MEAD NAT. REC. AREA
Nipomo
Bakersfield
Ridgecrest
Searchlight
Guadalupe
Santa Maria
Buena Vista Lake Bed
Tehachapi
Baker
MOJAVE NAT. PRESERVE
Mohave
Davis Dam
Kingman
Lompoc
Taft
Maricopa
Tehachapi Mts.
2692
Mojave
Yermo
Soda L.
Laughlin
Hualapai
Pt. Arguello
Lebec
Los Ang...
Lancaster
Barstow
Ludlow
New York Mts
Needles
Bullhead City
Pt. Conception
Solvang
Santa Barbara
Ojai
Palmdale
Victorville
Amboy
Bristol L.
Cadiz
Topock
Yucca
Carpinteria
Ventura
Oxnard
Simi Valley
Santa Clarita
3506 San Gorgonio Mt.
Twentynine Palms
Danby
L. Havasu
Lake Hava City
Santa Rosa I.
San Miguel I.
CHANNEL IS. NAT. PARK
Burbank
Glendale
Pasadena
Hesperia
Colorado River Aqueduct
Parker D.
Beverly Hills
Pomona
Apple Valley
Santa Cruz I.
Santa Monica
LOS ANGELES
Ontario
SAN BERNARDINO
JOSHUA TREE NAT. PARK
Parker
Inglewood
Anaheim
Riverside
Banning
Palm Springs
Indio
Desert Center
Salome
Long Beach
Huntington Beach
Corona
Santa Ana
Hemer
SANTA ROSA AND SAN JACINTO MTS. NAT. MON.
Coachella
Chocolate Mts.
Blythe
Quartzsite
San Nicolas I.
Newport Beach
Santa Catalina I.
San Clemente
Mission Viejo
Temecula
Vista
Coachella Canal
Sonoran Desert
San Clemente I.
Oceanside
Carlsbad
Escondido
Julian
Salton Sea
-72
Westmorland
Calipatria
Imperial Dam
Santa Catalina
Gulf of
Ramona
Brawley
Holtville
Yuma
SAN DIEGO
La Mesa
El Cajon
El Centro
Calexico
Somerton
San Luis
Wellton
Chula Vista
National City
Gila
American Canal
Sent
TIJUANA
Tecate
Mexicali
San Luis Río Colorado
Rosarito
Laguna Salada
PARQUE NACIONAL CONSTITUCIÓN DE 1857
Sierra de Juárez
Desierto de Altar
Ensenada
Pta. Santo Tomas
Santo Tomás
BAJA CALIFORNIA
C. Te
Cerro de la Encantada 3078
San Felipe
Puerto Peñasco
B. San Jor
C. Colonet
PARQUE NACIONAL SAN PEDRO MARTIR
Sierra de San Pedro Mártir
Golfo de Cali (Mar de Cortés)
San Telmo
Punta Prieta
Canal de las Ballenas
I. Ánge de la Guard
C. San Quintin
I. San Luis
El Rosario
Pta. Baja
Pta. San Antonio
Isla Cedros
B. Sebastián Vizcaíno

PACIFIC

OCEAN

Channel Is.

PACIFIC

OCEAN

Hawaiian Islands

Kapaa
Kaua'i
Lihue
Kauai Channel
O'ahu
Ni'ihau
Wahiawā
Kāne'ohe
Pearl City
Honolulu
Pearl Harbor
Kaunakakai
Moloka'i
Lāna'i
Kahului
Maui
Kaho'olawe
Wailuku
'Alenuihāhā Channel
Waimea (Kamuela)
Hawai'i
Mauna Kea 4205
Hilo
Kailua
Mauna Loa 4169
Mountain View
Kilauea
Pāhala

11 160 158 **12** 156 **13**
22
20

HAWAI'I

50 0 100 km
50 0 50 100 miles

Projection: Albers Equal Area with two standard parallels

ft m
12 000 4000
9000 3000
6000 2000
4500 1500
3000 1000
1200 400
600 200
0 0
200 600
2000 6000
4000 12 000
m ft

── Freeways   ⊡⊛ State Capitals   National Parks

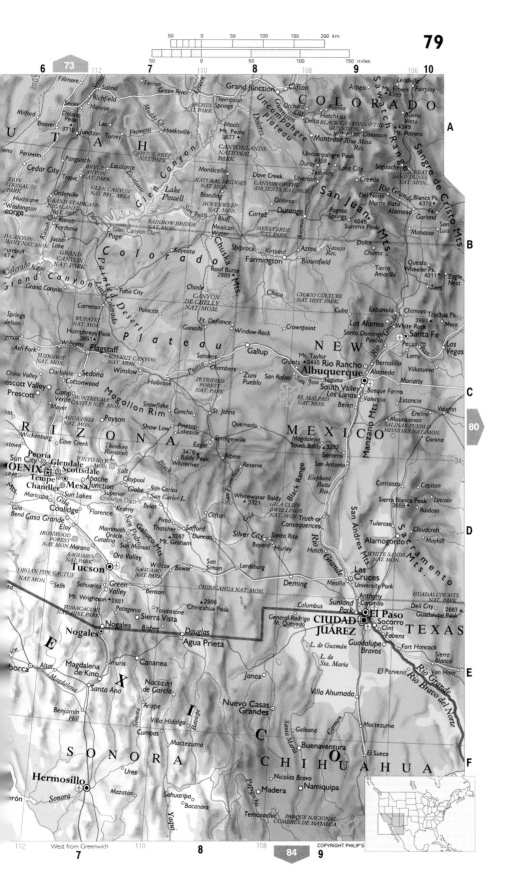

50 0 50 100 150 200 km
50   100   150 miles

6 75 94   **7** 92   **8** 90   **9**

Ohio

Yates Center Iola Moran Nevada El Dorado Springs Camdenton Rolla Bonne Terre Park Hills Chester Herrin Harrisburg Marion
ka Chanute Neosho Fort Scott Stockton Buffalo Lebanon Salem Farmington Perryville Fredericktown Jacksontown Anna Vienna Carbondale
Fredonia Neodesha Girard Lamar Bolivar Greenfield Ash Grove Houston Ironton Greenville Cape Girardeau Metropolis
Independence Parsons Pittsburg Carthage Republic Springfield Cabool Mountain Grove Van Buren Sikeston Charleston Paducah A
Sedan Columbus Webb City Nixa 510▲ Ava West Plains Doniphan Corning Poplar Bluff New Madrid Mayfield 82
Coffeyville Baxter Springs Joplin Aurora ○Ozark Thayer Pocahontas Malden Portageville Hickman Union City
Springs Broken Arrow Grand Lake O' The Cherokees Miami Neosho Monett Branson Bull Shoals L. Gainesville Norfork Black Kennett Caruthersville Tiptonville Martin McKenzie Dyersburg
rtlesville Nowata Vinita Bentonville Rogers Harrison Mountain Home Cherokee Village Walnut Ridge Paragould Blytheville Ripley Brownsville
Claremore MISSOURI Table Rock L. White Berryville 581▲ BUFFALO NAT. RIVER Newport Marked Tree Osceola Humboldt Jackson
M A Tulsa Pryor Siloam Springs Springdale Fayetteville Tahlequah Boston Mts. Mountain View Batesville Jonesboro Trumann TENNESSEE
inole Okmulgee Stilwell Little Red Heber Springs Searcy Augusta Wynne Earle West Memphis Covington Millington Bartlett Memphis Germantown Corinth

ARKANSAS Boonville

GULF OF MEXICO

● State Capitals   National Parks

A

Gainesville · Bull Shoals L. · Mountain Home · Doniphan · Poplar Bluff · Thayer · Dexter · New Madrid · Mayfield · Murray · L. Barkley · Hopkinsville · Russellville · Scottsville · Franklin · Monticello · L. Cumberland · Dale · Hollow L. · BIG SOUTH L. · NAT. REC. AREA

Marshall · Mountain View · Cherokee Village · Pocahontas · Piggott · Corning · Partageville · Hickman · Union City · Tiptonville · Paris · Kentucky L. · Clarksville · Henderson ville · Springfield · Gallatin · Lafayette · Livingston · BUFFALO NAT. RIVER

36 · White · Little Red · Walnut Ridge · Black · Kennett · Martin · McKenzie · Dyersburg · Nashville · Dickson · La Vergne · Lebanon · Cookeville · LAND BETWEEN THE LAKES NAT. REC. AREA

Clinton · Heber Springs · Newport · Trumann · Marked Tree · Osceola · Ripley · Jackson · Centerville · Columbia · Murfreesboro · McMinnville · Crossville · Har

B

TENNESSEE · Rock

Morrilton · Searcy · Augusta · Wynne · Forrest City · Millington · Henderson · Lawrenceburg · Savannah · Selmer · Pulaski · Elk · S. Pittsburg · Soddy-Daisy · Dayton · Sweet

ARKANSAS · Memphis · Germantown · Olive Branch · Corinth · Florence · Athens · Huntsville · Winchester · Cleve · RUSSELL CAVE NAT. MON. · Chattano · Dalton

Little Rock · Jacksonville · Brinkley · Southaven · Holly Springs · Sheffield · Tuscumbia · Muscle Shoals · Scottsboro · La Fayette

C

Pine Bluff · Rison · Clarksdale · Water Valley · Tupelo · Haleyville · Cullman · Arab · Albertville · Rome · Cartersville · Mari

Fordyce · Rosedale · Cleveland · Grenada · West Point · Aberdeen · Fayette · Jasper · Birmingham · Leeds · Talladega · ATLA

MISSISSIPPI · ALABAMA

D

LOUISIANA · New Orleans · Metairie · Chalmette · Chandeleur L. · GULF ISLANDS NAT. SEASHORE

E

GULF OF

F

MEXICO

Projection: Albers' Equal Area with two standard parallels · 88 · West from Greenwich · 86 · 5

ft m
6000 2000
4500 1500
3000 1000
1200 400
600 200
0 0
200 600
2000 6000
4000 12 000
m ft

30
28

2 3 4

═══ Freeways   ⊠ ✸ State Capitals   ▭ National Parks

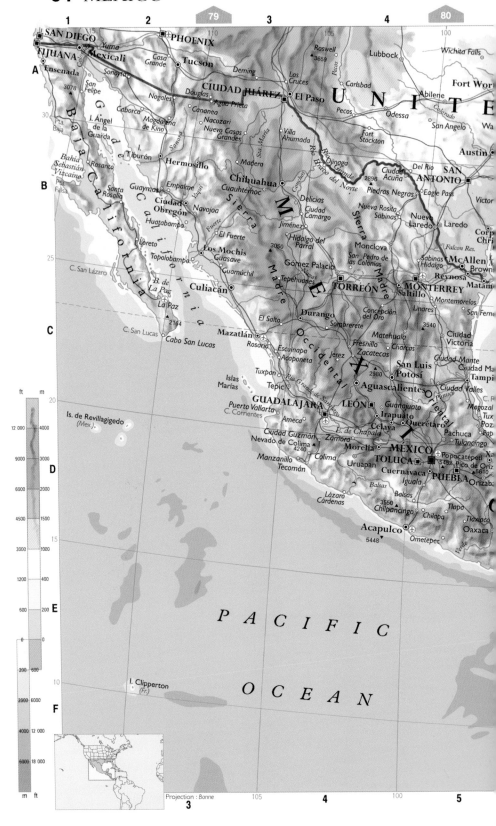

79 3 80

1 2 3 4

SAN DIEGO
Yuma
TIJUANA
Mexicali
Ensenada
PHOENIX
Casa
Grande
Tucson
Deming
Las
Cruces
Roswell
3659
Lubbock
Wichita Falls
Fort Wor
San
Felipe
Sonoyta
Nogales
Douglas
Agua Prieta
CIUDAD JUÁREZ
El Paso
Carlsbad
Abilene
A
3078
Caborca
Cananea
Nacozari
Pecos
Fort
Stockton
Odessa
San Angelo
Wa
Austin
Baja California
Pta.
Baja
I. Ángel
de la
Guarda
Magdalena
de Kino
Nuevo Casas
Grandes
Villa
Ahumada
Sta. María
Río Bravo del Norte
Ojinaga
Del Río
Ciudad
Acuña
SAN
ANTONIO
I.
Tiburón
Hermosillo
Madera
Chihuahua
Cuauhtémoc
Conchos
Piedras Negras
Eagle Pass
Victor
B
Bahía
Sebastián
Vizcaíno
Pta.
Falsa
Santa
Rosalía
Guaymas
Empalme
Ciudad
Obregón
Navojoa
Yaqui
M
Delicias
Ciudad
Camargo
Jiménez
Nueva Rosita
Sabinas
Monclova
Sabinas
Hidalgo
Nuevo
Laredo
Laredo
Corp
Chri
Falcon Res.
Huatabampa
Fuerte
El Fuerte
Hidalgo del
Parral
Sierra
Sierra
Madre
McAllen
Browns
C
C. San Lázaro
California
Loreto
Topolobampo
Los Mochis
Guasave
Guamúchil
3050
Tepehuanes
San Pedro de
las Colonias
Gómez Palacio
Reynosa
MONTERREY
Saltillo
Matam
B. de
La Paz
Culiacán
TORREÓN
Montemorelos
San Ferne
La Paz
2164
El Salto
Durango
Concepción
del Oro
Linares
Ciudad
Victoria
C. San Lucas
Cabo San Lucas
Mazatlán
Rosario
Sombrerete
3540
Matehuala
Ciudad
Mante
Ciudad Ma
Escuinapa
Acaponeta
Jerez
Fresnillo
Zacatecas
Charcas
E
Madre
San Luis
Potosí
Ciudad Valles
Tampi
2980
Tuxpan
Río Grande de Santiago
Islas
Marías
Tepic
Aguascalientes
Oriental
C. R
20
Puerto Vallarta
C. Corrientes
GUADALAJARA
LEÓN
Guanajuato
Ameca
Irapuato
Celaya
Querétaro
Pachuca
Tulancingo
Magozal
Tux
Poz
Pap
Is. de Revillagigedo
(Mex.)
Ciudad Guzmán
Nevado de Colima
4240
L. de Chapala
Zamora
Morelia
MÉXICO
TOLUCA
Popocatépetl
5452
Pico de Oriz
5610
D
Manzanillo
Tecomán
Colima
Uruapan
Cuernavaca
Iguala
PUEBLA
Orizab
Lázaro
Cárdenas
Balsas
Balsas
3550
Chilpancingo
Chilapa
Tlapa
Tlaxiaco
Oaxaca
15
Acapulco
5448
Ometepec
Verde

P A C I F I C
E

O C E A N
10
I. Clipperton
(Fr.)
F

Scale
ft m
12 000 4000
9000 3000
6000 2000
4500 1500
3000 1000
1200 400
600 200
0 0
200 600
2000 6000
4000 12 000
6000 18 000
m ft

Projection : Bonne

105 4 100 5

3

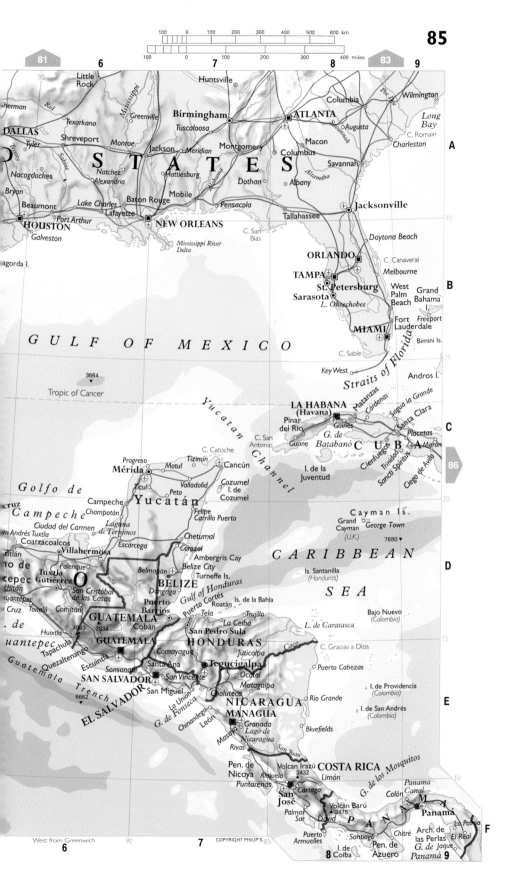

100 0 100 200 300 400 500 600 km
100 0 100 200 300 400 miles

95 90

Little Rock

Huntsville

Columbia

Wilmington

Long Bay

Sherman

Red

Birmingham

ATLANTA

Augusta

C. Romain

DALLAS

Tyler

Texarkana

Greenville

Tuscaloosa

Macon

Charleston

Savannah

A

Shreveport

Monroe

Jackson

Meridian

Montgomery

Columbus

Savannah

Nacogdoches

Natchez

Alexandria

Hattiesburg

Alabama

Dothan

Albany

Altamaha

Bryan

S T A T E S

Beaumont

Lake Charles

Baton Rouge

Mobile

Pensacola

Jacksonville

HOUSTON

Port Arthur

Lafayette

NEW ORLEANS

Tallahassee

30

Galveston

C. San Blas

Daytona Beach

agorda I.

Mississippi River Delta

ORLANDO

C. Canaveral

TAMPA

Melbourne

St. Petersburg

West Palm Beach

Grand Bahama I.

B

Sarasota

L. Okeechobee

Freeport

G U L F   O F   M E X I C O

MIAMI

Fort Lauderdale

Bimini Is.

3664

C. Sable

25

Tropic of Cancer

Key West

Straits of Florida

Andros I.

Yucatan

LA HABANA (Havana)

Matanzas

Cárdenas

Sagua la Grande

Pinar del Río

Güines

Santa Clara

Progreso

Tizimín

C. Catoche

C. San Antonio

Guane

G. de Batabanó

CUBA

Placetas

Morón

C

Mérida

Motul

Cancún

Channel

Cienfuegos

Trinidad

Sancti Spíritus

Ciego de Ávila

Golfo de

Ticul

Valladolid

Cozumel

I. de la Juventud

86

Campeche

Peto

Yucatán

I. de Cozumel

20

Campeche

Champotón

Felipe Carrillo Puerto

Cayman Is.

Ciudad del Carmen

Laguna de Términos

Grand Cayman

George Town

cruz

Ciudad del Carmen

Chetumal

(U.K.)

7680

Coatzacoalcos

Escárcega

Corozal

C A R I B B E A N

n Andrés Tuxtla

Villahermosa

Ambergris Cay

Is. Santanilla (Honduras)

D

itlán

Palenque

Belmopan

Belize City

Bajo Nuevo (Colombia)

no de

Tuxtla Gutiérrez

BELIZE

Turneffe Is.

S E A

tepec

San Cristóbal de las Casas

Dangriga

Gulf of Honduras

uantepec

Puerto Barrios

Is. de la Bahía

Cruz

Tonalá

Comitán

GUATEMALA

Tela

Roatán

Trujillo

L. de Caratasca

. de

Huixtla

4093 3834

Cobán

La Ceiba

C. Gracias a Dios

uantepec

Tapachula

GUATEMALA

San Pedro Sula

HONDURAS

Coco

Quezaltenango

Comayagua

Juticalpa

Puerto Cabezas

Guatemala Trench

Escuintla

Santa Ana

Tegucigalpa

Ocotal

I. de Providencia (Colombia)

E

Sonsonate

SAN SALVADOR

San Vincente

Matagalpa

Río Grande

I. de San Andrés (Colombia)

6662

San Miguel

Choluteca

NICARAGUA

EL SALVADOR

La Unión

MANAGUA

Bluefields

G. de Fonseca

Chinandega

León

Granada

Masaya

Lago de Nicaragua

Rivas

San Juan

G. de los Mosquitos

Pen. de Nicoya

Volcan Irazú 3432

COSTA RICA

Panama Canal

10

Atajuela

Limón

Colón

Puntarenas

Cartago

P A N A M A

Panamá

San José

Volcan Barú 3475

Arch. de las Perlas

La Palma

Palmar Sur

David

El Real

F

Puerto Armuelles

Santiago

Chitré

G. de Jaque

I. de Coiba

Pen. de Azuero

Panamá

100   0   100   200   300   400   500   600 km
100   0   100   200   300   400 miles

6   65   **7**   60   **8**   55

A

SARGASSO
SEA

B

ATLANTIC   OCEAN

Tropic of Cancer

guana I.

Turks & Caicos Is.
Cockburn (U.K.)
Town

Cap-Haitien
Port-de-Paix
Monte Christi
Puerto Plata
Gonaïves   Santiago de
La Vega   los Caballeros
San Francisco
de Macoris

9200   Puerto Rico   Trench

Arecibo   SAN JUAN
ITI   3175   Charlotte   Anguilla (U.K.)
St-Marc   DOMINICAN   La Romana   Amalie   Virgin Is.   St-Martin (Fr.)
San Juan   REP.   (U.S.A.)(U.K.)   St-Barthélemy (Fr.)
Bani   San Pedro de Macoris   Caguas   ST. KITTS & NEVIS
Barahona   SANTO DOMINGO   Ponce   St. Croix   St-Eustatius   ANTIGUA &
Mayagüez   (U.S.A.)   (Neth.)   St. John's   BARBUDA
PUERTO RICO   Basseterre   Montserrat (U.K.)
C
(U.S.A.)
Hispaniola   GUADELOUPE (Fr.)
t i l l e s   Leeward   Pointe-à-Pitre
Islands   Basse-Terre
L e s s e r   DOMINICA
Roseau

Fort-de-France   MARTINIQUE (Fr.)

B E A N   S E A   A n t i l l e s   Castries
ST. LUCIA
ST. VINCENT &   Kingstown   BARBADOS
THE GRENADINES   Bridgetown
W i n d w a r d
Islands   GRENADA   **D**
La Blanquilla   St. George's
:(Ven.)   Tobago

Pta. Gallinas   I. de Margarita
n. de la   Aruba (Neth.)   Porlamar
Guajira   Oranjestad   Curaçao   Güiria   Port of Spain
Punto   Willemstad   La Tortuga   Carúpano   TRINIDAD & TOBAGO
cha   Fijo   Bonaire   Cumaná   G. de   San Fernando
Nevada   Coro   NETH.   Paria
ta Marta   San   ANTILLES   Maiquetía   Puerto La   2596
MARACAIBO   Felipe   Puerto Cabello   CARACAS   Cruz   Maturín
lledupar   Cabimas   MARACAY
L. de   Barquisimeto   VALENCIA   Barcelona   El Tigre   Tucupita
Maracaibo   Acarigua   Orinoco   **E**
Merida   S   Ciudad
5007   Barinas   O   Guayana
uta   San Fernando   Caicara   Ciudad Bolívar   Georgetown
Wilches   San Cristóbal   Apure   de Apure   Embalse de Guri   Bartica
Pamplona   Arauca   Tumeremo   New Amsterdam   Linden
ucaramanga   Wismar
V E N E Z U E L A   Angel   G
Sogamoso   Meta   Puerto Carreño   Falls   U
Tunja   Mt. Roraima   Y
OTÁ   Puerto Ayacucho   2810   A
lavicencio   O M B I A   Vichada   Sierra Pacaraima   N
Orinoco   Serra   A
Puerto Inírida   Parima   **F**
Guaviare   Casiquiare   Boa Vista

SURINAME

92

B R A Z I L
Equator
COPYRIGHT PHILIP'S

5   70   **90**   **6**   65   **7**   60   **8**

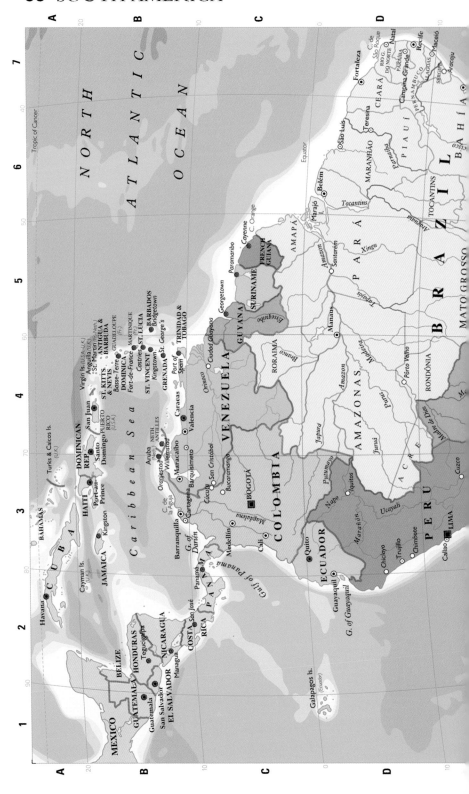

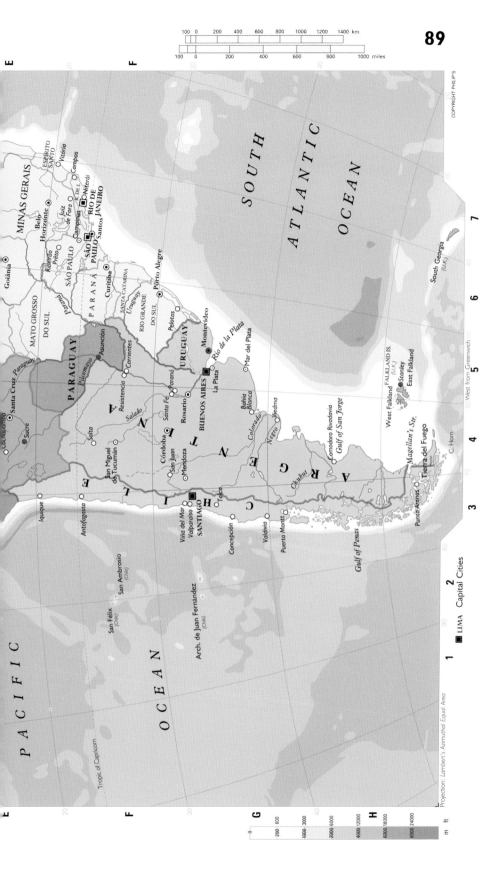

100 0   200   400   600   800   1000 1200 1400 km

100 0   200   400   600   800 1000 miles

COPYRIGHT PHILIP'S

Projection: *Lambert's Azimuthal Equal Area*

■ LIMA   Capital Cities

1   2   3   4   5   6   7

E   F   G   H

m   ft
0
200   600
1000   3000
2000   6000
4000   12000
6000   18000
8000   24000

PACIFIC

OCEAN

Tropic of Capricorn

San Félix *(Chile)*

San Ambrosio *(Chile)*

Arch. de Juan Fernández *(Chile)*

Iquique

Antofagasta

Viña del Mar
Valparaíso
■ SANTIAGO

Concepción

Valdivia

Puerto Montt

Gulf of Penas

Salta

San Miguel
de Tucumán

Córdoba

San Juan
Mendoza

Talca

Cochabamba
● Sucre

Santa Cruz

PARAGUAY

Pilcomayo

Paraguay

Asunción

Corrientes

Resistencia

Santa Fe
Paraná
Rosario

San Miguel

Salado

Córdoba

A   R   G   E   N   T   I   N   A

CHILE

Colorado

Negro

Chubut

Comodoro Rivadavia

Gulf of San Jorge

Puerto Arenas

Tierra del Fuego

Magellan's Str.

C. Horn

Bahía
Blanca

Mar del Plata

BUENOS AIRES
■
La Plata

Río de la Plata

Montevideo
URUGUAY

Pelotas

Porto Alegre

RIO GRANDE
DO SUL

SANTA CATARINA

Uruguay

Curitiba

PARANÁ

Paraná

MATO GROSSO
DO SUL

Goiânia

MINAS GERAIS

Belo
Horizonte

Ribeirão
Prêto

SÃO PAULO

■ SÃO
PAULO

Santos

Campinas

Juiz
de Fora

■ RIO DE
JANEIRO
Niterói

Campos

Vitória

ESPÍRITO
SANTO

SOUTH

ATLANTIC

OCEAN

South Georgia
(U.K.)

FALKLAND IS.
(U.K.)
West Falkland
● Stanley
East Falkland

West from Greenwich

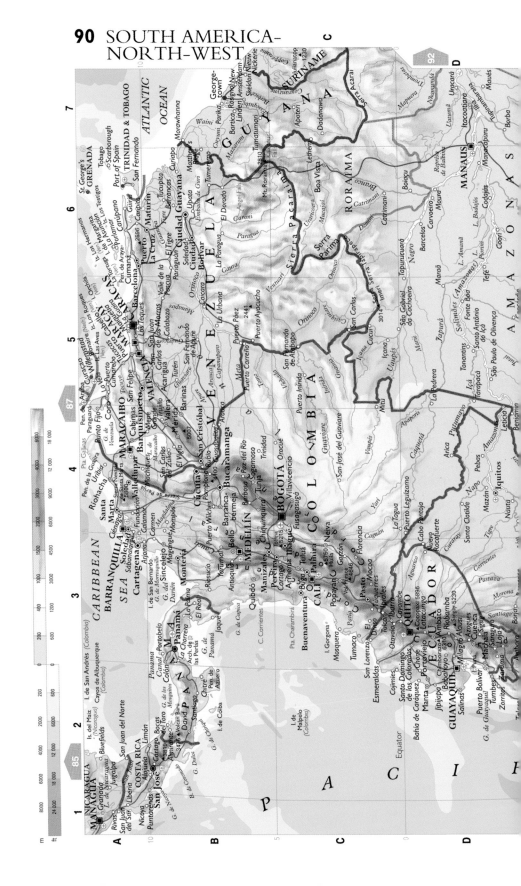

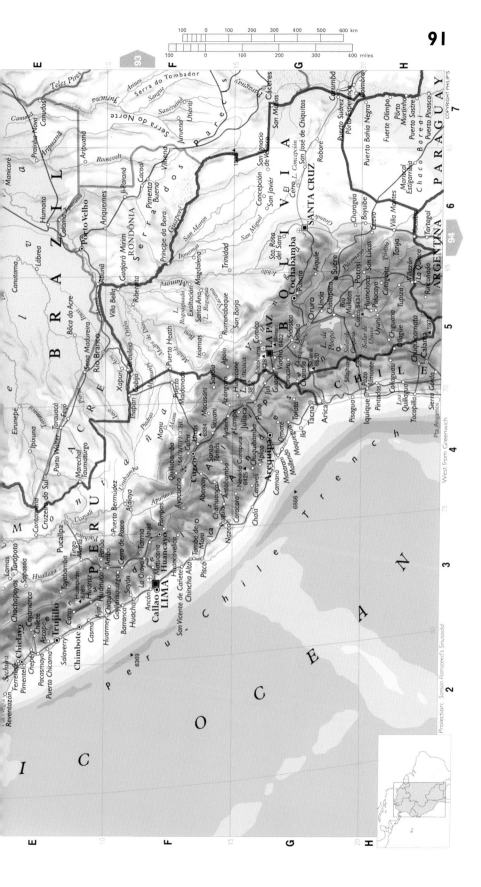

100 0 100 200 300 400 500 600 km
100 0 100 200 300 400 miles

COPYRIGHT PHILIP'S

93

E F G H

Teles Pires

Serra do Tombador
Annos
Aripuanã
Sangue
Sauéninga
Juruena
Cáceres

Serra do Norte
Utiarití
Iquirupãna

Camará
Prainha Nova
Canudos
Aripuanã
Juruena

Manicoré
Aripuanã
Roosevelt
San Ignacio
San Mátias

Humaitá
Calama
Jarama
Roosevelt
Vilhena
Juína
San Miguel

Canutama
Lábrea
Porto Velho
Ariquemes
Pimenta Bueno
Cacoal
Concepción
San Javier
Concepción
Santa Cruz
Puerto Suárez
Pôrto Esperança
Fuerte Olimpo
Puerto Sastre

BRAZIL
RONDÔNIA
Serra dos Parecis
Cerro L. Concepción
SANTA CRUZ
Roboré
San José de Chiquitos
Puerto Pinasco

PARAGUAY

ARGENTINA

94

PERU

BOLIVIA

CHILE

PACIFIC OCEAN

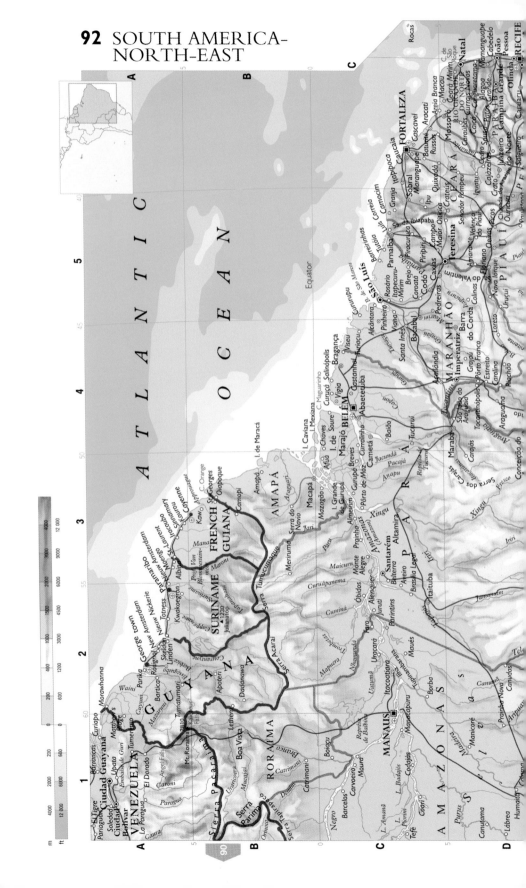

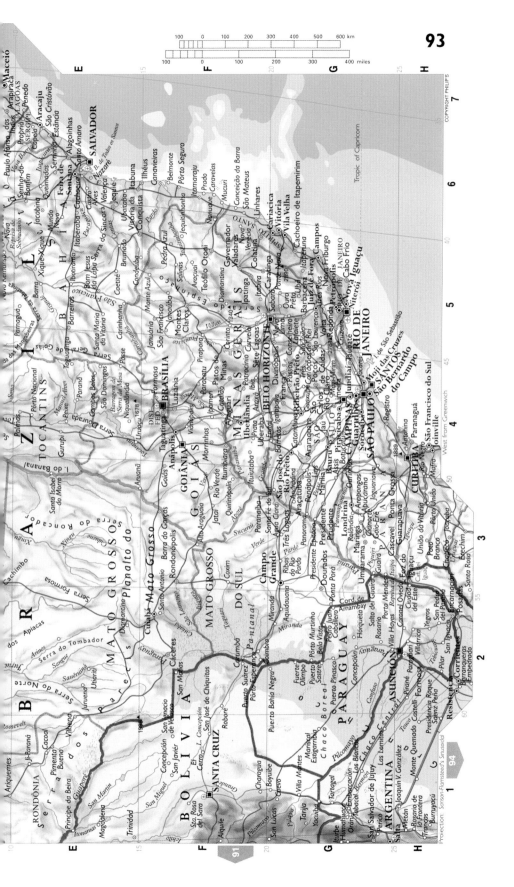

100 0 100 200 300 400 500 600 km
100   0   100   200   300   400 miles

Projection: Sanson-Flamsteed's Sinusoidal

West from Greenwich

Tropic of Capricorn

Maceió
Arapiraca
ALAGOAS
Propriá
Penedo
Aracaju
SERGIPE
São Cristóvão
Estância
Santo Amaro
SALVADOR
B. de Todos os Santos
Nazaré
Alagoinhas
Santana
Cachoeira
Valença
Jequié
Itabuna
Ilhéus
Canavieiras
Belmonte
Pôrto Seguro
Caravelas
Prado
Itamaraju
Mucuri
Conceição da Barra
São Mateus
Linhares
Vila Velha
VITÓRIA
Cachoeiro de Itapemirim
Cariacica
Colatina
ESPÍRITO SANTO
Nova Venécia
Campos
Cabo Frio
RIO DE JANEIRO
Nova Friburgo
Petrópolis
Niterói
Macaé
Volta Redonda
Barra Mansa
Barbacena
Juiz de Fora
Ubá
São João del Rei
Conselheiro Lafaiete
Ouro Prêto
Ponte Nova
Caratinga
Ipatinga
Governador Valadares
Teófilo Otoni
MINAS GERAIS
Diamantina
Araçuaí
Itaobim
Salinas
Montes Claros
Januária
Jequitinhonha
Nanuque
Almenara
BELO HORIZONTE
Itabira
Sabará
Sete Lagoas
Curvelo
Pirapora
Divinópolis
Bom Despacho
Patos de Minas
Patrocínio
Araxá
Uberaba
Uberlândia
Ituiutaba
Frutal
Catalão
Araguari
Itumbiara
Rio Verde
Jataí
Morrinhos
GOIÁS
GOIÂNIA
Anápolis
Luziânia
Formosa
BRASÍLIA
DISTRITO FEDERAL
Niquelândia
Pôrto Nacional
TOCANTINS
Gurupi
Palmas

São Francisco
Barreiras
Bom Jesus da Lapa
Serra do Espinhaço
Caetité
Brumado
Vitória da Conquista
Itaberaba
Feira de Santana
Jacobina
Senhor do Bonfim
Xique-Xique
Barra
Remanso
Juàzeiro
Petrolina

B A H I A

Carinhanha
Posse
Campos Belos
São Domingos
Paranã

Serra Geral de Goiás

Serra da Mesa
Barragem de
1678

Uruaçu

Aruanã

Rio Araguaia

Alto Araguaia

Barra do Garças

Aragarças

Barragem de

MATO GROSSO

Planalto do
Mato Grosso

Cuiabá
Rondonópolis
Diamantino
Nobres
Chapada dos Guimarães
Santo Antônio

Serra do Roncador

Xingu

Serra Formosa

Apiacás
Serra do Tombador

Arinos
Sauéruiná
Juína
Juruena

Vilhena
Pimenta Bueno
Cacoal
Ariquemes
Ji-Paraná
RONDÔNIA
Príncipe da Beira
Costa Marques

Guaporé

Roosevelt

Cáceres
San Matías
San Ignacio
San José de Chiquitos
Robore
BOLIVIA
SANTA CRUZ
Concepción
San Javier
Puerto Suárez
Corumbá
Pôrto Esperança
Ladário
Coimbra

Pantanal

MATO GROSSO DO SUL

Coxim
Miranda
Aquidauana
Campo Grande
Ponta Porã
Dourados
Mundo Novo
Naviraí
Amambaí

Cassilândia
Três Lagoas
Paranaíba
Água Clara
Ribas do Rio Pardo

Presidente Epitácio
Presidente Prudente

SÃO PAULO
Araçatuba
Penápolis
Birigui
Marília
Bauru
Jaú
Araraquara
Ribeirão Prêto
Franca
São Carlos
Rio Claro
Piracicaba
Limeira
CAMPINAS
Jundiaí
Guarulhos
SÃO PAULO
SANTOS
São Bernardo do Campo
São Vicente
Mojí das Cruzes
Sorocaba
Itapetininga
Registro

PARANÁ
Jacarezinho
Londrina
Maringá
Umuarama
Campo Mourão
Guarapuava
CURITIBA
Paranaguá
Ponta Grossa
União da Vitória
Mafra
Joinville
São Francisco do Sul
Foz do Iguaçu
Cascavel
Toledo

Ciudad del Este
Coronel Oviedo
PARAGUAY
ASUNCIÓN
Villarrica
San Pedro
Concepción
Pedro Juan Caballero
Fuerte Olimpo
Puerto Sastre
Bahía Negra
Puerto Pinasco
Puerto Casado
Pôrto Murtinho

Mariscal Estigarribia

Chaco Boreal

Gran Chaco

Los Lomitas
Formosa
Clorinda
Villa Hayes
San Ignacio
Encarnación
Posadas

Resistencia
Corrientes
Barranqueras
Empedrado
Goya
ARGENTINA

San Salvador de Jujuy
Perico
Salta
S. Pedro
Metán
Joaquín V. González
Monte Quemado
Castelli
Presidencia Roque Sáenz Peña

Pilcomayo
Bermejo

Tartagal
Yacuiba
Villa Montes
Camiri
Charagua
Boyuibe
Sta. Rosa del Sara

San Miguel
San Lucas
San José
Trinidad
Magdalena
Itonamas
Mamoré
Aiquile
Tarija

BRAZIL
BRASIL
GOIÁS
TOCANTINS
MATO GROSSO

Grande
Itacatu
Santa Rosa
Paranavaí
Apucarana

Pato Branco
Chapecó
Erechim
Ijuí

Rio Uruguai

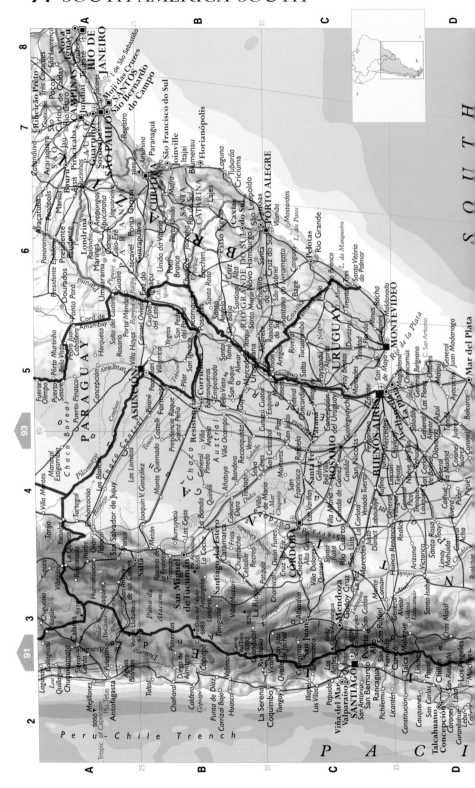

S O U T H

100 0 100 200 300 400 500 600 km
100 0 100 200 300 400 miles

COPYRIGHT PHILIP'S

Projection: Sanson-Flamsteed's Sinusoidal

ATLANTIC

OCEAN

South Georgia (UK)

FALKLAND ISLANDS
(ISLAS MALVINAS) (UK)
King George B.
West Falkland
Weddell I.
C. Dolphin
Stanley
Port Darwin
East Falkland
C. Meredith
Falkland Sd.

60° West from Greenwich 55

•5830

A T L A N T I C

Valdivia
La Unión
Osorno
L. Llanquihue
Puerto Montt
Ancud
Castro
I. de Chiloé
Quellón
C. Quilán
Boca del Guafo
Is. Guaitecas
Arch. de los Chonos
Pen. de Taitao
Pen. Tres Montes
G. de Penas
I. Campana
I. Wellington
I. Mornington
I. Madre de Dios
Arch. Reina Adelaida
Estrecho de Magallanes
(Magellan's Str.)
I. Hanover
Estrecho Nelson
I. Santa Inés

Apóstol
San Martín
de los Andes
Norquinco
Cholila
Esquel
Tecka
C. San Martín
de Bariloche
Lelequé
Gastre
Los Plumas
Paso de Indios
Coihaique
Mte. San Lorenzo
Mte. Fitzroy
Cerro
Cochrane
Balmaceda
Perito Moreno
Sarmiento
El Turbio
Puerto Natales
Punta Arenas
Porvenir
Río Grande
Tierra del Fuego
Ushuaia
I. Navarino
Is. Wollaston
C. de Hornos (C. Horn)
Pen. Hardy
I. Hoste
Canal Beagle
I. de Los Estados (Staten I.)
San Sebastián

El Cuy
Sierra Colorada
Maquinchao
Valcheta
San Antonio Oeste
Carmen de Patagones
Viedma
Golfo San Matías
Pen. Valdés
Puerto Madryn
Rawson
Trelew
Teleto
G. Nuevo
Puerto Lobos
C. Dos Bahías
Comodoro Rivadavia
Golfo San Jorge
C. Tres Puntas
Cabo Blanco
Pto. Medanosa
Puerto Deseado
Fitz Roy
Puerto San Julián
Puerto Santa Cruz
Bahía Grande
Río Gallegos
C. Vírgenes
Estrecho de Magallanes

m
ft
8000 6000 4000 2000 0
24 000 18 000 12 000 6000 0

200 400 600 1000 1500 2000 3000 4000 m
600 1200 3000 6000 9000 12 000 ft

P A C I F I C

O C E A N

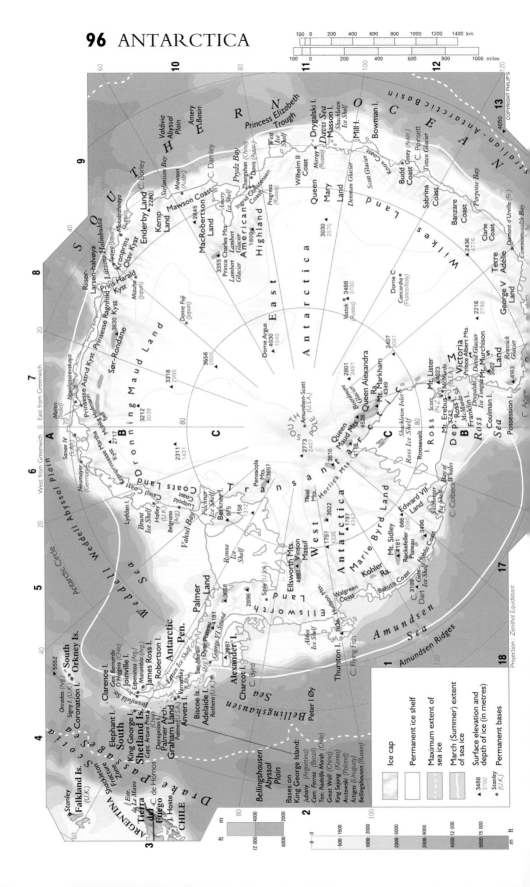

100 0   200   400   600   800   1000 1200 1400 km

100 0   200   400   600   800   1000 miles

COPYRIGHT PHILIP'S

Projection: Zenithal Equidistant

Legend

Ice cap

Permanent ice shelf

Maximum extent of sea ice

March (Summer) extent of ice

▲3488 Surface elevation and
3700   depth of ice (in metres)

● Stanley Permanent bases
 (U.K.)

Bases on
King George Island:
Jubany (Argentina)
Com. Ferraz (Brazil)
Ten. Rodolfo Marsh (Chile)
Great Wall (China)
King Sejong (Korea)
Arctowski (Poland)
Artigas (Uruguay)
Bellingshausen (Russia)

Selected labels

SOUTHERN OCEAN

Indian – Antarctic Basin

Princess Elizabeth Trough

Amery Abyssal Plain

Valdivia Abyssal Plain

Enderby Land

Kemp Land

MacRobertson Land

American Highland

Wilkes Land

Queen Mary Land

East Antarctica

Dronning Maud Land

Sør-Rondane

Coats Land

Transantarctic Mts.

Horlick Mts.

Ellsworth Mts.

West Antarctica

Marie Byrd Land

Ellsworth Land

Amundsen Sea

Amundsen Ridges

Ross Sea

Ross Ice Shelf

Victoria Land

George V Land

Terre Adélie

Commonwealth Bay

Bellingshausen Sea

Bellingshausen Abyssal Plain

Palmer Land

Antarctic Pen.

Alexander I.

Charcot I.

Peter I Øy

Weddell Sea

Weddell Abyssal Plain

South Orkney Is.

South Shetland Is.

Graham Land

Drake Passage

Falkland Is. (U.K.)

Tierra del Fuego

ARGENTINA

CHILE

SOUTH POLE

Amundsen–Scott (U.S.A.)

Vostok (Russia)

Dome C Concordia (France/Italy)

Dome Fuji (Japan)

Dome Argus

INDEX TO MAP PAGES

The index contains the names of all the principal places and features shown on the world maps. Physical features composed of a proper name (Erie) and a description (Lake) are positioned alphabetically by the proper name. The description is positioned after the proper name and is usually abbreviated:

Erie, L., *U.S.A.* **76 C5**

Where a description forms part of a settlement or administrative name, however, it is always written in full and put in its true alphabetical position:

Lake Charles, *U.S.A.* . **81 D7**

Names beginning St. are alphabetized under Saint, but Sankt, Sant, Santa and San are all spelt in full and are alphabetized accordingly.

The number in bold type which follows each name in the index refers to the number of the map page where that feature or place will be found. This is usually the largest scale at which the place or feature appears.

The letter and figure which are in bold type immediately after the page number give the grid square on the map page, within which the feature is situated.

Rivers are indexed to their mouths or confluences, and carry the symbol ➜ after their names. The following symbols are also used in the index: ∎ country, ☑ overseas territory or dependency, ☐ first order administrative area, △ national park.

A

A Coruña, *Spain* **18 A1**
A Estrada, *Spain* **18 A1**
A Fonsagrada, *Spain* **18 A2**
Aachen, *Germany* **14 C4**
Aalborg, *Denmark* **9 D7**
Aalen, *Germany* **14 D6**
Aarhus = Århus, *Denmark* ... **9 D8**
Aba, *Nigeria* **53 G7**
Abaco I., *Bahamas* **86 A4**
Ābādān, *Iran* **47 E7**
Ābādeh, *Iran* **44 D3**
Abadla, *Algeria* **52 B5**
Abaetetuba, *Brazil* **92 C4**
Abancay, *Peru* **91 F4**
Abarqū, *Iran* **44 D3**
Abashiri, *Japan* **32 A9**
Abashiri-Wan, *Japan* **32 B9**
Abay = Nîl el Azraq ➜, *Sudan* **55 E5**
Abay, *Kazakhstan* **29 E8**
Abaya, L., *Ethiopia* **57 C7**
Abbay = Nîl el Azraq ➜,
  Sudan **55 E5**
Abbeville, *France* **12 A4**
Abbot Ice Shelf, *Antarctica* .. **96 B2**
ABC Islands = Netherlands
  Antilles ☑, *W. Indies* **87 D6**
Abd al Kūrī, *Yemen* **49 E5**
Abéché, *Chad* **55 F3**
Abel Tasman △, *N.Z.* **64 D5**
Abeokuta, *Nigeria* **53 G6**
Abercorn, *Australia* **63 A5**
Aberdeen, *Australia* **63 B5**
Aberdeen, *U.K.* **10 C5**
Aberdeen, *S. Dak., U.S.A.* .. **74 C5**
Aberdeen, *Wash., U.S.A.* ... **72 C2**
Aberystwyth, *U.K.* **11 E4**
Abidjan, *Ivory C.* **53 G5**
Abilene, *U.S.A.* **80 C4**
Abitibi, L., *Canada* **71 E6**

Abkhazia ☐, *Georgia* **25 E5**
Abminga, *Australia* **62 A1**
Åbo = Turku, *Finland* **9 C10**
Abohar, *India* **42 D9**
Abomey, *Benin* **53 G6**
Abong-Mbang, *Cameroon* .. **56 D2**
Abou-Deïa, *Chad* **55 F2**
Absaroka Range, *U.S.A.* ... **73 D9**
Abū 'Alī, *Si. Arabia* **47 F7**
Abu Dhabi = Abū Ẓāby, *U.A.E.* **44 E3**
Abu Hamed, *Sudan* **55 E5**
Abū Kamāl, *Syria* **46 D5**
Abū Madd, Ra's, *Si. Arabia* .. **47 F4**
Abū Zabad, *Sudan* **55 F4**
Abū Ẓāby, *U.A.E.* **44 E3**
Abuja, *Nigeria* **53 G7**
Abunã, *Brazil* **91 E5**
Abunã ➜, *Brazil* **91 E5**
Abut Hd., *N.Z.* **65 E4**
Acaponeta, *Mexico* **84 C3**
Acapulco, *Mexico* **84 D5**
Acarigua, *Venezuela* **90 B5**
Accra, *Ghana* **53 G5**
Aceh ☐, *Indonesia* **38 D1**
Achalpur, *India* **43 J10**
Acharnes, *Greece* **23 E4**
Acheloos ➜, *Greece* **23 E3**
Achill I., *Ireland* **11 E1**
Achinsk, *Russia* **30 D7**
Acireale, *Italy* **21 F5**
Acklins I., *Bahamas* **86 B5**
Aconcagua, Cerro, *Argentina* **94 C3**
Aconquija, Mt., *Argentina* ... **94 B3**
Acraman, L., *Australia* **62 B2**
Acre = 'Akko, *Israel* **46 D3**
Acre ☐, *Brazil* **91 E4**
Acre ➜, *Brazil* **91 E5**
Ad Dahnā, *Si. Arabia* **47 F7**
Ad Dammām, *Si. Arabia* ... **47 F7**
Ad Dawādimī, *Si. Arabia* ... **47 F6**
Ad Dawḥah, *Qatar* **44 E2**
Ad Dilam, *Si. Arabia* **47 G6**
Ad Dīwānīyah, *Iraq* **47 E6**

Ada, *U.S.A.* **81 B5**
Adair, C., *Canada* **70 B6**
Adaja ➜, *Spain* **18 B3**
Adam, *Oman* **44 F4**
Adamaoua, Massif de l',
  Cameroon **55 G1**
Adamello, Mte., *Italy* **13 C9**
Adaminaby, *Australia* **63 C4**
Adams, Mt., *U.S.A.* **72 C3**
Adam's Bridge, *Sri Lanka* .. **43 Q11**
Adana, *Turkey* **46 C3**
Adapazarı = Sakarya, *Turkey* **25 E3**
Adarama, *Sudan* **55 E5**
Adare, C., *Antarctica* **96 B15**
Adaut, *Indonesia* **37 F4**
Adavale, *Australia* **63 A3**
Adda ➜, *Italy* **13 D8**
Addis Ababa = Addis Abeba,
  Ethiopia **49 F2**
Addis Abeba, *Ethiopia* **49 F2**
Adelaide, *Australia* **62 B2**
Adelaide I., *Antarctica* **96 A3**
Adelaide Pen., *Canada* **68 B10**
Adélie, Terre, *Antarctica* ... **96 A14**
Aden = Al 'Adan, *Yemen* ... **49 E4**
Aden, G. of, *Asia* **49 E4**
Adi, *Indonesia* **37 E4**
Adige ➜, *Italy* **20 B4**
Adilabad, *India* **43 K11**
Adirondack Mts., *U.S.A.* ... **77 C8**
Adis Abeba = Addis Abeba,
  Ethiopia **49 F2**
Admiralty I., *U.S.A.* **68 C6**
Admiralty Is., *Papua N. G.* ... **64 K9**
Adonara, *Indonesia* **37 F2**
Adoni, *India* **43 M10**
Adour ➜, *France* **12 E3**
Adra, *Spain* **18 D4**
Adrano, *Italy* **21 F5**
Adrar, *Algeria* **52 D6**
Adrar des Iforas, *Africa* **52 E6**
Adriatic Sea, *Medit. S.* **20 C5**
Adua, *Indonesia* **37 E3**

Adzhar Republic

Adzhar Republic = Ajaria □,
  Georgia 25 E5
Ægean Sea, Medit. S. 23 E5
Aerhtai Shan, Mongolia ... 34 B4
Afghanistan ■, Asia 45 C6
'Afif, Si. Arabia 47 G5
Afuá, Brazil 92 C3
Afyon, Turkey 46 C2
Afyonkarahisar = Afyon,
  Turkey 46 C2
Agadez, Niger 53 E7
Agadir, Morocco 52 B4
Agartala, India 41 F8
Agats, Indonesia 37 F5
Agboville, Ivory C. 53 G5
Agde, France 13 E5
Agen, France 12 D4
Aghios Efstratios, Greece ... 23 E5
Aghiou Orous, Kolpos, Greece 23 D5
Agra, India 42 F10
Ağri, Turkey 25 F5
Agri ➤, Italy 21 D6
Ağri Dağı, Turkey 25 F5
Ağri Karakose = Ağri, Turkey 25 F5
Agrigento, Italy 21 F4
Agrinio, Greece 23 E3
Água Clara, Brazil 93 G3
Agua Prieta, Mexico 84 A3
Aguarico ➤, Ecuador 90 D3
Aguas Blancas, Chile 94 A3
Aguascalientes, Mexico ... 84 C4
Aguilas, Spain 19 D5
Agulhas, C., S. Africa 58 E4
Agung, Gunung, Indonesia . . 39 F5
Agusan ➤, Phil. 36 C3
Ahaggar, Algeria 52 D7
Ahar, Iran 46 C6
Ahipara B., N.Z. 64 A5
Ahiri, India 43 K12
Ahmadabad, India 43 H8
Ahmadnagar, India 43 K9
Ahmadpur, Pakistan 42 E7
Ahmedabad = Ahmadabad,
  India 43 H8
Ahmednagar = Ahmadnagar,
  India 43 K9
Ahvāz, Iran 47 E7
Ahvenanmaa, Finland 9 C10
Aḥwar, Yemen 49 E4
Aigues-Mortes, France 13 E6
Aihui, China 35 A7
Aija, Peru 91 E3
Aikawa, Japan 33 D6
Aiken, U.S.A. 83 C7
Aimere, Indonesia 37 F2
Aïn Ben Tili, Mauritania ... 52 C4
Aïn Sefra, Algeria 52 B5
Aïr, Niger 53 E7
Air Force I., Canada 70 C6
Aisne ➤, France 13 B5
Aitutaki, Cook Is. 65 L14
Aix-en-Provence, France ... 13 E6
Aix-la-Chapelle = Aachen,
  Germany 14 C4
Aix-les-Bains, France 13 D6
Aizawl, India 41 F9
Aizuwakamatsu, Japan 33 E6
Ajaccio, France 13 F8
Ajanta Ra., India 43 J9
Ajaria □, Georgia 25 E5
Ajdābiyā, Libya 54 B3
Ajka, Hungary 16 E3
'Ajmān, U.A.E. 44 E3
Ajmer, India 42 F9
Ajo, C. de, Spain 18 A4
Akaroa, N.Z. 65 E5
Akelamo, Indonesia 37 D3
Aketi, Dem. Rep. of the Congo 56 D4
Akhisar, Turkey 23 E6
Akimiski I., Canada 71 D5
Akita, Japan 32 D7
Akjoujt, Mauritania 53 E3
Akkeshi, Japan 32 B9
'Akko, Israel 46 D3
Aklavik, Canada 68 B6
Akola, India 43 J10
Akordat, Eritrea 57 A7

Akpatok I., Canada 70 C7
Akranes, Iceland 8 C1
Akron, U.S.A. 76 D5
Aksai Chin, China 42 B11
Aksaray, Turkey 46 C3
Akşehir, Turkey 46 C2
Aksu, China 34 B3
Aktogay, Kazakhstan 29 E8
Aktsyabrski, Belarus 17 B9
Aktyubinsk = Aqtöbe,
  Kazakhstan 29 D6
Akure, Nigeria 53 G7
Akureyri, Iceland 8 B2
Akyab = Sittwe, Burma 41 G9
Al 'Adan, Yemen 49 E4
Al Aḥsā = Hasa, Si. Arabia . . 47 F7
Al Amādīyah, Iraq 46 C5
Al 'Amārah, Iraq 47 E6
Al 'Aqabah, Jordan 47 E3
Al 'Aramah, Si. Arabia 47 F6
Al Ashkhara, Oman 45 F4
Al Badi', Si. Arabia 47 G6
Al Baḥral Mayyit = Dead Sea,
  Asia 47 E3
Al Başrah, Iraq 47 E6
Al Baydā, Libya 54 B3
Al Faḍilī, Si. Arabia 47 F7
Al Fallūjah, Iraq 46 D5
Al Fāw, Iraq 47 E7
Al Fujayrah, U.A.E. 44 E4
Al Ḥaddār, Si. Arabia 47 G6
Al Ḥāmad, Si. Arabia 47 E4
Al Ḥamar, Si. Arabia 47 G6
Al Ḥamrā', Si. Arabia 47 F4
Al Ḥariq, Si. Arabia 47 G6
Al Ḥasakah, Syria 46 C5
Al Ḥayy, Iraq 47 D6
Al Ḥillah, Iraq 47 D6
Al Ḥillah, Si. Arabia 47 G6
Al Hoceïma, Morocco 52 A5
Al Ḥudaydah, Yemen 49 E3
Al Hufūf, Si. Arabia 47 F7
Al Ḥulwah, Si. Arabia 47 G6
Al Jāfūrah, Si. Arabia 47 F7
Al Jaghbūb, Libya 54 C3
Al Jahrah, Kuwait 47 E6
Al Jalāmīd, Si. Arabia 47 E4
Al Jawf, Libya 54 D3
Al Jawf, Si. Arabia 47 E4
Al Jazair = Algeria ■, Africa . 52 C6
Al Jazirah, Iraq 46 D5
Al Jubayl, Si. Arabia 47 F7
Al Jubaylah, Si. Arabia ... 47 F6
Al Junaynah, Sudan 55 F3
Al Khābūra, Oman 44 F4
Al Khalīl, West Bank 47 E3
Al Kharsānīyah, Si. Arabia . 47 F7
Al Khaṣab, Oman 44 E4
Al Kufrah, Libya 54 D3
Al Kūt, Iraq 47 D6
Al Kuwayt, Kuwait 47 E7
Al Lādhiqīyah, Syria 46 D3
Al Luḥayyah, Yemen 49 D3
Al Madīnah, Si. Arabia 47 F4
Al Maghreb = Morocco ■,
  N. Afr. 52 B4
Al Majma'ah, Si. Arabia ... 47 F6
Al Manāmah, Bahrain 44 E2
Al Marj, Libya 54 B3
Al Mawṣil, Iraq 46 C5
Al Midhnab, Si. Arabia ... 47 F6
Al Mubarraz, Si. Arabia ... 47 F7
Al Muḥarraq, Bahrain ... 44 E2
Al Mukallā, Yemen 49 E4
Al Mukhā, Yemen 49 E3
Al Musayyib, Iraq 47 D6
Al Muwayliḥ, Si. Arabia ... 47 F3
Al Qadīmah, Si. Arabia ... 47 G4
Al Qā'iyah, Si. Arabia 47 F5
Al Qāmishlī, Syria 46 C5
Al Qaşim □, Si. Arabia ... 47 F5
Al Qaṭīf, Si. Arabia 47 F7
Al Qaṭrūn, Libya 54 D2
Al Quds = Jerusalem,
  Israel/West Bank 47 E3
Al Qurnah, Iraq 47 E6
Al 'Ulā, Si. Arabia 47 F4

Al 'Uqayr, Si. Arabia 47 F7
Al 'Uwaynid, Si. Arabia 47 F6
Al 'Uwayqilah, Si. Arabia ... 47 E5
Al 'Uyūn, Si. Arabia 47 F5
Al Wakrah, Qatar 44 E2
Al Yamāmah, Si. Arabia ... 47 F6
Al Yaman = Yemen ■, Asia . 49 D4
Alabama □, U.S.A. 82 C4
Alabama ➤, U.S.A. 82 D4
Alaçam Dağları, Turkey ... 23 E7
Alacant = Alicante, Spain ... 19 C5
Alagoa Grande, Brazil 92 D6
Alagoas □, Brazil 93 D6
Alagoinhas, Brazil 93 E6
Alajuela, Costa Rica 86 D3
Alamosa, U.S.A. 79 B10
Åland = Ahvenanmaa, Finland 9 C10
Alania = North Ossetia □,
  Russia 25 E5
Alanya, Turkey 46 C2
Alapayevsk, Russia 29 D7
Alappuzha = Alleppey, India . 43 Q10
Alaşehir, Turkey 23 E7
Alaska □, U.S.A. 69 B4
Alaska, G. of, Pac. Oc. 69 C5
Alaska Peninsula, U.S.A. ... 69 C4
Alaska Range, U.S.A. 69 B4
Alatyr, Russia 24 C6
Alausi, Ecuador 90 D3
Alawoona, Australia 62 B3
Alba, Italy 13 D8
Albacete, Spain 19 C5
Albacutya, L., Australia 62 C3
Albanel, L., Canada 71 D6
Albania ■, Europe 23 D3
Albany, Australia 60 H2
Albany, Ga., U.S.A. 83 D5
Albany, N.Y., U.S.A. 77 C9
Albany, Oreg., U.S.A. 72 D2
Albany ➤, Canada 71 D5
Albardón, Argentina 94 C3
Albemarle, U.S.A. 83 B7
Alberche ➤, Spain 18 C3
Alberga ➤, Australia 62 A2
Albert, L., Africa 57 D6
Albert, L., Australia 62 C2
Albert Nile ➤, Uganda ... 57 D6
Albertville, France 13 D7
Albi, France 12 E5
Albina, Suriname 92 A3
Alborán, Medit. S. 18 E4
Ålborg = Aalborg, Denmark . 9 D7
Alborz, Reshteh-ye Kūhhā-ye,
  Iran 44 B3
Albuquerque, U.S.A. 79 C9
Albury, Australia 63 C4
Alcalá de Henares, Spain ... 18 B4
Alcalá la Real, Spain 18 D4
Álcamo, Italy 21 F4
Alcaníz, Spain 19 B5
Alcântara, Brazil 92 C5
Alcántara, Embalse de, Spain 18 C2
Alcantarilla, Spain 19 D5
Alcaraz, Sierra de, Spain ... 19 C4
Alcaudete, Spain 18 D3
Alcázar de San Juan, Spain . 18 C4
Alchevsk, Ukraine 25 D4
Alcira = Alzira, Spain 19 C5
Alcoy, Spain 19 C5
Aldabra Is., Seychelles 51 G8
Aldan ➤, Russia 31 C10
Alderney, U.K. 11 G5
Aleg, Mauritania 53 E3
Alegrete, Brazil 94 B5
Aleksandriya = Oleksandriya,
  Ukraine 17 C8
Alençon, France 12 B4
Aleppo = Ḥalab, Syria 46 C4
Alert, Canada 70 A7
Alès, France 13 D6
Alessándria, Italy 13 D8
Ålesund, Norway 8 C7
Aleutian Is., Pac. Oc. 69 C2
Alexander Arch., U.S.A. ... 69 C6
Alexander I., Antarctica ... 96 A3
Alexandra, Australia 63 C4
Alexandra, N.Z. 65 F3

Alexandria = El Iskandarîya, *Egypt* 54 B4
Alexandria, *Romania* 22 C5
Alexandria, *La., U.S.A.* 81 D7
Alexandria, *Va., U.S.A.* 77 E7
Alexandrina, L., *Australia* 62 C2
Alexandroupoli, *Greece* 22 D5
Aleysk, *Russia* 29 D9
Alga, *Kazakhstan* 29 E6
Algarve, *Portugal* 18 D1
Algeciras, *Spain* 18 D3
Algemesí, *Spain* 19 C5
Alger, *Algeria* 52 A6
Algeria ■, *Africa* 52 C6
Alghero, *Italy* 21 D2
Algiers = Alger, *Algeria* 52 A6
Alhucemas = Al Hoceïma, *Morocco* 52 A5
'Alī al Gharbī, *Iraq* 47 D6
'Alī Khēl, *Afghan.* 42 C6
Aliağa, *Turkey* 23 E6
Alicante, *Spain* 19 C5
Alice Springs, *Australia* 60 E5
Aligarh, *India* 42 F11
Alīgūdarz, *Iran* 46 D7
Alipur, *Pakistan* 42 E7
Alipur Duar, *India* 41 D7
Aliwal North, *S. Africa* 59 E5
Aljustrel, *Portugal* 18 D1
Alkmaar, *Neths.* 14 B3
All American Canal, *U.S.A.* 78 D5
Allahabad, *India* 40 E3
Allegheny →, *U.S.A.* 77 D5
Allegheny Mts., *U.S.A.* 77 F5
Allentown, *U.S.A.* 77 D8
Alleppey, *India* 43 Q10
Aller →, *Germany* 14 B5
Allier →, *France* 13 C5
Allora, *Australia* 63 A5
Alma Ata = Almaty, *Kazakhstan* 29 E8
Almada, *Portugal* 18 C1
Almadén, *Spain* 18 C3
Almansa, *Spain* 19 C5
Almanzor, Pico, *Spain* 18 B3
Almanzora →, *Spain* 19 D5
Almaty, *Kazakhstan* 29 E8
Almazán, *Spain* 19 B4
Almeirim, *Brazil* 92 C3
Almelo, *Neths.* 14 B4
Almendralejo, *Spain* 18 C2
Almería, *Spain* 19 D4
Almora, *India* 42 E11
Alnwick, *U.K.* 10 D6
Alon, *Burma* 41 F10
Alor, *Indonesia* 37 F2
Alor Setar, *Malaysia* 38 C2
Alps, *Europe* 14 E5
Alsace □, *France* 13 B7
Alsasua, *Spain* 19 A4
Alta Gracia, *Argentina* 94 C4
Altai = Aerhtai Shan, *Mongolia* 34 B4
Altai = Gorno-Altay □, *Russia* 29 D9
Altamira, *Brazil* 92 C3
Altamura, *Italy* 21 D6
Altanbulag, *Mongolia* 35 A5
Altay, *China* 34 B3
Altea, *Spain* 19 C5
Alto Araguaia, *Brazil* 93 F3
Alto Molocue, *Mozam.* 59 B7
Alton, *U.S.A.* 75 F9
Altoona, *U.S.A.* 77 D6
Altun Shan, *China* 34 C3
Alusi, *Indonesia* 37 F4
Alvear, *Argentina* 94 B5
Alwar, *India* 42 F10
Alxa Zuoqi, *China* 35 C5
Alzira, *Spain* 19 C5
Am Timan, *Chad* 55 F3
Amâdi, *Sudan* 55 G5
Amadjuak L., *Canada* 70 C6
Amagasaki, *Japan* 33 F4
Amahai, *Indonesia* 37 E3
Amakusa-Shotō, *Japan* 33 G2
Amaliada, *Greece* 23 F3
Amalner, *India* 43 J9
Amambay, Cordillera de, *S. Amer.* 94 A5
Amankeldi, *Kazakhstan* 29 D7
Amapá, *Brazil* 92 B3
Amapá □, *Brazil* 92 B3
Amarante, *Brazil* 92 D5
Amarillo, *U.S.A.* 80 B3
Amaro, Mte., *Italy* 20 C5
Amasra, *Turkey* 46 B3
Amazon = Amazonas →, *S. Amer.* 92 C3
Amazonas □, *Brazil* 90 D6
Amazonas →, *S. Amer.* 92 C3
Ambala, *India* 42 D10
Ambalavao, *Madag.* 59 C9
Ambanja, *Madag.* 59 A9
Ambato, *Ecuador* 90 D3
Ambatolampy, *Madag.* 59 B9
Ambatondrazaka, *Madag.* 59 B9
Amberg, *Germany* 15 D6
Ambergris Cay, *Belize* 85 D7
Amberley, *N.Z.* 65 E5
Ambikapur, *India* 40 F4
Ambilobé, *Madag.* 59 A9
Ambo, *Peru* 91 F3
Amboise, *France* 12 C4
Ambon, *Indonesia* 37 E3
Ambositra, *Madag.* 59 C9
Ambovombe, *Madag.* 59 D9
Amboyna Cay, *S. China Sea* 38 C4
Ambriz, *Angola* 56 F2
Amchitka I., *U.S.A.* 69 C1
Amderma, *Russia* 28 C7
Ameca, *Mexico* 84 C4
Ameland, *Neths.* 14 B3
American Highland, *Antarctica* 96 B10
American Samoa ⧄, *Pac. Oc.* 65 L13
Americus, *U.S.A.* 83 C5
Amery Ice Shelf, *Antarctica* 96 A10
Ames, *U.S.A.* 75 D8
Amherst, *Canada* 71 E7
Amiata, Mte., *Italy* 20 C3
Amiens, *France* 12 B5
'Ammān, *Jordan* 47 E3
Ammochostos = Famagusta, *Cyprus* 46 D3
Amorgos, *Greece* 23 F5
Amos, *Canada* 71 E6
Amoy = Xiamen, *China* 35 D6
Ampanihy, *Madag.* 59 C8
Ampenan, *Indonesia* 39 F5
Amper →, *Germany* 15 D6
Amravati, *India* 43 J10
Amreli, *India* 43 J7
Amritsar, *India* 42 D9
Amroha, *India* 42 E11
Amsterdam, *Neths.* 14 B3
Amstetten, *Austria* 15 D8
Amudarya →, *Uzbekistan* 29 E6
Amund Ringnes I., *Canada* 70 B4
Amundsen Gulf, *Canada* 68 A7
Amundsen Sea, *Antarctica* 96 B1
Amuntai, *Indonesia* 39 E5
Amur →, *Russia* 31 D12
Amurang, *Indonesia* 37 D2
Amyderya = Amudarya →, *Uzbekistan* 29 E6
An Nafūd, *Si. Arabia* 47 E5
An Najaf, *Iraq* 47 D6
An Nhon, *Vietnam* 38 B3
An Nu'ayrīyah, *Si. Arabia* 47 F7
Anabar →, *Russia* 30 B9
Anaconda, *U.S.A.* 73 C7
Anadolu, *Turkey* 25 F3
'Ānah, *Iraq* 46 D5
Anaheim, *U.S.A.* 78 D4
Anakapalle, *India* 40 J4
Anambas, Kepulauan, *Indonesia* 39 D3
Anamur, *Turkey* 46 C3
Anan, *Japan* 33 G4
Anantnag, *India* 42 C9
Ananyiv, *Ukraine* 17 E9
Anápolis, *Brazil* 93 F4
Anār, *Iran* 44 D3
Anārak, *Iran* 44 C3
Anatolia = Anadolu, *Turkey* 25 F3
Añatuya, *Argentina* 94 B4
Anchorage, *U.S.A.* 69 B5
Ancohuma, Nevado, *Bolivia* 91 G5
Ancón, *Peru* 91 F3
Ancona, *Italy* 20 C4
Ancud, *Chile* 95 E2
Ancud, G. de, *Chile* 95 E2
Andalgalá, *Argentina* 94 B3
Andalucía □, *Spain* 18 D3
Andalusia, *U.S.A.* 82 D4
Andaman Is., *Ind. Oc.* 27 G11
Andaman Sea, *Ind. Oc.* 38 B1
Andapa, *Madag.* 59 A9
Anderson, *U.S.A.* 76 D3
Anderson →, *Canada* 68 B7
Andes, Cord. de los, *S. Amer.* 91 G4
Andhra Pradesh □, *India* 43 L11
Andijon, *Uzbekistan* 29 E8
Andikíthira = Antikythira, *Greece* 23 G4
Andizhan = Andijon, *Uzbekistan* 29 E8
Andkhvoy, *Afghan.* 45 B6
Andoany, *Madag.* 59 A9
Andorra ■, *Europe* 19 A6
Andorra La Vella, *Andorra* 12 E4
Andreanof Is., *U.S.A.* 69 C2
Ándria, *Italy* 20 D6
Andros, *Greece* 23 F5
Andros I., *Bahamas* 86 B4
Andújar, *Spain* 18 C3
Andulo, *Angola* 56 G3
Aneto, Pico de, *Spain* 19 A6
Angara →, *Russia* 30 D7
Angarsk, *Russia* 30 D8
Angaston, *Australia* 62 B2
Ånge, *Sweden* 8 C9
Angeles, *Phil.* 36 A2
Ångermanälven →, *Sweden* 8 C9
Angers, *France* 12 C3
Anglesey, *U.K.* 11 E4
Ango, *Dem. Rep. of the Congo* 57 D5
Angoche, *Mozam.* 59 B7
Angola ■, *Africa* 58 A3
Angoulême, *France* 12 D4
Angoumois, *France* 12 D4
Angren, *Uzbekistan* 29 E8
Anguilla ⧄, *W. Indies* 87 C7
Anhui □, *China* 35 C6
Anjou, *France* 12 C3
Ankaboa, Tanjona, *Madag.* 59 C8
Ankang, *China* 35 C5
Ankara, *Turkey* 25 F3
Ankaratra, *Madag.* 59 B9
Ann Arbor, *U.S.A.* 76 C4
Annaba, *Algeria* 52 A7
Annan, *U.K.* 11 D5
Annapolis, *U.S.A.* 77 E7
Annecy, *France* 13 D7
Anning, *China* 34 D5
Anniston, *U.S.A.* 82 C5
Annobón, *Atl. Oc.* 51 G4
Anqing, *China* 35 C6
Ansbach, *Germany* 14 D6
Anshan, *China* 35 B7
Anshun, *China* 35 D5
Ansongo, *Mali* 53 E6
Ansudu, *Indonesia* 37 E5
Antabamba, *Peru* 91 F4
Antakya = Hatay, *Turkey* 46 C4
Antalaha, *Madag.* 59 A10
Antalya, *Turkey* 46 C2
Antalya Körfezi, *Turkey* 46 C2
Antananarivo, *Madag.* 59 B9
Antarctic Pen., *Antarctica* 96 A4
Antarctica 96 C
Antequera, *Spain* 18 D3
Anti Atlas, *Morocco* 52 C4
Antibes, *France* 13 E7
Anticosti, Î. d', *Canada* 71 E7
Antigonish, *Canada* 71 E7
Antigua & Barbuda ■, *W. Indies* 87 C7
Antikythira, *Greece* 23 G4
Antioquia, *Colombia* 90 B3
Antofagasta, *Chile* 94 A2

Antonina, *Brazil* 94 B7
Antrim, *U.K.* 11 D3
Antsirabe, *Madag.* 59 B9
Antsiranana, *Madag.* 59 A9
Antsohihy, *Madag.* 59 A9
Antwerpen, *Belgium* 14 C3
Anupgarh, *India* 42 E8
Anvers = Antwerpen, *Belgium* 14 C3
Anvers I., *Antarctica* 96 A3
Anxi, *China* 34 B4
Anxious B., *Australia* 62 B1
Anyang, *China* 35 C6
Anzhero-Sudzhensk, *Russia* . 29 D9
Ánzio, *Italy* 20 D4
Aoga-Shima, *Japan* 33 G6
Aomen = Macau, *China* 35 D6
Aomori, *Japan* 32 C7
Aoraki Mount Cook, *N.Z.* ... 65 E4
Aosta, *Italy* 13 D7
Aotearoa = New Zealand ■,
  Oceania 64 D7
Apalachicola ➤, *U.S.A.* 82 E5
Apaporis ➤, *Colombia* 90 D5
Aparri, *Phil.* 36 A2
Apeldoorn, *Neths.* 14 B3
Apennines = Appennini, *Italy* 20 B3
Apia, *Samoa* 65 L13
Apiacás, Serra dos, *Brazil* .. 91 E7
Aplao, *Peru* 91 G4
Apo, Mt., *Phil.* 36 C3
Apolo, *Bolivia* 91 F5
Apoteri, *Guyana* 90 C7
Appalachian Mts., *U.S.A.* ... 77 F5
Appennini, *Italy* 20 B3
Appleton, *U.S.A.* 76 B1
Aprília, *Italy* 20 D4
Apucarana, *Brazil* 94 A6
Apure ➤, *Venezuela* 90 B5
Apurímac ➤, *Peru* 91 F4
Aqaba = Al 'Aqabah, *Jordan* . 47 E3
Aqaba, G. of, *Red Sea* 47 E3
Âqchah, *Afghan.* 45 B6
'Aqrah, *Iraq* 46 C5
Aqtöbe, *Kazakhstan* 29 D6
Aquidauana, *Brazil* 93 G2
Aquitain, Bassin, *France* 12 D3
Ar Rachidiya = Er Rachidia,
  Morocco 52 B5
Ar Ramādī, *Iraq* 46 D5
Ar Raqqah, *Syria* 46 D4
Ar Rass, *Si. Arabia* 47 F5
Ar Rifā'ī, *Iraq* 47 E6
Ar Riyāḍ, *Si. Arabia* 47 F6
Ar Ruṭbah, *Iraq* 46 D5
Ar Ruwayḍah, *Si. Arabia* ... 47 G6
Ara, *India* 40 E5
'Arab, Bahr el ➤, *Sudan* 55 G4
Arab, Shatt al ➤, *Asia* 47 E7
Arabian Desert = Es Sahrâ'
  Esh Sharqîya, *Egypt* 54 C5
Arabian Gulf = Persian Gulf,
  Asia 44 E2
Arabian Sea, *Ind. Oc.* 26 G8
Araç, *Turkey* 46 B3
Aracaju, *Brazil* 93 E6
Aracati, *Brazil* 92 C6
Araçatuba, *Brazil* 93 G3
Aracena, *Spain* 18 D2
Araçuaí, *Brazil* 93 F5
Arad, *Romania* 16 E5
Arafura Sea, *E. Indies* 37 F4
Aragón □, *Spain* 19 B5
Aragón ➤, *Spain* 19 A5
Araguacema, *Brazil* 92 D4
Araguaia ➤, *Brazil* 92 D4
Araguari, *Brazil* 93 F4
Araguari ➤, *Brazil* 92 B4
Arak, *Algeria* 52 C6
Arakan Coast, *Burma* 41 H9
Arakan Yoma, *Burma* 41 H10
Araks = Aras, Rūd-e ➤, *Asia* 46 B7
Aral, *Kazakhstan* 29 E7
Aral Sea, *Asia* 29 E6
Aralsk = Aral, *Kazakhstan* .. 29 E7
Aralskoye More = Aral Sea,
  Asia 29 E6
Aran I., *Ireland* 10 D2

Aran Is., *Ireland* 11 E2
Aranda de Duero, *Spain* 18 B4
Aranjuez, *Spain* 18 B4
Arapgir, *Turkey* 46 C4
Arapiraca, *Brazil* 93 D6
Arapongas, *Brazil* 94 A6
Araraquara, *Brazil* 93 G4
Ararat, *Australia* 62 C3
Ararat, Mt. = Ağrı Dağı, *Turkey* 25 F5
Araripe, Chapada do, *Brazil* . 92 D6
Aras, Rūd-e ➤, *Asia* 46 B7
Arauca, *Colombia* 90 B4
Arauca ➤, *Venezuela* 90 B5
Araxá, *Brazil* 93 F4
Araya, Pen. de, *Venezuela* .. 90 A6
Árbatax, *Italy* 21 E2
Arbīl, *Iraq* 46 C6
Arbroath, *U.K.* 10 C5
Arcachon, *France* 12 D3
Archangel = Arkhangelsk,
  Russia 28 C5
Arckaringa Cr. ➤, *Australia* . 62 A2
Arcos de la Frontera, *Spain* . 18 D3
Arcot, *India* 43 N11
Arctic Bay, *Canada* 70 B5
Arctic Red River =
  Tsiigehtchic, *Canada* 68 B6
Arda ➤, *Bulgaria* 22 D6
Ardabīl, *Iran* 46 C7
Ardahan, *Turkey* 46 B5
Ardenne, *Belgium* 14 D3
Ardestān, *Iran* 44 C3
Ardlethan, *Australia* 63 B4
Ardmore, *U.S.A.* 80 B5
Ardrossan, *Australia* 62 B2
Arecibo, *Puerto Rico* 87 C6
Areia Branca, *Brazil* 92 C6
Arendal, *Norway* 9 D7
Arequipa, *Peru* 91 G4
Arévalo, *Spain* 18 B3
Arezzo, *Italy* 20 C3
Arganda, *Spain* 18 B4
Argentan, *France* 12 B3
Argentário, Mte., *Italy* 20 C3
Argentina ■, *S. Amer.* 94 D3
Argentino, L., *Argentina* ... 95 G2
Argeş ➤, *Romania* 22 B6
Arghandab ➤, *Afghan.* 42 D4
Argolikos Kolpos, *Greece* .. 23 F4
Argos, *Greece* 23 F4
Argostoli, *Greece* 23 E3
Århus, *Denmark* 9 D8
Ariadnoye, *Russia* 32 A4
Arica, *Chile* 91 G4
Arica, *Colombia* 90 D4
Arinos ➤, *Brazil* 91 F7
Aripuanã, *Brazil* 91 E6
Aripuanã ➤, *Brazil* 90 E6
Ariquemes, *Brazil* 91 E6
Arizona, *Argentina* 94 D3
Arizona □, *U.S.A.* 79 C7
Arjona, *Colombia* 90 A3
Arkalyk = Arqalyk, *Kazakhstan* 29 D7
Arkansas □, *U.S.A.* 81 B7
Arkansas ➤, *U.S.A.* 81 C8
Arkansas City, *U.S.A.* 80 A5
Arkhangelsk, *Russia* 28 C5
Arklow, *Ireland* 11 E3
Arkticheskiy, Mys, *Russia* ... 30 A7
Arlanzón ➤, *Spain* 18 A3
Arlbergpass, *Austria* 14 E6
Arles, *France* 13 E6
Arlington, *Va., U.S.A.* 77 E7
Arlington, *Wash., U.S.A.* ... 72 B2
Arlon, *Belgium* 14 D3
Armagh, *U.K.* 11 D3
Armavir, *Russia* 25 D5
Armenia, *Colombia* 90 C3
Armenia ■, *Asia* 25 E5
Armidale, *Australia* 63 B5
Arnaud ➤, *Canada* 70 C4
Arnauti, C., *Cyprus* 46 D3
Arnhem, *Neths.* 14 C3
Arnhem, C., *Australia* 60 C6
Arnhem Land, *Australia* ... 60 C5
Arno ➤, *Italy* 20 C3
Arno Bay, *Australia* 62 B2

Arnsberg, *Germany* 14 C5
Arqalyk, *Kazakhstan* 29 D7
Arrah = Ara, *India* 40 E5
Arran, *U.K.* 10 D4
Arras, *France* 13 A5
Arrecife, *Canary Is.* 52 C3
Arrée, Mts. d', *France* 12 B2
Arrowtown, *N.Z.* 65 F3
Arsenev, *Russia* 32 A3
Arta, *Greece* 23 E3
Artem, *Russia* 32 B3
Arthur ➤, *Australia* 62 D3
Arthur's Pass, *N.Z.* 65 E4
Arthur's Pass △, *N.Z.* 65 E4
Artigas, *Uruguay* 94 C5
Artois, *France* 12 A5
Artsyz, *Ukraine* 17 E9
Artvin, *Turkey* 25 E5
Aru, Kepulauan, *Indonesia* . 37 F4
Arua, *Uganda* 57 D6
Aruanã, *Brazil* 93 E3
Aruba ☐, *W. Indies* 87 D6
Arunachal Pradesh □, *India* . 41 C10
Arusha, *Tanzania* 57 E7
Aruwimi ➤, *Dem. Rep. of
  the Congo* 56 D4
Arviat, *Canada* 68 B10
Arxan, *China* 35 B6
Arys, *Kazakhstan* 29 E7
Arzamas, *Russia* 24 B5
As Saffānīyah, *Si. Arabia* .. 47 E7
As Samāwah, *Iraq* 47 E6
As Sohar = Şuḥār, *Oman* .. 44 E4
As Sulaymānīyah, *Iraq* 46 D6
As Sulaymānīyah, *Si. Arabia* 47 F6
As Summān, *Si. Arabia* ... 47 F6
As Sūq, *Si. Arabia* 47 G5
As Suwaydā', *Syria* 46 D4
As Şuwayrah, *Iraq* 47 D6
Asahigawa, *Japan* 32 B8
Asansol, *India* 40 F6
Ascension I., *Atl. Oc.* 51 G2
Aschaffenburg, *Germany* .. 14 D5
Aschersleben, *Germany* ... 15 C6
Áscoli Piceno, *Italy* 20 C4
Ascope, *Peru* 91 E3
Aseb, *Eritrea* 49 E3
Asenovgrad, *Bulgaria* 22 C5
Aşgabat = Ashgabat,
  Turkmenistan 29 F6
Ash Shāmiyah, *Iraq* 47 E6
Ash Shāriqah, *U.A.E.* 44 E3
Ash Shaṭrah, *Iraq* 47 E6
Ash Shu'bah, *Si. Arabia* ... 47 E6
Ashburton, *N.Z.* 65 E4
Asheville, *U.S.A.* 83 B6
Ashford, *Australia* 63 A5
Ashford, *U.K.* 11 F7
Ashgabat, *Turkmenistan* ... 29 F6
Ashizuri-Zaki, *Japan* 33 G3
Ashkhabad = Ashgabat,
  Turkmenistan 29 F6
Ashmyany, *Belarus* 17 A7
Ashqelon, *Israel* 47 E3
Ashtabula, *U.S.A.* 76 D5
Ashuanipi, L., *Canada* 71 D7
Asia, Kepulauan, *Indonesia* . 37 D4
Asifabad, *India* 43 K11
Asinara, *Italy* 20 D2
Asinara, G. dell', *Italy* 20 D2
Asino, *Russia* 29 D9
Asipovichy, *Belarus* 17 B9
'Asir, *Si. Arabia* 48 D3
Asir, Ras, *Somali Rep.* 49 E5
Asmera, *Eritrea* 57 A7
Aspiring, Mt., *N.Z.* 65 F3
Assab = Aseb, *Eritrea* 49 E3
Assam □, *India* 41 D9
Assen, *Neths.* 14 B4
Assiniboia, *Canada* 69 D9
Assiniboine ➤, *Canada* ... 69 D10
Assis, *Brazil* 94 A6
Assisi, *Italy* 20 C4
Astana, *Kazakhstan* 29 D8
Asti, *Italy* 13 D8
Astipalea, *Greece* 23 F6
Astorga, *Spain* 18 A2

Astoria, *U.S.A.* 72 C2
Astrakhan, *Russia* 25 D6
Asturias □, *Spain* 18 A3
Asunción, *Paraguay* 94 B5
Aswân, *Egypt* 54 D5
Aswan Dam = Sadd el Aali,
  Egypt 54 D5
Asyût, *Egypt* 54 C5
At Ṭafilah, *Jordan* 47 E3
Aṭ Ṭā'if, *Si. Arabia* 48 C3
Atacama, Desierto de, *Chile* . 94 A3
Atacama, Salar de, *Chile* 94 A3
Atalaya, *Peru* 91 F4
Atamyrat, *Turkmenistan* ... 29 F7
Atapupu, *E. Timor* 37 F2
Atâr, *Mauritania* 52 D3
Atasū, *Kazakhstan* 29 E8
Atauro, *E. Timor* 37 F3
Atbara, *Sudan* 55 E5
'Atbara, Nahr ➤, *Sudan* ... 55 E5
Atbasar, *Kazakhstan* 29 D7
Athabasca, *Canada* 69 C8
Athabasca ➤, *Canada* 68 C8
Athabasca, L., *Canada* 68 C8
Athens = Athina, *Greece* ... 23 F4
Athens, *Ala., U.S.A.* 82 B4
Athens, *Ga., U.S.A.* 83 C6
Athina, *Greece* 23 F4
Athínai = Athina, *Greece* ... 23 F4
Athlone, *Ireland* 11 E3
Athos, *Greece* 23 D5
Athy, *Ireland* 11 E3
Ati, *Chad* 55 F2
Atlanta, *U.S.A.* 83 C5
Atlantic City, *U.S.A.* 77 E8
Atlas Mts. = Haut Atlas,
  Morocco 52 B4
Atrek ➤, *Turkmenistan* 44 B3
Atsuta, *Japan* 32 B7
Attapu, *Laos* 38 B3
Attawapiskat, *Canada* 71 D5
Attawapiskat ➤, *Canada* ... 71 D5
Attock, *Pakistan* 42 C8
Attopeu = Attapu, *Laos* 38 B3
Attur, *India* 43 P11
Atuel ➤, *Argentina* 94 D3
Atyraū, *Kazakhstan* 29 E6
Aubagne, *France* 13 E6
Aube ➤, *France* 13 B5
Auburn, *U.S.A.* 82 C5
Auburn Ra., *Australia* 63 A5
Aubusson, *France* 12 D5
Auch, *France* 12 E4
Auckland, *N.Z.* 64 B6
Aude ➤, *France* 13 E5
Augathella, *Australia* 63 A4
Augsburg, *Germany* 14 D6
Augusta, *Italy* 21 F5
Augusta, *Ga., U.S.A.* 83 C7
Augusta, *Maine, U.S.A.* ... 77 B11
Aujuittuq = Grise Fiord,
  Canada 70 B5
Aunis, *France* 12 C3
Auponhia, *Indonesia* 37 E3
Aurangabad, *Bihar, India* ... 40 E5
Aurangabad, *Maharashtra,
  India* 43 K9
Aurich, *Germany* 14 B4
Aurillac, *France* 12 D5
Aurora, *Colo., U.S.A.* 74 F2
Aurora, *Ill., U.S.A.* 76 D1
Austin, *Minn., U.S.A.* 75 D8
Austin, *Tex., U.S.A.* 80 D5
Austral Is. = Tubuaï, Îs.,
  French Polynesia 65 M16
Austral Seamount Chain,
  Pac. Oc. 65 M16
Australia ■, *Oceania* 60 E6
Australian Capital Territory □,
  Australia 63 C4
Austria ■, *Europe* 15 E8
Autun, *France* 13 C6
Auvergne □, *France* 13 D5
Auvergne, Mts. d', *France* .. 13 D5
Auxerre, *France* 13 C5
Avallon, *France* 13 C5
Aveiro, *Brazil* 92 C2

Aveiro, *Portugal* 18 B1
Āvej, *Iran* 46 D7
Avellaneda, *Argentina* 94 C5
Avellino, *Italy* 21 D5
Aversa, *Italy* 21 D5
Avesta, *Sweden* 9 C9
Avezzano, *Italy* 20 C4
Aviemore, *U.K.* 10 C5
Avignon, *France* 13 E6
Ávila, *Spain* 18 B3
Avilés, *Spain* 18 A3
Avoca ➤, *Australia* 62 C3
Avola, *Italy* 21 F5
Avranches, *France* 12 B3
Awaji-Shima, *Japan* 33 F4
Awash, *Ethiopia* 49 F3
Awatere ➤, *N.Z.* 65 D6
Awbārī, *Libya* 54 C1
Awbārī, Idehan, *Libya* 54 C1
Awjilah, *Libya* 54 C3
Axel Heiberg I., *Canada* ... 70 B5
Axim, *Ghana* 53 H5
Axios ➤, *Greece* 23 D4
Ayabaca, *Peru* 90 D3
Ayabe, *Japan* 33 F4
Ayacucho, *Argentina* 94 D5
Ayacucho, *Peru* 91 F4
Ayaguz = Ayaköz, *Kazakhstan* 29 E9
Ayaköz, *Kazakhstan* 29 E9
Ayamonte, *Spain* 18 D2
Ayaviri, *Peru* 91 F4
Aydın, *Turkey* 23 F6
Ayers Rock = Uluru, *Australia* 60 F5
Aylmer, L., *Canada* 68 B8
Ayn Dār, *Si. Arabia* 47 F7
Ayr, *U.K.* 10 D4
Aytos, *Bulgaria* 22 C6
Ayu, Kepulauan, *Indonesia* . 37 D4
Ayvacık, *Turkey* 23 E6
Ayvalık, *Turkey* 23 E6
Az Zahrān, *Si. Arabia* 47 F7
Az Zarqā, *Jordan* 46 D4
Az Zilfī, *Si. Arabia* 47 F6
Az Zubayr, *Iraq* 47 E6
Azamgarh, *India* 40 D4
Azärbayjan = Azerbaijan ■,
  Asia 25 E6
Āzarbāyjān-e Gharbī □, *Iran* . 46 C6
Āzarbāyjān-e Sharqī □, *Iran* . 46 C6
Azare, *Nigeria* 53 F8
Azerbaijan ■, *Asia* 25 E6
Azbine = Aïr, *Niger* 53 E7
Azogues, *Ecuador* 90 D3
Azores, *Atl. Oc.* 50 C1
Azov, *Russia* 25 D4
Azov, Sea of, *Europe* 25 D4
Azuaga, *Spain* 18 C3
Azuero, Pen. de, *Panama* .. 86 E3
Azul, *Argentina* 94 D5

B

Ba Don, *Vietnam* 38 A3
Baardeere = Bardera,
  Somali Rep. 49 G3
Bab el Mandeb, *Red Sea* .. 49 E3
Bābā, Koh-i-, *Afghan.* 42 B5
Baba Burnu, *Turkey* 23 E6
Babadag, *Romania* 22 B7
Babaeski, *Turkey* 22 D6
Babahoyo, *Ecuador* 90 D3
Babar, *Indonesia* 37 F3
Babo, *Indonesia* 37 E4
Bābol, *Iran* 44 B3
Bābol Sar, *Iran* 44 B3
Babruysk, *Belarus* 17 B9
Babuyan Chan., *Phil.* 36 A2
Babylon, *Iraq* 46 D6
Bacabal, *Brazil* 92 C5
Bacan, Kepulauan, *Indonesia* 37 E3
Bacarra, *Phil.* 36 A2
Bacău, *Romania* 17 E8
Back ➤, *Canada* 68 B9
Bacolod, *Phil.* 36 B2

Bad Ischl, *Austria* 15 E7
Bad Kissingen, *Germany* ... 14 C6
Badagara, *India* 43 P9
Badajoz, *Spain* 18 C2
Badalona, *Spain* 19 B7
Badampahar, *India* 40 F6
Badanah, *Si. Arabia* 47 E5
Badarinath, *India* 42 D11
Badas, Kepulauan, *Indonesia* 39 D3
Baddo ➤, *Pakistan* 42 E4
Bade, *Indonesia* 37 F5
Baden, *Austria* 15 D9
Baden-Baden, *Germany* ... 14 D5
Baden-Württemberg □,
  Germany 14 D5
Badgastein, *Austria* 15 E7
Bādghīs □, *Afghan.* 42 B3
Badin, *Pakistan* 43 G6
Badlands, *U.S.A.* 74 D3
Baena, *Spain* 18 D3
Baeza, *Spain* 18 D4
Baffin B., *N. Amer.* 70 B7
Baffin I., *Canada* 70 C6
Bafing ➤, *Mali* 53 F3
Bafoulabé, *Mali* 53 F3
Bāfq, *Iran* 44 D3
Bāft, *Iran* 44 D4
Bafwasende, *Dem. Rep. of
  the Congo* 57 D5
Bagamoyo, *Tanzania* 57 F7
Baganga, *Phil.* 36 C3
Bagansiapiapi, *Indonesia* .. 39 D2
Bagdarin, *Russia* 30 D9
Bagé, *Brazil* 94 C6
Baghdād, *Iraq* 46 D6
Bagheria, *Italy* 21 E4
Baghlān, *Afghan.* 42 A6
Baghlān □, *Afghan.* 45 C7
Bago = Pegu, *Burma* 41 J11
Baguio, *Phil.* 36 A2
Bahamas ■, *N. Amer.* 86 A4
Baharampur, *India* 40 E7
Bahawalpur, *Pakistan* 42 E7
Bahía = Salvador, *Brazil* ... 93 E6
Bahía □, *Brazil* 93 E5
Bahía Blanca, *Argentina* ... 94 D4
Bahía de Caráquez, *Ecuador* . 90 D2
Bahía Laura, *Argentina* 95 F3
Bahía Negra, *Paraguay* 91 H7
Bahraich, *India* 40 D3
Bahrain ■, *Asia* 44 E2
Baia Mare, *Romania* 17 E6
Baïbokoum, *Chad* 55 G2
Baidoa, *Somali Rep.* 49 G3
Baie-Comeau, *Canada* 71 E7
Baie Verte, *Canada* 71 E8
Ba'ījī, *Iraq* 46 D5
Baikal, L. = Baykal, Oz., *Russia* 30 D8
Baikonur = Bayqongyr,
  Kazakhstan 29 E7
Baile Atha Cliath = Dublin,
  Ireland 11 E3
Băileşti, *Romania* 22 B4
Bā'ir, *Jordan* 47 E4
Bairiki = Tarawa, *Kiribati* ... 64 J12
Bairnsdale, *Australia* 63 C4
Baitadi, *Nepal* 40 C3
Baiyin, *China* 35 C5
Baja, *Hungary* 16 E4
Baja, Pta., *Mexico* 84 B1
Baja California, *Mexico* 84 A1
Bajimba, Mt., *Australia* 63 A5
Bakel, *Senegal* 53 F3
Baker, L., *Canada* 68 B10
Baker, Mt., *U.S.A.* 72 B3
Baker I., *Pac. Oc.* 64 J13
Baker Lake, *Canada* 68 B10
Bakers Dozen Is., *Canada* .. 71 D6
Bakersfield, *U.S.A.* 78 C3
Bākhtarān = Kermānshāh, *Iran* 46 D6
Bakı, *Azerbaijan* 25 E6
Bakony, *Hungary* 16 E3
Bakouma, *C.A.R.* 55 G3
Baku = Bakı, *Azerbaijan* ... 25 E6
Bakutis Coast, *Antarctica* .. 96 B1
Baky = Bakı, *Azerbaijan* ... 25 E6
Balabac I., *Phil.* 38 C5

Balabac Str., *E. Indies* 38 C5
Balabalangan, Kepulauan,
   Indonesia 39 E5
Balaghat Ra., *India* 43 K10
Balaguer, *Spain* 19 B6
Balaklava, *Ukraine* 25 E3
Balakovo, *Russia* 24 C6
Balashov, *Russia* 24 C5
Balasore = Baleshwar, *India* . 40 G6
Balaton, *Hungary* 16 E3
Balbina, Reprêsa de, *Brazil* .. 90 D7
Balchik, *Bulgaria* 22 C7
Balclutha, *N.Z.* 65 G3
Baleares, Is., *Spain* 19 C7
Balearic Is. = Baleares, Is.,
   Spain 19 C7
Baleine = Whale ➤, *Canada* . 70 D7
Baler, *Phil.* 36 A2
Baleshwar, *India* 40 G6
Bali, *Indonesia* 39 F5
Bali □, *Indonesia* 39 F5
Balikeşir, *Turkey* 23 E6
Balikpapan, *Indonesia* 39 E5
Balimbing, *Phil.* 36 C1
Balkan Mts. = Stara Planina,
   Bulgaria 22 C4
Balkanabat, *Turkmenistan* .. 29 F6
Balkh, *Afghan.* 45 B6
Balkhash = Balqash,
   Kazakhstan 29 E8
Balkhash, Ozero = Balqash
   Köl, *Kazakhstan* 29 E8
Ballarat, *Australia* 62 C3
Ballater, *U.K.* 10 C5
Ballina, *Australia* 63 A5
Ballina, *Ireland* 11 D2
Ballinasloe, *Ireland* 11 E2
Ballymena, *U.K.* 11 D3
Balmaceda, *Chile* 95 F2
Balmoral, *Australia* 62 C3
Balochistan = Baluchistan □,
   Pakistan 42 F4
Balonne ➤, *Australia* 63 A4
Balqash, *Kazakhstan* 29 E8
Balqash Köl, *Kazakhstan* 29 E8
Balrampur, *India* 40 D4
Balranald, *Australia* 62 B3
Balsas ➤, *Mexico* 84 D4
Balta, *Ukraine* 17 D9
Bălţi, *Moldova* 17 E8
Baltic Sea, *Europe* 9 D9
Baltimore, *U.S.A.* 77 E7
Baluchistan □, *Pakistan* 42 F4
Balya, *Turkey* 23 E6
Bam, *Iran* 44 D4
Bama, *Nigeria* 55 F1
Bamako, *Mali* 53 F4
Bambari, *C.A.R.* 55 G3
Bamberg, *Germany* 14 D6
Bamenda, *Cameroon* 53 G8
Bāmīān □, *Afghan.* 42 B5
Bampūr, *Iran* 45 E5
Ban Don = Surat Thani,
   Thailand 38 C1
Ban Kantang, *Thailand* 38 C1
Ban Mê Thuôt = Buon Ma
   Thuot, *Vietnam* 38 B3
Banaba, *Kiribati* 64 K11
Banalia, *Dem. Rep. of*
   the Congo 57 D5
Bananal, I. do, *Brazil* 93 E3
Banaras = Varanasi, *India* .. 40 E4
Bânâs, Ras, *Egypt* 54 D6
Band-e Torkestan, *Afghan.* .. 45 C6
Banda, Kepulauan, *Indonesia* 37 E3
Banda Aceh, *Indonesia* 38 C1
Banda Banda, Mt., *Australia* . 63 B5
Banda Elat, *Indonesia* 37 F4
Banda Sea, *Indonesia* 37 F3
Bandanaira, *Indonesia* 37 E3
Bandar = Machilipatnam,
   India 40 J3
Bandar-e Abbās, *Iran* 44 E4
Bandar-e Anzalī, *Iran* 46 C7
Bandar-e Bushehr = Būshehr,
   Iran 44 D2
Bandar-e Chārak, *Iran* 44 E3

Bandar-e Deylam, *Iran* 47 E7
Bandar-e Emām Khomeynī,
   Iran 47 E7
Bandar-e Lengeh, *Iran* 44 E3
Bandar-e Rīg, *Iran* 44 D2
Bandar-e Torkeman, *Iran* ... 44 B3
Bandar Lampung =
   Tanjungkarang
   Telukbetung, *Indonesia* ... 39 F3
Bandar Maharani = Muar,
   Malaysia 39 D2
Bandar Penggaram = Batu
   Pahat, *Malaysia* 39 D2
Bandar Seri Begawan, *Brunei* 38 D5
Bandar Sri Aman = Sriman,
   Malaysia 39 D4
Bandera, *Argentina* 94 B4
Bandırma, *Turkey* 23 D7
Bandjarmasin = Banjarmasin,
   Indonesia 39 E4
Bandon, *Ireland* 11 F2
Bandundu, *Dem. Rep. of*
   the Congo 56 E3
Bandung, *Indonesia* 39 F3
Banff, *Canada* 69 C8
Banff, *U.K.* 10 C5
Bang Saphan, *Thailand* 38 B1
Bangalore, *India* 43 N10
Bangassou, *C.A.R.* 56 D4
Banggai, Kepulauan,
   Indonesia 37 E2
Banggi, Pulau, *Malaysia* 38 C5
Banghāzī, *Libya* 54 B3
Bangka, *Sulawesi, Indonesia* 37 D3
Bangka, *Sumatera, Indonesia* 39 E3
Bangka, Selat, *Indonesia* ... 39 E3
Bangkinang, *Indonesia* 39 D2
Bangko, *Indonesia* 39 E2
Bangkok, *Thailand* 38 B2
Bangladesh ■, *Asia* 41 E7
Bangong Co, *China* 42 B11
Bangor, *Down, U.K.* 11 D4
Bangor, *Gwynedd, U.K.* 11 E4
Bangor, *U.S.A.* 77 B11
Bangued, *Phil.* 36 A2
Bangui, *C.A.R.* 56 D3
Bangweulu, L., *Zambia* 57 G6
Bani, *Dom. Rep.* 87 C5
Bāniyās, *Syria* 46 D3
Banja Luka, *Bos.-H.* 20 B6
Banjarmasin, *Indonesia* 39 E4
Banjul, *Gambia* 53 F2
Bankipore, *India* 40 E5
Banks I., *Canada* 68 A7
Banks Pen., *N.Z.* 65 E5
Banks Str., *Australia* 62 D4
Bankura, *India* 40 F6
Bannu, *Pakistan* 42 C7
Banswara, *India* 43 H9
Bantry, *Ireland* 11 F2
Banyak, Kepulauan, *Indonesia* 39 D1
Banzare Coast, *Antarctica* ... 96 A13
Baoding, *China* 35 C6
Baoji, *China* 35 C5
Baoshan, *China* 34 D4
Baotou, *China* 35 B6
Bapatla, *India* 40 K3
Ba'qūbah, *Iraq* 46 D6
Bar, *Serbia & M.* 22 C2
Bar, *Ukraine* 17 D8
Bar-le-Duc, *France* 13 B6
Barabai, *Indonesia* 39 E5
Baracoa, *Cuba* 86 B5
Barahona, *Dom. Rep.* 87 C5
Barail Range, *India* 41 E9
Barakaldo, *Spain* 19 A4
Barakpur, *India* 41 F7
Baramula, *India* 42 B9
Baran, *India* 43 G10
Baranavichy, *Belarus* 17 B8
Baranof I., *U.S.A.* 69 C6
Barapasi, *Indonesia* 37 E5
Barat Daya, Kepulauan,
   Indonesia 37 F3
Barbacena, *Brazil* 93 G5
Barbados ■, *W. Indies* 87 D8
Barbastro, *Spain* 19 A6

Barcellona Pozzo di Gotto,
   Italy 21 E5
Barcelona, *Spain* 19 B7
Barcelona, *Venezuela* 90 A6
Barcelos, *Brazil* 90 D6
Bardaï, *Chad* 54 D2
Barddhaman, *India* 40 F6
Bardera, *Somali Rep.* 49 G3
Bardīyah, *Libya* 54 B4
Bareilly, *India* 42 E11
Barfleur, Pte. de, *France* ... 12 B3
Barhi, *India* 40 E5
Bari, *Italy* 20 D6
Bari Doab, *Pakistan* 42 D8
Barīdī, Ra's, *Si. Arabia* 47 F4
Barinas, *Venezuela* 90 B4
Baring, C., *Canada* 68 B8
Barisal, *Bangla.* 41 F8
Barisan, Bukit, *Indonesia* ... 39 E2
Barito ➤, *Indonesia* 39 E4
Barkly Tableland, *Australia* .. 60 D6
Bârlad ➤, *Romania* 17 F8
Barlee, L., *Australia* 60 F2
Barletta, *Italy* 20 D6
Barmedman, *Australia* 63 B4
Barmer, *India* 42 G7
Barmera, *Australia* 62 B3
Barnaul, *Russia* 29 D9
Barnsley, *U.K.* 11 E6
Barnstaple, *U.K.* 11 F4
Baro, *Nigeria* 53 G7
Baroda = Vadodara, *India* .. 43 H8
Barotseland, *Zambia* 58 B4
Barpeta, *India* 41 D8
Barquísimeto, *Venezuela* ... 90 A5
Barra, *Brazil* 93 E5
Barra, *U.K.* 10 C3
Barra do Corda, *Brazil* 92 D4
Barra Falsa, Pta. da, *Mozam.* 59 C7
Barraba, *Australia* 63 B5
Barrackpur = Barakpur, *India* 41 F7
Barraigh = Barra, *U.K.* 10 C3
Barranca, *Lima, Peru* 91 F3
Barranca, *Loreto, Peru* 90 D3
Barrancabermeja, *Colombia* . 90 B4
Barrancas, *Venezuela* 90 B6
Barrancos, *Portugal* 18 C2
Barranqueras, *Argentina* ... 94 B5
Barranquilla, *Colombia* 90 A4
Barreiras, *Brazil* 93 E5
Barreirinhas, *Brazil* 92 C5
Barreiro, *Portugal* 18 C1
Barretos, *Brazil* 93 G4
Barrie, *Canada* 71 E6
Barrier Ra., *Australia* 62 B3
Barrington Tops, *Australia* .. 63 B5
Barringun, *Australia* 63 A4
Barrow, *U.S.A.* 69 A4
Barrow-in-Furness, *U.K.* 11 D5
Barry, *U.K.* 11 F5
Barsi, *India* 43 K9
Barsoi, *India* 40 E6
Barstow, *U.S.A.* 78 C4
Bartica, *Guyana* 90 B7
Bartin, *Turkey* 46 B3
Bartlesville, *U.S.A.* 81 A6
Barysaw, *Belarus* 17 A9
Bāsa'idū, *Iran* 44 E3
Basankusa, *Dem. Rep. of*
   the Congo 56 D3
Basarabeasca, *Moldova* 17 E9
Basarabia = Bessarabiya,
   Moldova 17 E9
Basel, *Switz.* 14 E4
Bashkortostan □, *Russia* ... 29 D6
Basilan, *Phil.* 36 C2
Basilan Str., *Phil.* 36 C2
Basildon, *U.K.* 11 F7
Basim = Washim, *India* 43 J10
Basingstoke, *U.K.* 11 F6
Basle = Basel, *Switz.* 14 E4
Basque Provinces = Pais
   Vasco □, *Spain* 19 A4
Basra = Al Başrah, *Iraq* 47 E6
Bass Str., *Australia* 61 H8
Bassano del Grappa, *Italy* .. 20 B3
Bassas da India, *Ind. Oc.* ... 59 C7

Basse-Terre, *Guadeloupe* ... 87 C7
Bassein, *Burma* 41 J10
Basseterre, *St. Kitts & Nevis* . 87 C7
Bastak, *Iran* 44 E3
Bastar, *India* 40 H3
Basti, *India* 40 D4
Bastia, *France* 13 E8
Bastogne, *Belgium* 14 C3
Bata, *Eq. Guin.* 56 D1
Bataan □, *Phil.* 36 B2
Batabanó, G. de, *Cuba* ... 86 B3
Batac, *Phil.* 36 A2
Batagai, *Russia* 31 C11
Batamay, *Russia* 31 C10
Batangafo, *C.A.R.* 55 G2
Batangas, *Phil.* 36 B2
Batanta, *Indonesia* 37 E4
Batdambang, *Cambodia* .. 38 B2
Batemans B., *Australia* ... 63 C5
Batemans Bay, *Australia* .. 63 C5
Bath, *U.K.* 11 F5
Bathurst, *Australia* 63 B4
Bathurst, *Canada* 71 E7
Bathurst, C., *Canada* 68 A7
Bathurst Harb., *Australia* . 62 D4
Bathurst I., *Australia* 70 B3
Bathurst Inlet, *Canada* ... 68 B9
Batlow, *Australia* 63 C4
Batman, *Turkey* 46 C5
Batna, *Algeria* 52 A7
Baton Rouge, *U.S.A.* 81 D8
Batouri, *Cameroon* 56 D2
Battambang = Batdambang,
  Cambodia 38 B2
Battipáglia, *Italy* 21 D5
Battle Creek, *U.S.A.* 76 C3
Batu, *Ethiopia* 49 F2
Batu, Kepulauan, *Indonesia* . 39 E1
Batu Pahat, *Malaysia* 39 D2
Batuata, *Indonesia* 37 F2
Batumi, *Georgia* 25 E5
Baturaja, *Indonesia* 39 E2
Baturité, *Brazil* 92 C6
Bau, *Malaysia* 39 D4
Baubau, *Indonesia* 37 F2
Baucau, *E. Timor* 37 F3
Bauchi, *Nigeria* 53 F7
Bauer, C., *Australia* 62 B1
Baukau = Baucau, *E. Timor* . 37 F3
Bauld, C., *Canada* 71 D8
Bauru, *Brazil* 93 G4
Bautzen, *Germany* 15 C8
Bavaria = Bayern □, *Germany* 15 D6
Bawdwin, *Burma* 41 F11
Bawean, *Indonesia* 39 F4
Bawku, *Ghana* 53 F5
Bawlake, *Burma* 41 H11
Bay City, *U.S.A.* 76 C4
Bay View, *N.Z.* 64 C7
Bayamo, *Cuba* 86 B4
Bayamón, *Puerto Rico* 87 C6
Bayan Har Shan, *China* ... 34 C4
Bayan Hot = Alxa Zuoqi, *China* 35 C5
Bayanaüyl, *Kazakhstan* ... 29 D8
Bayanhongor, *Mongolia* ... 35 B5
Baybay, *Phil.* 36 B2
Baydhabo = Baidoa,
  Somali Rep. 49 G3
Bayern □, *Germany* 15 D6
Bayeux, *France* 12 B3
Bayındır, *Turkey* 23 E6
Baykal, Oz., *Russia* 30 D8
Bayombong, *Phil.* 36 A2
Bayonne, *France* 12 E3
Bayovar, *Peru* 91 E2
Bayqongyr, *Kazakhstan* ... 29 E7
Baýramaly, *Turkmenistan* .. 29 F7
Bayramiç, *Turkey* 23 E6
Bayreuth, *Germany* 15 D6
Bayrūt, *Lebanon* 46 D3
Baytown, *U.S.A.* 81 E6
Baza, *Spain* 19 D4
Bazaruto, I. do, *Mozam.* ... 59 C7
Beachport, *Australia* 62 C2
Beagle, Canal, *S. Amer.* ... 95 G3
Beardmore Glacier, *Antarctica* 96 C14
Béarn, *France* 12 E3
Beauce, Plaine de la, *France* . 12 B4

Beaudesert, *Australia* 63 A5
Beaufort, *Malaysia* 38 C5
Beaufort Sea, *Arctic* 66 B6
Beaufort West, *S. Africa* ... 58 E4
Beaumont, *U.S.A.* 81 D6
Beaune, *France* 13 C6
Beauvais, *France* 12 B5
Beaver ➤, *Canada* 69 C9
Beawar, *India* 42 F9
Bečej, *Serbia & M.* 22 B3
Béchar, *Algeria* 52 B5
Bedford, *U.K.* 11 E6
Beenleigh, *Australia* 63 A5
Be'er Sheva, *Israel* 47 E3
Beersheba = Be'er Sheva,
  Israel 47 E3
Befale, *Dem. Rep. of
  the Congo* 56 D4
Bega, *Australia* 63 C4
Behbehān, *Iran* 47 E7
Behshahr, *Iran* 44 B3
Bei Jiang ➤, *China* 35 D6
Bei'an, *China* 35 B7
Beihai, *China* 35 D5
Beijing, *China* 35 C6
Beilpajah, *Australia* 63 B3
Beinn na Faoghla =
  Benbecula, *U.K.* 10 C3
Beira, *Mozam.* 59 B6
Beirut = Bayrūt, *Lebanon* .. 46 D3
Beitbridge, *Zimbabwe* 59 C6
Beja, *Portugal* 18 C2
Béja, *Tunisia* 54 A1
Bejaïa, *Algeria* 52 A7
Béjar, *Spain* 18 B3
Bejestān, *Iran* 44 C4
Békéscsaba, *Hungary* 16 E5
Bela, *India* 40 E4
Bela, *Pakistan* 42 F5
Bela Crkva, *Serbia & M.* ... 22 B3
Bela Vista, *Brazil* 94 A5
Bela Vista, *Mozam.* 59 D6
Belarus ■, *Europe* 24 C2
Belau = Palau ■, *Palau* 36 C4
Belawan, *Indonesia* 39 D1
Belaya Tserkov = Bila Tserkva,
  Ukraine 17 D10
Belcher Chan., *Canada* ... 70 B4
Belcher Is., *Canada* 71 D6
Beled Weyne = Belet Uen,
  Somali Rep. 49 G4
Belém, *Brazil* 92 C4
Belet Uen, *Somali Rep.* ... 49 G4
Belev, *Russia* 24 C4
Belfast, *U.K.* 11 D4
Belfort, *France* 13 C7
Belgaum, *India* 43 M9
Belgium ■, *Europe* 14 C3
Belgorod, *Russia* 24 C4
Belgorod-Dnestrovskiy =
  Bilhorod-Dnistrovskyy,
  Ukraine 25 D3
Belgrade = Beograd,
  Serbia & M. 22 B3
Beli Drim ➤, *Europe* 22 C3
Belinyu, *Indonesia* 39 E3
Belitung, *Indonesia* 39 E3
Belize ■, *Cent. Amer.* 85 D7
Belize City, *Belize* 85 D7
Belkovskiy, Ostrov, *Russia* . 30 B11
Bell Peninsula, *Canada* ... 70 C5
Bell Ville, *Argentina* 94 C4
Bella Unión, *Uruguay* 94 C5
Bella Vista, *Argentina* 94 B5
Bellary, *India* 43 M10
Bellata, *Australia* 63 A4
Belle-Île, *France* 12 C2
Belle Isle, *Canada* 71 D8
Belle Isle, Str. of, *Canada* .. 71 D8
Belleville, *Canada* 71 E6
Belleville, *U.S.A.* 75 F10
Bellin = Kangirsuk, *Canada* . 70 D7
Bellingen, *Australia* 63 B5
Bellingham, *U.S.A.* 72 B2
Bellingshausen Sea,
  Antarctica 96 A2
Bellinzona, *Switz.* 13 C8

Belluno, *Italy* 20 A4
Belmonte, *Brazil* 93 F6
Belmopan, *Belize* 85 D7
Belo Horizonte, *Brazil* 93 F5
Belo-Tsiribihina, *Madag.* ... 59 B8
Beloit, *U.S.A.* 75 D10
Belokorovichi, *Ukraine* 17 C9
Belomorsk, *Russia* 28 C4
Belonia, *India* 41 F8
Belorussia = Belarus ■,
  Europe 24 C2
Belovo, *Russia* 29 D9
Beloye, Ozero, *Russia* 24 A4
Beloye More, *Russia* 8 B13
Belozersk, *Russia* 24 A4
Beltana, *Australia* 62 B2
Belterra, *Brazil* 92 C3
Beltsy = Bălţi, *Moldova* ... 17 E8
Belukha, *Russia* 29 E9
Beluran, *Malaysia* 38 C5
Belyy, Ostrov, *Russia* 28 B8
Belyy Yar, *Russia* 29 D9
Bembéréke, *Benin* 53 F6
Bemidji, *U.S.A.* 75 B7
Ben Lomond, *N.S.W.,*
  Australia 63 B5
Ben Lomond, *Tas., Australia* 62 D4
Ben Nevis, *U.K.* 10 C4
Bena, *Nigeria* 53 F7
Benalla, *Australia* 63 C4
Benares = Varanasi, *India* .. 40 E4
Benavente, *Spain* 18 A3
Benbecula, *U.K.* 10 C3
Benbonyathe Hill, *Australia* . 62 B2
Bend, *U.S.A.* 72 D3
Bender Beila, *Somali Rep.* . 49 F5
Bendery = Tighina, *Moldova* 17 E9
Bendigo, *Australia* 63 C3
Benevento, *Italy* 20 D5
Bengal, Bay of, *Ind. Oc.* ... 41 J7
Bengalûru = Bangalore, *India* 43 N10
Bengbu, *China* 35 C6
Benghazi = Banghāzī, *Libya* . 54 B3
Bengkalis, *Indonesia* 39 D2
Bengkulu, *Indonesia* 39 E2
Bengkulu □, *Indonesia* 39 E2
Benguela, *Angola* 58 A2
Beni, *Dem. Rep. of the Congo* 57 D5
Beni ➤, *Bolivia* 91 F5
Beni Mellal, *Morocco* 52 B4
Beni Suef, *Egypt* 54 C5
Benidorm, *Spain* 19 C5
Benin ■, *Africa* 53 G6
Benin, Bight of, *W. Afr.* ... 53 H6
Benin City, *Nigeria* 53 G7
Benjamin Constant, *Brazil* .. 90 D4
Benoni, *S. Africa* 59 D5
Bent, *Iran* 44 E4
Benteng, *Indonesia* 37 F2
Benton Harbor, *U.S.A.* 76 C2
Benue ➤, *Nigeria* 53 G7
Benxi, *China* 35 B7
Beo, *Indonesia* 36 D3
Beograd, *Serbia & M.* 22 B3
Beppu, *Japan* 33 G2
Berat, *Albania* 23 D2
Berau, Teluk, *Indonesia* ... 37 E4
Berber, *Sudan* 55 E5
Berbera, *Somali Rep.* 49 E4
Berbérati, *C.A.R.* 56 D3
Berbice ➤, *Guyana* 90 B7
Berdichev = Berdychiv,
  Ukraine 17 D9
Berdsk, *Russia* 29 D9
Berdyansk, *Ukraine* 25 D4
Berdychiv, *Ukraine* 17 D9
Berebere, *Indonesia* 37 D3
Bereda, *Somali Rep.* 49 E5
Berehove, *Ukraine* 17 D6
Berekum, *Ghana* 53 G5
Berestechko, *Ukraine* 17 C7
Bereza = Byaroza, *Belarus* . 17 B7
Berezhany, *Ukraine* 17 D7
Berezina = Byarezina ➤,
  Belarus 17 B10
Berezniki, *Russia* 28 D6
Berezovo, *Russia* 28 C7

Berga, *Spain* **19 A6**
Bergama, *Turkey* **23 E6**
Bérgamo, *Italy* **13 D8**
Bergen, *Norway* **8 C7**
Bergerac, *France* **12 D4**
Berhala, Selat, *Indonesia* . . . **39 E2**
Berhampore = Baharampur,
    India **40 E7**
Berhampur = Brahmapur,
    India **40 H5**
Bering Sea, *Pac. Oc.* **69 C1**
Bering Strait, *Pac. Oc.* **69 B3**
Berja, *Spain* **19 D4**
Berkeley, *U.S.A.* **72 H2**
Berkner I., *Antarctica* **96 B4**
Berlin, *Germany* **15 B7**
Bermejo ➛, *Formosa,*
    Argentina **94 B5**
Bermejo ➛, *San Juan,*
    Argentina **94 C3**
Bermuda ⬚, *Atl. Oc.* **67 F13**
Bern, *Switz.* **14 E4**
Bernburg, *Germany* **15 C6**
Berne = Bern, *Switz.* **14 E4**
Bernina, Piz, *Switz.* **13 C8**
Beroun, *Czech Rep.* **16 D2**
Berri, *Australia* **62 B3**
Berry, *Australia* **63 B5**
Berry, *France* **12 C5**
Bershad, *Ukraine* **17 D9**
Bertoua, *Cameroon* **56 D2**
Berwick-upon-Tweed, *U.K.* . . **10 D6**
Besalampy, *Madag.* **59 B8**
Besançon, *France* **13 C7**
Besar, *Indonesia* **39 E5**
Bessarabiya, *Moldova* **17 E9**
Bessarabka = Basarabeasca,
    Moldova **17 E9**
Bessemer, *U.S.A.* **82 C4**
Betanzos, *Spain* **18 A1**
Bétaré Oya, *Cameroon* **56 C2**
Bethel, *U.S.A.* **69 B3**
Bethlehem, *S. Africa* **59 D5**
Bethlehem, *U.S.A.* **77 D8**
Béthune, *France* **13 A5**
Betong, *Malaysia* **39 D4**
Betroka, *Madag.* **59 C9**
Bettiah, *India* **40 D5**
Betul, *India* **43 J10**
Beverley, *U.K.* **11 E6**
Beverly Hills, *U.S.A.* **78 C3**
Beyneu, *Kazakhstan* **29 E6**
Beypazarı, *Turkey* **25 E3**
Beyşehir Gölü, *Turkey* **46 C2**
Béziers, *France* **13 E5**
Bezwada = Vijayawada, *India* **40 J3**
Bhachau, *India* **43 H7**
Bhadrakh, *India* **40 G6**
Bhadravati, *India* **43 N9**
Bhagalpur, *India* **40 E6**
Bhakra Dam, *India* **42 D10**
Bhamo, *Burma* **41 E11**
Bhandara, *India* **43 J11**
Bhanrer Ra., *India* **43 H11**
Bharat = India ◼, *Asia* **43 J10**
Bharatpur, *India* **42 F10**
Bhatpara, *India* **41 F7**
Bhavnagar, *India* **43 J8**
Bhawanipatna, *India* **40 H4**
Bhilai = Bhilainagar-Durg,
    India **40 G3**
Bhilainagar-Durg, *India* **40 G3**
Bhilsa = Vidisha, *India* **43 H10**
Bhilwara, *India* **43 G9**
Bhima ➛, *India* **43 L10**
Bhind, *India* **42 F11**
Bhiwandi, *India* **43 K8**
Bhiwani, *India* **42 E10**
Bhola, *Bangla.* **41 F8**
Bhopal, *India* **43 H10**
Bhubaneshwar, *India* **40 G5**
Bhuj, *India* **43 H6**
Bhusawal, *India* **43 J9**
Bhutan ◼, *Asia* **41 D8**
Biafra, B. of = Bonny, Bight of,
    Africa **56 D1**
Biak, *Indonesia* **37 E5**

Biała Podlaska, *Poland* **17 B6**
Białogard, *Poland* **16 A2**
Białystok, *Poland* **17 B6**
Biaro, *Indonesia* **37 D3**
Biarritz, *France* **12 E3**
Bibai, *Japan* **32 B7**
Biberach, *Germany* **14 D5**
Bida, *Nigeria* **53 G7**
Bidar, *India* **43 L10**
Biddeford, *U.S.A.* **77 C10**
Bié, Planalto de, *Angola* . . . **58 A3**
Bielefeld, *Germany* **14 B5**
Biella, *Italy* **13 D8**
Bielsk Podlaski, *Poland* **17 B6**
Bielsko-Biała, *Poland* **16 D4**
Bien Hoa, *Vietnam* **38 B3**
Bienville, L., *Canada* **71 D6**
Big Horn Mts. = Bighorn Mts.,
    U.S.A. **73 D10**
Big Spring, *U.S.A.* **80 C3**
Big Trout L., *Canada* **71 D5**
Biğa, *Turkey* **23 D6**
Bigadiç, *Turkey* **23 E7**
Biggar, *Canada* **69 C9**
Biggenden, *Australia* **63 A5**
Bighorn ➛, *U.S.A.* **73 C10**
Bighorn Mts., *U.S.A.* **73 D10**
Bihać, *Bos.-H.* **20 B5**
Bihar, *India* **40 E5**
Bihar ⬚, *India* **40 E5**
Bihor, Munţii, *Romania* **17 E6**
Bijagós, Arquipélago dos,
    Guinea-Biss. **53 F2**
Bijapur, *Chhattisgarh, India* . **40 H3**
Bijapur, *Karnataka, India* . . . **43 L9**
Bijār, *Iran* **46 D6**
Bijeljina, *Bos.-H.* **20 B7**
Bijnor, *India* **42 E11**
Bikaner, *India* **42 E8**
Bikini Atoll, *Marshall Is.* **64 H11**
Bila Tserkva, *Ukraine* **17 D10**
Bilara, *India* **42 F8**
Bilaspur, *India* **40 F4**
Bilauk Taungdan, *Thailand* . . **38 B1**
Bilbao, *Spain* **19 A4**
Bilbo = Bilbao, *Spain* **19 A4**
Bilecik, *Turkey* **25 E3**
Bilhorod-Dnistrovskyy,
    Ukraine **25 D3**
Billings, *U.S.A.* **73 D9**
Billiton Is. = Belitung,
    Indonesia **39 E3**
Bilma, *Niger* **55 E1**
Biloxi, *U.S.A.* **81 D9**
Biltine, *Chad* **55 F3**
Bima, *Indonesia* **37 F1**
Bina-Etawah, *India* **43 G11**
Binalbagan, *Phil.* **36 B2**
Binalong, *Australia* **63 B4**
Bīnālūd, Kūh-e, *Iran* **44 B4**
Binatang = Bintangau,
    Malaysia **39 D4**
Bindura, *Zimbabwe* **59 B6**
Bingara, *Australia* **63 A5**
Binghamton, *U.S.A.* **77 C8**
Bingöl, *Turkey* **46 C5**
Binh Dinh = An Nhon,
    Vietnam **38 B3**
Binh Son, *Vietnam* **38 A3**
Binjai, *Indonesia* **39 D1**
Binnaway, *Australia* **63 B4**
Binongko, *Indonesia* **37 F2**
Bintan, *Indonesia* **39 D2**
Bintangau, *Malaysia* **39 D4**
Bintulu, *Malaysia* **39 D4**
Bintuni, *Indonesia* **37 E4**
Binzert = Bizerte, *Tunisia* . . . **54 A1**
Bioko, *Eq. Guin.* **53 H7**
Bir, *India* **43 K9**
Bir Atrun, *Sudan* **55 E4**
Bîr Mogreïn, *Mauritania* **52 C3**
Birchip, *Australia* **62 C3**
Birecik, *Turkey* **46 C4**
Bireuen, *Indonesia* **38 C1**
Birmingham, *U.K.* **11 E6**
Birmingham, *U.S.A.* **82 C4**
Birmitrapur, *India* **40 F5**

Birni Nkonni, *Niger* **53 F7**
Birnin Kebbi, *Nigeria* **53 F6**
Birr, *Ireland* **11 E3**
Birrie ➛, *Australia* **63 A4**
Birsk, *Russia* **29 D6**
Birur, *India* **43 N9**
Bisa, *Indonesia* **37 E3**
Biscay, B. of, *Atl. Oc.* **12 D2**
Biscoe Is., *Antarctica* **96 A3**
Bishkek, *Kyrgyzstan* **29 E8**
Biskra, *Algeria* **52 B7**
Bismarck, *U.S.A.* **74 B4**
Bismarck Arch., *Papua N. G.* . **64 K9**
Bissagos = Bijagós,
    Guinea-Biss. **53 F2**
Bissau, *Guinea-Biss.* **53 F2**
Bistriţa, *Romania* **17 E7**
Bistriţa ➛, *Romania* **17 E8**
Bitlis, *Turkey* **46 C5**
Bitola, *Macedonia* **22 D3**
Bitolj = Bitola, *Macedonia* . . **22 D3**
Bitterfontein, *S. Africa* **58 E3**
Bitterroot Range, *U.S.A.* **73 D6**
Biu, *Nigeria* **55 F1**
Biwa-Ko, *Japan* **33 F5**
Biysk, *Russia* **29 D9**
Bizerte, *Tunisia* **54 A1**
Bjelovar, *Croatia* **20 B6**
Björneborg = Pori, *Finland* . . **8 C10**
Black Forest = Schwarzwald,
    Germany **14 D5**
Black Hills, *U.S.A.* **74 D3**
Black Sea, *Eurasia* **25 E3**
Black Volta ➛, *Africa* **53 G5**
Blackball, *N.Z.* **65 E4**
Blackburn, *U.K.* **11 E5**
Blackpool, *U.K.* **11 E5**
Blackwater ➛, *Ireland* **11 E2**
Blagodarnyy, *Russia* **25 D5**
Blagoevgrad, *Bulgaria* **22 C4**
Blagoveshchensk, *Russia* . . . **31 D10**
Blanc, Mont, *Europe* **13 D7**
Blanca, B., *Argentina* **95 D4**
Blanca Peak, *U.S.A.* **79 B10**
Blanche, C., *Australia* **62 B1**
Blanche, L., *Australia* **62 A2**
Blanes, *Spain* **19 B7**
Blantyre, *Malawi* **59 B6**
Blayney, *Australia* **63 B4**
Blenheim, *N.Z.* **65 D5**
Blida, *Algeria* **52 A6**
Bligh Sound, *N.Z.* **65 F1**
Bloemfontein, *S. Africa* **59 D5**
Bloemhof, *S. Africa* **59 D5**
Blois, *France* **12 C4**
Bloomington, *Ill., U.S.A.* **75 E10**
Bloomington, *Ind., U.S.A.* . . . **76 E2**
Blue Mts., *U.S.A.* **72 D4**
Blue Nile = Nîl el Azraq ➛,
    Sudan **55 E5**
Blue Ridge, *U.S.A.* **83 A7**
Bluefields, *Nic.* **86 D3**
Bluff, *N.Z.* **65 G3**
Blumenau, *Brazil* **94 B7**
Bo, *S. Leone* **53 G3**
Bo Hai, *China* **35 C6**
Boa Vista, *Brazil* **90 C6**
Bobadah, *Australia* **63 B4**
Bobbili, *India* **40 H4**
Bobo-Dioulasso, *Burkina Faso* **53 F5**
Bóbr ➛, *Poland* **16 B2**
Bobraomby, Tanjon' i, *Madag.* **59 A9**
Bobruysk = Babruysk, *Belarus* **17 B9**
Boby, Pic, *Madag.* **59 C9**
Bôca do Acre, *Brazil* **91 E5**
Boca Raton, *U.S.A.* **83 F7**
Bochum, *Germany* **14 C4**
Bodaybo, *Russia* **30 D9**
Boden, *Sweden* **8 B10**
Bodensee, *Europe* **13 C8**
Bodhan, *India* **43 K10**
Bodø, *Norway* **8 B8**
Bodrog ➛, *Hungary* **16 D5**
Bodrum, *Turkey* **23 F6**
Boende, *Dem. Rep. of*
    the Congo **56 E4**

Place	Page	Grid
Bogalusa, *U.S.A.*	81	D9
Bogan Gate, *Australia*	63	B4
Boggabilla, *Australia*	63	A5
Boggabri, *Australia*	63	B5
Bogo, *Phil.*	36	B2
Bogong, Mt., *Australia*	63	C4
Bogor, *Indonesia*	39	F3
Bogotá, *Colombia*	90	C4
Bogotol, *Russia*	29	D9
Bogra, *Bangla.*	41	E7
Bohemian Forest =		
Böhmerwald, *Germany*	15	D7
Böhmerwald, *Germany*	15	D7
Bohol □, *Phil.*	36	C2
Bohol Sea, *Phil.*	36	C2
Boise, *U.S.A.*	72	E5
Boise City, *U.S.A.*	80	A2
Bojador, C., *W. Sahara*	52	C3
Bojana ➜, *Albania*	22	D2
Bojnūrd, *Iran*	44	B4
Bokhara ➜, *Australia*	63	A4
Bokoro, *Chad*	55	F2
Bolan Pass, *Pakistan*	42	E5
Bolbec, *France*	12	B4
Bole, *China*	34	B3
Bolekhiv, *Ukraine*	17	D6
Bolesławiec, *Poland*	16	C2
Bolhrad, *Ukraine*	17	F9
Bolivia ■, *S. Amer.*	91	G6
Bollon, *Australia*	63	A4
Bolobo, *Dem. Rep. of*		
the Congo	56	E3
Bologna, *Italy*	20	B3
Bologoye, *Russia*	24	B3
Bolsena, L. di, *Italy*	20	C3
Bolshevik, Ostrov, *Russia*	30	B8
Bolshoy Begichev, Ostrov,		
Russia	30	B9
Bolshoy Kavkas = Caucasus		
Mountains, *Eurasia*	25	E5
Bolshoy Lyakhovskiy, Ostrov,		
Russia	31	B12
Bolton, *U.K.*	11	E5
Bolu, *Turkey*	25	E3
Bolvadin, *Turkey*	46	C2
Bolzano, *Italy*	20	A3
Bom Jesus da Lapa, *Brazil*	93	E5
Boma, *Dem. Rep. of*		
the Congo	56	F2
Bombala, *Australia*	63	C4
Bombay = Mumbai, *India*	43	K8
Bomboma, *Dem. Rep. of*		
the Congo	56	D3
Bomu ➜, *C.A.R.*	56	D4
Bon, C., *Tunisia*	21	F3
Bonaire, *Neth. Ant.*	87	D6
Bonang, *Australia*	63	C4
Bonavista, *Canada*	71	E8
Bondo, *Dem. Rep. of*		
the Congo	56	D4
Bondoukou, *Ivory C.*	53	G5
Bone, Teluk, *Indonesia*	37	E2
Bonerate, *Indonesia*	37	F2
Bonerate, Kepulauan,		
Indonesia	37	F2
Bong Son = Hoai Nhon,		
Vietnam	38	B3
Bongor, *Chad*	55	F2
Bonifacio, *France*	13	F8
Bonin Is., *Pac. Oc.*	27	G18
Bonn, *Germany*	14	C4
Bonney, L., *Australia*	62	C3
Bonny, Bight of, *Africa*	56	D1
Bonoi, *Indonesia*	37	E5
Bonthe, *S. Leone*	53	G3
Bontoc, *Phil.*	36	A2
Booligal, *Australia*	63	B3
Boonah, *Australia*	63	A5
Boorindal, *Australia*	63	B4
Boorowa, *Australia*	63	B4
Boosaaso = Bosaso,		
Somali Rep.	49	E4
Boothia, Gulf of, *Canada*	70	B5
Boothia Pen., *Canada*	68	A10
Booué, *Gabon*	56	E2
Bor, *Serbia & M.*	22	B4
Bôr, *Sudan*	55	G5
Borås, *Sweden*	9	D8
Boräzjän, *Iran*	44	D2
Borba, *Brazil*	90	D7
Borda, C., *Australia*	62	C2
Bordeaux, *France*	12	D3
Borden I., *Canada*	70	B2
Borden Pen., *Canada*	70	B5
Bordertown, *Australia*	62	C3
Bordj Fly Ste. Marie, *Algeria*	52	C5
Bordj-in-Eker, *Algeria*	52	D7
Bordj Omar Driss, *Algeria*	52	C7
Borger, *U.S.A.*	80	B3
Borhoyn Tal, *Mongolia*	35	B6
Borisoglebsk, *Russia*	24	C5
Borisov = Barysaw, *Belarus*	17	A9
Borja, *Peru*	90	D3
Borkou, *Chad*	55	E2
Borkum, *Germany*	14	B4
Borley, C., *Antarctica*	96	A9
Borneo, *E. Indies*	39	D4
Bornholm, *Denmark*	9	D9
Borongan, *Phil.*	36	B3
Borovichi, *Russia*	24	B3
Borşa, *Romania*	17	E7
Borūjerd, *Iran*	46	D7
Boryslav, *Ukraine*	17	D6
Bosa, *Italy*	21	D2
Bosanska Gradiška, *Bos.-H.*	20	B6
Bosaso, *Somali Rep.*	49	E4
Boshrüyeh, *Iran*	44	C4
Bosna ➜, *Bos.-H.*	20	B7
Bosnia-Herzegovina ■,		
Europe	20	B6
Bosnik, *Indonesia*	37	E5
Bosobolo, *Dem. Rep. of*		
the Congo	56	D3
Bosporus = İstanbul Boğazı,		
Turkey	22	D7
Bossangoa, *C.A.R.*	55	G2
Bosso, *Niger*	55	F1
Bosten Hu, *China*	34	B3
Boston, *U.K.*	11	E6
Boston, *U.S.A.*	77	C10
Bothnia, G. of, *Europe*	8	C10
Bothwell, *Australia*	62	D4
Botletle ➜, *Botswana*	58	C4
Botoşani, *Romania*	17	E8
Botswana ■, *Africa*	58	C4
Botucatu, *Brazil*	93	G4
Bouaké, *Ivory C.*	53	G4
Bouar, *C.A.R.*	56	C3
Bouârfa, *Morocco*	52	B5
Bougainville I., *Papua N. G.*	64	K10
Bougie = Bejaïa, *Algeria*	52	A7
Bougouni, *Mali*	53	F4
Boulder, *U.S.A.*	74	E2
Boulder Dam = Hoover Dam,		
U.S.A.	78	B5
Boulogne-sur-Mer, *France*	12	A4
Bouna, *Ivory C.*	53	G5
Boundiali, *Ivory C.*	53	G4
Bourbonnais, *France*	13	C5
Bourem, *Mali*	53	E5
Bourg-en-Bresse, *France*	13	C6
Bourg-St-Maurice, *France*	13	D7
Bourgas = Burgas, *Bulgaria*	22	C6
Bourges, *France*	12	C5
Bourgogne □, *France*	13	C6
Bourke, *Australia*	63	B4
Bournemouth, *U.K.*	11	F6
Bowen Mts., *Australia*	63	C4
Bowman I., *Antarctica*	96	A12
Bowral, *Australia*	63	B5
Bowraville, *Australia*	63	B5
Boyne ➜, *Ireland*	11	E3
Boyoma, Chutes, *Dem. Rep.*		
of the Congo	57	D5
Boz Dağları, *Turkey*	23	E7
Bozburun, *Turkey*	23	F7
Bozcaada, *Turkey*	23	E6
Bozdoğan, *Turkey*	23	F7
Bozeman, *U.S.A.*	73	D8
Bozen = Bolzano, *Italy*	20	A3
Bozoum, *C.A.R.*	55	G2
Bra, *Italy*	13	D7
Brač, *Croatia*	20	C6
Bracciano, L. di, *Italy*	20	C4
Brach, *Libya*	54	C1
Bräcke, *Sweden*	8	C9
Bradenton, *U.S.A.*	83	F6
Bradford, *U.K.*	11	E6
Braga, *Portugal*	18	B1
Bragança, *Brazil*	92	C4
Bragança, *Portugal*	18	B2
Brahestad = Raahe, *Finland*	8	C10
Brahmanbaria, *Bangla.*	41	F8
Brahmani ➜, *India*	40	G6
Brahmapur, *India*	40	H5
Brahmaputra ➜, *Asia*	41	F7
Braidwood, *Australia*	63	C4
Brăila, *Romania*	17	F8
Branco ➜, *Brazil*	90	D6
Brandenburg, *Germany*	15	B7
Brandenburg □, *Germany*	15	B7
Brandon, *Canada*	69	D10
Braniewo, *Poland*	16	A4
Bransfield Str., *Antarctica*	96	A4
Brantford, *Canada*	76	C5
Brasil = Brazil ■, *S. Amer.*	93	E4
Brasiléia, *Brazil*	91	F5
Brasília, *Brazil*	93	F4
Braşov, *Romania*	17	F7
Brassey, Banjaran, *Malaysia*	38	D5
Bratislava, *Slovak Rep.*	16	D3
Bratsk, *Russia*	30	D8
Braunau, *Austria*	15	D7
Braunschweig, *Germany*	14	B6
Bravo del Norte, Rio =		
Grande, Rio ➜, *N. Amer.*	85	B5
Brawley, *U.S.A.*	78	D5
Bray, *Ireland*	11	E3
Bray, Pays de, *France*	12	B4
Brazil ■, *S. Amer.*	93	E4
Brazos ➜, *U.S.A.*	81	E6
Brazzaville, *Congo*	56	E3
Brčko, *Bos.-H.*	20	B7
Breaksea Sd., *N.Z.*	65	F2
Bream B., *N.Z.*	64	A6
Bream Hd., *N.Z.*	64	A6
Brecon, *U.K.*	11	F5
Breda, *Neths.*	14	C3
Bredasdorp, *S. Africa*	58	E4
Bregenz, *Austria*	14	E5
Breiðafjörður, *Iceland*	8	B1
Brejo, *Brazil*	92	C5
Bremen, *Germany*	14	B5
Bremerhaven, *Germany*	14	B5
Bremerton, *U.S.A.*	72	C2
Brennerpass, *Austria*	15	E6
Bréscia, *Italy*	13	D9
Breslau = Wrocław, *Poland*	16	C3
Bressanone, *Italy*	20	A3
Brest, *Belarus*	17	B6
Brest, *France*	12	B1
Brest-Litovsk = Brest, *Belarus*	17	B6
Bretagne □, *France*	12	B2
Brett, C., *N.Z.*	64	A6
Brewarrina, *Australia*	63	A4
Bria, *C.A.R.*	55	G3
Briançon, *France*	13	D7
Bribie I., *Australia*	63	A5
Bridgeport, *U.S.A.*	77	D9
Bridgetown, *Barbados*	87	D8
Bridgewater, *Canada*	71	E7
Bridgewater, C., *Australia*	62	C3
Bridlington, *U.K.*	11	D6
Bridport, *Australia*	62	D4
Brigham City, *U.S.A.*	73	F7
Bright, *Australia*	63	C4
Brighton, *Australia*	62	C2
Brighton, *U.K.*	11	F6
Brindisi, *Italy*	21	D6
Brisbane, *Australia*	63	A5
Brisbane ➜, *Australia*	63	A5
Bristol, *U.K.*	11	F5
Bristol, *U.S.A.*	83	A6
Bristol B., *U.S.A.*	69	C3
Bristol Channel, *U.K.*	11	F4
British Indian Ocean Terr. =		
Chagos Arch. □, *Ind. Oc.*	26	J9
British Virgin Is. ☑, *W. Indies*	87	C7
Brittany = Bretagne □, *France*	12	B2
Brive-la-Gaillarde, *France*	12	D4

Brixen

Brixen = Bressanone, *Italy* .. **20 A3**
Brno, *Czech Rep.* **16 D3**
Brock I., *Canada* **70 B2**
Brocken, *Germany* **14 C6**
Brodeur Pen., *Canada* **70 B5**
Brodnica, *Poland* **16 B4**
Brody, *Ukraine* **17 C7**
Broken Hill, *Australia* **62 B3**
Brooks Range, *U.S.A.* **69 B5**
Broome, *Australia* **60 D3**
Broughton Island =
  Qikiqtarjuaq, *Canada* **70 C7**
Brown, Pt., *Australia* **62 B1**
Brownsville, *U.S.A.* **81 G5**
Brownwood, *U.S.A.* **80 D4**
Bruay-la-Buissière, *France* .. **13 A5**
Bruce, Mt., *Australia* **60 E2**
Bruck an der Mur, *Austria* ... **15 E8**
Bruges = Brugge, *Belgium* .. **14 C2**
Brugge, *Belgium* **14 C2**
Brumado, *Brazil* **93 E5**
Brunei = Bandar Seri
  Begawan, *Brunei* **38 D5**
Brunei ■, *Asia* **38 D4**
Brunner, L., *N.Z.* **65 E4**
Brunswick = Braunschweig,
  Germany **14 B6**
Brunswick, *U.S.A.* **83 D7**
Brunswick, Pen. de, *Chile* .. **95 G2**
Brussel, *Belgium* **14 C3**
Brussels = Brussel, *Belgium* . **14 C3**
Bruthen, *Australia* **63 C4**
Bruxelles = Brussel, *Belgium* **14 C3**
Bryan, *U.S.A.* **81 D5**
Bryan, Mt., *Australia* **62 B2**
Bryansk, *Russia* **24 C3**
Bu Craa, *W. Sahara* **52 C3**
Buapinang, *Indonesia* **37 E2**
Bucak, *Turkey* **46 C2**
Bucaramanga, *Colombia* ... **90 B4**
Buchach, *Ukraine* **17 D7**
Buchanan, *Liberia* **53 G3**
Bucharest = Bucureşti,
  Romania **22 B6**
Buckie, *U.K.* **10 C5**
Buckleboo, *Australia* **62 B2**
Bucureşti, *Romania* **22 B6**
Budalin, *Burma* **41 F10**
Budapest, *Hungary* **16 E4**
Budd Coast, *Antarctica* **96 A12**
Bude, *U.K.* **11 F4**
Budennovsk, *Russia* **25 E5**
Budgewoi, *Australia* **63 B5**
Budjala, *Dem. Rep. of
  the Congo* **56 D3**
Buenaventura, *Colombia* ... **90 C3**
Buenos Aires, *Argentina* ... **94 C5**
Buenos Aires, L., *Argentina* . **95 F2**
Buffalo, *U.S.A.* **77 C6**
Bug = Buh →, *Ukraine* **25 D3**
Bug →, *Poland* **16 B5**
Buga, *Colombia* **90 C3**
Bugel, Tanjung, *Indonesia* .. **39 F4**
Bugsuk I., *Phil.* **38 C5**
Bugun Shara, *Mongolia* ... **35 B5**
Buguruslan, *Russia* **29 D6**
Buh →, *Ukraine* **25 D3**
Buir Nur, *Mongolia* **35 B6**
Bujumbura, *Burundi* **57 E5**
Bukavu, *Dem. Rep. of
  the Congo* **57 E5**
Bukhara = Bukhoro,
  Uzbekistan **29 F7**
Bukhoro, *Uzbekistan* **29 F7**
Bukittinggi, *Indonesia* **39 E2**
Bukoba, *Tanzania* **57 E6**
Bula, *Indonesia* **37 E4**
Bulahdelah, *Australia* **63 B5**
Bulan, *Phil.* **36 B2**
Bulandshahr, *India* **42 E10**
Bulawayo, *Zimbabwe* **59 C5**
Buldan, *Turkey* **23 E7**
Bulgan, *Mongolia* **35 B5**
Bulgaria ■, *Europe* **22 C5**
Buli, Teluk, *Indonesia* **37 D3**
Buliluyan, C., *Phil.* **38 C5**
Bulloo →, *Australia* **63 A3**

Bulloo L., *Australia* **62 A3**
Bulls, *N.Z.* **64 D6**
Bulsar = Valsad, *India* **43 J8**
Bulukumba, *Indonesia* **37 F2**
Bulun, *Russia* **30 B10**
Bumba, *Dem. Rep. of
  the Congo* **56 D4**
Bumhpa Bum, *Burma* **41 D11**
Bunbury, *Australia* **60 G2**
Buncrana, *Ireland* **11 D3**
Bundaberg, *Australia* **63 A5**
Bundi, *India* **43 G9**
Bundoran, *Ireland* **11 D2**
Bungo Channel, *Japan* **33 G3**
Bunia, *Dem. Rep. of
  the Congo* **57 D6**
Bunji, *Pakistan* **42 B9**
Buntok, *Indonesia* **39 E4**
Bunyu, *Indonesia* **39 D5**
Buol, *Indonesia* **37 D2**
Buon Ma Thuot, *Vietnam* .. **38 B3**
Buorkhaya, Mys, *Russia* **31 B11**
Buqayq, *Si. Arabia* **47 F7**
Bur Acaba, *Somali Rep.* **49 G3**
Bûr Safâga, *Egypt* **54 C5**
Bûr Sa'îd, *Egypt* **54 B5**
Bûr Sûdân, *Sudan* **55 E6**
Burao, *Somali Rep.* **49 F4**
Buraydah, *Si. Arabia* **47 F6**
Burdur, *Turkey* **46 C2**
Burdwan = Barddhaman, *India* **40 F6**
Burgas, *Bulgaria* **22 C6**
Burgos, *Spain* **18 A4**
Burgundy = Bourgogne □,
  France **13 C6**
Burhaniye, *Turkey* **23 E6**
Burhanpur, *India* **43 J10**
Burias I., *Phil.* **36 B2**
Buriram, *Thailand* **38 A2**
Burkina Faso ■, *Africa* **53 F5**
Burlington, *Iowa, U.S.A.* **75 E9**
Burlington, *N.C., U.S.A.* **83 A8**
Burlington, *Vt., U.S.A.* **77 B9**
Burlyu-Tyube, *Kazakhstan* .. **29 E8**
Burma ■, *Asia* **41 G11**
Burnie, *Australia* **62 D4**
Burnley, *U.K.* **11 E5**
Burnside →, *Canada* **68 B9**
Burqān, *Kuwait* **47 E6**
Burqin, *China* **34 B3**
Burra, *Australia* **62 B2**
Burren Junction, *Australia* .. **63 B4**
Burrinjuck Res., *Australia* ... **63 C4**
Burruyacú, *Argentina* **94 B4**
Bursa, *Turkey* **23 D7**
Buru, *Indonesia* **37 E3**
Burundi ■, *Africa* **57 E6**
Burutu, *Nigeria* **53 G7**
Bury St. Edmunds, *U.K.* **11 E7**
Busan, *S. Korea* **35 C7**
Büshehr, *Iran* **44 D2**
Büshehr □, *Iran* **44 D2**
Bushire = Büshehr, *Iran* **44 D2**
Businga, *Dem. Rep. of
  the Congo* **56 D4**
Buşra ash Shām, *Syria* **46 D4**
Busto Arsízio, *Italy* **13 D8**
Busu Djanoa, *Dem. Rep. of
  the Congo* **56 D4**
Busuanga I., *Phil.* **36 B1**
Buta, *Dem. Rep. of the Congo* **57 D4**
Butare, *Rwanda* **57 E5**
Butaritari, *Kiribati* **64 J12**
Butembo, *Dem. Rep. of
  the Congo* **57 D5**
Butha Qi, *China* **35 B7**
Buton, *Indonesia* **37 E2**
Butte, *U.S.A.* **73 C7**
Butterworth = Gcuwa,
  S. Africa **59 E5**
Butterworth, *Malaysia* **38 C2**
Butuan, *Phil.* **36 C3**
Butung = Buton, *Indonesia* .. **37 E2**
Buturlinovka, *Russia* **24 C5**
Buur Hakaba = Bur Acaba,
  Somali Rep. **49 G3**
Buxoro = Bukhoro, *Uzbekistan* **29 F7**

Buxtehude, *Germany* **14 B5**
Buy, *Russia* **24 B5**
Buyant-Uhaa, *Mongolia* ... **35 B6**
Büyük Menderes →, *Turkey* . **23 F6**
Büyükçekmece, *Turkey* **22 D7**
Buzău, *Romania* **17 F8**
Buzău →, *Romania* **17 F8**
Buzen, *Japan* **33 G2**
Buzi →, *Mozam.* **59 B6**
Buzuluk, *Russia* **29 D6**
Byarezina →, *Belarus* **17 B10**
Byaroza, *Belarus* **17 B7**
Bydgoszcz, *Poland* **16 B3**
Byelorussia = Belarus ■,
  Europe **24 C2**
Bykhaw, *Belarus* **17 B10**
Bykhov = Bykhaw, *Belarus* .. **17 B10**
Bylot I., *Canada* **70 B6**
Byrd, C., *Antarctica* **96 A3**
Byrock, *Australia* **63 B4**
Byron Bay, *Australia* **63 A5**
Byrranga, Gory, *Russia* **30 B8**
Bytom, *Poland* **16 C4**
Bytów, *Poland* **16 A3**

C

Ca Mau, *Vietnam* **38 C3**
Caála, *Angola* **58 A3**
Cabanatuan, *Phil.* **36 A2**
Cabedelo, *Brazil* **92 D7**
Cabimas, *Venezuela* **90 A4**
Cabinda, *Angola* **56 F2**
Cabinda □, *Angola* **56 F2**
Cabinet Mts., *U.S.A.* **73 C6**
Cabo Blanco, *Argentina* ... **95 F3**
Cabo Frio, *Brazil* **93 G5**
Cabo Pantoja, *Peru* **90 D3**
Cabo Verde = Cape Verde
  Is. ■, *Atl. Oc.* **50 E1**
Cabonga, Réservoir, *Canada* **71 E6**
Caboolture, *Australia* **63 A5**
Cabora Bassa Dam = Cahora
  Bassa, Reprêsa de, *Mozam.* **59 B6**
Cabot Str., *Canada* **71 E8**
Cabra, *Spain* **18 D3**
Cabrera, *Spain* **19 C7**
Cabriel →, *Spain* **19 C5**
Čačak, *Serbia & M.* **22 C3**
Cáceres, *Brazil* **91 G7**
Cáceres, *Spain* **18 C2**
Cachimbo, Serra do, *Brazil* .. **93 D2**
Cachoeira, *Brazil* **93 E6**
Cachoeira do Sul, *Brazil* ... **94 C6**
Cachoeiro de Itapemirim,
  Brazil **93 G5**
Cacólo, *Angola* **56 G3**
Caconda, *Angola* **58 A3**
Cadibarrawirracanna, L.,
  Australia **62 A2**
Cadiz, *Phil.* **36 B2**
Cádiz, *Spain* **18 D2**
Cádiz, G. de, *Spain* **18 D2**
Cadney Park, *Australia* **62 A1**
Caen, *France* **12 B3**
Caetité, *Brazil* **93 E5**
Cagayan de Oro, *Phil.* **36 C2**
Cágliari, *Italy* **21 E2**
Cágliari, G. di, *Italy* **21 E2**
Caguas, *Puerto Rico* **87 C6**
Cahora Bassa, Reprêsa de,
  Mozam. **59 B6**
Cahors, *France* **12 D4**
Cahul, *Moldova* **17 F9**
Caicara, *Venezuela* **90 B5**
Caicó, *Brazil* **92 D6**
Caird Coast, *Antarctica* **96 B5**
Cairns, *Australia* **61 D8**
Cairo = El Qâhira, *Egypt* ... **54 B5**
Cairo, *U.S.A.* **81 A9**
Cajamarca, *Peru* **91 E3**
Cajàzeiras, *Brazil* **92 D6**
Calabar, *Nigeria* **53 H7**
Calábria □, *Italy* **21 E6**
Calafate, *Argentina* **95 G2**

106

Calahorra, *Spain* 19 A5
Calais, *France* 12 A4
Calama, *Brazil* 91 E6
Calama, *Chile* 94 A3
Calamar, *Colombia* 90 A4
Calamian Group, *Phil.* 36 B1
Calamocha, *Spain* 19 B5
Calang, *Indonesia* 38 D1
Calapan, *Phil.* 36 B2
Călăraşi, *Romania* 22 B6
Calatayud, *Spain* 19 B5
Calauag, *Phil.* 36 B2
Calavite, C., *Phil.* 36 B2
Calbayog, *Phil.* 36 B2
Calca, *Peru* 91 F4
Calcutta = Kolkata, *India* .. 41 F7
Caldas da Rainha, *Portugal* .. 18 C1
Caldera, *Chile* 94 B2
Caldwell, *U.S.A.* 72 E5
Caledon →, *S. Africa* 59 E5
Calgary, *Canada* 69 C8
Cali, *Colombia* 90 C3
Calicut, *India* 43 P9
California □, *U.S.A.* 78 B3
California, G. de, *Mexico* 84 B2
Calingasta, *Argentina* 94 C3
Callabonna, L., *Australia* .. 62 A3
Callao, *Peru* 91 F3
Caloundra, *Australia* 63 A5
Caltagirone, *Italy* 21 F5
Caltanissetta, *Italy* 21 F5
Calulo, *Angola* 56 G2
Calvi, *France* 13 E8
Calviá, *Spain* 19 C7
Calvinia, *S. Africa* 58 E3
Camabatela, *Angola* 56 F3
Camacupa, *Angola* 58 A3
Camagüey, *Cuba* 86 B4
Camaná, *Peru* 91 G4
Camargue, *France* 13 E6
Camarones, *Argentina* 95 E3
Cambay = Khambhat, *India* . 43 H8
Cambay, G. of = Khambhat, G.
  of, *India* 43 J8
Cambodia ■, *Asia* 38 B3
Cambrai, *France* 13 A5
Cambrian Mts., *U.K.* 11 E5
Cambridge, *N.Z.* 64 B6
Cambridge, *U.K.* 11 E7
Cambridge, *U.S.A.* 77 C10
Cambridge Bay = Ikaluktutiak,
  Canada 68 B9
Cambundi-Catembo, *Angola* 56 G3
Camden, *Ark., U.S.A.* 81 C7
Camden, *N.J., U.S.A.* 77 E8
Cameroon ■, *Africa* 56 C2
Cameroun, Mt., *Cameroon* .. 53 H7
Cametá, *Brazil* 92 C4
Caminha, *Portugal* 18 B1
Camira Creek, *Australia* ... 63 A5
Camocim, *Brazil* 92 C5
Campana, I., *Chile* 95 F1
Campánia □, *Italy* 21 D5
Campbell Town, *Australia* .. 62 D4
Campbellton, *Canada* 71 E7
Campbelltown, *Australia* ... 63 B5
Campbeltown, *U.K.* 10 D4
Campeche, *Mexico* 85 D6
Campeche, Golfo de, *Mexico* 85 D6
Camperdown, *Australia* 62 C3
Câmpina, *Romania* 17 F7
Campina Grande, *Brazil* ... 92 D6
Campinas, *Brazil* 94 A7
Campo Grande, *Brazil* 93 G3
Campo Maior, *Brazil* 92 C5
Campobasso, *Italy* 20 D5
Campos, *Brazil* 93 G5
Campos Belos, *Brazil* 93 E4
Câmpulung, *Romania* 17 F7
Camrose, *Canada* 69 C8
Çan, *Turkey* 23 D6
Can Tho, *Vietnam* 38 B3
Canada ■, *N. Amer.* 68 C8
Cañada de Gómez, *Argentina* 94 C4
Çanakkale, *Turkey* 23 D6
Çanakkale Boğazı, *Turkey* .. 23 D6
Cananea, *Mexico* 84 A2

Canarias, Is., *Atl. Oc.* 52 C2
Canary Is. = Canarias, Is.,
  Atl. Oc. 52 C2
Canavieiras, *Brazil* 93 F6
Canberra, *Australia* 63 C4
Candelo, *Australia* 63 C4
Candia = Iraklio, *Greece* ... 23 G5
Canea = Chania, *Greece* ... 23 G5
Canelones, *Uruguay* 94 C5
Cañete, *Chile* 94 D2
Cañete, *Peru* 91 F3
Cangas de Narcea, *Spain* .. 18 A2
Canguaretama, *Brazil* 92 D6
Canguçu, *Brazil* 94 C6
Caniapiscau →, *Canada* ... 70 D7
Caniapiscau, L. de, *Canada* . 71 D7
Canicattì, *Italy* 21 F4
Çankırı, *Turkey* 25 E3
Cann River, *Australia* 63 C4
Cannanore, *India* 43 P9
Cannes, *France* 13 E7
Canoas, *Brazil* 94 B6
Canora, *Canada* 69 C9
Canowindra, *Australia* 63 B4
Cantabria □, *Spain* 18 A4
Cantabrian Mts. = Cantábrica,
  Cordillera, *Spain* 18 A3
Cantábrica, Cordillera, *Spain* 18 A3
Cantal, Plomb du, *France* .. 13 D5
Canterbury, *U.K.* 11 F7
Canterbury Bight, *N.Z.* 65 F4
Canterbury Plains, *N.Z.* 65 E4
Canton = Guangzhou, *China* . 35 D6
Canton, *U.S.A.* 76 D5
Canudos, *Brazil* 91 E7
Canutama, *Brazil* 91 E6
Cap-Haïtien, *Haiti* 87 C5
Capanaparo →, *Venezuela* . 90 B5
Cape Barren I., *Australia* ... 62 D4
Cape Breton I., *Canada* 71 E7
Cape Coast, *Ghana* 53 G5
Cape Dorset, *Canada* 70 C6
Cape Girardeau, *U.S.A.* 81 A9
Cape Town, *S. Africa* 58 E3
Cape Verde Is. ■, *Atl. Oc.* ... 50 E1
Cape York Peninsula,
  Australia 61 C7
Capela, *Brazil* 93 E6
Capim →, *Brazil* 92 C4
Capraia, *Italy* 13 E8
Capri, *Italy* 21 D5
Caprivi Strip, *Namibia* 58 B4
Captain's Flat, *Australia* ... 63 C4
Caquetá →, *Colombia* 90 D5
Caracal, *Romania* 22 B5
Caracas, *Venezuela* 90 A5
Caracol, *Brazil* 93 D5
Carajás, Serra dos, *Brazil* .. 92 D3
Caransebeş, *Romania* 17 F6
Caratasca, L., *Honduras* ... 86 C3
Caratinga, *Brazil* 93 F5
Caraúbas, *Brazil* 92 D6
Caravaca de la Cruz, *Spain* . 19 C5
Caravelas, *Brazil* 93 F6
Caraveli, *Peru* 91 G4
Carballo, *Spain* 18 A1
Carbonara, C., *Italy* 21 E2
Carbondale, *U.S.A.* 81 A9
Carbonear, *Canada* 71 E8
Carbónia, *Italy* 21 E2
Carcassonne, *France* 12 E5
Carcross, *Canada* 68 B6
Cardamon Hills, *India* 43 Q10
Cárdenas, *Cuba* 86 B3
Cardiff, *U.K.* 11 F5
Cardigan B., *U.K.* 11 E4
Cardston, *Canada* 69 D8
Carei, *Romania* 17 E6
Caria, *Turkey* 23 F7
Cariacica, *Brazil* 93 G5
Caribbean Sea, *W. Indies* .. 86 D5
Cariboo Mts., *Canada* 69 C7
Carinda, *Australia* 63 B4
Carinhanha, *Brazil* 93 E5
Carinthia = Kärnten □, *Austria* 15 E7
Caripito, *Venezuela* 90 A6

Carlisle, *U.K.* 11 D5
Carlow, *Ireland* 11 E3
Carlsbad, *U.S.A.* 80 C1
Carmacks, *Canada* 68 B6
Carmarthen, *U.K.* 11 F4
Carmaux, *France* 12 D5
Carmen, *Colombia* 90 B3
Carmen de Patagones,
  Argentina 95 E4
Carmona, *Spain* 18 D3
Carnac, *France* 12 C2
Carnarvon, *Australia* 60 E1
Carnarvon, *S. Africa* 58 E4
Carnegie, L., *Australia* 60 F3
Carnot, *C.A.R.* 56 D3
Carnot, C., *Australia* 62 B2
Carolina, *Brazil* 92 D4
Caroline I., *Kiribati* 65 K15
Caroline Is., *Micronesia* 64 J10
Caroni →, *Venezuela* 90 B6
Caronie = Nébrodi, Monti,
  Italy 21 F5
Caroona, *Australia* 63 B5
Carpathians, *Europe* 16 D5
Carpaţii Meridionali, *Romania* 17 F7
Carpentaria, G. of, *Australia* . 60 C6
Carpentras, *France* 13 D6
Carpi, *Italy* 20 B3
Carrara, *Italy* 13 D9
Carrauntoohill, *Ireland* 11 E2
Carrick-on-Suir, *Ireland* 11 E3
Carrieton, *Australia* 62 B2
Carrizal Bajo, *Chile* 94 B2
Carson City, *U.S.A.* 72 G4
Cartagena, *Colombia* 90 A3
Cartagena, *Spain* 19 D5
Cartago, *Colombia* 90 C3
Cartago, *Costa Rica* 86 E3
Carterton, *N.Z.* 65 D6
Carthage, *U.S.A.* 81 A6
Cartwright, *Canada* 70 D8
Caruaru, *Brazil* 92 D6
Carúpano, *Venezuela* 90 A6
Carvoeiro, *Brazil* 90 D6
Carvoeiro, C., *Portugal* 18 C1
Casablanca, *Morocco* 52 B4
Cascade Ra., *U.S.A.* 72 C3
Cascais, *Portugal* 18 C1
Cascavel, *Brazil* 94 A6
Cáscina, *Italy* 20 C3
Caserta, *Italy* 20 D5
Caseyr, Raas = Asir, Ras,
  Somali Rep. 49 E5
Casiguran, *Phil.* 36 A2
Casilda, *Argentina* 94 C4
Casino, *Australia* 63 A5
Casiquiare →, *Venezuela* .. 90 C5
Casma, *Peru* 91 E3
Caspe, *Spain* 19 B5
Casper, *U.S.A.* 73 E10
Caspian Sea, *Eurasia* 29 E6
Castellammare di Stábia, *Italy* 21 D5
Castelló de la Plana, *Spain* . 19 C5
Castelo Branco, *Portugal* ... 18 C2
Castelsarrasin, *France* 12 D4
Castelvetrano, *Italy* 21 F4
Casterton, *Australia* 62 C3
Castilla-La Mancha □, *Spain* 18 C4
Castilla y Leon □, *Spain* ... 18 A3
Castlebar, *Ireland* 11 E2
Castleblaney, *Ireland* 11 D3
Castlemaine, *Australia* 63 C3
Castlereagh →, *Australia* .. 63 B4
Castres, *France* 12 E5
Castries, *St. Lucia* 87 D7
Castro, *Chile* 95 E2
Castro Alves, *Brazil* 93 E6
Castuera, *Spain* 18 C3
Cat I., *Bahamas* 86 B4
Catalão, *Brazil* 93 F4
Çatalca, *Turkey* 22 D7
Catalonia = Cataluña □, *Spain* 19 B6
Cataluña □, *Spain* 19 B6
Catamarca, *Argentina* 94 B3
Catanduanes □, *Phil.* 36 B2
Catanduva, *Brazil* 93 G4
Catánia, *Italy* 21 F5

Catanzaro

Catanzaro, *Italy*	21	E6
Catarman, *Phil.*	36	B2
Cateel, *Phil.*	36	C3
Catoche, C., *Mexico*	85	C7
Catrimani, *Brazil*	90	C6
Catskill Mts., *U.S.A.*	77	C8
Cauca →, *Colombia*	90	B4
Caucaia, *Brazil*	92	C6
Caucasus Mountains, *Eurasia*	25	E5
Caungula, *Angola*	56	F3
Cauquenes, *Chile*	94	D2
Caura →, *Venezuela*	90	B6
Cauvery →, *India*	43	P11
Caux, Pays de, *France*	12	B4
Cavan, *Ireland*	11	D3
Cavendish, *Australia*	62	C3
Caviana, I., *Brazil*	92	B3
Cavite, *Phil.*	36	B2
Cawndilla L., *Australia*	62	B3
Cawnpore = Kanpur, *India*	40	D3
Caxias, *Brazil*	92	C5
Caxias do Sul, *Brazil*	94	B6
Cayambe, *Ecuador*	90	C3
Cayenne, *Fr. Guiana*	92	A3
Cayman Is. ☑, *W. Indies*	86	C3
Cazombo, *Angola*	58	A4
Ceanannus Mor, *Ireland*	11	E3
Ceará = Fortaleza, *Brazil*	92	C6
Ceará ☐, *Brazil*	92	D6
Ceará Mirim, *Brazil*	92	D6
Cebollar, *Argentina*	94	B3
Cebu, *Phil.*	36	B2
Cecil Plains, *Australia*	63	A5
Cedar L., *Canada*	69	C10
Cedar Rapids, *U.S.A.*	75	E9
Cedro, *Brazil*	92	D6
Ceduna, *Australia*	62	B1
Ceerigaabo = Erigavo, *Somali Rep.*	49	E4
Cefalù, *Italy*	21	E5
Cegléd, *Hungary*	16	E4
Celaya, *Mexico*	84	C4
Celebes = Sulawesi, *Indonesia*	37	E2
Celebes Sea, *Indonesia*	37	D2
Celje, *Slovenia*	20	A5
Celle, *Germany*	14	B6
Celtic Sea, *Atl. Oc.*	11	F2
Central, Cordillera, *Colombia*	90	C3
Central African Rep. ■, *Africa*	56	C4
Central Makran Range, *Pakistan*	42	F4
Cephalonia = Kefalonia, *Greece*	23	E3
Ceram = Seram, *Indonesia*	37	E3
Ceram Sea = Seram Sea, *Indonesia*	37	E3
Ceres, *Argentina*	94	B4
Cerignola, *Italy*	20	D5
Cerigo = Kythira, *Greece*	23	F4
Çerkeş, *Turkey*	46	B3
Çerkezköy, *Turkey*	22	D6
Cervera, *Spain*	19	B6
Cesena, *Italy*	20	B4
Ceská Rep. = Czech Rep. ■, *Europe*	16	D2
České Budějovice, *Czech Rep.*	16	D2
Českomoravská Vrchovina, *Czech Rep.*	16	D2
Çeşme, *Turkey*	23	E6
Cessnock, *Australia*	63	B5
Cetinje, *Serbia & M.*	22	C2
Cetraro, *Italy*	21	E5
Ceuta, *N. Afr.*	18	E3
Cévennes, *France*	13	D5
Ceylon = Sri Lanka ■, *Asia*	43	R12
Chachapoyas, *Peru*	91	E3
Chachran, *Pakistan*	42	E7
Chad ■, *Africa*	55	E2
Chad, L. = Tchad, L., *Chad*	55	F1
Chadileuvú →, *Argentina*	94	D3
Chadyr-Lunga = Ciadâr-Lunga, *Moldova*	17	E9
Chagai Hills = Chāh Gay Hills, *Afghan.*	42	E3
Chagos Arch. ☑, *Ind. Oc.*	26	J9
Chāh Bahar, *Iran*	45	E5
Chāh Gay Hills, *Afghan.*	42	E3
Chahār Borjak, *Afghan.*	42	D3
Chaibasa, *India*	40	F5
Chakhānsūr, *Afghan.*	42	D3
Chakradharpur, *India*	40	F5
Chakwal, *Pakistan*	42	C8
Chala, *Peru*	91	G4
Chalcis = Halkida, *Greece*	23	E4
Chalhuanca, *Peru*	91	F4
Chalisgaon, *India*	43	J9
Chalky Inlet, *N.Z.*	65	G2
Challapata, *Bolivia*	91	G5
Chalon-sur-Saône, *France*	13	C6
Châlons-en-Champagne, *France*	13	B6
Chaman, *Pakistan*	42	D5
Chamba, *India*	42	C10
Chambal →, *India*	42	F11
Chambéry, *France*	13	D6
Chamical, *Argentina*	94	C3
Chamonix-Mont Blanc, *France*	13	D7
Champagne, *France*	13	B6
Champaign, *U.S.A.*	76	D1
Champlain, L., *U.S.A.*	77	B9
Chañaral, *Chile*	94	B2
Chandigarh, *India*	42	D10
Chandler, *Australia*	62	A1
Chandpur, *Bangla.*	41	F8
Chandrapur, *India*	43	K11
Chang Jiang →, *China*	35	C7
Changanacheri, *India*	43	Q10
Changane →, *Mozam.*	59	C6
Changchiak'ou = Zhangjiakou, *China*	35	B6
Ch'angchou = Changzhou, *China*	35	C6
Changchun, *China*	35	B7
Changde, *China*	35	D6
Changhai = Shanghai, *China*	35	C7
Changhua, *Taiwan*	35	D7
Changsha, *China*	35	D6
Changzhi, *China*	35	C6
Changzhou, *China*	35	C6
Chania, *Greece*	23	G5
Chanion, Kolpos, *Greece*	23	G4
Channapatna, *India*	43	N10
Channel Is., *U.K.*	11	G5
Channel-Port aux Basques, *Canada*	71	E8
Chantada, *Spain*	18	A2
Chanthaburi, *Thailand*	38	B2
Chantrey Inlet, *Canada*	68	B10
Chanute, *U.S.A.*	81	A6
Chao Phraya →, *Thailand*	38	B2
Chaozhou, *China*	35	D6
Chapala, L. de, *Mexico*	84	C4
Chapayevsk, *Russia*	24	C6
Chapleau, *Canada*	71	E5
Chapra = Chhapra, *India*	40	E5
Chara, *Russia*	31	D9
Charagua, *Bolivia*	91	G6
Charaña, *Bolivia*	91	G5
Chardzhou = Türkmenabat, *Turkmenistan*	29	F7
Charente →, *France*	12	D3
Chari →, *Chad*	55	F1
Chārīkār, *Afghan.*	42	B6
Chärjew = Türkmenabat, *Turkmenistan*	29	F7
Charleroi, *Belgium*	14	C3
Charles, C., *U.S.A.*	77	F8
Charleston, *S.C., U.S.A.*	83	C8
Charleston, *W. Va., U.S.A.*	76	E5
Charleville, *Australia*	63	A4
Charleville-Mézières, *France*	13	B6
Charlotte, *U.S.A.*	83	B7
Charlotte Amalie, *U.S. Virgin Is.*	87	C6
Charlottesville, *U.S.A.*	77	E6
Charlottetown, *Canada*	71	E7
Charlton, *Australia*	62	C3
Charlton I., *Canada*	71	D6
Charolles, *France*	13	C6
Charters Towers, *Australia*	61	E8
Chartres, *France*	12	B4
Chascomús, *Argentina*	94	D5
Châteaubriant, *France*	12	C3
Châteaulin, *France*	12	B1
Châteauroux, *France*	12	C4
Châtellerault, *France*	12	C4
Chatham = Miramichi, *Canada*	71	E7
Chatham, *U.K.*	11	F7
Chatrapur, *India*	40	H5
Châttagâm = Chittagong, *Bangla.*	41	F8
Chattahoochee →, *U.S.A.*	82	D5
Chattanooga, *U.S.A.*	82	B5
Chaukan Pass, *Burma*	41	D11
Chaumont, *France*	13	B6
Chaves, *Brazil*	92	C4
Chaves, *Portugal*	18	B2
Cheb, *Czech Rep.*	16	C1
Cheboksary, *Russia*	24	B6
Chech, Erg, *Africa*	52	D5
Chechenia ☐, *Russia*	25	E6
Chechnya = Chechenia ☐, *Russia*	25	E6
Cheduba I., *Burma*	41	H9
Cheepie, *Australia*	63	A4
Chegga, *Mauritania*	52	C4
Chegutu, *Zimbabwe*	59	B6
Chehalis, *U.S.A.*	72	C2
Cheju-do = Jeju-do, *S. Korea*	35	C7
Chekiang = Zhejiang ☐, *China*	35	D7
Cheleken = Hazar, *Turkmenistan*	29	F6
Chelforó, *Argentina*	95	D3
Chelkar = Shalqar, *Kazakhstan*	29	E6
Chelkar Tengiz, Solonchak, *Kazakhstan*	29	E7
Chełm, *Poland*	17	C6
Chełmno, *Poland*	16	B4
Chelmsford, *U.K.*	11	F7
Cheltenham, *U.K.*	11	F5
Chelyabinsk, *Russia*	29	D7
Chelyuskin, Mys, *Russia*	30	B8
Chemba, *Mozam.*	59	B6
Chemnitz, *Germany*	15	C7
Chenab →, *Pakistan*	42	D7
Chengchou = Zhengzhou, *China*	35	C6
Chengde, *China*	35	B6
Chengdu, *China*	35	C5
Chengjiang, *China*	34	D5
Ch'engtu = Chengdu, *China*	35	C5
Chennai, *India*	43	N12
Cheom Ksan, *Cambodia*	38	B2
Chepén, *Peru*	91	E3
Chepes, *Argentina*	94	C3
Cher →, *France*	12	C4
Cherbourg, *France*	12	B3
Cherdyn, *Russia*	28	C6
Cherepanovo, *Russia*	29	D9
Cherepovets, *Russia*	24	B4
Chergui, Chott ech, *Algeria*	52	B6
Cherikov = Cherykaw, *Belarus*	17	B10
Cherkasy, *Ukraine*	24	D3
Cherlak, *Russia*	29	D8
Chernaya, *Russia*	30	B6
Chernigov = Chernihiv, *Ukraine*	24	C3
Chernihiv, *Ukraine*	24	C3
Chernivtsi, *Ukraine*	17	D7
Chernobyl = Chornobyl, *Ukraine*	17	C10
Chernovtsy = Chernivtsi, *Ukraine*	17	D7
Cherrapunji, *India*	41	E8
Cherven, *Belarus*	17	B9
Chervonohrad, *Ukraine*	17	C7
Cherykaw, *Belarus*	17	B10
Chesapeake, *U.S.A.*	77	F7
Chesapeake B., *U.S.A.*	77	E7
Cheshskaya Guba, *Russia*	28	C5
Chester, *U.K.*	11	E5
Chester, *U.S.A.*	77	E8
Chesterfield, *U.K.*	11	E6
Chesterfield, Îs., *N. Cal.*	64	L10
Chesterfield Inlet, *Canada*	68	B10
Chesterton Ra., *Australia*	63	A4
Chetumal, *Mexico*	85	D7
Cheviot Hills, *U.K.*	10	D5
Chew Bahir, *Ethiopia*	55	H6
Cheyenne, *U.S.A.*	74	E2
Cheyenne →, *U.S.A.*	74	C4

Chhapra, *India* 40 E5
Chhatarpur, *India* 43 G11
Chhindwara, *India* 43 H11
Chi ➸, *Thailand* 38 A2
Chiai, *Taiwan* 35 D7
Chiávari, *Italy* 13 D8
Chiavenna, *Italy* 13 C8
Chiba, *Japan* 33 F7
Chibemba, *Angola* 58 B2
Chibia, *Angola* 58 B2
Chibougamau, *Canada* 71 E6
Chicacole = Srikakulam, *India* 40 H4
Chicago, *U.S.A.* 76 D2
Chichagof I., *U.S.A.* 69 C6
Ch'ich'ihaerh = Qiqihar, *China* 35 B7
Chickasha, *U.S.A.* 80 B5
Chiclana de la Frontera, *Spain* 18 D2
Chiclayo, *Peru* 91 E3
Chico, *U.S.A.* 72 G3
Chico ➸, *Chubut, Argentina* 95 E3
Chico ➸, *Santa Cruz,*
  Argentina 95 F3
Chicoutimi, *Canada* 71 E6
Chidambaram, *India* 43 P11
Chidley, C., *Canada* 70 C7
Chiemsee, *Germany* 15 E7
Chiese ➸, *Italy* 13 D9
Chieti, *Italy* 20 C5
Chiguana, *Bolivia* 91 H5
Chihli, G. of = Bo Hai, *China* . 35 C6
Chihuahua, *Mexico* 84 B3
Chiili = Shieli, *Kazakhstan* . . 29 E7
Chik Bollapur, *India* 43 N10
Chikmagalur, *India* 43 N9
Chilapa, *Mexico* 84 D5
Chilas, *Pakistan* 42 B9
Chilaw, *Sri Lanka* 43 R11
Childers, *Australia* 63 A5
Chile ■, *S. Amer.* 94 D2
Chilete, *Peru* 91 E3
Chililabombwe, *Zambia* 59 A5
Chilin = Jilin, *China* 35 B7
Chilka L., *India* 40 H5
Chillán, *Chile* 94 D2
Chiloé, I. de, *Chile* 95 E2
Chilpancingo, *Mexico* 84 D5
Chilung, *Taiwan* 35 D7
Chilwa, L., *Malawi* 59 B7
Chimbay, *Uzbekistan* 29 E6
Chimborazo, *Ecuador* 90 D3
Chimbote, *Peru* 91 E3
Chimkent = Shymkent,
  Kazakhstan 29 E7
Chimoio, *Mozam.* 59 B6
Chin □, *Burma* 41 F9
China ■, *Asia* 35 C5
Chinan = Jinan, *China* 35 C6
Chinandega, *Nic.* 85 E7
Chincha Alta, *Peru* 91 F3
Chinchilla, *Australia* 63 A5
Chinchou = Jinzhou, *China* . . 35 B7
Chinde, *Mozam.* 59 B7
Chindwin ➸, *Burma* 41 G10
Chingola, *Zambia* 59 A5
Ch'ingtao = Qingdao, *China* . 35 C7
Chinguetti, *Mauritania* 52 D3
Chinhoyi, *Zimbabwe* 59 B6
Chiniot, *Pakistan* 42 D8
Chinnampo = Namp'o,
  N. Korea 35 C7
Chinon, *France* 12 C4
Chióggia, *Italy* 20 B4
Chíos = Hios, *Greece* 23 E6
Chipata, *Zambia* 59 A6
Chiquián, *Peru* 91 F3
Chiquinquira, *Colombia* 90 B4
Chirchiq, *Uzbekistan* 29 E7
Chiredzi, *Zimbabwe* 59 C6
Chirmiri, *India* 40 F4
Chisasibi, *Canada* 71 D6
Chişinău, *Moldova* 17 E9
Chistopol, *Russia* 24 B7
Chita, *Russia* 30 D9
Chitral, *Pakistan* 42 B7
Chitré, *Panama* 86 E3
Chittagong, *Bangla.* 41 F8

Chittagong □, *Bangla.* 41 E8
Chittaurgarh, *India* 43 G9
Chittoor, *India* 43 N11
Chitungwiza, *Zimbabwe* 59 B6
Chiusi, *Italy* 20 C3
Chivasso, *Italy* 13 D7
Chivilcoy, *Argentina* 94 B4
Chkalov = Orenburg, *Russia* . 29 D6
Choele Choel, *Argentina* 95 D3
Chojnice, *Poland* 16 B3
Cholet, *France* 12 C3
Choluteca, *Honduras* 85 E7
Choma, *Zambia* 59 B5
Chomolungma = Everest, Mt.,
  Nepal 40 C6
Chomutov, *Czech Rep.* 16 C1
Chon Buri, *Thailand* 38 B2
Chone, *Ecuador* 90 D3
Ch'öngjin, *N. Korea* 35 B7
Chongqing, *China* 35 D5
Chonos, Arch. de los, *Chile* . . 95 F2
Chop, *Ukraine* 17 D6
Chora Sfakion, *Greece* 23 G5
Chornobyl, *Ukraine* 17 C10
Chortkiv, *Ukraine* 17 D7
Chorzów, *Poland* 16 C4
Chos-Malal, *Argentina* 94 D2
Choszczno, *Poland* 16 B2
Chotila, *India* 43 H7
Choybalsan, *Mongolia* 35 B6
Christchurch, *N.Z.* 65 E5
Christmas I. = Kiritimati,
  Kiribati 65 J15
Chū = Shū, *Kazakhstan* 29 E8
Ch'uanchou = Quanzhou,
  China 35 D6
Chubut ➸, *Argentina* 95 E3
Chudskoye, Ozero, *Russia* . . 24 B2
Chūgoku-Sanchi, *Japan* 33 F3
Chula Vista, *U.S.A.* 78 D4
Chulucanas, *Peru* 90 E2
Chulym ➸, *Russia* 29 D9
Chumbicha, *Argentina* 94 B3
Chumphon, *Thailand* 38 B1
Chuna ➸, *Russia* 30 D7
Chuncheon, *S. Korea* 35 C7
Chungking = Chongqing,
  China 35 D5
Chunya, *Tanzania* 57 F6
Chuquibamba, *Peru* 91 G4
Chuquicamata, *Chile* 94 A3
Chur, *Switz.* 13 C8
Churachandpur, *India* 41 E9
Churchill, *Canada* 68 C10
Churchill ➸, *Man., Canada* . . 68 C10
Churchill ➸, *Nfld. & L.,*
  Canada 71 D7
Churchill, C., *Canada* 68 C10
Churchill Falls, *Canada* 71 D7
Churchill L., *Canada* 69 C9
Churu, *India* 42 E9
Chushal, *India* 42 C11
Chusovoy, *Russia* 28 D6
Chuuk, *Micronesia* 64 J10
Chuvashia □, *Russia* 24 B6
Ciadâr-Lunga, *Moldova* 17 E9
Cicero, *U.S.A.* 76 D2
Ciechanów, *Poland* 16 B5
Ciego de Ávila, *Cuba* 86 B4
Ciénaga, *Colombia* 90 A4
Cienfuegos, *Cuba* 86 B3
Cieza, *Spain* 19 C5
Cijara, Embalse de, *Spain* . . 18 C3
Cill Chainnigh = Kilkenny,
  Ireland 11 E3
Cimişlia, *Moldova* 17 E9
Cimone, Mte., *Italy* 20 B3
Cinca ➸, *Spain* 19 B6
Cincar, *Bos.-H.* 20 C6
Cincinnati, *U.S.A.* 76 E3
Çine, *Turkey* 23 F7
Cinto, Mte., *France* 13 E8
Circle, *U.S.A.* 69 B5
Cirebon, *Indonesia* 39 F3
Citlaltépetl = Orizaba, Pico de,
  Mexico 84 D5

Città del Vaticano = Vatican
  City ■, *Europe* 20 D4
Città di Castello, *Italy* 20 C4
Ciudad Bolívar, *Venezuela* . . 90 B6
Ciudad de México, *Mexico* . . 84 D5
Ciudad del Carmen, *Mexico* . 85 D6
Ciudad Delicias = Delicias,
  Mexico 84 B3
Ciudad Guayana, *Venezuela* . 90 B6
Ciudad Juárez, *Mexico* 84 A3
Ciudad Madero, *Mexico* 84 C5
Ciudad Mante, *Mexico* 84 C5
Ciudad Obregón, *Mexico* . . . 84 B3
Ciudad Real, *Spain* 18 C4
Ciudad Rodrigo, *Spain* 18 B2
Ciudad Victoria, *Mexico* 84 C5
Civitanova Marche, *Italy* 20 C4
Civitavécchia, *Italy* 20 C3
Cizre, *Turkey* 46 C5
Clare, *Australia* 62 B2
Clarence ➸, *Australia* 63 A5
Clarence ➸, *N.Z.* 65 E5
Clarence, I., *Chile* 95 G2
Clarence I., *Antarctica* 96 A4
Clarie Coast, *Antarctica* 96 A13
Clarke I., *Australia* 62 D4
Clarksdale, *U.S.A.* 81 B8
Clarksville, *U.S.A.* 82 A4
Claveria, *Phil.* 36 A2
Clear, C., *Ireland* 11 F2
Clearwater, *U.S.A.* 83 F6
Clearwater Mts., *U.S.A.* 73 C6
Clermont-Ferrand, *France* . . . 13 D5
Cleveland, *U.S.A.* 76 D5
Clifden, *N.Z.* 65 G2
Clifton, *Australia* 63 A5
Clinton, *N.Z.* 65 G3
Clinton, *U.S.A.* 75 E9
Clinton Colden L., *Canada* . . 68 B9
Clones, *Ireland* 11 D3
Clonmel, *Ireland* 11 E3
Clovis, *U.S.A.* 80 B2
Cluj-Napoca, *Romania* 17 E6
Clunes, *Australia* 62 C3
Clutha ➸, *N.Z.* 65 G3
Clyde, *N.Z.* 65 F3
Clyde ➸, *U.K.* 10 D4
Clyde, Firth of, *U.K.* 10 D4
Clyde River, *Canada* 70 B7
Coari, *Brazil* 90 D6
Coast Mts., *Canada* 68 C7
Coast Ranges, *U.S.A.* 72 F2
Coats I., *Canada* 70 C5
Coats Land, *Antarctica* 96 B5
Coatzacoalcos, *Mexico* 85 D6
Cobar, *Australia* 63 B4
Cóbh, *Ireland* 11 F2
Cobija, *Bolivia* 91 F5
Cobram, *Australia* 63 C4
Coburg, *Germany* 15 C6
Cocanada = Kakinada, *India* . 40 J4
Cochabamba, *Bolivia* 91 G5
Cochin, *India* 43 Q10
Cochin China = Nam-Phan,
  Vietnam 38 B3
Cochrane, *Canada* 71 E5
Cochrane, L., *Chile* 95 F2
Cockburn, *Australia* 62 B3
Cockburn, Canal, *Chile* 95 G2
Coco ➸, *Cent. Amer.* 86 D3
Cocobeach, *Gabon* 56 D1
Cod, C., *U.S.A.* 77 C10
Codajás, *Brazil* 90 D6
Codó, *Brazil* 92 C5
Coeur d'Alene, *U.S.A.* 72 C5
Coffeyville, *U.S.A.* 81 A6
Coffin B., *Australia* 62 B2
Coffin Bay Peninsula,
  Australia 62 B2
Coffs Harbour, *Australia* 63 B5
Cognac, *France* 12 D3
Cohuna, *Australia* 63 C3
Coiba, I. de, *Panama* 86 E3
Coig ➸, *Argentina* 95 G3
Coihaique, *Chile* 95 F2
Coimbatore, *India* 43 P10

Coimbra

Coimbra, *Brazil* 91 G7
Coimbra, *Portugal* 18 B1
Coín, *Spain* 18 D3
Cojimies, *Ecuador* 90 C3
Colac, *Australia* 62 C3
Colatina, *Brazil* 93 F5
Colbeck, C., *Antarctica* 96 B17
Colchester, *U.K.* 11 F7
Coleraine, *Australia* 62 C3
Coleraine, *U.K.* 11 D3
Coleridge, L., *N.Z.* 65 E4
Colesberg, *S. Africa* 59 E5
Colhué Huapi, L., *Argentina* . 95 F3
Colima, *Mexico* 84 D4
Colinas, *Brazil* 92 D5
Coll, *U.K.* 10 C3
Collaguasi, *Chile* 91 H5
Collarenebri, *Australia* 63 A4
Collina, Passo di, *Italy* ... 20 B3
Collingwood, *N.Z.* 64 D5
Colmar, *France* 13 B7
Colo ⟶, *Australia* 63 B5
Cologne = Köln, *Germany* ... 14 C4
Colomb-Béchar = Béchar,
  Algeria 52 B5
Colombia ■, *S. Amer.* 90 C4
Colombo, *Sri Lanka* 43 R11
Colón, *Panama* 85 F9
Colonia Dora, *Argentina* ... 94 B4
Colonsay, *U.K.* 10 C3
Colorado □, *U.S.A.* 79 A10
Colorado ⟶, *Argentina* 95 D4
Colorado ⟶, *N. Amer.* 78 E5
Colorado Plateau, *U.S.A.* ... 79 B7
Colorado Springs, *U.S.A.* ... 74 F2
Columbia, *Mo., U.S.A.* 75 F8
Columbia, *S.C., U.S.A.* 83 B7
Columbia, *Tenn., U.S.A.* 82 B4
Columbia ⟶, *N. Amer.* 72 C1
Columbia, C., *Canada* 70 A7
Columbia, District of □, *U.S.A.* 77 E7
Columbia Basin, *U.S.A.* 72 C4
Columbretes, Is., *Spain* ... 19 C6
Columbus, *Ga., U.S.A.* 82 C5
Columbus, *Miss., U.S.A.* 82 C3
Columbus, *Ohio, U.S.A.* 76 E4
Colville ⟶, *U.S.A.* 69 A4
Colville, C., *N.Z.* 64 B6
Colwyn Bay, *U.K.* 11 E5
Comácchio, *Italy* 20 B4
Comallo, *Argentina* 95 E2
Comilla, *Bangla.* 41 F8
Comino, C., *Italy* 21 D2
Committee B., *Canada* 70 C5
Commonwealth B., *Antarctica* 96 A14
Commoron Cr. ⟶, *Australia* . 63 A5
Communism Pk. = imeni
  Ismail Samani, Pik,
  Tajikistan 29 F8
Como, *Italy* 13 D8
Como, Lago di, *Italy* 13 D8
Comodoro Rivadavia,
  Argentina 95 F3
Comorin, C., *India* 43 Q10
Comoros ■, *Ind. Oc.* 51 H8
Compiègne, *France* 13 B5
Comrat, *Moldova* 17 E9
Conakry, *Guinea* 53 G3
Conara, *Australia* 62 D4
Concarneau, *France* 12 C2
Conceição da Barra, *Brazil* .. 93 F6
Concepción, *Bolivia* 91 G6
Concepción, *Chile* 94 D2
Concepción, *Paraguay* 94 A5
Concepción, L., *Bolivia* 91 G6
Concepción del Oro, *Mexico* 84 C4
Concepción del Uruguay,
  Argentina 94 C5
Conchos ⟶, *Mexico* 84 B3
Concord, *N.C., U.S.A.* 83 B7
Concord, *N.H., U.S.A.* 77 C10
Concordia, *Argentina* 94 C5
Concórdia, *Brazil* 90 D5
Condamine, *Australia* 63 A5
Condeúba, *Brazil* 93 E5
Condobolin, *Australia* 63 B4

Conegliano, *Italy* 20 B4
Confuso ⟶, *Paraguay* 94 B5
Congo (Kinshasa) = Congo,
  Dem. Rep. of the ■, *Africa* 56 E4
Congo ■, *Africa* 56 E3
Congo ⟶, *Africa* 56 F2
Congo, Dem. Rep. of the ■,
  Africa 56 E4
Conjeeveram = Kanchipuram,
  India 43 N11
Conn, L., *Ireland* 11 D2
Connacht □, *Ireland* 11 E2
Connecticut □, *U.S.A.* 77 D9
Connecticut ⟶, *U.S.A.* 77 D9
Connemara, *Ireland* 11 E2
Conran, C., *Australia* 63 C4
Conselheiro Lafaiete, *Brazil* . 93 G5
Constance = Konstanz,
  Germany 14 E5
Constance, L. = Bodensee,
  Europe 13 C8
Constanţa, *Romania* 22 B7
Constantine, *Algeria* 52 A7
Constitución, *Chile* 94 D2
Contai, *India* 40 G6
Contamana, *Peru* 91 E4
Contas ⟶, *Brazil* 93 E6
Conway, L., *Australia* 62 A2
Coober Pedy, *Australia* 62 A1
Cooch Behar = Koch Bihar,
  India 41 D7
Cook, B., *Chile* 95 H2
Cook, Mt. = Aoraki Mount
  Cook, *N.Z.* 65 E4
Cook Inlet, *U.S.A.* 69 C4
Cook Is., *Pac. Oc.* 65 L14
Cook Strait, *N.Z.* 65 D6
Cooktown, *Australia* 61 D8
Coolabah, *Australia* 63 B4
Cooladdi, *Australia* 63 A4
Coolah, *Australia* 63 B4
Coolamon, *Australia* 63 B4
Cooma, *Australia* 63 C4
Coonabarabran, *Australia* .. 63 B4
Coonamble, *Australia* 63 B4
Coondapoor, *India* 43 N9
Cooninnie, L., *Australia* ... 62 A2
Cooper Cr. ⟶, *Australia* ... 62 A2
Coorong, The, *Australia* ... 62 C2
Cooroy, *Australia* 63 A5
Cootamundra, *Australia* ... 63 B4
Copenhagen = København,
  Denmark 9 D8
Copiapó, *Chile* 94 B2
Copiapó ⟶, *Chile* 94 B2
Coppermine = Kugluktuk,
  Canada 68 B8
Coppermine ⟶, *Canada* ... 68 B8
Coquimbo, *Chile* 94 C2
Corabia, *Romania* 22 C5
Coracora, *Peru* 91 G4
Coral Harbour, *Canada* 70 C5
Coral Sea, *Pac. Oc.* 64 L10
Corato, *Italy* 21 D6
Corby, *U.K.* 11 E6
Corcaigh = Cork, *Ireland* ... 11 F2
Corcubión, *Spain* 18 A1
Córdoba, *Argentina* 94 C4
Córdoba, *Spain* 18 D3
Córdoba, Sierra de, *Argentina* 94 C4
Cordova, *U.S.A.* 69 B5
Corfu = Kerkyra, *Greece* ... 23 E2
Coria, *Spain* 18 C2
Corigliano Cálabro, *Italy* 21 E6
Corinth = Korinthos, *Greece* . 23 F4
Corinth, G. of = Korinthiakos
  Kolpos, *Greece* 23 E4
Corinto, *Brazil* 93 F5
Cork, *Ireland* 11 F2
Çorlu, *Turkey* 22 D6
Corner Brook, *Canada* 71 E8
Corneşti, *Moldova* 17 E9
Cornwall, *Canada* 71 E6
Cornwall I., *Canada* 70 B4
Cornwallis I., *Canada* 70 B4
Corny Pt., *Australia* 62 B2

Coro, *Venezuela* 90 A5
Coroatá, *Brazil* 92 C5
Corocoro, *Bolivia* 91 G5
Coroico, *Bolivia* 91 G5
Coromandel, *N.Z.* 64 B6
Coronation Gulf, *Canada* ... 68 B8
Coronation I., *Antarctica* ... 96 A4
Coronel, *Chile* 94 D2
Coronel Dorrego, *Argentina* . 94 D4
Coronel Suárez, *Argentina* .. 94 D4
Corowa, *Australia* 63 C4
Corpus Christi, *U.S.A.* 80 F5
Corrib, L., *Ireland* 11 E2
Corrientes, *Argentina* 94 B5
Corrientes ⟶, *Peru* 90 D4
Corrientes, C., *Colombia* ... 90 B3
Corrientes, C., *Mexico* 84 C3
Corriverton = Skeldon,
  Guyana 90 B7
Corse □, *France* 13 E8
Corse, C., *France* 13 E8
Corsica = Corse □, *France* ... 13 E8
Corsicana, *U.S.A.* 81 C5
Corte, *France* 13 E8
Cortés, Mar de = California, G.
  de, *Mexico* 84 B2
Çorum, *Turkey* 25 E3
Corumbá, *Brazil* 91 G7
Corunna = A Coruña, *Spain* . 18 A1
Corvallis, *U.S.A.* 72 D2
Cosenza, *Italy* 21 E6
Costa Blanca, *Spain* 19 C5
Costa Brava, *Spain* 19 B7
Costa del Sol, *Spain* 18 D3
Costa Dorada, *Spain* 19 B6
Costa Rica ■, *Cent. Amer.* .. 86 E3
Cotabato, *Phil.* 36 C2
Cotagaita, *Bolivia* 91 H5
Côte d'Azur, *France* 13 E7
Côte-d'Ivoire = Ivory Coast ■,
  Africa 53 G4
Cotentin, *France* 12 B3
Cotonou, *Benin* 53 G6
Cotopaxi, *Ecuador* 90 D3
Cotswold Hills, *U.K.* 11 F5
Cottbus, *Germany* 15 C8
Couedic, C. du, *Australia* ... 62 C2
Coulman I., *Antarctica* 96 B15
Council Bluffs, *U.S.A.* 75 E7
Courantyne ⟶, *S. Amer.* ... 90 B7
Courtrai = Kortrijk, *Belgium* . 14 C2
Coventry, *U.K.* 11 E6
Covilhã, *Portugal* 18 B2
Covington, *U.S.A.* 76 E3
Cowal, L., *Australia* 63 B4
Cowangie, *Australia* 62 C3
Cowell, *Australia* 62 B2
Cowra, *Australia* 63 B4
Coxim, *Brazil* 93 F3
Cox's Bazar, *Bangla.* 41 G8
Cozumel, Isla, *Mexico* 85 C7
Cracow = Kraków, *Poland* ... 16 C4
Cracow, *Australia* 63 A5
Cradock, *S. Africa* 59 E5
Craigavon, *U.K.* 11 D3
Crailsheim, *Germany* 14 D6
Craiova, *Romania* 22 B4
Cranbrook, *Canada* 69 D8
Crateús, *Brazil* 92 D5
Crato, *Brazil* 92 D6
Crawley, *U.K.* 11 F6
Crazy Mts., *U.S.A.* 73 C8
Crema, *Italy* 13 D8
Cremona, *Italy* 13 D9
Cres, *Croatia* 20 B5
Crete = Kriti, *Greece* 23 G5
Créteil, *France* 12 B5
Creus, C. de, *Spain* 19 A7
Creuse ⟶, *France* 12 C4
Crewe, *U.K.* 11 E5
Criciúma, *Brazil* 94 B7
Crimean Pen. = Krymskyy
  Pivostriv, *Ukraine* 25 D3
Crişul Negru ⟶, *Romania* .. 16 E5
Crna ⟶, *Macedonia* 22 D3
Crna Gora = Montenegro □,
  Serbia & M. 22 C2

Crna Gora, *Macedonia* 22 C3
Croatia ■, *Europe* 20 B6
Crocker, Banjaran, *Malaysia* . 38 C5
Croker, C., *Australia* 60 C5
Cromer, *U.K.* 11 E7
Cromwell, *N.Z.* 65 F3
Crookwell, *Australia* 63 B4
Cross Sound, *U.S.A.* 69 C6
Crotone, *Italy* 21 E6
Crows Nest, *Australia* 63 A5
Crowsnest Pass, *Canada* 69 D8
Cruz Alta, *Brazil* 94 B6
Cruz del Eje, *Argentina* 94 C4
Cruzeiro do Sul, *Brazil* 91 E4
Crystal Brook, *Australia* 62 B2
Csongrád, *Hungary* 16 E5
Cuamba, *Mozam.* 59 A7
Cuando ➙, *Angola* 58 B4
Cuango = Kwango ➙,
  Dem. Rep. of the Congo .. 56 E3
Cuanza ➙, *Angola* 56 F2
Cuba ■, *W. Indies* 86 B4
Cubango ➙, *Africa* 58 B4
Cúcuta, *Colombia* 90 B4
Cuddalore, *India* 43 P11
Cuddapah, *India* 43 M11
Cuenca, *Ecuador* 90 D3
Cuenca, *Spain* 19 B4
Cuenca, Serranía de, *Spain* . 19 C5
Cuernavaca, *Mexico* 84 D5
Cuevas del Almanzora, *Spain* 19 D5
Cuevo, *Bolivia* 91 H6
Cuiabá, *Brazil* 93 F2
Cuiabá ➙, *Brazil* 93 F2
Cuito ➙, *Angola* 58 B4
Culcairn, *Australia* 63 C4
Culgoa ➙, *Australia* 63 A4
Culiacán, *Mexico* 84 C3
Culion, *Phil.* 36 B2
Cullarin Ra., *Australia* 63 B4
Cullera, *Spain* 19 C5
Culuene ➙, *Brazil* 93 E3
Culverden, *N.Z.* 65 E5
Cumaná, *Venezuela* 90 A6
Cumberland, *U.S.A.* 77 E6
Cumberland Pen., *Canada* .. 70 C7
Cumberland Plateau, *U.S.A.* . 76 F3
Cumberland Sd., *Canada* .. 70 C7
Cumborah, *Australia* 63 A4
Cumbum, *India* 43 M11
Cummins, *Australia* 62 B2
Cumnock, *Australia* 63 B4
Cunene ➙, *Angola* 58 B2
Cúneo, *Italy* 13 D7
Cunnamulla, *Australia* 63 A4
Cupica, G. de, *Colombia* ... 90 B3
Curaçao, *Neth. Ant.* 87 D6
Curaray ➙, *Peru* 90 D4
Curiapo, *Venezuela* 90 B6
Curicó, *Chile* 94 C2
Curitiba, *Brazil* 94 B7
Currabubula, *Australia* 63 B5
Currais Novos, *Brazil* 92 D6
Curralinho, *Brazil* 92 C4
Currie, *Australia* 62 C3
Curtea de Argeş, *Romania* .. 17 F7
Curtis Group, *Australia* 62 C4
Curuápanema ➙, *Brazil* ... 92 C2
Curuçá, *Brazil* 92 C4
Curup, *Indonesia* 39 E2
Cururupu, *Brazil* 92 C5
Curuzú Cuatiá, *Argentina* ... 94 B5
Cuttaburra ➙, *Australia* ... 63 A3
Cuttack, *India* 40 G5
Cuvier I., *N.Z.* 64 B6
Cuxhaven, *Germany* 14 B5
Cuyo, *Phil.* 36 B2
Cuzco, *Bolivia* 91 H5
Cuzco, *Peru* 91 F4
Cwmbran, *U.K.* 11 F5
Cyclades, *Greece* 23 F5
Cygnet, *Australia* 62 D4
Cyprus ■, *Asia* 46 D3
Cyrenaica, *Libya* 54 C3
Czech Rep. ■, *Europe* 16 D2
Częstochowa, *Poland* 16 C4

D

Da Hinggan Ling, *China* 35 B7
Da Lat, *Vietnam* 38 B3
Da Nang, *Vietnam* 38 A3
Da Qaidam, *China* 34 C4
Daba Shan, *China* 35 C5
Dabo = Pasirkuning, *Indonesia* 39 E2
Dabola, *Guinea* 53 F3
Dacca = Dhaka, *Bangla.* 41 F8
Dachau, *Germany* 15 D6
Dadanawa, *Guyana* 90 C7
Dadra & Nagar Haveli □, *India* 43 J8
Dadu, *Pakistan* 42 F5
Daegu, *S. Korea* 35 C7
Daejeon, *S. Korea* 35 C7
Daet, *Phil.* 36 B2
Dagana, *Senegal* 53 E2
Dagestan □, *Russia* 25 E6
Dagö = Hiiumaa, *Estonia* ... 24 B1
Dagupan, *Phil.* 36 A2
Dahlak Kebir, *Eritrea* 49 D3
Dahod, *India* 43 H9
Daió-Misaki, *Japan* 33 F5
Daisetsu-Zan, *Japan* 32 B8
Dakar, *Senegal* 53 F2
Dakhla, *W. Sahara* 52 D2
Dakhla, El Wâhât el-, *Egypt* .. 54 C4
Đakovica, *Serbia & M.* 22 C3
Dalälven ➙, *Sweden* 9 C9
Dalaman ➙, *Turkey* 23 F7
Dalandzadgad, *Mongolia* ... 35 B5
Dalap-Uliga-Darrit = Majuro,
  Marshall Is. 64 J12
Dālbandīn, *Pakistan* 42 E4
Dalby, *Australia* 63 A5
Dali, *China* 34 D5
Dalian, *China* 35 C7
Daliang Shan, *China* 34 D5
Dallas, *U.S.A.* 81 C5
Dalmacija, *Croatia* 20 C6
Dalmatia = Dalmacija, *Croatia* 20 C6
Dalnegorsk, *Russia* 32 A4
Daloa, *Ivory C.* 53 G4
Dalton, *U.S.A.* 82 B5
Daly Waters, *Australia* 60 D5
Daman, *India* 43 J8
Damanhûr, *Egypt* 54 B5
Damar, *Indonesia* 37 F3
Damaraland, *Namibia* 58 C3
Damascus = Dimashq, *Syria* . 46 D4
Damävand, *Iran* 44 C3
Damävand, Qolleh-ye, *Iran* .. 44 C3
Damba, *Angola* 56 F3
Dâmboviţa ➙, *Romania* ... 22 B6
Dämghän, *Iran* 44 B3
Damiel, *Spain* 18 C4
Damietta = Dumyât, *Egypt* .. 54 B5
Dammam = Ad Dammām,
  Si. Arabia 47 F7
Damoh, *India* 43 H11
Dampier, *Australia* 60 E2
Dampier, Selat, *Indonesia* ... 37 E4
Danbury, *U.S.A.* 77 D9
Dandeldhura, *Nepal* 40 C3
Dandeli, *India* 43 M9
Dandenong, *Australia* 63 C4
Dandong, *China* 35 B7
Danger Is. = Pukapuka,
  Cook Is. 65 L14
Dangla Shan = Tanggula
  Shan, *China* 34 C4
Danilov, *Russia* 24 B5
Dankhar Gompa, *India* 42 C11
Danmark = Denmark ■,
  Europe 9 D7
Dannevirke, *N.Z.* 64 D7
Danube = Dunărea ➙, *Europe* 17 F9
Danville, *U.S.A.* 83 A8
Danzig = Gdańsk, *Poland* .. 16 A4
Dar el Beida = Casablanca,
  Morocco 52 B4
Dar es Salaam, *Tanzania* ... 57 F7
Dārāb, *Iran* 44 D3
Daraj, *Libya* 54 B1
Darband, *Pakistan* 42 B8

Darbhanga, *India* 40 D5
Dardanelles = Çanakkale
  Boğazı, *Turkey* 23 D6
Dârfûr, *Sudan* 55 F3
Dargai, *Pakistan* 42 B7
Darganata, *Turkmenistan* ... 29 E7
Dargaville, *N.Z.* 64 A5
Darıca, *Turkey* 22 D7
Darién, G. del, *Colombia* ... 90 B3
Darjeeling = Darjiling, *India* . 40 D7
Darjiling, *India* 40 D7
Darling ➙, *Australia* 62 B3
Darling Downs, *Australia* ... 63 A5
Darling Ra., *Australia* 60 G2
Darlington, *U.K.* 11 D6
Darłowo, *Poland* 16 A3
Darmstadt, *Germany* 14 D5
Darnah, *Libya* 54 B3
Darnley, C., *Antarctica* 96 A10
Darnley B., *Canada* 68 B7
Dart, C., *Antarctica* 96 B18
Dartmoor, *U.K.* 11 F5
Dartmouth, *Canada* 71 E7
Dartmouth Res., *Australia* .. 63 A4
Darvaza, *Turkmenistan* 29 E6
Darvel, Teluk = Lahad Datu,
  Telok, *Malaysia* 36 D1
Darwha, *India* 43 J10
Darwin, *Australia* 60 C5
Daryoi Amu = Amudarya ➙,
  Uzbekistan 29 E6
Dās, *U.A.E.* 44 E3
Dashen, Ras, *Ethiopia* 57 B7
Dashoguz, *Turkmenistan* ... 29 E6
Dasht ➙, *Pakistan* 42 G2
Datça, *Turkey* 23 F6
Datia, *India* 43 G11
Datong, *China* 35 B6
Datu, Tanjung, *Indonesia* ... 39 D3
Datu Piang, *Phil.* 36 C2
Daugava ➙, *Latvia* 24 B1
Daugavpils, *Latvia* 24 B2
Daulpur, *India* 42 F10
Dauphin, *Canada* 69 C9
Dauphiné, *France* 13 D6
Davangere, *India* 43 M9
Davao, *Phil.* 36 C3
Davao G., *Phil.* 36 C3
Dävar Panāh = Sarāvān, *Iran* 45 E5
Davenport, *U.S.A.* 75 E9
David, *Panama* 86 E3
David Gorodok = Davyd
  Haradok, *Belarus* 17 B8
Davis Sea, *Antarctica* 96 A11
Davos, *Switz.* 13 C8
Davyd Haradok, *Belarus* ... 17 B8
Dawei = Tavoy, *Burma* 38 B1
Dawna Ra., *Burma* 41 J12
Dawson, *Canada* 68 B6
Dawson, I., *Chile* 95 G2
Dax, *France* 12 E3
Daxian, *China* 35 C5
Daxue Shan, *China* 34 C5
Daylesford, *Australia* 62 C3
Dayr az Zawr, *Syria* 46 D5
Dayton, *U.S.A.* 76 E3
Daytona Beach, *U.S.A.* 83 E7
De Aar, *S. Africa* 58 E4
Dead Sea, *Asia* 47 E3
Deal I., *Australia* 62 C4
Deán Funes, *Argentina* 94 C4
Death Valley, *U.S.A.* 78 B4
Debar, *Macedonia* 22 D3
Debre Markos, *Ethiopia* 55 F6
Debrecen, *Hungary* 16 E5
Decatur, Ala., *U.S.A.* 82 B4
Decatur, Ill., *U.S.A.* 75 F10
Deccan, *India* 43 L11
Děčín, *Czech Rep.* 16 C2
Dedéagach = Alexandroupoli,
  Greece 22 D5
Dee ➙, *U.K.* 10 C5
Deepwater, *Australia* 63 A5
Deer Lake, *Canada* 71 E8
Deggendorf, *Germany* 15 D7
Deh Bid, *Iran* 44 D3
Dehibat, *Tunisia* 54 B1

Dehra Dun, *India* 42 D11
Dej, *Romania* 17 E6
Dekese, *Dem. Rep. of*
  the Congo 56 E4
Delano, *U.S.A.* 78 C3
Delaware □, *U.S.A.* 77 E8
Delegate, *Australia* 63 C4
Delgado, C., *Mozam.* 57 G8
Delgo, *Sudan* 55 D5
Delhi, *India* 42 E10
Delicias, *Mexico* 84 B3
Déline, *Canada* 68 B7
Delmenhorst, *Germany* 14 B5
Deloraine, *Australia* 62 D4
Delungra, *Australia* 63 A5
Delvinë, *Albania* 23 E3
Demanda, Sierra de la, *Spain* 18 A4
Demavend = Damāvand,
  Qolleh-ye, *Iran* 44 C3
Dembidolo, *Ethiopia* 55 G5
Demini ➤, *Brazil* 90 D6
Demirci, *Turkey* 23 E7
Demirköy, *Turkey* 22 D6
Dempo, *Indonesia* 39 E2
Den Haag = 's-Gravenhage,
  Neths. 14 B3
Den Helder, *Neths.* 14 B3
Denali = McKinley, Mt., *U.S.A.* 69 B4
Denau, *Uzbekistan* 29 F7
Dendang, *Indonesia* 39 E3
Denia, *Spain* 19 C6
Denial B., *Australia* 62 B1
Deniliquin, *Australia* 63 C3
Denizli, *Turkey* 46 C2
Denman Glacier, *Antarctica* . 96 A11
Denmark ■, *Europe* 9 D7
Denmark Str., *Atl. Oc.* 66 C17
Denpasar, *Indonesia* 39 F5
Denton, *U.S.A.* 80 C5
D'Entrecasteaux Is.,
  Papua N. G. 61 B9
Denver, *U.S.A.* 74 F2
Deoghar, *India* 40 E6
Deolali, *India* 40 D4
Deoria, *India* 40 D4
Deosai Mts., *Pakistan* 42 B9
Dera Ghazi Khan, *Pakistan* .. 42 D7
Dera Ismail Khan, *Pakistan* .. 42 D7
Derbent, *Russia* 25 E6
Derby, *Australia* 60 D3
Derby, *U.K.* 11 E6
Derg, L., *Ireland* 11 E2
Derry = Londonderry, *U.K.* .. 11 D3
Des Moines, *U.S.A.* 75 E8
Des Moines ➤, *U.S.A.* 75 E9
Desaguadero ➤, *Bolivia* 91 G5
Dese, *Ethiopia* 49 E2
Desna ➤, *Ukraine* 17 C10
Desolación, I., *Chile* 95 G2
Despeñaperros, Paso, *Spain* . 18 C4
Dessau, *Germany* 15 C7
Dessye = Dese, *Ethiopia* ... 49 E2
D'Estrees B., *Australia* 62 C2
Detmold, *Germany* 14 C5
Detroit, *U.S.A.* 76 C4
Deutsche Bucht, *Germany* .. 14 A5
Deutschland = Germany ■,
  Europe 14 C6
Deva, *Romania* 17 F6
Devakottai, *India* 43 Q11
Deventer, *Neths.* 14 B4
Devon I., *Canada* 70 B5
Devonport, *Australia* 62 D4
Devonport, *N.Z.* 64 B6
Dewas, *India* 43 H10
Deyhūk, *Iran* 44 C4
Deyyer, *Iran* 44 E2
Dezfūl, *Iran* 47 D7
Dezhneva, Mys, *Russia* 31 C16
Dhahran = Aẓ Ẓahrān,
  Si. Arabia 47 F7
Dhaka, *Bangla.* 41 F8
Dhaka □, *Bangla.* 41 E8
Dhamtari, *India* 40 G3
Dhanbad, *India* 40 E6
Dhangarhi, *Nepal* 40 C3
Dhankuta, *Nepal* 40 D6

Dhar, *India* 43 H9
Dharmapuri, *India* 43 N11
Dhaulagiri, *Nepal* 40 C4
Dhenkanal, *India* 40 G5
Dhrol, *India* 43 H7
Dhuburi, *India* 41 D7
Dhule, *India* 43 J9
Diafarabé, *Mali* 53 F5
Diamantina, *Brazil* 93 F5
Diamantina ➤, *Australia* ... 62 A2
Diamantino, *Brazil* 93 E2
Diamond Harbour, *India* 40 F7
Dibaya-Lubue, *Dem. Rep. of*
  the Congo 56 E3
Dibrugarh, *India* 41 D10
Didiéni, *Mali* 53 F4
Diefenbaker, L., *Canada* 69 C9
Diego Suarez = Antsiranana,
  Madag. 59 A9
Dieppe, *France* 12 B4
Digby, *Canada* 71 E7
Dighinala, *Bangla.* 41 F9
Digne-les-Bains, *France* 13 D7
Digos, *Phil.* 36 C3
Digul ➤, *Indonesia* 37 F5
Dihang = Brahmaputra ➤,
  Asia 41 F7
Dijlah, Nahr ➤, *Asia* 47 E6
Dijon, *France* 13 C6
Dikson, *Russia* 28 B9
Dikti Oros, *Greece* 23 G5
Dili, *E. Timor* 37 F3
Dilli = Delhi, *India* 42 E10
Dillingham, *U.S.A.* 69 C4
Dilolo, *Dem. Rep. of*
  the Congo 56 G4
Dimashq, *Syria* 46 D4
Dimboola, *Australia* 62 C3
Dîmboviţa = Dâmboviţa ➤,
  Romania 22 B6
Dimitrovgrad, *Bulgaria* 22 C5
Dimitrovgrad, *Russia* 24 C6
Dimitrovo = Pernik, *Bulgaria* . 22 C4
Dinagat, *Phil.* 36 B3
Dinajpur, *Bangla.* 41 E7
Dinan, *France* 12 B2
Dinant, *Belgium* 14 C3
Dinar, *Turkey* 46 C2
Dīnār, Kūh-e, *Iran* 44 D2
Dinara Planina, *Croatia* 20 B6
Dinard, *France* 12 B2
Dinaric Alps = Dinara Planina,
  Croatia 20 B6
Dindigul, *India* 43 P11
Dingle, *Ireland* 11 E1
Dingwall, *U.K.* 10 C4
Dinosaur △, *U.S.A.* 73 F9
Dipolog, *Phil.* 36 C2
Dir, *Pakistan* 42 B7
Dire Dawa, *Ethiopia* 49 F3
Dirfis Oros, *Greece* 23 E4
Dirranbandi, *Australia* 63 A4
Disa, *India* 43 G8
Disappointment, L., *Australia* 60 E3
Disaster B., *Australia* 63 C4
Discovery B., *Australia* 62 C3
Disteghil Sar, *Pakistan* 42 A9
District of Columbia □, *U.S.A.* 77 E7
Distrito Federal □, *Brazil* ... 93 F4
Diu, *India* 43 J7
Divinópolis, *Brazil* 93 G5
Divnoye, *Russia* 25 D5
Diyarbakır, *Turkey* 46 C5
Djakarta = Jakarta, *Indonesia* 39 F3
Djambala, *Congo* 56 E2
Djanet, *Algeria* 52 D7
Djawa = Jawa, *Indonesia* ... 39 F3
Djelfa, *Algeria* 52 B6
Djerba, Î. de, *Tunisia* 54 B1
Djerid, Chott, *Tunisia* 52 B7
Djibouti, *Djibouti* 49 E3
Djibouti ■, *Africa* 49 E3
Djolu, *Dem. Rep. of the Congo* 56 D4
Djoum, *Cameroon* 56 D2
Djourab, Erg du, *Chad* 55 E2
Dmitriya Lapteva, Proliv,
  Russia 31 B12

Dnepr = Dnipro ➤, *Ukraine* . 25 D3
Dneprodzerzhinsk =
  Dniprodzerzhynsk, *Ukraine* 25 D3
Dnepropetrovsk =
  Dnipropetrovsk, *Ukraine* .. 25 D4
Dnestr = Dnister ➤, *Europe* . 17 E10
Dnieper = Dnipro ➤, *Ukraine* 25 D3
Dniester = Dnister ➤, *Europe* 17 E10
Dnipro ➤, *Ukraine* 25 D3
Dniprodzerzhynsk, *Ukraine* .. 25 D3
Dnipropetrovsk, *Ukraine* ... 25 D4
Dnister ➤, *Europe* 17 E10
Dnyapro = Dnipro ➤, *Ukraine* 25 D3
Doba, *Chad* 55 G2
Doberai, Jazirah, *Indonesia* . 37 E4
Dobo, *Indonesia* 37 F4
Doboj, *Bos.-H.* 20 B7
Dobrich, *Bulgaria* 22 C6
Dobruja, *Europe* 22 B7
Dobrush, *Belarus* 17 B10
Dodecanese, *Greece* 23 F6
Dodekanisa = Dodecanese,
  Greece 23 F6
Dodge City, *U.S.A.* 80 A3
Dodoma, *Tanzania* 57 F7
Doha = Ad Dawḥah, *Qatar* .. 44 E2
Dohazari, *Bangla.* 41 F9
Doi, *Indonesia* 37 D3
Dois Irmãos, Sa., *Brazil* 93 D5
Dolak, Pulau, *Indonesia* 37 F5
Dolbeau-Mistassini, *Canada* . 71 E6
Dole, *France* 13 C6
Dolomites = Dolomiti, *Italy* . 20 A3
Dolomiti, *Italy* 20 A3
Dolores, *Argentina* 94 D5
Dolphin, C., *Falk. Is.* 95 G5
Dolphin and Union Str.,
  Canada 68 B8
Dombarovskiy, *Russia* 29 D6
Dominica ■, *W. Indies* 87 C7
Dominican Rep. ■, *W. Indies* 87 C5
Domodóssola, *Italy* 13 C8
Domville, Mt., *Australia* 63 A5
Don ➤, *Russia* 25 D4
Don ➤, *U.K.* 10 C5
Don Benito, *Spain* 18 C3
Donald, *Australia* 62 C3
Donau = Dunărea ➤, *Europe* 17 F9
Donauwörth, *Germany* 14 D6
Doncaster, *U.K.* 11 E6
Dondo, Teluk, *Indonesia* ... 37 D2
Donegal, *Ireland* 11 D2
Donets ➤, *Russia* 25 D5
Donetsk, *Ukraine* 25 D4
Donggala, *Indonesia* 37 E1
Dongola, *Sudan* 55 E5
Dongting Hu, *China* 35 D6
Donington, C., *Australia* ... 62 B2
Donnelly's Crossing, *N.Z.* ... 64 A5
Donostia-San Sebastián,
  Spain 19 A5
Dora Báltea ➤, *Italy* 13 D8
Dorchester, C., *Canada* 70 C6
Dordogne ➤, *France* 12 D3
Dordrecht, *Neths.* 14 C3
Dori, *Burkina Faso* 53 F5
Dornbirn, *Austria* 14 E5
Doro, Kavo, *Greece* 23 E5
Dorohoi, *Romania* 17 E8
Döröö Nuur, *Mongolia* 34 B4
Dorrigo, *Australia* 63 B5
Dortmund, *Germany* 14 C4
Dos Bahías, C., *Argentina* .. 95 E3
Dos Hermanas, *Spain* 18 D3
Dosso, *Niger* 53 F6
Dothan, *U.S.A.* 82 D5
Douai, *France* 13 A5
Douala, *Cameroon* 53 H7
Double Island Pt., *Australia* . 63 A5
Doubs ➤, *France* 13 C6
Doubtful Sd., *N.Z.* 65 F2
Doubtless B., *N.Z.* 64 A5
Douglas, *I. of Man* 11 D4
Douglas, *U.S.A.* 79 E8
Dourados, *Brazil* 94 A6
Douro ➤, *Europe* 18 B1

Dover, Australia 62 D4
Dover, U.K. 11 F7
Dover, Str. of, Europe 11 F7
Dovrefjell, Norway 8 C7
Dowlat Yār, Afghan. 45 C6
Dowlatābād, Iran 44 D4
Drăgăşani, Romania 22 B5
Dragichyn, Belarus 17 B7
Dragoman, Prokhod, Bulgaria 22 C4
Draguignan, France 13 E7
Drakensberg, S. Africa 59 E5
Drama, Greece 22 D5
Drammen, Norway 9 D8
Drau = Drava ➤, Croatia 20 B7
Drava ➤, Croatia 20 B7
Dresden, Germany 15 C7
Dreux, France 12 B4
Drin ➤, Albania 22 C2
Drina ➤, Bos.-H. 20 B7
Drobeta-Turnu Severin,
  Romania 22 B4
Drochia, Moldova 17 D8
Drogheda, Ireland 11 E3
Drogichin = Dragichyn,
  Belarus 17 B7
Drogobych = Drohobych,
  Ukraine 17 D6
Drohobych, Ukraine 17 D6
Droichead Atha = Drogheda,
  Ireland 11 E3
Dromedary, C., Australia 63 C5
Dronning Maud Land,
  Antarctica 96 B7
Druk Yul = Bhutan ■, Asia .. 41 D8
Drumheller, Canada 69 C8
Drummond Pt., Australia .. 62 B2
Drut ➤, Belarus 17 B10
Drygalski I., Antarctica 96 A11
Dubā, Si. Arabia 47 F3
Dubai = Dubayy, U.A.E. 44 E3
Dubăsari, Moldova 17 E9
Dubăsari Vdkhr., Moldova .. 17 E9
Dubawnt ➤, Canada 68 B9
Dubawnt L., Canada 68 B9
Dubayy, U.A.E. 44 E3
Dubbo, Australia 63 B4
Dublin, Ireland 11 E3
Dublin, U.S.A. 83 C6
Dubno, Ukraine 17 C7
Dubossary = Dubăsari,
  Moldova 17 E9
Dubovka, Russia 24 D5
Dubréka, Guinea 53 G3
Dubrovnik, Croatia 20 C7
Dubrovytsya, Ukraine 17 C8
Dudhi, India 40 E4
Dudinka, Russia 30 C6
Duero = Douro ➤, Europe .. 18 B1
Dugi Otok, Croatia 20 B5
Duisburg, Germany 14 C4
Dukhān, Qatar 44 E2
Duki, Pakistan 42 D6
Dulce ➤, Argentina 94 C4
Duluth, U.S.A. 75 B8
Dum Duma, India 41 D10
Dumaguete, Phil. 36 C2
Dumai, Indonesia 39 D2
Dumaran, Phil. 36 B1
Dumfries, U.K. 11 D5
Dumyât, Egypt 54 B5
Dún Dealgan = Dundalk,
  Ireland 11 D3
Dún Laoghaire, Ireland 11 E3
Duna = Dunărea ➤, Europe . 17 F9
Dunaj = Dunărea ➤, Europe 17 F9
Dunakeszi, Hungary 16 E4
Dunărea ➤, Europe 17 F9
Dunaújváros, Hungary 16 E4
Dunav = Dunărea ➤, Europe 17 F9
Dunback, N.Z. 65 F4
Dunbar, U.K. 10 D5
Duncan, U.S.A. 80 B5
Dundalk, Ireland 11 D3
Dundee, U.K. 10 C5
Dunedin, N.Z. 65 F4
Dunfermline, U.K. 10 C5
Dungarvan, Ireland 11 E3

Dungog, Australia 63 B5
Dungu, Dem. Rep. of
  the Congo 57 D5
Dunhuang, China 34 B4
Dunkerque, France 12 A5
Dunkirk = Dunkerque, France 12 A5
Dúnleary = Dún Laoghaire,
  Ireland 11 E3
Dunolly, Australia 62 C3
Dunstan Mts., N.Z. 65 F3
Durance ➤, France 13 E6
Durango, Mexico 84 C4
Durazno, Uruguay 94 C5
Durazzo = Durrës, Albania .. 22 D2
Durban, S. Africa 59 D6
Düren, Germany 14 C4
Durg = Bhilainagar-Durg, India 40 G3
Durgapur, India 40 F6
Durham, U.K. 11 D6
Durham, U.S.A. 83 B8
Durmitor, Serbia & M. 22 C2
Durrës, Albania 22 D2
Dursunbey, Turkey 23 E7
D'Urville, Tanjung, Indonesia 37 E5
D'Urville I., N.Z. 65 D5
Dushak, Turkmenistan 29 F7
Dushanbe, Tajikistan 29 F7
Dusky Sd., N.Z. 65 F2
Düsseldorf, Germany 14 C4
Dutch Harbor, U.S.A. 69 C3
Duyun, China 35 D5
Dvina, Severnaya ➤, Russia 28 C5
Dvinsk = Daugavpils, Latvia . 24 B2
Dwarka, India 43 H6
Dyatlovo = Dzyatlava, Belarus 17 B7
Dyer, C., Canada 70 C7
Dyer Plateau, Antarctica .. 96 B3
Dyersburg, U.S.A. 81 A9
Dymer, Ukraine 17 C10
Dyushambe = Dushanbe,
  Tajikistan 29 F7
Dzerzhinsk, Russia 24 B5
Dzhambul = Taraz, Kazakhstan 29 E8
Dzhankoy, Ukraine 25 D3
Dzhezkazgan = Zhezqazghan,
  Kazakhstan 29 E7
Dzhizak = Jizzakh, Uzbekistan 29 E7
Działdowo, Poland 16 B5
Dzierżoniów, Poland 16 C3
Dzungaria = Junggar Pendi,
  China 34 B3
Dzungarian Basin = Junggar
  Pendi, China 34 B3
Dzuumod, Mongolia 35 B5
Dzyarzhynsk, Belarus 17 B8
Dzyatlava, Belarus 17 B7

E

Earnslaw, Mt., N.Z. 65 F3
East Bengal, Bangla. 41 E7
East Beskids = Vychodné
  Beskydy, Europe 17 D5
East C. = Dezhneva, Mys,
  Russia 31 C16
East C., N.Z. 64 B8
East China Sea, Asia 35 C7
East Falkland, Falk. Is. 95 G5
East Kilbride, U.K. 10 D4
East London, S. Africa 59 E5
East Main = Eastmain, Canada 71 D6
East Orange, U.S.A. 77 D8
East Sea = Japan, Sea of, Asia 32 D4
East Toorale, Australia 63 B4
Eastbourne, N.Z. 65 D6
Eastbourne, U.K. 11 F7
Eastern Ghats, India 43 N11
Eastmain, Canada 71 D6
Eastmain ➤, Canada 71 D6
Eau Claire, U.S.A. 75 C9
Eau Claire, L. à l', Canada .. 71 D6
Eberswalde-Finow, Germany 15 B7
Ebetsu, Japan 32 B7
Ebolowa, Cameroon 56 D2

Ebro ➤, Spain 19 B6
Eceabat, Turkey 23 D6
Ech Chéliff, Algeria 52 A6
Echo Bay, Canada 68 B8
Echuca, Australia 63 C3
Ecija, Spain 18 D3
Eclipse Sd., Canada 70 B6
Ecuador ■, S. Amer. 90 D3
Ed Dar el Beida = Casablanca,
  Morocco 52 B4
Ed Debba, Sudan 55 E5
Ed Dueim, Sudan 55 F5
Eddystone Pt., Australia 62 D4
Eden, Australia 63 C4
Eder ➤, Germany 14 C5
Edessa, Greece 23 D4
Édhessa = Edessa, Greece .. 23 D4
Edievale, N.Z. 65 F3
Edinburg, U.S.A. 80 F4
Edinburgh, U.K. 10 D5
Edineţ, Moldova 17 D8
Edirne, Turkey 22 D6
Edithburgh, Australia 62 C2
Edmonton, Canada 69 C8
Edmundston, Canada 71 E7
Edremit, Turkey 23 E6
Edremit Körfezi, Turkey ... 23 E6
Edson, Canada 69 C8
Edward ➤, Australia 62 C3
Edward, L., Africa 57 E5
Edward VII Land, Antarctica 96 C17
Edwards Plateau, U.S.A. ... 80 D3
Eesti = Estonia ■, Europe ... 24 B2
Égadi, Ísole, Italy 21 F4
Eger = Cheb, Czech Rep. ... 16 C1
Eger, Hungary 16 E5
Egio, Greece 23 E4
Eglinton I., Canada 70 B2
Egmont, C., N.Z. 64 C5
Egmont, Mt. = Taranaki, Mt.,
  N.Z. 64 C6
Egmont △, N.Z. 64 C6
Eğridir, Turkey 46 C2
Eğridir Gölü, Turkey 46 C2
Egypt ■, Africa 54 C5
Eibar, Spain 19 A4
Eidsvold, Australia 63 A5
Eifel, Germany 14 C4
Eigg, U.K. 10 C3
Eil, Somali Rep. 49 F4
Eildon, L., Australia 63 C4
Eindhoven, Neths. 14 C3
Eire = Ireland ■, Europe ... 11 E3
Eirunepé, Brazil 91 E5
Eisenach, Germany 14 C6
Eisenerz, Austria 15 E8
Eivissa, Spain 19 C6
Eketahuna, N.Z. 64 D6
Ekibastuz, Kazakhstan 29 D8
El Aaiún, W. Sahara 52 C3
El 'Alamein, Egypt 54 B4
El Asnam = Ech Chéliff,
  Algeria 52 A6
El Bayadh, Algeria 52 B6
El Centro, U.S.A. 78 D5
El Cerro, Bolivia 91 G6
El Cuy, Argentina 95 D3
El Dere, Somali Rep. 49 G4
El Diviso, Colombia 90 C3
El Djouf, Mauritania 53 D4
El Dorado, Ark., U.S.A. 81 C7
El Dorado, Kans., U.S.A. ... 80 A5
El Dorado, Venezuela 90 B6
El Escorial, Spain 18 B3
El Faiyûm, Egypt 54 C5
El Fâsher, Sudan 55 F4
El Ferrol = Ferrol, Spain ... 18 A1
El Fuerte, Mexico 84 B3
El Gal, Somali Rep. 49 E5
El Geneina = Al Junaynah,
  Sudan 55 F3
El Gîza, Egypt 54 C5
El Iskandarîya, Egypt 54 B4
El Jadida, Morocco 52 B4
El Khârga, Egypt 54 C5
El Khartûm, Sudan 55 E5

El Maestrazgo

El Maestrazgo, *Spain* 19 B5
El Mahalla el Kubra, *Egypt* .. 54 B5
El Mansûra, *Egypt* 54 B5
El Minyâ, *Egypt* 54 C5
El Obeid, *Sudan* 55 F5
El Odaiya, *Sudan* 55 F4
El Oued, *Algeria* 52 B7
El Paso, *U.S.A.* 79 E9
El Prat de Llobregat, *Spain* . 19 B7
El Puerto de Santa María,
  Spain 18 D2
El Qâhira, *Egypt* 54 B5
El Salvador ■, *Cent. Amer.* ... 85 E7
El Suweis, *Egypt* 54 C5
El Tigre, *Venezuela* 90 B6
El Turbio, *Argentina* 95 G2
El Uqsur, *Egypt* 54 C5
El Vigía, *Venezuela* 90 B4
El Wak, *Kenya* 57 D8
El Wuz, *Sudan* 55 E5
Elat, *Israel* 47 E3
Elâzığ, *Turkey* 46 C4
Elba, *Italy* 20 C3
Elbasan, *Albania* 22 D3
Elbe ➤, *Europe* 14 B5
Elbert, Mt., *U.S.A.* 79 A9
Elbeuf, *France* 12 B4
Elbing = Elbląg, *Poland* .. 16 A4
Elbląg, *Poland* 16 A4
Elbrus, *Asia* 25 E5
Elburz Mts. = Alborz, Reshteh-
  ye Kûhhâ-ye, *Iran* 44 B3
Elche, *Spain* 19 C5
Elda, *Spain* 19 C5
Elde ➤, *Germany* 15 B6
Eldoret, *Kenya* 57 D7
Elefantes ➤, *Africa* 59 C6
Elektrostal, *Russia* 24 B4
Elephant I., *Antarctica* ... 96 A4
Eleuthera, *Bahamas* 86 A4
Elgin, *U.K.* 10 C5
Elgin, *U.S.A.* 76 C1
Elgon, Mt., *Africa* 57 D6
Eliase, *Indonesia* 37 F4
Elista, *Russia* 25 D5
Elizabeth, *Australia* 62 B2
Elizabeth, *U.S.A.* 77 D8
Elizabeth City, *U.S.A.* ... 83 A9
Elizabethton, *U.S.A.* 83 A6
Ełk, *Poland* 16 B6
Elkhart, *U.S.A.* 76 D3
Elkhovo, *Bulgaria* 22 C6
Elko, *U.S.A.* 72 F6
Ellas = Greece ■, *Europe* . 23 E4
Ellef Ringnes I., *Canada* . 70 B3
Ellery, Mt., *Australia* ... 63 C4
Ellesmere, L., *N.Z.* 65 G5
Ellesmere I., *Canada* 70 B6
Ellice Is. = Tuvalu ■, *Pac. Oc.* 64 K12
Elliot Lake, *Canada* 71 E5
Elliston, *Australia* 62 B1
Ellore = Eluru, *India* 40 J3
Ellsworth Land, *Antarctica* . 96 B2
Ellsworth Mts., *Antarctica* . 96 B2
Elmore, *Australia* 63 C3
Elmshorn, *Germany* 14 B5
Eltham, *N.Z.* 64 C6
Eluru, *India* 40 J3
Elvas, *Portugal* 18 C2
Elx = Elche, *Spain* 19 C5
Ely, *U.K.* 11 E7
Emâmrûd, *Iran* 44 B3
Embarcación, *Argentina* . 94 A4
Embetsu, *Japan* 32 A7
Embi, *Kazakhstan* 29 E6
Embi ➤, *Kazakhstan* ... 29 E6
Embrun, *France* 13 D7
Emden, *Germany* 14 B4
Emet, *Turkey* 23 E7
Emi Koussi, *Chad* 55 E2
Emine, Nos, *Bulgaria* .. 22 C6
Emissi, Tarso, *Chad* ... 54 D2
Emmen, *Neths.* 14 B4
Empalme, *Mexico* 84 B2
Empangeni, *S. Africa* .. 59 D6
Empedrado, *Argentina* . 94 B5

Empty Quarter = Rub' al Khâlî,
  Si. Arabia 48 D4
Ems ➤, *Germany* 14 B4
En Nahud, *Sudan* 55 F4
Enare = Inarijärvi, *Finland* ... 8 B11
Enarotali, *Indonesia* 37 E5
Encarnación, *Paraguay* .. 94 B5
Encounter B., *Australia* .. 62 C2
Ende, *Indonesia* 37 F2
Enderby Land, *Antarctica* . 96 A9
Enewetak Atoll, *Marshall Is.* . 64 H11
Enez, *Turkey* 23 D6
Engaño, C., *Phil.* 36 A2
Engaru, *Japan* 32 A8
Engels, *Russia* 24 C6
Enggano, *Indonesia* 39 F2
England □, *U.K.* 11 E6
Englewood, *U.S.A.* 74 F2
English Bazar = Ingraj Bazar,
  India 40 E7
English Channel, *Europe* . 11 F5
Enid, *U.S.A.* 80 A5
Enna, *Italy* 21 F5
Ennedi, *Chad* 55 E3
Enngonia, *Australia* 63 A4
Ennis, *Ireland* 11 E2
Enniskillen, *U.K.* 11 D3
Enns ➤, *Austria* 15 D8
Enschede, *Neths.* 14 B4
Ensenada, *Mexico* 84 A1
Entebbe, *Uganda* 57 D6
Entroncamento, *Portugal* . 18 C1
Enugu, *Nigeria* 53 G7
Eólie, Ís., *Italy* 21 E5
Épernay, *France* 13 B5
Ephesus, *Turkey* 23 F6
Épinal, *France* 13 B7
Equatorial Guinea ■, *Africa* . 56 D1
Er Rachidia, *Morocco* ... 52 B5
Er Rahad, *Sudan* 55 F5
Er Rif, *Morocco* 52 A5
Erāwadī Myit = Irrawaddy ➤,
  Burma 41 K10
Erbil = Arbīl, *Iraq* 46 C6
Erciyaş Dağı, *Turkey* ... 46 C3
Érd, *Hungary* 16 E4
Erdek, *Turkey* 23 D6
Erebus, Mt., *Antarctica* .. 96 B15
Erechim, *Brazil* 94 B6
Ereğli, *Konya, Turkey* .. 46 C3
Ereğli, *Zonguldak, Turkey* ... 25 E3
Eresma ➤, *Spain* 18 B3
Erfurt, *Germany* 15 C6
Ergani, *Turkey* 46 C4
Érice, *Italy* 21 E4
Erie, *U.S.A.* 77 C5
Erie, L., *N. Amer.* 76 C5
Erigavo, *Somali Rep.* ... 49 E4
Erimanthos, *Greece* 23 F3
Erimo-misaki, *Japan* ... 32 C8
Eritrea ■, *Africa* 49 E2
Erlangen, *Germany* 15 D6
Ermenek, *Turkey* 46 C3
Erne, Lower L., *U.K.* ... 11 D3
Erode, *India* 43 P10
Eromanga, *Australia* ... 63 A3
Erramala Hills, *India* ... 43 M11
Ertis = Irtysh ➤, *Russia* . 28 C7
Erzgebirge, *Germany* ... 15 C7
Erzincan, *Turkey* 25 F4
Erzurum, *Turkey* 25 F5
Es Sahrâ' Esh Sharqîya, *Egypt* 54 C5
Es Sînâ', *Egypt* 54 C5
Esan-Misaki, *Japan* 32 C7
Esashi, *Hokkaidō, Japan* ... 32 A8
Esashi, *Hokkaidō, Japan* .. 32 C7
Esbjerg, *Denmark* 9 D7
Esbo = Espoo, *Finland* .. 9 C10
Esch-sur-Alzette, *Lux.* .. 13 B6
Escuinapa de Hidalgo, *Mexico* 84 C3
Esenguly, *Turkmenistan* . 29 F6
Eşfahān, *Iran* 44 C2
Esh Sham = Dimashq, *Syria* . 46 D4
Esil = Ishim ➤, *Russia* . 29 D8
Esker, *Canada* 71 D7
Eskilstuna, *Sweden* 9 D9

Eskimo Point = Arviat, *Canada* 68 B10
Eskişehir, *Turkey* 25 F3
Esla ➤, *Spain* 18 B2
Eslāmābād-e Gharb, *Iran* .. 46 D6
Eşme, *Turkey* 23 E7
Esmeraldas, *Ecuador* ... 90 C3
España = Spain ■, *Europe* .. 18 C4
Esperance, *Australia* ... 60 G3
Espichel, C., *Portugal* .. 18 C1
Espinazo, Sierra del =
  Espinhaço, Serra do, *Brazil* 93 F5
Espinhaço, Serra do, *Brazil* . 93 F5
Espírito Santo □, *Brazil* .. 93 G5
Espíritu Santo, *Vanuatu* ... 64 L11
Espoo, *Finland* 9 C10
Esquel, *Argentina* 95 E2
Esquina, *Argentina* 94 C5
Essaouira, *Morocco* 52 B4
Essen, *Germany* 14 C4
Essequibo ➤, *Guyana* .. 90 B7
Esslingen, *Germany* ... 14 D5
Estados, I. de Los, *Argentina* 95 G4
Estância, *Brazil* 93 E6
Estevan, *Canada* 69 D9
Estonia ■, *Europe* 24 B2
Estrela, Serra da, *Portugal* .. 18 B2
Estremoz, *Portugal* 18 C2
Estrondo, Serra do, *Brazil* .. 92 D4
Esztergom, *Hungary* ... 16 E4
Étampes, *France* 12 B5
Etawah, *India* 42 F11
eThekwini = Durban, *S. Africa* 59 D6
Ethiopia ■, *Africa* 49 F2
Ethiopian Highlands, *Ethiopia* 48 F2
Etna, *Italy* 21 F5
Etosha Pan, *Namibia* ... 58 B3
Euboea = Evia, *Greece* .. 23 E5
Eucumbene, L., *Australia* .. 63 C4
Eufaula, *U.S.A.* 82 D5
Eugene, *U.S.A.* 72 E2
Eugowra, *Australia* 63 B4
Eulo, *Australia* 63 A4
Euphrates = Furāt, Nahr al ➤,
  Asia 47 E6
Eureka, *Canada* 70 B5
Eureka, *U.S.A.* 72 F1
Euroa, *Australia* 63 C4
Europa, Île, *Ind. Oc.* ... 59 C8
Europa, Picos de, *Spain* . 18 A3
Europa, Pta. de, *Gib.* ... 18 D3
Evans Head, *Australia* .. 63 A5
Evanston, *U.S.A.* 76 C2
Evansville, *U.S.A.* 76 F2
Everard, L., *Australia* ... 62 B1
Everest, Mt., *Nepal* 40 C6
Everett, *U.S.A.* 72 C2
Everglades △, *U.S.A.* ... 83 G7
Évia, *Greece* 23 E5
Évora, *Portugal* 18 C2
Évreux, *France* 12 B4
Evros ➤, *Greece* 22 D6
Évry, *France* 12 B5
Évvoia = Evia, *Greece* .. 23 E5
Ewo, *Congo* 56 E2
Exaltación, *Bolivia* 91 F5
Exeter, *U.K.* 11 F5
Exmoor, *U.K.* 11 F5
Exmouth, *U.K.* 11 F5
Extremadura □, *Spain* .. 18 C2
Eyasi, L., *Tanzania* 57 E6
Eyre (North), L., *Australia* .. 62 A2
Eyre (South), L., *Australia* .. 62 A2
Eyre, L., *Australia* 60 F6
Eyre Mts., *N.Z.* 65 F3
Eyre Pen., *Australia* ... 62 B2
Ezine, *Turkey* 23 E6

F

F.Y.R.O.M. = Macedonia ■,
  Europe 22 D3
Fabriano, *Italy* 20 C4
Fada, *Chad* 55 E3
Fada-n-Gourma, *Burkina Faso* 53 F6
Faddeyevskiy, Ostrov, *Russia* 31 B12

Faenza, *Italy* 20 B3
Færoe Is. = Føroyar ⧄, *Atl. Oc.* 6 C4
Făgăraș, *Romania* 17 F7
Fagnano, L., *Argentina* 95 G3
Fahraj, *Iran* 45 D4
Fair Isle, *U.K.* 10 B6
Fairbanks, *U.S.A.* 69 B5
Fairfield, *Ala., U.S.A.* 82 C4
Fairfield, *Calif., U.S.A.* 72 G2
Fairlie, *N.Z.* 65 F4
Fairweather, Mt., *U.S.A.* 69 C6
Faisalabad, *Pakistan* 42 D8
Faizabad, *India* 40 D4
Fakfak, *Indonesia* 37 E4
Falaise, *France* 12 B3
Falam, *Burma* 41 F9
Falconara Maríttima, *Italy* .. 20 C4
Falcone, C. del, *Italy* 20 D2
Faleshty = Fălești, *Moldova* . 17 E8
Fălești, *Moldova* 17 E8
Falkland Is. ⧄, *Atl. Oc.* 95 G5
Falkland Sd., *Falk. Is.* 95 G5
Fall River, *U.S.A.* 77 D10
Falmouth, *U.K.* 11 F4
Fălticeni, *Romania* 17 E8
Falun, *Sweden* 9 C9
Famagusta, *Cyprus* 46 D3
Fano, *Italy* 20 C4
Fao = Al Fāw, *Iraq* 47 E7
Faradje, *Dem. Rep. of
  the Congo* 57 D5
Farafangana, *Madag.* 59 C9
Farāh, *Afghan.* 42 C3
Farāh □, *Afghan.* 42 C3
Faranah, *Guinea* 53 F3
Farasān, Jazā'ir, *Si. Arabia* .. 49 D3
Farasan Is. = Farasān, Jazā'ir,
  Si. Arabia 49 D3
Fareham, *U.K.* 11 F6
Farewell, C., *N.Z.* 64 D5
Farghona, *Uzbekistan* 29 E8
Fargo, *U.S.A.* 74 B6
Farīmān, *Iran* 45 C4
Farina, *Australia* 62 B2
Faro, *Brazil* 92 C2
Faro, *Portugal* 18 D2
Farrāshband, *Iran* 44 D3
Fārs □, *Iran* 44 D3
Farsala, *Greece* 23 E4
Fartak, Râs, *Si. Arabia* 47 E3
Fāryāb □, *Afghan.* 45 B6
Fasā, *Iran* 44 D3
Fasano, *Italy* 21 D6
Fastiv, *Ukraine* 17 C9
Fastov = Fastiv, *Ukraine* 17 C9
Fatagar, Tanjung, *Indonesia* . 37 E4
Fatehgarh, *India* 42 F11
Fatehpur, *Raj., India* 42 F9
Fatehpur, *Ut. P., India* 40 E3
Favara, *Italy* 21 F4
Favignana, *Italy* 21 F4
Faxaflói, *Iceland* 8 C1
Faya-Largeau, *Chad* 55 E2
Fayd, *Si. Arabia* 47 F5
Fayetteville, *Ark., U.S.A.* ... 81 A6
Fayetteville, *N.C., U.S.A.* ... 83 B8
Fazilka, *India* 42 D9
Fdérik, *Mauritania* 52 D3
Feather ➨, *U.S.A.* 72 G3
Featherston, *N.Z.* 65 D6
Fécamp, *France* 12 B4
Fehmarn, *Germany* 15 A6
Feilding, *N.Z.* 64 D6
Feira de Santana, *Brazil* 93 E6
Feldkirch, *Austria* 14 E5
Felipe Carrillo Puerto, *Mexico* 85 D7
Felixstowe, *U.K.* 11 F7
Fenoarivo Atsinanana,
  Madag. 59 B9
Fenyang, *China* 35 C6
Feodosiya, *Ukraine* 25 D4
Ferdows, *Iran* 44 C4
Ferfer, *Somali Rep.* 49 F4
Fergana = Farghona,
  Uzbekistan 29 E8
Fermo, *Italy* 20 C4

Fermont, *Canada* 71 D7
Fernando de Noronha, *Brazil* 92 C7
Fernando Póo = Bioko,
  Eq. Guin. 53 H7
Ferozepore = Firozpur, *India* . 42 D9
Ferrara, *Italy* 20 B3
Ferreñafe, *Peru* 91 E3
Ferret, C., *France* 12 D3
Ferrol, *Spain* 18 A1
Fès, *Morocco* 52 B5
Fetești, *Romania* 22 B6
Fetlar, *U.K.* 10 A6
Feuilles ➨, *Canada* 70 D6
Fez = Fès, *Morocco* 52 B5
Fezzan, *Libya* 54 C2
Fianarantsoa, *Madag.* 59 C9
Fier, *Albania* 23 D2
Figeac, *France* 12 D5
Figueira da Foz, *Portugal* ... 18 B1
Figueres, *Spain* 19 A7
Figuig, *Morocco* 52 B5
Fiji ■, *Pac. Oc.* 64 L12
Filiatra, *Greece* 23 F3
Filyos Cayi ➨, *Turkey* 46 B3
Fingoè, *Mozam.* 59 A6
Finike, *Turkey* 46 C2
Finisterre, C. = Fisterra, C.,
  Spain 18 A1
Finland ■, *Europe* 8 C11
Finland, G. of, *Europe* 9 D11
Finlay ➨, *Canada* 68 C7
Finley, *Australia* 63 C4
Finniss, C., *Australia* 62 B1
Fiora ➨, *Italy* 20 C3
Fiordland △, *N.Z.* 65 F2
Firat = Furāt, Nahr al ➨, *Asia* 47 E6
Firenze, *Italy* 20 C3
Firozabad, *India* 42 F11
Firozpur, *India* 42 D9
Fīrūzābād, *Iran* 44 D3
Fīrūzkūh, *Iran* 44 C3
Fish ➨, *Namibia* 58 D3
Fishguard, *U.K.* 11 E4
Fisterra, C., *Spain* 18 A1
Fitz Roy, *Argentina* 95 F3
Fiume = Rijeka, *Croatia* 20 B5
Fizi, *Dem. Rep. of the Congo* 57 E5
Flagstaff, *U.S.A.* 79 C7
Flåm, *Norway* 8 C7
Flaming Gorge Res., *U.S.A.* . 73 F9
Flamingo, Teluk, *Indonesia* . 37 F5
Flanders = Flandre, *Europe* .. 14 C2
Flandre, *Europe* 14 C2
Flathead L., *U.S.A.* 73 C7
Flattery, C., *U.S.A.* 72 B1
Flensburg, *Germany* 14 A5
Flers, *France* 12 B3
Flesko, Tanjung, *Indonesia* . 37 D2
Flin Flon, *Canada* 69 C9
Flinders ➨, *Australia* 61 D7
Flinders I., *Australia* 62 C4
Flinders Ranges, *Australia* .. 62 B2
Flint, *U.S.A.* 76 C4
Flint I., *Kiribati* 65 L15
Florence = Firenze, *Italy* 20 C3
Florence, *Ala., U.S.A.* 82 B4
Florence, *S.C., U.S.A.* 83 B8
Florence, L., *Australia* 62 A2
Flores, *Indonesia* 37 F2
Flores Sea, *Indonesia* 37 F2
Florești, *Moldova* 17 E9
Floriano, *Brazil* 92 D5
Florianópolis, *Brazil* 94 B7
Florida, *Uruguay* 94 C5
Florida □, *U.S.A.* 83 F6
Florida, Straits of, *U.S.A.* ... 86 B3
Florina, *Greece* 23 D3
Florø, *Norway* 8 C7
Fluk, *Indonesia* 37 E3
Flushing = Vlissingen, *Neths.* 14 C2
Fly ➨, *Papua N. G.* 61 B7
Flying Fish, C., *Antarctica* ... 96 B1
Foça, *Turkey* 23 E6
Focșani, *Romania* 17 F8
Fóggia, *Italy* 20 D5
Föhr, *Germany* 14 A5

Foix, *France* 12 E4
Folda, *Norway* 8 B8
Foligno, *Italy* 20 C4
Folkestone, *U.K.* 11 F7
Fond du Lac, *U.S.A.* 75 D10
Fondi, *Italy* 20 D4
Fongafale, *Tuvalu* 64 K12
Fonsagrada = A Fonsagrada,
  Spain 18 A2
Fonseca, G. de, *Cent. Amer.* . 85 E7
Fontainebleau, *France* 13 B5
Fonte Boa, *Brazil* 90 D5
Fontenay-le-Comte, *France* .. 12 C3
Foochow = Fuzhou, *China* .. 35 D6
Forbes, *Australia* 63 B4
Fords Bridge, *Australia* 63 A4
Forestier Pen., *Australia* 62 D4
Forfar, *U.K.* 10 C5
Forlì, *Italy* 20 B4
Formentera, *Spain* 19 C6
Formentor, C. de, *Spain* 19 C7
Fórmia, *Italy* 20 D4
Formosa = Taiwan ■, *Asia* . 35 D7
Formosa, *Argentina* 94 B5
Formosa, Serra, *Brazil* 93 E3
Føroyar ⧄, *Atl. Oc.* 6 C4
Forsayth, *Australia* 61 D7
Forst, *Germany* 15 C8
Fort Albany, *Canada* 71 D5
Fort Collins, *U.S.A.* 74 E2
Fort Dauphin = Taolanaro,
  Madag. 59 D9
Fort-de-France, *Martinique* .. 87 D7
Fort Dodge, *U.S.A.* 75 D7
Fort Franklin = Déline, *Canada* 68 B7
Fort George = Chisasibi,
  Canada 71 D6
Fort Good Hope, *Canada* ... 68 B7
Fort Lauderdale, *U.S.A.* 83 F7
Fort Liard, *Canada* 68 B7
Fort Macleod, *Canada* 69 D8
Fort McPherson, *Canada* ... 68 B6
Fort Myers, *U.S.A.* 83 F7
Fort Norman = Tulita, *Canada* 68 B7
Fort Peck L., *U.S.A.* 73 C10
Fort Pierce, *U.S.A.* 83 F7
Fort Providence, *Canada* ... 68 B8
Fort Resolution, *Canada* ... 68 B8
Fort Rupert = Waskaganish,
  Canada 71 D6
Fort Scott, *U.S.A.* 81 A6
Fort Shevchenko, *Kazakhstan* 29 E6
Fort Simpson, *Canada* 68 B7
Fort Smith, *Canada* 68 B8
Fort Smith, *U.S.A.* 81 B6
Fort Walton Beach, *U.S.A.* .. 82 D4
Fort Wayne, *U.S.A.* 76 D3
Fort William, *U.K.* 10 C4
Fort Worth, *U.S.A.* 80 C5
Fort Yukon, *U.S.A.* 69 B5
Fortaleza, *Brazil* 92 C6
Forūr, *Iran* 44 E3
Foshan, *China* 35 D6
Fossano, *Italy* 13 D7
Fougères, *France* 12 B3
Foula, *U.K.* 10 A5
Fourni, *Greece* 23 F6
Fouta Djallon, *Guinea* 53 F3
Foveaux Str., *N.Z.* 65 G3
Foxe Basin, *Canada* 70 C6
Foxe Chan., *Canada* 70 C5
Foxe Pen., *Canada* 70 C6
Foxton, *N.Z.* 64 D6
Foz do Iguaçu, *Brazil* 94 B6
Franca, *Brazil* 93 G4
Francavilla Fontana, *Italy* ... 21 D6
France ■, *Europe* 13 C5
Frances, *Australia* 62 C3
Franceville, *Gabon* 56 E2
Franche-Comté, *France* 13 C6
Francistown, *Botswana* 59 C5
Frankfurt, *Brandenburg,
  Germany* 15 B8
Frankfurt, *Hessen, Germany* . 14 C5
Fränkische Alb, *Germany* ... 15 D6
Franklin B., *Canada* 68 B7

Franklin I.

Franklin I., *Antarctica* 96 B15
Franklin Mts., *Canada* 68 B7
Franklin Str., *Canada* 68 A10
Frankston, *Australia* 63 C4
Frantsa Iosifa, Zemlya, *Russia* 28 A6
Fraser ➝, *Canada* 69 D7
Fraser I., *Australia* 63 A5
Fraserburgh, *U.K.* 10 C5
Fray Bentos, *Uruguay* 94 C5
Fredericksburg, *U.S.A.* 77 E7
Fredericton, *Canada* 71 E7
Frederikshavn, *Denmark* 9 D8
Fredrikstad, *Norway* 9 D8
Free State □, *S. Africa* 59 D5
Freeport, *Bahamas* 86 A4
Freeport, *U.S.A.* 75 D10
Freetown, *S. Leone* 53 G3
Fregenal de la Sierra, *Spain* . 18 C2
Freiburg, *Germany* 14 E4
Freire, *Chile* 95 D2
Freising, *Germany* 15 D6
Freistadt, *Austria* 15 D8
Fréjus, *France* 13 E7
Fremont, *U.S.A.* 78 B2
French Guiana □, *S. Amer.* . 92 B3
French Polynesia □, *Pac. Oc.* 65 M16
Fresco ➝, *Brazil* 92 D3
Freshfield, C., *Antarctica* . . 96 A14
Fresnillo, *Mexico* 84 C4
Fresno, *U.S.A.* 78 B3
Freycinet Pen., *Australia* . . 62 D4
Fria, C., *Namibia* 58 B2
Frías, *Argentina* 94 B3
Friedrichshafen, *Germany* . 14 E5
Friendly Is. = Tonga ■,
 Pac. Oc. 65 L13
Frobisher B., *Canada* 70 C7
Frobisher Bay = Iqaluit,
 Canada 70 C7
Frome ➝, *Australia* 62 A2
Frome, L., *Australia* 62 B2
Frosinone, *Italy* 20 D4
Frunze = Bishkek, *Kyrgyzstan* 29 E8
Frutal, *Brazil* 93 F4
Frýdek-Místek, *Czech Rep.* . . 16 D4
Fuchou = Fuzhou, *China* . . . 35 D6
Fuchū, *Japan* 33 F3
Fuengirola, *Spain* 18 D3
Fuentes de Oñoro, *Spain* . . 18 B2
Fuerte ➝, *Mexico* 84 B3
Fuerte Olimpo, *Paraguay* . . 91 H7
Fuerteventura, *Canary Is.* . . 52 C3
Fuhai, *China* 34 B3
Fuji, *Japan* 33 F6
Fuji-San, *Japan* 33 F6
Fujian □, *China* 35 D6
Fujiyama, Mt. = Fuji-San,
 Japan 33 F6
Fukien = Fujian □, *China* . . 35 D6
Fukuchiyama, *Japan* 33 F4
Fukue-Shima, *Japan* 33 G1
Fukui, *Japan* 33 E5
Fukuoka, *Japan* 33 G2
Fukushima, *Japan* 33 E7
Fukuyama, *Japan* 33 F3
Fulda, *Germany* 14 C5
Fulda ➝, *Germany* 14 C5
Funabashi, *Japan* 33 F7
Funafuti = Fongafale, *Tuvalu* 64 K12
Funchal, *Madeira* 52 B2
Fundación, *Colombia* 90 A4
Fundão, *Portugal* 18 B2
Fundy, B. of, *Canada* 71 E7
Funtua, *Nigeria* 53 F7
Furât, Nahr al ➝, *Asia* . . . 47 E6
Furneaux Group, *Australia* . 62 D4
Fürstenwalde, *Germany* . . . 15 B8
Fürth, *Germany* 14 D6
Furukawa, *Japan* 32 D7
Fury and Hecla Str., *Canada* . 70 C5
Fusagasuga, *Colombia* . . . 90 C4
Fushun, *China* 35 B7
Futuna, *Wall. & F. Is.* . . . 64 L12
Fuxin, *China* 35 B7
Fuzhou, *China* 35 D6
Fyn, *Denmark* 9 D8

G

Gabela, *Angola* 56 G2
Gabès, *Tunisia* 54 B1
Gabès, G. de, *Tunisia* 54 B1
Gabon ■, *Africa* 56 E2
Gaborone, *Botswana* 59 C5
Gabrovo, *Bulgaria* 22 C5
Gachsārān, *Iran* 44 D2
Gadag, *India* 43 M9
Gadarwara, *India* 43 H11
Gadhada, *India* 43 J7
Gadsden, *U.S.A.* 82 B4
Gadwal, *India* 43 L10
Gafsa, *Tunisia* 52 B7
Gagnoa, *Ivory C.* 53 G4
Gagnon, *Canada* 71 D7
Gaillimh = Galway, *Ireland* . . 11 E2
Gainesville, *Fla., U.S.A.* . . . 83 E6
Gainesville, *Ga., U.S.A.* . . . 83 B6
Gainesville, *Tex., U.S.A.* . . . 80 C5
Gairdner, L., *Australia* . . . 62 B2
Galashiels, *U.K.* 10 D5
Galați, *Romania* 17 F9
Galatina, *Italy* 21 D7
Galcaio, *Somali Rep.* 49 F4
Galdhøpiggen, *Norway* 8 C7
Galela, *Indonesia* 37 D3
Galesburg, *U.S.A.* 75 E9
Galich, *Russia* 24 B5
Galicia □, *Spain* 18 A2
Galilee, Sea of = Yam
 Kinneret, *Israel* 46 D3
Gállego ➝, *Spain* 19 B5
Gallegos ➝, *Argentina* . . . 95 G3
Gallinas, Pta., *Colombia* . . . 90 A4
Gallipoli = Gelibolu, *Turkey* . 23 D6
Gallípoli, *Italy* 21 D6
Gällivare, *Sweden* 8 B10
Galloway, Mull of, *U.K.* . . . 11 D4
Galveston, *U.S.A.* 81 E6
Gálvez, *Argentina* 94 C4
Galway, *Ireland* 11 E2
Galway B., *Ireland* 11 E2
Gambia ■, *W. Afr.* 53 F2
Gambia ➝, *W. Afr.* 53 F2
Gambier, Îs., *French Polynesia* 65 M17
Gambier Is., *Australia* 62 C2
Gamboma, *Congo* 56 E3
Gan Jiang ➝, *China* 35 D6
Ganāveh, *Iran* 44 D2
Gäncä, *Azerbaijan* 25 E6
Gand = Gent, *Belgium* 14 C2
Ganda, *Angola* 58 A2
Gandak ➝, *India* 40 E5
Gandava, *Pakistan* 42 E5
Gander, *Canada* 71 E8
Gandhi Sagar, *India* 43 G9
Gandía, *Spain* 19 C5
Ganedidalem = Gani,
 Indonesia 37 E3
Ganga ➝, *India* 41 F8
Ganganagar, *India* 42 E8
Gangaw, *Burma* 41 F10
Gangdisê Shan, *China* 40 B3
Ganges = Ganga ➝, *India* . . 41 F8
Gangneung, *S. Korea* 35 C7
Gangtok, *India* 41 D7
Gani, *Indonesia* 37 E3
Gansu □, *China* 34 C5
Ganta, *Liberia* 53 G4
Gantheaume, C., *Australia* . 62 C2
Gantsevichi = Hantsavichy,
 Belarus 17 B8
Ganyem = Genyem, *Indonesia* 37 E6
Ganzhou, *China* 35 D6
Gaoua, *Burkina Faso* 53 F5
Gaoual, *Guinea* 53 F3
Gaoxiong = Kaohsiung,
 Taiwan 35 D7
Gap, *France* 13 D7
Gar, *China* 34 C2
Garabogazköl Aylagy,
 Turkmenistan 29 E6
Garagum, *Turkmenistan* . . . 29 F6
Garanhuns, *Brazil* 92 D6

Garda, L. di, *Italy* 20 B3
Garden City, *U.S.A.* 80 A3
Gardēz, *Afghan.* 42 C6
Gardo, *Somali Rep.* 49 F4
Garigliano ➝, *Italy* 20 D4
Garland, *U.S.A.* 73 F7
Garm, *Tajikistan* 29 F8
Garmisch-Partenkirchen,
 Germany 14 E6
Garmsār, *Iran* 44 C3
Garoe, *Somali Rep.* 49 F4
Garonne ➝, *France* 12 D3
Garoowe = Garoe,
 Somali Rep. 49 F4
Garoua, *Cameroon* 55 G1
Garrison Res. = Sakakawea,
 L., *U.S.A.* 74 B4
Garry, L., *Canada* 68 B9
Garvie Mts., *N.Z.* 65 F3
Garwa = Garoua, *Cameroon* . 55 G1
Gary, *U.S.A.* 76 D2
Garzê, *China* 34 C5
Garzón, *Colombia* 90 C3
Gasan Kuli = Esenguly,
 Turkmenistan 29 F6
Gascogne, *France* 12 E4
Gascogne, G. de, *Europe* . . . 12 D2
Gascony = Gascogne, *France* 12 E4
Gaspé, *Canada* 71 E7
Gaspésie, Pén. de la, *Canada* 71 E7
Gasteiz = Vitoria-Gasteiz,
 Spain 19 A4
Gastonia, *U.S.A.* 83 B7
Gastre, *Argentina* 95 E3
Gata, C. de, *Spain* 19 D4
Gata, Sierra de, *Spain* 18 B2
Gateshead, *U.K.* 11 D6
Gauhati = Guwahati, *India* . . 41 D8
Gavāter, *Iran* 45 E5
Gavdos, *Greece* 23 G5
Gävle, *Sweden* 9 C9
Gawilgarh Hills, *India* 43 J10
Gawler, *Australia* 62 B2
Gaxun Nur, *China* 34 B5
Gaya, *India* 40 E5
Gaya, *Niger* 53 F6
Gayndah, *Australia* 63 A5
Gaysin = Haysyn, *Ukraine* . . 17 D9
Gayvoron = Hayvoron,
 Ukraine 17 D9
Gaza, *Gaza Strip* 47 E3
Gaziantep, *Turkey* 46 C4
Gazimağosa = Famagusta,
 Cyprus 46 D3
Gcuwa, *S. Africa* 59 E5
Gdańsk, *Poland* 16 A4
Gdańska, Zatoka, *Poland* . . . 16 A4
Gdov, *Russia* 24 B2
Gdynia, *Poland* 16 A4
Gebe, *Indonesia* 37 D3
Gebze, *Turkey* 22 D7
Gedaref, *Sudan* 55 F6
Gediz ➝, *Turkey* 23 E6
Gedser, *Denmark* 9 E8
Geelong, *Australia* 63 C3
Geesthacht, *Germany* 14 B6
Geidam, *Nigeria* 55 F1
Gejiu, *China* 34 D5
Gela, *Italy* 21 F5
Gelibolu, *Turkey* 23 D6
Gelsenkirchen, *Germany* . . . 14 C4
Gemena, Dem. Rep. of
 the Congo 56 D3
Gemerek, *Turkey* 46 C4
Gemlik, *Turkey* 23 D7
General Acha, *Argentina* . . . 94 D4
General Alvear, B. Aires,
 Argentina 94 D5
General Alvear, Mendoza,
 Argentina 94 D3
General Belgrano, *Argentina* 94 D5
General Juan Madariaga,
 Argentina 94 D5
General La Madrid, *Argentina* 94 D4
General MacArthur, *Phil.* . . . 36 B3
General Pico, *Argentina* . . . 94 D4
General Pinedo, *Argentina* . . 94 B4

General Santos, *Phil.* 36 C3
General Villegas, *Argentina* . 94 D4
Geneva = Genève, *Switz.* ... 14 E4
Geneva, L. = Léman, L.,
Europe 13 C7
Genève, *Switz.* 14 E4
Genil ➝, *Spain* 18 D3
Gennargentu, Mti. del, *Italy* . 21 D2
Genoa = Génova, *Italy* 13 D8
Genoa, *Australia* 63 C4
Génova, *Italy* 13 D8
Génova, G. di, *Italy* 20 C2
Gent, *Belgium* 14 C2
Genyem, *Indonesia* 37 E6
Georga, Zemlya, *Russia* 28 A5
George, *S. Africa* 58 E4
George ➝, *Canada* 70 D7
George, L., *N.S.W., Australia* 63 C4
George, L., *S. Austral.,*
Australia 62 C3
George River =
Kangiqsualujjuaq, *Canada* 70 D7
George Sound, *N.Z.* 65 F2
George Town, *Cayman Is.* .. 86 C3
George Town, *Malaysia* 38 C2
George V Land, *Antarctica* . 96 A14
George VI Sound, *Antarctica* 96 B3
Georgetown = Janjanbureh,
Gambia 53 F3
Georgetown, *Guyana* 90 B7
Georgia □, *U.S.A.* 83 C6
Georgia ■, *Asia* 25 E5
Georgian B., *Canada* 71 E5
Georgiyevsk, *Russia* 25 E5
Gera, *Germany* 15 C7
Geral de Goiás, Serra, *Brazil* . 93 E4
Geraldton, *Australia* 60 F1
Gerede, *Turkey* 46 B3
Gereshk, *Afghan.* 42 D4
Germany ■, *Europe* 14 C6
Germiston, *S. Africa* 59 D5
Gernika-Lumo, *Spain* 19 A4
Gerona = Girona, *Spain* ... 19 B7
Geser, *Indonesia* 37 E4
Getafe, *Spain* 18 B4
Gettysburg, *U.S.A.* 77 E7
Getxo, *Spain* 19 A4
Getz Ice Shelf, *Antarctica* .. 96 B18
Ghaghara ➝, *India* 40 E5
Ghana ■, *W. Afr.* 53 G5
Ghanzi, *Botswana* 58 C4
Ghardaïa, *Algeria* 52 B6
Gharyān, *Libya* 54 B1
Ghat, *Libya* 54 D1
Ghats, Eastern, *India* 43 N11
Ghats, Western, *India* 43 N9
Ghawdex = Gozo, *Malta* ... 21 F5
Ghayl, *Si. Arabia* 47 G6
Ghazal, Bahr el ➝, *Chad* ... 55 F2
Ghazâl, Bahr el ➝, *Sudan* .. 55 G5
Ghaziabad, *India* 42 E10
Ghazipur, *India* 40 E4
Ghazni, *Afghan.* 42 C6
Ghazni □, *Afghan.* 42 C6
Ghent = Gent, *Belgium* 14 C2
Gheorghe Gheorghiu-Dej =
Oneşti, *Romania* 17 E8
Ghowr □, *Afghan.* 42 C4
Ghugus, *India* 43 K11
Ghūriān, *Afghan.* 42 B2
Gia Lai = Plei Ku, *Vietnam* .. 38 B3
Gianitsa, *Greece* 23 D4
Giarabub = Al Jaghbūb, *Libya* 54 C3
Giarre, *Italy* 21 F5
Gibeon, *Namibia* 58 D3
Gibraltar ☑, *Europe* 18 D3
Gibraltar, Str. of, *Medit. S.* .. 18 E3
Gibson Desert, *Australia* ... 60 E4
Giebnegáisi = Kebnekaise,
Sweden 8 B9
Giessen, *Germany* 14 C5
Gifu, *Japan* 33 F5
Gíglio, *Italy* 20 C3
Gijón, *Spain* 18 A3
Gila ➝, *U.S.A.* 78 D5
Gīlān □, *Iran* 46 C7
Gilbert Is., *Kiribati* 64 J12

Gilgandra, *Australia* 63 B4
Gilgit, *India* 42 B9
Gilles, L., *Australia* 62 B2
Gin Gin, *Australia* 63 A5
Ginir, *Ethiopia* 49 F3
Giona, Oros, *Greece* 23 E4
Giresun, *Turkey* 25 E4
Girga, *Egypt* 54 C5
Giridih, *India* 40 E6
Girne = Kyrenia, *Cyprus* ... 46 D3
Giron = Kiruna, *Sweden* ... 8 B10
Girona, *Spain* 19 B7
Gironde ➝, *France* 12 D3
Girvan, *U.K.* 10 D4
Gisborne, *N.Z.* 64 C8
Gisenyi, *Rwanda* 57 E5
Gitega, *Burundi* 57 E5
Githio, *Greece* 23 F4
Giuba ➝, *Somali Rep.* 49 G3
Giurgiu, *Romania* 22 C5
Giza = El Gîza, *Egypt* 54 C5
Gizab, *Afghan.* 42 C4
Giżycko, *Poland* 16 A5
Gjirokastër, *Albania* 23 D3
Gjoa Haven, *Canada* 68 B10
Glace Bay, *Canada* 71 E8
Gladstone, *Queens., Australia* 61 E9
Gladstone, *S. Austral.,*
Australia 62 B2
Glâma = Glomma ➝, *Norway* 9 C8
Glasgow, *U.K.* 10 D4
Glazov, *Russia* 28 D6
Gleiwitz = Gliwice, *Poland* .. 16 C4
Glen Canyon △, *U.S.A.* 79 B7
Glen Innes, *Australia* 63 A5
Glendale, *U.S.A.* 78 C3
Glenelg ➝, *Australia* 62 C3
Glenmorgan, *Australia* 63 A4
Glenorchy, *Australia* 62 D4
Glenreagh, *Australia* 63 B5
Glenrothes, *U.K.* 10 C5
Glens Falls, *U.S.A.* 77 C9
Gliwice, *Poland* 16 C4
Głogów, *Poland* 16 C3
Glomma ➝, *Norway* 9 C8
Glorieuses, Îs., *Ind. Oc.* 59 A9
Gloucester, *Australia* 63 B5
Gloucester, *U.K.* 11 F5
Glusk, *Belarus* 17 B9
Gmünd, *Austria* 15 D8
Gmunden, *Austria* 15 E7
Gniezno, *Poland* 16 B3
Goa, *India* 43 M8
Goa □, *India* 43 M8
Goalen Hd., *Australia* 63 C5
Goalpara, *India* 41 D8
Goba, *Ethiopia* 49 F2
Gobabis, *Namibia* 58 C3
Gobi, *Asia* 35 B6
Godavari ➝, *India* 40 J4
Godavari Pt., *India* 40 J4
Godhra, *India* 43 H8
Gods ➝, *Canada* 69 C10
Gods L., *Canada* 69 C10
Goeie Hoop, Kaap die = Good
Hope, C. of, *S. Africa* ... 58 E3
Gogra = Ghaghara ➝, *India* . 40 E5
Goiânia, *Brazil* 93 F4
Goiás, *Brazil* 93 F3
Goiás □, *Brazil* 93 E4
Goio-Erê, *Brazil* 94 A6
Gojra, *Pakistan* 42 D8
Gökçeada, *Turkey* 23 D5
Gökova Körfezi, *Turkey* 23 F6
Goktelk, *Burma* 41 F11
Gold Coast, *Australia* 63 A5
Golden B., *N.Z.* 64 D5
Golden Gate, *U.S.A.* 72 H2
Goldsboro, *U.S.A.* 83 B9
Goleniów, *Poland* 16 B2
Golfo Aranci, *Italy* 20 D2
Golspie, *U.K.* 10 C5
Goma, Dem. Rep. of
the Congo 57 E5
Gomel = Homyel, *Belarus* ... 17 B10
Gomera, *Canary Is.* 52 C2
Gómez Palacio, *Mexico* 84 B4

Gomogomo, *Indonesia* 37 F4
Gomoh, *India* 40 F6
Gompa = Ganta, *Liberia* ... 53 G4
Gonābād, *Iran* 44 C4
Gonaïves, *Haiti* 87 C5
Gonbad-e Kāvūs, *Iran* 44 B3
Gonda, *India* 40 D3
Gonder, *Ethiopia* 55 F6
Gönen, *Turkey* 23 D6
Gonghe, *China* 34 C5
Gongolgon, *Australia* 63 B4
Good Hope, C. of, *S. Africa* . 58 E3
Goodooga, *Australia* 63 A4
Goolgowi, *Australia* 63 B4
Goondiwindi, *Australia* 63 A5
Gop, *India* 43 H6
Göppingen, *Germany* 14 D5
Gorakhpur, *India* 40 D4
Goražde, *Bos.-H.* 20 C7
Gordon ➝, *Australia* 62 D4
Gore, *Ethiopia* 55 G6
Gore, *N.Z.* 65 G3
Gorgān, *Iran* 44 B3
Gorgona, I., *Colombia* 90 C3
Gorízia, *Italy* 20 B4
Gorkiy = Nizhniy Novgorod,
Russia 24 B5
Gorkovskoye Vdkhr., *Russia* . 24 B5
Görlitz, *Germany* 15 C8
Gorlovka = Horlivka, *Ukraine* 25 D4
Gorna Dzhumayo =
Blagoevgrad, *Bulgaria* ... 22 C4
Gorna Oryakhovitsa, *Bulgaria* 22 C5
Gorno-Altay □, *Russia* 29 D9
Gorno-Altaysk, *Russia* 29 D9
Gornyy, *Russia* 32 A3
Gorodenka = Horodenka,
Ukraine 17 D7
Gorodok = Horodok, *Ukraine* 17 D6
Gorokhov = Horokhiv, *Ukraine* 17 C7
Gorontalo, *Indonesia* 37 D2
Gorzów Wielkopolski, *Poland* 16 B2
Gosford, *Australia* 63 B5
Goshogawara, *Japan* 32 C7
Goslar, *Germany* 14 C6
Gospič, *Croatia* 20 B5
Göta kanal, *Sweden* 9 D9
Göteborg, *Sweden* 9 D8
Gotha, *Germany* 14 C6
Gothenburg = Göteborg,
Sweden 9 D8
Gotland, *Sweden* 9 D9
Gotō-Rettō, *Japan* 33 G1
Göttingen, *Germany* 14 C5
Gottwaldov = Zlín, *Czech Rep.* 16 D3
Gouda, *Neths.* 14 B3
Gouin, Rés., *Canada* 71 E6
Goulburn, *Australia* 63 B4
Governador Valadares, *Brazil* 93 F5
Goya, *Argentina* 94 B5
Goyder Lagoon, *Australia* .. 62 A2
Goyllarisquisga, *Peru* 91 F3
Goz Beïda, *Chad* 55 F3
Gozo, *Malta* 21 F5
Graaff-Reinet, *S. Africa* 58 E4
Gračac, *Croatia* 20 B5
Gracias a Dios, C., *Honduras* 86 D3
Grado, *Spain* 18 A2
Grafton, *Australia* 63 A5
Graham Bell, Ostrov = Greem-
Bell, Ostrov, *Russia* 28 A7
Graham Land, *Antarctica* ... 96 A3
Grahamstown, *S. Africa* ... 59 E5
Grajaú, *Brazil* 92 D4
Grajaú ➝, *Brazil* 92 C5
Grampian Mts., *U.K.* 10 C4
Grampians, The, *Australia* .. 62 C3
Gran Canaria, *Canary Is.* ... 52 C2
Gran Chaco, *S. Amer.* 94 B4
Gran Paradiso, *Italy* 13 D7
Gran Sasso d'Itália, *Italy* ... 20 C4
Granada, *Nic.* 85 E7
Granada, *Spain* 18 D4
Granby, *Canada* 71 E6
Grand Bahama I., *Bahamas* . 86 A4
Grand Bassam, *Ivory C.* 53 G5
Grand Canyon, *U.S.A.* 79 B6

Grand Cayman, *Cayman Is.* . 86 C3
Grand Coulee Dam, *U.S.A.* . . 72 C4
Grand Falls, *Canada* 71 E7
Grand Falls-Windsor, *Canada* 71 E8
Grand Forks, *U.S.A.* 74 B6
Grand Island, *U.S.A.* 74 E5
Grand Rapids, *Canada* 69 C10
Grand Rapids, *U.S.A.* 76 C3
Grand St-Bernard, Col du,
  Europe 13 D7
Grand Teton, *U.S.A.* 73 E8
Grande →, *Bolivia* 91 G6
Grande →, *Bahia, Brazil* . . . 93 E5
Grande →, *Minas Gerais,*
  Brazil 93 G3
Grande, B., *Argentina* 95 G3
Grande, Rio →, *N. Amer.* . . . 85 B5
Grande Baleine, R. de la →,
  Canada 71 D6
Granite City, *U.S.A.* 75 F9
Granity, *N.Z.* 65 D4
Granja, *Brazil* 92 C5
Granollers, *Spain* 19 B7
Grantham, *U.K.* 11 E6
Granville, *France* 12 B3
Grasse, *France* 13 E7
Graulhet, *France* 12 E4
's-Gravenhage, *Neths.* 14 B3
Gravesend, *Australia* 63 A5
Graz, *Austria* 15 E8
Great Abaco I. = Abaco I.,
  Bahamas 86 A4
Great Australian Bight,
  Australia 60 G4
Great Barrier I., *N.Z.* 64 B6
Great Barrier Reef, *Australia* . 61 D8
Great Basin, *U.S.A.* 72 G5
Great Bear →, *Canada* 68 B7
Great Bear L., *Canada* 68 B7
Great Belt = Store Bælt,
  Denmark 9 D8
Great Divide, The = Great
  Dividing Ra., *Australia* . . . 61 E8
Great Dividing Ra., *Australia* 61 E8
Great Falls, *U.S.A.* 73 C8
Great Inagua I., *Bahamas* . . 86 B5
Great Indian Desert = Thar
  Desert, *India* 42 F7
Great Karoo, *S. Africa* 58 E4
Great Khingan Mts. = Da
  Hinggan Ling, *China* 35 B7
Great Lake, *Australia* 62 D4
Great Ouse →, *U.K.* 11 E7
Great Ruaha →, *Tanzania* . . 57 F7
Great Saint Bernard Pass =
  Grand St-Bernard, Col du,
  Europe 13 D7
Great Salt Desert = Kavir,
  Dasht-e, *Iran* 44 C3
Great Salt L., *U.S.A.* 73 F7
Great Salt Lake Desert, *U.S.A.* 73 F7
Great Sandy Desert, *Australia* 60 E3
Great Sangi = Sangihe, Pulau,
  Indonesia 37 D3
Great Slave L., *Canada* 68 B8
Great Smoky Mts. △, *U.S.A.* . 83 B6
Great Victoria Desert,
  Australia 60 F4
Great Wall, *China* 35 C5
Great Yarmouth, *U.K.* 11 E7
Great Zab = Zāb al Kabīr →,
  Iraq 46 C5
Greater Antilles, *W. Indies* . . 86 C5
Greater Sudbury = Sudbury,
  Canada 71 E5
Greater Sunda Is., *Indonesia* 39 F4
Gredos, Sierra de, *Spain* . . . 18 B3
Greece ■, *Europe* 23 E4
Greeley, *U.S.A.* 74 E2
Greely Fd., *Canada* 70 A5
Greem-Bell, Ostrov, *Russia* . 28 A7
Green →, *U.S.A.* 79 A8
Green Bay, *U.S.A.* 76 B2
Green C., *Australia* 63 C5
Greenland ☑, *N. Amer.* 66 C9
Greenock, *U.K.* 10 D4
Greensboro, *U.S.A.* 83 A8

Greenville, *Ala., U.S.A.* 82 D4
Greenville, *Miss., U.S.A.* 81 C8
Greenville, *N.C., U.S.A.* 83 B9
Greenville, *S.C., U.S.A.* 83 B6
Greenwood, *Miss., U.S.A.* . . . 81 C8
Greenwood, *S.C., U.S.A.* . . . 83 B6
Gregory, L., *Australia* 62 A2
Greifswald, *Germany* 15 A7
Greiz, *Germany* 15 C7
Gremikha, *Russia* 28 C4
Grenada ■, *W. Indies* 87 D7
Grenfell, *Australia* 63 B4
Grenoble, *France* 13 D6
Grey →, *N.Z.* 65 E4
Grey Ra., *Australia* 63 A3
Greymouth, *N.Z.* 65 E4
Greytown, *N.Z.* 65 D6
Griffin, *U.S.A.* 83 C5
Griffith, *Australia* 63 B4
Grimaylov = Hrymayliv,
  Ukraine 17 D8
Grimsby, *U.K.* 11 E6
Gris-Nez, C., *France* 12 A4
Grise Fiord, *Canada* 70 B5
Grodno = Hrodna, *Belarus* . . 17 B6
Grodzyanka = Hrodzyanka,
  Belarus 17 B9
Grójec, *Poland* 16 C5
Groningen, *Neths.* 14 B4
Grootfontein, *Namibia* 58 B3
Grosser Arber, *Germany* 15 D7
Grosseto, *Italy* 20 C3
Grossglockner, *Austria* 15 E7
Groznyy, *Russia* 25 E6
Grudziądz, *Poland* 16 B4
Gryazi, *Russia* 24 C4
Gryazovets, *Russia* 28 D5
Gua, *India* 40 F5
Guadalajara, *Mexico* 84 C4
Guadalajara, *Spain* 18 B4
Guadalcanal, *Solomon Is.* . . . 64 K11
Guadalete →, *Spain* 18 D2
Guadalquivir →, *Spain* 18 D2
Guadalupe = Guadeloupe ☑,
  W. Indies 87 C7
Guadalupe, Sierra de, *Spain* . 18 C3
Guadarrama, Sierra de, *Spain* 18 B4
Guadeloupe ☑, *W. Indies* . . . 87 C7
Guadiana →, *Portugal* 18 D2
Guadix, *Spain* 18 D4
Guafo, Boca del, *Chile* 95 E2
Guaíra, *Brazil* 94 A6
Guaitecas, Is., *Chile* 95 E2
Guajará-Mirim, *Brazil* 91 F5
Guajira, Pen. de la, *Colombia* 90 A4
Gualeguaychú, *Argentina* . . . 94 C5
Guam ☑, *Pac. Oc.* 64 H9
Guamúchil, *Mexico* 84 B3
Guanahani = San Salvador I.,
  Bahamas 86 B5
Guanajuato, *Mexico* 84 C4
Guandacol, *Argentina* 94 B3
Guane, *Cuba* 86 B3
Guangdong ☐, *China* 35 D6
Guangxi Zhuangzu Zizhiqu ☐,
  China 35 D5
Guangzhou, *China* 35 D6
Guanipa →, *Venezuela* 90 B6
Guantánamo, *Cuba* 86 B4
Guaporé →, *Brazil* 91 F5
Guaqui, *Bolivia* 91 G5
Guarapuava, *Brazil* 94 B6
Guarda, *Portugal* 18 B2
Guardafui, C. = Asir, Ras,
  Somali Rep. 49 E5
Guasdualito, *Venezuela* 90 B4
Guatemala, *Guatemala* 85 E6
Guatemala ■, *Cent. Amer.* . . 85 D6
Guaviare →, *Colombia* 90 C5
Guaxupé, *Brazil* 93 G4
Guayaquil, *Ecuador* 90 D3
Guayaquil, G. de, *Ecuador* . . 90 D2
Guaymas, *Mexico* 84 B2
Guddu Barrage, *Pakistan* . . . 42 E6
Gudur, *India* 43 M11
Guecho = Getxo, *Spain* 19 A4
Guelph, *Canada* 76 C5

Guéret, *France* 12 C4
Guernica = Gernika-Lumo,
  Spain 19 A4
Guernsey, *U.K.* 11 G5
Guidónia-Montecélio, *Italy* . . 20 C4
Guijá, *Mozam.* 59 C6
Guildford, *U.K.* 11 F6
Guilin, *China* 35 D6
Guimarães, *Portugal* 18 B1
Guimaras ☐, *Phil.* 36 B2
Guinea ■, *W. Afr.* 53 F3
Guinea, Gulf of, *Atl. Oc.* 51 F3
Guinea-Bissau ■, *Africa* 53 F3
Guingamp, *France* 12 B2
Güiria, *Venezuela* 90 A6
Guiuan, *Phil.* 36 B3
Guiyang, *China* 35 D5
Guizhou ☐, *China* 35 D5
Gujarat ☐, *India* 43 H7
Gujranwala, *Pakistan* 42 C9
Gujrat, *Pakistan* 42 C9
Gulbarga, *India* 43 L10
Gulf, The = Persian Gulf, *Asia* 44 E2
Gulgong, *Australia* 63 B4
Güllük, *Turkey* 23 F6
Gülshat, *Kazakhstan* 29 E8
Gulu, *Uganda* 57 D6
Gümüşhane, *Turkey* 46 B4
Gumzai, *Indonesia* 37 F4
Guna, *India* 43 G10
Gunnedah, *Australia* 63 B5
Gunningbar Cr. →, *Australia* . 63 B4
Gunsan, *S. Korea* 35 C7
Guntakal, *India* 43 M10
Guntur, *India* 40 J3
Gunungapi, *Indonesia* 37 F3
Gunungsitoli, *Indonesia* 39 D1
Gunza, *Angola* 56 G2
Gupis, *Pakistan* 42 A8
Gurdaspur, *India* 42 C9
Gurkha, *Nepal* 40 C5
Gurley, *Australia* 63 A4
Gurupá, *Brazil* 92 C3
Gurupá, I. Grande de, *Brazil* . 92 C3
Gurupi →, *Brazil* 92 C4
Guryev = Atyraū, *Kazakhstan* 29 E6
Gusau, *Nigeria* 53 F7
Güstrow, *Germany* 15 B7
Gütersloh, *Germany* 14 C5
Guthrie, *U.S.A.* 80 B5
Guwahati, *India* 41 D8
Guyana ■, *S. Amer.* 90 B7
Guyane française = French
  Guiana ☑, *S. Amer.* 92 B3
Guyenne, *France* 12 D4
Guyra, *Australia* 63 B5
Güzelyurt = Morphou, *Cyprus* 46 D3
Gwa, *Burma* 41 J10
Gwabegar, *Australia* 63 B4
Gwädar, *Pakistan* 42 G3
Gwalior, *India* 42 F11
Gwanda, *Zimbabwe* 59 C5
Gwangju, *S. Korea* 35 C7
Gwanju = Gwangju, *S. Korea* 35 C7
Gweru, *Zimbabwe* 59 B5
Gwydir →, *Australia* 63 A4
Gyandzha = Gäncä, *Azerbaijan* 25 E6
Gyaring Hu, *China* 34 C4
Gydanskiy Poluostrov, *Russia* 28 B8
Gympie, *Australia* 63 A5
Gyöngyös, *Hungary* 16 E4
Győr, *Hungary* 16 E3
Gyula, *Hungary* 16 E5
Gyumri, *Armenia* 25 E5
Gyzylarbat = Serdar,
  Turkmenistan 29 F6

H

Haarlem, *Neths.* 14 B3
Haast →, *N.Z.* 65 E3
Haboro, *Japan* 32 A7
Hachijō-Jima, *Japan* 33 G6
Hachinohe, *Japan* 32 C7
Hadarba, Ras, *Sudan* 54 D6

Ḥadd, Ra's al, *Oman* 45 F4
Hadejia, *Nigeria* 53 F7
Ḥadera, *Israel* 46 D3
Haḍramawt, *Yemen* 49 D4
Haeju, *N. Korea* 35 C7
Haerhpin = Harbin, *China* ... 35 B7
Hafar al Bāṭin, *Si. Arabia* 47 E6
Hafizabad, *Pakistan* 42 C8
Haflong, *India* 41 E9
Haft Gel, *Iran* 47 E7
Hagen, *Germany* 14 C4
Hagerstown, *U.S.A.* 77 E7
Hagi, *Japan* 33 F2
Hagondange, *France* 13 B7
Hague, C. de la, *France* 12 B3
Hague, The = 's-Gravenhage,
  Neths. 14 B3
Haguenau, *France* 13 B7
Haidarâbâd = Hyderabad,
  India 43 L11
Haifa = Ḥefa, *Israel* 46 D3
Haikou, *China* 35 D6
Ḥa'il, *Si. Arabia* 47 F5
Hailar, *China* 35 B6
Hailuoto, *Finland* 8 B10
Hainan □, *China* 35 E5
Haiphong, *Vietnam* 35 D5
Haiti ■, *W. Indies* 87 C5
Haiya, *Sudan* 55 E6
Hajdúböszörmény, *Hungary* . 16 E5
Hajnówka, *Poland* 17 B6
Hakodate, *Japan* 32 C7
Hala, *Pakistan* 42 G6
Ḥalab, *Syria* 46 C4
Ḥalabjah, *Iraq* 46 D6
Halaib, *Sudan* 54 D6
Halberstadt, *Germany* 15 C6
Halcombe, *N.Z.* 64 D6
Halcon, *Phil.* 36 B2
Halden, *Norway* 9 D8
Haldwani, *India* 42 E11
Halfmoon Bay, *N.Z.* 65 G3
Halifax, *Canada* 71 E7
Halifax, *U.K.* 11 E6
Halīl →, *Iran* 44 E4
Halkida, *Greece* 23 E4
Hall Beach = Sanirajak,
  Canada 70 C5
Hall Pen., *Canada* 70 C7
Hallāniyat, Jazā'ir al, *Oman* . 49 D6
Halle, *Germany* 15 C6
Hallett, *Australia* 62 B2
Halmahera, *Indonesia* 37 D3
Halmstad, *Sweden* 9 D8
Hälsingborg = Helsingborg,
  Sweden 9 D8
Ḥālūl, *Qatar* 44 E3
Hamada, *Japan* 33 F3
Hamadān, *Iran* 46 D7
Hamadān □, *Iran* 46 D7
Ḥamāh, *Syria* 46 D4
Hamamatsu, *Japan* 33 F5
Hamar, *Norway* 8 C8
Hamburg, *Germany* 14 B5
Hämeenlinna, *Finland* 8 C10
Hameln, *Germany* 14 B5
Hamersley Ra., *Australia* ... 60 E2
Hamhŭng, *N. Korea* 35 C7
Hami, *China* 34 B4
Hamilton, *Australia* 62 C3
Hamilton, *Canada* 71 E6
Hamilton, *N.Z.* 64 B6
Hamilton, *U.K.* 10 D4
Hamilton →, *Australia* 62 A2
Hamley Bridge, *Australia* ... 62 B2
Hamlin = Hameln, *Germany* . 14 B5
Hamm, *Germany* 14 C4
Hammerfest, *Norway* 8 A10
Hammond, *U.S.A.* 76 D2
Hampden, *N.Z.* 65 F4
Hampton, *U.S.A.* 77 F7
Han Pijesak, *Bos.-H.* 20 B7
Hanamaki, *Japan* 32 D7
Hanau, *Germany* 14 C5
Handan, *China* 35 C6
Hangayn Nuruu, *Mongolia* .. 34 B4
Hangchou = Hangzhou, *China* 35 C7

Hangzhou, *China* 35 C7
Hangzhou Wan, *China* 35 C7
Hania = Chania, *Greece* 23 G5
Ḥanīsh, *Yemen* 49 E3
Hankö, *Finland* 9 D10
Hanle, *India* 42 C11
Hanmer Springs, *N.Z.* 65 E5
Hanna, *Canada* 69 C8
Hannibal, *U.S.A.* 75 F9
Hannover, *Germany* 14 B5
Hanoi, *Vietnam* 35 D5
Hanover = Hannover,
  Germany 14 B5
Hanover, I., *Chile* 95 G2
Hansi, *India* 42 E9
Hanson, L., *Australia* 62 B2
Hantsavichy, *Belarus* 17 B8
Hanzhong, *China* 35 C5
Haora, *India* 40 F7
Haparanda, *Sweden* 8 B10
Happy Valley-Goose Bay,
  Canada 71 D7
Hapur, *India* 42 E10
Ḥaql, *Si. Arabia* 47 E3
Har, *Indonesia* 37 F4
Har Hu, *China* 34 C4
Har Us Nuur, *Mongolia* 34 B4
Ḥaraḍ, *Si. Arabia* 47 F7
Haranomachi, *Japan* 33 E7
Harare, *Zimbabwe* 59 B6
Harbin, *China* 35 B7
Hardangerfjorden, *Norway* .. 8 C7
Hardwar = Haridwar, *India* .. 42 E11
Hardy, Pen., *Chile* 95 H3
Harer, *Ethiopia* 49 F3
Hargeisa, *Somali Rep.* 49 F3
Hari →, *Indonesia* 39 E2
Haridwar, *India* 42 E11
Haringhat →, *Bangla.* 41 G7
Harirūd →, *Asia* 42 A2
Harlingen, *U.S.A.* 80 F5
Harlow, *U.K.* 11 F7
Harney Basin, *U.S.A.* 72 E4
Härnösand, *Sweden* 8 C9
Harricana →, *Canada* 71 D6
Harris, *U.K.* 10 C3
Harris, L., *Australia* 62 B2
Harrisburg, *U.S.A.* 77 D7
Harrison, C., *Canada* 70 D8
Harrogate, *U.K.* 11 D6
Hart, L., *Australia* 62 B2
Hartford, *U.S.A.* 77 D9
Hartlepool, *U.K.* 11 D6
Harvey, *U.S.A.* 76 D2
Harwich, *U.K.* 11 F7
Haryana □, *India* 42 E10
Haryn →, *Belarus* 17 B8
Harz, *Germany* 14 C6
Hasa, *Si. Arabia* 47 F7
Haskovo = Khaskovo, *Bulgaria* 22 D5
Hassi Messaoud, *Algeria* ... 52 B7
Hastings, *N.Z.* 64 C7
Hastings, *U.K.* 11 F7
Hastings, *U.S.A.* 74 E5
Hastings Ra., *Australia* 63 B5
Hatay, *Turkey* 46 C4
Hatfield P.O., *Australia* 62 B3
Hatgal, *Mongolia* 34 A5
Hathras, *India* 42 F11
Hatia, *Bangla.* 41 F8
Hattah, *Australia* 62 B3
Hatteras, C., *U.S.A.* 83 B10
Hattiesburg, *U.S.A.* 81 D9
Hatvan, *Hungary* 16 E4
Haugesund, *Norway* 9 D7
Hauraki G., *N.Z.* 64 B6
Haut Atlas, *Morocco* 52 B4
Havana = La Habana, *Cuba* .. 86 B3
Havant, *U.K.* 11 F6
Havel →, *Germany* 15 B7
Havelock, *N.Z.* 65 D5
Haverfordwest, *U.K.* 11 F4
Havlíčkův Brod, *Czech Rep.* . 16 D2
Havre, *U.S.A.* 73 B9
Havre-St.-Pierre, *Canada* ... 71 D7
Havza, *Turkey* 46 B3
Hawai'i □, *U.S.A.* 78 H12

Hawaiian Is., *Pac. Oc.* 78 H12
Hawea, L., *N.Z.* 65 F3
Hawera, *N.Z.* 64 C6
Hawick, *U.K.* 10 D5
Hawke B., *N.Z.* 64 C7
Hawker, *Australia* 62 B2
Hay, *Australia* 63 B3
Hay River, *Canada* 68 B8
Haya = Tehoru, *Indonesia* .. 37 E3
Hayastan = Armenia ■, *Asia* . 25 E5
Hayes →, *Canada* 69 C10
Hayrabolu, *Turkey* 22 D6
Haysyn, *Ukraine* 17 D9
Hayvoron, *Ukraine* 17 D9
Hazar, *Turkmenistan* 29 F6
Hazārān, Kūh-e, *Iran* 44 D4
Hazaribag, *India* 40 F5
Healesville, *Australia* 63 C4
Hearst, *Canada* 71 E5
Hebei □, *China* 35 C6
Hebel, *Australia* 63 A4
Hebron = Al Khalīl, *West Bank* 47 E3
Hebron, *Canada* 70 D7
Hechi, *China* 35 D5
Hechuan, *China* 35 C5
Heerlen, *Neths.* 13 A6
Ḥefa, *Israel* 46 D3
Hefei, *China* 35 C6
Hegang, *China* 35 B8
Heidelberg, *Germany* 14 D5
Heilbronn, *Germany* 14 D5
Heilongjiang □, *China* 35 B7
Heimaey, *Iceland* 8 C1
Hejaz = Ḥijāz, *Si. Arabia* ... 47 F4
Hekimhan, *Turkey* 46 C4
Hekou, *China* 34 D5
Helena, Ark., *U.S.A.* 81 B8
Helena, Mont., *U.S.A.* 73 C7
Helensville, *N.Z.* 64 B6
Helgoland, *Germany* 14 A4
Heligoland B. = Deutsche
  Bucht, *Germany* 14 A5
Hellas = Greece ■, *Europe* .. 23 E4
Hellespont = Çanakkale
  Boğazı, *Turkey* 23 D6
Hellín, *Spain* 19 C5
Helmand □, *Afghan.* 42 D3
Helmand →, *Afghan.* 42 D2
Helmsdale, *U.K.* 10 B5
Helsingborg, *Sweden* 9 D8
Helsinki, *Finland* 9 C11
Helwân, *Egypt* 54 C5
Hemel Hempstead, *U.K.* ... 11 F6
Henan □, *China* 35 C6
Henares →, *Spain* 18 B4
Henashi-Misaki, *Japan* 32 C6
Henderson, *U.S.A.* 83 A8
Hengyang, *China* 35 D6
Henrietta Maria, C., *Canada* . 71 D5
Hentiyn Nuruu, *Mongolia* ... 35 B5
Henty, *Australia* 63 C4
Henzada, *Burma* 41 J10
Heraklion = Iraklio, *Greece* .. 23 G5
Herāt, *Afghan.* 42 B3
Herāt □, *Afghan.* 42 B3
Herceg-Novi, *Serbia & M.* .. 22 C2
Hereford, *U.K.* 11 E5
Herford, *Germany* 14 B5
Hermidale, *Australia* 63 B4
Hermite, I., *Chile* 95 H3
Hermon, Mt. = Shaykh, J. ash,
  Lebanon 46 D3
Hermosillo, *Mexico* 84 B2
Hernád →, *Hungary* 16 E5
Heroica Nogales = Nogales,
  Mexico 84 A2
's-Hertogenbosch, *Neths.* ... 14 C3
Hessen □, *Germany* 14 C5
Hexham, *U.K.* 11 D5
Heywood, *Australia* 62 C3
Hialeah, *U.S.A.* 83 G7
Hibbing, *U.S.A.* 75 B8
Hibbs B., *Australia* 62 D4
Hickory, *U.S.A.* 83 B7
Hicks, Pt., *Australia* 63 C4
Hidalgo del Parral, *Mexico* .. 84 B3
Higashiajima-San, *Japan* ... 33 E7

Higashiōsaka, *Japan* 33 F4
High Point, *U.S.A.* 83 B8
High River, *Canada* 69 C8
High Tatra = Tatry,
   Slovak Rep. 16 D4
High Wycombe, *U.K.* 11 F6
Hiiumaa, *Estonia* 24 B1
Ḥijārah, Ṣaḥrā' al, *Iraq* ... 47 E6
Ḥijāz, *Si. Arabia* 47 F4
Hijo = Tagum, *Phil.* 36 C3
Hikurangi, *Gisborne, N.Z.* .. 64 C7
Hikurangi, *Northland, N.Z.* ... 64 A6
Hildesheim, *Germany* 14 B5
Hillston, *Australia* 63 B4
Hilo, *U.S.A.* 78 J13
Hilversum, *Neths.* 14 B3
Himachal Pradesh □, *India* . 42 D10
Himalaya, *Asia* 40 C5
Himatnagar, *India* 43 H8
Himeji, *Japan* 33 F4
Himi, *Japan* 33 E5
Ḥimṣ, *Syria* 46 D4
Hindmarsh, L., *Australia* ... 62 C3
Hindu Bagh, *Pakistan* 42 D5
Hindu Kush, *Asia* 42 B7
Hindupur, *India* 43 N10
Hinganghat, *India* 43 J11
Hingoli, *India* 43 K10
Hinna = Imi, *Ethiopia* 49 F3
Hinojosa del Duque, *Spain* .. 18 C3
Hinthada = Henzada, *Burma* . 41 J10
Hios, *Greece* 23 E6
Hirakud Dam, *India* 40 G4
Hiroo, *Japan* 32 B8
Hirosaki, *Japan* 32 C7
Hiroshima, *Japan* 33 F3
Hisar, *India* 42 E9
Hispaniola, *W. Indies* 87 C5
Hitachi, *Japan* 33 E7
Hjälmaren, *Sweden* 9 D9
Hkakabo Razi, *Burma* 41 C11
Hlyboka, *Ukraine* 17 D7
Ho Chi Minh City = Thanh Pho
   Ho Chi Minh, *Vietnam* 38 B3
Hoai Nhon, *Vietnam* 38 B3
Hoare B., *Canada* 70 C7
Hobart, *Australia* 62 D4
Hobbs Coast, *Antarctica* .. 96 B18
Hodaka-Dake, *Japan* 33 E5
Hodeida = Al Ḥudaydah,
   Yemen 49 E3
Hodgson, *Canada* 69 C10
Hódmezővásárhely, *Hungary* 16 E5
Hodna, Chott el, *Algeria* ... 52 A6
Hodonín, *Czech Rep.* 16 D3
Hoek van Holland, *Neths.* ... 14 B3
Hof, *Germany* 15 C6
Hofsjökull, *Iceland* 8 C2
Hōfu, *Japan* 33 F2
Hogan Group, *Australia* ... 62 C4
Hoggar = Ahaggar, *Algeria* . 52 D7
Hoh Xil Shan, *China* 34 C3
Hoher Rhön = Rhön, *Germany* 14 C5
Hohhot, *China* 35 B6
Hoi An, *Vietnam* 38 A3
Hokianga Harbour, *N.Z.* ... 64 A5
Hokitika, *N.Z.* 65 E4
Hokkaidō □, *Japan* 32 B8
Holbrook, *Australia* 63 C4
Holguín, *Cuba* 86 B4
Hollywood, *U.S.A.* 83 G7
Holman, *Canada* 68 A8
Holstebro, *Denmark* 9 D7
Holyhead, *U.K.* 11 E4
Homalin, *Burma* 41 E10
Hombori, *Mali* 53 E5
Home B., *Canada* 70 C7
Homer, *U.S.A.* 69 C4
Homs = Ḥimṣ, *Syria* 46 D4
Homyel, *Belarus* 17 B10
Hon Chong, *Vietnam* 38 B2
Honan = Henan □, *China* .. 35 C6
Honbetsu, *Japan* 32 B8
Honduras ■, *Cent. Amer.* .. 85 E7
Honduras, G. de, *Caribbean* . 85 D7
Hønefoss, *Norway* 9 C8
Honfleur, *France* 12 B4

Hong Kong □, *China* 35 D6
Hongjiang, *China* 35 D5
Hongshui He →, *China* 35 D5
Hongze Hu, *China* 35 C6
Honiara, *Solomon Is.* 64 K10
Honjō, *Japan* 32 D7
Honolulu, *U.S.A.* 78 H12
Honshū, *Japan* 33 F4
Hood, Mt., *U.S.A.* 72 D3
Hooghly = Hugli →, *India* .. 40 G7
Hook of Holland = Hoek van
   Holland, *Neths.* 14 B3
Hoorn, *Neths.* 14 B5
Hoover Dam, *U.S.A.* 78 B5
Hope, L., *Australia* 62 A2
Hopedale, *Canada* 70 D7
Hopei = Hebei □, *China* 35 C6
Hopetoun, *Australia* 62 C3
Hopetown, *S. Africa* 58 D4
Hoquiam, *U.S.A.* 72 C2
Horlick Mts., *Antarctica* ... 96 C1
Horlivka, *Ukraine* 25 D4
Hormoz, *Iran* 44 E3
Hormoz, Jaz.-ye, *Iran* 44 E4
Hormozgān □, *Iran* 44 E3
Hormuz, Str. of, *The Gulf* .. 44 E4
Horn, *Austria* 15 D8
Horn, Cape = Hornos, C. de,
   Chile 95 H3
Hornavan, *Sweden* 8 B9
Hornos, C. de, *Chile* 95 H3
Horodenka, *Ukraine* 17 D7
Horodok, *Khmelnytskyy,
   Ukraine* 17 D8
Horodok, *Lviv, Ukraine* 17 D6
Horokhiv, *Ukraine* 17 C7
Horqin Youyi Qianqi, *China* . 35 B7
Horqueta, *Paraguay* 94 A5
Horsham, *Australia* 62 C3
Horton →, *Canada* 68 B7
Hoshangabad, *India* 43 H10
Hoshiarpur, *India* 42 D9
Hospet, *India* 43 M10
Hoste, I., *Chile* 95 H3
Hot Springs, *U.S.A.* 81 B7
Hotan, *China* 34 C2
Hotazel, *S. Africa* 58 D4
Houhora Heads, *N.Z.* 64 A5
Houlton, *U.S.A.* 77 A12
Houma, *U.S.A.* 81 E8
Houston, *U.S.A.* 81 E6
Hovd □, *Mongolia* 34 B4
Hövsgöl Nuur, *Mongolia* ... 34 A5
Howard, *Australia* 63 A5
Howe, C., *Australia* 63 C5
Howitt, L., *Australia* 62 A2
Howrah = Haora, *India* 40 F7
Höxter, *Germany* 14 C5
Hoy, *U.K.* 10 B5
Høyanger, *Norway* 8 C7
Hoyerswerda, *Germany* 15 C8
Hpa-an = Pa-an, *Burma* 41 J11
Hpunan Pass, *Burma* 41 D11
Hradec Králové, *Czech Rep.* . 16 C2
Hrodna, *Belarus* 17 B6
Hrodzyanka, *Belarus* 17 B9
Hrvatska = Croatia ■, *Europe* 20 B6
Hrymayliv, *Ukraine* 17 D8
Hsenwi, *Burma* 41 F11
Hsiamen = Xiamen, *China* .. 35 D6
Hsian = Xi'an, *China* 35 C5
Hsinhailien = Lianyungang,
   China 35 C6
Hsüchou = Xuzhou, *China* .. 35 C6
Hua Hin, *Thailand* 38 B1
Huacho, *Peru* 91 F3
Huai He →, *China* 35 C6
Huainan, *China* 35 C6
Huallaga →, *Peru* 90 E3
Huambo, *Angola* 58 A3
Huancabamba, *Peru* 91 E3
Huancane, *Peru* 91 G5
Huancavelica, *Peru* 91 F3
Huancayo, *Peru* 91 F3
Huang Hai = Yellow Sea,
   China 35 C7
Huang He →, *China* 35 C6

Huangshan, *China* 35 D6
Huangshi, *China* 35 C6
Huánuco, *Peru* 91 E3
Huaraz, *Peru* 91 E3
Huarmey, *Peru* 91 F3
Huascarán, Nevado, *Peru* ... 91 E3
Huasco, *Chile* 94 B2
Huatabampo, *Mexico* 84 B3
Hubei □, *China* 35 C6
Hubli, *India* 43 M9
Huddersfield, *U.K.* 11 E6
Hudiksvall, *Sweden* 8 C9
Hudson →, *U.S.A.* 77 D8
Hudson Bay, *Canada* 70 C5
Hudson Mts., *Antarctica* ... 96 B2
Hudson Str., *Canada* 70 C7
Hue, *Vietnam* 38 A3
Huelva, *Spain* 18 D2
Huesca, *Spain* 19 A5
Hughenden, *Australia* 61 E7
Hugli →, *India* 40 G7
Huila, Nevado del, *Colombia* 90 C3
Huinca Renancó, *Argentina* . 94 C4
Huize, *China* 34 D5
Hukawng Valley, *Burma* ... 41 D11
Ḥulayfā', *Si. Arabia* 47 F5
Hull = Kingston upon Hull,
   U.K. 11 E6
Hull, *Canada* 71 E6
Hulun Nur, *China* 35 B6
Humahuaca, *Argentina* 94 A3
Humaitá, *Brazil* 91 E6
Humber →, *U.K.* 11 E6
Humboldt, *Canada* 69 C9
Humboldt →, *U.S.A.* 72 F4
Hume, L., *Australia* 63 C4
Hūn, *Libya* 54 C2
Húnaflói, *Iceland* 8 B1
Hunan □, *China* 35 D6
Hunedoara, *Romania* 17 F6
Hungary ■, *Europe* 16 E4
Hungerford, *Australia* 63 A3
Hŭngnam, *N. Korea* 35 C7
Hunsrück, *Germany* 14 D4
Hunter I., *Australia* 62 D3
Hunter Ra., *Australia* 63 B5
Hunterville, *N.Z.* 64 C6
Huntington, *U.S.A.* 76 E4
Huntington Beach, *U.S.A.* . 78 D3
Huntly, *N.Z.* 64 B6
Huntly, *U.K.* 10 C5
Huntsville, *Canada* 71 E6
Huntsville, *U.S.A.* 82 B4
Huonville, *Australia* 62 D4
Hupeh = Hubei □, *China* ... 35 C6
Huron, L., *U.S.A.* 76 B4
Hurunui →, *N.Z.* 65 E5
Húsavík, *Iceland* 8 B2
Huşi, *Romania* 17 E9
Hutchinson, *U.S.A.* 80 A5
Hutton, Mt., *Australia* 63 A4
Hvar, *Croatia* 20 C6
Hwang Ho = Huang He →,
   China 35 C6
Hwange, *Zimbabwe* 59 B5
Hyargas Nuur, *Mongolia* ... 34 B4
Hyderabad, *India* 43 L11
Hyderabad, *Pakistan* 42 G6
Hydra, *Greece* 23 F4
Hyères, *France* 13 E7
Hyères, Îs. d', *France* 13 E7
Hyūga, *Japan* 33 G2

I

I-n-Gall, *Niger* 53 E7
Iaco →, *Brazil* 91 E5
Ialomiţa →, *Romania* 22 B6
Iaşi, *Romania* 17 E8
Iba, *Phil.* 36 A2
Ibadan, *Nigeria* 53 G6
Ibagué, *Colombia* 90 C3
Ibar →, *Serbia & M.* 22 C3
Ibarra, *Ecuador* 90 C3
Ibiá, *Brazil* 93 F4

Ibiapaba, Sa. da, *Brazil* 92 C5
Ibiza = Eivissa, *Spain* 19 C6
Ibonma, *Indonesia* 37 E4
Ibotirama, *Brazil* 93 E5
Ibu, *Indonesia* 37 D3
Ibusuki, *Japan* 33 H2
Ica, *Peru* 91 F3
Iça →, *Brazil* 90 D5
Içana, *Brazil* 90 C5
İçel, *Turkey* 46 C3
Iceland ■, *Europe* 8 B2
Ich'ang = Yichang, *China* . . . 35 C6
Ichchapuram, *India* 40 H5
Ichihara, *Japan* 33 F7
Ichilo →, *Bolivia* 91 G6
Ichinomiya, *Japan* 33 F5
Ichinoseki, *Japan* 32 D7
Idaho □, *U.S.A.* 73 D7
Idaho Falls, *U.S.A.* 73 E7
Idar-Oberstein, *Germany* . . . 14 D4
Idensalmi = Iisalmi, *Finland* . 8 C11
Idfû, *Egypt* 54 D5
Ídhra = Hydra, *Greece* 23 F4
Idi, *Indonesia* 38 C1
Idi, Oros = Psiloritis, Oros,
  Greece 23 G5
Idiofa, *Dem. Rep. of
  the Congo* 56 E3
Idlib, *Syria* 46 D4
Ierapetra, *Greece* 23 G5
Iesi, *Italy* 20 C4
Ife, *Nigeria* 53 G6
Iforas, Adrar des, *Africa* . . . 52 E6
Igarapava, *Brazil* 93 G4
Igarka, *Russia* 28 C9
Iglésias, *Italy* 21 E2
Igloolik, *Canada* 70 C5
Igluligaarjuk = Chesterfield
  Inlet, *Canada* 68 B10
Iglulik = Igloolik, *Canada* . . . 70 C5
İğneada Burnu, *Turkey* 22 D7
Igoumenitsa, *Greece* 23 E3
Iguaçu →, *Brazil* 94 B6
Iguaçu, Cat. del, *Brazil* 94 B6
Iguala, *Mexico* 84 D5
Igualada, *Spain* 19 B6
Iguassu = Iguaçu →, *Brazil* . . 94 B6
Iguatu, *Brazil* 92 D6
Iharana, *Madag.* 59 A10
Ihosy, *Madag.* 59 C9
Iida, *Japan* 33 F5
Iisalmi, *Finland* 8 C11
Ijebu-Ode, *Nigeria* 53 G6
IJsselmeer, *Neths.* 14 B3
Ikaluktutiak, *Canada* 68 B9
Ikaria, *Greece* 23 F6
Ikeda, *Japan* 33 F3
Ikela, *Dem. Rep. of the Congo* 56 E4
Iki, *Japan* 33 G1
Ikopa →, *Madag.* 59 B9
Ikparjuk = Arctic Bay, *Canada* 70 B5
Ilagan, *Phil.* 36 A2
Îlām, *Iran* 46 D6
Iława, *Poland* 16 B4
Ile →, *Kazakhstan* 29 E8
Île-de-France □, *France* 12 B5
Ilebo, *Dem. Rep. of the Congo* 56 E4
Ilesha, *Nigeria* 53 G6
Ilhéus, *Brazil* 93 E6
Ili = Ile →, *Kazakhstan* 29 E8
Iligan, *Phil.* 36 C2
Illampu = Ancohuma, Nevado,
  Bolivia 91 G5
Illana B., *Phil.* 36 C2
Illapel, *Chile* 94 C2
Iller →, *Germany* 14 D5
Illimani, Nevado, *Bolivia* . . . 91 G5
Ilmen, Ozero, *Russia* 24 B3
Ilo, *Peru* 91 G4
Iloilo, *Phil.* 36 B2
Ilorin, *Nigeria* 53 G6
Ilwaki, *Indonesia* 37 F3
Imabari, *Japan* 33 F3
Imandra, Ozero, *Russia* 28 C4
Imari, *Japan* 33 G1
Imatra, *Finland* 8 C11

imeni 26 Bakinskikh
  Komissarov = Neftçala,
  Azerbaijan 46 C7
imeni Ismail Samani, Pik,
  Tajikistan 29 F8
Imeri, Serra, *Brazil* 90 C5
Imi, *Ethiopia* 49 F3
Ímola, *Italy* 20 B3
Imperatriz, *Brazil* 92 D4
Impéria, *Italy* 13 E8
Imperial Dam, *U.S.A.* 78 D5
Impfondo, *Congo* 56 D3
Imphal, *India* 41 E9
İmroz = Gökçeada, *Turkey* . 23 D5
Imuruan B., *Phil.* 36 B1
In Salah, *Algeria* 52 C6
Ina, *Japan* 33 F5
Inangahua, *N.Z.* 65 D4
Inanwatan, *Indonesia* 37 E4
Iñapari, *Peru* 91 F5
Inari, *Finland* 8 B11
Inarijärvi, *Finland* 8 B11
Inca, *Spain* 19 C7
İnce Burun, *Turkey* 25 E3
Incheon, *S. Korea* 35 C7
İncirliova, *Turkey* 23 F6
Incomáti →, *Mozam.* 59 D6
Indalsälven →, *Sweden* 8 C9
Indaw, *Burma* 41 E11
Independence, *Kans., U.S.A.* 81 A6
Independence, *Mo., U.S.A.* . . 75 F7
India ■, *Asia* 43 J10
Indian →, *U.S.A.* 83 F7
Indiana □, *U.S.A.* 76 D3
Indianapolis, *U.S.A.* 76 E2
Indigirka →, *Russia* 31 B12
Indira Gandhi Canal, *India* . . 42 F8
Indonesia ■, *Asia* 39 E4
Indore, *India* 43 H9
Indravati →, *India* 40 H3
Indre →, *France* 12 C4
Indus →, *Pakistan* 43 G5
İnebolu, *Turkey* 25 E3
Inglewood, *Queens., Australia* 63 A5
Inglewood, *Vic., Australia* . . 62 C3
Inglewood, *N.Z.* 64 C6
Ingolstadt, *Germany* 15 D6
Ingraj Bazar, *India* 40 E7
Ingrid Christensen Coast,
  Antarctica 96 A10
Ingulec = Inhulec, *Ukraine* . . 25 D3
Inhambane, *Mozam.* 59 C7
Inharrime, *Mozam.* 59 C7
Inhulec, *Ukraine* 25 D3
Ining = Yining, *China* 29 E9
Inírida →, *Colombia* 90 C5
Injune, *Australia* 63 A4
Inland Kaikoura Ra., *N.Z.* . . . 65 D5
Inland Sea, *Japan* 33 F3
Inle L., *Burma* 41 G11
Inn →, *Austria* 15 D7
Innamincka, *Australia* 62 A3
Inner Hebrides, *U.K.* 10 C3
Inner Mongolia = Nei
  Monggol Zizhiqu □, *China* 35 B6
Innsbruck, *Austria* 15 E6
Inongo, *Dem. Rep. of
  the Congo* 56 E3
Inouçdjouac = Inukjuak,
  Canada 70 D6
Inowrocław, *Poland* 16 B4
Insein, *Burma* 41 J11
International Falls, *U.S.A.* . . . 75 A8
Inukjuak, *Canada* 70 D6
Inútil, B., *Chile* 95 G2
Inuvik, *Canada* 68 B6
Invercargill, *N.Z.* 65 G3
Inverell, *Australia* 63 A5
Invergordon, *U.K.* 10 C4
Inverness, *U.K.* 10 C4
Inverurie, *U.K.* 10 C5
Investigator Group, *Australia* 62 B1
Investigator Str., *Australia* . . 62 C2
Inya, *Russia* 29 D9
Inza, *Russia* 24 C6
Ioannina, *Greece* 23 E3

Ionian Is. = Iónioi Nísoi,
  Greece 23 E3
Ionian Sea, *Medit. S.* 21 F6
Iónioi Nísoi, *Greece* 23 E3
Ios, *Greece* 23 F5
Iowa □, *U.S.A.* 75 D8
Iowa City, *U.S.A.* 75 E9
Ipameri, *Brazil* 93 F4
Ipatinga, *Brazil* 93 F5
Ipiales, *Colombia* 90 C3
Ipin = Yibin, *China* 35 D5
Ipixuna, *Brazil* 91 E4
Ipoh, *Malaysia* 38 D2
Ippy, *C.A.R.* 55 G3
İpsala, *Turkey* 22 D6
Ipswich, *Australia* 63 A5
Ipswich, *U.K.* 11 E7
Ipu, *Brazil* 92 C5
Iqaluit, *Canada* 70 C7
Iquique, *Chile* 91 H4
Iquitos, *Peru* 90 D4
Iracoubo, *Fr. Guiana* 92 A3
Iraklio, *Greece* 23 G5
Iráklion = Iraklio, *Greece* . . . 23 G5
Iran ■, *Asia* 44 C3
Iran, Pegunungan, *Malaysia* . 39 D4
Îránshahr, *Iran* 45 E5
Irapuato, *Mexico* 84 C4
Iraq ■, *Asia* 46 D5
Ireland ■, *Europe* 11 E3
Irian Jaya = Papua □,
  Indonesia 37 E5
Iringa, *Tanzania* 57 F7
Iriri →, *Brazil* 92 C3
Irish Republic = Ireland ■,
  Europe 11 E3
Irish Sea, *Europe* 11 E4
Irkutsk, *Russia* 30 D8
Irō-Zaki, *Japan* 33 F6
Iron Baron, *Australia* 62 B2
Iron Gate = Portile de Fier,
  Europe 22 B4
Iron Knob, *Australia* 62 B2
Ironwood, *U.S.A.* 75 B9
Irpin, *Ukraine* 17 C10
Irrara Cr. →, *Australia* 63 A4
Irrawaddy □, *Burma* 41 J10
Irrawaddy →, *Burma* 41 K10
Irrawaddy, Mouths of the,
  Burma 41 K10
Irtysh →, *Russia* 28 C7
Irún, *Spain* 19 A5
Irunea = Pamplona, *Spain* . . 19 A5
Irvine, *U.K.* 10 D4
Irymple, *Australia* 62 B3
Isabela, *Phil.* 36 C2
Ísafjörður, *Iceland* 8 B1
Isahaya, *Japan* 33 G2
Isar →, *Germany* 15 D7
Íschia, *Italy* 21 D4
Ise-Wan, *Japan* 33 F5
Isère →, *France* 13 D6
Isérnia, *Italy* 20 D5
Isfahan = Eşfahān, *Iran* 44 C2
Ishikari-Gawa →, *Japan* 32 B7
Ishikari-Wan, *Japan* 32 B7
Ishim →, *Russia* 29 D8
Ishinomaki, *Japan* 32 D7
Ishkuman, *Pakistan* 42 A8
Isil Kul, *Russia* 29 D8
Isiro, *Dem. Rep. of the Congo* 57 D5
İskenderun, *Turkey* 46 C4
İskūr →, *Bulgaria* 22 C5
Islamabad, *Pakistan* 42 C8
Island = Iceland ■, *Europe* . 8 B2
Island L., *Canada* 69 C10
Island Lagoon, *Australia* . . . 62 B2
Islands, B. of, *N.Z.* 64 A6
Islay, *U.K.* 10 D3
Isle →, *France* 12 D3
Isle of Wight □, *U.K.* 11 F6
Ismail = Izmayil, *Ukraine* . . . 17 F9
Ismâ'ilîya, *Egypt* 47 E3
İsparta, *Turkey* 46 C2
Íspica, *Italy* 21 F5
Israel ■, *Asia* 46 E3
Issoire, *France* 13 D5

121

Issyk-Kul, Ozero = Ysyk-Köl,
  Kyrgyzstan 29 E8
İstanbul, *Turkey* 22 D7
İstanbul Boğazı, *Turkey* 22 D7
Istiea, *Greece* 23 E4
Istra, *Croatia* 20 B4
Istres, *France* 13 E6
Istria = Istra, *Croatia* 20 B4
Itaberaba, *Brazil* 93 E5
Itabira, *Brazil* 93 F5
Itabuna, *Brazil* 93 E6
Itaipú, Reprêsa de, *Brazil* .. 94 B6
Itaituba, *Brazil* 92 C2
Itajaí, *Brazil* 94 B7
Italy ■, *Europe* 20 C4
Itapecuru-Mirim, *Brazil* 92 C5
Itaperuna, *Brazil* 93 G5
Itapicuru →, *Bahia, Brazil* ... 93 E6
Itapicuru →, *Maranhão, Brazil* 92 C5
Itapipoca, *Brazil* 92 C6
Itaquí, *Brazil* 94 B5
Ithaca = Ithaki, *Greece* 23 E3
Ithaki, *Greece* 23 E3
Itō, *Japan* 33 F6
Itonamas →, *Bolivia* 91 F6
Ituiutaba, *Brazil* 93 F4
Itumbiara, *Brazil* 93 F4
Iturbe, *Argentina* 94 A3
Itzehoe, *Germany* 14 B5
Ivanava, *Belarus* 17 B7
Ivanhoe, *Australia* 63 B3
Ivano-Frankivsk, *Ukraine* ... 17 D7
Ivanovo = Ivanava, *Belarus* . 17 B7
Ivanovo, *Russia* 24 B5
Ivatsevichy, *Belarus* 17 B7
Ivory Coast ■, *Africa* 53 G4
Ivrea, *Italy* 13 D7
Ivujivik, *Canada* 70 C6
Iwaizumi, *Japan* 32 D7
Iwaki, *Japan* 33 E7
Iwakuni, *Japan* 33 F3
Iwamizawa, *Japan* 32 B7
Iwanai, *Japan* 32 B7
Iwata, *Japan* 33 F5
Iwate-San, *Japan* 32 D7
Iwo, *Nigeria* 53 G6
Ixiamas, *Bolivia* 91 F5
Izhevsk, *Russia* 28 D6
Izmayil, *Ukraine* 17 F9
İzmir, *Turkey* 23 E6
İzmit = Kocaeli, *Turkey* 25 E2
İznik Gölü, *Turkey* 23 D7
Izu-Shotō, *Japan* 33 F7
Izumi-Sano, *Japan* 33 F4
Izumo, *Japan* 33 F3
Izyaslav, *Ukraine* 17 C8

J

Jabalpur, *India* 43 H11
Jablah, *Syria* 46 D4
Jablonec nad Nisou,
  Czech Rep. 16 C2
Jaboatão, *Brazil* 92 D6
Jaca, *Spain* 19 A5
Jacarei, *Brazil* 94 A7
Jackson, *Mich., U.S.A.* 76 C3
Jackson, *Miss., U.S.A.* 81 C8
Jackson, *Tenn., U.S.A.* 82 B3
Jackson B., *N.Z.* 65 E3
Jacksons, *N.Z.* 65 E4
Jacksonville, *Fla., U.S.A.* ... 83 D7
Jacksonville, *Ill., U.S.A.* 75 F9
Jacksonville, *N.C., U.S.A.* ... 83 B9
Jacmel, *Haiti* 87 C5
Jacobabad, *Pakistan* 42 E6
Jacobina, *Brazil* 93 E5
Jacundá →, *Brazil* 92 C3
Jade Mt. = Yü Shan, *Taiwan* . 35 D7
Jaén, *Peru* 91 E3
Jaén, *Spain* 18 D4
Jaffa = Tel Aviv-Yafo, *Israel* . 46 D3
Jaffa, C., *Australia* 62 C2
Jaffna, *Sri Lanka* 43 Q12
Jagadhri, *India* 42 D10

Jagdalpur, *India* 40 H3
Jagodina, *Serbia & M.* 22 B3
Jagraon, *India* 42 D9
Jagtial, *India* 43 K11
Jaguariaíva, *Brazil* 94 A7
Jaguaribe →, *Brazil* 92 C6
Jahrom, *Iran* 44 D3
Jailolo, *Indonesia* 37 D3
Jailolo, Selat, *Indonesia* 37 D3
Jaipur, *India* 42 F9
Jakarta, *Indonesia* 39 F3
Jalālābād, *Afghan.* 42 B7
Jalapa Enríquez = Xalapa,
  Mexico 84 D5
Jalgaon, *India* 43 J9
Jalna, *India* 43 K9
Jalón →, *Spain* 19 B5
Jalpaiguri, *India* 41 D7
Jaluit I., *Marshall Is.* 64 J11
Jamaica ■, *W. Indies* 86 C4
Jamalpur, *Bangla.* 41 E7
Jamalpur, *India* 40 E6
Jamanxim →, *Brazil* 92 C2
Jambi, *Indonesia* 39 E2
Jambi □, *Indonesia* 39 E2
Jambongan, Pulau, *Malaysia* 38 C5
James →, *U.S.A.* 74 D6
James B., *Canada* 71 D5
James Ross I., *Antarctica* ... 96 A4
Jamestown, *Australia* 62 B2
Jamestown, *N. Dak., U.S.A.* . 74 B5
Jamestown, *N.Y., U.S.A.* ... 77 C6
Jamkhandi, *India* 43 L9
Jammu, *India* 42 C9
Jammu & Kashmir □, *India* . 42 B10
Jamnagar, *India* 43 H7
Jamshedpur, *India* 40 F6
Jand, *Pakistan* 42 C8
Jandaq, *Iran* 44 C3
Jandowae, *Australia* 63 A5
Janesville, *U.S.A.* 75 D10
Janjanbureh, *Gambia* 53 F3
Januária, *Brazil* 93 F5
Jaora, *India* 43 H9
Japan ■, *Asia* 33 F5
Japan, Sea of, *Asia* 32 D4
Japen = Yapen, *Indonesia* .. 37 E5
Japurá →, *Brazil* 90 D5
Jaqué, *Panama* 90 B3
Jarama →, *Spain* 18 B4
Jarvis I., *Pac. Oc.* 65 K15
Jarwa, *India* 40 D4
Jäsk, *Iran* 44 E4
Jasper, *U.S.A.* 82 C4
Jászberény, *Hungary* 16 E4
Jataí, *Brazil* 93 F3
Játiva = Xátiva, *Spain* 19 C5
Jaú, *Brazil* 93 G4
Jauja, *Peru* 91 F3
Jaunpur, *India* 40 E4
Java = Jawa, *Indonesia* 39 F3
Java Sea, *Indonesia* 39 E3
Jawa, *Indonesia* 39 F3
Jaya, Puncak, *Indonesia* ... 37 E5
Jayanti, *India* 41 D7
Jayapura, *Indonesia* 37 E6
Jayawijaya, Pegunungan,
  Indonesia 37 E5
Jaynagar, *India* 40 D6
Jebel, Bahr el →, *Sudan* ... 55 G5
Jedburgh, *U.K.* 10 D5
Jedda = Jiddah, *Si. Arabia* . 47 G4
Jędrzejów, *Poland* 16 C5
Jefferson City, *U.S.A.* 75 F8
Jega, *Nigeria* 53 F6
Jeju-do, *S. Korea* 35 C7
Jelenia Góra, *Poland* 16 C2
Jelgava, *Latvia* 24 B1
Jena, *Germany* 15 C6
Jeonju, *S. Korea* 35 C7
Jeparit, *Australia* 62 C3
Jequié, *Brazil* 93 E5
Jequitinhonha, *Brazil* 93 F5
Jequitinhonha →, *Brazil* ... 93 F6
Jérémie, *Haiti* 86 C5
Jerez de la Frontera, *Spain* . 18 D2
Jerez de los Caballeros, *Spain* 18 C2

Jerid, Chott el = Djerid, Chott,
  Tunisia 52 B7
Jerilderie, *Australia* 63 C4
Jersey, *U.K.* 11 G5
Jersey City, *U.S.A.* 77 D8
Jerusalem, *Israel/West Bank* 47 E3
Jervis B., *Australia* 63 C5
Jervis I. = Iesi, *Italy* 20 C4
Jessore, *Bangla.* 41 F7
Jeypore, *India* 40 H4
Jhal Jhao, *Pakistan* 42 F4
Jhalawar, *India* 43 G10
Jhang Maghiana, *Pakistan* .. 42 D8
Jhansi, *India* 43 G11
Jharsuguda, *India* 40 G5
Jhelum, *Pakistan* 42 C8
Jhelum →, *Pakistan* 42 D8
Jhunjhunu, *India* 42 E9
Jiamusi, *China* 35 B8
Ji'an, *China* 35 D6
Jiangmen, *China* 35 D6
Jiangsu □, *China* 35 C6
Jiangxi □, *China* 35 D6
Jiaxing, *China* 35 C7
Jiayi = Chiai, *Taiwan* 35 D7
Jibuti = Djibouti ■, *Africa* .. 49 E3
Jiddah, *Si. Arabia* 47 G4
Jido, *India* 41 C10
Jihlava, *Czech Rep.* 16 D2
Jihlava →, *Czech Rep.* 16 D3
Jijiga, *Ethiopia* 49 F3
Jilin, *China* 35 B7
Jilong = Chilung, *Taiwan* ... 35 D7
Jima, *Ethiopia* 55 G6
Jiménez, *Mexico* 84 B4
Jinan, *China* 35 C6
Jindabyne, *Australia* 63 C4
Jindřichův Hradec, *Czech Rep.* 16 D2
Jingdezhen, *China* 35 D6
Jinggu, *China* 34 D5
Jinhua, *China* 35 D6
Jining, Nei Monggol Zizhiqu,
  China 35 B6
Jining, Shandong, *China* ... 35 C6
Jinja, *Uganda* 57 D6
Jinnah Barrage, *Pakistan* ... 42 C7
Jinzhou, *China* 35 B7
Jiparaná →, *Brazil* 91 E6
Jipijapa, *Ecuador* 90 D2
Jiu →, *Romania* 22 C4
Jiujiang, *China* 35 D6
Jixi, *China* 35 B8
Jizzakh, *Uzbekistan* 29 E7
Joaçaba, *Brazil* 94 B6
João Pessoa, *Brazil* 92 D7
Joaquín V. González,
  Argentina 94 B4
Jodhpur, *India* 42 F8
Joensuu, *Finland* 8 C11
Jogjakarta = Yogyakarta,
  Indonesia 39 F4
Johannesburg, *S. Africa* 59 D5
Johnson City, *U.S.A.* 83 A6
Johnston Falls = Mambilima
  Falls, *Zambia* 57 G5
Johnstown, *U.S.A.* 77 D6
Johor Bahru, *Malaysia* 39 D2
Joinville, *Brazil* 94 B7
Joinville I., *Antarctica* 96 A4
Joliet, *U.S.A.* 76 D1
Joliette, *Canada* 71 E6
Jolo, *Phil.* 36 C2
Jones Sound, *Canada* 70 B5
Jonesboro, *U.S.A.* 81 B8
Jönköping, *Sweden* 9 D8
Jonquière, *Canada* 71 E6
Joplin, *U.S.A.* 81 A6
Jordan ■, *Asia* 47 E4
Jorhat, *India* 41 D10
Jorong, *Indonesia* 39 E4
Jos, *Nigeria* 53 G7
Jotunheimen, *Norway* 8 C7
Jowzjān □, *Afghan.* 45 B6
Juan de Fuca, Str of.,
  N. Amer. 72 B1
Juan Fernández, Arch. de,
  Pac. Oc. 89 G3

Juárez, *Argentina* 94 D5
Juàzeiro, *Brazil* 93 D5
Juàzeiro do Norte, *Brazil* 92 D6
Juba = Giuba ➤, *Somali Rep.* 49 G3
Jubbulpore = Jabalpur, *India* 43 H11
Juby, C., *Morocco* 52 C3
Júcar = Xúquer ➤, *Spain* . . . 19 C5
Juchitán de Zaragoza, *Mexico* 85 D5
Jugoslavia = Serbia &
Montenegro ■, *Europe* . . . 22 B3
Juiz de Fora, *Brazil* 93 G5
Juli, *Peru* 91 G5
Juliaca, *Peru* 91 G4
Jullundur, *India* 42 D9
Jumilla, *Spain* 19 C5
Jumla, *Nepal* 40 C4
Jumna = Yamuna ➤, *India* . . 40 E3
Junagadh, *India* 43 J7
Jundiaí, *Brazil* 94 A7
Juneau, *U.S.A.* 69 C6
Junee, *Australia* 63 B4
Junggar Pendi, *China* 34 B3
Junin, *Argentina* 94 C4
Junín de los Andes, *Argentina* 95 D2
Jūniyah, *Lebanon* 46 D3
Jur, Nahr el ➤, *Sudan* 55 G4
Jura = Jura, Mts. du, *Europe* 13 C7
Jura = Schwäbische Alb,
Germany 14 D5
Jura, *U.K.* 10 D4
Jura, Mts. du, *Europe* 13 C7
Juruá ➤, *Brazil* 90 D5
Juruena ➤, *Brazil* 91 E7
Juruti, *Brazil* 92 C2
Justo Daract, *Argentina* 94 C3
Jutland = Jylland, *Denmark* . 9 D7
Juventud, I. de la, *Cuba* 86 B3
Jwaneng, *Botswana* 58 C4
Jylland, *Denmark* 9 D7
Jyväskylä, *Finland* 8 C11

K

K2, *Pakistan* 42 B10
Kaapstad = Cape Town,
S. Africa 58 E3
Kabaena, *Indonesia* 37 F2
Kabala, *S. Leone* 53 G3
Kabale, *Uganda* 57 E6
Kabalo, *Dem. Rep. of
the Congo* 57 F5
Kabanjahe, *Indonesia* 39 D1
Kabardino-Balkaria □, *Russia* 25 E5
Kabarega Falls = Murchison
Falls, *Uganda* 57 D6
Kabasalan, *Phil.* 36 C2
Kabompo ➤, *Zambia* 58 A4
Kabongo, *Dem. Rep. of
the Congo* 57 F5
Kabūd Gonbad, *Iran* 44 B4
Kābul, *Afghan.* 42 B6
Kābul □, *Afghan.* 42 B6
Kābul ➤, *Pakistan* 42 C8
Kaburuang, *Indonesia* 37 D3
Kabwe, *Zambia* 59 A5
Kachchh, Gulf of, *India* 43 H6
Kachchh, Rann of, *India* . . . 43 G6
Kachin □, *Burma* 41 D11
Kachiry, *Kazakhstan* 29 D8
Kaçkar, *Turkey* 25 E5
Kadan Kyun, *Burma* 38 B1
Kadina, *Australia* 62 B2
Kadiyevka = Stakhanov,
Ukraine 25 D4
Kadoma, *Zimbabwe* 59 B5
Kâdugli, *Sudan* 55 F4
Kaduna, *Nigeria* 53 F7
Kaédi, *Mauritania* 53 E3
Kaesŏng, *N. Korea* 35 C7
Kāf, *Si. Arabia* 47 E4
Kafan = Kapan, *Armenia* . . . 25 F6
Kafanchan, *Nigeria* 53 G7
Kafue ➤, *Zambia* 59 B5
Kaga Bandoro, *C.A.R.* 55 G2
Kagan, *Uzbekistan* 29 F7

Kağızman, *Turkey* 46 B5
Kagoshima, *Japan* 33 H2
Kagul = Cahul, *Moldova* . . . 17 F9
Kahayan ➤, *Indonesia* 39 E4
Kahnūj, *Iran* 44 E4
Kahoʻolawe, *U.S.A.* 78 H12
Kahramanmaraş, *Turkey* . . . 46 C4
Kahurangi △, *N.Z.* 65 D5
Kai, Kepulauan, *Indonesia* . . 37 F4
Kai Besar, *Indonesia* 37 F4
Kai Kecil, *Indonesia* 37 F4
Kaiapoi, *N.Z.* 65 E5
Kaieteur Falls, *Guyana* 90 B7
Kaifeng, *China* 35 C6
Kaikohe, *N.Z.* 64 A5
Kaikoura, *N.Z.* 65 E5
Kaimana, *Indonesia* 37 E4
Kaimanawa Mts., *N.Z.* 64 C6
Kainji Res., *Nigeria* 53 F6
Kaipara Harbour, *N.Z.* 64 B6
Kaironi, *Indonesia* 37 E4
Kairouan, *Tunisia* 54 A1
Kaiserslautern, *Germany* . . . 14 D4
Kaitaia, *N.Z.* 64 A5
Kaitangata, *N.Z.* 65 G3
Kajaani, *Finland* 8 C11
Kajabbi, *Australia* 61 D6
Kajo Kaji, *Sudan* 55 H5
Kakamega, *Kenya* 57 D6
Kakanui Mts., *N.Z.* 65 F4
Kakhovka, *Ukraine* 25 D3
Kakhovske Vdskh., *Ukraine* . 25 D3
Kakinada, *India* 40 J4
Kalaallit Nunaat =
Greenland ☑, *N. Amer.* . . 66 C9
Kalabagh, *Pakistan* 42 C7
Kalabahi, *Indonesia* 37 F2
Kalach, *Russia* 24 C5
Kaladan ➤, *Burma* 41 G9
Kalahari, *Africa* 58 C4
Kalakan, *Russia* 31 D9
Kalamata, *Greece* 23 F4
Kalamazoo, *U.S.A.* 76 C3
Kalan, *Turkey* 46 C4
Kalao, *Indonesia* 37 F2
Kalaotoa, *Indonesia* 37 F2
Kalat, *Pakistan* 42 E5
Kalce, *Slovenia* 20 B5
Kale, *Turkey* 23 F7
Kalegauk Kyun, *Burma* 41 K11
Kalemie, *Dem. Rep. of
the Congo* 57 F5
Kalewa, *Burma* 41 F10
Kalgoorlie-Boulder, *Australia* 60 G3
Kaliakra, Nos, *Bulgaria* 22 C7
Kalianda, *Indonesia* 39 F3
Kalibo, *Phil.* 36 B2
Kalima, *Dem. Rep. of
the Congo* 57 E5
Kalimantan, *Indonesia* 39 E4
Kalimantan Barat □,
Indonesia 39 D4
Kalimantan Selatan □,
Indonesia 39 E5
Kalimantan Tengah □,
Indonesia 39 E4
Kalimantan Timur □,
Indonesia 39 D5
Kálimnos, *Greece* 23 F6
Kaliningrad, *Russia* 24 C1
Kalinkavichy, *Belarus* 17 B9
Kalispell, *U.S.A.* 73 B6
Kalisz, *Poland* 16 C4
Kallsjön, *Sweden* 8 C8
Kalmar, *Sweden* 9 D9
Kalmykia □, *Russia* 25 D6
Kalocsa, *Hungary* 16 E4
Kaluga, *Russia* 24 C4
Kalush, *Ukraine* 17 D7
Kalutara, *Sri Lanka* 43 R11
Kamaishi, *Japan* 32 D7
Kamarän, *Yemen* 49 D3
Kamchatka, Poluostrov,
Russia 31 D13
Kamchatka Pen. = Kamchatka,
Poluostrov, *Russia* 31 D13
Kamchiya ➤, *Bulgaria* 22 C6

Kamen, *Russia* 29 D9
Kamen-Rybolov, *Russia* 32 A3
Kamenjak, Rt, *Croatia* 20 B4
Kamenka Bugskaya =
Kamyanka-Buzka, *Ukraine* . 17 C7
Kamensk Uralskiy, *Russia* . . . 29 D7
Kamin-Kashyrskyy, *Ukraine* . 17 C7
Kamina, *Dem. Rep. of
the Congo* 57 F5
Kamloops, *Canada* 69 C7
Kampala, *Uganda* 57 D6
Kampar ➤, *Indonesia* 39 D2
Kampen, *Neths.* 14 B3
Kampong Chhnang,
Cambodia 38 B2
Kampong Saom, *Cambodia* . 38 B2
Kampot, *Cambodia* 38 B2
Kampuchea = Cambodia ■,
Asia 38 B3
Kampungbaru = Tolitoli,
Indonesia 37 D2
Kamrau, Teluk, *Indonesia* . . . 37 E4
Kamui-Misaki, *Japan* 32 B7
Kamyanets-Podilskyy, *Ukraine* 17 D8
Kamyanka-Buzka, *Ukraine* . . 17 C7
Kamyshin, *Russia* 24 C6
Kanaaupscow, *Canada* 71 D6
Kanagi, *Japan* 32 C7
Kananga, *Dem. Rep. of
the Congo* 56 F4
Kanash, *Russia* 24 B6
Kanastraíon, Ákra = Paliouri,
Akra, *Greece* 23 E4
Kanazawa, *Japan* 33 E5
Kanchanaburi, *Thailand* 38 B1
Kanchenjunga, *Nepal* 40 D7
Kanchipuram, *India* 43 N11
Kandahar = Qandahār,
Afghan. 42 D4
Kandalaksha, *Russia* 8 B12
Kandangan, *Indonesia* 39 E5
Kandi, *Benin* 53 F6
Kandla, *India* 43 H7
Kandos, *Australia* 63 B4
Kandy, *Sri Lanka* 43 R12
Kangaroo I., *Australia* 62 C2
Kangāvar, *Iran* 46 D7
Kangean, Kepulauan,
Indonesia 39 F5
Kangiqliniq = Rankin Inlet,
Canada 68 B10
Kangiqsualujjuaq, *Canada* . . 70 D7
Kangiqsujuaq, *Canada* 70 C6
Kangiqtugaapik = Clyde River,
Canada 70 B7
Kangirsuk, *Canada* 70 D7
Kangto, *China* 41 D9
Kaniapiskau = Caniapiscau ➤,
Canada 70 D7
Kaniapiskau, L. = Caniapiscau,
L. de, *Canada* 71 D7
Kanin, Poluostrov, *Russia* . . . 28 C5
Kanin Nos, Mys, *Russia* 28 C5
Kaniva, *Australia* 62 C3
Kankakee, *U.S.A.* 76 D2
Kankan, *Guinea* 53 F4
Kankendy = Xankändi,
Azerbaijan 25 F6
Kanker, *India* 40 G3
Kannapolis, *U.S.A.* 83 B7
Kannauj, *India* 42 F11
Kannod, *India* 43 H10
Kano, *Nigeria* 53 F7
Kanowit, *Malaysia* 39 D4
Kanoya, *Japan* 33 H2
Kanpetlet, *Burma* 41 G9
Kanpur, *India* 40 D3
Kansas □, *U.S.A.* 74 F5
Kansas City, *Kans., U.S.A.* . . 75 F7
Kansas City, *Mo., U.S.A.* . . . 75 F7
Kansk, *Russia* 30 D7
Kansu = Gansu □, *China* . . . 34 C5
Kanye, *Botswana* 59 C5
Kaohsiung, *Taiwan* 35 D7
Kaolack, *Senegal* 53 F2
Kapan, *Armenia* 25 F6

Kapanga

Kapanga, *Dem. Rep. of the Congo* ... 56 F4
Kapchagai = Qapshaghay, *Kazakhstan* ... 29 E8
Kapela = Velika Kapela, *Croatia* ... 20 B5
Kapfenberg, *Austria* ... 15 E8
Kapiri Mposhi, *Zambia* ... 59 A5
Käpisä □, *Afghan.* ... 45 C7
Kapit, *Malaysia* ... 39 D4
Kapiti I., *N.Z.* ... 65 D6
Kapoeta, *Sudan* ... 55 H5
Kaposvár, *Hungary* ... 16 E3
Kaptai L., *Bangla.* ... 41 F9
Kapuas ➙, *Indonesia* ... 39 E3
Kapuas Hulu, Pegunungan, *Malaysia* ... 39 D4
Kapunda, *Australia* ... 62 B2
Kapuni, *N.Z.* ... 64 C6
Kaputar, Mt., *Australia* ... 63 B5
Kara, *Russia* ... 28 C7
Kara Bogaz Gol, Zaliv = Garabogazköl Aylagy, *Turkmenistan* ... 29 E6
Kara Kalpak Republic = Qoraqalpoghistan □, *Uzbekistan* ... 29 E6
Kara Kum = Garagum, *Turkmenistan* ... 29 F6
Kara Sea, *Russia* ... 28 B8
Karabiğa, *Turkey* ... 23 D6
Karabük, *Turkey* ... 46 B3
Karaburun, *Turkey* ... 23 E6
Karabutak = Qarabutaq, *Kazakhstan* ... 29 E7
Karacabey, *Turkey* ... 23 D7
Karacasu, *Turkey* ... 23 F7
Karachi, *Pakistan* ... 43 G5
Karad, *India* ... 43 L9
Karaganda = Qaraghandy, *Kazakhstan* ... 29 E8
Karagayly = Qaraghayly, *Kazakhstan* ... 29 E8
Karaikal, *India* ... 43 P11
Karaikkudi, *India* ... 43 P11
Karakalpakstan = Qoraqalpoghistan □, *Uzbekistan* ... 29 E6
Karakelong, *Indonesia* ... 36 D3
Karakitang, *Indonesia* ... 37 D3
Karakol, *Kyrgyzstan* ... 29 E8
Karakoram Pass, *Asia* ... 42 B10
Karakoram Ra., *Pakistan* ... 42 B10
Karalon, *Russia* ... 30 D9
Karaman, *Turkey* ... 46 C3
Karamay, *China* ... 34 B3
Karambu, *Indonesia* ... 39 E5
Karamea Bight, *N.Z.* ... 65 D4
Karasburg, *Namibia* ... 58 D3
Karasino, *Russia* ... 28 C9
Karasuk, *Russia* ... 29 D8
Karatau, Khrebet = Qarataū, *Kazakhstan* ... 29 E7
Karatsu, *Japan* ... 33 G2
Karawanken, *Europe* ... 20 A5
Karazhal, *Kazakhstan* ... 29 E8
Karbalā', *Iraq* ... 47 D6
Karcag, *Hungary* ... 16 E5
Karditsa, *Greece* ... 23 E3
Karelia □, *Russia* ... 8 C12
Kargasok, *Russia* ... 29 D9
Kargat, *Russia* ... 29 D9
Kargil, *India* ... 42 B10
Kariba, L., *Zimbabwe* ... 59 B5
Kariba Dam, *Zimbabwe* ... 59 B5
Kariba Gorge, *Zambia* ... 59 B5
Karimata, Kepulauan, *Indonesia* ... 39 E3
Karimata, Selat, *Indonesia* ... 39 E3
Karimnagar, *India* ... 43 K11
Karimunjawa, Kepulauan, *Indonesia* ... 39 F4
Karin, *Somali Rep.* ... 49 E4
Karkaralinsk = Qarqaraly, *Kazakhstan* ... 29 E8
Karkinitska Zatoka, *Ukraine* ... 25 D3

Karkinitskiy Zaliv = Karkinitska Zatoka, *Ukraine* ... 25 D3
Karkuk = Kirkūk, *Iraq* ... 46 D6
Karlovac, *Croatia* ... 20 B5
Karlovo, *Bulgaria* ... 22 C5
Karlovy Vary, *Czech Rep.* ... 16 C1
Karlsbad = Karlovy Vary, *Czech Rep.* ... 16 C1
Karlskrona, *Sweden* ... 9 D9
Karlsruhe, *Germany* ... 14 D5
Karlstad, *Sweden* ... 9 D8
Karnal, *India* ... 42 E10
Karnali ➙, *Nepal* ... 40 C3
Karnaphuli Res. = Kaptai L., *Bangla.* ... 41 F9
Karnataka □, *India* ... 43 N10
Kärnten □, *Austria* ... 15 E7
Karonga, *Malawi* ... 57 F6
Karoonda, *Australia* ... 62 C2
Karora, *Sudan* ... 55 E6
Karpathos, *Greece* ... 23 G6
Kars, *Turkey* ... 25 E5
Karsakpay, *Kazakhstan* ... 29 E7
Karshi = Qarshi, *Uzbekistan* ... 29 F7
Karufa, *Indonesia* ... 37 E4
Karungu, *Kenya* ... 57 E6
Karviná, *Czech Rep.* ... 16 D4
Karwar, *India* ... 43 M9
Kasai ➙, *Dem. Rep. of the Congo* ... 56 E3
Kasama, *Zambia* ... 57 G6
Kasandra Kolpos, *Greece* ... 23 D4
Kasaragod, *India* ... 43 N9
Kasba L., *Canada* ... 68 B9
Kasempa, *Zambia* ... 59 A5
Kasenga, *Dem. Rep. of the Congo* ... 57 G5
Kāshān, *Iran* ... 44 C2
Kashgar = Kashi, *China* ... 34 C2
Kashi, *China* ... 34 C2
Kashk-e Kohneh, *Afghan.* ... 42 B3
Kāshmar, *Iran* ... 44 C4
Kashun Noerh = Gaxun Nur, *China* ... 34 B5
Kasimov, *Russia* ... 24 C5
Kasiruta, *Indonesia* ... 37 E3
Kasongo, *Dem. Rep. of the Congo* ... 57 E5
Kasongo Lunda, *Dem. Rep. of the Congo* ... 56 F3
Kasos, *Greece* ... 23 G6
Kassalâ, *Sudan* ... 55 E6
Kassel, *Germany* ... 14 C5
Kastamonu, *Turkey* ... 25 E3
Kasur, *Pakistan* ... 42 D9
Katanga □, *Dem. Rep. of the Congo* ... 57 F4
Katangi, *India* ... 43 J11
Katerini, *Greece* ... 23 D4
Katha, *Burma* ... 41 E11
Kathiawar, *India* ... 43 H7
Kathmandu = Katmandu, *Nepal* ... 40 D5
Katihar, *India* ... 40 E6
Katima Mulilo, *Zambia* ... 58 B4
Katingan = Mendawai ➙, *Indonesia* ... 39 E4
Katiola, *Ivory C.* ... 53 G4
Katmandu, *Nepal* ... 40 D5
Katoomba, *Australia* ... 63 B5
Katowice, *Poland* ... 16 C4
Katsina, *Nigeria* ... 53 F7
Kattegat, *Denmark* ... 9 D8
Kaua'i, *U.S.A.* ... 78 G11
Kaunas, *Lithuania* ... 24 C1
Kavala, *Greece* ... 22 D5
Kavalerovo, *Russia* ... 32 A4
Kavīr, Dasht-e, *Iran* ... 44 C3
Kaw, *Fr. Guiana* ... 92 B3
Kawagoe, *Japan* ... 33 F6
Kawaguchi, *Japan* ... 33 F6
Kawardha, *India* ... 40 G3
Kawasaki, *Japan* ... 33 F6
Kawasi, *Indonesia* ... 37 E3
Kawawachikamach, *Canada* ... 71 D7
Kawerau, *N.Z.* ... 64 C7
Kawhia, *N.Z.* ... 64 C6

Kawhia Harbour, *N.Z.* ... 64 C6
Kawio, Kepulauan, *Indonesia* ... 36 D3
Kawnro, *Burma* ... 41 F12
Kawthoolei = Kayin □, *Burma* ... 41 H11
Kawthule = Kayin □, *Burma* ... 41 H11
Kaya, *Burkina Faso* ... 53 F5
Kayah □, *Burma* ... 41 H11
Kayan ➙, *Indonesia* ... 39 D5
Kayeli, *Indonesia* ... 37 E3
Kayes, *Mali* ... 53 F3
Kayin □, *Burma* ... 41 H11
Kayoa, *Indonesia* ... 37 D3
Kayseri, *Turkey* ... 46 C3
Kazachye, *Russia* ... 31 B11
Kazakhstan ■, *Asia* ... 29 E7
Kazan, *Russia* ... 24 B6
Kazanlŭk, *Bulgaria* ... 22 C5
Kazatin = Kozyatyn, *Ukraine* ... 17 D9
Kāzerūn, *Iran* ... 44 D2
Kazym ➙, *Russia* ... 28 C7
Kea, *Greece* ... 23 F5
Kebnekaise, *Sweden* ... 8 B9
Kebri Dehar, *Ethiopia* ... 49 F3
Kecskemét, *Hungary* ... 16 E4
Kediri, *Indonesia* ... 39 F4
Keelung = Chilung, *Taiwan* ... 35 D7
Keetmanshoop, *Namibia* ... 58 D3
Kefalonia, *Greece* ... 23 E3
Kefamenanu, *Indonesia* ... 37 F2
Keffi, *Nigeria* ... 53 G7
Keflavík, *Iceland* ... 8 C1
Keighley, *U.K.* ... 11 E6
Keimoes, *S. Africa* ... 58 D4
Keith, *Australia* ... 62 C3
Kekri, *India* ... 42 G9
Kelang = Klang, *Malaysia* ... 39 D2
Kells = Ceanannus Mor, *Ireland* ... 11 E3
Kelowna, *Canada* ... 69 D8
Kelso, *N.Z.* ... 65 F3
Keluang = Kluang, *Malaysia* ... 39 D2
Kem, *Russia* ... 28 C4
Kema, *Indonesia* ... 37 D3
Kemah, *Turkey* ... 46 C4
Kemerovo, *Russia* ... 29 D9
Kemi, *Finland* ... 8 B10
Kemi älv = Kemijoki ➙, *Finland* ... 8 B10
Kemi träsk = Kemijärvi, *Finland* ... 8 B11
Kemijärvi, *Finland* ... 8 B11
Kemijoki ➙, *Finland* ... 8 B10
Kemp Land, *Antarctica* ... 96 A9
Kempsey, *Australia* ... 63 B5
Kempten, *Germany* ... 14 E6
Kendal, *Indonesia* ... 39 F4
Kendall, *Australia* ... 63 B5
Kendari, *Indonesia* ... 37 E2
Kendawangan, *Indonesia* ... 39 E4
Kendrapara, *India* ... 40 G6
Kenema, *S. Leone* ... 53 G3
Keng Tawng, *Burma* ... 41 G12
Keng Tung, *Burma* ... 41 G12
Kenitra, *Morocco* ... 52 B4
Kennewick, *U.S.A.* ... 72 C4
Kenogami ➙, *Canada* ... 71 D5
Kenosha, *U.S.A.* ... 76 C2
Kent Group, *Australia* ... 62 C4
Kent Pen., *Canada* ... 68 B9
Kentaū, *Kazakhstan* ... 29 E7
Kentucky □, *U.S.A.* ... 76 F3
Kentville, *Canada* ... 71 E7
Kenya ■, *Africa* ... 57 D7
Kenya, Mt., *Kenya* ... 57 E7
Kepi, *Indonesia* ... 37 F5
Kerala □, *India* ... 43 P10
Kerang, *Australia* ... 62 C3
Kerch, *Ukraine* ... 25 D4
Kericho, *Kenya* ... 57 E7
Kerinci, *Indonesia* ... 39 E2
Kerki = Atamyrat, *Turkmenistan* ... 29 F7
Kerkyra, *Greece* ... 23 E2
Kermadec Is., *Pac. Oc.* ... 64 M13
Kermadec Trench, *Pac. Oc.* ... 65 N13
Kermān, *Iran* ... 44 D4
Kermān □, *Iran* ... 44 D4

Kermānshāh, *Iran* 46 D6
Kerrobert, *Canada* 69 C9
Kerulen ➡, *Asia* 35 B6
Kerzaz, *Algeria* 52 C5
Keşan, *Turkey* 22 D6
Kesennuma, *Japan* 32 D7
Kestenga, *Russia* 28 C4
Ket ➡, *Russia* 29 D9
Ketapang, *Indonesia* 39 E4
Ketchikan, *U.S.A.* 69 C6
Kętrzyn, *Poland* 16 A5
Key West, *U.S.A.* 86 B3
Khabarovsk, *Russia* 31 E11
Khābūr ➡, *Syria* 46 D5
Khairpur, *Pakistan* 42 F6
Khakassia ☐, *Russia* 30 D6
Khalkhāl, *Iran* 46 C7
Khalkís = Halkida, *Greece* 23 E4
Khalmer Yu, *Russia* 28 C7
Khalturin, *Russia* 24 B6
Khalūf, *Oman* 48 C6
Khambhat, *India* 43 H8
Khambhat, G. of, *India* 43 J8
Khamir, *Yemen* 49 D3
Khānābād, *Afghan.* 45 B7
Khānaqin, *Iraq* 46 D6
Khandwa, *India* 43 J10
Khanewal, *Pakistan* 42 D7
Khaniá = Chania, *Greece* 23 G5
Khanka, L., *Asia* 32 A3
Khankendy = Xankändi,
  Azerbaijan 25 F6
Khanty-Mansiysk, *Russia* 29 C7
Khapcheranga, *Russia* 30 E9
Kharagpur, *India* 40 F6
Kharan Kalat, *Pakistan* 42 E4
Kharānaq, *Iran* 44 C3
Kharda, *India* 43 K9
Kharg = Khārk, Jazireh-ye,
  Iran 47 E7
Khârga, El Wâhât-el, *Egypt* 54 C5
Khargon, *India* 43 J9
Khārk, Jazireh-ye, *Iran* 47 E7
Kharkiv, *Ukraine* 24 D4
Kharkov = Kharkiv, *Ukraine* 24 D4
Kharovsk, *Russia* 24 B5
Kharta, *Turkey* 22 D7
Khartoum = El Khartûm,
  Sudan 55 E5
Khasan, *Russia* 32 B2
Khāsh, *Iran* 42 E2
Khashm el Girba, *Sudan* 55 F6
Khaskovo, *Bulgaria* 22 D5
Khatanga, *Russia* 30 B8
Khatanga ➡, *Russia* 30 B8
Khaybar, Ḥarrat, *Si. Arabia* 47 F5
Khed Brahma, *India* 43 G8
Khemmarat, *Thailand* 38 A3
Khenchela, *Algeria* 52 A7
Kherson, *Ukraine* 25 D3
Kheta ➡, *Russia* 30 B8
Khilok, *Russia* 30 D9
Khíos = Hios, *Greece* 23 E6
Khiuma = Hiiumaa, *Estonia* 24 B1
Khiva, *Uzbekistan* 29 E7
Khīyāv, *Iran* 46 C6
Khmelnik, *Ukraine* 17 D8
Khmelnytskyy, *Ukraine* 17 D8
Khodoriv, *Ukraine* 17 D7
Khodzent = Khŭjand,
  Tajikistan 29 E7
Khojak Pass, *Afghan.* 42 D5
Kholm, *Afghan.* 45 B6
Kholm, *Russia* 24 B3
Khomeyn, *Iran* 44 C2
Khon Kaen, *Thailand* 38 A2
Khorat = Nakhon Ratchasima,
  Thailand 38 B2
Khorramābād, *Iran* 46 D7
Khorrāmshahr, *Iran* 47 E7
Khotyn, *Ukraine* 17 D8
Khouribga, *Morocco* 52 B4
Khowst, *Afghan.* 42 C6
Khoyniki, *Belarus* 17 C9
Khu Khan, *Thailand* 38 B2
Khudzhand = Khŭjand,
  Tajikistan 29 E7

Khūgīānī, *Afghan.* 42 D4
Khŭjand, *Tajikistan* 29 E7
Khulna, *Bangla.* 41 F7
Khulna ☐, *Bangla.* 41 F7
Khūr, *Iran* 44 C4
Khush, *Afghan.* 42 C3
Khushab, *Pakistan* 42 C8
Khust, *Ukraine* 17 D6
Khuzdar, *Pakistan* 42 F5
Khvor, *Iran* 44 C3
Khvormūj, *Iran* 44 D2
Khvoy, *Iran* 46 C6
Khyber Pass, *Afghan.* 42 B7
Kiama, *Australia* 63 B5
Kiamba, *Phil.* 36 C2
Kiangsi = Jiangxi ☐, *China* 35 D6
Kiangsu = Jiangsu ☐, *China* 35 C6
Kibombo, *Dem. Rep. of
  the Congo* 57 E5
Kíbris = Cyprus ■, *Asia* 46 D3
Kibwezi, *Kenya* 57 E7
Kicking Horse Pass, *Canada* 69 C8
Kidal, *Mali* 53 E6
Kidnappers, C., *N.Z.* 64 C7
Kiel, *Germany* 14 A6
Kiel Canal = Nord-Ostsee-
  Kanal, *Germany* 14 A5
Kielce, *Poland* 16 C5
Kieler Bucht, *Germany* 14 A6
Kiev = Kyyiv, *Ukraine* 17 C10
Kiffa, *Mauritania* 53 E3
Kifrī, *Iraq* 46 D6
Kigali, *Rwanda* 57 E6
Kigoma-Ujiji, *Tanzania* 57 E5
Kii Channel, *Japan* 33 F5
Kikinda, *Serbia & M.* 22 B3
Kikládhes = Cyclades, *Greece* 23 F5
Kikwit, *Dem. Rep. of
  the Congo* 56 E3
Kilcoy, *Australia* 63 A5
Kilimanjaro, *Tanzania* 57 E7
Kilis, *Turkey* 46 C4
Kiliya, *Ukraine* 17 F9
Kilkenny, *Ireland* 11 E3
Kilkis, *Greece* 23 D4
Killarney, *Australia* 63 A5
Killarney, *Ireland* 11 E2
Killeen, *U.S.A.* 80 D5
Killini, *Greece* 23 F4
Kilmarnock, *U.K.* 10 D4
Kilmore, *Australia* 63 C3
Kilosa, *Tanzania* 57 F7
Kilrush, *Ireland* 11 E2
Kilwa Kivinje, *Tanzania* 57 F7
Kimaam, *Indonesia* 37 F5
Kimba, *Australia* 62 B2
Kimberley, *Australia* 60 D4
Kimberley, *S. Africa* 58 D4
Kimmirut, *Canada* 70 C7
Kimry, *Russia* 24 B4
Kinabalu, Gunung, *Malaysia* 38 C5
Kindia, *Guinea* 53 F3
Kindu, *Dem. Rep. of
  the Congo* 57 E5
King George B., *Falk. Is.* 95 G4
King George I., *Antarctica* 96 A4
King George Is., *Canada* 71 D5
King I. = Kadan Kyun, *Burma* 38 B1
King I., *Australia* 62 C3
King William I., *Canada* 68 B10
Kingait = Cape Dorset, *Canada* 70 C6
Kingaok = Bathurst Inlet,
  Canada 68 B9
Kingaroy, *Australia* 63 A5
Kingoonya, *Australia* 62 B2
Kings Canyon △, *U.S.A.* 78 B3
King's Lynn, *U.K.* 11 E7
Kingscote, *Australia* 62 C2
Kingsport, *U.S.A.* 83 A6
Kingston, *Canada* 71 E6
Kingston, *Jamaica* 86 C4
Kingston, *N.Z.* 65 F3
Kingston South East, *Australia* 62 C2
Kingston upon Hull, *U.K.* 11 E6
Kingstown, *St. Vincent* 87 D7
Kingsville, *U.S.A.* 80 F5

Kınık, *Turkey* 23 E6
Kinkala, *Congo* 56 E2
Kinleith, *N.Z.* 64 C6
Kinsale, *Ireland* 11 F2
Kinsha = Chang Jiang ➡,
  China 35 C7
Kinshasa, *Dem. Rep. of
  the Congo* 56 E3
Kinston, *U.S.A.* 83 B9
Kiparissia, *Greece* 23 F3
Kiparissiakos Kolpos, *Greece* 23 F3
Kipushi, *Dem. Rep. of
  the Congo* 59 A5
Kirghizia = Kyrgyzstan ■, *Asia* 29 E8
Kiribati ■, *Pac. Oc.* 64 K12
Kırıkkale, *Turkey* 25 F3
Kirillov, *Russia* 24 B4
Kirin = Jilin, *China* 35 B7
Kirinyaga = Kenya, Mt., *Kenya* 57 E7
Kiritimati, *Kiribati* 65 J15
Kirkcaldy, *U.K.* 10 C5
Kirkcudbright, *U.K.* 11 D4
Kirkee, *India* 43 K8
Kirkland Lake, *Canada* 71 E5
Kırklareli, *Turkey* 22 D6
Kirkūk, *Iraq* 46 D6
Kirkwall, *U.K.* 10 B5
Kirov, *Russia* 28 D5
Kirovabad = Gäncä,
  Azerbaijan 25 E6
Kirovohrad, *Ukraine* 25 D3
Kirovskiy, *Russia* 32 A3
Kirsanov, *Russia* 24 C5
Kırşehir, *Turkey* 25 F3
Kirthar Range, *Pakistan* 42 F5
Kiruna, *Sweden* 8 B10
Kiryū, *Japan* 33 E6
Kisangani, *Dem. Rep. of
  the Congo* 57 D5
Kisar, *Indonesia* 37 F3
Kishanganj, *India* 40 D7
Kishangarh, *India* 42 F7
Kishb, Ḥarrat al, *Si. Arabia* 47 G5
Kishinev ≠ Chişinău, *Moldova* 17 E9
Kishtwar, *India* 42 C9
Kisii, *Kenya* 57 E6
Kiskőrös, *Hungary* 16 E4
Kiskunfélegyháza, *Hungary* 16 E4
Kiskunhalas, *Hungary* 16 E4
Kislovodsk, *Russia* 25 E5
Kiso-Gawa ➡, *Japan* 33 F5
Kissidougou, *Guinea* 53 G3
Kisumu, *Kenya* 57 E6
Kita, *Mali* 53 F4
Kitaibaraki, *Japan* 33 E7
Kitakyūshū, *Japan* 33 G2
Kitale, *Kenya* 57 D7
Kitami, *Japan* 32 B8
Kitchener, *Canada* 71 E5
Kitega = Gitega, *Burundi* 57 E5
Kíthira = Kythira, *Greece* 23 F4
Kíthnos, *Greece* 23 F5
Kittakittaooloo, L., *Australia* 62 A2
Kitui, *Kenya* 57 E7
Kitwe, *Zambia* 59 A5
Kivertsi, *Ukraine* 17 C7
Kivu, L., *Dem. Rep. of
  the Congo* 57 E5
Kiyev = Kyyiv, *Ukraine* 17 C10
Kiyevskoye Vdkhr. = Kyyivske
  Vdskh., *Ukraine* 17 C10
Kızıl Irmak ➡, *Turkey* 25 E4
Kizlyar, *Russia* 25 E6
Kizyl-Arvat = Serdar,
  Turkmenistan 29 F6
Kladno, *Czech Rep.* 16 C2
Klagenfurt, *Austria* 15 E8
Klaipėda, *Lithuania* 24 B1
Klamath Falls, *U.S.A.* 72 E3
Klamath Mts., *U.S.A.* 72 F2
Klang, *Malaysia* 39 D2
Klarälven ➡, *Sweden* 9 C8
Klatovy, *Czech Rep.* 16 D1
Klerksdorp, *S. Africa* 59 D5
Kletsk = Klyetsk, *Belarus* 17 B8
Kłodzko, *Poland* 16 C3
Klouto, *Togo* 53 G6

Kluane L.

Kluane L., Canada 68 B6
Kluang, Malaysia 39 D2
Kluczbork, Poland 16 C4
Klyetsk, Belarus 17 B8
Knossos, Greece 23 G5
Knox Coast, Antarctica 96 A12
Knoxville, U.S.A. 83 B6
Koartac = Quaqtaq, Canada . 70 C7
Koba, Indonesia 37 F4
Kobarid, Slovenia 20 A4
Kōbe, Japan 33 F4
København, Denmark 9 D8
Koblenz, Germany 14 C4
Kobryn, Belarus 17 B7
Kocaeli, Turkey 25 E2
Kočani, Macedonia 22 D4
Koch Bihar, India 41 D7
Kochi = Cochin, India 43 Q10
Kōchi, Japan 33 G3
Kochiu = Gejiu, China 34 D5
Kodiak, U.S.A. 69 C4
Kodiak I., U.S.A. 69 C4
Kofiau, Indonesia 37 E3
Koforidua, Ghana 53 G5
Kōfu, Japan 33 F6
Kohat, Pakistan 42 C7
Kohima, India 41 E10
Kohkīlūyeh va Būyer
  Aḥmadi □, Iran 44 D2
Kohler Ra., Antarctica 96 B1
Kokand = Qūqon, Uzbekistan 29 E8
Kokas, Indonesia 37 E4
Kokchetav = Kökshetaū,
  Kazakhstan 29 D7
Koko Kyunzu, Burma 41 K9
Kokomo, U.S.A. 76 D2
Kökshetaū, Kazakhstan ... 29 D7
Koksoak →, Canada 70 D7
Kokstad, S. Africa 59 E5
Kola, Indonesia 37 F4
Kola Pen. = Kolskiy
  Poluostrov, Russia 8 B13
Kolaka, Indonesia 37 E2
Kolar, India 43 N11
Kolar Gold Fields, India 43 N11
Kolayat, India 42 F8
Kolepom = Dolak, Pulau,
  Indonesia 37 F5
Kolguyev, Ostrov, Russia ... 28 C5
Kolhapur, India 43 L9
Kolín, Czech Rep. 16 C2
Kolkata, India 41 F7
Kollam = Quilon, India 43 Q10
Köln, Germany 14 C4
Koło, Poland 16 B4
Kołobrzeg, Poland 16 A2
Kolomna, Russia 24 B4
Kolomyya, Ukraine 17 D7
Kolonodale, Indonesia 37 E2
Kolosib, India 41 E9
Kolpashevo, Russia 29 D9
Kolpino, Russia 24 B3
Kolskiy Poluostrov, Russia .. 8 B13
Kolwezi, Dem. Rep. of
  the Congo 57 G5
Kolyma →, Russia 31 C13
Komatsu, Japan 33 E5
Komi □, Russia 28 C6
Kommunarsk = Alchevsk,
  Ukraine 25 D4
Kommunizma, Pik = imeni
  Ismail Samani, Pik,
  Tajikistan 29 F8
Komodo, Indonesia 37 F1
Komoran, Pulau, Indonesia . 37 F5
Komotini, Greece 22 D5
Kompong Cham, Cambodia . 38 B3
Kompong Chhnang =
  Kampong Chhnang,
  Cambodia 38 B2
Kompong Som = Kampong
  Saom, Cambodia 38 B2
Komrat = Comrat, Moldova . 17 E9
Komsomolets, Ostrov, Russia 30 A7
Kon Tum, Vietnam 38 B3
Konarhā □, Afghan. 42 B7
Konch, India 42 G11

Kondoa, Tanzania 57 E7
Köneürgench, Turkmenistan 29 E6
Kong, Ivory C. 53 G5
Kong, Koh, Cambodia 38 B2
Konglu, Burma 41 D11
Kongolo, Dem. Rep. of
  the Congo 57 F5
Konin, Poland 16 B4
Konjic, Bos.-H. 20 C6
Konosha, Russia 28 C5
Konotop, Ukraine 24 C3
Końskie, Poland 16 C5
Konstanz, Germany 14 E5
Kontagora, Nigeria 53 F7
Konya, Turkey 46 C3
Konya Ovası, Turkey 46 C3
Koonibba, Australia 62 B1
Koorawatha, Australia 63 B4
Kootenay L., Canada 69 D8
Kopaonik, Serbia & M. 22 C3
Koper, Slovenia 20 B4
Kopi, Australia 62 B2
Koprivnica, Croatia 20 A6
Kopychyntsi, Ukraine 17 D7
Korab, Macedonia 22 D3
Korçë, Albania 23 D3
Korčula, Croatia 20 C6
Kordestan = Kurdistan, Asia . 46 D5
Kordestān □, Iran 46 D6
Kordofân, Sudan 55 F4
Korea, North ■, Asia 35 C7
Korea, South ■, Asia 35 C7
Korea Bay, Korea 35 C7
Korea Strait, Asia 35 C7
Korets, Ukraine 17 C8
Korhogo, Ivory C. 53 G4
Korinthiakos Kolpos, Greece 23 E4
Korinthos, Greece 23 F4
Kōriyama, Japan 33 E7
Korneshty = Corneşti,
  Moldova 17 E9
Koro, Ivory C. 53 G4
Korogwe, Tanzania 57 F7
Koror, Palau 36 C4
Körös →, Hungary 16 E5
Korosten, Ukraine 17 C9
Korostyshev, Ukraine 17 C9
Kortrijk, Belgium 14 C2
Kos, Greece 23 F6
Kościan, Poland 16 B3
Kosciuszko, Mt., Australia .. 63 C4
Kosha, Sudan 54 D5
K'oshih = Kashi, China 34 C2
Koshiki-Rettō, Japan 33 H1
Košice, Slovak Rep. 16 D5
Kosovo □, Serbia & M. 22 C3
Kosovska Mitrovica,
  Serbia & M. 22 C3
Kôstî, Sudan 55 F5
Kostopil, Ukraine 17 C8
Kostroma, Russia 24 B5
Kostrzyn, Poland 16 B2
Koszalin, Poland 16 A3
Kota, India 43 G9
Kota Belud, Malaysia 38 C5
Kota Bharu, Malaysia 38 C2
Kota Kinabalu, Malaysia ... 38 C5
Kota Kubu Bharu, Malaysia . 39 D2
Kota Tinggi, Malaysia 39 D2
Kotaagung, Indonesia 39 F2
Kotabaru, Indonesia 39 E5
Kotabumi, Indonesia 39 E2
Kotamobagu, Indonesia ... 37 D2
Kotelnich, Russia 24 B6
Kotelnyy, Ostrov, Russia .. 31 B11
Kotka, Finland 9 C11
Kotlas, Russia 28 C5
Kotor, Serbia & M. 22 C2
Kotovsk, Ukraine 17 E9
Kotri, Pakistan 42 G6
Kotturu, India 43 M10
Kotuy →, Russia 30 B8
Kotzebue, U.S.A. 69 B3
Koudougou, Burkina Faso . 53 F5
Kouilou →, Congo 56 E2
Koula Moutou, Gabon 56 E2
Koulen = Kulen, Cambodia .. 38 B2

Koumra, Chad 55 G2
Kounradskiy, Kazakhstan ... 29 E8
Kousseri, Cameroon 55 F1
Kouvola, Finland 8 C11
Kovel, Ukraine 17 C7
Kovrov, Russia 24 B5
Koyampattur = Coimbatore,
  India 43 P10
Köyceğiz, Turkey 23 F7
Kozan, Turkey 46 C3
Kozani, Greece 23 D3
Kozhikode = Calicut, India .. 43 P9
Kozyatyn, Ukraine 17 D9
Kra, Isthmus of = Kra, Kho
  Khot, Thailand 38 B1
Kra, Kho Khot, Thailand ... 38 B1
Kracheh, Cambodia 38 B3
Kragujevac, Serbia & M. 22 B3
Krakatau = Rakata, Pulau,
  Indonesia 39 F3
Kraków, Poland 16 C4
Kraljevo, Serbia & M. 22 C3
Kramatorsk, Ukraine 25 D4
Kranj, Slovenia 20 A5
Kraśnik, Poland 16 C6
Krasnoarmeysk, Russia ... 29 D5
Krasnodar, Russia 25 D4
Krasnoperekopsk, Ukraine .. 25 D3
Krasnoselkup, Russia 28 C9
Krasnoturinsk, Russia 28 D7
Krasnoyarsk, Russia 30 D7
Krasnyy Luch, Ukraine 25 D4
Krasnyy Yar, Russia 25 D6
Kratie = Kracheh, Cambodia . 38 B3
Krau, Indonesia 37 E6
Krefeld, Germany 14 C4
Kremen, Croatia 20 B5
Kremenchuk, Ukraine 24 D3
Kremenchuksk Vdskh.,
  Ukraine 24 D3
Kremenets, Ukraine 17 C7
Krems, Austria 15 D8
Kribi, Cameroon 56 D1
Krichev = Krychaw, Belarus . 17 B10
Krishna →, India 40 K3
Krishnanagar, India 41 F7
Kristiansand, Norway 9 D7
Kristiansund, Norway 8 C7
Kriti, Greece 23 G5
Krivoy Rog = Kryvyy Rih,
  Ukraine 25 D3
Krk, Croatia 20 B5
Kronprins Olav Kyst,
  Antarctica 96 A9
Kronshtadt, Russia 24 B2
Kroonstad, S. Africa 59 D5
Kropotkin, Russia 25 D5
Krotoszyn, Poland 16 C3
Krung Thep = Bangkok,
  Thailand 38 B2
Krupki, Belarus 17 A9
Kruševac, Serbia & M. 22 C3
Krychaw, Belarus 17 B10
Krymskyy Pivostriv, Ukraine . 25 D3
Kryvyy Rih, Ukraine 25 D3
Ksar el Kebir, Morocco 52 B4
Ksar es Souk = Er Rachidia,
  Morocco 52 B5
Kuala Lipis, Malaysia 39 D2
Kuala Lumpur, Malaysia ... 39 D2
Kuala Sepetang, Malaysia .. 38 D2
Kuala Terengganu, Malaysia 38 C2
Kualajelai, Indonesia 39 E4
Kualakapuas, Indonesia ... 39 E4
Kualakurun, Indonesia 39 E4
Kualapembuang, Indonesia . 39 E4
Kualasimpang, Indonesia .. 39 D1
Kuandang, Indonesia 37 D2
Kuangchou = Guangzhou,
  China 35 D6
Kuantan, Malaysia 39 D2
Kuba = Quba, Azerbaijan .. 25 E6
Kuban →, Russia 25 D4
Kuching, Malaysia 39 D4
Kucing = Kuching, Malaysia . 39 D4
Kuda, India 43 H7
Kudat, Malaysia 38 C5

Kudymkar, *Russia* 28 D6
Kueiyang = Guiyang, *China* . 35 D5
Kufra Oasis = Al Kufrah, *Libya* 54 D3
Kufstein, *Austria* 15 E7
Kugaaruk = Pelly Bay, *Canada* 70 C5
Kugluktuk, *Canada* 68 B8
Küh-e Sorkh, *Iran* 44 C4
Kühak, *Iran* 42 F3
Kühhä-ye-Bashäkerd, *Iran* . . . 45 E4
Kühpäyeh, *Iran* 44 C3
Kuito, *Angola* 58 A3
Kuji, *Japan* 32 C7
Kukës, *Albania* 22 C3
Kula, *Turkey* 23 E7
Kulasekarappattinam, *India* . 43 Q11
Kulen, *Cambodia* 38 B2
Külob, *Tajikistan* 29 F7
Kulsary, *Kazakhstan* 29 E6
Kulunda, *Russia* 29 D8
Kulwin, *Australia* 62 C3
Kulyab = Külob, *Tajikistan* . . 29 F7
Kuma ➤, *Russia* 25 E6
Kumagaya, *Japan* 33 E6
Kumai, *Indonesia* 39 E4
Kumamba, Kepulauan,
    Indonesia 37 E5
Kumamoto, *Japan* 33 G2
Kumanovo, *Macedonia* 22 C3
Kumara, *N.Z.* 65 E4
Kumasi, *Ghana* 53 G5
Kumba, *Cameroon* 53 H7
Kumbakonam, *India* 43 P11
Kumbarilla, *Australia* 63 A5
Kumon Bum, *Burma* 41 D11
Kungrad = Qŭnghirot,
    Uzbekistan 29 E6
Kungur, *Russia* 29 D6
Kunlong, *Burma* 41 F12
Kunlun Shan, *Asia* 34 C3
Kunming, *China* 34 D5
Kunya-Urgench =
    Köneürgench, *Turkmenistan* 29 E6
Kuopio, *Finland* 8 C11
Kupa ➤, *Croatia* 20 B6
Kuqa, *China* 34 B3
Kür ➤, *Azerbaijan* 25 E6
Kura = Kür ➤, *Azerbaijan* . . 25 E6
Kurdistan, *Asia* 46 D5
Kürdzhali, *Bulgaria* 22 D5
Kure, *Japan* 33 F3
Kurgan, *Russia* 29 D7
Kuria Maria Is. = Hallāniyat,
    Jazā'ir al, *Oman* 49 D6
Kurigram, *Bangla.* 41 E7
Kuril Is. = Kurilskiye Ostrova,
    Russia 31 E12
Kurilskiye Ostrova, *Russia* . . 31 E12
Kurnool, *India* 43 L11
Kurow, *N.Z.* 65 F4
Kurri Kurri, *Australia* 63 B5
Kursk, *Russia* 24 C4
Kuruktag, *China* 34 B3
Kuruman, *S. Africa* 58 D4
Kurume, *Japan* 33 G2
Kus Gölü, *Turkey* 23 D6
Kuşadası, *Turkey* 23 F6
Kushimoto, *Japan* 33 G4
Kushiro, *Japan* 32 B9
Kushtia, *Bangla.* 41 F7
Kuskokwim B., *U.S.A.* 69 C3
Kustanay = Qostanay,
    Kazakhstan 29 D7
Kütahya, *Turkey* 25 F3
Kutaisi, *Georgia* 25 E5
Kutaraja = Banda Aceh,
    Indonesia 38 C1
Kutch, Gulf of = Kachchh, Gulf
    of, *India* 43 H6
Kutch, Rann of = Kachchh,
    Rann of, *India* 43 G6
Kutno, *Poland* 16 B4
Kutu, *Dem. Rep. of the Congo* 56 E3
Kutum, *Sudan* 55 F3
Kuujjuaq, *Canada* 70 D7
Kuujjuarapik, *Canada* 71 D6
Kuusamo, *Finland* 8 B11
Kuwait = Al Kuwayt, *Kuwait* . 47 E7

Kuwait ■, *Asia* 47 E6
Kuybyshev = Samara, *Russia* 24 C7
Kuybyshev, *Russia* 29 D8
Kuybyshevskoye Vdkhr.,
    Russia 24 B6
Kuyumba, *Russia* 30 C7
Kuzey Anadolu Dağları,
    Turkey 25 E4
Kuznetsk, *Russia* 24 C6
Kvarner, *Croatia* 20 B5
Kvarnerič, *Croatia* 20 B5
Kwajalein, *Marshall Is.* 64 J11
Kwakoegron, *Suriname* 92 A2
KwaMashu, *S. Africa* 59 D6
Kwando ➤, *Africa* 58 B4
Kwangchow = Guangzhou,
    China 35 D6
Kwango ➤, *Dem. Rep. of*
    the Congo 56 E3
Kwangsi-Chuang = Guangxi
    Zhuangzu Zizhiqu □, *China* 35 D5
Kwangtung = Guangdong □,
    China 35 D6
Kwatisore, *Indonesia* 37 E4
KwaZulu Natal □, *S. Africa* . 59 D6
Kweichow = Guizhou □, *China* 35 D5
Kwekwe, *Zimbabwe* 59 B5
Kwidzyn, *Poland* 16 B4
Kwoka, *Indonesia* 37 E4
Kyabra Cr. ➤, *Australia* 63 A3
Kyabram, *Australia* 63 C4
Kyancutta, *Australia* 62 B2
Kyaukpadaung, *Burma* 41 G10
Kyaukpyu, *Burma* 41 H9
Kyaukse, *Burma* 41 G11
Kyneton, *Australia* 63 C3
Kyō-ga-Saki, *Japan* 33 F4
Kyoga, L., *Uganda* 57 D6
Kyogle, *Australia* 63 A5
Kyongpyaw, *Burma* 41 J10
Kyōto, *Japan* 33 F4
Kypros = Cyprus ■, *Asia* . . . 46 D3
Kyrenia, *Cyprus* 46 D3
Kyrgyzstan ■, *Asia* 29 E8
Kystatyam, *Russia* 30 C10
Kythira, *Greece* 23 F4
Kyunhla, *Burma* 41 F10
Kyūshū, *Japan* 33 G2
Kyustendil, *Bulgaria* 22 C4
Kyusyur, *Russia* 30 B10
Kyyiv, *Ukraine* 17 C10
Kyyivske Vdskh., *Ukraine* . . . 17 C10
Kyzyl Kum, *Uzbekistan* 29 E7
Kyzyl-Kyya, *Kyrgyzstan* 29 E8
Kyzyl-Orda = Qyzylorda,
    Kazakhstan 29 E7

L

La Alcarria, *Spain* 19 B4
La Asunción, *Venezuela* 90 A6
La Banda, *Argentina* 94 B4
La Carlota, *Argentina* 94 C4
La Ceiba, *Honduras* 85 D7
La Cocha, *Argentina* 94 B3
La Coruña = A Coruña, *Spain* 18 A1
La Crosse, *U.S.A.* 75 D9
La Estrada = A Estrada, *Spain* 18 A1
La Grande ➤, *Canada* 71 D6
La Grange, *U.S.A.* 82 C5
La Guaira, *Venezuela* 90 A5
La Habana, *Cuba* 86 B3
La Línea de la Concepción,
    Spain 18 D3
La Mancha, *Spain* 19 C4
La Palma, *Canary Is.* 52 C2
La Palma del Condado, *Spain* 18 D2
La Paragua, *Venezuela* 90 B6
La Paz, *Entre Ríos, Argentina* 94 C5
La Paz, *San Luis, Argentina* . 94 C3
La Paz, *Bolivia* 91 G5
La Paz, *Mexico* 84 C2
La Pedrera, *Colombia* 90 D5
La Plata, *Argentina* 94 D5

La Quiaca, *Argentina* 94 A3
La Rioja, *Argentina* 94 B3
La Rioja □, *Spain* 19 A4
La Robla, *Spain* 18 A3
La Roche-sur-Yon, *France* . . . 12 C3
La Rochelle, *France* 12 C3
La Roda, *Spain* 19 C4
La Romana, *Dom. Rep.* 87 C6
La Serena, *Chile* 94 B2
La Seu d'Urgell, *Spain* 19 A6
La Seyne-sur-Mer, *France* . . . 13 E6
La Spézia, *Italy* 13 D8
La Tortuga, *Venezuela* 87 D6
La Tuque, *Canada* 71 E6
La Unión, *Chile* 95 E2
La Urbana, *Venezuela* 90 B5
La Vall d'Uixó, *Spain* 19 C5
La Vega, *Dom. Rep.* 87 C5
Laas Caanood = Las Anod,
    Somali Rep. 49 F4
Labe = Elbe ➤, *Europe* 14 B5
Labé, *Guinea* 53 F3
Laboulaye, *Argentina* 94 C4
Labrador, *Canada* 71 D7
Labrador City, *Canada* 71 D7
Labrador Sea, *Atl. Oc.* 70 D8
Lábrea, *Brazil* 91 E6
Labuan, *Malaysia* 38 C5
Labuan, Pulau, *Malaysia* 38 C5
Labuha, *Indonesia* 37 E3
Labuhanbajo, *Indonesia* 37 F2
Labuk, Telok, *Malaysia* 38 C5
Labyrinth, L., *Australia* 62 B2
Labytnangi, *Russia* 28 C7
Lac La Biche, *Canada* 69 C8
Lac la Martre = Wha Ti,
    Canada 68 B8
Lacanau, *France* 12 D3
Laccadive Is. = Lakshadweep
    Is., *India* 26 G9
Lacepede B., *Australia* 62 C2
Lachlan ➤, *Australia* 63 B3
Lacombe, *Canada* 69 C8
Ladakh Ra., *India* 42 B10
Lādīz, *Iran* 45 D5
Ladoga, L. = Ladozhskoye
    Ozero, *Russia* 8 C12
Ladozhskoye Ozero, *Russia* . 8 C12
Ladysmith, *S. Africa* 59 D5
Lae, *Papua N. G.* 61 B8
Lafayette, *U.S.A.* 81 D7
Lafia, *Nigeria* 53 G7
Laghmän □, *Afghan.* 45 C7
Laghouat, *Algeria* 52 B6
Lagonoy G., *Phil.* 36 B2
Lagos, *Nigeria* 53 G6
Lagos, *Portugal* 18 D1
Laguna, *Brazil* 94 B7
Lagunas, *Peru* 90 E3
Lahad Datu, *Malaysia* 36 C1
Lahad Datu, Telok, *Malaysia* . 36 D1
Lahat, *Indonesia* 39 E2
Lahewa, *Indonesia* 39 D1
Lähijän, *Iran* 46 C7
Lahn ➤, *Germany* 14 C4
Lahore, *Pakistan* 42 D9
Lahti, *Finland* 8 C11
Lahtis = Lahti, *Finland* 8 C11
Laï, *Chad* 55 G2
Laila = Layla, *Si. Arabia* 47 G6
Lairg, *U.K.* 10 B4
Laizhou, *China* 35 C6
Lajes, *Brazil* 94 B6
Lake Cargelligo, *Australia* . . . 63 B4
Lake Charles, *U.S.A.* 81 D7
Lake City, *U.S.A.* 83 D6
Lake Harbour = Kimmirut,
    Canada 70 C7
Lake Worth, *U.S.A.* 83 F7
Lakeland, *U.S.A.* 83 E7
Lakes Entrance, *Australia* . . . 63 C4
Lakewood, *U.S.A.* 76 D5
Lakhnau = Lucknow, *India* . . 40 D3
Lakonikos Kolpos, *Greece* . . . 23 F4
Lakor, *Indonesia* 37 F3
Lakota, *Ivory C.* 53 G4

Lakshadweep Is.

Lakshadweep Is., *India* 26 G9
Lalaghat, *India* 41 E9
L'Albufera, *Spain* 19 C5
Lalín, *Spain* 18 A1
Lamaing, *Burma* 41 K11
Lamas, *Peru* 91 E3
Lambaréné, *Gabon* 56 E2
Lambert Glacier, *Antarctica* . 96 B10
Lamego, *Portugal* 18 B2
Lameroo, *Australia* 62 C3
Lamia, *Greece* 23 E4
Lamon B., *Phil.* 36 B2
Lampa, *Peru* 91 G4
Lampedusa, *Medit. S.* 21 G4
Lampione, *Medit. S.* 21 G4
Lampung □, *Indonesia* 39 F2
Lamu, *Kenya* 57 E8
Lāna'i, *U.S.A.* 78 H12
Lanak La, *China* 42 B11
Lancaster, *U.K.* 11 D5
Lancaster, *U.S.A.* 77 D7
Lancaster Sd., *Canada* 70 B5
Lanchow = Lanzhou, *China* .. 35 C5
Lanciano, *Italy* 20 C5
Landeck, *Austria* 14 E6
Landes, *France* 12 D3
Landi Kotal, *Pakistan* 42 B7
Land's End, *U.K.* 11 F4
Landshut, *Germany* 15 D7
La'nga Co, *China* 40 B3
Langjökull, *Iceland* 8 C2
Langkawi, Pulau, *Malaysia* .. 38 C1
Langkon, *Malaysia* 38 C5
Langreo, *Spain* 18 A3
Langres, *France* 13 C6
Langres, Plateau de, *France* . 13 C6
Langsa, *Indonesia* 38 D1
Languedoc, *France* 13 E5
Lannion, *France* 12 B2
Lansdowne, *Australia* 63 B5
Lansing, *U.S.A.* 76 C3
Lanusei, *Italy* 21 E2
Lanzarote, *Canary Is.* 52 C3
Lanzhou, *China* 35 C5
Laoag, *Phil.* 36 A2
Laoang, *Phil.* 36 B3
Laon, *France* 13 B5
Laos ■, *Asia* 38 A3
Lappland, *Europe* 8 B10
Lapseki, *Turkey* 23 D6
Laptev Sea, *Russia* 30 B10
L'Áquila, *Italy* 20 C4
Lār, *Iran* 44 E3
Laramie, *U.S.A.* 74 E2
Larantuka, *Indonesia* 37 F2
Larat, *Indonesia* 37 F4
Laredo, *U.S.A.* 80 F4
Lariang, *Indonesia* 37 E1
Larisa, *Greece* 23 E4
Larnaca, *Cyprus* 46 D3
Larne, *U.K.* 11 D4
Larrimah, *Australia* 60 D5
Larsen Ice Shelf, *Antarctica* . 96 A3
Larvik, *Norway* 9 D8
Las Anod, *Somali Rep.* 49 F4
Las Cruces, *U.S.A.* 79 D9
Las Flores, *Argentina* 94 D5
Las Lajas, *Argentina* 94 D2
Las Lomitas, *Argentina* 94 A4
Las Palmas, *Canary Is.* 52 C2
Las Plumas, *Argentina* 95 E3
Las Varillas, *Argentina* 94 C4
Las Vegas, *U.S.A.* 78 B5
Lash-e Joveyn, *Afghan.* 42 D2
Lashio, *Burma* 41 F11
Lassen Pk., *U.S.A.* 72 F3
Lastoursville, *Gabon* 56 E2
Lastovo, *Croatia* 20 C6
Latacunga, *Ecuador* 90 D3
Latakia = Al Lādhiqīyah, *Syria* 46 D3
Latina, *Italy* 20 D4
Latium = Lazio □, *Italy* 20 C4
Latrobe, *Australia* 62 D4
Latvia ■, *Europe* 24 B1
Lauchhammer, *Germany* ... 15 C7
Launceston, *Australia* 62 D4

Laurel, *U.S.A.* 81 D9
Lauria, *Italy* 21 D5
Lausanne, *Switz.* 14 E4
Laut, *Indonesia* 38 D3
Laut Kecil, Kepulauan,
  Indonesia 39 E5
Laval, *France* 12 B3
Lavrio, *Greece* 23 F5
Lawas, *Malaysia* 38 D5
Lawele, *Indonesia* 37 F2
Lawrence, *N.Z.* 65 F3
Lawrence, *U.S.A.* 75 F7
Lawton, *U.S.A.* 80 B4
Layla, *Si. Arabia* 47 G6
Lazio □, *Italy* 20 C4
Lazo, *Russia* 32 B3
Le Creusot, *France* 13 C6
Le Havre, *France* 12 B4
Le Mans, *France* 12 C4
Le Mont-St-Michel, *France* .. 12 B3
Le Puy-en-Velay, *France* ... 13 D5
Le Touquet-Paris-Plage,
  France 12 A4
Le Tréport, *France* 12 A4
Le Verdon-sur-Mer, *France* . 12 D3
Leamington Spa = Royal
  Leamington Spa, *U.K.* ... 11 E6
Leavenworth, *U.S.A.* 75 F7
Lebak, *Phil.* 36 C2
Lebanon ■, *Asia* 46 D3
Lębork, *Poland* 16 A3
Lebrija, *Spain* 18 D2
Lebu, *Chile* 94 D2
Lecce, *Italy* 21 D7
Lecco, *Italy* 13 D8
Lech →, *Germany* 14 D6
Łęczyca, *Poland* 16 B4
Leeds, *U.K.* 11 E6
Leer, *Germany* 14 B4
Leeton, *Australia* 63 B4
Leeuwarden, *Neths.* 14 B3
Leeuwin, C., *Australia* 60 G2
Leeward Is., *Atl. Oc.* 87 C7
Lefkada, *Greece* 23 E3
Leganés, *Spain* 18 B4
Legazpi, *Phil.* 36 B2
Leghorn = Livorno, *Italy* ... 20 C3
Legionowo, *Poland* 16 B5
Legnago, *Italy* 20 B3
Legnica, *Poland* 16 C3
Leh, *India* 42 B10
Leicester, *U.K.* 11 E6
Leiden, *Neths.* 14 B3
Leie →, *Belgium* 14 C2
Leine →, *Germany* 14 B5
Leinster □, *Ireland* 11 E3
Leipzig, *Germany* 15 C7
Leiria, *Portugal* 18 C1
Leitrim, *Ireland* 11 D2
Leizhou Bandao, *China* 35 D6
Lekva Oros, *Greece* 23 G5
Leleque, *Argentina* 95 E2
Léman, L., *Europe* 13 C7
Lemhi Ra., *U.S.A.* 73 D7
Lena →, *Russia* 30 B10
Leninogorsk, *Kazakhstan* ... 29 D9
Leninsk, *Russia* 25 D6
Leninsk-Kuznetskiy, *Russia* .. 29 D9
Lenmalu, *Indonesia* 37 E4
Lens, *France* 13 A5
Lentini, *Italy* 21 F5
Leoben, *Austria* 15 E8
Leodhas = Lewis, *U.K.* 10 B3
León, *Mexico* 84 C4
León, *Nic.* 85 E7
León, *Spain* 18 A3
León, Montes de, *Spain* ... 18 A2
Leongatha, *Australia* 63 C4
Leova, *Moldova* 17 E9
Lepel = Lyepyel, *Belarus* ... 24 C2
Lérida = Lleida, *Spain* 19 B6
Lerwick, *U.K.* 10 A6
Les Cayes, *Haiti* 86 C5
Les Sables-d'Olonne, *France* 12 C3
Lesbos, *Greece* 23 E6
Leskovac, *Serbia & M.* 22 C3

Lesotho ■, *Africa* 59 D5
Lesozavodsk, *Russia* 32 A3
Lesser Antilles, *W. Indies* ... 87 D7
Lesser Sunda Is., *Indonesia* . 37 F2
Lésvos = Lesbos, *Greece* ... 23 E6
Leszno, *Poland* 16 C3
Lethbridge, *Canada* 69 D8
Leti, Kepulauan, *Indonesia* .. 37 F3
Leticia, *Colombia* 90 D4
Letpadan, *Burma* 41 J10
Letpan, *Burma* 41 H10
Letterkenny, *Ireland* 11 D3
Leuser, G., *Indonesia* 39 D1
Leuven, *Belgium* 14 C3
Levanger, *Norway* 8 C3
Levin, *N.Z.* 64 D6
Lévis, *Canada* 71 E6
Levkás = Lefkada, *Greece* .. 23 E3
Levkôsia = Nicosia, *Cyprus* . 46 D3
Levskigrad = Karlovo, *Bulgaria* 22 C3
Lewis, *U.K.* 10 B3
Lewisporte, *Canada* 71 E8
Lewiston, Idaho, *U.S.A.* 72 C5
Lewiston, Maine, *U.S.A.* ... 77 B10
Lexington, Ky., *U.S.A.* 76 E3
Lexington, N.C., *U.S.A.* 83 B7
Leyte □, *Phil.* 36 B2
Lezhë, *Albania* 22 D2
Lhasa, *China* 34 D4
Lhazê, *China* 34 D3
Lhokkruet, *Indonesia* 38 D1
Lhokseumawe, *Indonesia* .. 38 C1
L'Hospitalet de Llobregat,
  Spain 19 B7
Liancourt Rocks = Tok-do,
  Asia 33 E2
Lianga, *Phil.* 36 C3
Lianyungang, *China* 35 C6
Liaoning □, *China* 35 B7
Liaoyuan, *China* 35 B7
Liard →, *Canada* 68 B7
Libau = Liepāja, *Latvia* 24 B1
Libenge, Dem. Rep. of
  the Congo 56 D3
Liberal, *U.S.A.* 80 A3
Liberec, *Czech Rep.* 16 C2
Liberia ■, *W. Afr.* 53 G4
Liberia, *Costa Rica* 54 C4
Lîbîya, Sahrâ', *Africa* 54 C4
Libobo, Tanjung, *Indonesia* . 37 E3
Libourne, *France* 12 D3
Libreville, *Gabon* 56 D1
Libya ■, *N. Afr.* 54 C2
Libyan Desert = Lîbîya, Sahrâ',
  Africa 54 C4
Licantén, *Chile* 94 D2
Licata, *Italy* 21 F4
Lichinga, *Mozam.* 59 A7
Lida, *Belarus* 17 B7
Liechtenstein ■, *Europe* ... 14 E5
Liège, *Belgium* 14 C3
Liegnitz = Legnica, *Poland* .. 16 C3
Lienyünchiangshih =
  Lianyungang, *China* 35 C6
Lienz, *Austria* 15 E7
Liepāja, *Latvia* 24 B1
Lietuva = Lithuania ■, *Europe* 24 B1
Liffey →, *Ireland* 11 E3
Lifford, *Ireland* 11 D3
Lightning Ridge, *Australia* .. 63 A4
Liguria □, *Italy* 13 D8
Ligurian Sea, *Medit. S.* 20 C2
Lijiang, *China* 34 D5
Likasi, Dem. Rep. of
  the Congo 57 G5
Lille, *France* 13 A5
Lillehammer, *Norway* 8 C8
Lilongwe, *Malawi* 59 A6
Liloy, *Phil.* 36 C2
Lim →, *Bos.-H.* 20 C7
Lima, *Indonesia* 37 E3
Lima, *Peru* 91 F3
Lima, *U.S.A.* 76 D3
Lima →, *Portugal* 18 B1
Limassol, *Cyprus* 46 D3
Limay Mahuida, *Argentina* .. 94 D3
Limbang, *Brunei* 38 D5

Limbe, Cameroon ... 53 H7
Limburg, Germany ... 14 C5
Limeira, Brazil ... 93 G4
Limerick, Ireland ... 11 E2
Limfjorden, Denmark ... 9 D7
Limia = Lima →, Portugal ... 18 B1
Limnos, Greece ... 23 E5
Limoges, France ... 12 D4
Limón, Costa Rica ... 86 E3
Limousin □, France ... 12 D4
Limoux, France ... 12 E5
Limpopo →, Africa ... 59 D6
Limuru, Kenya ... 57 E7
Linares, Chile ... 94 D2
Linares, Mexico ... 84 C5
Linares, Spain ... 18 C4
Lincoln, Argentina ... 94 C4
Lincoln, N.Z. ... 65 E5
Lincoln, U.K. ... 11 E6
Lincoln, U.S.A. ... 75 E6
Linden, Guyana ... 90 B7
Lindesnes, Norway ... 9 D7
Lindi, Tanzania ... 57 F7
Lindos, Greece ... 23 F7
Lingayen, Phil. ... 36 A2
Lingayen G., Phil. ... 36 A2
Lingen, Germany ... 14 B4
Lingga, Indonesia ... 39 E2
Lingga, Kepulauan, Indonesia 39 E2
Linguère, Senegal ... 53 E2
Linhai, China ... 35 D7
Linhares, Brazil ... 93 F5
Linköping, Sweden ... 9 D9
Linosa, Medit. S. ... 21 G4
Lins, Brazil ... 93 G4
Linxia, China ... 34 C5
Linz, Austria ... 15 D8
Lion, G. du, France ... 13 E6
Lipa, Phil. ... 36 B2
Lipari, Italy ... 21 E5
Lipcani, Moldova ... 17 D8
Lipetsk, Russia ... 24 C4
Lipkany = Lipcani, Moldova . 17 D8
Lipovets, Ukraine ... 17 D9
Lippe →, Germany ... 14 C4
Liptrap, C., Australia ... 63 C4
Lira, Uganda ... 57 D6
Liria = Lliria, Spain ... 19 C5
Lisala, Dem. Rep. of
  the Congo ... 56 D4
Lisboa, Portugal ... 18 C1
Lisbon = Lisboa, Portugal ... 18 C1
Lisburn, U.K. ... 11 D3
Lisichansk = Lysychansk,
  Ukraine ... 25 D4
Lisieux, France ... 12 B4
Liski, Russia ... 24 C4
Lismore, Australia ... 63 A5
Lister, Mt., Antarctica ... 96 B15
Liston, Australia ... 63 A5
Listowel, Ireland ... 11 E2
Litani →, Lebanon ... 46 D3
Lithgow, Australia ... 63 B5
Lithino, Akra, Greece ... 23 G5
Lithuania ■, Europe ... 24 B1
Litoměřice, Czech Rep. ... 16 C2
Little Barrier I., N.Z. ... 64 B6
Little Khingan Mts. = Xiao
  Hinggan Ling, China ... 35 B7
Little Missouri →, U.S.A. ... 74 B3
Little River, N.Z. ... 65 E5
Little Rock, U.S.A. ... 81 B7
Little Zab = Zāb aş Şaghīr →,
  Iraq ... 46 D5
Liukang Tenggaja = Sabalana,
  Kepulauan, Indonesia 37 F1
Liuwa Plain, Zambia ... 58 A4
Liuzhou, China ... 35 D5
Livadia, Greece ... 23 E4
Liverpool, Canada ... 71 D7
Liverpool, U.K. ... 11 E5
Liverpool Ra., Australia ... 63 B5
Livingstone, Zambia ... 59 B5
Livny, Russia ... 24 C4
Livorno, Italy ... 20 C3
Ljubljana, Slovenia ... 20 A5

Llancanelo, Salina, Argentina 94 D3
Llanelli, U.K. ... 11 F4
Llanes, Spain ... 18 A3
Llano Estacado, U.S.A. ... 80 C2
Llanos, S. Amer. ... 90 C4
Lleida, Spain ... 19 B6
Lliria, Spain ... 19 C5
Llobregat →, Spain ... 19 B7
Lloret de Mar, Spain ... 19 B7
Llucmajor, Spain ... 19 C7
Llullaillaco, Volcán, S. Amer. 94 A3
Loa →, Chile ... 94 A2
Lobatse, Botswana ... 59 D5
Lobería, Argentina ... 94 D5
Lobito, Angola ... 58 A2
Locarno, Switz. ... 13 C8
Loch Garman = Wexford,
  Ireland ... 11 E3
Loches, France ... 12 C4
Lock, Australia ... 62 B2
Lodhran, Pakistan ... 42 E7
Lodi, Italy ... 13 D8
Lodi, U.S.A. ... 72 G3
Lodja, Dem. Rep. of
  the Congo ... 56 E4
Lodwar, Kenya ... 57 D7
Łódź, Poland ... 16 C4
Lofoten, Norway ... 8 B9
Logan, U.S.A. ... 73 F8
Logan, Mt., Canada ... 68 B5
Logone →, Chad ... 55 F2
Logroño, Spain ... 19 A4
Lohardaga, India ... 40 F5
Loi-kaw, Burma ... 41 H11
Loir →, France ... 12 C3
Loire →, France ... 12 C2
Loja, Ecuador ... 90 D3
Loja, Spain ... 18 D3
Loji = Kawasi, Indonesia ... 37 E3
Lokitaung, Kenya ... 57 D7
Lokkan tekojärvi, Finland ... 8 B11
Lokoja, Nigeria ... 53 G7
Lom, Bulgaria ... 22 C4
Lomami →, Dem. Rep. of
  the Congo ... 56 D4
Lombárdia □, Italy ... 13 D8
Lomblen, Indonesia ... 37 F2
Lombok, Indonesia ... 39 F5
Lomé, Togo ... 53 G6
Lomela, Dem. Rep. of
  the Congo ... 56 E4
Lomela →, Dem. Rep. of
  the Congo ... 56 E4
Lomond, L., U.K. ... 10 C4
Lompobatang, Indonesia ... 37 F1
Łomża, Poland ... 16 B6
Loncoche, Chile ... 95 D2
Londa, India ... 43 M9
London, Canada ... 71 E5
London, U.K. ... 11 F6
Londonderry, U.K. ... 11 D3
Londonderry, C., Australia ... 60 C4
Londonderry, I., Chile ... 95 H2
Londrina, Brazil ... 94 A6
Long Beach, U.S.A. ... 78 D3
Long I., Bahamas ... 86 B4
Long I., U.S.A. ... 77 D9
Long Xuyen, Vietnam ... 38 B3
Longford, Australia ... 62 D4
Longford, Ireland ... 11 E3
Longiram, Indonesia ... 39 E5
Longnawan, Indonesia ... 39 D4
Longreach, Australia ... 61 E7
Longview, Tex., U.S.A. ... 81 C6
Longview, Wash., U.S.A. ... 72 C2
Lons-le-Saunier, France ... 13 C6
Lop Nor, China ... 34 B4
Lopez, C., Gabon ... 56 E1
Lora →, Afghan. ... 42 D4
Lora, Hämün-i-, Pakistan ... 42 E4
Lora Cr. →, Australia ... 62 A2
Lora del Río, Spain ... 18 D3
Lorain, U.S.A. ... 76 D4
Loralai, Pakistan ... 42 D6
Lorca, Spain ... 19 D5
Lord Howe I., Pac. Oc. ... 64 N10

Lord Howe Rise, Pac. Oc. ... 64 N11
Lorestän □, Iran ... 46 D6
Loreto, Brazil ... 92 D4
Lorient, France ... 12 C2
Lorne, Australia ... 62 C3
Lorraine □, France ... 13 B7
Los Alamos, U.S.A. ... 79 C9
Los Andes, Chile ... 94 C2
Los Angeles, Chile ... 94 D2
Los Angeles, U.S.A. ... 78 C3
Los Blancos, Argentina ... 94 A4
Los Hermanos Is., Venezuela 90 A6
Los Mochis, Mexico ... 84 B3
Los Roques Is., Venezuela .. 90 A5
Los Testigos, Is., Venezuela . 90 A6
Los Vilos, Chile ... 94 C2
Lošinj, Croatia ... 20 B5
Lot →, France ... 12 D4
Lota, Chile ... 94 D2
Loubomo, Congo ... 56 E2
Louga, Senegal ... 53 E2
Lougheed I., Canada ... 70 B3
Louis Trichardt, S. Africa ... 59 C5
Louis XIV, Pte., Canada ... 71 D6
Louisiade Arch., Papua N. G. 61 C9
Louisiana □, U.S.A. ... 81 D8
Louisville, U.S.A. ... 76 E3
Loulé, Portugal ... 18 D1
Lourdes, France ... 12 E3
Louth, Australia ... 63 B4
Louth, U.K. ... 11 E6
Louvain = Leuven, Belgium . 14 C3
Lovech, Bulgaria ... 22 C5
Lowell, U.S.A. ... 77 C10
Lower California = Baja
  California, Mexico ... 84 A1
Lower Hutt, N.Z. ... 65 D6
Lower Saxony =
  Niedersachsen □, Germany 14 B5
Lower Tunguska = Tunguska,
  Nizhnyaya →, Russia ... 30 C6
Lowestoft, U.K. ... 11 E7
Lowgar □, Afghan. ... 45 C7
Łowicz, Poland ... 16 B4
Loxton, Australia ... 62 B3
Loyalty Is. = Loyauté, Îs.,
  N. Cal. ... 64 M11
Loyang = Luoyang, China ... 35 C6
Loyauté, Îs., N. Cal. ... 64 M11
Loyew, Belarus ... 17 C10
Luachimo, Angola ... 56 F4
Lualaba →, Dem. Rep. of
  the Congo ... 57 D5
Luanda, Angola ... 56 F2
Luangwa →, Zambia ... 59 A6
Luanshya, Zambia ... 59 A5
Luapula →, Africa ... 57 F5
Luarca, Spain ... 18 A2
Luau, Angola ... 56 G4
Lubang Is., Phil. ... 36 B2
Lubango, Angola ... 58 A2
Lubbock, U.S.A. ... 80 C3
Lübeck, Germany ... 15 B6
Lubero = Luofu, Dem. Rep. of
  the Congo ... 57 E5
Lubin, Poland ... 16 C3
Lublin, Poland ... 17 C6
Lubnän = Lebanon ■, Asia ... 46 D3
Lubuklinggau, Indonesia ... 39 E2
Lubuksikaping, Indonesia ... 39 D2
Lubumbashi, Dem. Rep. of
  the Congo ... 59 A5
Lubutu, Dem. Rep. of
  the Congo ... 57 E5
Lucca, Italy ... 20 C3
Lucena, Phil. ... 36 B2
Lucena, Spain ... 18 D3
Lucerne = Luzern, Switz. ... 13 C8
Luckenwalde, Germany ... 15 B7
Lucknow, India ... 40 D3
Lüda = Dalian, China ... 35 C7
Lüderitz, Namibia ... 58 D3
Ludhiana, India ... 42 D9
Ludwigsburg, Germany ... 14 D5
Ludwigshafen, Germany ... 14 D5
Lufira →, Dem. Rep. of
  the Congo ... 57 F5

Lufkin

Lufkin, *U.S.A.* 81 D6
Luga, *Russia* 24 B2
Lugano, *Switz.* 13 C8
Lugansk = Luhansk, *Ukraine* . 25 D4
Lugh Ganana, *Somali Rep.* . . 49 G3
Lugo, *Italy* 20 B3
Lugo, *Spain* 18 A2
Lugoj, *Romania* 17 F5
Lugovoy = Qulan, *Kazakhstan* 29 E8
Luhansk, *Ukraine* 25 D4
Luichow Pen. = Leizhou
  Bandao, *China* 35 D6
Luimneach = Limerick, *Ireland* 11 E2
Luís Correia, *Brazil* 92 C5
Luitpold Coast, *Antarctica* . . . 96 B5
Luiza, *Dem. Rep. of the Congo* 56 F4
Lukanga Swamp, *Zambia* . . . 59 A5
Lukenie →, *Dem. Rep. of
  the Congo* 56 E3
Łuków, *Poland* 17 C6
Luleå, *Sweden* 8 B10
Luleälven →, *Sweden* 8 B10
Lüleburgaz, *Turkey* 22 D6
Lulonga →, *Dem. Rep. of
  the Congo* 56 D3
Lulua →, *Dem. Rep. of
  the Congo* 56 E4
Lumbala N'guimbo, *Angola* . 58 A4
Lumsden, *N.Z.* 65 F3
Lumut, Tanjung, *Indonesia* . . 39 E3
Lund, *Sweden* 8 D8
Lundazi, *Zambia* 59 A6
Lundu, *Malaysia* 39 D3
Lüneburg, *Germany* 14 B6
Lüneburger Heide, *Germany* . 14 B6
Lunéville, *France* 13 B7
Lunglei, *India* 41 F9
Luni, *India* 42 G8
Luni →, *India* 43 G7
Luninyets, *Belarus* 17 B8
Luofu, *Dem. Rep. of
  the Congo* 57 E5
Luoyang, *China* 35 C6
Lurgan, *U.K.* 11 D3
Lusaka, *Zambia* 59 B5
Lusambo, *Dem. Rep. of
  the Congo* 56 E4
Lushnjë, *Albania* 23 D2
Luta = Dalian, *China* 35 C7
Lutherstadt Wittenberg,
  Germany 15 C7
Luton, *U.K.* 11 F6
Łutselk'e, *Canada* 68 B8
Lutsk, *Ukraine* 17 C7
Lützow Holmbukta, *Antarctica* 96 A8
Luuq = Lugh Ganana,
  Somali Rep. 49 G3
Luwuk, *Indonesia* 37 E2
Luxembourg, *Lux.* 13 B7
Luxembourg ■, *Europe* 14 D4
Luxor = El Uqsur, *Egypt* 54 C5
Luza, *Russia* 24 A6
Luzern, *Switz.* 13 C8
Luzhou, *China* 35 D5
Luziânia, *Brazil* 93 F4
Luzon, *Phil.* 36 A2
Lviv, *Ukraine* 17 D7
Lvov = Lviv, *Ukraine* 17 D7
Lyakhavichy, *Belarus* 17 B8
Lyakhovskiye, Ostrova, *Russia* 31 B12
Lydenburg, *S. Africa* 59 D6
Lydia, *Turkey* 23 E7
Lyell, *U.K.* 65 D5
Lyepyel, *Belarus* 24 C2
Łyna →, *Poland* 16 A5
Lynchburg, *U.S.A.* 77 F6
Lynd Ra., *Australia* 63 A4
Lyndhurst, *Australia* 62 B2
Lynn Lake, *Canada* 69 C9
Lyon, *France* 13 D6
Lyonnais, *France* 13 D6
Lys = Leie →, *Belgium* 14 C2
Lysychansk, *Ukraine* 25 D4
Lyttelton, *N.Z.* 65 E5
Lyubertsy, *Russia* 24 B4
Lyuboml, *Ukraine* 17 C7

M

Ma'ān, *Jordan* 47 E3
Ma'anshan, *China* 35 C6
Ma'arrat an Nu'mān, *Syria* . . 46 D4
Maas →, *Neths.* 14 C3
Maastricht, *Neths.* 13 A6
McAllen, *U.S.A.* 80 F4
Macao = Macau, *China* 35 D6
Macapá, *Brazil* 92 B3
Macau, *Brazil* 92 D6
Macau, *China* 35 D6
M'Clintock Chan., *Canada* . . . 68 A9
M'Clure Str., *Canada* 70 B2
McComb, *U.S.A.* 81 D8
MacDonnell Ranges, *Australia* 60 E5
Macedonia □, *Greece* 23 D4
Macedonia ■, *Europe* 22 D3
Maceió, *Brazil* 93 D6
Macerata, *Italy* 20 C4
Macfarlane, L., *Australia* 62 B2
Macgillycuddy's Reeks,
  Ireland 11 F2
McGregor Ra., *Australia* 62 A3
Mach, *Pakistan* 42 E5
Machado = Jiparaná →, *Brazil* 91 E6
Machakos, *Kenya* 57 E7
Machala, *Ecuador* 90 D3
Machilipatnam, *India* 40 J3
Machiques, *Venezuela* 90 A4
Machupicchu, *Peru* 91 F4
Macintyre →, *Australia* 63 A5
Mackay, *Australia* 61 E8
Mackay, L., *Australia* 60 E4
Mackenzie →, *Canada* 68 B6
Mackenzie City = Linden,
  Guyana 90 B7
Mackenzie King I., *Canada* . . 70 B2
Mackenzie Mts., *Canada* 68 B6
McKinley, Mt., *U.S.A.* 69 B4
McKinney, *U.S.A.* 81 C5
Macksville, *Australia* 63 B5
Maclean, *Australia* 63 A5
Maclear, *S. Africa* 59 E5
Macleay →, *Australia* 63 B5
McMurdo Sd., *Antarctica* . . . 96 B15
Mâcon, *France* 13 C6
Macon, *U.S.A.* 83 C6
McPherson Ra., *Australia* . . . 63 A5
Macquarie Harbour, *Australia* 62 D4
MacRobertson Land,
  Antarctica 96 B10
Macumba →, *Australia* 62 A2
Madadeni, *S. Africa* 59 D6
Madagascar ■, *Africa* 59 C9
Madā'in Sālih, *Si. Arabia* 47 F4
Madama, *Niger* 54 D1
Madang, *Papua N. G.* 61 B8
Madaripur, *Bangla.* 41 F8
Madauk, *Burma* 41 J11
Madaya, *Burma* 41 F11
Maddalena, *Italy* 20 D2
Madeira, *Atl. Oc.* 52 B2
Madeira →, *Brazil* 90 D7
Madeleine, Îs. de la, *Canada* . 71 E7
Madha, *India* 43 L9
Madhya Pradesh □, *India* . . . 43 H10
Madikeri, *India* 43 N9
Madimba, *Dem. Rep. of
  the Congo* 56 E3
Madingou, *Congo* 56 E2
Madison, *U.S.A.* 75 D10
Madiun, *Indonesia* 39 F4
Madras = Chennai, *India* 43 N12
Madras = Tamil Nadu □, *India* 43 P10
Madre, L., *U.S.A.* 80 F5
Madre, Sierra, *Phil.* 36 A2
Madre de Dios →, *Bolivia* . . . 91 F5
Madre de Dios, I., *Chile* 95 G1
Madre Occidental, Sierra,
  Mexico 84 B3
Madrid, *Spain* 18 B4
Madurai, *India* 43 Q11
Madurantakam, *India* 43 N11
Mae Sot, *Thailand* 38 A1
Maebashi, *Japan* 33 E6

Maevatanana, *Madag.* 59 B9
Mafeteng, *Lesotho* 59 D5
Maffra, *Australia* 63 C4
Mafia I., *Tanzania* 57 F7
Mafra, *Brazil* 94 B7
Mafra, *Portugal* 18 C1
Magadan, *Russia* 31 D13
Magallanes, Estrecho de,
  Chile 95 G2
Magangué, *Colombia* 90 B4
Magdalen Is. = Madeleine, Îs.
  de la, *Canada* 71 E7
Magdalena, *Argentina* 94 D5
Magdalena, *Bolivia* 91 F6
Magdalena →, *Colombia* 90 A4
Magdeburg, *Germany* 15 B6
Magelang, *Indonesia* 39 F4
Magellan's Str. = Magallanes,
  Estrecho de, *Chile* 95 G2
Maggiore, Lago, *Italy* 13 D8
Magnetic Pole (North),
  Canada 70 A2
Magnetic Pole (South),
  Antarctica 96 A13
Magnitogorsk, *Russia* 29 D6
Magosa = Famagusta, *Cyprus* 46 D3
Maguarinho, C., *Brazil* 92 C4
Magusa = Famagusta, *Cyprus* 46 D3
Magwe, *Burma* 41 G10
Magyarorszag = Hungary ■,
  Europe 16 E4
Mahābād, *Iran* 46 C6
Mahabo, *Madag.* 59 C8
Mahajanga, *Madag.* 59 B9
Mahakam →, *Indonesia* 39 E5
Mahalapye, *Botswana* 59 C5
Maḥallāt, *Iran* 44 C2
Mahanadi →, *India* 40 G6
Maharashtra □, *India* 43 J9
Mahbubnagar, *India* 43 L10
Mahdia, *Tunisia* 54 A1
Mahenge, *Tanzania* 57 F7
Maheno, *N.Z.* 65 F4
Mahesana, *India* 43 H8
Mahia Pen., *N.Z.* 64 C7
Mahilyow, *Belarus* 17 B10
Mahinerangi, L., *N.Z.* 65 F3
Mahón = Maó, *Spain* 19 C8
Mai-Ndombe, L., *Dem. Rep. of
  the Congo* 56 E3
Maicurú →, *Brazil* 92 C3
Maidstone, *U.K.* 11 F7
Maiduguri, *Nigeria* 55 F1
Maijdi, *Bangla.* 41 F8
Maikala Ra., *India* 40 G3
Main →, *Germany* 14 D5
Maine, *France* 12 C3
Maingkwan, *Burma* 41 D11
Mainit, L., *Phil.* 36 C3
Mainland, Orkney, *U.K.* 10 B5
Mainland, Shet., *U.K.* 10 A6
Mainz, *Germany* 14 C5
Maipú, *Argentina* 94 D5
Maiquetía, *Venezuela* 90 A5
Mairabari, *India* 41 D9
Maitland, N.S.W., *Australia* . . 63 B5
Maitland, S. Austral., *Australia* 62 B2
Maizuru, *Japan* 33 F4
Majene, *Indonesia* 37 E1
Majorca = Mallorca, *Spain* . . 19 C7
Majuro, *Marshall Is.* 64 J12
Makale, *Indonesia* 37 E1
Makarikari = Makgadikgadi
  Salt Pans, *Botswana* 59 C5
Makasar = Ujung Pandang,
  Indonesia 37 F1
Makasar, Selat, *Indonesia* . . . 37 E1
Makasar, Str. of = Makasar,
  Selat, *Indonesia* 37 E1
Makat = Maqat, *Kazakhstan* . 29 E6
Makedonija = Macedonia ■,
  Europe 22 D3
Makeyevka = Makiyivka,
  Ukraine 25 D4
Makgadikgadi Salt Pans,
  Botswana 59 C5
Makhachkala, *Russia* 25 E6

Makhado = Louis Trichardt,
S. Africa 59 C5
Makian, *Indonesia* 37 D3
Makinsk, *Kazakhstan* 29 D8
Makiyivka, *Ukraine* 25 D4
Makkah, *Si. Arabia* 47 G4
Makó, *Hungary* 16 E5
Makokou, *Gabon* 56 D2
Makrai, *India* 43 H10
Makran, *Asia* 45 E5
Makran Coast Range, *Pakistan* 42 G4
Mākū, *Iran* 46 C6
Makurazaki, *Japan* 33 H2
Makurdi, *Nigeria* 53 G7
Malabar Coast, *India* 43 P9
Malacca, Straits of, *Indonesia* 38 D1
Maladzyechna, *Belarus* 17 A8
Málaga, *Spain* 18 D3
Malagasy Rep. =
  Madagascar ■, *Africa* 59 C9
Malakâl, *Sudan* 55 G5
Malakand, *Pakistan* 42 B7
Malang, *Indonesia* 39 F4
Malanje, *Angola* 56 F3
Mälaren, *Sweden* 9 D9
Malargüe, *Argentina* 94 D3
Malaryta, *Belarus* 17 C7
Malatya, *Turkey* 46 C4
Malawi ■, *Africa* 59 A6
Malawi, L., *Africa* 59 A6
Malay Pen., *Asia* 38 C2
Malaybalay, *Phil.* 36 C3
Malåyer, *Iran* 46 D7
Malaysia ■, *Asia* 38 D4
Malazgirt, *Turkey* 25 F5
Malbooma, *Australia* 62 B1
Malbork, *Poland* 16 A4
Malden I., *Kiribati* 65 K15
Maldives ■, *Ind. Oc.* 26 H9
Maldonado, *Uruguay* 94 C6
Maleas, Akra, *Greece* 23 F4
Malegaon, *India* 43 J9
Malema, *Mozam.* 59 A7
Malha, *Sudan* 55 E4
Mali ■, *Africa* 53 E5
Mali →, *Burma* 41 E11
Maliku, *Indonesia* 37 E2
Malili, *Indonesia* 37 E2
Malin Hd., *Ireland* 10 D3
Malindi, *Kenya* 57 E8
Malines = Mechelen, *Belgium* 14 C3
Malino, *Indonesia* 37 D2
Malita, *Phil.* 36 C3
Malkara, *Turkey* 22 D6
Mallacoota Inlet, *Australia* . 63 C4
Mallaig, *U.K.* 10 C4
Mallawi, *Egypt* 54 C5
Mallorca, *Spain* 19 C7
Mallow, *Ireland* 11 E2
Malmö, *Sweden* 9 D8
Malolos, *Phil.* 36 B2
Malpelo, I. de, *Colombia* ... 90 C2
Malta ■, *Europe* 21 G5
Maltahöhe, *Namibia* 58 C3
Maluku, *Indonesia* 37 E3
Maluku □, *Indonesia* 37 E3
Maluku Sea = Molucca Sea,
  Indonesia 37 E2
Malvan, *India* 43 L8
Malvinas, Is. = Falkland Is. ⊘,
  Atl. Oc. 95 G5
Malyn, *Ukraine* 17 C9
Malyy Lyakhovskiy, Ostrov,
  Russia 31 B12
Mamanguape, *Brazil* 92 D6
Mamasa, *Indonesia* 37 E1
Mamberamo →, *Indonesia* . 37 E5
Mambilima Falls, *Zambia* .. 57 G5
Mamburao, *Phil.* 36 B2
Mamoré →, *Bolivia* 91 F5
Mamou, *Guinea* 53 F3
Mamuju, *Indonesia* 37 E1
Man, *Ivory C.* 53 G4
Man, I. of, *U.K.* 11 D4
Man Na, *Burma* 41 F11
Manaar, G. of = Mannar, G. of,
  Asia 43 Q11

Manacapuru, *Brazil* 90 D6
Manacor, *Spain* 19 C7
Manado, *Indonesia* 37 D2
Managua, *Nic.* 85 E7
Manakara, *Madag.* 59 C9
Manama = Al Manāmah,
  Bahrain 44 E2
Mananjary, *Madag.* 59 C9
Manaos = Manaus, *Brazil* .. 90 D7
Manapouri, *N.Z.* 65 F2
Manapouri, L., *N.Z.* 65 F2
Manas, *China* 34 B3
Manas →, *India* 41 D8
Manaung, *Burma* 41 H9
Manaus, *Brazil* 90 D7
Manchester, *U.K.* 11 E5
Manchester, *U.S.A.* 77 C10
Mand →, *Iran* 44 D3
Mandal, *Norway* 9 D7
Mandala, Puncak, *Indonesia* . 37 E6
Mandalay, *Burma* 41 F11
Mandalī, *Iraq* 46 D6
Mandar, Teluk, *Indonesia* .. 37 E1
Mandaue, *Phil.* 36 B2
Mandi, *India* 42 D10
Mandimba, *Mozam.* 59 A7
Mandioli, *Indonesia* 37 E3
Mandla, *India* 40 F3
Mandritsara, *Madag.* 59 B9
Mandsaur, *India* 43 G9
Mandvi, *India* 43 H6
Mandya, *India* 43 N10
Manfalûṭ, *Egypt* 54 C5
Manfredónia, *Italy* 20 D5
Mangalia, *Romania* 22 C7
Mangalore, *India* 43 N9
Mangaweka, *N.Z.* 64 C6
Manggar, *Indonesia* 39 E3
Manggawitu, *Indonesia* ... 37 E4
Mangghystaü Tübegi,
  Kazakhstan 29 E6
Mangkalihat, Tanjung,
  Indonesia 37 D1
Mangla Dam, *Pakistan* 42 C8
Mangnai, *China* 34 C4
Mango, *Togo* 53 F6
Mangoche, *Malawi* 59 A7
Mangoky →, *Madag.* 59 C8
Mangole, *Indonesia* 37 E3
Mangonui, *N.Z.* 64 A5
Mangueira, L. da, *Brazil* .. 94 C6
Mangyshlak, Poluostrov =
  Mangghystaü Tübegi,
  Kazakhstan 29 E6
Manica, *Mozam.* 59 B6
Manicoré, *Brazil* 91 E6
Manicouagan →, *Canada* .. 71 E7
Manicouagan, Rés., *Canada* . 71 D7
Manīfah, *Si. Arabia* 47 F7
Manihiki, *Cook Is.* 65 L14
Manila, *Phil.* 36 B2
Manila B., *Phil.* 36 B2
Manilla, *Australia* 63 B5
Manipur □, *India* 41 E9
Manipur →, *Burma* 41 F10
Manisa, *Turkey* 23 E6
Manitoba □, *Canada* 69 C10
Manitoba, L., *Canada* 69 C10
Manitoulin I., *Canada* 71 E5
Manitowoc, *U.S.A.* 76 B2
Manizales, *Colombia* 90 B3
Manjhand, *Pakistan* 42 G6
Manjra →, *India* 43 K10
Manmad, *India* 43 J9
Mannahill, *Australia* 62 B3
Mannar, *Sri Lanka* 43 Q11
Mannar, G. of, *Asia* 43 Q11
Mannar I., *Sri Lanka* 43 Q11
Mannheim, *Germany* 14 D5
Mannum, *Australia* 62 B2
Manokwari, *Indonesia* 37 E4
Manono, Dem. Rep. of
  the Congo 57 F5
Manosque, *France* 13 E6
Manresa, *Spain* 19 B6
Mansa, *Zambia* 57 G5

Mansel I., *Canada* 70 C5
Mansfield, *Australia* 63 C4
Mansfield, *U.K.* 11 E6
Mansfield, *U.S.A.* 76 D4
Manta, *Ecuador* 90 D2
Mantalingajan, Mt., *Phil.* ... 38 C5
Mantes-la-Jolie, *France* 12 B4
Manthani, *India* 43 K11
Mántova, *Italy* 20 B3
Manu, *Peru* 91 F4
Manuel Alves →, *Brazil* ... 93 E4
Manui, *Indonesia* 37 E2
Manukau, *N.Z.* 64 B6
Manych-Gudilo, Ozero, *Russia* 25 D5
Manzai, *Pakistan* 42 C7
Manzanares, *Spain* 18 C4
Manzanillo, *Cuba* 86 B4
Manzanillo, *Mexico* 84 D4
Manzhouli, *China* 35 B6
Mao, *Chad* 55 F2
Maó, *Spain* 19 C8
Maoke, Pegunungan,
  Indonesia 37 E5
Maoming, *China* 35 D6
Mapam Yumco, *China* 40 B3
Mapia, Kepulauan, *Indonesia* 37 D4
Mapuera →, *Brazil* 90 D7
Maputo, *Mozam.* 59 D6
Maqat, *Kazakhstan* 29 E6
Maqnā, *Si. Arabia* 47 E3
Maquan He =
  Brahmaputra →, *Asia* .. 41 F7
Maquela do Zombo, *Angola* . 56 F3
Maquinchao, *Argentina* 95 E3
Mar Chiquita, L., *Argentina* . 94 C4
Mar del Plata, *Argentina* ... 94 D5
Mar Menor, *Spain* 19 D5
Maraã, *Brazil* 90 D5
Marabá, *Brazil* 92 D4
Maracá, I. de, *Brazil* 92 B3
Maracaibo, *Venezuela* 90 A4
Maracaibo, L. de, *Venezuela* . 90 B4
Maracay, *Venezuela* 90 A5
Maradi, *Niger* 53 F7
Marägheh, *Iran* 46 C6
Marāh, *Si. Arabia* 47 F6
Marajó, I. de, *Brazil* 92 C4
Marand, *Iran* 46 C6
Maranguape, *Brazil* 92 C6
Maranhão = São Luís, *Brazil* . 92 C5
Maranhão □, *Brazil* 92 D4
Maranoa →, *Australia* 63 A4
Marañón →, *Peru* 90 D4
Marão, *Mozam.* 59 C6
Maraş = Kahramanmaraş,
  Turkey 46 C4
Maratua, *Indonesia* 37 D1
Marbella, *Spain* 18 D3
Marburg, *Germany* 14 C5
Marche, *France* 12 C4
Marchena, *Spain* 18 D3
Mardan, *Pakistan* 42 B8
Mardin, *Turkey* 46 C5
Marek = Stanke Dimitrov,
  Bulgaria 22 C4
Margarita, I. de, *Venezuela* . 90 A6
Margaritovo, *Russia* 32 B4
Margate, *U.K.* 11 F7
Märgow, Dasht-e, *Afghan.* . 42 D3
Mari El □, *Russia* 24 B6
Maria I., *Australia* 62 D4
Maria van Diemen, C., *N.Z.* . 64 A5
Mariana Trench, *Pac. Oc.* .. 64 H9
Maribor, *Slovenia* 20 A5
Marie Byrd Land, *Antarctica* . 96 B18
Mariecourt = Kangiqsujuaq,
  Canada 70 C6
Mariental, *Namibia* 58 C3
Mariinsk, *Russia* 29 D9
Marília, *Brazil* 93 G3
Marín, *Spain* 18 A1
Marinduque, *Phil.* 36 B2
Maringá, *Brazil* 94 A6
Marion, *U.S.A.* 81 A9
Mariscal Estigarribia,
  Paraguay 91 H6
Maritimes, Alpes, *Europe* ... 13 D7

131

Maritsa

Maritsa = Evros ➤, *Greece* .. 22 D6
Mariupol, *Ukraine* 25 D4
Marīvān, *Iran* 46 D6
Marka = Merca, *Somali Rep.* . 49 G3
Markham, Mt., *Antarctica* ... 96 C15
Marks, *Russia* 24 C6
Marla, *Australia* 62 A1
Marmagao, *India* 43 M8
Marmara, *Turkey* 23 D6
Marmara Denizi, *Turkey* 22 D7
Marmaris, *Turkey* 23 F7
Marmolada, Mte., *Italy* 20 A3
Marne ➤, *France* 12 B5
Maroantsetra, *Madag.* 59 B9
Marondera, *Zimbabwe* 59 B6
Maroni ➤, *Fr. Guiana* 92 A3
Maroochydore, *Australia* .. 63 A5
Maroona, *Australia* 62 C3
Maroua, *Cameroon* 55 F1
Marovoay, *Madag.* 59 B9
Marquises, Îs., *French*
  Polynesia 65 K17
Marrakech, *Morocco* 52 B4
Marrawah, *Australia* 62 D3
Marree, *Australia* 62 A2
Marrowie Cr. ➤, *Australia* .. 63 B4
Marrupa, *Mozam.* 59 A7
Marsá Matrûh, *Egypt* 54 B4
Marsabit, *Kenya* 57 D7
Marsala, *Italy* 21 F4
Marsden, *Australia* 63 B4
Marseille, *France* 13 E6
Marshall, *U.S.A.* 81 C6
Marshall Is. ■, *Pac. Oc.* 64 J12
Marshalltown, *U.S.A.* 75 D8
Martaban, *Burma* 41 J11
Martaban, G. of, *Burma* ... 41 J11
Martapura, *Kalimantan,*
  Indonesia 39 E4
Martapura, *Sumatera,*
  Indonesia 39 E2
Martigues, *France* 13 E6
Martinborough, *N.Z.* 65 D6
Martinique ☑, *W. Indies* ... 87 D7
Martinsville, *U.S.A.* 83 A8
Marton, *N.Z.* 64 D6
Martos, *Spain* 18 D4
Marudi, *Malaysia* 39 D4
Maruf, *Afghan.* 42 D5
Marugame, *Japan* 33 F3
Marwar, *India* 42 G8
Mary, *Turkmenistan* 29 F7
Maryborough = Port Laoise,
  Ireland 11 E3
Maryborough, *Queens.,*
  Australia 63 A5
Maryborough, *Vic., Australia* 62 C3
Maryland ☐, *U.S.A.* 77 C7
Marystown, *Canada* 71 E8
Marzūq, *Libya* 54 C1
Marzūq, Idehān, *Libya* 54 D1
Masaka, *Uganda* 57 E6
Masalembo, Kepulauan,
  Indonesia 39 F4
Masalima, Kepulauan,
  Indonesia 39 F5
Masamba, *Indonesia* 37 E2
Masan, *S. Korea* 35 C7
Masandam, Ra's, *Oman* ... 44 E4
Masasi, *Tanzania* 57 G7
Masaya, *Nic.* 85 E7
Masbate, *Phil.* 36 B2
Mascara, *Algeria* 52 A6
Masela, *Indonesia* 37 F3
Maseru, *Lesotho* 59 D5
Mashābih, *Si. Arabia* 47 F4
Mashhad, *Iran* 44 B4
Mäshkel, Hämûn-i-, *Pakistan* 42 E3
Mashki Chāh, *Pakistan* ... 42 E3
Mashonaland, *Zimbabwe* ... 59 B6
Masindi, *Uganda* 57 D6
Masjed Soleyman, *Iran* ... 47 E7
Mask, L., *Ireland* 11 E2
Maskin, *Oman* 44 F4
Masoala, Tanjon' i, *Madag.* . 59 B10
Masohi = Amahai, *Indonesia* 37 E3
Mason City, *U.S.A.* 75 D8

Masqat, *Oman* 45 F4
Massa, *Italy* 13 D9
Massachusetts ☐, *U.S.A.* ... 77 C9
Massakory, *Chad* 55 F2
Massangena, *Mozam.* 59 C6
Massena, *U.S.A.* 77 B8
Massénya, *Chad* 55 F2
Massif Central, *France* 13 D5
Massinga, *Mozam.* 59 C7
Masson I., *Antarctica* 96 A11
Mastanli = Momchilgrad,
  Bulgaria 22 D5
Masterton, *N.Z.* 65 D6
Mastuj, *Pakistan* 42 A8
Mastung, *Pakistan* 42 E5
Masty, *Belarus* 17 B7
Masuda, *Japan* 33 F2
Masvingo, *Zimbabwe* 59 C6
Mata-au = Clutha ➤, *N.Z.* .. 65 G3
Matabeleland, *Zimbabwe* ... 59 B5
Matadi, *Dem. Rep. of*
  the Congo 56 F2
Matagalpa, *Nic.* 85 E7
Matagami, *Canada* 71 E6
Matagami, L., *Canada* 71 E6
Matak, *Indonesia* 39 D3
Matam, *Senegal* 53 E3
Matamoros, *Coahuila, Mexico* 84 B4
Matamoros, *Tamaulipas,*
  Mexico 84 B5
Ma'ṭan as Sarra, *Libya* 54 D3
Matane, *Canada* 71 E7
Matanzas, *Cuba* 86 B3
Matapan, C. = Tenaro, Akra,
  Greece 23 F4
Mataram, *Indonesia* 39 F5
Matarani, *Peru* 91 G4
Mataró, *Spain* 19 B7
Mataura, *N.Z.* 65 G3
Matehuala, *Mexico* 84 C4
Matera, *Italy* 21 D6
Mathraki, *Greece* 21 E7
Mathura, *India* 42 F10
Mati, *Phil.* 36 C3
Matiri Ra., *N.Z.* 65 D5
Mato Grosso ☐, *Brazil* 93 E3
Mato Grosso, Planalto do,
  Brazil 93 F3
Mato Grosso do Sul ☐, *Brazil* 93 F3
Matochkin Shar, *Russia* ... 28 B6
Matosinhos, *Portugal* 18 B1
Maṭruḥ, *Oman* 45 F4
Matsue, *Japan* 33 F3
Matsumae, *Japan* 32 C7
Matsumoto, *Japan* 33 E6
Matsusaka, *Japan* 33 F5
Matsuyama, *Japan* 33 G3
Mattagami ➤, *Canada* 71 D5
Mattancheri, *India* 43 Q10
Matthews Ridge, *Guyana* . 90 B6
Matucana, *Peru* 91 F3
Matûn = Khowst, *Afghan.* ... 42 C6
Maturín, *Venezuela* 90 B6
Mau Ranipur, *India* 43 G11
Maubeuge, *France* 13 A5
Maude, *Australia* 63 B3
Maudin Sun, *Burma* 90 D7
Maués, *Brazil* 40 E3
Mauganj, *India* 78 H12
Maui, *U.S.A.* 78 H12
Maulamyaing = Moulmein,
  Burma 41 J11
Maumere, *Indonesia* 37 F2
Maun, *Botswana* 58 B4
Maungmagan Kyunzu, *Burma* 41 K11
Mauritania ■, *Africa* 53 E3
Mauritius ■, *Ind. Oc.* 51 H9
Mawk Mai, *Burma* 41 G11
Mawlaik, *Burma* 41 F10
Mawlamyine = Moulmein,
  Burma 41 J11
Mawson Coast, *Antarctica* . 96 A10
Mayaguana, *Bahamas* ... 87 B5
Mayagüez, *Puerto Rico* ... 87 C6
Maydena, *Australia* 62 D4
Mayenne ➤, *France* 12 C3
Maykop, *Russia* 25 E5

Mayo, *Canada* 68 B6
Mayon Volcano, *Phil.* 36 B2
Mayor I., *N.Z.* 64 B7
Mayotte ☑, *Ind. Oc.* 59 A9
Mayu, *Indonesia* 37 D3
Mazabuka, *Zambia* 59 B5
Mazagán = El Jadida,
  Morocco 52 B4
Mazagão, *Brazil* 92 C3
Mazán, *Peru* 90 D4
Māzandarān ☐, *Iran* 44 B3
Mazār-e Sharīf, *Afghan.* ... 45 B6
Mazara del Vallo, *Italy* 21 F4
Mazarrón, *Spain* 19 D5
Mazaruni ➤, *Guyana* 90 B7
Mazatlán, *Mexico* 84 C3
Māzhān, *Iran* 44 C4
Mazinān, *Iran* 44 B4
Mazoe ➤, *Mozam.* 59 B6
Mazurski, Pojezierze, *Poland* 16 B5
Mazyr, *Belarus* 17 C9
Mbabane, *Swaziland* 59 D6
Mbaïki, *C.A.R.* 56 D3
Mbala, *Zambia* 57 F6
Mbale, *Uganda* 57 D6
Mbalmayo, *Cameroon* ... 56 D2
Mbandaka, *Dem. Rep. of*
  the Congo 56 D3
Mbanza Congo, *Angola* ... 56 F2
Mbanza Ngungu, *Dem. Rep.*
  of the Congo 56 F2
Mbarara, *Uganda* 57 E6
Mbeya, *Tanzania* 57 F6
Mbini = Río Muni ☐, *Eq. Guin.* 56 D2
Mbour, *Senegal* 53 F2
Mbuji-Mayi, *Dem. Rep. of*
  the Congo 56 F4
Mdantsane, *S. Africa* 59 E5
Mead, L., *U.S.A.* 78 B5
Mearim ➤, *Brazil* 92 C5
Meaux, *France* 13 B5
Mecca = Makkah, *Si. Arabia* . 47 G4
Mechelen, *Belgium* 14 C3
Mecheria, *Algeria* 52 B5
Mecklenburg, *Germany* ... 15 B6
Mecklenburger Bucht,
  Germany 15 A6
Medan, *Indonesia* 39 D1
Medanosa, Pta., *Argentina* . 95 F3
Médéa, *Algeria* 52 A6
Medellín, *Colombia* 90 B3
Medford, *U.S.A.* 72 E2
Medgidia, *Romania* 22 B7
Medicine Bow Mts., *U.S.A.* . 73 F10
Medicine Hat, *Canada* 69 C8
Medina = Al Madīnah,
  Si. Arabia 47 F4
Medina del Campo, *Spain* . 18 B3
Medina Sidonia, *Spain* 18 D3
Medinipur, *India* 40 F6
Mediterranean Sea, *Europe* . 50 C5
Médoc, *France* 12 D3
Medveditsa ➤, *Russia* 24 D5
Medvezhyegorsk, *Russia* .. 28 C4
Meekatharra, *Australia* ... 60 F2
Meerut, *India* 42 E10
Megara, *Greece* 23 F4
Meghalaya ☐, *India* 41 E8
Meighen I., *Canada* 70 B4
Meiktila, *Burma* 41 G10
Meissen, *Germany* 15 C7
Meizhou, *China* 35 D6
Mejillones, *Chile* 94 A2
Mekhtar, *Pakistan* 42 D6
Meknès, *Morocco* 52 B4
Mekong ➤, *Asia* 38 C3
Mekongga, *Indonesia* 37 E2
Mekvari = Kür ➤, *Azerbaijan* 25 E6
Melagiri Hills, *India* 43 N10
Melaka, *Malaysia* 39 D2
Melalap, *Malaysia* 38 C5
Melanesia, *Pac. Oc.* 64 K10
Melbourne, *Australia* 63 C3
Melbourne, *U.S.A.* 83 E7
Mélèzes ➤, *Canada* 70 D6
Melfort, *Canada* 69 C9
Melilla, *N. Afr.* 19 E4

Modimolle

Melitopol, *Ukraine* 25 D4
Melk, *Austria* 15 D8
Melo, *Uruguay* 94 C6
Melolo, *Indonesia* 37 F2
Melrose, *Australia* 63 B4
Melun, *France* 13 B5
Melville, *Canada* 69 C9
Melville I., *Australia* 60 C5
Melville I., *Canada* 70 B2
Melville Pen., *Canada* 70 C5
Memboro, *Indonesia* 37 F1
Memel = Klaipėda, *Lithuania* 24 B1
Memmingen, *Germany* .. 14 E6
Mempawah, *Indonesia* 39 D3
Memphis, *Tenn., U.S.A.* ... 82 B3
Memphis, *Tex., U.S.A.* 80 B3
Ménaka, *Mali* 53 E6
Menan = Chao Phraya →,
  Thailand 38 B2
Mendawai →, *Indonesia* ... 39 E4
Mende, *France* 13 D5
Mendocino, C., *U.S.A.* 72 F1
Mendoza, *Argentina* 94 C3
Mene Grande, *Venezuela* .. 90 B4
Menemen, *Turkey* 23 E6
Menggala, *Indonesia* 39 E3
Mengzi, *China* 34 D5
Menindee, *Australia* 62 B3
Menindee L., *Australia* 62 B3
Meningie, *Australia* 62 C2
Menominee, *U.S.A.* 76 B2
Menongue, *Angola* 58 A3
Menorca, *Spain* 19 C7
Mentawai, Kepulauan,
  Indonesia 39 E1
Menton, *France* 13 E7
Meppel, *Neths.* 14 B4
Merano, *Italy* 20 A3
Merauke, *Indonesia* 37 F6
Merbein, *Australia* 62 B3
Merca, *Somali Rep.* 49 G3
Merced, *U.S.A.* 78 B2
Mercedes, *B. Aires, Argentina* 94 C5
Mercedes, *Corrientes,*
  Argentina 94 B5
Mercedes, *San Luis,*
  Argentina 94 C3
Mercedes, *Uruguay* 94 C5
Mercer, *N.Z.* 64 B6
Mercy, C., *Canada* 70 C7
Meredith, C., *Falk. Is.* 95 G4
Mergui Arch. = Myeik Kyunzu,
  Burma 38 B1
Mérida, *Mexico* 85 C7
Mérida, *Spain* 18 C2
Mérida, *Venezuela* 90 B4
Meridian, *U.S.A.* 82 C3
Merirumã, *Brazil* 92 B3
Merriwa, *Australia* 63 B5
Merseburg, *Germany* 15 C6
Mersin = İçel, *Turkey* 46 C3
Mersing, *Malaysia* 39 D2
Merthyr Tydfil, *U.K.* 11 F5
Mértola, *Portugal* 18 D2
Meru, *Kenya* 57 D7
Mesa, *U.S.A.* 79 D7
Meshed = Mashhad, *Iran* .. 44 B4
Mesologi, *Greece* 23 E3
Mesopotamia = Al Jazirah,
  Iraq 46 D5
Messina = Musina, *S. Africa* . 59 C6
Messina, *Italy* 21 E5
Messina, Str. di, *Italy* 21 E5
Messini, *Greece* 23 F4
Messiniakos Kolpos, *Greece* . 23 F4
Mesta →, *Bulgaria* 22 D5
Meta →, *S. Amer.* 90 B5
Meta Incognita Pen., *Canada* 70 C7
Metairie, *U.S.A.* 81 E8
Metán, *Argentina* 94 B4
Methven, *N.Z.* 65 E4
Metlakatla, *U.S.A.* 69 C6
Metz, *France* 13 B7
Meulaboh, *Indonesia* 39 D1
Meureudu, *Indonesia* 38 C1
Meuse →, *Europe* 13 A6
Mexiana, I., *Brazil* 92 C4

Mexicali, *Mexico* 84 A1
México, *Mexico* 84 D5
Mexico ■, *Cent. Amer.* 84 C4
México, Ciudad de, *Mexico* . 84 D5
Mexico, G. of, *Cent. Amer.* .. 85 B7
Meymaneh, *Afghan.* 42 B4
Mezen, *Russia* 28 C5
Mezen →, *Russia* 28 C5
Mézenc, Mt., *France* 13 D6
Mezőkövesd, *Hungary* 16 E5
Mezőtúr, *Hungary* 16 E5
Mhow, *India* 43 H9
Miami, *U.S.A.* 83 G7
Miami Beach, *U.S.A.* 83 G7
Miāndowāb, *Iran* 46 C6
Miandrivazo, *Madag.* 59 B9
Miāneh, *Iran* 46 C6
Mianwali, *Pakistan* 42 C7
Miass, *Russia* 29 D7
Michigan □, *U.S.A.* 76 C3
Michigan, L., *U.S.A.* 76 C2
Michurin, *Bulgaria* 22 C6
Michurinsk, *Russia* 24 C5
Micronesia, *Pac. Oc.* 64 H11
Micronesia, Federated States
  of ■, *Pac. Oc.* 64 J10
Middelburg, *S. Africa* 58 E5
Middlesbrough, *U.K.* 11 D6
Midi, Canal du →, *France* .. 12 E4
Midland, *U.S.A.* 80 D3
Midyat, *Turkey* 46 C5
Midžōr, *Bulgaria* 22 C4
Międzychód, *Poland* 16 B2
Międzyrzec Podlaski, *Poland* 17 C6
Mielec, *Poland* 16 C5
Mieres, *Spain* 18 A3
Mikhaylovgrad = Montana,
  Bulgaria 22 C4
Mikines, *Greece* 23 F4
Mikonos = Mykonos, *Greece* 23 F5
Milagro, *Ecuador* 90 D3
Milan = Milano, *Italy* 13 D8
Milano, *Italy* 13 D8
Milâs, *Turkey* 23 F6
Milazzo, *Italy* 21 E5
Mildura, *Australia* 62 B3
Miles, *Australia* 63 A5
Miletus, *Turkey* 23 F6
Milford Haven, *U.K.* 11 F4
Milford Sd., *N.Z.* 65 F2
Milford Sound, *N.Z.* 65 F2
Milḥ, Baḥr al =
  Buḥayrat ar, *Iraq* 47 D5
Mill I., *Antarctica* 96 A12
Millau, *France* 13 D5
Millennium I. = Caroline I.,
  Kiribati 65 K15
Millicent, *Australia* 62 C3
Millinocket, *U.S.A.* 77 B11
Millmerran, *Australia* 63 A5
Milos, *Greece* 23 F5
Milparinka, *Australia* 62 A3
Milton, *N.Z.* 65 G3
Milton Keynes, *U.K.* 11 E6
Milwaukee, *U.S.A.* 76 C2
Min Jiang →, *Fujian, China* . 35 D6
Min Jiang →, *Sichuan, China* 35 D5
Minā Su'ud, *Kuwait* 47 E7
Mīnā'al Aḥmadī, *Kuwait* ... 47 E7
Minamata, *Japan* 33 G2
Minas, *Uruguay* 94 C5
Minas Gerais □, *Brazil* 93 F4
Minbu, *Burma* 41 G10
Mindanao, *Phil.* 36 C2
Mindanao Sea = Bohol Sea,
  Phil. 36 C2
Mindanao Trench, *Pac. Oc.* .. 36 B3
Minden, *Germany* 14 B5
Mindiptana, *Indonesia* 37 F6
Mindoro, *Phil.* 36 B2
Mindoro Str., *Phil.* 36 B2
Mingäçevir Su Anbarı,
  Azerbaijan 25 E6
Mingin, *Burma* 41 F10
Mingteke Daban = Mintaka
  Pass, *Pakistan* 42 A9
Minho = Miño →, *Spain* ... 18 B1

Minho, *Portugal* 18 B1
Minna, *Nigeria* 53 G7
Minneapolis, *U.S.A.* 75 C8
Minnesota □, *U.S.A.* 75 B7
Minnipa, *Australia* 62 B2
Miño →, *Spain* 18 B1
Minorca = Menorca, *Spain* .. 19 C7
Minot, *U.S.A.* 74 A4
Minsk, *Belarus* 24 C2
Mińsk Mazowiecki, *Poland* .. 16 B5
Mintaka Pass, *Pakistan* 42 A9
Minto, L., *Canada* 70 D6
Minutang, *India* 41 C11
Mira, *Italy* 20 B4
Mirabello, Kolpos, *Greece* .. 23 G5
Miraj, *India* 43 L9
Miram Shah, *Pakistan* 42 C7
Miramichi, *Canada* 71 E7
Miranda, *Brazil* 93 G2
Miranda de Ebro, *Spain* ... 19 A4
Miranda do Douro, *Portugal* . 18 B2
Miri, *Malaysia* 38 D4
Mirim, L., *S. Amer.* 94 C6
Mirpur Khas, *Pakistan* 42 G6
Mirzapur, *India* 40 E4
Mish'āb, Ra's al, *Si. Arabia* . 47 E7
Mishan, *China* 35 B8
Miskolc, *Hungary* 16 D5
Misool, *Indonesia* 37 E4
Miṣr = Egypt ■, *Africa* 54 C5
Miṣrātah, *Libya* 54 B2
Missinaibi →, *Canada* 71 D5
Mississippi □, *U.S.A.* 81 C9
Mississippi →, *U.S.A.* 81 E9
Mississippi River Delta, *U.S.A.* 81 E9
Missoula, *U.S.A.* 73 C7
Missouri □, *U.S.A.* 75 F8
Missouri →, *U.S.A.* 75 F9
Mistassini, L., *Canada* 71 D6
Misurata = Miṣrātah, *Libya* . 54 B2
Mitchell, *Australia* 63 A4
Mitchell, *U.S.A.* 74 D5
Mitchell →, *Australia* 61 D7
Mitilini, *Greece* 23 E6
Mito, *Japan* 33 E7
Mitrovica = Kosovska
  Mitrovica, *Serbia & M.* ... 22 C3
Mittagong, *Australia* 63 B5
Mittimatalik = Pond Inlet,
  Canada 70 B6
Mitú, *Colombia* 90 C4
Mitumba, Mts., *Dem. Rep. of*
  the Congo 57 F5
Mitwaba, *Dem. Rep. of*
  the Congo 57 F5
Miyake-Jima, *Japan* 33 F6
Miyako, *Japan* 32 D7
Miyakonojō, *Japan* 33 H2
Miyazaki, *Japan* 33 H2
Miyet, Bahr el = Dead Sea,
  Asia 47 E3
Mizdah, *Libya* 54 B1
Mizoram □, *India* 41 F9
Mjøsa, *Norway* 8 C8
Mladá Boleslav, *Czech Rep.* . 16 C2
Mlanje, Pic, *Malawi* 59 B7
Mława, *Poland* 16 B5
Mljet, *Croatia* 20 C6
Mmabatho, *S. Africa* 59 D5
Mo i Rana, *Norway* 8 B8
Moa, *Indonesia* 37 F3
Mobaye, *C.A.R.* 56 D4
Mobayi, *Dem. Rep. of*
  the Congo 56 D4
Mobile, *U.S.A.* 82 D3
Moçambique ■, *Africa* 59 B7
Moçambique, *Mozam.* 59 B8
Mochudi, *Botswana* 59 C5
Mocimboa da Praia, *Mozam.* 57 G8
Mocoa, *Colombia* 90 C3
Mocuba, *Mozam.* 59 B7
Modane, *France* 13 D7
Módena, *Italy* 20 B3
Modesto, *U.S.A.* 78 B2
Módica, *Italy* 21 F5
Modimolle, *S. Africa* 59 C5

133

Moe

Place	Page	Grid
Moe, *Australia*	63	C4
Moengo, *Suriname*	92	A3
Mogadishu = Muqdisho, *Somali Rep.*	49	G4
Mogador = Essaouira, *Morocco*	52	B4
Mogami-Gawa →, *Japan*	32	D7
Mogaung, *Burma*	41	E11
Mogi das Cruzes, *Brazil*	94	A7
Mogilev = Mahilyow, *Belarus*	17	B10
Mogilev-Podolskiy = Mohyliv-Podilskyy, *Ukraine*	17	D8
Mogok, *Burma*	41	F11
Mohács, *Hungary*	16	F4
Moḥammadābād, *Iran*	44	B4
Mohyliv-Podilskyy, *Ukraine*	17	D8
Moisie →, *Canada*	71	D7
Mojave Desert, *U.S.A.*	78	C4
Mokai, *N.Z.*	64	C6
Mokau, *N.Z.*	64	C6
Mokokchung, *India*	41	D10
Mokopane, *S. Africa*	59	C5
Mokra Gora, *Serbia & M.*	22	C3
Molchanovo, *Russia*	29	D9
Moldavia = Moldova ■, *Europe*	17	E9
Molde, *Norway*	8	C7
Moldova ■, *Europe*	17	E9
Moldoveanu, Vf., *Romania*	17	F7
Molepolole, *Botswana*	59	C5
Molfetta, *Italy*	20	D6
Moline, *U.S.A.*	75	E9
Mollendo, *Peru*	91	G4
Molodechno = Maladzyechna, *Belarus*	17	A8
Moloka'i, *U.S.A.*	78	H12
Molong, *Australia*	63	B4
Molopo →, *Africa*	58	D4
Molu, *Indonesia*	37	F4
Molucca Sea, *Indonesia*	37	E2
Moluccas = Maluku, *Indonesia*	37	E3
Moma, *Mozam.*	59	B7
Mombasa, *Kenya*	57	E7
Mombetsu, *Japan*	32	A8
Momchilgrad, *Bulgaria*	22	D5
Mompós, *Colombia*	90	B4
Mona Passage, *W. Indies*	87	C6
Monaco ■, *Europe*	13	E7
Monahans, *U.S.A.*	80	D2
Monastir = Bitola, *Macedonia*	22	D3
Moncayo, Sierra del, *Spain*	19	B5
Mönchengladbach, *Germany*	14	C4
Monchique, *Portugal*	18	D1
Monclova, *Mexico*	84	B4
Moncton, *Canada*	71	E7
Mondego →, *Portugal*	18	B1
Mondeodo, *Indonesia*	37	E2
Mondovi, *Italy*	13	D7
Monforte de Lemos, *Spain*	18	A2
Mong Hsu, *Burma*	41	G12
Mong Kung, *Burma*	41	G11
Mong Nai, *Burma*	41	G11
Mong Pawk, *Burma*	41	F12
Mong Ton, *Burma*	41	G12
Mong Wa, *Burma*	41	G13
Mong Yai, *Burma*	41	F12
Mongalla, *Sudan*	55	G5
Monghyr = Munger, *India*	40	E6
Mongibello = Etna, *Italy*	21	F5
Mongo, *Chad*	55	F2
Mongolia ■, *Asia*	35	B5
Mongu, *Zambia*	58	B4
Monkoto, *Dem. Rep. of the Congo*	56	E4
Monópoli, *Italy*	21	D6
Monroe, La., *U.S.A.*	81	C7
Monroe, N.C., *U.S.A.*	83	B7
Monrovia, *Liberia*	53	G3
Mons, *Belgium*	14	C2
Monse, *Indonesia*	37	E2
Mont-de-Marsan, *France*	12	E3
Mont-Laurier, *Canada*	71	E6
Mont-St-Michel, Le, *France*	12	B3
Montalbán, *Spain*	19	B5
Montana, *Bulgaria*	22	C4
Montana □, *U.S.A.*	73	C9
Montargis, *France*	13	C5
Montauban, *France*	12	D4
Montbéliard, *France*	13	C7
Montceau-les-Mines, *France*	13	C6
Monte Alegre, *Brazil*	92	C3
Monte Azul, *Brazil*	93	F5
Monte-Carlo, *Monaco*	13	E7
Monte Caseros, *Argentina*	94	C5
Monte Comán, *Argentina*	94	C3
Monte Santu, C. di, *Italy*	21	D2
Montecristo, *Italy*	20	C3
Montego Bay, *Jamaica*	86	C4
Montélimar, *France*	13	D6
Montemorelos, *Mexico*	84	B5
Montenegro □, *Serbia & M.*	22	C2
Montepuez, *Mozam.*	59	A7
Monterey, *U.S.A.*	78	B2
Montería, *Colombia*	90	B3
Monterrey, *Mexico*	84	B4
Montes Claros, *Brazil*	93	F5
Montesilvano, *Italy*	20	C5
Montevideo, *Uruguay*	94	C5
Montgomery, *U.S.A.*	82	C4
Montilla, *Spain*	18	D3
Montluçon, *France*	13	C5
Montmorillon, *France*	12	C4
Montoro, *Spain*	18	C3
Montpellier, *France*	13	E5
Montréal, *Canada*	71	E6
Montrose, *U.K.*	10	C5
Montrose, *U.S.A.*	79	A9
Montserrat ☑, *W. Indies*	87	C7
Monywa, *Burma*	41	F10
Monza, *Italy*	13	D8
Monze, *Zambia*	59	B5
Monze, C., *Pakistan*	43	G5
Monzón, *Spain*	19	B6
Moonie, *Australia*	63	A5
Moonie →, *Australia*	63	A4
Moonta, *Australia*	62	B2
Moose Jaw, *Canada*	69	C9
Moosomin, *Canada*	69	C9
Moosonee, *Canada*	71	D5
Mopti, *Mali*	53	F5
Moquegua, *Peru*	91	G4
Mora, *Sweden*	8	C8
Moradabad, *India*	42	E11
Morafenobe, *Madag.*	59	B8
Moramanga, *Madag.*	59	B9
Moratuwa, *Sri Lanka*	43	R11
Morava →, *Serbia & M.*	22	B3
Morava →, *Slovak Rep.*	16	D3
Moravian Hts. = Českomoravská Vrchovina, *Czech Rep.*	16	D2
Morawhanna, *Guyana*	90	B7
Moray Firth, *U.K.*	10	C5
Morden, *Canada*	69	D10
Mordvinia □, *Russia*	24	C5
Moree, *Australia*	63	A4
Morelia, *Mexico*	84	D4
Morella, *Spain*	19	B5
Morena, Sierra, *Spain*	18	C3
Moreton I., *Australia*	63	A5
Morgan City, *U.S.A.*	81	E8
Morioka, *Japan*	32	D7
Morlaix, *France*	12	B2
Mornington, *Australia*	63	C4
Mornington, I., *Chile*	95	F1
Moro G., *Phil.*	36	C2
Morocco ■, *N. Afr.*	52	B4
Morogoro, *Tanzania*	57	F7
Morombe, *Madag.*	59	C8
Morón, *Cuba*	86	B4
Morón de la Frontera, *Spain*	18	D3
Morondava, *Madag.*	59	C8
Morotai, *Indonesia*	37	D3
Moroto, *Uganda*	57	D6
Morphou, *Cyprus*	46	D3
Morrinhos, *Brazil*	93	F4
Morrinsville, *N.Z.*	64	B6
Morristown, *U.S.A.*	83	A6
Morshansk, *Russia*	24	C5
Morteros, *Argentina*	94	C4
Mortlake, *Australia*	62	C3
Morundah, *Australia*	63	B4
Moruya, *Australia*	63	C5
Morvan, *France*	13	C6
Morven, *Australia*	63	A4
Morwell, *Australia*	63	C4
Moscos Is., *Burma*	41	L11
Moscow = Moskva, *Russia*	24	B4
Moscow, *U.S.A.*	72	C5
Mosel →, *Europe*	13	A7
Moselle = Mosel →, *Europe*	13	A7
Mosgiel, *N.Z.*	65	F4
Moshi, *Tanzania*	57	E7
Mosjøen, *Norway*	8	B8
Moskva, *Russia*	24	B4
Mosonmagyaróvár, *Hungary*	16	E3
Mosquera, *Colombia*	90	C3
Moss Vale, *Australia*	63	B5
Mossburn, *N.Z.*	65	F3
Mosselbaai, *S. Africa*	58	E4
Mossendjo, *Congo*	56	E2
Mossgiel, *Australia*	63	B3
Mossoró, *Brazil*	92	D6
Most, *Czech Rep.*	16	C1
Mostaganem, *Algeria*	52	A6
Mostar, *Bos.-H.*	20	C6
Mostardas, *Brazil*	94	C6
Mosty = Masty, *Belarus*	17	B7
Mostyska, *Ukraine*	17	D6
Mosul = Al Mawşil, *Iraq*	46	C5
Motihari, *India*	40	D5
Motril, *Spain*	18	D4
Motueka, *N.Z.*	65	D5
Motueka →, *N.Z.*	65	D5
Moudros, *Greece*	23	E5
Mouila, *Gabon*	56	E2
Moulamein, *Australia*	63	C3
Moulins, *France*	13	C5
Moulmein, *Burma*	41	J11
Moundou, *Chad*	55	G2
Mount Aspiring △, *N.Z.*	65	F3
Mount Barker, *Australia*	62	C2
Mount Cook, *N.Z.*	65	E4
Mount Gambier, *Australia*	62	C3
Mount Hope, N.S.W., *Australia*	63	B4
Mount Hope, S. Austral., *Australia*	62	B2
Mount Isa, *Australia*	61	E6
Mount Lofty Ranges, *Australia*	62	B2
Mount Maunganui, *N.Z.*	64	B7
Mount Perry, *Australia*	63	A5
Moura, *Brazil*	90	D6
Moura, *Portugal*	18	C2
Mourdi, Dépression du, *Chad*	55	E3
Moussoro, *Chad*	55	F2
Moutong, *Indonesia*	37	D2
Moyale, *Kenya*	49	G2
Moyen Atlas, *Morocco*	52	B4
Moyo, *Indonesia*	39	F5
Moyyero →, *Russia*	30	C8
Moyynty, *Kazakhstan*	29	E8
Mozambique = Moçambique, *Mozam.*	59	B8
Mozambique ■, *Africa*	59	B7
Mozambique Chan., *Africa*	51	H8
Mozdok, *Russia*	25	E6
Mozyr = Mazyr, *Belarus*	17	C9
Mpanda, *Tanzania*	57	F6
Mpika, *Zambia*	59	A6
Mpwapwa, *Tanzania*	57	F7
Mthatha, *S. Africa*	59	E5
Mu Us Shamo, *China*	35	C5
Muar, *Malaysia*	39	D2
Muarabungo, *Indonesia*	39	E2
Muaraenim, *Indonesia*	39	E2
Muarajuloi, *Indonesia*	39	E4
Muarakaman, *Indonesia*	39	E5
Muaratebo, *Indonesia*	39	E2
Muaratembesi, *Indonesia*	39	E2
Muaratewe, *Indonesia*	39	E4
Mubarraz = Al Mubarraz, *Si. Arabia*	47	F7
Mubi, *Nigeria*	55	F1
Muckadilla, *Australia*	63	A4
Mucuri, *Brazil*	93	F6
Mudanjiang, *China*	35	B7
Mudanya, *Turkey*	23	D7
Mudgee, *Australia*	63	B4
Mufulira, *Zambia*	59	A5
Mugi, *Japan*	33	G4

Muğla, Turkey 23 F7
Mugu, Nepal 40 C4
Muhammad Qol, Sudan 54 D6
Mühlhausen, Germany 14 C6
Mühlig Hofmann fjell,
 Antarctica 96 B7
Mujnak = Muynak, Uzbekistan 29 E6
Mukacheve, Ukraine 17 D6
Mukah, Malaysia 39 D4
Mukden = Shenyang, China . 35 B7
Mukoınuko, Indonesia 39 E2
Muktsar, India 42 D9
Mula, Spain 19 C5
Mulchén, Chile 94 D2
Mulde →, Germany 15 C7
Mulhacén, Spain 18 D4
Mulhouse, France 13 C7
Mull, U.K. 10 C4
Muller, Pegunungan,
 Indonesia 39 D4
Mullingar, Ireland 11 E3
Mullumbimby, Australia .. 63 A5
Multan, Pakistan 42 D7
Mumbai, India 43 K8
Muna, Indonesia 37 F2
München, Germany 15 D6
Munchen-Gladbach =
 Mönchengladbach,
 Germany 14 C4
Muncie, U.S.A. 76 D3
Münden, Germany 14 C5
Mundo Novo, Brazil 93 E5
Mungallala, Australia 63 A4
Mungallala Cr. →, Australia . 63 A4
Mungbere, Dem. Rep. of
 the Congo 57 D5
Munger, India 40 E6
Munich = München, Germany 15 D6
Muñoz Gamero, Pen., Chile . 95 G2
Münster, Germany 14 C4
Munster □, Ireland 11 E2
Muntok, Indonesia 39 E3
Muqdisho, Somali Rep. ... 49 G4
Murallón, Cerro, Chile 95 F2
Murang'a, Kenya 57 E7
Murashi, Russia 24 B6
Muratlı, Turkey 22 D6
Murchison →, Australia ... 60 F1
Murchison, Mt., Antarctica .. 96 B15
Murchison Falls, Uganda .. 57 D6
Murcia, Spain 19 C5
Murcia □, Spain 19 D5
Mureş →, Romania 22 A3
Murfreesboro, U.S.A. 82 B4
Murgap, Tajikistan 29 F8
Murghob = Murgap, Tajikistan 29 F8
Murgon, Australia 63 A5
Müritz, Germany 15 B7
Murmansk, Russia 8 B12
Murom, Russia 24 B5
Muroran, Japan 32 B7
Muroto, Japan 33 G4
Muroto-Misaki, Japan 33 G4
Murray →, Australia 62 C2
Murray Bridge, Australia ... 62 C2
Murrumbidgee →, Australia 62 B3
Murrumburrah, Australia .. 63 B4
Murrurundi, Australia 63 B5
Murtoa, Australia 62 C3
Murwara, India 40 F3
Murwillumbah, Australia .. 63 A5
Mürzzuschlag, Austria 15 E8
Muş, Turkey 46 C5
Mûsa, Gebel, Egypt 47 E3
Musa Khel, Pakistan 42 D6
Mûsa Qal'eh, Afghan. 42 C4
Musala, Bulgaria 22 C4
Musala, Indonesia 39 D1
Muscat = Masqat, Oman ... 45 F4
Muscatine, U.S.A. 75 E9
Musgrave Ranges, Australia . 60 F5
Mushie, Dem. Rep. of
 the Congo 56 E3
Musi →, Indonesia 39 E2
Musina, S. Africa 59 C6
Muskogee, U.S.A. 81 B6
Musoma, Tanzania 57 E6

Mussoorie, India 42 D11
Mustafakemalpaşa, Turkey .. 23 D7
Mustang, Nepal 40 C4
Musters, L., Argentina 95 F3
Muswellbrook, Australia 63 B5
Mût, Egypt 54 C4
Mut, Turkey 46 C3
Mutare, Zimbabwe 59 B6
Muting, Indonesia 37 F6
Mutoray, Russia 30 C8
Mutsu, Japan 32 C7
Mutsu-Wan, Japan 32 C7
Muynak, Uzbekistan 29 E6
Muzaffarabad, Pakistan 42 B8
Muzaffargarh, Pakistan 42 D7
Muzaffarnagar, India 42 E10
Muzaffarpur, India 40 D5
Muzhi, Russia 28 C7
Mvuma, Zimbabwe 59 B6
Mwanza, Dem. Rep. of
 the Congo 57 F5
Mwanza, Tanzania 57 E6
Mweka, Dem. Rep. of
 the Congo 56 E4
Mweru, L., Zambia 57 F5
Mwinilunga, Zambia 58 A4
My Tho, Vietnam 38 B3
Myanaung, Burma 41 H10
Myanmar = Burma ■, Asia . 41 G11
Myaungmya, Burma 41 J10
Mycenæ = Mikines, Greece . 23 F4
Myeik Kyunzu, Burma 38 B1
Myingyan, Burma 41 G10
Myitkyina, Burma 41 E11
Mykolayiv, Ukraine 25 D3
Mykonos, Greece 23 F5
Mymensingh, Bangla. 41 E8
Mýrdalsjökull, Iceland 8 C2
Mysia, Turkey 23 E6
Mysore = Karnataka □, India 43 N10
Mysore, India 43 N10
Myszków, Poland 16 C4
Mytishchi, Russia 24 B4

N

Na Hearadh = Harris, U.K. ... 10 C3
Naab →, Germany 15 D7
Nababeep, S. Africa 58 D3
Naberezhnyye Chelny, Russia 29 D6
Nabeul, Tunisia 54 A1
Nabire, Indonesia 37 E5
Nåblus = Nābulus, West Bank 46 D3
Nābulus, West Bank 46 D3
Nacala, Mozam. 59 A8
Nachingwea, Tanzania 57 G7
Nacogdoches, U.S.A. 81 D6
Nacozari de García, Mexico . 84 A3
Nadiad, India 43 H8
Nadüshan, Iran 44 C3
Nadvirna, Ukraine 17 D7
Nadym, Russia 28 C8
Nadym →, Russia 28 C8
Nafpaktos, Greece 23 E3
Nafplio, Greece 23 F4
Nafud Desert = An Nafūd,
 Si. Arabia 47 E5
Naga, Phil. 36 B2
Nagaland □, India 41 E10
Nagano, Japan 33 E6
Nagaoka, Japan 33 E6
Nagappattinam, India 43 P11
Nagar Parkar, Pakistan 43 G7
Nagasaki, Japan 33 G1
Nagaur, India 42 F8
Nagercoil, India 43 Q10
Nagîneh, Iran 44 C4
Nagoya, Japan 33 F5
Nagpur, India 43 J11
Nagykanizsa, Hungary 16 E3
Nagykörös, Hungary 16 E4
Naha, Japan 35 D7
Nahävand, Iran 46 D7
Nain, Canada 70 D7
Nā'īn, Iran 44 C3

Nairn, U.K. 10 C5
Nairobi, Kenya 57 E7
Najaf = An Najaf, Iraq 47 D6
Najafābād, Iran 44 C2
Najd, Si. Arabia 47 F5
Najibabad, India 42 E11
Nakamura, Japan 33 G3
Nakashibetsu, Japan 32 B9
Nakhichevan = Naxçıvan,
 Azerbaijan 25 F6
Nakhichevan Rep. =
 Naxçıvan □, Azerbaijan ... 25 F6
Nakhodka, Russia 32 B3
Nakhon Phanom, Thailand .. 38 A2
Nakhon Ratchasima, Thailand 38 B2
Nakhon Sawan, Thailand .. 38 A2
Nakhon Si Thammarat,
 Thailand 38 C2
Nakina, Canada 71 D5
Nakuru, Kenya 57 E7
Nal →, Pakistan 42 G4
Nalchik, Russia 25 E5
Nalgonda, India 43 L11
Nallamalai Hills, India 43 M11
Nam Co, China 34 C4
Nam-Phan, Vietnam 38 B3
Namak, Daryächeh-ye, Iran . 44 C3
Namak, Kavir-e, Iran 44 C4
Namaland, Namibia 58 D3
Namangan, Uzbekistan ... 29 E8
Namapa, Mozam. 59 A7
Namber, Indonesia 37 E4
Nambour, Australia 63 A5
Nambucca Heads, Australia . 63 B5
Namib Desert, Namibia 58 C2
Namibe, Angola 58 B2
Namibia ■, Africa 58 C3
Namlea, Indonesia 37 E3
Namoi →, Australia 63 B4
Nampa, U.S.A. 72 E5
Nampo, N. Korea 35 C7
Nampō-Shotō, Japan 33 H7
Nampula, Mozam. 59 B7
Namrole, Indonesia 37 E3
Namse Shankou, China ... 40 C4
Namtu, Burma 41 F11
Namur, Belgium 14 C3
Nan-ch'ang = Nanchang,
 China 35 D6
Nanaimo, Canada 69 D7
Nanango, Australia 63 A5
Nanao, Japan 33 E5
Nanchang, China 35 D6
Nanching = Nanjing, China . 35 C6
Nanchong, China 35 C5
Nancy, France 13 B7
Nanda Devi, India 42 D11
Nanded, India 43 K10
Nandewar Ra., Australia .. 63 B5
Nandurbar, India 43 J9
Nandyal, India 43 M11
Nanga-Eboko, Cameroon .. 56 D2
Nanga Parbat, Pakistan ... 42 B9
Nangapinoh, Indonesia 39 E4
Nangarhär □, Afghan. 42 B7
Nangatayap, Indonesia 39 E4
Nanjing, China 35 C6
Nanking = Nanjing, China ... 35 C6
Nanning, China 35 D5
Nanping, China 35 D6
Nansei-Shotō = Ryūkyū-rettō,
 Japan 35 D7
Nansen Sd., Canada 70 A4
Nantes, France 12 C3
Nantucket I., U.S.A. 77 D10
Nanuque, Brazil 93 F5
Nanusa, Kepulauan, Indonesia 36 D3
Nanyang, China 35 C6
Nanyuki, Kenya 57 D7
Nao, C. de la, Spain 19 C6
Napa, U.S.A. 72 G2
Napier, N.Z. 64 C7
Naples = Nápoli, Italy 21 D5
Naples, U.S.A. 83 F7
Napo →, Peru 90 D4
Nápoli, Italy 21 D5
Nara, Mali 53 E4

Naracoorte

Entry	Page	Ref
Naracoorte, *Australia*	62	C3
Naradhan, *Australia*	63	B4
Narasapur, *India*	40	J3
Narathiwat, *Thailand*	38	C2
Narayanganj, *Bangla.*	41	F8
Narayanpet, *India*	43	L10
Narbonne, *France*	13	E5
Nardò, *Italy*	21	D7
Narew ➤, *Poland*	16	B5
Narin, *Afghan.*	42	A6
Narmada ➤, *India*	43	J8
Narodnaya, *Russia*	28	C6
Narooma, *Australia*	63	C5
Narrabri, *Australia*	63	B4
Narran ➤, *Australia*	63	A4
Narrandera, *Australia*	63	B4
Narromine, *Australia*	63	B4
Narsimhapur, *India*	43	H11
Naruto, *Japan*	33	F4
Narva, *Estonia*	24	B2
Narvik, *Norway*	8	B9
Naryan-Mar, *Russia*	28	C6
Narym, *Russia*	29	D9
Naryn, *Kyrgyzstan*	29	E8
Naseby, *N.Z.*	65	F4
Naser, Buheirat en, *Egypt*	54	D5
Nashville, *U.S.A.*	82	A4
Nasik, *India*	43	K8
Nasirabad, *India*	42	F9
Nassau, *Bahamas*	86	A4
Nassau, B., *Chile*	95	H3
Nasser, L. = Naser, Buheirat en, *Egypt*	54	D5
Natal, *Brazil*	92	D6
Natal, *Indonesia*	39	D1
Naṭanz, *Iran*	44	C2
Natashquan, *Canada*	71	D7
Natashquan ➤, *Canada*	71	D7
Natchez, *U.S.A.*	81	D8
Nathalia, *Australia*	63	C4
Nathdwara, *India*	43	G8
Natitingou, *Benin*	53	F6
Natkyizin, *Burma*	41	K11
Natron, L., *Tanzania*	57	E7
Natuna Besar, Kepulauan, *Indonesia*	39	D3
Natuna Selatan, Kepulauan, *Indonesia*	39	D3
Naturaliste, C., *Australia*	62	D4
Naujaat = Repulse Bay, *Canada*	70	C5
Naumburg, *Germany*	15	C6
Nauru ■, *Pac. Oc.*	64	K11
Naushahra = Nowshera, *Pakistan*	42	B8
Nauta, *Peru*	90	D4
Nautanwa, *India*	40	D4
Navahrudak, *Belarus*	17	B7
Navalmoral de la Mata, *Spain*	18	C3
Navarino, I., *Chile*	95	H3
Navarra □, *Spain*	19	A5
Năvodari, *Romania*	22	B7
Navoi = Nawoiy, *Uzbekistan*	29	E7
Navojoa, *Mexico*	84	B3
Navsari, *India*	43	J8
Nawabshah, *Pakistan*	42	F6
Nawakot, *Nepal*	40	D5
Nawalgarh, *India*	42	F9
Nawāsif, Ḥarrat, *Si. Arabia*	47	G5
Nawoiy, *Uzbekistan*	29	E7
Naxçıvan, *Azerbaijan*	25	F6
Naxçıvan □, *Azerbaijan*	25	F6
Naxos, *Greece*	23	F5
Nãy Band, *Iran*	44	E3
Nayoro, *Japan*	32	A8
Nazas ➤, *Mexico*	84	B4
Nazilli, *Turkey*	23	F7
Ndalatando, *Angola*	56	F2
Ndélé, *C.A.R.*	55	G3
Ndjamena, *Chad*	55	F1
Ndola, *Zambia*	59	A5
Neagh, Lough, *U.K.*	11	D3
Neales ➤, *Australia*	62	A2
Near Is., *U.S.A.*	69	C1
Neath, *U.K.*	11	F5
Nebine Cr. ➤, *Australia*	63	A4
Nebitdag = Balkanabat, *Turkmenistan*	29	F6
Nebraska □, *U.S.A.*	74	E5
Nébrodi, Monti, *Italy*	21	F5
Neckar ➤, *Germany*	14	D5
Necochea, *Argentina*	94	D5
Nederland = Netherlands ■, *Europe*	14	B3
Neemuch = Nimach, *India*	43	G9
Neepawa, *Canada*	69	C10
Neftçala, *Azerbaijan*	46	C7
Negapatam = Nagappattinam, *India*	43	P11
Negele, *Ethiopia*	49	F2
Negombo, *Sri Lanka*	43	R11
Negotin, *Serbia & M.*	22	B4
Negrais, C. = Maudin Sun, *Burma*	41	K10
Negro ➤, *Argentina*	95	E4
Negro ➤, *Brazil*	90	D6
Negro ➤, *Uruguay*	94	C5
Negros, *Phil.*	36	C2
Nei Monggol Zizhiqu □, *China*	35	B6
Neijiang, *China*	35	D5
Neiva, *Colombia*	90	C3
Nejd = Najd, *Si. Arabia*	47	F5
Nellore, *India*	43	M11
Nelson, *Canada*	69	D8
Nelson, *N.Z.*	65	D5
Nelson ➤, *Canada*	69	C10
Nelson, C., *Australia*	62	C3
Nelson, Estrecho, *Chile*	95	G2
Nelson Lakes △, *N.Z.*	65	D5
Nelspruit, *S. Africa*	59	D6
Néma, *Mauritania*	53	E4
Neman = Nemunas ➤, *Lithuania*	24	B1
Nemunas ➤, *Lithuania*	24	B1
Nemuro, *Japan*	32	B9
Nemuro Str., *Japan*	32	B9
Nenagh, *Ireland*	11	E2
Nenjiang, *China*	35	B7
Nepal ■, *Asia*	40	D5
Nepalganj, *Nepal*	40	C3
Neretva ➤, *Croatia*	20	C6
Ness, L., *U.K.*	10	C4
Nesterov, *Ukraine*	17	C6
Nesvizh = Nyasvizh, *Belarus*	17	B8
Netherlands ■, *Europe*	14	B3
Netherlands Antilles ☑, *W. Indies*	87	D6
Nettilling L., *Canada*	70	C6
Neubrandenburg, *Germany*	15	B7
Neumünster, *Germany*	14	A5
Neunkirchen, *Germany*	14	D4
Neuquén, *Argentina*	94	D3
Neuruppin, *Germany*	15	B7
Neustrelitz, *Germany*	15	B7
Neva ➤, *Russia*	24	B3
Nevada □, *U.S.A.*	72	G5
Nevers, *France*	13	C5
Nevertire, *Australia*	63	B4
Nevinnomyssk, *Russia*	25	E5
Nevşehir, *Turkey*	46	C3
New Amsterdam, *Guyana*	90	B7
New Angledool, *Australia*	63	A4
New Bedford, *U.S.A.*	77	D10
New Bern, *U.S.A.*	83	B9
New Brighton, *N.Z.*	65	E5
New Britain, *Papua N. G.*	64	K10
New Britain, *U.S.A.*	77	D9
New Brunswick □, *Canada*	71	E7
New Caledonia ☑, *Pac. Oc.*	64	M11
New Castile = Castilla-La Mancha □, *Spain*	18	C4
New Delhi, *India*	42	E10
New England Ra., *Australia*	63	B5
New Glasgow, *Canada*	71	E7
New Hampshire □, *U.S.A.*	77	C10
New Haven, *U.S.A.*	77	D9
New Hebrides = Vanuatu ■, *Pac. Oc.*	64	L11
New Ireland, *Papua N. G.*	64	K10
New Jersey □, *U.S.A.*	77	E9
New Liskeard, *Canada*	71	E6
New London, *U.S.A.*	77	D9
New Mexico □, *U.S.A.*	79	C9
New Norfolk, *Australia*	62	D4
New Orleans, *U.S.A.*	81	E8
New Plymouth, *N.Z.*	64	C6
New Providence, *Bahamas*	86	A4
New Siberian Is. = Novosibirskiye Ostrova, *Russia*	31	B12
New South Wales □, *Australia*	63	B4
New York, *U.S.A.*	77	D9
New York □, *U.S.A.*	77	C8
New Zealand ■, *Oceania*	64	D7
Newark, *U.S.A.*	77	D8
Newburgh, *U.S.A.*	77	D8
Newbury, *U.K.*	11	F6
Newcastle, *Australia*	63	B5
Newcastle-upon-Tyne, *U.K.*	11	D6
Newfoundland & Labrador □, *Canada*	71	D8
Newman, *Australia*	60	E2
Newport, I. of W., *U.K.*	11	F6
Newport, *Newport, U.K.*	11	F5
Newport, *U.S.A.*	77	D10
Newport News, *U.S.A.*	77	F7
Newquay, *U.K.*	11	F4
Newry, *U.K.*	11	D3
Neya, *Russia*	24	B5
Neyrīz, *Iran*	44	D3
Neyshābūr, *Iran*	44	B4
Nezhin = Nizhyn, *Ukraine*	24	C3
Ngabang, *Indonesia*	39	D3
Ngabordamlu, Tanjung, *Indonesia*	37	F4
Nganglong Kangri, *China*	40	A3
Ngaoundéré, *Cameroon*	56	C2
Ngapara, *N.Z.*	65	F4
Ngoring Hu, *China*	34	C4
Nguigmi, *Niger*	55	F1
Nha Trang, *Vietnam*	38	B3
Nhill, *Australia*	62	C3
Niagara Falls, *Canada*	71	E6
Niagara Falls, *U.S.A.*	77	C6
Niah, *Malaysia*	39	D4
Niamey, *Niger*	53	F6
Nias, *Indonesia*	39	D1
Nicaragua ■, *Cent. Amer.*	85	E7
Nicaragua, L. de, *Nic.*	85	E7
Nicastro, *Italy*	21	E6
Nice, *France*	13	E7
Nichinan, *Japan*	33	H2
Nicobar Is., *Ind. Oc.*	27	H11
Nicosia, *Cyprus*	46	D3
Nicoya, Pen. de, *Costa Rica*	85	F7
Niedersachsen □, *Germany*	14	B5
Niemen = Nemunas ➤, *Lithuania*	24	B1
Nienburg, *Germany*	14	B5
Nieuw Amsterdam, *Suriname*	92	A2
Nieuw Nickerie, *Suriname*	92	A2
Niğde, *Turkey*	46	C3
Niger ■, *W. Afr.*	53	E7
Niger ➤, *W. Afr.*	53	G7
Nigeria ■, *W. Afr.*	53	G7
Nightcaps, *N.Z.*	65	F3
Nihon = Japan ■, *Asia*	33	F5
Nii-Jima, *Japan*	33	F6
Niigata, *Japan*	33	E6
Niʻihau, *U.S.A.*	78	H10
Niitsu, *Japan*	33	E6
Nijmegen, *Neths.*	14	C3
Nikiniki, *Indonesia*	37	F2
Nikolayev = Mykolayiv, *Ukraine*	25	D3
Nikolayevsk, *Russia*	24	C6
Nikopol, *Ukraine*	25	D3
Nīkshahr, *Iran*	45	E5
Nikšić, *Serbia & M.*	22	C2
Nîl, Nahr en ➤, *Africa*	54	B5
Nîl el Abyad ➤, *Sudan*	55	E5
Nîl el Azraq ➤, *Sudan*	55	E5
Nile = Nîl, Nahr en ➤, *Africa*	54	B5
Nimach, *India*	43	G9
Nîmes, *France*	13	E6
Nimfaíon, Ákra = Pines, Akra, *Greece*	23	D5
Nimmitabel, *Australia*	63	C4
Nīmrūz □, *Afghan.*	45	D5
Nīnawá, *Iraq*	46	C4

Nindigully, *Australia*	63	A4
Nineveh = Ninawá, *Iraq*	46	C5
Ningbo, *China*	35	D7
Ningxia Huizu Zizhiqu □, *China*	35	C5
Niobrara →, *U.S.A.*	74	D5
Nioro du Sahel, *Mali*	53	E4
Niort, *France*	12	C3
Nipawin, *Canada*	69	C9
Nipigon, L., *Canada*	71	E5
Nipissing, L., *Canada*	71	E6
Nippon = Japan ■, *Asia*	33	F5
Niquelândia, *Brazil*	93	E4
Nirmal, *India*	43	K11
Nirmali, *India*	40	D6
Niš, *Serbia & M.*	22	C3
Nişâb, *Si. Arabia*	47	E6
Nişâb, *Yemen*	49	E4
Nistru = Dnister →, *Europe*	17	E10
Niterói, *Brazil*	93	G5
Niue, *Cook Is.*	65	L14
Niut, *Indonesia*	39	D4
Nivernais, *France*	13	C5
Nizamabad, *India*	43	K11
Nizamghat, *India*	41	C10
Nizhnevartovsk, *Russia*	29	C8
Nizhniy Novgorod, *Russia*	24	B5
Nizhniy Tagil, *Russia*	29	D6
Nizhyn, *Ukraine*	24	C3
Nkhotakota, *Malawi*	59	A6
Nkongsamba, *Cameroon*	53	H7
Nmai →, *Burma*	41	E11
Noakhali = Maijdi, *Bangla.*	41	F8
Nobeoka, *Japan*	33	G2
Nocera Inferiore, *Italy*	21	D5
Nogales, *Mexico*	84	A2
Nogales, *U.S.A.*	79	E7
Nögata, *Japan*	33	G2
Noginsk, *Russia*	30	C7
Noires, Mts., *France*	12	B2
Noirmoutier, Î. de, *France*	12	C2
Nojima-Zaki, *Japan*	33	F6
Nok Kundi, *Pakistan*	42	E3
Nola, *C.A.R.*	56	D3
Nome, *U.S.A.*	69	B3
Nong Khai, *Thailand*	38	A2
Noranda = Rouyn-Noranda, *Canada*	71	E6
Nord-Ostsee-Kanal, *Germany*	14	A5
Norderney, *Germany*	14	B4
Norderstedt, *Germany*	14	B5
Nordfriesische Inseln, *Germany*	14	A5
Nordhausen, *Germany*	14	C6
Nordkapp, *Norway*	8	A11
Nordrhein-Westfalen □, *Germany*	14	C4
Nordvik, *Russia*	30	B9
Norfolk, *U.S.A.*	77	F7
Norfolk I., *Pac. Oc.*	64	M11
Norge = Norway ■, *Europe*	8	C8
Norilsk, *Russia*	30	C6
Norman, *U.S.A.*	80	B5
Norman Wells, *Canada*	68	B7
Normandie, *France*	12	B4
Normanton, *Australia*	61	D7
Norquinco, *Argentina*	95	E2
Norrköping, *Sweden*	9	D9
Norrland, *Sweden*	8	C9
Norseman, *Australia*	60	G3
North, C., *Canada*	71	E7
North Battleford, *Canada*	69	C9
North Bay, *Canada*	71	E6
North Bend, *U.S.A.*	72	E1
North C., *N.Z.*	64	A5
North Cape = Nordkapp, *Norway*	8	A11
North Carolina □, *U.S.A.*	83	B7
North Channel, *U.K.*	11	D4
North Dakota □, *U.S.A.*	74	B4
North East Frontier Agency = Arunachal Pradesh □, *India*	41	C10
North Frisian Is. = Nordfriesische Inseln, *Germany*	14	A5
North I., *N.Z.*	64	B5
North Korea ■, *Asia*	35	C7
North Lakhimpur, *India*	41	D10
North Magnetic Pole, *Canada*	70	A2
North Minch, *U.K.*	10	B4
North Ossetia □, *Russia*	25	E5
North Platte, *U.S.A.*	74	E4
North Platte →, *U.S.A.*	74	E4
North Rhine Westphalia = Nordrhein-Westfalen □, *Germany*	14	C4
North Saskatchewan →, *Canada*	69	C8
North Sea, *Europe*	10	D8
North Sporades = Vories Sporades, *Greece*	23	E4
North Taranaki Bight, *N.Z.*	64	C6
North Thompson →, *Canada*	69	C7
North Uist, *U.K.*	10	C3
North West C., *Australia*	60	E1
North West Frontier □, *Pakistan*	42	B8
North West Highlands, *U.K.*	10	C4
North West River, *Canada*	71	D7
Northampton, *U.K.*	11	E6
Northern Circars, *India*	40	J4
Northern Ireland □, *U.K.*	11	D3
Northern Marianas ☑, *Pac. Oc.*	64	H9
Northern Territory □, *Australia*	60	D5
Northland □, *N.Z.*	64	A5
Northumberland, C., *Australia*	62	C3
Northumberland Str., *Canada*	71	E7
Northwest Territories □, *Canada*	68	B9
Norton Sd., *U.S.A.*	69	B3
Norway ■, *Europe*	8	C8
Norway House, *Canada*	69	C10
Norwegian B., *Canada*	70	B5
Norwegian Sea, *Atl. Oc.*	6	B5
Norwich, *U.K.*	11	E7
Noshiro, *Japan*	32	C7
Noşratābād, *Iran*	45	D4
Nossob →, *S. Africa*	58	D4
Nosy Barren, *Madag.*	59	B8
Nosy Bé, *Madag.*	59	A9
Nosy Boraha, *Madag.*	59	B9
Nosy Varika, *Madag.*	59	C9
Noteć →, *Poland*	16	B2
Notre Dame B., *Canada*	71	E8
Notre-Dame-de-Koartac = Quaqtaq, *Canada*	70	C7
Notre-Dame-d'Ivugivic = Ivujivik, *Canada*	70	C6
Nottaway →, *Canada*	71	D6
Nottingham, *U.K.*	11	E6
Nottingham I., *Canada*	70	C6
Nouâdhibou, *Mauritania*	52	D2
Nouâdhibou, Ras, *Mauritania*	52	D2
Nouakchott, *Mauritania*	53	E2
Nouméa, *N. Cal.*	64	M11
Nouveau Comptoir = Wemindji, *Canada*	71	D6
Nouvelle-Calédonie = New Caledonia ☑, *Pac. Oc.*	64	M11
Nova Casa Nova, *Brazil*	93	D5
Nova Friburgo, *Brazil*	93	G5
Nova Iguaçu, *Brazil*	93	G5
Nova Iorque, *Brazil*	92	D5
Nova Lima, *Brazil*	93	F5
Nova Scotia □, *Canada*	71	E7
Nova Venécia, *Brazil*	93	F5
Nova Zagora, *Bulgaria*	22	C5
Novara, *Italy*	13	D8
Novaya Ladoga, *Russia*	24	A3
Novaya Lyalya, *Russia*	29	D7
Novaya Zemlya, *Russia*	28	B6
Novgorod, *Russia*	24	B3
Novhorod-Siverskyy, *Ukraine*	24	C3
Novi Lígure, *Italy*	13	D8
Novi Pazar, *Serbia & M.*	22	C3
Novi Sad, *Serbia & M.*	22	B2
Novo Mesto, *Slovenia*	20	B5
Novo Remanso, *Brazil*	93	D5
Novoaltaysk, *Russia*	29	D9
Novocherkassk, *Russia*	25	D5
Novogrudok = Navahrudak, *Belarus*	17	B7
Novohrad-Volynskyy, *Ukraine*	17	C8
Novokachalinsk, *Russia*	32	A3
Novokuybyshevsk, *Russia*	24	C6
Novokuznetsk, *Russia*	29	D9
Novomoskovsk, *Russia*	24	C4
Novorossiysk, *Russia*	25	E4
Novorybnoye, *Russia*	30	B8
Novoselytsya, *Ukraine*	17	D8
Novoshakhtinsk, *Russia*	25	D4
Novosibirsk, *Russia*	29	D9
Novosibirskiye Ostrova, *Russia*	31	B12
Novotroitsk, *Russia*	29	D6
Novouzensk, *Russia*	24	C6
Novovolynsk, *Ukraine*	17	C7
Novska, *Croatia*	20	B6
Novyy Port, *Russia*	28	C8
Nowa Sól, *Poland*	16	C2
Nowgong, *India*	41	D9
Nowra, *Australia*	63	B5
Nowshera, *Pakistan*	42	B8
Nowy Targ, *Poland*	16	D5
Nowy Tomyśl, *Poland*	16	B3
Noyon, *France*	13	B5
Nsanje, *Malawi*	59	B7
Nubian Desert = Nûbîya, Es Sahrâ en, *Sudan*	54	D5
Nûbîya, Es Sahrâ en, *Sudan*	54	D5
Nuboai, *Indonesia*	37	E5
Nueltin L., *Canada*	68	B10
Nueva Rosita, *Mexico*	84	B4
Nuéve de Julio, *Argentina*	94	D4
Nuevitas, *Cuba*	86	B4
Nuevo, G., *Argentina*	95	E4
Nuevo Laredo, *Mexico*	84	B5
Nugget Pt., *N.Z.*	65	G3
Nuhaka, *N.Z.*	64	C7
Nukey Bluff, *Australia*	62	B2
Nuku'alofa, *Tonga*	65	M13
Nukus, *Uzbekistan*	29	E6
Nullarbor Plain, *Australia*	60	G4
Numalla, L., *Australia*	63	A3
Numan, *Nigeria*	55	G1
Numazu, *Japan*	33	F6
Numfoor, *Indonesia*	37	E4
Numurkah, *Australia*	63	C4
Nunavut □, *Canada*	70	C5
Nuneaton, *U.K.*	11	E6
Nunivak I., *U.S.A.*	69	B3
Nunkun, *India*	42	C10
Núoro, *Italy*	21	D2
Nuremberg = Nürnberg, *Germany*	15	D6
Nuriootpa, *Australia*	62	B2
Nürnberg, *Germany*	15	D6
Nurran, L. = Terewah, L., *Australia*	63	A4
Nusa Tenggara Barat □, *Indonesia*	39	F5
Nusa Tenggara Timur □, *Indonesia*	37	F2
Nushki, *Pakistan*	42	E5
Nuwakot, *Nepal*	40	C4
Nuweveldberge, *S. Africa*	58	E4
Nuyts Arch., *Australia*	62	B1
Nyahururu, *Kenya*	57	D7
Nyainqentanglha Shan, *China*	34	C4
Nyâlâ, *Sudan*	55	F3
Nyasa, L. = Malawi, L., *Africa*	59	A6
Nyasvizh, *Belarus*	17	B8
Nyda, *Russia*	28	C8
Nyíregyháza, *Hungary*	17	E5
Nylstroom = Modimolle, *S. Africa*	59	C5
Nymagee, *Australia*	63	B4
Nyngan, *Australia*	63	B4
Nyoman = Nemunas →, *Lithuania*	24	B1
Nysa, *Poland*	16	C3
Nysa →, *Europe*	16	B2
Nyslott = Savonlinna, *Finland*	8	C11
Nystad = Uusikaupunki, *Finland*	9	C10
Nyurba, *Russia*	30	C9
Nzega, *Tanzania*	57	E6
Nzérékoré, *Guinea*	53	G4
Nzeto, *Angola*	56	F2

O

Ō-Shima, *Japan* 33 F6
Oahe, L., *U.S.A.* 74 C4
O'ahu, *U.S.A.* 78 H12
Oak Ridge, *U.S.A.* 83 A5
Oakey, *Australia* 63 A5
Oakland, *U.S.A.* 78 B1
Oamaru, *N.Z.* 65 F4
Oates Land, *Antarctica* 96 A15
Oaxaca, *Mexico* 84 D5
Ob ➜, *Russia* 28 C7
Oba, *Canada* 71 E5
Oban, *U.K.* 10 C4
Obbia, *Somali Rep.* 49 F4
Oberhausen, *Germany* 14 C4
Oberon, *Australia* 63 B4
Obi, Kepulauan, *Indonesia* . . 37 E3
Óbidos, *Brazil* 92 C2
Obihiro, *Japan* 32 B8
Obilatu, *Indonesia* 37 E3
Obo, *C.A.R.* 57 C5
Obozerskiy, *Russia* 28 C5
Obskaya Guba, *Russia* 28 C8
Obuasi, *Ghana* 53 G5
Ocala, *U.S.A.* 83 E6
Ocaña, *Spain* 18 C4
Occidental, Cordillera,
   Colombia 90 C3
Ocean I. = Banaba, *Kiribati* . 64 K11
Oceanside, *U.S.A.* 78 D4
Ocniţa, *Moldova* 17 D8
Ōda, *Japan* 33 F3
Odate, *Japan* 32 C7
Odawara, *Japan* 33 F6
Ödemiş, *Turkey* 23 E7
Odense, *Denmark* 9 D8
Oder ➜, *Europe* 15 B8
Odesa, *Ukraine* 25 D3
Odessa, *U.S.A.* 80 D2
Odienné, *Ivory C.* 53 G4
Odintsovo, *Russia* 24 B4
Odra = Oder ➜, *Europe* 15 B8
Odzi, *Zimbabwe* 59 B6
Oeiras, *Brazil* 92 D5
Ofanto ➜, *Italy* 20 D6
Offa, *Nigeria* 53 G6
Offenbach, *Germany* 14 C5
Offenburg, *Germany* 14 D4
Oga, *Japan* 32 D6
Oga-Hantō, *Japan* 32 D6
Ōgaki, *Japan* 33 F5
Ogbomosho, *Nigeria* 53 G6
Ogden, *U.S.A.* 73 F7
Ogdensburg, *U.S.A.* 77 B8
Oglio ➜, *Italy* 20 B3
Ogooué ➜, *Gabon* 56 E1
Ohai, *N.Z.* 65 F2
Ohakune, *N.Z.* 64 C6
Ohanet, *Algeria* 52 C7
Ohata, *Japan* 32 C7
Ohau, L., *N.Z.* 65 F3
Ohio □, *U.S.A.* 76 D4
Ohio ➜, *U.S.A.* 76 F1
Ohře ➜, *Czech Rep.* 16 C2
Ohrid, *Macedonia* 22 D3
Ohridsko Jezero, *Macedonia* 23 D3
Oise ➜, *France* 12 B5
Ōita, *Japan* 33 G2
Oiticica, *Brazil* 92 D5
Ojos del Salado, Cerro,
   Argentina 94 B3
Oka ➜, *Russia* 28 D5
Okaba, *Indonesia* 37 F5
Okahandja, *Namibia* 58 C2
Okanogan ➜, *U.S.A.* 72 B4
Okara, *Pakistan* 42 D8
Okavango Delta, *Botswana* . 58 B4
Okayama, *Japan* 33 F3
Okazaki, *Japan* 33 F5
Okeechobee, L., *U.S.A.* 83 F7
Okefenokee Swamp, *U.S.A.* . 83 D6
Okhotsk, Sea of, *Asia* 31 D12
Oki-Shotō, *Japan* 33 E3
Okinawa-Jima, *Japan* 35 D7
Oklahoma □, *U.S.A.* 80 B5

Oklahoma City, *U.S.A.* 80 B5
Okmulgee, *U.S.A.* 81 B6
Oknitsa = Ocniţa, *Moldova* . . 17 D8
Oksibil, *Indonesia* 37 E6
Oktyabrsk, *Kazakhstan* 29 E6
Oktyabrskiy = Aktsyabrski,
   Belarus 17 B9
Oktyabrskoy Revolyutsii,
   Ostrov, *Russia* 30 B7
Okuru, *N.Z.* 65 E3
Okushiri-Tō, *Japan* 32 B6
Öland, *Sweden* 9 D9
Olary, *Australia* 62 B3
Olavarría, *Argentina* 94 D4
Oława, *Poland* 16 C3
Ólbia, *Italy* 20 D2
Old Castile = Castilla y
   Leon □, *Spain* 18 A3
Old Crow, *Canada* 68 B6
Oldenburg, *Germany* 14 B5
Oldham, *U.K.* 11 E5
Olekma ➜, *Russia* 31 C10
Olekminsk, *Russia* 31 C10
Oleksandriya, *Ukraine* 17 C8
Olenek, *Russia* 30 C9
Olenek ➜, *Russia* 30 B10
Oléron, Î. d', *France* 12 D3
Oleśnica, *Poland* 16 C3
Olevsk, *Ukraine* 17 C8
Olhão, *Portugal* 18 D2
Olifants = Elefantes ➜, *Africa* 59 C6
Ólimbos, Óros = Olympos
   Oros, *Greece* 23 D4
Olinda, *Brazil* 92 D7
Olivenza, *Spain* 18 C2
Ollagüe, *Chile* 91 H5
Olomouc, *Czech Rep.* 16 D3
Olongapo, *Phil.* 36 B2
Olot, *Spain* 19 A7
Olsztyn, *Poland* 16 B5
Olt ➜, *Romania* 22 C5
Olteniţa, *Romania* 22 B6
Olymbos Oros, *Greece* 23 D4
Olympia, *Greece* 23 F3
Olympia, *U.S.A.* 72 C2
Olympic Mts., *U.S.A.* 72 C2
Olympus, Mt. = Olymbos
   Oros, *Greece* 23 D4
Olympus, Mt. = Uludağ,
   Turkey 23 D7
Om ➜, *Russia* 29 D8
Ōmagari, *Japan* 32 D7
Omagh, *U.K.* 11 D3
Omaha, *U.S.A.* 75 E7
Oman ■, *Asia* 48 C6
Oman, G. of, *Asia* 45 E4
Omaruru, *Namibia* 58 C3
Omate, *Peru* 91 G4
Ombai, Selat, *Indonesia* . . . 37 F2
Omboué, *Gabon* 56 E1
Ombrone ➜, *Italy* 20 C3
Omdurmân, *Sudan* 55 E5
Ometepec, *Mexico* 84 D5
Omo ➜, *Ethiopia* 55 G6
Omsk, *Russia* 29 D8
Ōmu, *Japan* 32 A8
Omul, Vf., *Romania* 17 F7
Omuramba Omatako ➜,
   Namibia 58 B4
Ōmuta, *Japan* 33 G2
Onang, *Indonesia* 37 E1
Onda, *Spain* 19 C5
Ondangwa, *Namibia* 58 B3
Onega, *Russia* 28 C4
Onega, L. = Onezhskoye
   Ozero, *Russia* 8 C13
Oneşti, *Romania* 17 E8
Onezhskoye Ozero, *Russia* . . 8 C13
Ongarue, *N.Z.* 64 C6
Onilahy ➜, *Madag.* 59 C8
Onitsha, *Nigeria* 53 G7
Ontario □, *Canada* 71 E5
Ontario, L., *N. Amer.* 77 C7
Oodnadatta, *Australia* 62 A2
Oostende, *Belgium* 14 C2
Ootacamund =
   Udagamandalam, *India* . . . 43 P10

Opala, *Dem. Rep. of
   the Congo* 56 E4
Opava, *Czech Rep.* 16 D3
Opole, *Poland* 16 C3
Oporto = Porto, *Portugal* . . . 18 B1
Opotiki, *N.Z.* 64 C7
Opua, *N.Z.* 64 A6
Opunake, *N.Z.* 64 C5
Oradea, *Romania* 17 E5
Öræfajökull, *Iceland* 8 C2
Orai, *India* 42 G11
Oral = Zhayyq ➜, *Kazakhstan* 29 E6
Oral, *Kazakhstan* 24 C7
Oran, *Algeria* 52 A5
Orange, *Australia* 63 B4
Orange, *France* 13 D6
Orange, *U.S.A.* 81 D7
Orange ➜, *S. Africa* 58 D3
Orange, C., *Brazil* 92 B3
Orange Free State = Free
   State □, *S. Africa* 59 D5
Orangeburg, *U.S.A.* 83 C7
Oranienburg, *Germany* 15 B7
Oranje = Orange ➜, *S. Africa* 58 D3
Orapa, *Botswana* 59 C5
Oras, *Phil.* 36 B3
Orbetello, *Italy* 20 C3
Orbost, *Australia* 63 C4
Orchila, I., *Venezuela* 90 A5
Ordos = Mu Us Shamo, *China* 35 C5
Ordu, *Turkey* 46 B4
Ore Mts. = Erzgebirge,
   Germany 15 C7
Örebro, *Sweden* 9 D9
Oregon □, *U.S.A.* 72 E3
Orekhovo-Zuyevo, *Russia* . . 24 B4
Orel, *Russia* 24 C4
Ören, *Turkey* 23 F6
Orenburg, *Russia* 29 D6
Orense = Ourense, *Spain* . . . 18 A2
Orepuki, *N.Z.* 65 G2
Orfanos Kolpos, *Greece* . . . 23 D5
Orgaz, *Spain* 18 C4
Orgeyev = Orhei, *Moldova* . . 17 E9
Orhaneli, *Turkey* 23 E7
Orhangazi, *Turkey* 23 D7
Orhei, *Moldova* 17 E9
Orhon Gol ➜, *Mongolia* 35 A5
Oriental, Cordillera, *Colombia* 90 B4
Orihuela, *Spain* 19 C5
Orinoco ➜, *Venezuela* 90 B6
Orissa □, *India* 40 G5
Oristano, *Italy* 21 E2
Oristano, G. di, *Italy* 21 E2
Orizaba, *Mexico* 84 D5
Orizaba, Pico de, *Mexico* . . . 84 D5
Orkney Is., *U.K.* 10 B5
Orlando, *U.S.A.* 83 E7
Orléanais, *France* 12 C5
Orléans, *France* 12 C4
Ormara, *Pakistan* 42 G4
Ormoc, *Phil.* 36 B2
Ormond, *N.Z.* 64 C7
Örnsköldsvik, *Sweden* 8 C9
Orocué, *Colombia* 90 C4
Orol Dengizi = Aral Sea, *Asia* 29 E6
Oroquieta, *Phil.* 36 C2
Orosháza, *Hungary* 16 E5
Orroroo, *Australia* 62 B2
Orsha, *Belarus* 24 C3
Orsk, *Russia* 29 D6
Orşova, *Romania* 22 B4
Ortaca, *Turkey* 23 F7
Ortegal, C., *Spain* 18 A2
Orthez, *France* 12 E3
Ortigueira, *Spain* 18 A2
Ortles, *Italy* 13 C9
Ortón ➜, *Bolivia* 91 F5
Orūmīyeh, *Iran* 46 C6
Orūmīyeh, Daryācheh-ye, *Iran* 46 C6
Oruro, *Bolivia* 91 G5
Oruzgān □, *Afghan.* 42 C5
Orvieto, *Italy* 20 C4
Oryakhovo, *Bulgaria* 22 C4
Ōsaka, *Japan* 33 F4
Ösel = Saaremaa, *Estonia* . . 24 B1
Osh, *Kyrgyzstan* 29 E8

Oshakati, *Namibia* 58 B3
Oshawa, *Canada* 71 E6
Oshkosh, *U.S.A.* 74 E3
Oshmyany = Ashmyany,
  Belarus 17 A7
Oshogbo, *Nigeria* 53 G6
Oshwe, *Dem. Rep. of*
  the Congo 56 E3
Osijek, *Croatia* 20 B7
Osipovichi = Asipovichy,
  Belarus 17 B9
Osizweni, *S. Africa* 59 D6
Oskarshamn, *Sweden* 9 D9
Öskemen, *Kazakhstan* 29 E9
Oslo, *Norway* 9 D8
Oslofjorden, *Norway* 9 D8
Osmanabad, *India* 43 K10
Osmaniye, *Turkey* 46 C4
Osnabrück, *Germany* 14 B5
Osorno, *Chile* 95 E2
Ossa, Mt., *Australia* 62 D4
Ossa, Óros, *Greece* 23 E4
Ostend = Oostende, *Belgium* 14 C2
Oster, *Ukraine* 17 C10
Österdalälven, *Sweden* 8 C8
Österreich = Austria ■,
  Europe 15 E8
Östersund, *Sweden* 8 C8
Ostfriesische Inseln, *Germany* 14 B4
Ostrava, *Czech Rep.* 16 D4
Ostróda, *Poland* 16 B4
Ostroh, *Ukraine* 17 C8
Ostrołęka, *Poland* 16 B5
Ostrów Mazowiecka, *Poland* 16 B5
Ostrów Wielkopolski, *Poland* 16 C3
Ostrowiec-Świętokrzyski,
  Poland 16 C5
Ostuni, *Italy* 21 D6
Osuna, *Spain* 18 D3
Oswego, *U.S.A.* 77 C7
Otago □, *N.Z.* 65 F3
Otago Harbour, *N.Z.* 65 F4
Otaki, *N.Z.* 64 D6
Otaru, *Japan* 32 B7
Otaru-Wan = Ishikari-Wan,
  Japan 32 B7
Otavalo, *Ecuador* 90 C3
Otjiwarongo, *Namibia* 58 C3
Otoineppu, *Japan* 32 A8
Otorohanga, *N.Z.* 64 C6
Otranto, *Italy* 21 D7
Otranto, C. d', *Italy* 21 D7
Otranto, Str. of, *Italy* 21 D7
Ōtsu, *Japan* 33 F4
Ottawa = Outaouais ⇝,
  Canada 71 E6
Ottawa, *Canada* 71 E6
Ottawa Is., *Canada* 70 D5
Ottumwa, *U.S.A.* 75 E8
Oturkpo, *Nigeria* 53 G7
Otway, B., *Chile* 95 G2
Otway, C., *Australia* 62 C3
Otwock, *Poland* 16 B5
Ouachita Mts., *U.S.A.* 81 B6
Ouagadougou, *Burkina Faso* 53 F5
Ouahran = Oran, *Algeria* ... 52 A5
Ouallene, *Algeria* 52 D6
Ouargla, *Algeria* 52 B7
Ouarzazate, *Morocco* 52 B4
Oubangi ⇝, *Dem. Rep. of*
  the Congo 56 E3
Oudtshoorn, *S. Africa* 58 E4
Ouessant, Î. d', *France* 12 B1
Ouesso, *Congo* 56 D3
Ouezzane, *Morocco* 52 B4
Oujda, *Morocco* 52 B5
Oulu, *Finland* 8 B11
Oulujärvi, *Finland* 8 C11
Oulujoki ⇝, *Finland* 8 B11
Oum Chalouba, *Chad* 55 E3
Oum Hadjer, *Chad* 55 F2
Ounianga Sérir, *Chad* 55 E3
Ourense, *Spain* 18 A2
Ouricuri, *Brazil* 92 D5
Ouro Prêto, *Brazil* 93 G5
Outaouais ⇝, *Canada* 71 E6
Outer Hebrides, *U.K.* 10 C3

Outjo, *Namibia* 58 C3
Ouyen, *Australia* 62 C3
Ovalle, *Chile* 94 C2
Ovamboland, *Namibia* 58 B3
Oviedo, *Spain* 18 A3
Ovruch, *Ukraine* 17 C9
Owaka, *N.Z.* 65 G3
Owambo = Ovamboland,
  Namibia 58 B3
Owase, *Japan* 33 F5
Owbeh, *Afghan.* 42 B3
Owen Sound, *Canada* 71 E5
Owen Stanley Ra.,
  Papua N. G. 61 B8
Owo, *Nigeria* 53 G7
Owyhee ⇝, *U.S.A.* 72 E5
Oxford, *N.Z.* 65 E5
Oxford, *U.K.* 11 F6
Oxnard, *U.S.A.* 78 C3
Oxus = Amudarya ⇝,
  Uzbekistan 29 E6
Oya, *Malaysia* 39 D4
Oyama, *Japan* 33 E6
Oyem, *Gabon* 56 D2
Oyo, *Nigeria* 53 G6
Ozamiz, *Phil.* 36 C2
Ozark Plateau, *U.S.A.* 81 A8
Özd, *Hungary* 16 D5

P

Pa-an, *Burma* 41 J11
Paarl, *S. Africa* 58 E3
Pab Hills, *Pakistan* 42 F5
Pabianice, *Poland* 16 C4
Pabna, *Bangla.* 41 E7
Pacaja ⇝, *Brazil* 92 C3
Pacaraima, Sa., *S. Amer.* ... 90 C6
Pacasmayo, *Peru* 91 E3
Pachpadra, *India* 42 G8
Pachuca, *Mexico* 84 C5
Padaido, Kepulauan,
  Indonesia 37 E5
Padang, *Indonesia* 39 E2
Padangpanjang, *Indonesia* . 39 E2
Padangsidempuan, *Indonesia* 39 D1
Paderborn, *Germany* 14 C5
Pádova, *Italy* 20 B3
Padua = Pádova, *Italy* 20 B3
Paducah, *U.S.A.* 76 F1
Paeroa, *N.Z.* 64 B6
Pag, *Croatia* 20 B5
Pagadian, *Phil.* 36 C2
Pagai Selatan, Pulau,
  Indonesia 39 E2
Pagai Utara, Pulau, *Indonesia* 39 E2
Pagalu = Annobón, *Atl. Oc.* . 51 G4
Pagastikos Kolpos, *Greece* .. 23 E4
Pagatan, *Indonesia* 39 E5
Pahiatua, *N.Z.* 64 D6
Päijänne, *Finland* 8 C11
Painan, *Indonesia* 39 E2
Paint Hills = Wemindji,
  Canada 71 D6
Painted Desert, *U.S.A.* 79 C7
País Vasco □, *Spain* 19 A4
Paisley, *U.K.* 10 D4
Paita, *Peru* 90 E2
Pajares, Puerto de, *Spain* .. 18 A3
Pakistan ■, *Asia* 42 E7
Pakokku, *Burma* 41 G10
Paktiā □, *Afghan.* 42 C6
Pakxe, *Laos* 38 A3
Pala, *Chad* 55 G2
Palagruža, *Croatia* 20 C6
Palam, *India* 43 K10
Palampur, *India* 42 C10
Palana, *Australia* 62 C4
Palanan, *Phil.* 36 A2
Palanan Pt., *Phil.* 36 A2
Palangkaraya, *Indonesia* .. 39 E4
Palani Hills, *India* 43 P10
Palanpur, *India* 43 G8
Palapye, *Botswana* 59 C5
Palau ■, *Palau* 36 C4

Palawan, *Phil.* 38 C5
Palayankottai, *India* 43 Q10
Paleleh, *Indonesia* 37 D2
Palembang, *Indonesia* 39 E2
Palencia, *Spain* 18 A3
Palermo, *Italy* 21 E4
Palestine, *U.S.A.* 81 D6
Paletwa, *Burma* 41 G9
Palghat, *India* 43 P10
Pali, *India* 42 G8
Palikir, *Micronesia* 64 J10
Paliouri, Akra, *Greece* 23 E4
Palitana, *India* 43 J7
Palk Bay, *Asia* 43 Q11
Palk Strait, *Asia* 43 Q11
Pallanza = Verbánia, *Italy* .. 13 D8
Palm Springs, *U.S.A.* 78 D4
Palma, B. de, *Spain* 19 C7
Palma de Mallorca, *Spain* .. 19 C7
Palmares, *Brazil* 92 D6
Palmas, C., *Liberia* 53 H4
Pálmas, G. di, *Italy* 21 E2
Palmeira dos Índios, *Brazil* . 93 D6
Palmer, *U.S.A.* 69 B5
Palmer Arch., *Antarctica* ... 96 A3
Palmer Land, *Antarctica* ... 96 B3
Palmerston, *N.Z.* 65 F4
Palmerston North, *N.Z.* 64 D6
Palmi, *Italy* 21 E5
Palmira, *Colombia* 90 C3
Palmyra = Tudmur, *Syria* .. 46 D4
Palopo, *Indonesia* 37 E2
Palos, C. de, *Spain* 19 D5
Palu, *Indonesia* 37 E1
Palu, *Turkey* 46 C5
Pamiers, *France* 12 E4
Pamir, *Tajikistan* 29 F8
Pamlico Sd., *U.S.A.* 83 B10
Pampa, *U.S.A.* 80 B3
Pampanua, *Indonesia* 37 E2
Pampas, *Argentina* 94 D4
Pampas, *Peru* 91 F4
Pamplona, *Colombia* 90 B4
Pamplona, *Spain* 19 A5
Panaji, *India* 43 M8
Panamá, *Panama* 85 F9
Panama ■, *Cent. Amer.* ... 86 E4
Panamá, G. de, *Panama* ... 86 E4
Panama Canal, *Panama* ... 86 E4
Panama City, *U.S.A.* 82 D5
Panão, *Peru* 91 E3
Panay, *Phil.* 36 B2
Panay G., *Phil.* 36 B2
Pančevo, *Serbia & M.* 22 B3
Pandan, *Phil.* 36 B2
Pandharpur, *India* 43 L9
Pando, L. = Hope, L., *Australia* 62 A2
Panevėžys, *Lithuania* 24 B1
Pang-Long, *Burma* 41 F12
Pang-Yang, *Burma* 41 F12
Pangani, *Tanzania* 57 F7
Pangfou = Bengbu, *China* .. 35 C6
Pangkajene, *Indonesia* 37 E1
Pangkalanbrandan, *Indonesia* 39 D1
Pangkalanbuun, *Indonesia* . 39 E4
Pangkalpinang, *Indonesia* .. 39 E3
Pangnirtung, *Canada* 70 C7
Pangutaran Group, *Phil.* ... 36 C2
Panjgur, *Pakistan* 42 F4
Panjim = Panaji, *India* 43 M8
Panjnad Barrage, *Pakistan* . 42 E7
Pannirtuuq = Pangnirtung,
  Canada 70 C7
Panorama, *Brazil* 94 A6
Pantar, *Indonesia* 37 F2
Pante Macassar, *E. Timor* ... 37 F2
Pantelleria, *Italy* 21 F3
Paoting = Baoding, *China* .. 35 C6
Paot'ou = Baotou, *China* ... 35 B6
Pápa, *Hungary* 16 E3
Papakura, *N.Z.* 64 B6
Papantla, *Mexico* 84 C5
Papar, *Malaysia* 38 C5
Paparoa △, *N.Z.* 65 E4
Papeete, *Tahiti* 65 L16
Papua □, *Indonesia* 37 E5

Papua New Guinea

Papua New Guinea ■,
Oceania 64 K9
Papudo, *Chile* 94 C2
Papun, *Burma* 41 H11
Pará = Belém, *Brazil* 92 C4
Pará □, *Brazil* 92 C3
Paracatu, *Brazil* 93 F4
Paracel Is., *S. China Sea* 38 A4
Parachilna, *Australia* 62 B2
Paradip, *India* 40 G6
Parado, *Indonesia* 37 F1
Paragua ➜, *Venezuela* 90 B6
Paraguaçu ➜, *Brazil* 93 E6
Paraguaná, Pen. de,
Venezuela 90 A4
Paraguarí, *Paraguay* 94 B5
Paraguay ■, *S. Amer.* 94 A5
Paraguay ➜, *Paraguay* 94 B5
Paraíba = João Pessoa, *Brazil* 92 D7
Paraíba □, *Brazil* 92 D6
Parakou, *Benin* 53 G6
Paramaribo, *Suriname* 92 A2
Paraná, *Argentina* 94 C4
Paraná, *Brazil* 93 E4
Paraná □, *Brazil* 94 A6
Paraná ➜, *Argentina* 94 C5
Paranaguá, *Brazil* 94 B7
Paranaíba, *Brazil* 93 F3
Paranaíba ➜, *Brazil* 93 G3
Paranapanema ➜, *Brazil* ... 94 A6
Parang, *Maguindanao, Phil.* . 36 C2
Parang, *Sulu, Phil.* 36 C2
Parângul Mare, Vf., *Romania* 17 F6
Paraparaumu, *N.Z.* 64 D6
Parbhani, *India* 43 K10
Parchim, *Germany* 15 B6
Pardo ➜, *Bahia, Brazil* 93 F6
Pardo ➜, *Mato Grosso, Brazil* 93 G3
Pardubice, *Czech Rep.* 16 C2
Parecis, Serra dos, *Brazil* ... 91 F7
Parepare, *Indonesia* 37 E1
Parga, *Greece* 23 E3
Pariaguán, *Venezuela* 90 B6
Parigi, *Indonesia* 37 E2
Parika, *Guyana* 90 B7
Parima, Serra, *Brazil* 90 C6
Parinari, *Peru* 90 D4
Parintins, *Brazil* 92 C2
Pariparit Kyun, *Burma* 41 K9
Paris, *France* 12 B5
Paris, *U.S.A.* 81 C6
Park Range, *U.S.A.* 73 G10
Parkersburg, *U.S.A.* 76 E5
Parkes, *Australia* 63 B4
Parla, *Spain* 18 B4
Parma, *Italy* 13 D9
Parnaguá, *Brazil* 93 E5
Parnaíba, *Brazil* 92 C5
Parnaíba ➜, *Brazil* 92 C5
Parnassos, *Greece* 23 E4
Pärnu, *Estonia* 24 B1
Paroo ➜, *Australia* 63 B3
Paros, *Greece* 23 F5
Parral, *Chile* 94 D2
Parry Is., *Canada* 70 B3
Parry Sound, *Canada* 71 E6
Partinico, *Italy* 21 E4
Paru ➜, *Brazil* 92 C3
Parvän □, *Afghan.* 42 B6
Parvatipuram, *India* 40 H4
Pas, The, *Canada* 69 C9
Pasadena, Calif., U.S.A. 78 C3
Pasadena, Tex., U.S.A. 81 E6
Pascagoula, *U.S.A.* 81 D9
Paşcani, *Romania* 17 E8
Pasco, *U.S.A.* 72 C4
Pasco, Cerro de, *Peru* 91 F3
Pasirkuning, *Indonesia* 39 E2
Pašman, *Croatia* 20 C5
Pasni, *Pakistan* 42 G3
Paso de Indios, *Argentina* ... 95 E3
Passau, *Germany* 15 D7
Passero, C., *Italy* 21 F5
Passo Fundo, *Brazil* 94 B6
Passos, *Brazil* 93 G4
Pastaza ➜, *Peru* 90 D3
Pasto, *Colombia* 90 C3

Patagonia, *Argentina* 95 F3
Patan, *India* 43 H8
Patani, *Indonesia* 37 D3
Patchewollock, *Australia* 62 C3
Patea, *N.Z.* 64 C6
Paternò, *Italy* 21 F5
Paterson, *U.S.A.* 77 D8
Pathankot, *India* 42 C9
Pathein = Bassein, *Burma* .. 41 J10
Patiala, *India* 42 D10
Patkai Bum, *India* 41 D10
Patmos, *Greece* 23 F6
Patna, *India* 40 E5
Patos, L. dos, *Brazil* 94 C6
Patos de Minas, *Brazil* 93 F4
Patquía, *Argentina* 94 C3
Patra, *Greece* 23 E3
Patraikos Kolpos, *Greece* ... 23 E3
Patras = Patra, *Greece* 23 E3
Patrocínio, *Brazil* 93 F4
Pattani, *Thailand* 38 C2
Patuakhali, *Bangla.* 41 F8
Pau, *France* 12 E3
Pauk, *Burma* 41 G10
Paulistana, *Brazil* 92 D5
Paulo Afonso, *Brazil* 93 D6
Pavia, *Italy* 13 D8
Pavlodar, *Kazakhstan* 29 D8
Pavlohrad, *Ukraine* 25 D4
Pavlovo, *Russia* 24 B5
Pavlovsk, *Russia* 24 C5
Pawtucket, *U.S.A.* 77 D10
Paxi, *Greece* 23 E3
Payakumbuh, *Indonesia* ... 39 E2
Payne Bay = Kangirsuk,
Canada 70 D7
Payne L., *Canada* 70 D6
Paysandú, *Uruguay* 94 C5
Paz, B. de la, *Mexico* 84 C2
Pazar, *Turkey* 46 B5
Pazardzhik, *Bulgaria* 22 C5
Peace ➜, *Canada* 68 C8
Peak Hill, *Australia* 63 B4
Peake Cr. ➜, *Australia* 62 A2
Peawanuck, *Canada* 71 D5
Pebane, *Mozam.* 59 B7
Pebas, *Peru* 90 D4
Peć, *Serbia & M.* 22 C3
Pechenga, *Russia* 28 C4
Pechenizhyn, *Ukraine* 17 D7
Pechora ➜, *Russia* 28 C6
Pechorskaya Guba, *Russia* .. 28 C6
Pecos ➜, *U.S.A.* 80 E3
Pécs, *Hungary* 16 E4
Pedder, L., *Australia* 62 D4
Pedirka, *Australia* 62 A2
Pedra Azul, *Brazil* 93 F5
Pedreiras, *Brazil* 92 C5
Pedro Afonso, *Brazil* 93 D4
Pedro Juan Caballero,
Paraguay 94 A5
Peebinga, *Australia* 62 B3
Peel ➜, *Australia* 63 B5
Peel ➜, *Canada* 68 B6
Peera Peera Poolanna L.,
Australia 62 A2
Pegasus Bay, *N.Z.* 65 E5
Pegu, *Burma* 41 J11
Pegu Yoma, *Burma* 41 H10
Pehuajó, *Argentina* 94 D4
Peine, *Germany* 14 B6
Peip'ing = Beijing, *China* ... 35 C6
Peipus, L. = Chudskoye,
Ozero, *Russia* 24 B2
Peixe, *Brazil* 93 E4
Pekalongan, *Indonesia* 39 F3
Pekanbaru, *Indonesia* 39 D2
Pekin, *U.S.A.* 75 E10
Peking = Beijing, *China* 35 C6
Pelagie, Is., *Italy* 21 G4
Pelaihari, *Indonesia* 39 E4
Peleaga, Vf., *Romania* 17 F6
Peleng, *Indonesia* 37 E2
Pelješac, *Croatia* 20 C6
Pelly ➜, *Canada* 68 B6
Pelly Bay, *Canada* 70 C5
Peloponnese □, *Greece* 23 F4

Pelorus Sd., *N.Z.* 65 D5
Pelotas, *Brazil* 94 C6
Pelvoux, Massif du, *France* . 13 D7
Pematangsiantar, *Indonesia* . 39 D1
Pemba, *Mozam.* 59 A8
Pemba I., *Tanzania* 57 F7
Pembroke, *Canada* 71 E6
Pembroke, *U.K.* 11 F4
Penang = Pinang, *Malaysia* .. 38 C2
Penápolis, *Brazil* 94 A6
Peñarroya-Pueblonuevo,
Spain 18 C3
Peñas, C. de, *Spain* 18 A3
Peñas, G. de, *Chile* 95 F2
Pench'i = Benxi, *China* 35 B7
Pend Oreille, L., *U.S.A.* 72 C5
Pendembu, *S. Leone* 53 G3
Pendleton, *U.S.A.* 72 D4
Penedo, *Brazil* 93 E6
Penguin, *Australia* 62 D4
Peniche, *Portugal* 18 C1
Penida, Nusa, *Indonesia* ... 39 F5
Peninsular Malaysia □,
Malaysia 39 D2
Penmarch, Pte. de, *France* .. 12 C1
Pennines, *U.K.* 11 D5
Pennsylvania □, *U.S.A.* 77 D7
Penny Str., *Canada* 70 B4
Penola, *Australia* 62 C3
Penong, *Australia* 60 G5
Penrhyn, *Cook Is.* 65 K15
Penrith, *Australia* 63 B5
Pensacola, *U.S.A.* 82 D4
Pensacola Mts., *Antarctica* . 96 C4
Penshurst, *Australia* 62 C3
Penticton, *Canada* 69 D8
Pentland Firth, *U.K.* 10 B5
Penza, *Russia* 24 C6
Penzance, *U.K.* 11 F4
Peoria, *U.S.A.* 75 E10
Perabumulih, *Indonesia* 39 E2
Perche, Collines du, *France* . 12 B4
Perdido, Mte., *Spain* 19 A6
Perdu, Mt. = Perdido, Mte.,
Spain 19 A6
Pereira, *Colombia* 90 C3
Pereyaslav-Khmelnytskyy,
Ukraine 24 C3
Pergamino, *Argentina* 94 C4
Péribonka ➜, *Canada* 71 E6
Perico, *Argentina* 94 A3
Périgueux, *France* 12 D4
Perijá, Sierra de, *Colombia* .. 90 B4
Perlas, Arch. de las, *Panama* 86 E4
Perm, *Russia* 29 D6
Pernambuco = Recife, *Brazil* . 92 D7
Pernatty Lagoon, *Australia* .. 62 B2
Pernik, *Bulgaria* 22 C4
Perpignan, *France* 13 E5
Persepolis, *Iran* 44 D3
Pershotravensk, *Ukraine* ... 17 C8
Persia = Iran ■, *Asia* 44 C3
Persian Gulf, *Asia* 44 E2
Perth, *Australia* 60 G2
Perth, *U.K.* 10 C5
Perth Amboy, *U.S.A.* 77 D8
Peru ■, *S. Amer.* 90 C3
Perúgia, *Italy* 20 C4
Pervomaysk, *Ukraine* 25 D3
Pervouralsk, *Russia* 29 D6
Pésaro, *Italy* 20 C4
Pescara, *Italy* 20 C5
Peshawar, *Pakistan* 42 B7
Peshkopi, *Albania* 22 D3
Pesqueira, *Brazil* 92 D6
Petah Tiqwa, *Israel* 46 D3
Petauke, *Zambia* 59 A6
Peter I. Øy, *Antarctica* 96 A2
Peterborough, *Australia* 62 B2
Peterborough, *Canada* 71 E6
Peterborough, *U.K.* 11 E6
Peterhead, *U.K.* 10 C6
Petersburg, *Alaska, U.S.A.* .. 69 C6
Petersburg, *Va., U.S.A.* 77 F7
Petitsikapau L., *Canada* 71 D7
Petlad, *India* 43 H8
Peto, *Mexico* 85 C7

Petone, N.Z. 65 D6
Petra Velikogo, Zaliv, Russia 32 B3
Petrich, Bulgaria 22 D4
Petrikov = Pyetrikaw, Belarus 17 B9
Petrolândia, Brazil 93 D6
Petrolina, Brazil 93 D5
Petropavl, Kazakhstan 29 D7
Petropavlovsk-Kamchatskiy,
Russia 31 D13
Petrópolis, Brazil 93 G5
Petroșani, Romania 17 F6
Petrovaradin, Serbia & M. 22 B2
Petrovsk, Russia 24 C6
Petrozavodsk, Russia 8 C12
Peureulak, Indonesia 38 D1
Pforzheim, Germany 14 D5
Phagwara, India 42 D9
Phalodi, India 42 F8
Phan Rang, Vietnam 38 B3
Phangan, Ko, Thailand 38 C2
Phangnga, Thailand 38 C1
Phatthalung, Thailand 38 C2
Phetchabun, Thailand 38 A2
Philadelphia, U.S.A. 77 E8
Philippine Trench = Mindanao
Trench, Pac. Oc. 36 B3
Philippines ■, Asia 36 B2
Philippopolis = Plovdiv,
Bulgaria 22 C5
Phillip I., Australia 63 C4
Phitsanulok, Thailand 38 A2
Phnom Dangrek, Thailand 38 B2
Phnom Penh, Cambodia 38 B2
Phoenix, U.S.A. 79 D6
Phra Nakhon Si Ayutthaya,
Thailand 38 B2
Phuket, Thailand 38 C1
Piacenza, Italy 13 D8
Pian Cr. ➤, Australia 63 B4
Pianosa, Italy 20 C3
Piatra Neamţ, Romania 17 E8
Piauí □, Brazil 92 D5
Piave ➤, Italy 20 B4
Pibor Post, Sudan 55 G5
Picardie □, France 13 B5
Pichilemu, Chile 94 C2
Pico Truncado, Argentina 95 F3
Picton, Australia 63 B5
Picton, N.Z. 65 D6
Picún Leufú, Argentina 95 D3
Piedmont = Piemonte □, Italy 13 D7
Piedras, R. de las ➤, Peru 91 F5
Piedras Negras, Mexico 84 B4
Pielinen, Finland 8 C11
Piemonte □, Italy 13 D7
Piet Retief, S. Africa 59 D6
Pietermaritzburg, S. Africa 59 D6
Pietersburg = Polokwane,
S. Africa 59 C5
Pietrosul, Vf., Maramureș,
Romania 17 E7
Pietrosul, Vf., Suceava,
Romania 17 E7
Pigüe, Argentina 94 D4
Piła, Poland 16 B3
Pilar, Paraguay 94 B5
Pilcomayo ➤, Paraguay 94 B5
Pilibhit, India 42 E11
Pilica ➤, Poland 16 C5
Pilipinas = Philippines ■, Asia 36 B2
Pilos, Greece 23 F3
Pimba, Australia 62 B2
Pimenta Bueno, Brazil 91 F6
Pimentel, Peru 91 E3
Pinang, Malaysia 38 C2
Pinar del Río, Cuba 86 B3
Pınarhisar, Turkey 22 D6
Pińczów, Poland 16 C5
Pindos Oros, Greece 23 E3
Pindus Mts. = Pindos Oros,
Greece 23 E3
Pine Bluff, U.S.A. 81 B7
Pine Point, Canada 68 B8
Pinega ➤, Russia 28 C5
Pinerolo, Italy 13 D7
Pines, Akra, Greece 23 D5
Ping ➤, Thailand 38 A2

Pingdong, Taiwan 35 D7
Pingliang, China 35 C5
Pingxiang, China 35 D5
Pinhel, Portugal 18 B2
Pini, Indonesia 39 D1
Pinios ➤, Greece 23 E4
Pinnaroo, Australia 62 C3
Pinrang, Indonesia 37 E1
Pinsk, Belarus 17 B8
Pintados, Chile 91 H5
Pinyug, Russia 24 A6
Piombino, Italy 20 C3
Pioner, Ostrov, Russia 30 B7
Piopiotaki = Milford Sd., N.Z. 65 F2
Piorini, L., Brazil 90 D6
Piotrków Trybunalski, Poland 16 C4
Pip, Iran 45 E5
Piquiri ➤, Brazil 94 A6
Piracicaba, Brazil 94 A7
Piracuruca, Brazil 92 C5
Piræus = Pireas, Greece 23 F4
Piraiévs = Pireas, Greece 23 F4
Pirané, Argentina 94 B5
Pirapora, Brazil 93 F5
Pireas, Greece 23 F4
Pírgos, Greece 23 F3
Pirin Planina, Bulgaria 22 D4
Pirineos = Pyrénées, Europe 12 E4
Piripiri, Brazil 92 C5
Pirmasens, Germany 14 D4
Pirot, Serbia & M. 22 C4
Piru, Indonesia 37 E3
Pisa, Italy 20 C3
Pisagua, Chile 91 G4
Pisco, Peru 91 F3
Písek, Czech Rep. 16 D2
Pishan, China 34 C2
Pising, Indonesia 37 F2
Pistóia, Italy 20 C3
Pisuerga ➤, Spain 18 B3
Pitarpunga L., Australia 62 B3
Pitcairn I., Pac. Oc. 65 M17
Piteå, Sweden 8 B10
Pitești, Romania 22 B5
Pithapuram, India 40 J4
Pittsburg, U.S.A. 81 A6
Pittsburgh, U.S.A. 77 D5
Pittsworth, Australia 63 A5
Piura, Peru 90 E2
Placentia, Canada 71 E8
Placentia B., Canada 71 E8
Plainview, U.S.A. 80 B3
Plaka, Akra, Greece 23 G6
Plasencia, Spain 18 B2
Plastun, Russia 32 A5
Plata, Río de la ➤, S. Amer. 94 C5
Plátani ➤, Italy 21 F4
Platte ➤, U.S.A. 75 F7
Plauen, Germany 15 C7
Plei Ku, Vietnam 38 B3
Plenty, B. of, N.Z. 64 B7
Plevlja, Serbia & M. 22 C2
Plevlja, Serbia & M. 22 C2
Płock, Poland 16 B4
Plöckenstein, Germany 15 D7
Ploiești, Romania 22 B6
Plovdiv, Bulgaria 22 C5
Plumtree, Zimbabwe 59 C5
Plymouth, U.K. 11 F4
Plzeň, Czech Rep. 16 D1
Po ➤, Italy 20 B4
Po Hai = Bo Hai, China 35 C6
Pobedy, Pik, Kyrgyzstan 29 E8
Pocatello, U.S.A. 73 E7
Poços de Caldas, Brazil 93 G4
Podgorica, Serbia & M. 22 C2
Podilska Vysochyna, Ukraine 17 D8
Podolsk, Russia 24 B4
Poh, Indonesia 37 E2
Pohnpei, Micronesia 64 J10
Poinsett, C., Antarctica 96 A12
Pointe-à-Pitre, Guadeloupe 87 C7
Pointe-Noire, Congo 56 E2
Poitiers, France 12 C4
Poitou, France 12 C3
Pokaran, India 42 F7
Pokataroo, Australia 63 A4

Pola = Pula, Croatia 20 B4
Polan, Iran 45 E5
Poland ■, Europe 16 B5
Polatsk, Belarus 24 B2
Polesye = Pripet Marshes,
Europe 17 B9
Police, Poland 16 B2
Poligiros, Greece 23 D4
Polillo Is., Phil. 36 B2
Pollachi, India 43 P10
Polnovat, Russia 28 C7
Polokwane, S. Africa 59 C5
Polonne, Ukraine 17 C8
Poltava, Ukraine 24 D3
Polunochnoye, Russia 28 C7
Polynesia, Pac. Oc. 65 L15
Polynésie française = French
Polynesia ☑, Pac. Oc. 65 M16
Pombal, Portugal 18 C1
Pomézia, Italy 20 D4
Pomorskie, Pojezierze, Poland 16 B3
Ponape = Pohnpei, Micronesia 64 J10
Ponca City, U.S.A. 80 A5
Ponce, Puerto Rico 87 C6
Pond Inlet, Canada 70 B6
Pondicherry, India 43 P11
Ponferrada, Spain 18 A2
Ponnani, India 43 P9
Ponta Grossa, Brazil 94 B6
Ponta Pora, Brazil 94 A5
Pontarlier, France 13 C7
Pontchartrain, L., U.S.A. 81 D8
Ponte Nova, Brazil 93 G5
Pontevedra, Spain 18 A1
Pontiac, U.S.A. 76 C4
Pontianak, Indonesia 39 E3
Pontine Is. = Ponziane, Ísole,
Italy 21 D4
Pontine Mts. = Kuzey Anadolu
Dağları, Turkey 25 E4
Pontivy, France 12 B2
Pontoise, France 12 B5
Ponziane, Ísole, Italy 21 D4
Poochera, Australia 62 B1
Poole, U.K. 11 F6
Poona = Pune, India 43 K8
Pooncarie, Australia 62 B3
Poopelloe L., Australia 63 B3
Poopó, L. de, Bolivia 91 G5
Popayán, Colombia 90 C3
Popiltah L., Australia 62 B3
Popio L., Australia 62 B3
Poplar Bluff, U.S.A. 81 A8
Popocatépetl, Volcán, Mexico 84 D5
Popokabaka, Dem. Rep. of
the Congo 56 F3
Porbandar, India 43 J6
Porcupine ➤, U.S.A. 69 B5
Pordenone, Italy 20 B4
Pori, Finland 8 C10
Porlamar, Venezuela 90 A6
Poroshiri-Dake, Japan 32 B8
Porpoise B., Antarctica 96 A13
Port Alberni, Canada 69 D7
Port Angeles, U.S.A. 72 B2
Port Arthur, Australia 62 D4
Port Arthur, U.S.A. 81 E7
Port-au-Prince, Haiti 87 C5
Port Augusta, Australia 62 B2
Port Broughton, Australia 62 B2
Port-Cartier, Canada 71 D7
Port Chalmers, N.Z. 65 F4
Port Darwin, Falk. Is. 95 G5
Port Davey, Australia 62 D4
Port Dickson, Malaysia 39 D2
Port Elizabeth, S. Africa 59 E5
Port Fairy, Australia 62 C3
Port-Gentil, Gabon 56 E1
Port Harcourt, Nigeria 53 H7
Port Harrison = Inukjuak,
Canada 70 D6
Port Hawkesbury, Canada 71 E7
Port Hedland, Australia 60 E2
Port Hope Simpson, Canada 71 D8
Port Huron, U.S.A. 76 C4
Port Kenny, Australia 62 B1

Port Lairge

Port Lairge = Waterford, Ireland ... 11 E3
Port Laoise, Ireland ... 11 E3
Port Lincoln, Australia ... 62 B2
Port Loko, S. Leone ... 53 G3
Port Louis, Mauritius ... 51 J9
Port MacDonnell, Australia .. 62 C3
Port Macquarie, Australia ... 63 B5
Port Moresby, Papua N. G. ... 61 B8
Port Nolloth, S. Africa ... 58 D3
Port Nouveau-Québec = Kangiqsualujjuaq, Canada 70 D7
Port of Spain, Trin. & Tob. .. 87 D7
Port Pegasus, N.Z. ... 65 G2
Port Phillip B., Australia ... 63 C3
Port Pirie, Australia ... 62 B2
Port Safaga = Bûr Safâga, Egypt ... 54 C5
Port Said = Bûr Sa'îd, Egypt . 54 B5
Port St. Johns = Umzimvubu, S. Africa ... 59 E5
Port Shepstone, S. Africa ... 59 E6
Port Stanley = Stanley, Falk. Is. ... 95 G5
Port Sudan = Bûr Sûdân, Sudan ... 55 E6
Port Talbot, U.K. ... 11 F5
Port-Vendres, France ... 13 E5
Port Vila, Vanuatu ... 64 L11
Port Wakefield, Australia ... 62 B2
Porta Orientalis, Romania ... 22 B4
Portadown, U.K. ... 11 D3
Portage la Prairie, Canada . 69 D10
Portalegre, Portugal ... 18 C2
Portbou, Spain ... 19 A7
Portile de Fier, Europe ... 22 B4
Portimão, Portugal ... 18 D1
Portland, N.S.W., Australia .. 63 B4
Portland, Vic., Australia ... 62 C3
Portland, Maine, U.S.A. ... 77 C10
Portland, Oreg., U.S.A. ... 72 D2
Portland B., Australia ... 62 C3
Porto, Portugal ... 18 B1
Pôrto Alegre, Brazil ... 94 C6
Pôrto de Móz, Brazil ... 92 C3
Porto Empédocle, Italy ... 21 F4
Pôrto Esperança, Brazil ... 91 G7
Pôrto Franco, Brazil ... 92 D4
Pôrto Mendes, Brazil ... 94 A6
Pôrto Murtinho, Brazil ... 91 H7
Pôrto Nacional, Brazil ... 93 E4
Porto-Novo, Benin ... 53 G6
Porto Santo, I. de, Madeira . 52 B2
Pôrto Seguro, Brazil ... 93 F6
Porto Tórres, Italy ... 20 D2
Pôrto União, Brazil ... 94 B6
Pôrto Válter, Brazil ... 91 E4
Porto-Vecchio, France ... 13 F8
Pôrto Velho, Brazil ... 91 E6
Portoferráio, Italy ... 20 C3
Portoscuso, Italy ... 21 E2
Portoviejo, Ecuador ... 90 D2
Portree, U.K. ... 10 C3
Portsmouth, U.K. ... 11 F6
Portsmouth, U.S.A. ... 77 F7
Porttipahdan tekojärvi, Finland ... 8 B11
Portugal ■, Europe ... 18 C1
Porvenir, Chile ... 95 G2
Posadas, Argentina ... 94 B5
Poso, Indonesia ... 37 E2
Posse, Brazil ... 93 E4
Possession I., Antarctica ... 96 B15
Poste-de-la-Baleine = Kuujjuarapik, Canada ... 71 D6
Postmasburg, S. Africa ... 58 D4
Postojna, Slovenia ... 20 B5
Potchefstroom, S. Africa ... 59 D5
Potenza, Italy ... 21 D5
Poteriteri, L., N.Z. ... 65 G2
Potgietersrus = Mokopane, S. Africa ... 59 C5
Poti, Georgia ... 25 E5
Potomac ➤, U.S.A. ... 77 E7
Potosí, Bolivia ... 91 G5
Pototan, Phil. ... 36 B2
Potrerillos, Chile ... 94 B3

Potsdam, Germany ... 15 B7
Poughkeepsie, U.S.A. ... 77 D9
Považská Bystrica, Slovak Rep. ... 16 D4
Poverty B., N.Z. ... 64 C8
Póvoa de Varzim, Portugal .. 18 B1
Povungnituk = Puvirnituq, Canada ... 70 C6
Powder ➤, U.S.A. ... 74 B2
Powell, L., U.S.A. ... 79 B7
Poyang Hu, China ... 35 D6
Požarevac, Serbia & M. ... 22 B3
Poznań, Poland ... 16 B3
Pozo Almonte, Chile ... 91 H5
Pozoblanco, Spain ... 18 C3
Pozzuoli, Italy ... 21 D5
Prachuap Khiri Khan, Thailand 38 B1
Prado, Brazil ... 93 F6
Prague = Praha, Czech Rep. . 16 C2
Praha, Czech Rep. ... 16 C2
Prainha, Amazonas, Brazil .. 91 E6
Prainha, Pará, Brazil ... 92 C3
Prapat, Indonesia ... 39 D1
Prata, Brazil ... 93 F4
Prato, Italy ... 20 C3
Pravia, Spain ... 18 A2
Praya, Indonesia ... 39 F5
Preobrazheniye, Russia ... 32 B3
Preparis North Channel, Ind. Oc. ... 41 K9
Preparis South Channel, Ind. Oc. ... 41 K9
Přerov, Czech Rep. ... 16 D3
Preservation Inlet, N.Z. ... 65 G2
Presidencia Roque Saenz Peña, Argentina ... 94 B4
Presidente Epitácio, Brazil .. 93 G3
Presidente Prudente, Brazil .. 93 G3
Prespansko Jezero, Macedonia ... 23 D3
Presque Isle, U.S.A. ... 77 A11
Preston, U.K. ... 11 E5
Pretoria, S. Africa ... 59 D5
Preveza, Greece ... 23 E3
Příbram, Czech Rep. ... 16 D2
Prichard, U.S.A. ... 82 D3
Prieska, S. Africa ... 58 D4
Prilep, Macedonia ... 22 D3
Priluki = Pryluky, Ukraine ... 24 C3
Prime Seal I., Australia ... 62 D4
Prince Albert, Canada ... 69 C9
Prince Albert Mts., Antarctica 96 B15
Prince Albert Pen., Canada .. 68 A8
Prince Albert Sd., Canada ... 68 A8
Prince Alfred, C., Canada ... 70 B1
Prince Charles I., Canada ... 70 C6
Prince Charles Mts., Antarctica ... 96 B10
Prince Edward I. □, Canada . 71 E7
Prince of Wales I., Canada .. 68 A10
Prince Patrick I., Canada ... 70 B2
Principe da Beira, Brazil ... 91 F6
Prins Harald Kyst, Antarctica 96 B8
Prinsesse Astrid Kyst, Antarctica ... 96 B7
Prinsesse Ragnhild Kyst, Antarctica ... 96 B8
Pripet = Prypyat ➤, Europe . 17 C10
Pripet Marshes, Europe ... 17 B9
Priština, Serbia & M. ... 22 C3
Privas, France ... 13 D6
Privolzhskaya Vozvyshennost, Russia ... 24 C6
Prizren, Serbia & M. ... 22 C3
Proddatur, India ... 43 M11
Progreso, Mexico ... 85 C7
Prokopyevsk, Russia ... 29 D9
Prokuplje, Serbia & M. ... 22 C3
Prome, Burma ... 41 H10
Propriá, Brazil ... 93 E6
Prosna ➤, Poland ... 16 B3
Prostějov, Czech Rep. ... 16 D3
Proston, Australia ... 63 A5
Provence, France ... 13 E6
Providence, U.S.A. ... 77 D10
Providencia, I. de, Colombia . 86 D3
Provins, France ... 13 B5

Provo, U.S.A. ... 73 F8
Pruszków, Poland ... 16 B5
Prut ➤, Romania ... 17 F9
Pruzhany, Belarus ... 17 B7
Prydz B., Antarctica ... 96 A10
Pryluky, Ukraine ... 24 C3
Prypyat ➤, Europe ... 17 C10
Przhevalsk = Karakol, Kyrgyzstan ... 29 E8
Psara, Greece ... 23 E5
Psiloritis, Oros, Greece ... 23 G5
Pskov, Russia ... 24 B2
Ptsich ➤, Belarus ... 17 B9
Puán, Argentina ... 94 D4
Pucallpa, Peru ... 91 E4
Puduchcheri = Pondicherry, India ... 43 P11
Pudukkottai, India ... 43 P11
Puebla, Mexico ... 84 D5
Pueblo, U.S.A. ... 74 F2
Puelches, Argentina ... 94 D3
Puente Alto, Chile ... 94 C2
Puente-Genil, Spain ... 18 D3
Puerto Aisén, Chile ... 95 F2
Puerto Ayacucho, Venezuela 90 B5
Puerto Barrios, Guatemala .. 85 D7
Puerto Bermúdez, Peru ... 91 F4
Puerto Bolívar, Ecuador ... 90 D3
Puerto Cabello, Venezuela . 90 A5
Puerto Cabezas, Nic. ... 86 D3
Puerto Carreño, Colombia . 90 B5
Puerto Chicama, Peru ... 91 E3
Puerto Coig, Argentina ... 95 G3
Puerto Cortés, Honduras ... 85 D7
Puerto Cumarebo, Venezuela 90 A5
Puerto Deseado, Argentina . 95 F3
Puerto Heath, Bolivia ... 91 F5
Puerto La Cruz, Venezuela .. 90 A6
Puerto Leguízamo, Colombia 90 D4
Puerto Lobos, Argentina ... 95 E3
Puerto Madryn, Argentina .. 95 E3
Puerto Maldonado, Peru ... 91 F5
Puerto Montt, Chile ... 95 E2
Puerto Natales, Chile ... 95 G2
Puerto Páez, Venezuela ... 90 B5
Puerto Pinasco, Paraguay .. 94 A5
Puerto Plata, Dom. Rep. ... 87 C5
Puerto Princesa, Phil. ... 36 C1
Puerto Rico ☑, W. Indies ... 87 C6
Puerto Sastre, Paraguay ... 91 H7
Puerto Suárez, Bolivia ... 91 G7
Puerto Wilches, Colombia . 90 B4
Puertollano, Spain ... 18 C3
Pueyrredón, L., Argentina .. 95 F2
Pugachev, Russia ... 24 C6
Puget Sound, U.S.A. ... 72 C2
Puigcerdà, Spain ... 19 A6
Pukaki, L., N.Z. ... 65 F4
Pukapuka, Cook Is. ... 65 L14
Pukekohe, N.Z. ... 64 B6
Pula, Croatia ... 20 B4
Puławy, Poland ... 16 C5
Pullman, U.S.A. ... 72 C5
Pulog, Mt., Phil. ... 36 A2
Pułtusk, Poland ... 16 B5
Puná, I., Ecuador ... 90 D2
Punakaiki, N.Z. ... 65 E4
Punakha Dzong, Bhutan ... 41 D7
Punata, Bolivia ... 91 G5
Punch, India ... 42 C7
Pune, India ... 43 K8
Punjab □, India ... 42 D9
Punjab □, Pakistan ... 42 D8
Puno, Peru ... 91 G4
Punta Alta, Argentina ... 94 D4
Punta Arenas, Chile ... 95 G2
Punta de Diaz, Chile ... 94 B2
Puntarenas, Costa Rica ... 86 E3
Punto Fijo, Venezuela ... 90 A4
Puquio, Peru ... 91 F4
Pur ➤, Russia ... 28 C8
Puracé, Vol., Colombia ... 90 C3
Puralia = Puruliya, India ... 40 F6
Puri, India ... 40 H5
Purnia, India ... 40 E6
Purukcahu, Indonesia ... 39 E4
Puruliya, India ... 40 F6

Purus ⇥, *Brazil* 90 D6
Pusan = Busan, *S. Korea* 35 C7
Pushkino, *Russia* 24 C6
Putao, *Burma* 41 D11
Putaruru, *N.Z.* 64 C6
Putignano, *Italy* 21 D6
Puting, Tanjung, *Indonesia* .. 39 E4
Putorana, Gory, *Russia* 30 C7
Puttalam, *Sri Lanka* 43 Q11
Puttgarden, *Germany* 15 A6
Putumayo ⇥, *S. Amer.* 90 D5
Putussibau, *Indonesia* 39 D4
Puvirnituq, *Canada* 70 C6
Puy-de-Dôme, *France* 13 D5
Pwllheli, *U.K.* 11 E4
Pyapon, *Burma* 41 J10
Pyasina ⇥, *Russia* 30 B6
Pyatigorsk, *Russia* 25 E5
Pyè = Prome, *Burma* 41 H10
Pyetrikaw, *Belarus* 17 B9
Pyinmana, *Burma* 41 H11
P'yŏngyang, *N. Korea* 35 C7
Pyrénées, *Europe* 12 E4
Pyu, *Burma* 41 H11

Q

Qā'emshahr, *Iran* 44 B3
Qahremānshahr =
  Kermānshāh, *Iran* 46 D6
Qaidam Pendi, *China* 34 C4
Qal'at al Akhḍar, *Si. Arabia* .. 47 E4
Qalāt-i-Ghilzai, *Afghan.* 45 C6
Qamani'tuaq = Baker Lake,
  Canada 68 B10
Qamruddin Karez, *Pakistan* . 42 D6
Qandahār, *Afghan.* 42 D4
Qandahār ☐, *Afghan.* 42 D4
Qapshaghay, *Kazakhstan* 29 E8
Qarabutaq, *Kazakhstan* 29 E7
Qaraghandy, *Kazakhstan* ... 29 E8
Qaraghayly, *Kazakhstan* ... 29 E8
Qarataū, *Kazakhstan* 29 E7
Qarataū, *Zhambyl, Kazakhstan* 29 E8
Qardho = Gardo, *Somali Rep.* 49 F4
Qarqan He ⇥, *China* 34 C3
Qarqaraly, *Kazakhstan* 29 E8
Qarshi, *Uzbekistan* 29 F7
Qaşr-e Qand, *Iran* 45 E5
Qasr Farâfra, *Egypt* 54 C4
Qatar ■, *Asia* 44 E2
Qattâra, Munkhafed el, *Egypt* 54 C4
Qattâra Depression = Qattâra,
  Munkhafed el, *Egypt* 54 C4
Qausuittuq = Resolute,
  Canada 70 B4
Qāyen, *Iran* 44 C4
Qazaqstan = Kazakhstan ■,
  Asia 29 E7
Qazvīn, *Iran* 46 C7
Qena, *Egypt* 54 C5
Qeshm, *Iran* 44 E4
Qikiqtarjuaq, *Canada* 70 C7
Qila Saifullāh, *Pakistan* ... 42 D6
Qilian Shan, *China* 34 C4
Qingdao, *China* 35 C7
Qinghai ☐, *China* 34 C4
Qinghai Hu, *China* 34 C5
Qinhuangdao, *China* 35 C6
Qinzhou, *China* 35 D5
Qiqihar, *China* 35 B7
Qitai, *China* 34 B3
Qom, *Iran* 44 C2
Qomolangma Feng = Everest,
  Mt., *Nepal* 40 C6
Qomsheh, *Iran* 44 C2
Qondūz, *Afghan.* 45 B7
Qondūz ☐, *Afghan.* 45 B7
Qoqon = Qūqon, *Uzbekistan* . 29 E8
Qoraqalpoghistan ☐,
  Uzbekistan 29 E6
Qostanay, *Kazakhstan* 29 D7
Quambatook, *Australia* 62 C3
Quambone, *Australia* 63 B4

Quan Long = Ca Mau,
  Vietnam 38 C3
Quang Ngai, *Vietnam* 38 A3
Quanzhou, *China* 35 D6
Quaqtaq, *Canada* 70 C7
Quartu Sant'Élena, *Italy* ... 21 E2
Quba, *Azerbaijan* 25 E6
Qüchān, *Iran* 44 B4
Queanbeyan, *Australia* 63 C4
Québec, *Canada* 71 E6
Québec ☐, *Canada* 71 E6
Queen Alexandra Ra.,
  Antarctica 96 C15
Queen Charlotte Is., *Canada* . 68 C6
Queen Charlotte Sd., *Canada* 69 C7
Queen Elizabeth Is., *Canada* . 66 B9
Queen Mary Land, *Antarctica* 96 B11
Queen Maud G., *Canada* ... 68 B9
Queen Maud Land = Dronning
  Maud Land, *Antarctica* .. 96 B7
Queen Maud Mts., *Antarctica* 96 C16
Queenscliff, *Australia* 63 C3
Queensland ☐, *Australia* ... 61 E7
Queenstown, *Australia* 62 D4
Queenstown, *N.Z.* 65 F3
Queenstown, *S. Africa* 59 E5
Queimadas, *Brazil* 93 E6
Quelimane, *Mozam.* 59 B7
Quelpart = Jeju-do, *S. Korea* 35 C7
Querétaro, *Mexico* 84 C4
Quetta, *Pakistan* 42 D5
Quezon City, *Phil.* 36 B2
Qui Nhon, *Vietnam* 38 B3
Quibaxe, *Angola* 56 F2
Quibdo, *Colombia* 90 B3
Quiberon, *France* 12 C2
Quilán, C., *Chile* 95 E2
Quillabamba, *Peru* 91 F4
Quillagua, *Chile* 91 H5
Quillota, *Chile* 94 C2
Quilon, *India* 43 Q10
Quilpie, *Australia* 63 A3
Quimilí, *Argentina* 94 B4
Quimper, *France* 12 B1
Quimperlé, *France* 12 C2
Quincy, *U.S.A.* 75 F9
Quines, *Argentina* 94 C3
Quintanar de la Orden, *Spain* 18 C4
Quirindi, *Australia* 63 B5
Quissanga, *Mozam.* 59 A8
Quito, *Ecuador* 90 D3
Quixadá, *Brazil* 92 C6
Qulan, *Kazakhstan* 29 E8
Qünghirot, *Uzbekistan* 29 E6
Quorn, *Australia* 62 B2
Qüqon, *Uzbekistan* 29 E8
Quseir, *Egypt* 54 C5
Quzhou, *China* 35 D6
Qyzylorda, *Kazakhstan* 29 E7

R

Raahe, *Finland* 8 C10
Raba, *Indonesia* 37 F1
Rába ⇥, *Hungary* 16 E3
Rabat, *Malta* 21 G5
Rabat, *Morocco* 52 B4
Rabaul, *Papua N. G.* 64 K10
Rābigh, *Si. Arabia* 47 G4
Râbnița, *Moldova* 17 E9
Race, C., *Canada* 71 E8
Rach Gia, *Vietnam* 38 B3
Racine, *U.S.A.* 76 C2
Rădăuți, *Romania* 17 E7
Radekhiv, *Ukraine* 17 C7
Radom, *Poland* 16 C5
Radomsko, *Poland* 16 C4
Radomyshl, *Ukraine* 17 C9
Radstock, C., *Australia* ... 62 B1
Rae, *Canada* 68 B8
Rae Bareli, *India* 40 D3
Rae Isthmus, *Canada* ... 70 C5
Raetihi, *N.Z.* 64 C6
Rafaela, *Argentina* 94 C4
Rafḥā, *Si. Arabia* 47 E5

Rafsanjän, *Iran* 44 D4
Ragachow, *Belarus* 17 B10
Ragama, *Sri Lanka* 43 R11
Raglan, *N.Z.* 64 B6
Ragusa, *Italy* 21 F5
Raha, *Indonesia* 37 E2
Rahimyar Khan, *Pakistan* . 42 E7
Raichur, *India* 43 L10
Raigarh, *India* 40 G4
Railton, *Australia* 62 D4
Rainier, Mt., *U.S.A.* 72 C3
Raipur, *India* 40 G3
Ra'is, *Si. Arabia* 47 G4
Raj Nandgaon, *India* 40 G3
Raja, Ujung, *Indonesia* .. 39 D1
Raja Ampat, Kepulauan,
  Indonesia 37 E3
Rajahmundry, *India* 40 J3
Rajang ⇥, *Malaysia* 39 D4
Rajapalaiyam, *India* 43 Q10
Rajasthan ☐, *India* 42 F8
Rajasthan Canal = Indira
  Gandhi Canal, *India* ... 42 F8
Rajgarh, *India* 43 G10
Rajkot, *India* 43 H7
Rajpipla, *India* 43 J8
Rajshahi, *Bangla.* 41 E7
Rakaia, *N.Z.* 65 E5
Rakaia ⇥, *N.Z.* 65 E5
Rakan, Ra's, *Qatar* 44 E2
Rakaposhi, *Pakistan* 42 A9
Rakata, Pulau, *Indonesia* .. 39 F3
Rakhiv, *Ukraine* 17 D7
Rakitnoye, *Russia* 32 A4
Rakiura △, *N.Z.* 65 G2
Raleigh, *U.S.A.* 83 B8
Ramanathapuram, *India* .. 43 Q11
Rame Hd., *Australia* 63 C4
Ramechhap, *Nepal* 40 D6
Ramgarh, *Jharkhand, India* . 40 F5
Ramgarh, *Raj., India* 42 F7
Ramnad = Ramanathapuram,
  India 43 Q11
Râmnicu Sărat, *Romania* .. 17 F8
Râmnicu Vâlcea, *Romania* .. 17 F7
Rampur, *India* 42 E11
Rampur Hat, *India* 40 E6
Ramree I., *Burma* 41 H9
Ramtek, *India* 43 J11
Ranaghat, *India* 41 F7
Ranau, *Malaysia* 38 C5
Rancagua, *Chile* 94 C2
Ranchi, *India* 40 F5
Randers, *Denmark* 9 D8
Rangaunu B., *N.Z.* 64 A5
Rangia, *India* 41 D8
Rangiora, *N.Z.* 65 E5
Rangitaiki ⇥, *N.Z.* 64 B7
Rangitata ⇥, *N.Z.* 65 E4
Rangitoto ke te tonga =
  D'Urville I., *N.Z.* 65 D5
Rangon ⇥, *Burma* 41 J11
Rangoon, *Burma* 41 J11
Rangpur, *Bangla.* 41 E7
Ranibennur, *India* 43 M9
Raniganj, *India* 40 F6
Raniwara, *India* 43 G8
Rankin Inlet, *Canada* ... 68 B10
Rankins Springs, *Australia* . 63 B4
Ranohira, *Madag.* 59 C9
Ranong, *Thailand* 38 C1
Ransiki, *Indonesia* 37 E4
Rantauprapat, *Indonesia* .. 39 D1
Rantemario, *Indonesia* ... 37 E1
Rapa, *French Polynesia* .. 65 M16
Rapallo, *Italy* 13 D8
Rāpch, *Iran* 45 E4
Raper, C., *Canada* 70 C7
Rapid City, *U.S.A.* 74 C3
Rarotonga, *Cook Is.* 65 M14
Ra's al Khaymah, *U.A.E.* .. 44 E4
Rasht, *Iran* 46 C7
Rat Islands, *U.S.A.* 69 C1
Ratangarh, *India* 42 E9
Rathenow, *Germany* 15 B7
Ratlam, *India* 43 H9
Ratnagiri, *India* 43 L8

Raukumara Ra., N.Z. 64 C7
Rauma, Finland 8 C10
Raumo = Rauma, Finland ... 8 C10
Raurkela, India 40 F5
Rausu-Dake, Japan 32 A9
Rava-Ruska, Ukraine 17 C6
Rāvar, Iran 44 D4
Ravenna, Italy 20 B4
Ravensburg, Germany 14 E5
Ravi ➡, Pakistan 42 D7
Rawalpindi, Pakistan 42 C8
Rawāndūz, Iraq 46 C6
Rawene, N.Z. 64 A5
Rawlins, U.S.A. 73 F10
Rawson, Argentina 95 E3
Ray, C., Canada 71 E8
Rayadurg, India 43 M10
Rayagada, India 40 H4
Raz, Pte. du, France 12 B1
Razāzah, Buḥayrat ar, Iraq .. 47 D5
Razazah, L. = Razāzah,
  Buḥayrat ar, Iraq 47 D5
Razdel'naya = Rozdilna,
  Ukraine 17 E10
Razgrad, Bulgaria 22 C6
Razim, Lacul, Romania 22 B7
Ré, Î. de, France 12 C3
Reading, U.K. 11 F6
Reading, U.S.A. 77 D8
Realicó, Argentina 94 D4
Rebi, Indonesia 37 F4
Rebiana, Libya 54 D3
Rebun-Tō, Japan 32 A7
Rechytsa, Belarus 17 B10
Recife, Brazil 92 D7
Reconquista, Argentina ... 94 B5
Recreo, Argentina 94 B3
Red ➡, U.S.A. 81 D8
Red Cliffs, Australia 62 B3
Red Deer, Canada 69 C8
Red River of the North ➡,
  N. Amer. 74 A6
Red Sea, Asia 48 C2
Red Tower Pass = Turnu
  Roşu, P., Romania 17 F7
Redcar, U.K. 11 D6
Redcliffe, Australia 63 A5
Redding, U.S.A. 72 F2
Redditch, U.K. 11 E6
Redon, France 12 C2
Redondela, Spain 18 A1
Redwood City, U.S.A. 78 B1
Ree, L., Ireland 11 E3
Reefton, N.Z. 65 E4
Regensburg, Germany 15 D7
Reggâne = Zaouiet Reggâne,
  Algeria 52 C6
Réggio di Calábria, Italy .. 21 E5
Réggio nell'Emília, Italy ... 20 B3
Reghin, Romania 17 E7
Regina, Canada 69 C9
Rehoboth, Namibia 58 C3
Rehovot, Israel 46 E3
Reichenbach, Germany ... 15 C7
Reidsville, U.S.A. 83 A8
Reigate, U.K. 11 F6
Reims, France 13 B6
Reina Adelaida, Arch., Chile . 95 G2
Reindeer L., Canada 69 C9
Reinga, C., N.Z. 64 A5
Reinosa, Spain 18 A3
Remarkable, Mt., Australia . 62 B2
Remeshk, Iran 45 E4
Rendsburg, Germany 14 A5
Rengat, Indonesia 39 E2
Reni, Ukraine 17 F9
Renmark, Australia 62 B3
Rennes, France 12 B3
Reno, U.S.A. 72 G4
Reno ➡, Italy 20 B4
Rentería, Spain 19 A5
Republican ➡, U.S.A. ... 74 F6
Repulse Bay, Canada 70 C5
Requena, Peru 90 E4
Requena, Spain 19 C5
Reşadiye = Datça, Turkey .. 23 F6
Resht = Rasht, Iran 46 C7

Resistencia, Argentina 94 B5
Reşiţa, Romania 17 F5
Resolute, Canada 70 B4
Resolution I., Canada 70 C7
Resolution I., N.Z. 65 F2
Rethimno, Greece 23 G5
Réunion ☑, Ind. Oc. 51 J9
Reus, Spain 19 B6
Reutlingen, Germany 14 D5
Revelstoke, Canada 69 C8
Revillagigedo, Is. de, Pac. Oc. 84 D2
Rewa, India 40 E3
Rewari, India 42 E10
Rey Malabo, Eq. Guin. ... 53 H7
Reykjavík, Iceland 8 C1
Reynosa, Mexico 84 B5
Rhein ➡, Europe 14 C4
Rhein-Main-Donau-Kanal,
  Germany 15 D6
Rheine, Germany 14 B4
Rheinland-Pfalz ☐, Germany 14 C4
Rhine = Rhein ➡, Europe ... 14 C4
Rhineland-Palatinate =
  Rheinland-Pfalz ☐, Germany 14 C4
Rhode Island ☐, U.S.A. 77 D10
Rhodes, Greece 23 F7
Rhodope Mts. = Rhodopi
  Planina, Bulgaria 22 D5
Rhodopi Planina, Bulgaria .. 22 D5
Rhön, Germany 14 C5
Rhondda, U.K. 11 F5
Rhône ➡, France 13 E6
Rhum, U.K. 10 C3
Riachão, Brazil 92 D4
Riasi, India 42 C9
Riau ☐, Indonesia 39 E2
Riau, Kepulauan, Indonesia . 39 D2
Ribadeo, Spain 18 A2
Ribeirão Prêto, Brazil 93 G4
Riberalta, Bolivia 91 F5
Riccarton, N.Z. 65 E5
Richards Bay, S. Africa ... 59 D6
Richland, U.S.A. 72 C4
Richmond, N.Z. 65 D5
Richmond, Calif., U.S.A. .. 72 H2
Richmond, Va., U.S.A. ... 77 F7
Richmond Ra., Australia .. 63 A5
Ridder = Leninogorsk,
  Kazakhstan 29 D9
Ried, Austria 15 D7
Riesa, Germany 15 C7
Rieti, Italy 20 C4
Rif = Er Rif, Morocco 52 A5
Riga, Latvia 24 B1
Riga, G. of, Latvia 24 B1
Rigestān, Afghan. 42 D4
Rigolet, Canada 70 D8
Riiser-Larsen-halvøya,
  Antarctica 96 A8
Rijeka, Croatia 20 B5
Rimah, Wadi ar ➡, Si. Arabia 47 F5
Rimini, Italy 20 B4
Rimouski, Canada 71 E7
Rinca, Indonesia 37 F1
Rinconada, Argentina ... 94 A3
Rinjani, Indonesia 39 F5
Rio Branco, Brazil 91 E5
Río Branco, Uruguay 94 C6
Río Cuarto, Argentina ... 94 C4
Rio de Janeiro, Brazil 93 G5
Rio de Janeiro ☐, Brazil .. 93 G5
Rio do Sul, Brazil 94 B7
Río Gallegos, Argentina .. 95 G3
Río Grande, Argentina ... 95 G3
Rio Grande, Brazil 94 C6
Rio Grande ➡, N. Amer. .. 85 B5
Río Grande de Santiago ➡,
  Mexico 84 C3
Rio Grande do Norte ☐, Brazil 92 D6
Rio Grande do Sul ☐, Brazil . 94 B6
Rio Largo, Brazil 93 D6
Rio Mulatos, Bolivia 91 G5
Río Muni ☐, Eq. Guin. ... 56 D2
Rio Negro, Brazil 94 B7
Rio Verde, Brazil 93 F3
Riobamba, Ecuador 90 D3
Ríohacha, Colombia 90 A4

Ríosucio, Caldas, Colombia . 90 B3
Ríosucio, Choco, Colombia .. 90 B3
Rishiri-Tō, Japan 32 A7
Riva del Garda, Italy 20 B3
Rivadavia, Chile 94 B2
Rivera, Uruguay 94 C5
Riverside, U.S.A. 78 D4
Riverton, Australia 62 B2
Riverton, N.Z. 65 G2
Riviera di Levante, Italy ... 13 D8
Riviera di Ponente, Italy ... 13 D8
Rivière-du-Loup, Canada .. 71 E7
Rivne, Ukraine 17 C8
Rívoli, Italy 13 D7
Rivoli B., Australia 62 C3
Riyadh = Ar Riyāḍ, Si. Arabia 47 F6
Rize, Turkey 25 E5
Rizzuto, C., Italy 21 E6
Roanne, France 13 C6
Roanoke, U.S.A. 77 F6
Robbins I., Australia 62 D4
Robertson I., Antarctica ... 96 A4
Robertstown, Australia .. 62 B2
Roberval, Canada 71 E6
Robinvale, Australia 62 B3
Roboré, Bolivia 91 G7
Robson, Mt., Canada 69 C8
Roca, C. da, Portugal 18 C1
Rocas, I., Brazil 92 C7
Rocha, Uruguay 94 C6
Rochefort, France 12 D3
Rochester, Minn., U.S.A. .. 75 C8
Rochester, N.Y., U.S.A. ... 77 C7
Rock, The, Australia 63 C4
Rock Hill, U.S.A. 83 B7
Rock Island, U.S.A. 75 E9
Rock Springs, U.S.A. 73 F9
Rockefeller Plateau, Antarctica 96 C18
Rockford, U.S.A. 75 D10
Rockhampton, Australia ... 61 E9
Rocky Mount, U.S.A. 83 B9
Rocky Mts., N. Amer. ... 68 C7
Rod, Pakistan 42 E3
Rodez, France 13 D5
Ródhos = Rhodes, Greece .. 23 F7
Rodney, C., N.Z. 64 B6
Roes Welcome Sd., Canada . 70 C5
Rogachev = Ragachow,
  Belarus 17 B10
Rogagua, L., Bolivia 91 F5
Rogatyn, Ukraine 17 D7
Rogoaguado, L., Bolivia .. 91 F5
Rohri, Pakistan 42 F6
Rohtak, India 42 E10
Roi Et, Thailand 38 A2
Rojo, C., Mexico 84 C5
Rokan ➡, Indonesia 39 D2
Rolândia, Brazil 94 A6
Roma, Australia 63 A4
Roma, Italy 20 D4
Romaine ➡, Canada 71 D7
Roman, Romania 17 E8
Romang, Indonesia 37 F3
Romania ■, Europe 22 B5
Romans-sur-Isère, France .. 13 D6
Romblon, Phil. 36 B2
Rome = Roma, Italy 20 D4
Rome, U.S.A. 82 B5
Romorantin-Lanthenay,
  France 12 C4
Roncador, Serra do, Brazil . 93 E3
Ronda, Spain 18 D3
Rondônia ☐, Brazil 91 F6
Rondonópolis, Brazil 93 F3
Ronge, L. la, Canada 69 C9
Ronne Ice Shelf, Antarctica . 96 B3
Roorkee, India 42 E10
Roosevelt ➡, Brazil 91 E6
Roosevelt I., Antarctica ... 96 B16
Roquetas de Mar, Spain ... 19 D4
Roraima ☐, Brazil 90 C6
Roraima, Mt., Venezuela .. 90 B6
Rosa, Monte, Europe 13 D7
Rosario, Argentina 94 C4
Rosário, Brazil 92 C5
Rosario, Mexico 84 C3
Rosario, Paraguay 94 A4

Rosario de la Frontera,
  Argentina 94 B3
Rosário do Sul, Brazil 94 C6
Roscommon, Ireland 11 E2
Roseau, Dominica 87 C7
Roseau, U.S.A. 75 A7
Rosebery, Australia 62 D4
Roseburg, U.S.A. 72 E2
Rosenheim, Germany 15 E7
Roses, G. de, Spain 19 A7
Rosetown, Canada 69 C9
Roseville, U.S.A. 72 G3
Rosewood, Australia 63 A5
Rosignano Maríttimo, Italy .. 20 C3
Rosignol, Guyana 90 B7
Roşiori de Vede, Romania .. 22 B5
Roslavl, Russia 24 C3
Ross, Australia 62 D4
Ross, N.Z. 65 E4
Ross I., Antarctica 96 B15
Ross Ice Shelf, Antarctica .. 96 C16
Ross Sea, Antarctica 96 B15
Rossano, Italy 21 E6
Rosslare, Ireland 11 E3
Rosso, Mauritania 53 E2
Rossosh, Russia 24 C4
Rostock, Germany 15 A7
Rostov, Don, Russia 25 D4
Rostov, Sverdlovsk, Russia .. 24 B4
Roswell, U.S.A. 80 C1
Rotherham, U.K. 11 E6
Rotondo, Mte., France 13 E8
Rotoroa, L., N.Z. 65 D5
Rotorua, N.Z. 64 C7
Rotorua, L., N.Z. 64 C7
Rotterdam, Neths. 14 C3
Rottweil, Germany 14 D5
Rotuma, Fiji 64 L12
Roubaix, France 13 A5
Rouen, France 12 B4
Round Mt., Australia 63 B5
Rousse = Ruse, Bulgaria 22 C5
Roussillon, France 13 E5
Rouyn-Noranda, Canada 71 E6
Rovaniemi, Finland 8 B11
Rovereto, Italy 20 B3
Rovigo, Italy 20 B3
Rovinj, Croatia 20 B4
Rovno = Rivne, Ukraine ... 17 C8
Rovuma = Ruvuma ➡,
  Tanzania 57 G8
Rowena, Australia 63 A4
Roxas, Phil. 36 B2
Roxburgh, N.Z. 65 F3
Royal Leamington Spa, U.K. . 11 E6
Royan, France 12 D3
Rozdilna, Ukraine 17 E10
Rozhyshche, Ukraine 17 C7
Rtishchevo, Russia 24 C5
Ruahine Ra., N.Z. 64 C7
Ruapehu, N.Z. 64 C6
Ruapuke I., N.Z. 65 G3
Rub' al Khālī, Si. Arabia 48 D4
Rubio, Venezuela 90 B4
Rubtsovsk, Russia 29 D9
Rudall, Australia 62 B2
Rudolfa, Ostrov, Russia 28 A6
Rufiji ➡, Tanzania 57 F7
Rufino, Argentina 94 C4
Rugby, U.K. 11 E6
Rügen, Germany 15 A7
Ruhr ➡, Germany 14 C4
Rukwa, L., Tanzania 57 F6
Rum = Rhum, U.K. 10 C3
Rumāḥ, Si. Arabia 47 F6
Rumania = Romania ■,
  Europe 22 B5
Rumbêk, Sudan 55 G4
Rumia, Poland 16 A4
Rumoi, Japan 32 B7
Runanga, N.Z. 65 E4
Runaway, C., N.Z. 64 B7
Rundu, Namibia 58 B3
Ruoqiang, China 34 C3
Rupa, India 41 D9
Rupat, Indonesia 39 D2

Rupert ➡, Canada 71 D6
Rupert House = Waskaganish,
  Canada 71 D6
Rurrenabaque, Bolivia 91 F5
Ruse, Bulgaria 22 C5
Russas, Brazil 92 C6
Russellkonda, India 40 H5
Rustavi, Georgia 25 E6
Rustenburg, S. Africa 59 D5
Ruteng, Indonesia 37 F2
Ruvuma ➡, Tanzania 57 G8
Ruwenzori, Africa 57 D5
Rwanda ■, Africa 57 E6
Ryazan, Russia 24 C4
Ryazhsk, Russia 24 C5
Rybachye, Kazakhstan 29 E9
Rybinsk, Russia 24 B4
Rybinskoye Vdkhr., Russia .. 24 B4
Rybnitsa = Râbniţa, Moldova 17 E9
Rylstone, Australia 63 B4
Ryōtsu, Japan 32 D6
Rypin, Poland 16 B4
Ryukyu Is. = Ryūkyū-rettō,
  Japan 35 D7
Ryūkyū-rettō, Japan 35 D7
Rzeszów, Poland 16 C5
Rzhev, Russia 24 B3

S

Sa Dec, Vietnam 38 B3
Sa'ādatābād, Iran 44 D3
Saale ➡, Germany 15 C6
Saalfeld, Germany 15 C6
Saar ➡, Europe 13 B7
Saarbrücken, Germany 14 D4
Saaremaa, Estonia 24 B1
Šabac, Serbia & M. 22 B2
Sabadell, Spain 19 B7
Sabah □, Malaysia 38 C5
Şabāḥ, Wadi ➡, Si. Arabia .. 47 G7
Sabalān, Kūhhā-ye, Iran 46 C6
Sabalana, Kepulauan,
  Indonesia 37 F1
Sábanalarga, Colombia 90 A4
Sabang, Indonesia 38 C1
Sabará, Brazil 93 F5
Saberania, Indonesia 37 E5
Sabhā, Libya 54 C1
Sabinas, Mexico 84 B4
Sabinas Hidalgo, Mexico ... 84 B4
Sablayan, Phil. 36 B2
Sable, C., Canada 71 E7
Sable, C., U.S.A. 86 A3
Sable I., Canada 71 E8
Sabrina Coast, Antarctica .. 96 A12
Sabulubbek, Indonesia 39 E1
Sabzevār, Iran 44 B4
Sabzvārān, Iran 44 D4
Săcele, Romania 17 F7
Sachsen □, Germany 15 C7
Sachsen-Anhalt □, Germany . 15 C7
Sacramento, U.S.A. 72 G3
Sacramento ➡, U.S.A. ... 72 G3
Sacramento Mts., U.S.A. 79 D10
Sadd el Aali, Egypt 54 D5
Sado, Japan 32 E6
Safi, Morocco 52 B4
Safid Kūh, Afghan. 42 B3
Saga, Japan 33 G2
Sagar, India 43 M9
Sagarmatha = Everest, Mt.,
  Nepal 40 C6
Saginaw, U.S.A. 76 C4
Saglouc = Salluit, Canada ... 70 C5
Sagua la Grande, Cuba ... 86 B3
Sagunt, Spain 19 C5
Sahagún, Spain 18 A3
Sahand, Kūh-e, Iran 46 C6
Sahara, Africa 52 D6
Saharanpur, India 42 E10
Saharien, Atlas, Algeria ... 52 B6
Sahiwal, Pakistan 42 D8
Sahrawi = Western Sahara ■,
  Africa 52 D3

Sa'id Bundâs, Sudan 55 G3
Sa'īdābād = Sīrjān, Iran 44 D3
Sa'īdīyeh, Iran 46 C7
Saidpur, Bangla. 41 E7
Saidu Sharif, Pakistan 42 B8
Saigon = Thanh Pho Ho Chi
  Minh, Vietnam 38 B3
Saikhoa Ghat, India 41 D10
Saiki, Japan 33 G2
Sailolof, Indonesia 37 E4
Saimaa, Finland 8 C11
Saimen = Saimaa, Finland . 8 C11
St. Andrews, U.K. 10 C5
St. Anthony, Canada 71 D8
St. Arnaud, Australia 62 C3
St-Augustin, Canada 71 D8
St. Augustine, U.S.A. 83 E7
St. Austell, U.K. 11 F4
St-Brieuc, France 12 B2
St. Catharines, Canada ... 77 C6
St-Chamond, France 13 D6
St. Christopher-Nevis = St.
  Kitts & Nevis ■, W. Indies . 87 C7
St. Cloud, U.S.A. 75 C7
St. Croix, U.S. Virgin Is. 87 C7
St-Denis, France 12 B5
St-Dizier, France 13 B6
St. Elias, Mt., U.S.A. 68 B5
St-Étienne, France 13 D6
St-Flour, France 13 D5
St-Gaudens, France 12 E4
St. George, Australia 63 A4
St-Georges, Fr. Guiana ... 92 B3
St. George's, Grenada 87 D7
St. George's Channel, Europe 11 F3
St. Georges Hd., Australia .. 63 C5
St. Gotthard P. = San
  Gottardo, P. del, Switz. ... 13 C8
St. Helena, Atl. Oc. 51 H3
St. Helena B., S. Africa 58 E3
St. Helens, Australia 62 D4
St. Helier, U.K. 11 G5
St-Hyacinthe, Canada 71 E6
St-Jean, L., Canada 71 E6
St. John, Canada 71 E7
St. John's, Antigua & B. 87 C7
St. John's, Canada 71 E8
St. Johns ➡, U.S.A. 83 D7
St. Joseph, U.S.A. 75 F7
St. Joseph, L., Canada 71 D4
St. Kilda, U.K. 10 C2
St. Kitts & Nevis ■, W. Indies 87 C7
St-Laurent, Fr. Guiana 92 A3
St. Lawrence ➡, Canada ... 71 E7
St. Lawrence, Gulf of, Canada 71 E7
St. Lawrence I., U.S.A. 69 B2
St-Lô, France 12 B3
St. Louis, Senegal 53 E2
St. Louis, U.S.A. 75 F9
St. Lucia ■, W. Indies 87 D7
St-Malo, France 12 B2
St-Marc, Haiti 87 C5
St. Mary Pk., Australia 62 B2
St. Marys, Australia 62 D4
St-Mathieu, Pte., France ... 12 B1
St-Nazaire, France 12 C2
St-Omer, France 12 A5
St. Paul, U.S.A. 75 C8
St. Peter Port, U.K. 11 G5
St. Petersburg = Sankt-
  Peterburg, Russia 24 B3
St. Petersburg, U.S.A. 83 F6
St-Pierre-et-Miquelon ☑,
  N. Amer. 71 E8
St-Quentin, France 13 B5
St-Tropez, France 13 E7
St. Vincent, G., Australia ... 62 C2
St. Vincent & the
  Grenadines ■, W. Indies . 87 D7
Ste-Marie, Ile = Nosy Boraha,
  Madag. 59 B9
Saintes, France 12 D3
Saintonge, France 12 D3
Saipan, N. Marianas 64 H9
Sairang, India 41 F9
Sajama, Bolivia 91 G5
Sajószentpéter, Hungary 16 D5

Sakākah

Sakākah, Si. Arabia 47 E5
Sakakawea, L., U.S.A. 74 B4
Sakartvelo = Georgia ■, Asia 25 E5
Sakarya, Turkey 25 E3
Sakata, Japan 32 D6
Sakhalin, Russia 31 D12
Sakon Nakhon, Thailand 38 A2
Sala, Sweden 9 D9
Sala Consilina, Italy 21 D5
Saladillo, Argentina 94 D5
Salado →, B. Aires, Argentina 94 D5
Salado →, La Pampa,
  Argentina 94 D3
Salado →, Santa Fe,
  Argentina 94 C4
Salaga, Ghana 53 G5
Salālah, Oman 49 D5
Salamanca, Chile 94 C2
Salamanca, Spain 18 B3
Salamina, Greece 23 F4
Salar de Atacama, Chile 94 A3
Salar de Uyuni, Bolivia 91 H5
Salaverry, Peru 91 E3
Salawati, Indonesia 37 E4
Salayar, Indonesia 37 F2
Saldanha, S. Africa 58 E3
Sale, Australia 63 C4
Salé, Morocco 52 B4
Salekhard, Russia 28 C7
Salem, India 43 P11
Salem, U.S.A. 72 D2
Salerno, Italy 21 D5
Salgótarján, Hungary 16 D4
Salihli, Turkey 23 E7
Salihorsk, Belarus 17 B8
Salima, Malawi 59 A6
Salina, Italy 21 E5
Salina, U.S.A. 74 F6
Salina Cruz, Mexico 85 D5
Salinas, Brazil 93 F5
Salinas, Ecuador 90 D2
Salinas, U.S.A. 78 B2
Salinas Grandes, Argentina . 94 C3
Salinópolis, Brazil 92 C4
Salisbury, Australia 62 B2
Salisbury, U.K. 11 F6
Salisbury, U.S.A. 83 B7
Salisbury I., Canada 70 C6
Salliq = Coral Harbour,
  Canada 70 C5
Salluit, Canada 70 C6
Salmās, Iran 46 C6
Salmon →, U.S.A. 72 D5
Salmon River Mts., U.S.A. .. 73 D6
Salon-de-Provence, France .. 13 E6
Salonica = Thessaloniki,
  Greece 23 D4
Salonta, Romania 16 E5
Salsk, Russia 25 D5
Salso →, Italy 21 F4
Salt L., Australia 62 B3
Salt Lake City, U.S.A. 73 F8
Salta, Argentina 94 A3
Saltillo, Mexico 84 B4
Salto, Uruguay 94 C5
Salto →, Italy 20 C4
Salton Sea, U.S.A. 78 D5
Salûm, Egypt 54 B4
Salur, India 40 H4
Salvador, Brazil 93 E6
Salvador, El ■, Cent. Amer. . 85 E7
Salween →, Burma 41 J11
Salyan, Azerbaijan 25 F6
Salzach →, Austria 15 D7
Salzburg, Austria 15 E7
Salzgitter, Germany 14 B6
Salzwedel, Germany 15 B6
Sama de Langreo = Langreo,
  Spain 18 A3
Samales Group, Phil. 36 C2
Samangān □, Afghan. 45 B7
Samani, Japan 32 B8
Samar, Phil. 36 B3
Samara, Russia 24 C7
Samarinda, Indonesia 39 E5
Samarkand = Samarqand,
  Uzbekistan 29 F7

Samarqand, Uzbekistan 29 F7
Sāmarrā', Iraq 46 D5
Sambalpur, India 40 G5
Sambar, Tanjung, Indonesia 39 E4
Sambas, Indonesia 39 D3
Sambhal, India 42 E11
Sambhar, India 42 F9
Sambiase, Italy 21 E6
Sambir, Ukraine 17 D6
Samoa ■, Pac. Oc. 65 L13
Samokov, Bulgaria 22 C4
Samos, Greece 23 F6
Samothráki = Mathraki,
  Greece 21 E7
Samothraki, Greece 23 D5
Sampit, Indonesia 39 E4
Sampit, Teluk, Indonesia .. 39 E4
Samsun, Turkey 25 E4
Samui, Ko, Thailand 38 C2
Samut Prakan, Thailand ... 38 B2
Samut Songkhram, Thailand 38 B2
San, Mali 53 F5
San Agustin, C., Phil. 36 C3
San Andrés, I. de, Caribbean 86 D3
San Andrés Tuxtla, Mexico . 85 D5
San Angelo, U.S.A. 80 D3
San Antonio, Chile 94 C2
San Antonio, U.S.A. 80 E4
San Antonio, C., Argentina . 94 D5
San Antonio Oeste, Argentina 95 E4
San Benedetto del Tronto,
  Italy 20 C4
San Bernardino, U.S.A. 78 C4
San Bernardino Str., Phil. .. 36 B2
San Bernardo, Chile 94 C2
San Bernardo, I. de, Colombia 90 B3
San Borja, Bolivia 91 F5
San Buenaventura = Ventura,
  U.S.A. 78 C3
San Carlos, Argentina 94 C3
San Carlos, Chile 94 D2
San Carlos, Phil. 36 B2
San Carlos, Amazonas,
  Venezuela 90 C5
San Carlos, Cojedes,
  Venezuela 90 B5
San Carlos de Bariloche,
  Argentina 95 E2
San Carlos del Zulia,
  Venezuela 90 B4
San Cristóbal, Argentina ... 94 C4
San Cristóbal, Venezuela .. 90 B4
San Cristóbal de las Casas,
  Mexico 85 D6
San Diego, U.S.A. 78 D4
San Diego, C., Argentina ... 95 G3
San Felipe, Chile 94 C2
San Felipe, Venezuela 90 A5
San Fernando, Chile 94 C2
San Fernando, La Union, Phil. 36 A2
San Fernando, Pampanga,
  Phil. 36 A2
San Fernando, Spain 18 D2
San Fernando, Trin. & Tob. . 87 D7
San Fernando de Apure,
  Venezuela 90 B5
San Fernando de Atabapo,
  Venezuela 90 C5
San Francisco, Argentina .. 94 C4
San Francisco, U.S.A. 78 B1
San Francisco de Macorís,
  Dom. Rep. 87 C5
San Gottardo, P. del, Switz. . 13 C8
San Ignacio, Bolivia 91 G6
San Ignacio, Paraguay 94 B5
San Ildefonso, C., Phil. 36 A2
San Javier, Bolivia 91 G6
San Joaquin →, U.S.A. 78 A2
San Jorge, G., Argentina ... 95 F3
San José, Costa Rica 86 E3
San Jose, Mind. Occ., Phil. . 36 B2
San Jose, Nueva Ecija, Phil. . 36 A2
San Jose, U.S.A. 78 B2
San José de Chiquitos, Bolivia 91 G6
San José de Jáchal, Argentina 94 C3
San José de Mayo, Uruguay 94 C5

San José del Guaviare,
  Colombia 90 C4
San Juan, Argentina 94 C3
San Juan, Puerto Rico 87 C6
San Juan →, Nic. 86 D3
San Juan de los Morros,
  Venezuela 90 B5
San Juan Mts., U.S.A. 79 B9
San Justo, Argentina 94 C4
San Lorenzo, Ecuador 90 C3
San Lorenzo, Mte., Argentina 95 F2
San Lucas, Bolivia 91 H5
San Lucas, C., Mexico 84 C2
San Luis, Argentina 94 C3
San Luis Obispo, U.S.A. 78 C2
San Luis Potosí, Mexico ... 84 C4
San Marino ■, Europe 20 C4
San Marino, San Marino ... 20 C4
San Martín, L., Argentina ... 95 F2
San Matías, Bolivia 91 G7
San Matías, G., Argentina .. 95 E4
San Miguel, El Salv. 85 E7
San Miguel →, Bolivia 91 F6
San Miguel de Tucumán,
  Argentina 94 B3
San Nicolás de los Arroyas,
  Argentina 94 C4
San Pédro, Ivory C. 53 H4
San Pedro de las Colonias,
  Mexico 84 B4
San Pedro de Macorís,
  Dom. Rep. 87 C6
San Pedro del Paraná,
  Paraguay 94 B5
San Pedro Sula, Honduras .. 85 D7
San Pietro, Italy 21 E2
San Rafael, Argentina 94 C3
San Rafael, U.S.A. 72 H2
San Remo, Italy 13 E7
San Roque, Argentina 94 B5
San Roque, Spain 18 D3
San Rosendo, Chile 94 D2
San Salvador, El Salv. 85 E7
San Salvador de Jujuy,
  Argentina 94 A4
San Salvador I., Bahamas ... 86 B5
San Sebastián = Donostia-San
  Sebastián, Spain 19 A5
San Sebastián, Argentina .. 95 G3
San Severo, Italy 20 D5
San Valentin, Mte., Chile 95 F2
San Vicente de la Barquera,
  Spain 18 A3
Sana', Yemen 49 D3
Sana →, Bos.-H. 20 B7
Sanaga →, Cameroon 56 D1
Sanana, Indonesia 37 E3
Sanandaj, Iran 46 D6
Sancti Spíritus, Cuba 86 B4
Sancy, Puy de, France 13 D5
Sandakan, Malaysia 38 C5
Sandanski, Bulgaria 22 D4
Sanday, U.K. 10 B5
Sandía, Peru 91 F5
Sandıklı, Turkey 46 C2
Sandoa, Dem. Rep. of
  the Congo 56 F4
Sandomierz, Poland 16 C5
Sandoway = Thandwe, Burma 41 H10
Sandusky, U.S.A. 76 D4
Sandy C., Australia 62 D3
Sandy L., Canada 69 C10
Sanford, Fla., U.S.A. 83 E7
Sanford, N.C., U.S.A. 83 B8
Sanford, Mt., U.S.A. 69 B5
Sanga →, Congo 56 E3
Sangamner, India 43 K9
Sangar, Russia 31 C10
Sangeang, Indonesia 37 F1
Sangerhausen, Germany ... 15 C6
Sanggau, Indonesia 39 D4
Sanghe, Pulau, Indonesia .. 37 D3
Sangkapura, Indonesia 39 F4
Sangli, India 43 L9
Sangmélima, Cameroon ... 56 D2
Sangre de Cristo Mts., U.S.A. 80 A1
Sanikiluaq, Canada 71 D6

Sanirajak, *Canada* 70 C5
Sanjo, *Japan* 33 E6
Sankt Gallen, *Switz.* 13 C8
Sankt Moritz, *Switz.* 13 C8
Sankt-Peterburg, *Russia* ... 24 B3
Sankt Pölten, *Austria* 15 D8
Sankuru �, *Dem. Rep. of
the Congo* 56 E4
Sanliurfa, *Turkey* 46 C4
Sanlúcar de Barrameda, *Spain* 18 D2
Sanmenxia, *China* 35 C6
Sannicandro Gargánico, *Italy* 20 D5
Sant Antoni Abat, *Spain* ... 19 C6
Sant Feliu de Guíxols, *Spain* 19 B7
Sant Jordi, G. de, *Spain* 19 B6
Santa Ana, *Bolivia* 91 F5
Santa Ana, *El Salv.* 85 E7
Santa Ana, *U.S.A.* 78 D4
Sant' Antíoco, *Italy* 21 E2
Santa Barbara, *U.S.A.* 78 C3
Santa Catalina I., *U.S.A.* ... 78 D3
Santa Catarina ☐, *Brazil* ... 94 B7
Santa Clara, *Cuba* 86 B4
Santa Clotilde, *Peru* 90 D4
Santa Coloma de Gramenet,
Spain 19 B7
Santa Cruz, *Argentina* 95 G3
Santa Cruz, *Bolivia* 91 G6
Santa Cruz, *Phil.* 36 B2
Santa Cruz, *U.S.A.* 78 B1
Santa Cruz ➱, *Argentina* ... 95 G3
Santa Cruz de Tenerife,
Canary Is. 52 C2
Santa Cruz do Sul, *Brazil* ... 94 B6
Santa Cruz Is., *Solomon Is.* .. 64 L11
Santa Fé, *Argentina* 94 C4
Santa Fe, *U.S.A.* 79 C10
Santa Filomena, *Brazil* 93 D4
Santa Inés, I., *Chile* 95 G2
Santa Isabel, *Argentina* 94 D3
Santa Isabel do Morro, *Brazil* 93 E3
Santa Lucia Range, *U.S.A.* .. 78 C2
Santa Maria, *Brazil* 94 B6
Santa Maria, *U.S.A.* 78 C2
Santa María ➱, *Mexico* 84 A3
Santa Maria da Vitória, *Brazil* 93 E5
Santa Maria di Léuca, C., *Italy* 21 E7
Santa Marta, *Colombia* 90 A4
Santa Marta, Sierra Nevada
de, *Colombia* 90 A4
Santa Maura = Lefkada,
Greece 23 E3
Santa Rosa, *La Pampa,
Argentina* 94 D4
Santa Rosa, *San Luis,
Argentina* 94 C3
Santa Rosa, *Brazil* 94 B6
Santa Rosa, *U.S.A.* 72 G2
Santa Vitória do Palmar, *Brazil* 94 C6
Santai, *China* 35 C5
Santana, Coxilha de, *Brazil* . 94 C5
Santana do Livramento, *Brazil* 94 C5
Santander, *Spain* 18 A4
Santarém, *Brazil* 92 C3
Santarém, *Portugal* 18 C1
Santiago, *Brazil* 94 B6
Santiago, *Chile* 94 C2
Santiago ➱, *Peru* 90 D3
Santiago de Compostela,
Spain 18 A1
Santiago de Cuba, *Cuba* ... 86 C4
Santiago de los Caballeros,
Dom. Rep. 87 C5
Santiago del Estero,
Argentina 94 B4
Santo Amaro, *Brazil* 93 E6
Santo Ângelo, *Brazil* 94 B6
Santo Antônio do Leverger,
Brazil 93 F2
Santo Domingo, *Dom. Rep.* . 87 C6
Santo Tomás, *Peru* 91 F4
Santo Tomé, *Argentina* 94 B5
Santo Tomé de Guayana =
Ciudad Guayana, *Venezuela* 90 B6
Santoña, *Spain* 18 A4
Santorini, *Greece* 23 F5
Santos, *Brazil* 94 A7

São Bernardo do Campo,
Brazil 93 G4
São Borja, *Brazil* 94 B5
São Carlos, *Brazil* 94 A7
São Cristóvão, *Brazil* 93 E6
São Domingos, *Brazil* 93 E4
São Francisco, *Brazil* 93 F5
São Francisco ➱, *Brazil* 93 E6
São Francisco do Sul, *Brazil* . 94 B7
São Gabriel, *Brazil* 94 C6
São João da Madeira,
Portugal 18 B1
São João del Rei, *Brazil* ... 93 G5
São João do Araguaia, *Brazil* 92 D4
São João do Piauí, *Brazil* .. 92 D5
São José do Rio Prêto, *Brazil* 93 G4
São Leopoldo, *Brazil* 94 B6
São Lourenço, *Brazil* 93 G4
São Lourenço ➱, *Brazil* ... 93 F2
São Luís, *Brazil* 92 C5
São Marcos ➱, *Brazil* 93 F4
São Marcos, B. de, *Brazil* .. 92 C5
São Mateus, *Brazil* 93 F6
São Paulo, *Brazil* 94 A7
São Paulo ☐, *Brazil* 94 A7
São Roque, C. de, *Brazil* ... 92 D6
São Sebastião, I. de, *Brazil* . 94 A7
São Tomé & Príncipe ■,
Africa 51 F4
São Vicente, C. de, *Portugal* . 18 D1
Saône ➱, *France* 13 D6
Saonek, *Indonesia* 37 E4
Saparua, *Indonesia* 37 E3
Sapele, *Nigeria* 53 G7
Saposoa, *Peru* 91 E3
Sapporo, *Japan* 32 B7
Sapulpa, *U.S.A.* 81 B5
Saqqez, *Iran* 46 C6
Sar-e Pol, *Afghan.* 45 B6
Sar-e Pol ☐, *Afghan.* 45 B6
Sar Planina, *Macedonia* ... 22 C3
Sarāb, *Iran* 46 C6
Saragossa = Zaragoza, *Spain* 19 B5
Saraguro, *Ecuador* 90 D3
Sarajevo, *Bos.-H.* 20 C7
Saran, Gunung, *Indonesia* . 39 E4
Sarangani B., *Phil.* 36 C3
Sarangani Is., *Phil.* 36 C3
Sarangarh, *India* 40 G4
Saransk, *Russia* 24 C6
Sarapul, *Russia* 29 D6
Sarasota, *U.S.A.* 83 F6
Saratov, *Russia* 24 C6
Sarāvān, *Iran* 45 E5
Saravane, *Laos* 38 A3
Sarawak ☐, *Malaysia* 39 D4
Saray, *Turkey* 22 D6
Saraykóy, *Turkey* 23 F7
Sarbāz, *Iran* 45 E5
Sarbīsheh, *Iran* 45 C4
Sarda ➱, *India* 40 D3
Sardarshahr, *India* 42 E9
Sardegna ☐, *Italy* 21 D2
Sardinia = Sardegna ☐, *Italy* . 21 D2
Sardis, *Turkey* 23 E7
Sargodha, *Pakistan* 42 C8
Sarh, *Chad* 55 G2
Sārī, *Iran* 44 B3
Sarıgöl, *Turkey* 23 E7
Sarikamiş, *Turkey* 46 B5
Sarikei, *Malaysia* 39 D4
Sark, *U.K.* 11 G5
Şarköy, *Turkey* 23 D6
Sarlat-la-Canéda, *France* ... 12 D4
Sarmi, *Indonesia* 37 E5
Sarmiento, *Argentina* 95 F3
Sarnia, *Canada* 71 E5
Sarolangun, *Indonesia* 39 E2
Saronikos Kolpos, *Greece* .. 23 F4
Sarre = Saar ➱, *Europe* 13 B7
Sarreguemines, *France* 13 B7
Sarthe ➱, *France* 12 C3
Sarvestān, *Iran* 44 D3
Sary-Tash, *Kyrgyzstan* 29 F8
Saryshaghan, *Kazakhstan* .. 29 E8
Sasaram, *India* 40 E5
Sasebo, *Japan* 33 G1

Saser, *India* 42 B10
Saskatchewan ☐, *Canada* ... 69 C9
Saskatchewan ➱, *Canada* .. 69 C9
Saskatoon, *Canada* 69 C9
Saskylakh, *Russia* 30 B9
Sasovo, *Russia* 24 C5
Sassandra, *Ivory C.* 53 H4
Sassandra ➱, *Ivory C.* 53 H4
Sássari, *Italy* 21 D2
Sassnitz, *Germany* 15 A7
Sassuolo, *Italy* 20 B3
Sasyk, Ozero, *Ukraine* 17 F9
Sata-Misaki, *Japan* 33 H2
Satadougou, *Mali* 53 F3
Satara, *India* 43 L8
Satmala Hills, *India* 43 J9
Satna, *India* 40 E3
Sátoraljaújhely, *Hungary* ... 16 D5
Satpura Ra., *India* 43 J10
Satu Mare, *Romania* 17 E6
Satui, *Indonesia* 39 E5
Saturnina ➱, *Brazil* 91 F7
Sauðarkrókur, *Iceland* 8 B2
Saudi Arabia ■, *Asia* 47 F6
Sauerland, *Germany* 14 C4
Sault Ste. Marie, *Canada* ... 71 E5
Sault Ste. Marie, *U.S.A.* 76 A3
Saumlaki, *Indonesia* 37 F4
Saumur, *France* 12 C3
Saunders, C., *N.Z.* 65 F4
Saurimo, *Angola* 56 F4
Sava ➱, *Serbia & M.* 22 B3
Savage I. = Niue, *Cook Is.* .. 65 L14
Savalou, *Benin* 53 G6
Savannah, *U.S.A.* 83 C7
Savannah ➱, *U.S.A.* 83 C7
Savannakhet, *Laos* 38 A2
Save ➱, *Mozam.* 59 C6
Sāveh, *Iran* 46 D7
Savelugu, *Ghana* 53 G5
Savoie ☐, *France* 13 D7
Savona, *Italy* 13 D8
Savonlinna, *Finland* 8 C11
Savoy = Savoie ☐, *France* .. 13 D7
Sawahlunto, *Indonesia* 39 E2
Sawai, *Indonesia* 37 E3
Sawai Madhopur, *India* 42 F10
Sawatch Range, *U.S.A.* 79 A9
Sawu, *Indonesia* 37 F2
Sawu Sea, *Indonesia* 37 F2
Saxony = Sachsen ☐,
Germany 15 C7
Saxony, Lower =
Niedersachsen ☐, *Germany* 14 B5
Sayán, *Peru* 91 F3
Sayan, Zapadnyy, *Russia* .. 30 D7
Saydā, *Lebanon* 46 D3
Sayghān, *Afghan.* 45 C6
Sayhūt, *Yemen* 49 D5
Saylac = Zeila, *Somali Rep.* . 49 E3
Saynshand = Buyant-Uhaa,
Mongolia 35 B6
Sazanit, *Albania* 23 D2
Sázava ➱, *Czech Rep.* 16 D2
Sazin, *Pakistan* 42 B8
Scandicci, *Italy* 20 C3
Scandinavia, *Europe* 8 C8
Scarborough, *U.K.* 11 D6
Scebeli, Wabi ➱, *Somali Rep.* 49 G3
Schaffhausen, *Switz.* 13 C8
Schefferville =
Kawawachikamach, *Canada* 71 D7
Schelde ➱, *Belgium* 14 C3
Schenectady, *U.S.A.* 77 C9
Schiermonnikoog, *Neths.* ... 14 B4
Schio, *Italy* 20 B3
Schleswig, *Germany* 14 A5
Schleswig-Holstein ☐,
Germany 14 A5
Schouten I., *Australia* 62 D4
Schouten Is. = Supiori,
Indonesia 37 E5
Schwäbische Alb, *Germany* . 14 D5
Schwaner, Pegunungan,
Indonesia 39 E4
Schwarzwald, *Germany* ... 14 D5
Schwedt, *Germany* 15 B8

Schweinfurt, *Germany* 14 C6
Schweiz = Switzerland ■,
  Europe 13 C8
Schwenningen = Villingen-
  Schwenningen, *Germany* . 14 D5
Schwerin, *Germany* 15 B6
Schwyz, *Switz.* 13 C8
Sciacca, *Italy* 21 F4
Scilla, *Italy* 21 E5
Scilly, Isles of, *U.K.* 11 G3
Scone, *Australia* 63 B5
Scotland □, *U.K.* 10 C4
Scott Glacier, *Antarctica* ... 96 A12
Scottsbluff, *U.S.A.* 74 E3
Scottsdale, *Australia* 62 D4
Scranton, *U.S.A.* 77 D8
Scunthorpe, *U.K.* 11 E6
Scutari = Shkodër, *Albania* .. 22 C2
Seaspray, *Australia* 63 C4
Seattle, *U.S.A.* 72 C2
Sebastopol = Sevastopol,
  Ukraine 25 E3
Sebha = Sabhā, *Libya* 54 C1
Şebinkarahisar, *Turkey* 46 B4
Sebta = Ceuta, *N. Afr.* 18 E3
Sebuku, *Indonesia* 39 E5
Sebuku, Teluk, *Malaysia* ... 39 D5
Secretary I., *N.Z.* 65 F2
Secunderabad, *India* 43 L11
Sedalia, *U.S.A.* 75 F8
Sedan, *France* 13 B6
Seddon, *N.Z.* 65 D6
Seddonville, *N.Z.* 65 D5
Sédhiou, *Senegal* 53 F2
Sedova, Pik, *Russia* 28 B6
Seferihisar, *Turkey* 23 E6
Segamat, *Malaysia* 39 D2
Segesta, *Italy* 21 F4
Seget, *Indonesia* 37 E4
Ségou, *Mali* 53 F4
Segovia = Coco ➤,
  Cent. Amer. 86 D3
Segovia, *Spain* 18 B3
Segre ➤, *Spain* 19 B6
Séguéla, *Ivory C.* 53 G4
Segura ➤, *Spain* 19 C5
Sehore, *India* 43 H10
Seinäjoki ➤, *Finland* 8 C10
Seine ➤, *France* 12 B4
Seistan = Sīstān, *Asia* 45 D5
Sekayu, *Indonesia* 39 E2
Sekondi-Takoradi, *Ghana* ... 53 H5
Selaru, *Indonesia* 37 F4
Selçuk, *Turkey* 23 F6
Sele ➤, *Italy* 21 D5
Selebi-Pikwe, *Botswana* ... 59 C5
Selenga = Selenge Mörön ➤,
  Asia 35 A5
Selenge Mörön ➤, *Asia* ... 35 A5
Seletan, Tanjung, *Indonesia* . 39 E4
Sélibabi, *Mauritania* 53 E3
Selīma, El Wâhât el, *Sudan* . 54 D4
Selkirk, *Canada* 69 C10
Selkirk Mts., *Canada* 69 C8
Selma, *U.S.A.* 83 B8
Selpele, *Indonesia* 37 E4
Selu, *Indonesia* 37 F4
Selva, *Argentina* 94 B4
Selvas, *Brazil* 91 E5
Seman ➤, *Albania* 23 D2
Semarang, *Indonesia* 39 F4
Semey, *Kazakhstan* 29 D9
Semipalatinsk = Semey,
  Kazakhstan 29 D9
Semirara Is., *Phil.* 36 B2
Semitau, *Indonesia* 39 D4
Semiyarka, *Kazakhstan* 29 D8
Semmering P., *Austria* 15 E8
Semnān, *Iran* 44 C3
Semnān □, *Iran* 44 C3
Semporna, *Malaysia* 36 D1
Semuda, *Indonesia* 39 E4
Sena Madureira, *Brazil* 91 E5
Senador Pompeu, *Brazil* ... 92 D6
Senanga, *Zambia* 58 B4
Sendai, *Kagoshima, Japan* . 33 H2
Sendai, *Miyagi, Japan* 32 D7

Sendai-Wan, *Japan* 32 D7
Senegal ■, *W. Afr.* 53 F3
Sénégal ➤, *W. Afr.* 53 E2
Senge Khambab = Indus ➤,
  Pakistan 43 G5
Senhor-do-Bonfim, *Brazil* ... 93 E5
Senigállia, *Italy* 20 C4
Senj, *Croatia* 20 B5
Senja, *Norway* 8 B9
Senlis, *France* 13 B5
Senmonorom, *Cambodia* ... 38 B3
Sens, *France* 13 B5
Senta, *Serbia & M.* 22 B3
Sentani, *Indonesia* 37 E6
Seo de Urgel = La Seu
  d'Urgell, *Spain* 19 A6
Seoul, *S. Korea* 35 C7
Sept-Îles, *Canada* 71 D7
Sequoia △, *U.S.A.* 78 B3
Seram, *Indonesia* 37 E3
Seram Sea, *Indonesia* 37 E3
Serasan, *Indonesia* 39 D3
Serbia □, *Serbia & M.* 22 C3
Serbia & Montenegro ■,
  Europe 22 B3
Serdar, *Turkmenistan* 29 F6
Serdobsk, *Russia* 24 C5
Seremban, *Malaysia* 39 D2
Sereth = Siret ➤, *Romania* . 17 F9
Sergipe □, *Brazil* 93 E6
Sergiyev Posad, *Russia* 24 B4
Seria, *Brunei* 38 D4
Serian, *Malaysia* 39 D4
Seribu, Kepulauan, *Indonesia* 39 F3
Serifos, *Greece* 23 F5
Sermata, *Indonesia* 37 F3
Serov, *Russia* 28 D7
Serowe, *Botswana* 59 C5
Serpukhov, *Russia* 24 C4
Serres, *Greece* 22 D4
Serrinha, *Brazil* 93 E6
Serua, *Indonesia* 37 F4
Serui, *Indonesia* 37 E5
Sesepe, *Indonesia* 37 E3
Setana, *Japan* 32 B6
Sète, *France* 13 E5
Sete Lagôas, *Brazil* 93 F5
Sétif, *Algeria* 52 A7
Settat, *Morocco* 52 B4
Setúbal, *Portugal* 18 C1
Setúbal, B. de, *Portugal* 18 C1
Sevana Lich, *Armenia* 25 E6
Sevastopol, *Ukraine* 25 E3
Severn ➤, *Canada* 71 D5
Severn ➤, *U.K.* 11 F5
Severnaya Zemlya, *Russia* .. 30 B7
Severnyye Uvaly, *Russia* ... 24 B6
Severo-Yeniseyskiy, *Russia* . 30 C7
Severodvinsk, *Russia* 28 C4
Sevilla, *Spain* 18 D2
Sevlievo, *Bulgaria* 22 C5
Seward, *U.S.A.* 69 B5
Seward Peninsula, *U.S.A.* .. 69 B3
Sewer, *Indonesia* 37 F4
Seychelles ■, *Ind. Oc.* 26 J7
Seyðisfjörður, *Iceland* 8 B3
Seymour, *Australia* 63 C4
Sfântu Gheorghe, *Romania* . 17 F7
Sfax, *Tunisia* 54 B1
Shaanxi □, *China* 35 C5
Shaba = Katanga □,
  Dem. Rep. of the Congo . 57 F4
Shaballe = Scebeli, Wabi ➤,
  Somali Rep. 49 G3
Shache, *China* 34 C2
Shackleton Ice Shelf,
  Antarctica 96 A11
Shackleton Inlet, *Antarctica* . 96 C15
Shadrinsk, *Russia* 29 D7
Shahdād, *Iran* 44 D4
Shahdād, Namakzār-e, *Iran* . 44 D4
Shahdadkot, *Pakistan* 42 F2
Shahgarh, *India* 42 F6
Shahjahanpur, *India* 42 F11
Shahrig, *Pakistan* 42 D5
Shajapur, *India* 43 H10
Shakhty, *Russia* 25 D5

Shakhunya, *Russia* 24 B6
Shaki, *Nigeria* 53 G6
Shalqar, *Kazakhstan* 29 E6
Shām, Bādiyat ash, *Asia* ... 47 D4
Shām, J. ash, *Oman* 44 F4
Shamīl, *Iran* 44 E4
Shammar, Jabal, *Si. Arabia* . 47 F5
Shamo = Gobi, *Asia* 35 B6
Shamo, L., *Ethiopia* 55 G6
Shan □, *Burma* 41 G12
Shandong □, *China* 35 C6
Shangani ➤, *Zimbabwe* ... 59 B5
Shanghai, *China* 35 C7
Shangqiu, *China* 35 C6
Shangrao, *China* 35 D6
Shangshui, *China* 35 C6
Shannon, *N.Z.* 64 D6
Shannon ➤, *Ireland* 11 E2
Shansi = Shanxi □, *China* ... 35 C6
Shantou, *China* 35 D6
Shantung = Shandong □,
  China 35 C6
Shanxi □, *China* 35 C6
Shaoguan, *China* 35 D6
Shaoxing, *China* 35 C7
Shaoyang, *China* 35 D6
Shaqra', *Si. Arabia* 47 F6
Shaqrā', *Yemen* 49 E4
Shari, *Japan* 32 B9
Sharjah = Ash Shāriqah,
  U.A.E. 44 E3
Sharon, *U.S.A.* 76 D5
Sharya, *Russia* 24 B6
Shashi, *China* 35 C6
Shasta, Mt., *U.S.A.* 72 F2
Shatt al Arab, *Asia* 47 E7
Shawinigan, *Canada* 71 E6
Shaykh, J. ash, *Lebanon* 46 D3
Shchūchīnsk, *Kazakhstan* ... 29 D8
Shebele = Scebeli, Wabi ➤,
  Somali Rep. 49 G3
Sheboygan, *U.S.A.* 76 C2
Sheffield, *U.K.* 11 E6
Shekhupura, *Pakistan* 42 D8
Shelby, *U.S.A.* 83 B7
Shelbyville, *U.S.A.* 82 B4
Shellharbour, *Australia* 63 B5
Shenandoah ➤, *U.S.A.* 77 E7
Shendam, *Nigeria* 53 G7
Shendi, *Sudan* 55 E5
Shensi = Shaanxi □, *China* . 35 C5
Shenyang, *China* 35 B7
Sheopur Kalan, *India* 42 G10
Shepetivka, *Ukraine* 17 C8
Shepparton, *Australia* 63 C4
Sherbro I., *S. Leone* 53 G3
Sherbrooke, *Canada* 71 E6
Sheridan, *U.S.A.* 73 D10
Sherman, *U.S.A.* 81 C5
Shetland Is., *U.K.* 10 A6
Shibām, *Yemen* 49 D4
Shibata, *Japan* 33 E6
Shibecha, *Japan* 32 B9
Shibetsu, *Japan* 32 A8
Shīeli, *Kazakhstan* 29 E7
Shijiazhuang, *China* 35 C6
Shikarpur, *Pakistan* 42 F6
Shikoku □, *Japan* 33 G3
Shikotsu-Ko, *Japan* 32 B7
Shiliguri, *India* 40 D7
Shillong, *India* 41 E8
Shimla, *India* 42 D10
Shimoga, *India* 43 N9
Shimonoseki, *Japan* 33 G2
Shindand, *Afghan.* 42 C3
Shingū, *Japan* 33 G4
Shinyanga, *Tanzania* 57 E6
Shio-no-Misaki, *Japan* 33 G4
Shipchenski Prokhod,
  Bulgaria 22 C5
Shiquan He = Indus ➤,
  Pakistan 43 G5
Shīr Kūh, *Iran* 44 D3
Shiragami-Misaki, *Japan* ... 32 C7
Shīrāz, *Iran* 44 D3
Shire ➤, *Africa* 59 B7
Shiriya-Zaki, *Japan* 32 C7

Shirvān, Iran 44 B4
Shirwa, L. = Chilwa, L.,
Malawi 59 B7
Shivpuri, India 43 G10
Shizuoka, Japan 33 F6
Shklow, Belarus 17 A10
Shkodër, Albania 22 C2
Shkumbini ➤, Albania 23 D2
Shmidta, Ostrov, Russia ... 30 A7
Sholapur = Solapur, India ... 43 L9
Shoshone Mts., U.S.A. 72 G5
Shqipëria = Albania ■, Europe 23 D3
Shreveport, U.S.A. 81 C7
Shrewsbury, U.K. 11 E5
Shrirampur, India 40 F7
Shū, Kazakhstan 29 E8
Shuangyashan, China 35 B8
Shule, China 34 C2
Shumagin Is., U.S.A. 69 C4
Shumen, Bulgaria 22 C6
Shūr ➤, Iran 44 D3
Shurugwi, Zimbabwe 59 B6
Shūsf, Iran 45 D5
Shūshtar, Iran 47 D7
Shwebo, Burma 41 F10
Shwegu, Burma 41 E11
Shweli ➤, Burma 41 F11
Shymkent, Kazakhstan 29 E7
Shyok, India 42 B11
Shyok ➤, Pakistan 42 B9
Si Kiang = Xi Jiang ➤, China 35 D6
Si-ngan = Xi'an, China 35 C5
Siahan Range, Pakistan 42 F4
Siaksriindrapura, Indonesia . 39 D2
Sialkot, Pakistan 42 C9
Siam = Thailand ■, Asia .. 38 A2
Sian = Xi'an, China 35 C5
Siantan, Indonesia 39 D3
Siargao I., Phil. 36 C3
Siasi, Phil. 36 C2
Siau, Indonesia 37 D3
Šiauliai, Lithuania 24 B1
Šibenik, Croatia 20 C5
Siberia, Russia 30 C8
Siberut, Indonesia 39 E1
Sibi, Pakistan 42 E5
Sibil = Oksibil, Indonesia ... 37 E6
Sibirtsevo, Russia 32 A3
Sibiti, Congo 56 E2
Sibiu, Romania 17 F7
Sibolga, Indonesia 39 D1
Sibsagar, India 41 D10
Sibu, Malaysia 39 D4
Sibuco, Phil. 36 C2
Sibuguey B., Phil. 36 C2
Sibut, C.A.R. 55 G2
Sibutu, Phil. 36 D1
Sibutu Passage, E. Indies ... 36 D1
Sibuyan I., Phil. 36 B2
Sibuyan Sea, Phil. 36 B2
Sichuan □, China 34 C5
Sicilia, Italy 21 F5
Sicily = Sicilia, Italy 21 F5
Sicuani, Peru 91 F4
Siddipet, India 43 K11
Sidi-bel-Abbès, Algeria 52 A5
Sidi Ifni, Morocco 52 C3
Sidley, Mt., Antarctica 96 B18
Sidon = Saydā, Lebanon .. 46 D3
Sidra, G. of = Surt, Khalīj,
Libya 54 B2
Siedlce, Poland 17 B6
Sieg ➤, Germany 14 C4
Siegen, Germany 14 C5
Siemreab, Cambodia 38 B2
Siena, Italy 20 C3
Sieradz, Poland 16 C4
Sierra Colorada, Argentina . 95 E3
Sierra Gorda, Chile 94 A3
Sierra Leone ■, W. Afr. 53 G3
Sierra Madre Occidental,
Mexico 84 B3
Sierra Nevada, Spain 18 D4
Sierra Nevada, U.S.A. 72 G3
Sifnos, Greece 23 F5
Sighetu-Marmației, Romania 17 E6
Sigli, Indonesia 38 C1

Siglufjörður, Iceland 8 B2
Sigsig, Ecuador 90 D3
Sigüenza, Spain 19 B4
Siguiri, Guinea 53 F4
Sikar, India 42 F9
Sikasso, Mali 53 F4
Sikhote Alin, Khrebet, Russia 32 A5
Sikinos, Greece 23 F5
Sikkim □, India 40 D7
Sil ➤, Spain 18 A2
Silchar, India 41 E9
Silesia = Śląsk, Poland 16 C3
Silgarhi Doti, Nepal 40 C3
Silghat, India 41 D9
Silifke, Turkey 46 C3
Siliguri = Shiliguri, India 40 D7
Siling Co, China 34 C3
Silistra, Bulgaria 22 B6
Silivri, Turkey 22 D7
Sillajhuay, Cordillera, Chile . 91 G5
Simanggang = Sri Aman,
Malaysia 39 D4
Simav, Turkey 23 E7
Simbirsk, Russia 24 C6
Simeria, Romania 17 F6
Simeulue, Indonesia 39 D1
Simferopol, Ukraine 25 E3
Simi, Greece 23 F6
Simikot, Nepal 40 C3
Simla = Shimla, India 42 D10
Simpson Desert, Australia .. 60 F6
Simpson Pen., Canada 70 C5
Sinabang, Indonesia 39 D1
Sinadogo, Somali Rep. 49 F4
Sinai = Es Sînâ', Egypt 54 C5
Sinai, Mt. = Mûsa, Gebel,
Egypt 47 E3
Sincelejo, Colombia 90 B3
Sincorá, Serra do, Brazil ... 93 E5
Sind = Sindh □, Pakistan .. 42 F6
Sind Sagar Doab, Pakistan . 42 D7
Sindangan, Phil. 36 C2
Sindh □, Pakistan 42 F6
Sines, Portugal 18 D1
Sines, C. de, Portugal 18 D1
Singa, Sudan 55 F5
Singapore ■, Asia 39 D2
Singaraja, Indonesia 39 F5
Singida, Tanzania 57 E6
Singkaling Hkamti, Burma .. 41 E10
Singkang, Indonesia 37 E2
Singkawang, Indonesia 39 D3
Singleton, Australia 63 B5
Singora = Songkhla, Thailand 38 C2
Sinjai, Indonesia 37 F2
Sinjār, Iraq 46 C5
Sinkat, Sudan 55 E6
Sinkiang = Xinjiang Uygur
Zizhiqu □, China 34 B3
Sinni ➤, Italy 21 D6
Sinop, Turkey 25 E4
Sintang, Indonesia 39 D4
Sintra, Portugal 18 C1
Siocon, Phil. 36 C2
Siófok, Hungary 16 E4
Sioux City, U.S.A. 75 D6
Sioux Falls, U.S.A. 74 D6
Sioux Lookout, Canada 69 C10
Siping, China 35 B7
Sipura, Indonesia 39 E1
Siquijor, Phil. 36 C2
Siracusa, Italy 21 F5
Sirajganj, Bangla. 41 E7
Siret ➤, Romania 17 F9
Sīrjān, Iran 44 D3
Sirohi, India 43 G8
Sironj, India 43 G10
Síros = Syros, Greece 23 F5
Sirsa, India 42 E9
Sisak, Croatia 20 B6
Sisaket, Thailand 38 A2
Sisophon, Cambodia 38 B2
Sistān, Asia 45 D5
Sīstān, Daryācheh-ye, Iran .. 45 D5
Sīstān va Balūchestān □, Iran 45 E5
Sitapur, India 40 D3
Sitges, Spain 19 B6

Sitia, Greece 23 G6
Sitka, U.S.A. 69 C6
Sittang Myit ➤, Burma 41 J11
Sittoung = Sittang Myit ➤,
Burma 41 J11
Sittwe, Burma 41 G9
Siuri, India 40 F6
Sivas, Turkey 25 F4
Siverek, Turkey 46 C4
Sivrihisar, Turkey 25 F3
Sîwa, Egypt 54 C4
Siwalik Range, Nepal 40 D4
Siwan, India 40 D5
Sjælland, Denmark 9 D8
Sjumen = Shumen, Bulgaria . 22 C6
Skadarsko Jezero,
Serbia & M. 22 C2
Skagen, Denmark 9 D8
Skagerrak, Denmark 9 D7
Skagway, U.S.A. 69 C6
Skala-Podilska, Ukraine 17 D8
Skalat, Ukraine 17 D7
Skardu, Pakistan 42 B9
Skarżysko-Kamienna, Poland 16 C5
Skeena ➤, Canada 68 C6
Skegness, U.K. 11 E7
Skeldon, Guyana 90 B7
Skeleton Coast, Namibia ... 58 C2
Skellefteå, Sweden 8 C10
Skellefteälven ➤, Sweden .. 8 C10
Skiathos, Greece 23 E4
Skien, Norway 9 D7
Skierniewice, Poland 16 C5
Skikda, Algeria 52 A7
Skiros, Greece 23 E5
Skole, Ukraine 17 D6
Skopelos, Greece 23 E4
Skopje, Macedonia 22 C3
Skvyra, Ukraine 17 D9
Skye, U.K. 10 C3
Skyros = Skiros, Greece 23 E5
Śląsk, Poland 16 C3
Slatina, Romania 22 B5
Slave ➤, Canada 68 B8
Slavgorod, Russia 29 D8
Slavonski Brod, Croatia 20 B7
Slavuta, Ukraine 17 C8
Slavyanka, Russia 32 B2
Slavyansk = Slovyansk,
Ukraine 25 D4
Slawharad, Belarus 17 B10
Sleaford B., Australia 62 B2
Sleeper Is., Canada 70 D5
Sligeach = Sligo, Ireland 11 D2
Sligo, Ireland 11 D2
Sliven, Bulgaria 22 C6
Slobodskoy, Russia 24 B7
Slobozia, Romania 22 B6
Slonim, Belarus 17 B7
Slough, U.K. 11 F6
Slovak Rep. ■, Europe 16 D4
Slovakian Ore Mts. =
Slovenské Rudohorie,
Slovak Rep. 16 D4
Slovenia ■, Europe 20 B5
Slovenska = Slovak Rep. ■,
Europe 16 D4
Slovenské Rudohorie,
Slovak Rep. 16 D4
Slovyansk, Ukraine 25 D4
Sluch ➤, Ukraine 17 C8
Słupsk, Poland 16 A3
Slutsk, Belarus 17 B8
Smallwood Res., Canada ... 71 D7
Smarhon, Belarus 17 A8
Smederevo, Serbia & M. ... 22 B3
Smithton, Australia 62 D4
Smoky Bay, Australia 62 B1
Smolensk, Russia 24 C3
Smolikas, Oros, Greece 23 D3
Smolyan, Bulgaria 23 D5
Smorgon = Smarhon, Belarus 17 A8
Smyrna = İzmir, Turkey 23 E6
Snake ➤, U.S.A. 72 C4
Snake I., Australia 63 C4
Snake River Plain, U.S.A. ... 73 E7
Sneek, Neths. 14 B3

Sněžka

Sněžka, Europe 16 C2
Snøhetta, Norway 8 C7
Snowdon, U.K. 11 E4
Snowdrift = Łutselk'e, Canada 68 B8
Snowtown, Australia 62 B2
Snowy ➤, Australia 63 C4
Snowy Mts., Australia 63 C4
Snyatyn, Ukraine 17 D7
Snyder, U.S.A. 80 C3
Sobat, Nahr ➤, Sudan ... 55 G5
Sobral, Brazil 92 C5
Soc Trang, Vietnam 38 C3
Soch'e = Shache, China 34 C2
Sochi, Russia 25 E4
Société, Îs. de la, French
  Polynesia 65 L15
Society Is. = Société, Îs. de la,
  French Polynesia 65 L15
Socompa, Portezuelo de,
  Chile 94 A3
Socotra, Yemen 49 E5
Söderhamn, Sweden 8 C9
Sodiri, Sudan 55 F4
Sofia = Sofiya, Bulgaria ... 22 C4
Sofia ➤, Madag. 59 B9
Sofiya, Bulgaria 22 C4
Sogamoso, Colombia 90 B4
Sognefjorden, Norway 8 C7
Sohâg, Egypt 54 C5
Soissons, France 13 B5
Sokal, Ukraine 17 C7
Söke, Turkey 23 F6
Sokhumi, Georgia 25 E5
Sokodé, Togo 53 G6
Sokol, Russia 24 B5
Sokółka, Poland 17 B6
Sokołów Podlaski, Poland ... 17 B6
Sokoto, Nigeria 53 F7
Solander I., N.Z. 65 G2
Solano, Phil. 36 A2
Solapur, India 43 L9
Soledad, Venezuela 90 B6
Soligalich, Russia 24 B5
Soligorsk = Salihorsk, Belarus 17 B8
Solikamsk, Russia 28 D6
Solimões = Amazonas ➤,
  S. Amer. 92 C3
Solingen, Germany 14 C4
Sóller, Spain 19 C7
Sologne, France 12 C4
Solok, Indonesia 39 E2
Solomon Is. ■, Pac. Oc. ... 64 K10
Solomon Sea, Papua N. G. . 61 B9
Solon, China 35 B7
Solor, Indonesia 37 F2
Šolta, Croatia 20 C6
Solţānābād, Iran 44 B4
Solunska Glava, Macedonia . 22 D3
Solwezi, Zambia 59 A5
Sōma, Japan 32 E7
Soma, Turkey 23 E6
Somali Rep. ■, Africa 49 F4
Sombor, Serbia & M. 22 B2
Sombrerete, Mexico 84 C4
Somerset I., Canada 68 A10
Someş ➤, Romania 17 E6
Somme ➤, France 12 A4
Somosierra, Puerto de, Spain 18 B4
Somport, Puerto de, Spain . . 12 E3
Sóndrio, Italy 13 C8
Sonepur, India 40 G4
Song Cau, Vietnam 38 B3
Songea, Tanzania 57 G7
Songhua Jiang ➤, China .. 35 B8
Songkhla, Thailand 38 C2
Songo, Mozam. 59 B6
Songpan, China 34 C5
Sonipat, India 42 E10
Sonmiani, Pakistan 42 G5
Sono ➤, Brazil 93 D4
Sonora ➤, Mexico 84 B2
Sonsonate, El Salv. 85 E7
Soochow = Suzhou, China . 35 C7
Soomaaliya = Somali Rep. ■,
  Africa 49 F4
Sopi, Indonesia 37 D3
Sopot, Poland 16 A4

Sopron, Hungary 16 E3
Sør-Rondane, Antarctica 96 B8
Sórgono, Italy 21 D2
Soria, Spain 19 B4
Sorkh, Kuh-e, Iran 44 C4
Soroca, Moldova 17 D9
Sorocaba, Brazil 94 A7
Soroki = Soroca, Moldova .. 17 D9
Sorong, Indonesia 37 E4
Soroti, Uganda 57 D6
Sørøya, Norway 8 A10
Sorsogon, Phil. 36 B2
Sosnowiec, Poland 16 C4
Souanké, Congo 56 D2
Soudas, Ormos, Greece 23 G5
Sŏul = Seoul, S. Korea 35 C7
Sources, Mt. aux, Lesotho .. 59 D5
Soure, Brazil 92 C4
Souris ➤, Canada 69 D10
Sousa, Brazil 92 D6
Sousse, Tunisia 54 A1
South Africa ■, Africa 58 E4
South Australia □, Australia . 62 B2
South Bend, U.S.A. 76 D2
South Carolina □, U.S.A. .. 83 C7
South China Sea, Asia 38 C4
South Dakota □, U.S.A. 74 C4
South East C., Australia ... 62 D4
South Horr, Kenya 57 D7
South I., N.Z. 65 E3
South Invercargill, N.Z. 65 G3
South Korea ■, Asia 35 C7
South Magnetic Pole,
  Antarctica 96 A13
South Nahanni ➤, Canada .. 68 B7
South Orkney Is., Antarctica . 96 A4
South Platte ➤, U.S.A. 74 E4
South Pole, Antarctica ..... 96 C
South Ronaldsay, U.K. 10 B5
South Saskatchewan ➤,
  Canada 69 C9
South Shetland Is., Antarctica 96 A4
South Shields, U.K. 11 D6
South Taranaki Bight, N.Z. .. 64 C6
South Uist, U.K. 10 C3
South West C., Australia ... 62 D4
South West C., N.Z. 65 G2
Southampton, U.K. 11 F6
Southampton I., Canada ... 70 C5
Southbridge, N.Z. 65 E5
Southend-on-Sea, U.K. 11 F7
Southern Alps, N.Z. 65 E4
Southern Indian L., Canada . 69 C10
Southern Ocean, Antarctica . 96 A9
Southern Uplands, U.K. 10 D5
Southland □, N.Z. 65 F3
Southport, Australia 63 A5
Sovetsk, Kaliningrad, Russia 24 B1
Sovetsk, Kirov, Russia 24 B6
Soweto, S. Africa 59 D5
Sozh ➤, Belarus 17 C10
Spain ■, Europe 18 C4
Spalding, Australia 62 B2
Spanish Town, Jamaica 86 C4
Sparta = Sparti, Greece 23 F4
Spartanburg, U.S.A. 83 B7
Sparti, Greece 23 F4
Spartivento, C., Calabria, Italy 21 F6
Spartivento, C., Sard., Italy . 21 E2
Spassk Dalniy, Russia 32 A3
Spatha, Akra, Greece 23 G4
Spence Bay = Taloyoak,
  Canada 68 B10
Spencer, C., Australia 62 C2
Spencer G., Australia 62 B2
Spenser Mts., N.Z. 65 E5
Spey ➤, U.K. 10 C5
Speyer, Germany 14 D5
Split, Croatia 20 C6
Spokane, U.S.A. 72 C5
Spoleto, Italy 20 C4
Sporyy Navolok, Mys, Russia 28 B7
Spratly Is., S. China Sea ... 38 C4
Spree ➤, Germany 15 B7
Springfield, N.Z. 65 E4
Springfield, Ill., U.S.A. 75 F10
Springfield, Mass., U.S.A. ... 77 C9

Springfield, Mo., U.S.A. 81 A7
Springfield, Ohio, U.S.A. ... 76 E4
Springfield, Oreg., U.S.A. .. 72 D2
Springs, S. Africa 59 D5
Srbija = Serbia □, Serbia & M. 22 C3
Sre Ambel, Cambodia 38 B2
Srebrenica, Bos.-H. 20 B7
Sredinnyy Khrebet, Russia .. 31 D14
Śrem, Poland 16 B3
Sremska Mitrovica,
  Serbia & M. 22 B2
Sri Aman, Malaysia 39 D4
Sri Lanka ■, Asia 43 R12
Srikakulam, India 40 H4
Srinagar, India 42 B9
Stade, Germany 14 B5
Stafford, U.K. 11 E5
Stakhanov, Ukraine 25 D4
Stalowa Wola, Poland 17 C6
Stamford, U.S.A. 77 D9
Stamford, U.K. 11 E7
Stanke Dimitrov, Bulgaria .. 22 C4
Stanley, Australia 62 D4
Stanley, Falk. Is. 95 G5
Stanovoy Khrebet, Russia .. 31 D10
Stanthorpe, Australia 63 A5
Stara Planina, Bulgaria 22 C4
Stara Zagora, Bulgaria 22 C5
Starachowice, Poland 16 C5
Staraya Russa, Russia 24 B3
Starbuck I., Kiribati 65 K15
Stargard Szczeciński, Poland 16 B2
Staritsa, Russia 24 B3
Starogard Gdański, Poland . . 16 B4
Starokonstyantyniv, Ukraine 17 D8
Staryy Chartoriysk, Ukraine . 17 C7
Staryy Oskol, Russia 24 C4
State College, U.S.A. 77 D7
Staten, I. = Estados, I. de Los,
  Argentina 95 G4
Statesville, U.S.A. 83 B7
Stavanger, Norway 9 D7
Staveley, N.Z. 65 E4
Stavropol, Russia 25 D5
Stawell, Australia 62 C3
Stefanie L. = Chew Bahir,
  Ethiopia 55 H6
Stefansson Bay, Antarctica . 96 A9
Steiermark □, Austria 15 E8
Steinkjer, Norway 8 C8
Stendal, Germany 15 B6
Steornabhaigh = Stornoway,
  U.K. 10 B3
Stepanakert = Xankändi,
  Azerbaijan 25 F6
Stephens Creek, Australia .. 62 B3
Stephenville, Canada 71 E8
Sterlitamak, Russia 29 D6
Stettin = Szczecin, Poland .. 16 B2
Stettiner Haff, Germany 15 B8
Stettler, Canada 69 C8
Steubenville, U.S.A. 76 D5
Stevenage, U.K. 11 F6
Stevenson ➤, Australia ... 62 A2
Stewart ➤, Canada 88 B6
Stewart, I., Chile 95 G2
Stewart I., N.Z. 65 G2
Steyr, Austria 15 D8
Stillwater, N.Z. 65 E4
Stillwater, U.S.A. 80 A5
Štip, Macedonia 22 D4
Stirling, U.K. 10 C5
Stockerau, Austria 15 D9
Stockholm, Sweden 9 D9
Stockport, U.K. 11 E5
Stockton, U.S.A. 78 B2
Stockton-on-Tees, U.K. 11 D6
Stoeng Treng, Cambodia .. 38 B3
Stoke-on-Trent, U.K. 11 E5
Stokes Pt., Australia 62 D3
Stolac, Bos.-H. 20 C6
Stolbovoy, Ostrov, Russia .. 30 B11
Stolbtsy = Stowbtsy, Belarus 17 B8
Stolin, Belarus 17 C8
Stonehaven, U.K. 10 C5
Stony Tunguska = Tunguska,
  Podkamennaya ➤, Russia 30 C7
Stora Lulevatten, Sweden ... 8 B9

Storavan, *Sweden* 8 B9
Store Bælt, *Denmark* 9 D8
Storm B., *Australia* 62 D4
Stormberge, *S. Africa* 59 E5
Stornoway, *U.K.* 10 B3
Storozhynets, *Ukraine* 17 D7
Storsjön, *Sweden* 8 C8
Storuman, *Sweden* 8 B9
Stowbtsy, *Belarus* 17 B8
Strahan, *Australia* 62 D4
Stralsund, *Germany* 15 A7
Stranraer, *U.K.* 11 D4
Strasbourg, *France* 13 B7
Stratford, *Canada* 76 C5
Stratford, *N.Z.* 64 C6
Strathalbyn, *Australia* 62 C2
Straubing, *Germany* 15 D7
Streaky B., *Australia* 62 B1
Streaky Bay, *Australia* 62 B1
Strelka, *Russia* 30 D7
Strezhevoy, *Russia* 29 C8
Strimonas ➤, *Greece* 23 D4
Strómboli, *Italy* 21 E5
Stronsay, *U.K.* 10 B5
Stroud Road, *Australia* 63 B5
Strumica, *Macedonia* 22 D4
Stryy, *Ukraine* 17 D6
Strzelecki Cr. ➤, *Australia* . 62 A2
Stuart Ra., *Australia* 62 A1
Stung Treng = Stoeng Treng,
Cambodia 38 B3
Stuttgart, *Germany* 14 D5
Styria = Steiermark ☐, *Austria* 15 E8
Suakin, *Sudan* 55 E6
Subansiri ➤, *India* 41 D9
Subi, *Indonesia* 39 D3
Subotica, *Serbia & M.* 16 E4
Suceava, *Romania* 17 E8
Suchou = Suzhou, *China* ... 35 C7
Süchow = Xuzhou, *China* .. 35 C6
Sucre, *Bolivia* 91 G5
Sudan ■, *Africa* 55 E4
Sudbury, *Canada* 71 E5
Sûdd, *Sudan* 55 G4
Sudeten Mts. = Sudety,
Europe 16 C3
Sudety, *Europe* 16 C3
Sudirman, Pegunungan,
Indonesia 37 E5
Sueca, *Spain* 19 C5
Suez = El Suweis, *Egypt* ... 54 C5
Suez, G. of = Suweis, Khalîg
el, *Egypt* 54 C5
Sugluk = Salluit, *Canada* ... 70 C6
Şuḩār, *Oman* 44 E4
Suhl, *Germany* 14 C6
Suihua, *China* 35 B7
Suisse = Switzerland ■,
Europe 13 C8
Sukadana, *Indonesia* 39 E3
Sukagawa, *Japan* 33 F7
Sukaraja, *Indonesia* 39 E4
Sukhona ➤, *Russia* 28 C5
Sukhumi = Sokhumi, *Georgia* 25 E5
Sukkur, *Pakistan* 42 F6
Sukkur Barrage, *Pakistan* .. 42 F6
Sukumo, *Japan* 33 G3
Sula, Kepulauan, *Indonesia* . 37 E3
Sulaiman Range, *Pakistan* .. 42 D6
Sulawesi, *Indonesia* 37 E2
Sulawesi Sea = Celebes Sea,
Indonesia 37 D2
Sulawesi Tengah ☐, *Indonesia* 37 E2
Sulawesi Tenggara ☐,
Indonesia 37 E2
Sulima, *S. Leone* 53 G3
Sulina, *Romania* 17 F9
Sullana, *Peru* 90 D2
Sultanpur, *India* 40 D4
Sulu Arch., *Phil.* 36 C2
Sulu Sea, *E. Indies* 36 C2
Suluq, *Libya* 54 B3
Sulzberger Ice Shelf,
Antarctica 96 B17
Sumalata, *Indonesia* 37 D2
Sumatera, *Indonesia* 39 D2

Sumatra = Sumatera,
Indonesia 39 D2
Sumba, *Indonesia* 37 F1
Sumba, Selat, *Indonesia* ... 37 F1
Sumbawa, *Indonesia* 39 F5
Sumbawa Besar, *Indonesia* . 39 F5
Sumbe, *Angola* 56 G2
Šumen = Shumen, *Bulgaria* . 22 C6
Sumgait = Sumqayıt,
Azerbaijan 25 E6
Summerside, *Canada* 71 E7
Šumperk, *Czech Rep.* 16 D3
Sumqayıt, *Azerbaijan* 25 E6
Sumter, *U.S.A.* 83 C7
Sumy, *Ukraine* 24 C3
Sunbury, *Australia* 63 C3
Sunda, Selat, *Indonesia* ... 39 F3
Sunda Str. = Sunda, Selat,
Indonesia 39 F3
Sundarbans, *Asia* 41 G7
Sundargarh, *India* 40 F5
Sunderland, *U.K.* 11 D6
Sundsvall, *Sweden* 8 C9
Sungaigerong, *Indonesia* .. 39 E2
Sungailiat, *Indonesia* 39 E3
Sungaipenuh, *Indonesia* ... 39 E2
Sungari = Songhua Jiang ➤,
China 35 B8
Sungurlu, *Turkey* 46 B3
Sunnyvale, *U.S.A.* 78 B1
Suntar, *Russia* 30 C9
Suomi = Finland ■, *Europe* . 8 C11
Supaul, *India* 40 D6
Superior, *U.S.A.* 75 B8
Superior, L., *N. Amer.* 71 E5
Suphan Dağı, *Turkey* 46 C5
Supiori, *Indonesia* 37 E5
Suqutra = Socotra, *Yemen* . 49 E5
Sür, *Lebanon* 46 D3
Şūr, *Oman* 45 F4
Sura ➤, *Russia* 24 B6
Surabaya, *Indonesia* 39 F4
Surakarta, *Indonesia* 39 F4
Surat, *Australia* 63 A4
Surat, *India* 43 J8
Surat Thani, *Thailand* 38 C1
Suratgarh, *India* 42 E8
Surgut, *Russia* 29 C8
Suriapet, *India* 43 L11
Surigao, *Phil.* 36 C3
Suriname ■, *S. Amer.* 92 B2
Suriname ➤, *Suriname* 92 A2
Surt, *Libya* 54 B2
Surt, Khalîj, *Libya* 54 B2
Surtsey, *Iceland* 8 C1
Suruga-Wan, *Japan* 33 F6
Süsangerd, *Iran* 47 E7
Susanville, *U.S.A.* 72 F3
Susquehanna ➤, *U.S.A.* ... 77 E7
Susques, *Argentina* 94 A3
Susunu, *Indonesia* 37 E4
Susurluk, *Turkey* 23 E7
Sutherland, *S. Africa* 58 E4
Sutherland Falls, *N.Z.* 65 F2
Sutlej ➤, *Pakistan* 42 E7
Suttsu, *Japan* 32 B7
Suva, *Fiji* 64 L12
Suva Planina, *Serbia & M.* .. 22 C4
Suvorov Is. = Suwarrow Is.,
Cook Is. 65 L14
Suwałki, *Poland* 17 A6
Suwarrow Is., *Cook Is.* 65 L14
Suweis, Khalîg el, *Egypt* ... 54 C5
Suzdal, *Russia* 24 B5
Suzhou, *China* 35 C7
Suzu, *Japan* 33 E5
Suzu-Misaki, *Japan* 33 E5
Svealand ☐, *Sweden* 9 D9
Sverdrup Chan., *Canada* ... 70 B4
Sverdrup Is., *Canada* 70 B4
Sverige = Sweden ■, *Europe* 9 D9
Svetlogorsk = Svyetlahorsk,
Belarus 17 B9
Svishtov, *Bulgaria* 22 C5
Svislach, *Belarus* 17 B7
Svizzera = Switzerland ■,
Europe 13 C8

Svyetlahorsk, *Belarus* 17 B9
Swabian Alps = Schwäbische
Alb, *Germany* 14 D5
Swakopmund, *Namibia* 58 C2
Swan Hill, *Australia* 62 C3
Swansea, *U.K.* 11 F5
Swatow = Shantou, *China* . 35 D6
Swaziland ■, *Africa* 59 D6
Sweden ■, *Europe* 9 D9
Sweetwater, *U.S.A.* 80 C3
Swellendam, *S. Africa* 58 E4
Świdnica, *Poland* 16 C3
Świdnik, *Poland* 17 C6
Świebodzin, *Poland* 16 B2
Świecie, *Poland* 16 B4
Swift Current, *Canada* 69 C9
Swindon, *U.K.* 11 F6
Swinemünde = Świnoujście,
Poland 16 B2
Świnoujście, *Poland* 16 B2
Switzerland ■, *Europe* 13 C8
Sydney, *Australia* 63 B5
Sydney, *Canada* 71 E7
Sydra, G. of = Surt, Khalîj,
Libya 54 B2
Syktyvkar, *Russia* 28 C6
Sylhet, *Bangla.* 41 E8
Sylt, *Germany* 14 A5
Sym, *Russia* 29 C9
Syracuse, *U.S.A.* 77 C7
Syrdarya ➤, *Kazakhstan* .. 29 E7
Syria ■, *Asia* 46 D4
Syrian Desert = Shām, Bādiyat
ash, *Asia* 47 D4
Syros, *Greece* 23 F5
Syzran, *Russia* 24 C6
Szczecin, *Poland* 16 B2
Szczecinek, *Poland* 16 B3
Szczeciński, Zalew = Stettiner
Haff, *Germany* 15 B8
Szczytno, *Poland* 16 B5
Szechwan = Sichuan ☐, *China* 34 C5
Szeged, *Hungary* 16 E5
Székesfehérvár, *Hungary* ... 16 E4
Szekszárd, *Hungary* 16 E4
Szentes, *Hungary* 16 E5
Szolnok, *Hungary* 16 E5
Szombathely, *Hungary* 16 E3

T

Tabacal, *Argentina* 94 A4
Tabaco, *Phil.* 36 B2
Ţābah, *Si. Arabia* 47 F5
Ţabas, *Khorāsān, Iran* 45 C5
Ţabas, *Yazd, Iran* 44 C4
Tabatinga, Serra da, *Brazil* . 93 E5
Tablas, *Phil.* 36 B2
Table B., *S. Africa* 58 E3
Table Mt., *S. Africa* 58 E3
Tábor, *Czech Rep.* 16 D2
Tabora, *Tanzania* 57 F6
Tabou, *Ivory C.* 53 H4
Tabriz, *Iran* 46 C6
Tabūk, *Si. Arabia* 47 E4
Tacheng, *China* 34 B3
Tacloban, *Phil.* 36 B2
Tacna, *Peru* 91 G4
Tacoma, *U.S.A.* 72 C2
Tacuarembó, *Uruguay* 94 C5
Tademaït, Plateau du, *Algeria* 52 C6
Tadjoura, *Djibouti* 49 E3
Tadmor, *N.Z.* 65 D5
Tadzhikistan = Tajikistan ■,
Asia 29 F8
Taegu = Daegu, *S. Korea* .. 35 C7
Taejŏn = Daejeon, *S. Korea* . 35 C7
Tafalla, *Spain* 19 A5
Tafelbaai = Table B., *S. Africa* 58 E3
Tafermaar, *Indonesia* 37 F4
Taft, *Phil.* 36 B3
Taftan, *Pakistan* 42 E2
Taftān, Küh-e, *Iran* 45 D5
Taga Dzong, *Bhutan* 41 D7
Taganrog, *Russia* 25 D4

Tagbilaran

Tagbilaran, Phil. ... 36 C2
Tagliamento →, Italy ... 20 B4
Taguatinga, Brazil ... 93 E5
Tagum, Phil. ... 36 C3
Tagus = Tejo →, Europe ... 18 C1
Tahakopa, N.Z. ... 65 G3
Tahan, Gunung, Malaysia ... 38 D2
Tahat, Algeria ... 52 D7
Tāherī, Iran ... 44 E3
Tahiti, French Polynesia ... 65 L16
Tahoe, L., U.S.A. ... 72 G3
Tahoua, Niger ... 53 F7
Tahta, Egypt ... 54 C5
Tahulandang, Indonesia ... 37 D3
Tahuna, Indonesia ... 37 D3
Taibei = T'aipei, Taiwan ... 35 D7
T'aichung, Taiwan ... 35 D7
Taieri →, N.Z. ... 65 G4
Taihape, N.Z. ... 64 C6
Tailem Bend, Australia ... 62 C2
Taimyr Peninsula = Taymyr, Poluostrov, Russia ... 30 B7
Tain, U.K. ... 10 C4
T'ainan, Taiwan ... 35 D7
T'aipei, Taiwan ... 35 D7
Taiping, Malaysia ... 38 D2
Taitao, Pen. de, Chile ... 95 F1
Taiwan ■, Asia ... 35 D7
Taiyuan, China ... 35 C6
Taizhong = T'aichung, Taiwan 35 D7
Ta'izz, Yemen ... 49 E3
Tajikistan ■, Asia ... 29 F8
Tajima, Japan ... 33 E6
Tajo = Tejo →, Europe ... 18 C1
Tak, Thailand ... 38 A1
Takada, Japan ... 33 E6
Takaka, N.Z. ... 65 D5
Takamatsu, Japan ... 33 F4
Takaoka, Japan ... 33 E5
Takapuna, N.Z. ... 64 B6
Takasaki, Japan ... 33 E6
Takayama, Japan ... 33 E5
Takefu, Japan ... 33 F5
Takengon, Indonesia ... 38 D1
Takeshima = Tok-do, Asia ... 33 E2
Tākestān, Iran ... 46 D7
Takev, Cambodia ... 38 B2
Takhār □, Afghan. ... 45 B7
Takikawa, Japan ... 32 B7
Takla Makan, China ... 34 C3
Taklamakan Shamo = Takla Makan, China ... 34 C3
Talara, Peru ... 90 D2
Talas, Kyrgyzstan ... 29 E8
Talaud, Kepulauan, Indonesia 36 D3
Talavera de la Reina, Spain . 18 C3
Talayan, Phil. ... 36 C2
Talbragar →, Australia ... 63 B4
Talca, Chile ... 94 D2
Talcahuano, Chile ... 94 D2
Talcher, India ... 40 G5
Taldyqorghan, Kazakhstan ... 29 E8
Tālesh, Kūhhā-ye, Iran ... 46 C7
Tali Post, Sudan ... 55 G5
Talibon, Phil. ... 36 B2
Taliwang, Indonesia ... 39 F5
Tall 'Afar, Iraq ... 46 C5
Talladega, U.S.A. ... 82 C4
Tallahassee, U.S.A. ... 83 D5
Tallangatta, Australia ... 63 C4
Tallinn, Estonia ... 24 B1
Taloyoak, Canada ... 68 B10
Taltal, Chile ... 94 B2
Talwood, Australia ... 63 A4
Talyawalka Cr. →, Australia . 62 B3
Tamale, Ghana ... 53 G5
Tamanrasset, Algeria ... 52 D7
Tamatave = Toamasina, Madag. ... 59 B9
Tambacounda, Senegal ... 53 F3
Tambelan, Kepulauan, Indonesia ... 39 D3
Tambo de Mora, Peru ... 91 F3
Tambora, Indonesia ... 39 F5
Tambov, Russia ... 24 C5
Tâmega →, Portugal ... 18 B1
Tamenglong, India ... 41 E9

Tamil Nadu □, India ... 43 P10
Tammerfors = Tampere, Finland ... 8 C10
Tamo Abu, Banjaran, Malaysia ... 39 D5
Tampa, U.S.A. ... 83 F6
Tampere, Finland ... 8 C10
Tampico, Mexico ... 84 C5
Tamu, Burma ... 41 E10
Tamworth, Australia ... 63 B5
Tana →, Kenya ... 57 E8
Tana →, Norway ... 8 A11
Tana, L., Ethiopia ... 55 F6
Tanabe, Japan ... 33 G4
Tanahbala, Indonesia ... 39 E1
Tanahgrogot, Indonesia ... 39 E5
Tanahjampea, Indonesia ... 37 F2
Tanahmasa, Indonesia ... 39 E1
Tanahmerah, Indonesia ... 37 F6
Tanakura, Japan ... 33 E7
Tanami Desert, Australia ... 60 D5
Tanana →, U.S.A. ... 69 B4
Tananarive = Antananarivo, Madag. ... 59 B9
Tánaro →, Italy ... 13 D8
Tandag, Phil. ... 36 C3
Tandil, Argentina ... 94 D5
Tando Adam, Pakistan ... 42 G6
Tandou L., Australia ... 62 B3
Taneatua, N.Z. ... 64 C7
Tanen Tong Dan = Dawna Ra., Burma ... 41 J12
Tanezrouft, Algeria ... 52 D6
Tanga, Tanzania ... 57 F7
Tanganyika, L., Africa ... 57 F5
Tanger, Morocco ... 52 A4
Tanggula Shan, China ... 34 C4
Tanghla Range = Tanggula Shan, China ... 34 C4
Tangier = Tanger, Morocco . 52 A4
Tangshan, China ... 35 C6
Tanimbar, Kepulauan, Indonesia ... 37 F4
Taninthari = Tenasserim, Burma ... 38 B1
Tanjay, Phil. ... 36 C2
Tanjore = Thanjavur, India . 43 P11
Tanjung, Phil. ... 39 E5
Tanjungbalai, Indonesia ... 39 D1
Tanjungbatu, Indonesia ... 39 D5
Tanjungkarang Telukbetung, Indonesia ... 39 F3
Tanjungpandan, Indonesia .. 39 E3
Tanjungpinang, Indonesia .. 39 D2
Tanjungredeb, Indonesia ... 39 D5
Tanjungselor, Indonesia ... 39 D5
Tanout, Niger ... 53 F7
Tanta, Egypt ... 54 B5
Tantung = Dandong, China .. 35 B7
Tanunda, Australia ... 62 B2
Tanzania ■, Africa ... 57 F6
Taolanaro, Madag. ... 59 D9
Taoudenni, Mali ... 52 D5
Tapa Shan = Daba Shan, China ... 35 C5
Tapajós →, Brazil ... 92 C3
Tapaktuan, Indonesia ... 39 D1
Tapanui, N.Z. ... 65 F3
Tapauá →, Brazil ... 91 E6
Tapeta, Liberia ... 53 G4
Tapirapecó, Serra, Venezuela 90 C6
Tapti →, India ... 43 J8
Tapuae-o-Uenuku, N.Z. ... 65 D5
Tapul Group, Phil. ... 36 C2
Taquari →, Brazil ... 91 G7
Tara, Australia ... 63 A5
Tara, Russia ... 29 D8
Tara →, Serbia & M. ... 22 C2
Tarābulus, Lebanon ... 46 D3
Tarābulus, Libya ... 54 B1
Tarakan, Indonesia ... 39 D5
Taranaki □, N.Z. ... 64 C6
Taranaki, Mt., N.Z. ... 64 C6
Tarancón, Spain ... 19 B4
Táranto, Italy ... 21 D6
Táranto, G. di, Italy ... 21 D6
Tarapacá, Colombia ... 90 D5

Tararua Ra., N.Z. ... 64 D6
Tarashcha, Ukraine ... 17 D10
Tarauacá, Brazil ... 91 E4
Tarauacá →, Brazil ... 91 E5
Tarawa, Kiribati ... 64 J12
Tarawera, N.Z. ... 64 C7
Tarawera, L., N.Z. ... 64 C7
Taraz, Kazakhstan ... 29 E8
Tarazona, Spain ... 19 B5
Tarbagatay, Khrebet, Kazakhstan ... 29 E9
Tarbela Dam, Pakistan ... 42 B8
Tarbes, France ... 12 E4
Tarcoola, Australia ... 62 B1
Tarcoon, Australia ... 63 B4
Taree, Australia ... 63 B5
Tarfaya, Morocco ... 52 C3
Târgoviște, Romania ... 22 B5
Târgu-Jiu, Romania ... 17 F6
Târgu Mureș, Romania ... 17 E7
Tarifa, Spain ... 18 D3
Tarija, Bolivia ... 94 A4
Tariku →, Indonesia ... 37 E5
Tarim Basin = Tarim Pendi, China ... 34 C3
Tarim He →, China ... 34 C3
Tarim Pendi, China ... 34 C3
Taritatu →, Indonesia ... 37 E5
Tarkhankut, Mys, Ukraine ... 25 D3
Tarko Sale, Russia ... 28 C8
Tarkwa, Ghana ... 53 G5
Tarlac, Phil. ... 36 A2
Tarma, Peru ... 91 F3
Tarn →, France ... 12 D4
Tarnobrzeg, Poland ... 16 C5
Tarnów, Poland ... 16 C5
Tarnowskie Góry, Poland ... 16 C4
Taroom, Australia ... 63 A4
Taroudannt, Morocco ... 52 B4
Tarragona, Spain ... 19 B6
Tarrasa = Terrassa, Spain ... 19 B7
Tarsus, Turkey ... 46 C3
Tartagal, Argentina ... 94 A4
Tartu, Estonia ... 24 B2
Tarțūs, Syria ... 46 D3
Tarutung, Indonesia ... 39 D1
Tash-Kömür, Kyrgyzstan ... 29 E8
Tashauz = Dashoguz, Turkmenistan ... 29 E6
Tashi Chho Dzong = Thimphu, Bhutan ... 41 D7
Tashkent = Toshkent, Uzbekistan ... 29 E7
Tashtagol, Russia ... 29 D9
Tasman B., N.Z. ... 65 D5
Tasman Mts., N.Z. ... 65 D5
Tasman Pen., Australia ... 62 D4
Tasmania □, Australia ... 62 D4
Tatabánya, Hungary ... 16 E4
Tatarbunary, Ukraine ... 17 F9
Tatarsk, Russia ... 29 D8
Tatarstan □, Russia ... 29 D6
Tateyama, Japan ... 33 F6
Tathra, Australia ... 63 C4
Tatnam, C., Canada ... 71 D4
Tatra = Tatry, Slovak Rep. .. 16 D4
Tatry, Slovak Rep. ... 16 D4
Tatta, Pakistan ... 43 G5
Tat'ung = Datong, China ... 35 B6
Tatvan, Turkey ... 46 C4
Taubaté, Brazil ... 94 A7
Tauern, Austria ... 15 E7
Taumarunui, N.Z. ... 64 C6
Taumaturgo, Brazil ... 91 E4
Taungdwingyi, Burma ... 41 G10
Taunggyi, Burma ... 41 G11
Taungup, Burma ... 41 H10
Taunton, U.K. ... 11 F5
Taunus, Germany ... 14 C5
Taupo, N.Z. ... 64 C7
Taupo, L., N.Z. ... 64 C6
Tauranga, N.Z. ... 64 B7
Tauranga Harb., N.Z. ... 64 B7
Taurianova, Italy ... 21 E6
Taurus Mts. = Toros Dağları, Turkey ... 46 C3

Tavastehus = Hämeenlinna, Finland 8 C10
Tavda, Russia 29 D7
Tavda ➤, Russia 29 D7
Tavira, Portugal 18 D2
Tavoy, Burma 38 B1
Tawau, Malaysia 38 D5
Tawitawi, Phil. 36 C2
Tay ➤, U.K. 10 C5
Tayabamba, Peru 91 E3
Taygetos Oros, Greece 23 F4
Taylakova, Russia 29 D8
Taymā, Si. Arabia 47 F4
Taymyr, Oz., Russia 30 B8
Taymyr, Poluostrov, Russia 30 B7
Taytay, Phil. 36 B1
Taz ➤, Russia 28 C8
Taza, Morocco 52 B5
Tazovskiy, Russia 28 C8
Tbilisi, Georgia 25 E5
Tchad = Chad ■, Africa 55 E2
Tchad, L., Chad 55 F1
Tch'eng-tou = Chengdu, China 35 C5
Tchibanga, Gabon 56 E2
Tch'ong-k'ing = Chongqing, China 35 D5
Tczew, Poland 16 A4
Te Anau, L., N.Z. 65 F2
Te Aroha, N.Z. 64 B6
Te Awamutu, N.Z. 64 C6
Te Ika a Maui = North I., N.Z. 64 B5
Te Kuiti, N.Z. 64 C6
Te Puke, N.Z. 64 B7
Te Waewae B., N.Z. 65 G2
Te Wai Pounamu = South I., N.Z. 65 E3
Tebakang, Malaysia 39 D4
Tébessa, Algeria 52 A7
Tebicuary ➤, Paraguay 94 B5
Tebingtinggi, Indonesia 39 D1
Tecuci, Romania 22 B6
Tedzhen = Tejen, Turkmenistan 29 F7
Tefé, Brazil 90 D6
Tegal, Indonesia 39 F3
Tegucigalpa, Honduras 85 E7
Tehachapi, U.S.A. 78 C3
Teheran = Tehrān, Iran 44 C2
Tehoru, Indonesia 37 E3
Tehrān, Iran 44 C2
Tehuantepec, Mexico 85 D5
Tehuantepec, G. de, Mexico 85 D5
Tehuantepec, Istmo de, Mexico 85 D6
Tejen, Turkmenistan 29 F7
Tejo ➤, Europe 18 C1
Tekapo, L., N.Z. 65 E4
Tekeli, Kazakhstan 29 E8
Tekirdağ, Turkey 22 D6
Tekkali, India 40 H5
Tel Aviv-Yafo, Israel 46 D3
Tela, Honduras 85 D7
Telanaipura = Jambi, Indonesia 39 E2
Telavi, Georgia 25 E6
Telekhany = Tsyelyakhany, Belarus 17 B7
Teles Pires ➤, Brazil 91 E7
Telford, U.K. 11 E5
Tellicherry, India 43 P9
Telsen, Argentina 95 E3
Teluk Anson = Teluk Intan, Malaysia 39 D2
Teluk Betung = Tanjungkarang Telukbetung, Indonesia 39 F3
Teluk Intan, Malaysia 39 D2
Telukbutun, Indonesia 39 D3
Telukdalem, Indonesia 39 D1
Tema, Ghana 53 G5
Temerloh, Malaysia 39 D2
Temir, Kazakhstan 29 E6
Temirtau, Kazakhstan 29 D8
Temirtau, Russia 29 D9
Tempe, U.S.A. 79 D7
Temple, U.S.A. 80 D5
Temuco, Chile 94 D2

Temuka, N.Z. 65 F4
Tenali, India 40 J3
Tenaro, Akra, Greece 23 F4
Tenasserim, Burma 38 B1
Tenda, Colle di, France 13 D7
Tendaho, Ethiopia 49 E3
Tenerife, Canary Is. 52 C2
Tengah, Kepulauan, Indonesia 39 F5
Tengchong, China 34 D4
Tenggarong, Indonesia 39 E5
Tengiz Köli, Kazakhstan 29 D7
Tenkasi, India 43 Q10
Tennessee □, U.S.A. 82 B4
Tennessee ➤, U.S.A. 76 F1
Tenom, Malaysia 38 C5
Tenterfield, Australia 63 A5
Teófilo Otoni, Brazil 93 F5
Tepa, Indonesia 37 F3
Tepic, Mexico 84 C4
Teplice, Czech Rep. 16 C1
Ter ➤, Spain 19 A7
Téramo, Italy 20 C4
Terang, Australia 62 C3
Terebovlya, Ukraine 17 D7
Terek ➤, Russia 25 E6
Teresina, Brazil 92 D5
Terewah, L., Australia 63 A4
Teridgerie Cr. ➤, Australia 63 B4
Términi Imerese, Italy 21 F4
Termiz, Uzbekistan 29 F7
Térmoli, Italy 20 C5
Ternate, Indonesia 37 D3
Terney, Russia 32 A5
Terni, Italy 20 C4
Ternopil, Ukraine 17 D7
Terowie, Australia 62 B2
Terracina, Italy 20 D4
Terralba, Italy 21 E2
Terrassa, Spain 19 B7
Terre Haute, U.S.A. 76 E2
Terschelling, Neths. 14 B3
Teruel, Spain 19 B5
Teryaweynya L., Australia 62 B3
Teshio, Japan 32 A7
Teshio-Gawa ➤, Japan 32 A7
Tesiyn Gol ➤, Mongolia 34 A4
Teslin, Canada 68 B6
Tessalit, Mali 52 D6
Tetas, Pta., Chile 94 A2
Tete, Mozam. 59 B6
Teterev ➤, Ukraine 17 C10
Teteven, Bulgaria 22 C5
Tetiyev, Ukraine 17 D9
Tétouan, Morocco 52 A4
Tetovo, Macedonia 22 C3
Teuco ➤, Argentina 94 B4
Teun, Malaysia 37 F3
Teutoburger Wald, Germany 14 B5
Tevere ➤, Italy 20 C4
Tewantin, Australia 63 A5
Texarkana, U.S.A. 81 C6
Texas, Australia 63 A5
Texas □, U.S.A. 80 D4
Texas City, U.S.A. 81 E6
Texel, Neths. 14 B3
Teyvareh, Afghan. 45 C6
Tezpur, India 41 D9
Thabana Ntlenyana, Lesotho 59 D5
Thabazimbi, S. Africa 59 C5
Thailand ■, Asia 38 A2
Thailand, G. of, Asia 38 B2
Thakhek, Laos 38 A2
Thal, Pakistan 42 C7
Thala La = Hkakabo Razi, Burma 41 C11
Thallon, Australia 63 A4
Thames, N.Z. 64 B6
Thames ➤, U.K. 11 F7
Thandwe, Burma 41 H10
Thane, India 43 K8
Thanh Pho Ho Chi Minh, Vietnam 38 B3
Thanjavur, India 43 P11
Thar Desert, India 42 F7
Tharad, India 43 G7
Thargomindah, Australia 63 A3
Tharrawaddy, Burma 41 J10

Thasos, Greece 23 D5
Thaton, Burma 41 J11
Thaungdut, Burma 41 E10
Thayetmyo, Burma 41 H10
Thazi, Burma 41 G11
The Gulf = Persian Gulf, Asia 44 E2
The Hague = 's-Gravenhage, Neths. 14 B3
The Pas, Canada 69 C9
The Wash, U.K. 11 E7
Thebes = Thiva, Greece 23 E4
Theebine, Australia 63 A5
Thermopiles, Greece 23 E4
Thermopylae P. = Thermopiles, Greece 23 E4
Thessaloniki, Greece 23 D4
Thessaloníki, Gulf of = Thessaloniki Kolpos, Greece 23 D4
Thessaloniki Kolpos, Greece 23 D4
Thetford, U.K. 11 E7
Thetford Mines, Canada 71 E6
Thevenard, Australia 62 B1
Thiel Mts., Antarctica 96 C2
Thiers, France 13 D5
Thiès, Senegal 53 F2
Thika, Kenya 57 E7
Thimphu, Bhutan 41 D7
Thionville, France 13 B7
Thira = Santorini, Greece 23 F5
Thiruvananthapuram = Trivandrum, India 43 Q10
Thistle I., Australia 62 C2
Thiva, Greece 23 E4
Þjórsá ➤, Iceland 8 C1
Thohoyandou, S. Africa 59 C6
Thomas, L., Australia 62 A2
Thomasville, Ga., U.S.A. 83 D6
Thomasville, N.C., U.S.A. 83 B7
Thompson, Canada 69 C10
Thrace, Turkey 22 D6
Three Hummock I., Australia 62 D3
Three Points, C., Ghana 53 H5
Thunder Bay, Canada 71 E5
Thung Song, Thailand 38 C1
Thunkar, Bhutan 41 D8
Thüringer Wald, Germany 14 C6
Thurles, Ireland 11 E3
Thurso, U.K. 10 B5
Thurston I., Antarctica 96 B2
Tian Shan, Asia 34 B3
Tianjin, China 35 C6
Tianshui, China 35 C5
Tiaret, Algeria 52 A6
Tiber = Tevere ➤, Italy 20 D4
Tiberias, L. = Yam Kinneret, Israel 46 D3
Tibesti, Chad 54 D2
Tibet = Xizang Zizhiqu □, China 34 C3
Tibooburra, Australia 62 A3
Tiburón, I., Mexico 84 B2
Ticino ➤, Italy 13 D8
Tiddim, Burma 41 F9
Tidjikja, Mauritania 53 E3
Tidore, Indonesia 37 D3
Tien Shan = Tian Shan, Asia 34 B3
Tientsin = Tianjin, China 35 C6
Tierra de Campos, Spain 18 A3
Tierra del Fuego, I. Gr. de, Argentina 95 G3
Tiétar ➤, Spain 18 C2
Tifu, Indonesia 37 E3
Tighina, Moldova 17 E9
Tigre ➤, Peru 90 D4
Tigris = Dijlah, Nahr ➤, Asia 47 E6
Tigyaing, Burma 41 F11
Tijuana, Mexico 84 A1
Tikamgarh, India 43 G11
Tikhoretsk, Russia 25 D5
Tikiraqjuaq = Whale Cove, Canada 68 B10
Tikrīt, Iraq 46 D5
Tiksi, Russia 30 B10
Tilamuta, Indonesia 37 D2
Tilburg, Neths. 14 C3
Tilos, Greece 23 F6
Tilpa, Australia 63 B3

Timaru

Timaru, N.Z. 65 F4
Timbuktu = Tombouctou, Mali 53 E5
Timimoun, Algeria 52 C6
Timirist, Râs, Mauritania 53 E2
Timişoara, Romania 16 F5
Timmins, Canada 71 E5
Timok →, Serbia & M. 22 B4
Timor, Asia 37 F2
Tinaca Pt., Phil. 36 C3
Tindouf, Algeria 52 C4
Tingo Maria, Peru 91 E3
Tinian, N. Marianas 64 H9
Tinnevelly = Tirunelveli, India 43 Q10
Tinogasta, Argentina 94 B3
Tinos, Greece 23 F5
Tintinara, Australia 62 C3
Tioman, Pulau, Malaysia . . . 39 D2
Tipperary, Ireland 11 E2
Tīrān, Iran 44 C2
Tiranë, Albania 22 D2
Tiraspol, Moldova 17 E9
Tire, Turkey 23 E6
Tirebolu, Turkey 25 E4
Tiree, U.K. 10 C3
Tîrgovişte = Târgovişte,
   Romania 22 B5
Tîrgu-Jiu = Târgu-Jiu,
   Romania 17 F6
Tîrgu Mureş = Târgu Mureş,
   Romania 17 E7
Tirich Mir, Pakistan 42 A7
Tiritiri o te Moana = Southern
   Alps, N.Z. 65 E4
Tírnavos, Greece 23 E4
Tirodi, India 43 J11
Tirol □, Austria 14 E6
Tirso →, Italy 21 E2
Tiruchchirappalli, India 43 P11
Tirunelveli, India 43 Q10
Tirupati, India 43 N11
Tiruppur, India 43 P10
Tiruvannamalai, India 43 N11
Tisa →, Serbia & M. 22 B3
Tisdale, Canada 69 C9
Tisza = Tisa →, Serbia & M. . 22 B3
Tit-Ary, Russia 30 B10
Titicaca, L., S. Amer. 91 G5
Titule, Dem. Rep. of
   the Congo 57 D5
Tivaouane, Senegal 53 F2
Tívoli, Italy 20 D4
Tiwī, Oman 45 F4
Tizi-Ouzou, Algeria 52 A6
Tjirebon = Cirebon, Indonesia 39 F3
Tlaxiaco, Mexico 84 D5
Tlemcen, Algeria 52 B5
Toamasina, Madag. 59 B9
Toay, Argentina 94 D4
Toba Kakar, Pakistan 42 D6
Tobago, Trin. & Tob. 87 D7
Tobelo, Indonesia 37 D3
Tobermory, U.K. 10 C3
Toboali, Indonesia 39 E3
Tobol →, Russia 29 D7
Tobol□, Indonesia 37 E2
Tobolsk, Russia 29 D7
Tobruk = Tubruq, Libya 54 B3
Tobyl = Tobol →, Russia . . . 29 D7
Tocantinópolis, Brazil 92 D4
Tocantins □, Brazil 93 E4
Tocantins →, Brazil 92 C4
Tocumwal, Australia 63 C4
Tocuyo →, Venezuela 90 A5
Todeli, Indonesia 37 E2
Todos os Santos, B. de, Brazil 93 E6
Togian, Kepulauan, Indonesia 37 E2
Togliatti, Russia 24 C6
Togo ■, W. Afr. 53 G6
Toinya, Sudan 55 G4
Tojikiston = Tajikistan ■, Asia 29 F8
Tojo, Indonesia 37 E2
Tok-do, Asia 33 E2
Tokala, Indonesia 37 E2
Tōkamachi, Japan 33 E6
Tokanui, N.Z. 65 G3
Tokarahi, N.Z. 65 F4
Tokat, Turkey 46 B4
Tokelau Is., Pac. Oc. 65 K13

Tokmak, Kyrgyzstan 29 E8
Tokushima, Japan 33 F4
Tokuyama, Japan 33 F2
Tōkyō, Japan 33 F6
Tolaga Bay, N.Z. 64 C8
Tolbukhin = Dobrich, Bulgaria 22 C6
Toledo, Spain 18 C3
Toledo, U.S.A. 76 D4
Toledo, Montes de, Spain . . . 18 C3
Toliara, Madag. 59 C8
Tolima, Colombia 90 C3
Tolitoli, Indonesia 37 D2
Tolo, Teluk, Indonesia 37 E2
Toluca, Mexico 84 D5
Tomakomai, Japan 32 B7
Tomar, Portugal 18 C1
Tomaszów Mazowiecki,
   Poland 16 C4
Tombouctou, Mali 53 E5
Tombua, Angola 58 B2
Tomelloso, Spain 18 C4
Tomini, Indonesia 37 D2
Tomini, Teluk, Indonesia . . . 37 E2
Tomsk, Russia 29 D9
Tonantins, Brazil 90 D5
Tondano, Indonesia 37 D2
Tonekābon, Iran 44 B2
Tonga ■, Pac. Oc. 65 L13
Tonga Trench, Pac. Oc. 65 L13
Tongareva = Penrhyn, Cook Is. 65 K15
Tongariro △, N.Z. 64 C6
Tongchuan, China 35 C5
Tonghua, China 35 B7
Tongking, G. of = Tonkin, G.
   of, Asia 35 D5
Tongoy, Chile 94 C2
Tongsa Dzong, Bhutan 41 D8
Tongue →, U.S.A. 74 B2
Tonk, India 42 F9
Tonkin, G. of, Asia 35 D5
Tonle Sap, Cambodia 38 B2
Toompine, Australia 63 A3
Toora, Australia 63 C4
Toowoomba, Australia 63 A5
Topeka, U.S.A. 75 F7
Topolobampo, Mexico 84 B3
Torata, Peru 91 G4
Torbalı, Turkey 23 E6
Torbat-e Heydārīyeh, Iran . . 44 C4
Torbat-e Jām, Iran 45 C5
Torbay □, U.K. 11 F5
Tordesillas, Spain 18 B3
Torgau, Germany 15 C7
Torino, Italy 13 D7
Torit, Sudan 55 H5
Tormes →, Spain 18 B2
Torneå = Tornio, Finland . . . 8 E12
Torneälven →, Europe 8 B10
Torneträsk, Sweden 8 B9
Tornio, Finland 8 E12
Tornionjoki = Torneälven →,
   Europe 8 B10
Tornquist, Argentina 94 D4
Toro, Cerro del, Chile 94 B3
Toronto, Canada 71 E6
Toropets, Russia 24 B3
Tororo, Uganda 57 D6
Toros Dağları, Turkey 46 C3
Torre de Moncorvo, Portugal 18 B2
Torre del Greco, Italy 21 D5
Torrejón de Ardoz, Spain . . . 18 B4
Torrelavega, Spain 18 A3
Torremolinos, Spain 18 D3
Torrens, L., Australia 62 B2
Torrent, Spain 19 C5
Torreón, Mexico 84 B4
Torres Vedras, Portugal 18 C1
Torrevieja, Spain 19 D5
Tortosa, Spain 19 B6
Tortosa, C., Spain 19 B6
Ţorūd, Iran 44 C3
Toruń, Poland 16 B4
Tosa-Wan, Japan 33 G3
Toscana □, Italy 20 C3
Toshkent, Uzbekistan 29 E7
Tostado, Argentina 94 B4
Tosya, Turkey 46 B3
Totma, Russia 24 A5

Totten Glacier, Antarctica . . . 96 A12
Tottenham, Australia 63 B4
Tottori, Japan 33 F4
Toubkal, Djebel, Morocco . . 52 B4
Tougan, Burkina Faso 53 F5
Touggourt, Algeria 52 B7
Toul, France 13 B6
Toulon, France 13 E6
Toulouse, France 12 E4
Toummo, Niger 54 D1
Toungoo, Burma 41 H11
Touraine, France 12 C4
Tourcoing, France 13 A5
Touriñán, C., Spain 18 A1
Tournai, Belgium 14 C2
Tournon-sur-Rhône, France . 13 D6
Tours, France 12 C4
Towada, Japan 32 C7
Towada-Ko, Japan 32 C7
Townsville, Australia 61 D8
Toya-Ko, Japan 32 B7
Toyama, Japan 33 E5
Toyama-Wan, Japan 33 E5
Toyohashi, Japan 33 F5
Toyooka, Japan 33 F4
Toyota, Japan 33 F5
Tozeur, Tunisia 52 B7
Tozkhurmato, Iraq 46 D6
Trá Li = Tralee, Ireland 11 E2
Trabzon, Turkey 25 E4
Trafalgar, C., Spain 18 D2
Trail, Canada 69 D8
Tralee, Ireland 11 E2
Trancas, Argentina 94 B3
Trang, Thailand 38 C1
Trangan, Indonesia 37 F4
Trangie, Australia 63 B4
Trani, Italy 20 D6
Transantarctic Mts., Antarctica 96 C3
Transilvania, Romania 17 F7
Transilvanian Alps = Carpaţii
   Meridionali, Romania 17 F7
Trápani, Italy 21 E4
Traralgon, Australia 63 C4
Trasimeno, L., Italy 20 C4
Traun, Austria 15 D8
Travemünde, Germany 15 B6
Travers, Mt., N.Z. 65 E5
Travnik, Bos.-H. 20 B6
Trébbia →, Italy 13 D8
Třebíč, Czech Rep. 16 D2
Trebinje, Bos.-H. 20 C7
Treinta y Tres, Uruguay 94 C6
Trelew, Argentina 95 E3
Tremp, Spain 19 A6
Trenque Lauquen, Argentina 94 D4
Trent →, U.K. 11 E6
Trento, Italy 20 A3
Trenton, U.S.A. 77 D8
Tres Arroyos, Argentina 94 D4
Três Lagoas, Brazil 93 G3
Tres Montes, C., Chile 95 F1
Tres Puntas, C., Argentina . . 95 F3
Três Rios, Brazil 93 G5
Treviso, Italy 20 B4
Triabunna, Australia 62 D4
Trichinopoly =
   Tiruchchirappalli, India . . . 43 P11
Trichur, India 43 P10
Trida, Australia 63 B4
Trier, Germany 14 D4
Trieste, Italy 20 B4
Triglav, Slovenia 20 A4
Trikala, Greece 23 E3
Trikora, Puncak, Indonesia . . 37 E5
Trinidad, Bolivia 91 F6
Trinidad, Cuba 86 B3
Trinidad, Uruguay 94 C5
Trinidad, U.S.A. 80 A1
Trinidad & Tobago ■,
   W. Indies 87 D7
Trinity →, U.S.A. 81 E6
Trinity B., Canada 71 E8
Trinity Range, U.S.A. 72 F4
Trinkitat, Sudan 55 E6
Tripoli = Tarābulus, Lebanon 46 D3
Tripoli = Tarābulus, Libya . . . 54 B1
Trípolis, Greece 23 F4

Tripura □, India 41 F8
Trivandrum, India 43 Q10
Troglav, Croatia 20 C6
Trois-Rivières, Canada 71 E6
Troitsko Pechorsk, Russia .. 28 C6
Trollhättan, Sweden 9 D8
Tromsø, Norway 8 B9
Tronador, Mte., Argentina . 95 E2
Trondheim, Norway 8 C8
Trondheimsfjorden, Norway 8 C8
Trout L., Canada 68 B7
Trouville-sur-Mer, France ... 12 B4
Troy, Turkey 23 E6
Troy, Ala., U.S.A. 82 D5
Troy, N.Y., U.S.A. 77 C9
Troyes, France 13 B6
Trudovoye, Russia 32 B3
Trujillo, Honduras 85 D7
Trujillo, Peru 91 E3
Trujillo, Spain 18 C3
Trujillo, Venezuela 90 B4
Truk = Chuuk, Micronesia .. 64 J10
Trundle, Australia 63 B4
Truro, Canada 71 E7
Truro, U.K. 11 F4
Truskavets, Ukraine 17 D6
Trutnov, Czech Rep. 16 C2
Tsaratanana, Madag. 59 B9
Tsetserleg, Mongolia 34 B5
Tshabong, Botswana 58 D4
Tshane, Botswana 58 C4
Tshela, Dem. Rep. of
  the Congo 56 E2
Tshikapa, Dem. Rep. of
  the Congo 56 F4
Tshwane = Pretoria, S. Africa 59 D5
Tsiigehtchic, Canada 68 B6
Tsimlyanskoye Vdkhr., Russia 25 D5
Tsinan = Jinan, China 35 C6
Tsinghai = Qinghai □, China . 34 C4
Tsingtao = Qingdao, China .. 35 C7
Tsirigo = Kythira, Greece .. 23 F4
Tskhinvali, Georgia 25 E5
Tsna →, Russia 24 C5
Tsuchiura, Japan 33 E7
Tsugaru Str., Japan 32 C7
Tsumeb, Namibia 58 B3
Tsuruga, Japan 33 F5
Tsuruoka, Japan 32 D6
Tsushima, Japan 33 F1
Tsuyama, Japan 33 F4
Tsyelyakhany, Belarus 17 B7
Tual, Indonesia 37 F4
Tuamotu, Îs., French
  Polynesia 65 L16
Tuamotu Ridge, Pac. Oc. .. 65 M17
Tuao, Phil. 36 A2
Tuapse, Russia 25 E4
Tuatapere, N.Z. 65 G2
Tubarão, Brazil 94 B7
Tübingen, Germany 14 D5
Tubruq, Libya 54 B3
Tubuaï, Îs., French Polynesia 65 M16
Tucacas, Venezuela 90 A5
Tucson, U.S.A. 79 D7
Tucumcari, U.S.A. 80 B2
Tucupita, Venezuela 90 B6
Tucuruí, Brazil 92 C4
Tucuruí, Reprêsa de, Brazil .. 92 C4
Tudela, Spain 19 A5
Tudmur, Syria 46 D4
Tuguegarao, Phil. 36 A2
Tui, Spain 18 A1
Tukangbesi, Kepulauan,
  Indonesia 37 F2
Tuktoyaktuk, Canada 68 B6
Tukuyu, Tanzania 57 F6
Tula, Russia 24 C4
Tūlak, Afghan. 45 C5
Tulare, U.S.A. 78 B3
Tulcán, Ecuador 90 C3
Tulcea, Romania 17 F9
Tulchyn, Ukraine 17 D9
Tulita, Canada 68 B7
Tullamore, Australia 63 B4
Tullamore, Ireland 11 E3
Tulle, France 12 D4
Tulsa, U.S.A. 81 A6

Tulua, Colombia 90 C3
Tumaco, Colombia 90 C3
Tumatumari, Guyana 90 B7
Tumba, L., Dem. Rep. of
  the Congo 56 E3
Tumbarumba, Australia ... 63 C4
Tumbes, Peru 90 D2
Tumby Bay, Australia 62 B2
Tumeremo, Venezuela 90 B6
Tumkur, India 43 N10
Tump, Pakistan 42 F3
Tumpat, Malaysia 38 C2
Tumu, Ghana 53 F5
Tumucumaque, Serra, Brazil 92 B3
Tumut, Australia 63 C4
Tuncurry, Australia 63 B5
Tundzha →, Bulgaria 22 D6
Tungabhadra →, India 43 M11
Tunguska, Nizhnyaya →,
  Russia 30 C6
Tunguska, Podkamennaya →,
  Russia 30 C7
Tunis, Tunisia 50 A1
Tunisia ■, Africa 50 B1
Tunja, Colombia 90 B4
Tunuyán →, Argentina 94 C3
Tupelo, U.S.A. 82 B3
Tupinambaranas, Brazil ... 90 D7
Tupiza, Bolivia 94 A3
Tupungato, Cerro, S. Amer. . 94 C3
Túquerres, Colombia 90 C3
Tura, Russia 30 C8
Turabah, Si. Arabia 47 E5
Tūrān, Iran 44 C4
Ţurayf, Si. Arabia 47 E4
Turek, Poland 16 B4
Turfan = Turpan, China 34 B3
Turfan Basin = Turpan Pendi,
  China 34 B3
Tŭrgovishte, Bulgaria 22 C6
Turgutlu, Turkey 23 E6
Turhal, Turkey 46 B4
Turia →, Spain 19 C5
Turiaçu, Brazil 92 C4
Turiaçu →, Brazil 92 C4
Turin = Torino, Italy 13 D7
Turkana, L., Africa 57 D7
Turkestan = Türkistan,
  Kazakhstan 29 E7
Turkey ■, Eurasia 25 F4
Türkistan, Kazakhstan 29 E7
Türkmenabat, Turkmenistan 29 F7
Türkmenbashi, Turkmenistan 29 E6
Turkmenistan ■, Asia 29 F6
Turks & Caicos Is. ☑,
  W. Indies 87 B5
Turku, Finland 9 C10
Turnagain, C., N.Z. 64 D7
Turneffe Is., Belize 85 D7
Turnhout, Belgium 14 C3
Tŭrnovo = Veliko Tŭrnovo,
  Bulgaria 22 C5
Turnu Măgurele, Romania .. 22 C5
Turnu Roşu, P., Romania ... 17 F7
Turpan, China 34 B3
Turpan Pendi, China 34 B3
Turukhansk, Russia 30 C6
Tuscaloosa, U.S.A. 82 C4
Tuscany = Toscana □, Italy .. 20 C4
Tuticorin, India 43 Q11
Tutóia, Brazil 92 C5
Tutong, Brunei 38 D4
Tutrakan, Bulgaria 22 B6
Tuttlingen, Germany 14 E5
Tutuala, E. Timor 37 F3
Tutuila, Amer. Samoa 65 L13
Tutume, Botswana 59 C5
Tuvalu ■, Pac. Oc. 64 K12
Tuxpan, Mexico 84 C5
Tuxtla Gutiérrez, Mexico ... 85 D6
Tuy = Tui, Spain 18 A1
Tuz Gölü, Turkey 46 C3
Ţūz Khurmātū = Tozkhurmato,
  Iraq 46 D6
Tuzla, Bos.-H. 20 B7
Tver, Russia 24 B4
Tweed Heads, Australia ... 63 A5
Twin Falls, U.S.A. 73 E6

Twofold B., Australia 63 C4
Tyachiv, Ukraine 17 D6
Tychy, Poland 16 C4
Tyler, U.S.A. 81 C6
Tyre = Sūr, Lebanon 46 D3
Tyrol = Tirol □, Austria 14 E6
Tyrrell →, Australia 62 C3
Tyrrell, L., Australia 62 C3
Tyrrhenian Sea, Medit. S. .. 21 E4
Tyumen, Russia 29 D7
Tzaneen, S. Africa 59 C6
Tzukong = Zigong, China ... 35 D5

U

U.S.A. = United States of
  America ■, N. Amer. 67 F10
Uatumã →, Brazil 90 D7
Uaupés, Brazil 90 D5
Uaupés →, Brazil 90 C5
Ubá, Brazil 93 G5
Ubaitaba, Brazil 93 E6
Ubangi = Oubangi →,
  Dem. Rep. of the Congo .. 56 E3
Ubauro, Pakistan 42 E6
Ube, Japan 33 G2
Úbeda, Spain 18 C4
Uberaba, Brazil 93 F4
Uberlândia, Brazil 93 F4
Ubon Ratchathani, Thailand . 38 A2
Ubort →, Belarus 17 B9
Ubundu, Dem. Rep. of
  the Congo 57 E5
Ucayali →, Peru 90 D4
Uchiura-Wan, Japan 32 B7
Udagamandalam, India ... 43 P10
Udaipur, India 43 G8
Udaipur Garhi, Nepal 40 D6
Udgir, India 43 K10
Udhampur, India 42 C9
Údine, Italy 20 A4
Udmurtia □, Russia 28 D6
Udon Thani, Thailand 38 A2
Udupi, India 43 N9
Uele →, Dem. Rep. of
  the Congo 57 D4
Uelzen, Germany 14 B6
Ufa, Russia 29 D6
Ugab →, Namibia 58 C2
Ugalla →, Tanzania 57 F6
Uganda ■, Africa 57 D6
Ugljan, Croatia 20 B5
Uibhist a Deas = South Uist,
  U.K. 10 C3
Uibhist a Tuath = North Uist,
  U.K. 10 C3
Uíge, Angola 56 F2
Uinta Mts., U.S.A. 73 F8
Uitenhage, S. Africa 59 E5
Ujjain, India 43 H9
Ujung Pandang, Indonesia . 37 F1
Ukhrul, India 41 E10
Ukhta, Russia 28 C6
Ukraine ■, Europe 25 D3
Ulaanbaatar, Mongolia ... 35 B5
Ulaangom, Mongolia 34 A4
Ulaanjirem, Mongolia 35 B5
Ulan Bator = Ulaanbaatar,
  Mongolia 35 B5
Ulan Ude, Russia 30 D8
Ulcinj, Serbia & M. 22 D2
Ule älv = Oulujoki →, Finland 8 B11
Ule träsk = Oulujärvi, Finland 8 C11
Uleåborg = Oulu, Finland ... 8 B11
Ulhasnagar, India 43 K8
Uliastay, Mongolia 34 B4
Ulladulla, Australia 63 C5
Ullapool, U.K. 10 C4
Ulleungdo, S. Korea 33 E2
Ulm, Germany 14 D5
Ulmarra, Australia 63 A5
Ulster □, U.K. 11 D3
Ulubat Gölü, Turkey 23 D7
Uludağ, Turkey 23 D7
Ulungur He →, China 34 B3
Uluru, Australia 60 F5

Ulutau, *Kazakhstan* 29 E7
Ulverstone, *Australia* 62 D4
Ulyanovsk = Simbirsk, *Russia* 24 C6
Ulyasutay = Uliastay,
  Mongolia 34 B4
Umala, *Bolivia* ■ 91 G5
'Umān = Oman ■, *Asia* 48 C6
Uman, *Ukraine* 17 D10
Umaria, *India* 40 F3
Umarkot, *Pakistan* 43 G6
Umbrella Mts., *N.Z.* 65 F3
Umeå, *Sweden* 8 C10
Umeälven ➡, *Sweden* 8 C10
Umera, *Indonesia* 37 E3
Umlazi, *S. Africa* 59 E6
Umm al Qaywayn, *U.A.E.* ... 44 E3
Umm Durman = Omdurmân,
  Sudan 55 E5
Umm Lajj, *Si. Arabia* 47 F4
Umm Ruwaba, *Sudan* 55 F5
Umnak I., *U.S.A.* 69 C3
Umniati ➡, *Zimbabwe* 59 B5
Umtata = Mthatha, *S. Africa* . 59 E5
Umuarama, *Brazil* 93 G3
Umzimvubu, *S. Africa* 59 E5
Una ➡, *Bos.-H.* 20 B6
Unalaska, *U.S.A.* 69 C3
Uncía, *Bolivia* 91 G5
Underbool, *Australia* 62 C3
Ungarie, *Australia* 63 B4
Ungarra, *Australia* 62 B2
Ungava, Pén. d', *Canada* ... 70 C6
Ungava B., *Canada* 70 D7
Ungeny = Ungheni, *Moldova* 17 E8
Ungheni, *Moldova* 17 E8
União da Vitória, *Brazil* ... 94 B6
Unimak I., *U.S.A.* 69 C3
United Arab Emirates ■, *Asia* 44 F3
United Kingdom ■, *Europe* . 11 D5
United States of America ■,
  N. Amer. 67 F10
Unnao, *India* 40 D3
Unst, *U.K.* 10 A6
Ünye, *Turkey* 46 B4
Upata, *Venezuela* 90 B6
Upemba, L., *Dem. Rep. of*
  the Congo 57 F5
Upington, *S. Africa* 58 D4
Upper Hutt, *N.Z.* 65 D6
Uppsala, *Sweden* 9 D9
Uqsuqtuuq = Gjoa Haven,
  Canada 68 B10
Ur, *Iraq* 47 E6
Ural = Zhayyq ➡, *Kazakhstan* 29 E6
Ural, *Australia* 63 B4
Ural Mts. = Uralskie Gory,
  Eurasia 28 D6
Uralla, *Australia* 63 B5
Uralsk = Oral, *Kazakhstan* ... 24 C7
Uralskie Gory, *Eurasia* 28 D6
Uray, *Russia* 29 C7
Urbana, *U.S.A.* 76 D1
Urbino, *Italy* 20 C4
Urbión, Picos de, *Spain* ... 19 A4
Urcos, *Peru* 91 F4
Urewera △, *N.Z.* 64 C7
Urfa = Sanliurfa, *Turkey* ... 46 C4
Urganch, *Uzbekistan* 29 E7
Uribia, *Colombia* 90 A4
Urla, *Turkey* 23 E6
Urmia = Orūmīyeh, *Iran* ... 46 C6
Urmia, L. = Orūmīyeh,
  Daryācheh-ye, *Iran* 46 C6
Uroševac, *Serbia & M.* 22 C3
Urubamba ➡, *Peru* 91 F4
Uruçara, *Brazil* 90 D7
Uruçuí, *Brazil* 92 D5
Uruguai ➡, *Brazil* 94 B6
Uruguaiana, *Brazil* 94 B5
Uruguay ■, *S. Amer.* 94 C5
Uruguay ➡, *S. Amer.* 94 C5
Ürümqi, *China* 29 E9
Ürzhar, *Kazakhstan* 29 E9
Usakos, *Namibia* 58 C3
Usedom, *Germany* 15 B8
Ushant = Ouessant, Î. d',
  France 12 B1
Ushibuka, *Japan* 33 G2

Üshtöbe, *Kazakhstan* 29 E8
Ushuaia, *Argentina* 95 G3
Usman, *Russia* 24 C4
Uspallata, P. de, *Argentina* . 94 C3
Uspenskiy, *Kazakhstan* 29 E8
Ussuriysk, *Russia* 32 B2
Ust-Ishim, *Russia* 29 D8
Ust-Kamenogorsk = Öskemen,
  Kazakhstan 29 E9
Ust-Kuyga, *Russia* 31 B11
Ust-Olenek, *Russia* 30 B10
Ust-Port, *Russia* 28 C9
Ust-Tsilma, *Russia* 28 C6
Ust Urt = Ustyurt Plateau, *Asia* 29 E6
Ústí nad Labem, *Czech Rep.* . 16 C2
Ústica, *Italy* 21 E4
Ustinov = Izhevsk, *Russia* ... 28 D6
Ustyurt Plateau, *Asia* 29 E6
Usu, *China* 34 B3
Usumacinta ➡, *Mexico* ... 85 D6
Usumbura = Bujumbura,
  Burundi 57 E5
Uta, *Indonesia* 37 E5
Utah □, *U.S.A.* 73 G8
Utiariti, *Brazil* 91 F7
Utica, *U.S.A.* 77 C8
Utrecht, *Neths.* 14 B3
Utrera, *Spain* 18 D3
Utsunomiya, *Japan* 33 E6
Uttar Pradesh □, *India* 42 F11
Uttaradit, *Thailand* 38 A2
Uusikaupunki, *Finland* 9 C10
Uvat, *Russia* 29 D7
Uvinza, *Tanzania* 57 F6
Uvira, *Dem. Rep. of the Congo* 57 E5
Uvs Nuur, *Mongolia* 34 A4
'Uwairidh, Ḥarrat al, *Si. Arabia* 47 F4
Uwajima, *Japan* 33 G3
Uyuni, *Bolivia* 91 H5
Uzbekistan ■, *Asia* 29 E7
Uzerche, *France* 12 D4
Uzh ➡, *Ukraine* 17 C10
Uzhgorod = Uzhhorod,
  Ukraine 17 D6
Uzhhorod, *Ukraine* 17 D6
Užice, *Serbia & M.* 22 C2
Uzunköprü, *Turkey* 22 D6

V

Vaal ➡, *S. Africa* 58 D4
Vaasa, *Finland* 8 C10
Vác, *Hungary* 16 E4
Vach = Vakh ➡, *Russia* ... 29 C8
Vadodara, *India* 43 H8
Vadsø, *Norway* 8 D13
Vaduz, *Liech.* 13 C8
Vahsel B., *Antarctica* 96 B5
Váhtjer = Gällivare, *Sweden* . 8 B10
Vaigach, *Russia* 28 B6
Vakh ➡, *Russia* 29 C8
Val-d'Or, *Canada* 71 E6
Valahia, *Romania* 22 B5
Valandovo, *Macedonia* 22 D4
Valcheta, *Argentina* 95 E3
Valdai Hills = Valdayskaya
  Vozvyshennost, *Russia* .. 24 B3
Valdayskaya Vozvyshennost,
  Russia 24 B3
Valdepeñas, *Spain* 18 C4
Valdés, Pen., *Argentina* 95 E4
Valdez, *U.S.A.* 69 B5
Valdivia, *Chile* 95 D2
Valdosta, *U.S.A.* 83 D6
Valença, *Brazil* 93 E6
Valença do Piauí, *Brazil* ... 92 D5
Valence, *France* 13 D6
Valencia, *Spain* 19 C5
Valencia, *Venezuela* 90 A5
Valencia □, *Spain* 19 C5
Valencia, G. de, *Spain* 19 C6
Valencia de Alcántara, *Spain* 18 C2
Valencia I., *Ireland* 11 F1
Valenciennes, *France* 13 A5
Valentim, Sa. do, *Brazil* ... 92 D5
Valera, *Venezuela* 90 B4

Valjevo, *Serbia & M.* 22 B2
Vall de Uxó = La Vall d'Uixó,
  Spain 19 C5
Valladolid, *Mexico* 85 C7
Valladolid, *Spain* 18 B3
Valle de la Pascua, *Venezuela* 90 B5
Valledupar, *Colombia* 90 A4
Vallejo, *U.S.A.* 72 G2
Vallenar, *Chile* 94 B2
Valletta, *Malta* 21 G5
Valls, *Spain* 19 B6
Valognes, *France* 12 B3
Valona = Vlorë, *Albania* ... 23 D2
Valozhyn, *Belarus* 17 A8
Valparaíso, *Chile* 94 C2
Vals, Tanjung, *Indonesia* ... 37 F5
Valsad, *India* 43 J8
Valverde del Camino, *Spain* . 18 D2
Van, *Turkey* 46 C5
Van, L. = Van Gölü, *Turkey* . 46 C5
Van Gölü, *Turkey* 46 C5
Van Rees, Pegunungan,
  Indonesia 37 E5
Vanadzor, *Armenia* 25 E5
Vancouver, *Canada* 69 D7
Vancouver, *U.S.A.* 72 D2
Vancouver I., *Canada* 69 D7
Vänern, *Sweden* 9 D8
Vangaindrano, *Madag.* 59 C9
Vännäs, *Sweden* 8 C9
Vannes, *France* 12 C2
Vanrhynsdorp, *S. Africa* ... 58 E3
Vantaa ➡, *Finland* 9 C11
Vanua Levu, *Fiji* 64 L12
Vanuatu ■, *Pac. Oc.* 64 L11
Vapnyarka, *Ukraine* 17 D9
Varanasi, *India* 40 E4
Varangerfjorden, *Norway* ... 8 A11
Varaždin, *Croatia* 20 A6
Varberg, *Sweden* 9 D8
Vardak □, *Afghan.* 45 C7
Vardar = Axios ➡, *Greece* . 23 D4
Varese, *Italy* 13 D8
Varna, *Bulgaria* 22 C6
Varzaneh, *Iran* 44 C3
Vasa = Vaasa, *Finland* 8 C10
Vasa Barris ➡, *Brazil* 93 E6
Vascongadas = País Vasco □,
  Spain 19 A4
Vasht = Khāsh, *Iran* 42 E2
Vasilevichi, *Belarus* 17 B9
Vasilkov = Vasylkiv, *Ukraine* . 17 C10
Västerås, *Sweden* 9 D9
Västerdalälven ➡, *Sweden* . 8 C8
Västervik, *Sweden* 9 D9
Vasto, *Italy* 20 C5
Vasylkiv, *Ukraine* 17 C10
Vatican City ■, *Europe* ... 20 D4
Vatnajökull, *Iceland* 8 C2
Vatra-Dornei, *Romania* 17 E7
Vättern, *Sweden* 9 D8
Vaupés = Uaupés ➡, *Brazil* . 90 C5
Vawkavysk, *Belarus* 17 B7
Vaygach, Ostrov, *Russia* ... 28 C6
Vedea ➡, *Romania* 22 C5
Vega, *Norway* 8 B8
Vegreville, *Canada* 69 C8
Vejer de la Frontera, *Spain* . 18 D3
Velebit Planina, *Croatia* ... 20 B5
Veles, *Macedonia* 22 D3
Vélez-Málaga, *Spain* 18 D3
Vélez Rubio, *Spain* 19 D4
Velhas ➡, *Brazil* 93 F5
Velika Kapela, *Croatia* 20 B5
Velikaya ➡, *Russia* 24 B2
Veliki Ustyug, *Russia* 24 A6
Velikiye Luki, *Russia* 24 B3
Veliko Tŭrnovo, *Bulgaria* ... 22 C5
Velikonda Range, *India* 43 M11
Velletri, *Italy* 20 D4
Vellore, *India* 43 N11
Venado Tuerto, *Argentina* . 94 C4
Vendée □, *France* 12 C3
Vendôme, *France* 12 C4
Venézia, *Italy* 20 B4
Venézia, G. di, *Italy* 20 B4
Venezuela ■, *S. Amer.* 90 B5

Venezuela, G. de, *Venezuela* . 90 A4
Vengurla, *India* 43 M8
Venice = Venézia, *Italy* 20 B4
Venkatapuram, *India* 40 H3
Ventoténe, *Italy* 21 D4
Ventoux, Mt., *France* 13 D6
Ventspils, *Latvia* 24 B1
Ventuarí ➝, *Venezuela* ... 90 C5
Ventura, *U.S.A.* 78 C3
Venus B., *Australia* 63 C4
Vera, *Argentina* 94 B4
Vera, *Spain* 19 D5
Veracruz, *Mexico* 84 D5
Veraval, *India* 43 J7
Verbánia, *Italy* 13 D8
Vercelli, *Italy* 13 D8
Verde ➝, *Argentina* 95 E3
Verden, *Germany* 14 B5
Verdun, *France* 13 B6
Vereeniging, *S. Africa* 59 D5
Verga, C., *Guinea* 53 F3
Veria, *Greece* 23 D4
Verín, *Spain* 18 B2
Verkhnevilyuysk, *Russia* ... 30 C10
Verkhniy Baskunchak, *Russia* 25 D6
Verkhoyansk, *Russia* 31 C11
Verkhoyanskiy Khrebet,
  Russia 31 C10
Vermont □, *U.S.A.* 77 C9
Vernon, *Canada* 69 C8
Vernon, *U.S.A.* 80 B4
Véroia = Veria, *Greece* 23 D4
Verona, *Italy* 20 B3
Versailles, *France* 12 B5
Vert, C., *Senegal* 53 F2
Verviers, *Belgium* 14 C3
Veselovskoye Vdkhr., *Russia* 25 D5
Vesoul, *France* 13 C7
Vesterålen, *Norway* 8 B9
Vestfjorden, *Norway* 8 B8
Vesuvio, *Italy* 21 D5
Vesuvius, Mt. = Vesuvio, *Italy* 21 D5
Veszprém, *Hungary* 16 E3
Vettore, Mte., *Italy* 20 C4
Vezhen, *Bulgaria* 22 C5
Viacha, *Bolivia* 91 G5
Viamão, *Brazil* 94 C6
Viana, *Brazil* 92 C5
Viana do Alentejo, *Portugal* . 18 C2
Viana do Castelo, *Portugal* . 18 B1
Viangchan = Vientiane, *Laos* 38 A2
Vianópolis, *Brazil* 93 F4
Viaréggio, *Italy* 20 C3
Vibo Valéntia, *Italy* 21 E6
Vic, *Spain* 19 B7
Vicenza, *Italy* 20 B3
Vich = Vic, *Spain* 19 B7
Vichy, *France* 13 C5
Vicksburg, *U.S.A.* 81 C8
Victor, *India* 43 J7
Victor Harbor, *Australia* ... 62 C2
Victoria, *Canada* 69 D7
Victoria, *Chile* 94 D2
Victoria □, *Australia* 62 C3
Victoria, L., *Africa* 57 E6
Victoria, L., *Australia* 62 B3
Victoria, Mt., *Burma* 41 G9
Victoria de Durango =
  Durango, *Mexico* 84 C4
Victoria Falls, *Zimbabwe* ... 59 B5
Victoria I., *Canada* 68 A8
Victoria Ld., *Antarctica* ... 96 B14
Victorica, *Argentina* 94 D3
Vicuña, *Chile* 94 C2
Vidin, *Bulgaria* 22 C4
Vidisha, *India* 43 H10
Viedma, *Argentina* 95 E4
Viedma, L., *Argentina* 95 F2
Vienna = Wien, *Austria* ... 15 D9
Vienne, *France* 13 D6
Vienne ➝, *France* 12 C4
Vientiane, *Laos* 38 A2
Vietnam ■, *Asia* 38 A3
Vigan, *Phil.* 36 A2
Vigévano, *Italy* 13 D8
Vigia, *Brazil* 92 C4

Vigo, *Spain* 18 A1
Vijayawada, *India* 40 J3
Vijosë ➝, *Albania* 23 D2
Vikeke = Viqueque, *E. Timor* . 37 F3
Vikna, *Norway* 8 C8
Vila do Bispo, *Portugal* 18 D1
Vila Franca de Xira, *Portugal* 18 C1
Vila Nova de Gaia, *Portugal* . 18 B1
Vila Real, *Portugal* 18 B2
Vila-real de los Infantes, *Spain* 19 C5
Vila Real de Santo António,
  Portugal 18 D2
Vila Velha, *Brazil* 93 G5
Vilagarcía de Arousa, *Spain* . 18 A1
Vilaine ➝, *France* 12 C2
Vilanculos, *Mozam.* 59 C7
Vilanova i la Geltrú, *Spain* .. 19 B6
Vileyka, *Belarus* 17 A8
Vilhelmina, *Sweden* 8 C9
Vilhena, *Brazil* 91 F6
Vilkitskogo, Proliv, *Russia* .. 30 B8
Vilkovo = Vylkove, *Ukraine* . 17 F9
Villa Ahumada, *Mexico* 84 A3
Villa Ángela, *Argentina* 94 B4
Villa Bella, *Bolivia* 91 F5
Villa de María, *Argentina* .. 94 B4
Villa Dolores, *Argentina* ... 94 C3
Villa Hayes, *Paraguay* 94 B5
Villa María, *Argentina* 94 C4
Villa Mazán, *Argentina* 94 B3
Villa Montes, *Bolivia* 94 A4
Villa Ocampo, *Argentina* .. 94 B5
Villacarrillo, *Spain* 18 C4
Villach, *Austria* 15 E7
Villaguay, *Argentina* 94 C5
Villahermosa, *Mexico* 85 D6
Villajoyosa, *Spain* 19 C5
Villalba, *Spain* 18 A2
Villanueva de la Serena, *Spain* 18 C3
Villanueva y Geltrú = Vilanova
  i la Geltrú, *Spain* 19 B6
Villarreal = Vila-real de los
  Infantes, *Spain* 19 C5
Villarrica, *Chile* 95 D2
Villarrica, *Paraguay* 94 B5
Villarrobledo, *Spain* 19 C4
Villavicencio, *Colombia* 90 C4
Villaviciosa, *Spain* 18 A3
Villazón, *Bolivia* 94 A3
Villena, *Spain* 19 C5
Villeneuve-d'Ascq, *France* .. 13 A5
Villeneuve-sur-Lot, *France* .. 12 D4
Villingen-Schwenningen,
  Germany 14 D5
Vilnius, *Lithuania* 24 C2
Vilyuy ➝, *Russia* 31 C10
Vilyuysk, *Russia* 31 C10
Viña del Mar, *Chile* 94 C2
Vinarós, *Spain* 19 B6
Vindhya Ra., *India* 43 H10
Vineland, *U.S.A.* 77 E8
Vinkovci, *Croatia* 20 B7
Vinnitsa = Vinnytsya, *Ukraine* 17 D9
Vinnytsya, *Ukraine* 17 D9
Viqueque, *E. Timor* 37 F3
Virac, *Phil.* 36 B2
Viramgam, *India* 43 H8
Virden, *Canada* 69 D9
Vire, *France* 12 B3
Vírgenes, C., *Argentina* ... 95 G3
Virgin Is., *W. Indies* 87 C7
Virginia, *S. Africa* 59 D5
Virginia □, *U.S.A.* 77 F6
Virginia Beach, *U.S.A.* 77 F8
Virovitica, *Croatia* 20 B6
Virudunagar, *India* 43 Q10
Vis, *Croatia* 20 C6
Visalia, *U.S.A.* 78 B3
Visayan Sea, *Phil.* 36 B2
Visby, *Sweden* 9 D9
Viscount Melville Sd., *Canada* 70 B3
Viseu, *Portugal* 18 B2
Vishakhapatnam, *India* 40 J4
Viso, Mte., *Italy* 13 D7

Vistula = Wisła ➝, *Poland* .. 16 A4
Vitebsk = Vitsyebsk, *Belarus* . 24 B3
Viterbo, *Italy* 20 C4
Viti Levu, *Fiji* 64 L12
Vitigudino, *Spain* 18 B2
Vitória, *Brazil* 93 G5
Vitória da Conquista, *Brazil* . 93 E5
Vitoria-Gasteiz, *Spain* 19 A4
Vitsyebsk, *Belarus* 24 B3
Vittória, *Italy* 21 F5
Vittório Véneto, *Italy* 20 B4
Viveiro, *Spain* 18 A2
Vize, *Turkey* 22 D6
Vizianagaram, *India* 40 H4
Vladikavkaz, *Russia* 25 E5
Vladimir, *Russia* 24 B5
Vladimir Volynskiy =
  Volodymyr-Volynskyy,
  Ukraine 17 C7
Vladivostok, *Russia* 32 B2
Vlissingen, *Neths.* 14 C2
Vlorë, *Albania* 23 D2
Vltava ➝, *Czech Rep.* 16 C2
Vogelkop = Doberai, Jazirah,
  Indonesia 37 E4
Vogelsberg, *Germany* 14 C5
Voghera, *Italy* 13 D8
Vohimarina = Iharana, *Madag.* 59 A10
Vohimena, Tanjon' i, *Madag.* 59 D9
Voi, *Kenya* 57 E7
Voiron, *France* 13 D6
Vojvodina □, *Serbia & M.* .. 22 B2
Volga ➝, *Russia* 25 D6
Volga Hts. = Privolzhskaya
  Vozvyshennost, *Russia* .. 24 C6
Volgodonsk, *Russia* 25 D5
Volgograd, *Russia* 25 D5
Volgogradskoye Vdkhr.,
  Russia 24 C6
Volkhov ➝, *Russia* 24 A3
Volkovysk = Vawkavysk,
  Belarus 17 B7
Volochanka, *Russia* 30 B7
Volodymyr-Volynskyy,
  Ukraine 17 C7
Vologda, *Russia* 24 B4
Volos, *Greece* 23 E4
Volovets, *Ukraine* 17 D6
Volozhin = Valozhyn, *Belarus* 17 A8
Volsk, *Russia* 24 C6
Volta ➝, *Ghana* 53 G6
Volta Redonda, *Brazil* 93 G5
Volterra, *Italy* 20 C3
Volturno ➝, *Italy* 20 D4
Volzhskiy, *Russia* 25 D5
Vorïes Sporades, *Greece* .. 23 E4
Vorkuta, *Russia* 28 C7
Voronezh, *Russia* 24 C4
Vosges, *France* 13 B7
Vostok I., *Kiribati* 65 L15
Vouga ➝, *Portugal* 18 B1
Voznesensk, *Ukraine* 25 D3
Vrangelya, Ostrov, *Russia* .. 31 B15
Vranje, *Serbia & M.* 22 C3
Vratsa, *Bulgaria* 22 C4
Vrbas ➝, *Bos.-H.* 20 B6
Vršac, *Serbia & M.* 22 B3
Vryburg, *S. Africa* 58 D4
Vryheid, *S. Africa* 59 D6
Vukovar, *Croatia* 20 B7
Vulcan, *Romania* 17 F6
Vulcaneşti, *Moldova* 17 F9
Vulcano, *Italy* 21 E5
Vulkaneshty = Vulcaneşti,
  Moldova 17 F9
Vung Tau, *Vietnam* 38 B3
Vyatka = Kirov, *Russia* 28 D5
Vyatskiye Polyany, *Russia* .. 24 B7
Vyazma, *Russia* 24 B3
Vyborg, *Russia* 28 C3
Vychegda ➝, *Russia* 28 C5
Vychodné Beskydy, *Europe* . 17 D5
Vylkove, *Ukraine* 17 F9
Vynohradiv, *Ukraine* 17 D6
Vyshniy Volochek, *Russia* .. 24 B3
Vyškov, *Czech Rep.* 16 D3

W

Waal ➜, *Neths.* 14 C3
Wabash ➜, *U.S.A.* 76 F1
Waco, *U.S.A.* 80 D5
Wad Hamid, *Sudan* 55 E5
Wad Medanî, *Sudan* 55 F5
Waddington, Mt., *Canada* .. 69 C7
Waddy Pt., *Australia* 63 A5
Wadi Halfa, *Sudan* 54 D5
Wafrah, *Si. Arabia* 47 E6
Wager B., *Canada* 70 C5
Wagga Wagga, *Australia* ... 63 C4
Waghete, *Indonesia* 37 E5
Wah, *Pakistan* 42 C8
Wahai, *Indonesia* 37 E3
Waiau ➜, *N.Z.* 65 E5
Waibeem, *Indonesia* 37 E4
Waigeo, *Indonesia* 37 E4
Waihi, *N.Z.* 64 B6
Waihou ➜, *N.Z.* 64 B6
Waikabubak, *Indonesia* ... 37 F1
Waikaremoana, L., *N.Z.* 64 C7
Waikari, *N.Z.* 65 E5
Waikato ➜, *N.Z.* 64 B6
Waikerie, *Australia* 62 B2
Waikokopu, *N.Z.* 64 C7
Waikouaiti, *N.Z.* 65 F4
Waimakariri ➜, *N.Z.* 65 E5
Waimate, *N.Z.* 65 F4
Wainganga ➜, *India* 43 K11
Waingapu, *Indonesia* 37 F2
Waiouru, *N.Z.* 64 C6
Waipara, *N.Z.* 65 E5
Waipawa, *N.Z.* 64 C7
Waipiro, *N.Z.* 64 C8
Waipoua Forest, *N.Z.* 64 A5
Waipu, *N.Z.* 64 A6
Waipukurau, *N.Z.* 64 D7
Wairakei, *N.Z.* 64 C7
Wairarapa, L., *N.Z.* 65 D6
Wairoa, *N.Z.* 64 C7
Waitaki ➜, *N.Z.* 65 F4
Waitangi, *N.Z.* 64 A6
Waitara, *N.Z.* 64 C6
Waitomo Caves, *N.Z.* 64 C6
Waiuku, *N.Z.* 64 B6
Wajima, *Japan* 33 E5
Wajir, *Kenya* 57 D8
Wakasa-Wan, *Japan* 33 F4
Wakatipu, L., *N.Z.* 65 F3
Wakayama, *Japan* 33 F4
Wakefield, *N.Z.* 65 D5
Wakkanai, *Japan* 32 A7
Wakool, *Australia* 63 C3
Wakool ➜, *Australia* 62 C3
Wakre, *Indonesia* 37 E4
Wałbrzych, *Poland* 16 C3
Walcha, *Australia* 63 B5
Wałcz, *Poland* 16 B3
Wales □, *U.K.* 11 E4
Walgett, *Australia* 63 A4
Walgreen Coast, *Antarctica* . 96 B1
Walla Walla, *U.S.A.* 72 C4
Wallachia = Valahia, *Romania* 22 B5
Wallal, *Australia* 63 A4
Wallaroo, *Australia* 62 B2
Wallis & Futuna, Is., *Pac. Oc.* 64 L13
Wallowa Mts., *U.S.A.* 72 D5
Wallumbilla, *Australia* 63 A4
Walvis Bay, *Namibia* 58 C2
Wamba, *Dem. Rep. of
the Congo* 57 D5
Wamena, *Indonesia* 37 E5
Wamulan, *Indonesia* 37 E3
Wana, *Pakistan* 42 C6
Wanaaring, *Australia* 63 A3
Wanaka, *N.Z.* 65 F3
Wanaka, L., *N.Z.* 65 F3
Wandoan, *Australia* 63 A4
Wangal, *Indonesia* 37 F4
Wanganella, *Australia* 63 C3
Wanganui, *N.Z.* 64 C6
Wangaratta, *Australia* 63 C4
Wangary, *Australia* 62 B2
Wangerooge, *Germany* 14 B4

Wangiwangi, *Indonesia* 37 F2
Warangal, *India* 43 L11
Waratah, *Australia* 62 D4
Waratah B., *Australia* 63 C4
Warburton, *Australia* 63 C4
Warburton ➜, *Australia* ... 62 A2
Ward, *N.Z.* 65 D6
Ward ➜, *Australia* 63 A4
Wardha, *India* 43 J11
Wardha ➜, *India* 43 K11
Warialda, *Australia* 63 A5
Wariap, *Indonesia* 37 E4
Warkopi, *Indonesia* 37 E4
Warner Mts., *U.S.A.* 72 F3
Warracknabeal, *Australia* .. 62 C3
Warragul, *Australia* 63 C4
Warrego ➜, *Australia* 63 B4
Warren, *Australia* 63 B4
Warren, *U.S.A.* 76 C4
Warri, *Nigeria* 53 G7
Warrina, *Australia* 62 A2
Warrington, *U.K.* 11 E5
Warrington, *U.S.A.* 82 D4
Warrnambool, *Australia* ... 62 C3
Warsa, *Indonesia* 37 E5
Warsaw = Warszawa, *Poland* 16 B5
Warszawa, *Poland* 16 B5
Warta ➜, *Poland* 16 B2
Waru, *Indonesia* 37 E4
Warwick, *Australia* 63 A5
Wasatch Ra., *U.S.A.* 73 F8
Wash, The, *U.K.* 11 E7
Washim, *India* 43 J10
Washington, *U.S.A.* 77 E7
Washington □, *U.S.A.* 72 C3
Washington, Mt., *U.S.A.* .. 77 B10
Wasian, *Indonesia* 37 E4
Wasior, *Indonesia* 37 E4
Waskaganish, *Canada* 71 D6
Wasserkuppe, *Germany* ... 14 C5
Watampone, *Indonesia* 37 E2
Waterbury, *U.S.A.* 77 D9
Waterford, *Ireland* 11 E3
Waterloo, *U.S.A.* 75 D8
Watertown, *U.S.A.* 77 C8
Waterville, *U.S.A.* 77 B11
Watford, *U.K.* 11 F6
Watling I. = San Salvador I.,
Bahamas 86 B5
Watrous, *Canada* 69 C9
Watsa, *Dem. Rep. of
the Congo* 57 D5
Watson Lake, *Canada* 68 B7
Watsonville, *U.S.A.* 78 B2
Wattiwarriganna Cr. ➜,
Australia 62 A2
Watuata = Batuata, *Indonesia* 37 F2
Watubela, Kepulauan,
Indonesia 37 E4
Wau = Wâw, *Sudan* 55 G4
Wauchope, *Australia* 63 B5
Waukegan, *U.S.A.* 76 C2
Waukesha, *U.S.A.* 76 C1
Wausau, *U.S.A.* 75 C10
Wauwatosa, *U.S.A.* 76 C2
Waverley, *N.Z.* 64 C6
Wâw, *Sudan* 55 G4
Wâw al Kabīr, *Libya* 54 C2
Waxahachie, *U.S.A.* 81 C5
Waycross, *U.S.A.* 83 D6
Wazirabad, *Pakistan* 42 C9
We, *Indonesia* 38 C1
Weda, *Indonesia* 37 D3
Weda, Teluk, *Indonesia* ... 37 D3
Weddell I., *Falk. Is.* 95 G4
Weddell Sea, *Antarctica* .. 96 A4
Wedderburn, *Australia* 62 C3
Wee Waa, *Australia* 63 B4
Weiden, *Germany* 15 D7
Weifang, *China* 35 C6
Weimar, *Germany* 15 C6
Weipa, *Australia* 61 C7
Weir ➜, *Australia* 63 A4
Wejherowo, *Poland* 16 A4
Welkom, *S. Africa* 59 D5
Wellesley Is., *Australia* ... 60 D6
Wellington, *Australia* 63 B4

Wellington, *N.Z.* 65 D6
Wellington, I., *Chile* 95 F1
Wellington, L., *Australia* ... 63 C4
Wellington Chan., *Canada* . 70 B4
Wels, *Austria* 15 D8
Welshpool, *U.K.* 11 E5
Wemindji, *Canada* 71 D6
Wenatchee, *U.S.A.* 72 C3
Wenchi, *Ghana* 53 G5
Wenchow = Wenzhou, *China* 35 D7
Wendesi, *Indonesia* 37 E4
Wensu, *China* 34 B3
Wentworth, *Australia* 62 B3
Wenut, *Indonesia* 37 E4
Wenzhou, *China* 35 D7
Weri, *Indonesia* 37 E4
Werra ➜, *Germany* 14 C5
Werrimull, *Australia* 62 B3
Werris Creek, *Australia* ... 63 B5
Weser ➜, *Germany* 14 B5
Wesiri, *Indonesia* 37 F3
West Bengal □, *India* 40 F7
West Beskids = Západné
Beskydy, *Europe* 16 D4
West Falkland, *Falk. Is.* ... 95 G4
West Fjord = Vestfjorden,
Norway 8 B8
West Ice Shelf, *Antarctica* . 96 A11
West Palm Beach, *U.S.A.* .. 83 F7
West Pt., *Australia* 62 C2
West Virginia □, *U.S.A.* ... 76 E5
West Wyalong, *Australia* .. 63 B4
Westall, Pt., *Australia* 62 B1
Westbury, *Australia* 62 D4
Westerland, *Germany* 14 A5
Western Australia □, *Australia* 60 F3
Western Dvina = Daugava ➜,
Latvia 24 B1
Western Ghats, *India* 43 N9
Western Sahara ■, *Africa* .. 52 D3
Western Samoa = Samoa ■,
Pac. Oc. 65 L13
Western Sierra Madre =
Madre Occidental, Sierra,
Mexico 84 B3
Westerwald, *Germany* 14 C4
Westland △, *N.Z.* 65 E4
Westland Bight, *N.Z.* 65 E4
Weston-super-Mare, *U.K.* . 11 F5
Westport, *Ireland* 11 E2
Westport, *N.Z.* 65 D4
Westray, *U.K.* 10 B5
Wetar, *Indonesia* 37 F3
Wetaskiwin, *Canada* 69 C8
Wetzlar, *Germany* 14 C5
Wexford, *Ireland* 11 E3
Weyburn, *Canada* 69 D9
Weymouth, *U.K.* 11 F5
Wha Ti, *Canada* 68 B8
Whakaari = White I., *N.Z.* . 64 B7
Whakatane, *N.Z.* 64 B7
Whale ➜, *Canada* 70 D7
Whale Cove, *Canada* 68 B10
Whales, B. of, *Antarctica* .. 96 B16
Whangamata, *N.Z.* 64 B6
Whangamomona, *N.Z.* ... 64 C6
Whanganui △, *N.Z.* 64 C6
Whangarei, *N.Z.* 64 A6
Whangarei Harb., *N.Z.* ... 64 A6
Wheeling, *U.S.A.* 76 D5
White ➜, *Ark., U.S.A.* 81 C8
White ➜, *Ind., U.S.A.* 76 E2
White Cliffs, *Australia* 62 B3
White I., *N.Z.* 64 B7
White Nile = Nîl el Abyaḍ ➜,
Sudan 55 E5
White Russia = Belarus ■,
Europe 24 C2
White Sea = Beloye More,
Russia 8 B13
Whitecliffs, *N.Z.* 65 E4
Whitehaven, *U.K.* 11 D5
Whitehorse, *Canada* 68 B6
Whitemark, *Australia* 62 D4
Whitianga, *N.Z.* 64 B6
Whitney, Mt., *U.S.A.* 78 B3

Whittlesea, *Australia* 63 C4
Wholdaia L., *Canada* 68 B9
Whyalla, *Australia* 62 B2
Wichita, *U.S.A.* 80 A5
Wichita Falls, *U.S.A.* 80 C4
Wick, *U.K.* 10 B5
Wickham, C., *Australia* 62 C3
Wicklow Mts., *Ireland* 11 E3
Wieluń, *Poland* 16 C4
Wien, *Austria* 15 D9
Wiener Neustadt, *Austria* ... 15 E9
Wiesbaden, *Germany* 14 C5
Wight, I. of, *U.K.* 11 F6
Wilcannia, *Australia* 62 B3
Wildspitze, *Austria* 14 E6
Wilhelm, Mt., *Papua N. G.* .. 61 B8
Wilhelm II Coast, *Antarctica* . 96 A11
Wilhelmshaven, *Germany* .. 14 B5
Wilkes-Barre, *U.S.A.* 77 D8
Willandra Creek →, *Australia* 63 B4
Willemstad, *Neth. Ant.* 87 D6
William Creek, *Australia* 62 A2
Williams Lake, *Canada* 69 C7
Williamsburg, *U.S.A.* 77 F7
Williamsport, *U.S.A.* 77 D7
Williamstown, *Australia* 63 C3
Williston, *U.S.A.* 74 A3
Willunga, *Australia* 62 C2
Wilmington, *Australia* 62 B2
Wilmington, *Del., U.S.A.* 77 E8
Wilmington, *N.C., U.S.A.* ... 83 B9
Wilpena Cr. →, *Australia* ... 62 B2
Wilson, *U.S.A.* 83 B9
Wilsons Promontory,
   Australia 63 C4
Wimmera →, *Australia* 62 C3
Winchester, *U.K.* 11 F6
Wind River Range, *U.S.A.* ... 73 E9
Windau = Ventspils, *Latvia* .. 24 B1
Windhoek, *Namibia* 58 C3
Windsor, *Australia* 63 B5
Windsor, *Canada* 71 E5
Wingham, *Australia* 63 B5
Winisk →, *Canada* 71 D5
Winnipeg, *Canada* 69 D10
Winnipeg, L., *Canada* 69 C10
Winnipegosis L., *Canada* ... 69 C9
Winona, *U.S.A.* 75 C9
Winston-Salem, *U.S.A.* 83 A7
Winterthur, *Switz.* 13 C8
Winton, *Australia* 61 E7
Winton, *N.Z.* 65 G3
Wirrulla, *Australia* 62 B1
Wisconsin □, *U.S.A.* 75 C10
Wisła →, *Poland* 16 A4
Wismar, *Germany* 15 B6
Witbank, *S. Africa* 59 D5
Wittenberge, *Germany* 15 B6
Wkra →, *Poland* 16 B5
Włocławek, *Poland* 16 B4
Włodawa, *Poland* 17 C6
Wokam, *Indonesia* 37 F4
Wolfsberg, *Austria* 15 E8
Wolfsburg, *Germany* 15 B6
Wolin, *Poland* 16 B2
Wollaston, Is., *Chile* 95 H3
Wollaston Pen., *Canada* ... 68 B8
Wollongong, *Australia* 63 B5
Wolverhampton, *U.K.* 11 E5
Wondai, *Australia* 63 A5
Wongalarroo L., *Australia* ... 63 B3
Wŏnsan, *N. Korea* 35 C7
Wonthaggi, *Australia* 63 C4
Woodenbong, *Australia* 63 A5
Woodend, *Australia* 63 C3
Woodland, *U.S.A.* 72 G3
Woodroffe, Mt., *Australia* ... 60 F5
Woods, L. of the, *Canada* ... 69 D10
Woodstock, *Canada* 71 E7
Woodville, *N.Z.* 64 D6
Woolamai, C., *Australia* 63 C4
Woolgoolga, *Australia* 63 B5
Woomera, *Australia* 62 B2
Worcester, *S. Africa* 58 E3
Worcester, *U.K.* 11 E5
Worcester, *U.S.A.* 77 C10

Workington, *U.K.* 11 D5
Worms, *Germany* 14 D5
Worthing, *U.K.* 11 F6
Wosi, *Indonesia* 37 E3
Wou-han = Wuhan, *China* .. 35 C6
Wousi = Wuxi, *China* 35 C7
Wowoni, *Indonesia* 37 E2
Wrangel I. = Vrangelya,
   Ostrov, *Russia* 31 B15
Wrangell, *U.S.A.* 69 C6
Wrangell Mts., *U.S.A.* 69 B5
Wrath, C., *U.K.* 10 B4
Wrexham, *U.K.* 11 E5
Wrigley, *Canada* 68 B7
Wrocław, *Poland* 16 C3
Września, *Poland* 16 B3
Wu Jiang →, *China* 35 D5
Wuhan, *China* 35 C6
Wuhsi = Wuxi, *China* 35 C7
Wuhu, *China* 35 C6
Wukari, *Nigeria* 53 G7
Wuliaru, *Indonesia* 37 F4
Wulumuchi = Ürümqi, *China* 29 E9
Wuntho, *Burma* 41 F10
Wuppertal, *Germany* 14 C4
Würzburg, *Germany* 14 D5
Wutongqiao, *China* 34 D5
Wuwei, *China* 34 C5
Wuxi, *China* 35 C7
Wuyi Shan, *China* 35 D6
Wuzhong, *China* 35 C5
Wuzhou, *China* 35 D6
Wyandotte, *U.S.A.* 76 C4
Wyandra, *Australia* 63 A4
Wyangala, L., *Australia* 63 B4
Wyara, L., *Australia* 63 A3
Wycheproof, *Australia* 62 C3
Wyndham, *Australia* 60 D4
Wyndham, *N.Z.* 65 G3
Wynyard, *Australia* 62 D4
Wyoming □, *U.S.A.* 73 E10
Wyong, *Australia* 63 B5

X

Xaafuun, *Somali Rep.* 49 E5
Xaafuun, Ras, *Somali Rep.* .. 49 E5
Xai-Xai, *Mozam.* 59 D6
Xainza, *China* 34 C3
Xalapa, *Mexico* 84 D5
Xangongo, *Angola* 58 B3
Xankändi, *Azerbaijan* 25 F6
Xanthi, *Greece* 22 D5
Xapuri, *Brazil* 91 F5
Xàtiva, *Spain* 19 C5
Xi Jiang →, *China* 35 D6
Xiaguan, *China* 34 D5
Xiamen, *China* 35 D6
Xi'an, *China* 35 C5
Xiang Jiang →, *China* 35 D6
Xiangfan, *China* 35 C6
Xianggang = Hong Kong □,
   China 35 D6
Xiangquan He = Sutlej →,
   Pakistan 42 E7
Xiangtan, *China* 35 D6
Xiao Hinggan Ling, *China* ... 35 B7
Xichang, *China* 34 D5
Xigazê, *China* 34 D3
Xing'an, *China* 35 D6
Xingu →, *Brazil* 92 C3
Xining, *China* 34 C5
Xinjiang Uygur Zizhiqu □,
   China 34 B3
Xinxiang, *China* 35 C6
Xinyang, *China* 35 C6
Xique-Xique, *Brazil* 93 E5
Xisha Qundao = Paracel Is.,
   S. China Sea 38 A4
Xixabangma Feng, *China* ... 40 C5
Xizang Zizhiqu □, *China* ... 34 C3
Xuanhua, *China* 35 B6
Xúquer →, *Spain* 19 C5
Xuzhou, *China* 35 C6

Y

Ya'an, *China* 34 D5
Yaapeet, *Australia* 62 C3
Yablonovyy Khrebet, *Russia* . 30 D9
Yablonovyy Ra. = Yablonovyy
   Khrebet, *Russia* 30 D9
Yacuiba, *Bolivia* 94 A4
Yadgir, *India* 43 L10
Yahuma, *Dem. Rep. of
   the Congo* 56 D4
Yakima, *U.S.A.* 72 C3
Yakovlevka, *Russia* 32 A3
Yakumo, *Japan* 32 B7
Yakutat, *U.S.A.* 69 C6
Yakutsk, *Russia* 31 C10
Yala, *Thailand* 38 C2
Yalinga, *C.A.R.* 55 G3
Yalong Jiang →, *China* 34 D5
Yalova, *Turkey* 22 D7
Yalta, *Ukraine* 25 E3
Yam Ha Melaḥ = Dead Sea,
   Asia 47 E3
Yam Kinneret, *Israel* 46 D3
Yamagata, *Japan* 32 D7
Yamaguchi, *Japan* 33 F2
Yamal, Poluostrov, *Russia* .. 28 B8
Yamantau, Gora, *Russia* ... 29 D6
Yamba, *Australia* 63 A5
Yâmbiô, *Sudan* 55 H4
Yambol, *Bulgaria* 22 C6
Yamdena, *Indonesia* 37 F4
Yamethin, *Burma* 41 G11
Yamma Yamma, L., *Australia* 62 A3
Yamoussoukro, *Ivory C.* 53 G4
Yampil, *Moldova* 17 D9
Yampol = Yampil, *Moldova* . 17 D9
Yamuna →, *India* 40 E3
Yamzho Yumco, *China* 34 D4
Yana →, *Russia* 31 B11
Yanbu 'al Baḥr, *Si. Arabia* .. 47 F4
Yanco Cr. →, *Australia* 63 C4
Yandoon, *Burma* 41 J10
Yangambi, *Dem. Rep. of
   the Congo* 56 D4
Yangch'ü = Taiyuan, *China* . 35 C6
Yangjiang, *China* 35 D6
Yangon = Rangoon, *Burma* . 41 J11
Yangquan, *China* 35 C6
Yangtse = Chang Jiang →,
   China 35 C7
Yangtze Kiang = Chang
   Jiang →, *China* 35 C7
Yanji, *China* 35 B7
Yanqi, *China* 34 B3
Yantabulla, *Australia* 63 A4
Yantai, *China* 35 C7
Yaoundé, *Cameroon* 56 D2
Yapen, *Indonesia* 37 E5
Yapen, Selat, *Indonesia* 37 E5
Yaqui →, *Mexico* 84 B2
Yar-Sale, *Russia* 28 C8
Yaraka, *Australia* 61 E7
Yaransk, *Russia* 24 B6
Yaremcha, *Ukraine* 17 D7
Yarensk, *Russia* 28 C5
Yarí →, *Colombia* 90 D4
Yarkand = Shache, *China* .. 34 C2
Yarkhun →, *Pakistan* 42 A8
Yarlung Ziangbo Jiang =
   Brahmaputra →, *Asia* .. 41 F7
Yarmouth, *Canada* 71 E7
Yaroslavl, *Russia* 24 B4
Yarram, *Australia* 63 C4
Yarraman, *Australia* 63 A5
Yarras, *Australia* 63 B5
Yartsevo, *Russia* 30 C7
Yaselda, *Belarus* 17 B8
Yasinya, *Ukraine* 17 D7
Yass, *Australia* 63 B4
Yatağan, *Turkey* 23 F7
Yathkyed L., *Canada* 68 B10
Yatsushiro, *Japan* 33 G2
Yauri, *Peru* 90 D4
Yavatmal, *India* 43 J11
Yavoriv, *Ukraine* 17 D6

Yawatahama, Japan 33 G3
Yazd, Iran 44 D3
Yazd □, Iran 44 C3
Yazdān, Iran 45 C5
Yazoo �, U.S.A. 81 C8
Yebyu, Burma 41 K12
Yecla, Spain 19 C5
Yedintsy = Edineţ, Moldova . 17 D8
Yegros, Paraguay 94 B5
Yei, Sudan 55 H5
Yekaterinburg, Russia 29 D7
Yelarbon, Australia 63 A5
Yelets, Russia 24 C4
Yelizavetgrad = Kirovohrad,
  Ukraine 25 D3
Yell, U.K. 10 A6
Yellow Sea, China 35 C7
Yellowhead Pass, Canada ... 69 C8
Yellowknife, Canada 68 B8
Yellowstone ➜, U.S.A. 74 B3
Yellowstone △, U.S.A. 73 D9
Yelsk, Belarus 17 C9
Yemen ■, Asia 49 D4
Yenangyaung, Burma 41 G10
Yenbo = Yanbu 'al Baḥr,
  Si. Arabia 47 F4
Yenda, Australia 63 B4
Yenice, Turkey 23 E6
Yenisey ➜, Russia 28 B9
Yeniseysk, Russia 30 D7
Yeniseyskiy Zaliv, Russia .. 28 B9
Yenyuka, Russia 31 D10
Yeola, India 43 J9
Yeovil, U.K. 11 F5
Yerbent, Turkmenistan ... 29 F6
Yerevan, Armenia 25 E5
Yermak, Kazakhstan 29 D8
Yershov, Russia 24 C6
Yerushalayim = Jerusalem,
  Israel/West Bank 47 E3
Yessey, Russia 30 C8
Yeu, Î. d', France 12 C2
Yevpatoriya, Ukraine 25 D3
Yeysk, Russia 25 D4
Yezd = Yazd, Iran 44 D3
Yibin, China 35 D5
Yichang, China 35 C6
Yichun, China 35 B7
Yıldız Dağları, Turkey 22 D6
Yinchuan, China 35 C5
Yingkou, China 35 B7
Yining, China 29 E9
Yinmabin, Burma 41 F10
Yishan, China 35 D5
Yiyang, China 35 D6
Yog Pt., Phil. 36 B2
Yogyakarta, Indonesia 39 F4
Yokadouma, Cameroon ... 56 D2
Yokkaichi, Japan 33 F5
Yokohama, Japan 33 F6
Yokosuka, Japan 33 F6
Yola, Nigeria 55 G1
Yonago, Japan 33 F3
Yonibana, S. Leone 53 G3
Yonkers, U.S.A. 77 D9
Yonne ➜, France 13 B5
York, U.K. 11 E6
York, U.S.A. 77 E7
York, C., Australia 61 C7
Yorke Pen., Australia 62 B2
Yorkton, Canada 69 C9
Yos Sudarso, Pulau = Dolak,
  Pulau, Indonesia 37 F5
Yosemite △, U.S.A. 78 B3
Yoshkar Ola, Russia 24 B6
Youghal, Ireland 11 F3
Young, Australia 63 B4
Younghusband, L., Australia 62 B2
Younghusband Pen., Australia 62 C2
Youngstown, U.S.A. 76 D5
Yozgat, Turkey 25 F3
Ysyk-Köl, Kyrgyzstan 29 E8
Yu Jiang ➜, China 35 D6
Yü Shan, Taiwan 35 D7
Yuan Jiang ➜, China 35 D6
Yuba City, U.S.A. 72 G3
Yūbetsu, Japan 32 A8

Yucatán □, Mexico 85 C7
Yucatán, Canal de, Caribbean 85 C7
Yucatán, Península de,
  Mexico 85 D7
Yuci, China 35 C6
Yugoslavia = Serbia &
  Montenegro ■, Europe ... 22 B3
Yukon ➜, U.S.A. 69 B3
Yukon Territory □, Canada .. 68 B6
Yukta, Russia 30 C8
Yuma, U.S.A. 78 D5
Yumen, China 34 C4
Yungas, Bolivia 91 G5
Yunnan □, China 34 D5
Yunta, Australia 62 B2
Yurga, Russia 29 D9
Yurimaguas, Peru 91 E3
Yushu, China 34 C4
Yuzhno-Sakhalinsk, Russia . 31 E12
Yvetot, France 12 B4

Z

Zāb al Kabīr ➜, Iraq 46 C5
Zāb aş Şaghir ➜, Iraq 46 D5
Zābol □, Afghan. 45 D6
Zābolī, Iran 45 E5
Zabrze, Poland 16 C4
Zacatecas, Mexico 84 C4
Zadar, Croatia 20 B5
Zadetkyi Kyun, Burma 38 C1
Zafra, Spain 18 C2
Żagań, Poland 16 C2
Zagazig, Egypt 54 B5
Zagreb, Croatia 20 B6
Zagros, Kūhhā-ye, Iran 44 C2
Zagros Mts. = Zāgros, Kūhhā-
  ye, Iran 44 C2
Zāhedān, Iran 45 D5
Zahlah, Lebanon 46 D3
Zaïre = Congo ➜, Africa ... 56 F2
Zaječar, Serbia & M. 22 C4
Zakhodnaya Dzvina =
  Daugava ➜, Latvia 24 B1
Zākhū, Iraq 46 C5
Zákinthos = Zakynthos,
  Greece 23 F3
Zakynthos, Greece 23 F3
Zalaegerszeg, Hungary ... 16 E3
Zalău, Romania 17 E6
Zaleshchiki = Zalishchyky,
  Ukraine 17 D7
Zalew Wiślany, Poland 16 A4
Zalingei, Sudan 55 F3
Zalishchyky, Ukraine 17 D7
Zambeze ➜, Africa 59 B7
Zambezi = Zambeze ➜, Africa 59 B7
Zambezi, Zambia 58 A4
Zambia ■, Africa 59 B5
Zamboanga, Phil. 36 C2
Zamora, Mexico 84 D4
Zamora, Spain 18 B3
Zamość, Poland 17 C6
Zanesville, U.S.A. 76 E4
Zanjān, Iran 46 C7
Zanjān □, Iran 46 C7
Zante = Zakynthos, Greece .. 23 F3
Zanzibar, Tanzania 57 F7
Zaouiet El-Kala = Bordj Omar
  Driss, Algeria 52 C7
Zaouiet Reggâne, Algeria ... 52 C6
Zap Suyu = Zāb al Kabīr ➜,
  Iraq 46 C5
Zapadnaya Dvina =
  Daugava ➜, Latvia 24 B1
Západné Beskydy, Europe .. 16 D4
Zaporizhzhya, Ukraine 25 D4
Zara, Turkey 46 C4
Zaragoza, Spain 19 B5
Zarand, Iran 44 D4
Zaranj, Afghan. 42 D2
Zaria, Nigeria 53 F7
Zaruma, Ecuador 90 D3
Żary, Poland 16 C2
Zarzis, Tunisia 54 B1
Zaskar Mts., India 42 C10

Zavāreh, Iran 44 C3
Zawiercie, Poland 16 C4
Zāwiyat al Bayḑā = Al Bayḑā,
  Libya 54 B3
Zāyandeh ➜, Iran 44 C3
Zaysan, Kazakhstan 29 E9
Zaysan Köl, Kazakhstan ... 29 E9
Zbarazh, Ukraine 17 D7
Zboriv, Ukraine 17 C8
Zduńska Wola, Poland 16 C4
Zeebrugge, Belgium 14 C2
Zeehan, Australia 62 D4
Zeila, Somali Rep. 49 E3
Zeitz, Germany 15 C7
Zelenograd, Russia 24 B4
Zemun, Serbia & M. 22 B3
Zenica, Bos.-H. 20 B6
Žepče, Bos.-H. 20 B7
Zêzere ➜, Portugal 18 C1
Zgorzelec, Poland 16 C2
Zhabinka, Belarus 17 B7
Zhailma, Kazakhstan 29 D7
Zhambyl = Taraz, Kazakhstan 29 E8
Zhangaqazaly, Kazakhstan . 29 E7
Zhangjiakou, China 35 B6
Zhangye, China 34 C5
Zhangzhou, China 35 D6
Zhanjiang, China 35 D6
Zhanyi, China 34 D5
Zhaotong, China 34 D5
Zharkent, Kazakhstan 29 E9
Zhashkiv, Ukraine 17 D10
Zhayyq ➜, Kazakhstan ... 29 E6
Zhdanov = Mariupol, Ukraine 25 D4
Zhejiang □, China 35 D7
Zhengzhou, China 35 C6
Zhezqazghan, Kazakhstan . 29 E7
Zhigansk, Russia 30 C10
Zhilinda, Russia 30 B9
Zhitomir = Zhytomyr, Ukraine 17 C9
Zhlobin, Belarus 17 B10
Zhmerynka, Ukraine 17 D9
Zhob, Pakistan 42 D6
Zhodzina, Belarus 17 A9
Zhongdian, China 34 D4
Zhumadian, China 35 C6
Zhytomyr, Ukraine 17 C9
Zibo, China 35 C6
Zielona Góra, Poland 16 C2
Zigey, Chad 55 F2
Zigong, China 35 D5
Ziguinchor, Senegal 53 F2
Zile, Turkey 46 B3
Zillah, Libya 54 C2
Zimbabwe ■, Africa 59 B5
Zimnicea, Romania 22 C5
Zinder, Niger 53 F7
Zion △, U.S.A. 79 B6
Zirreh, Gowd-e, Afghan. ... 42 E3
Zlatograd, Bulgaria 22 D5
Zlatoust, Russia 29 D6
Zlín, Czech Rep. 16 D3
Zmeinogorsk, Kazakhstan . 29 D9
Znojmo, Czech Rep. 16 D3
Zolochiv, Ukraine 17 D7
Zomba, Malawi 59 B7
Zongo, Dem. Rep. of
  the Congo 56 D3
Zonguldak, Turkey 25 E3
Zorritos, Peru 90 D2
Zouar, Chad 54 D2
Zouîrât, Mauritania 52 D3
Zrenjanin, Serbia & M. ... 22 B3
Zufar, Oman 48 D5
Zug, Switz. 13 C8
Zugspitze, Germany 14 E6
Zumbo, Mozam. 59 B6
Zunyi, China 35 D5
Zürich, Switz. 13 C8
Zuwārah, Libya 54 B1
Zvishavane, Zimbabwe ... 59 C6
Zwelitsha, S. Africa 59 E5
Zwettl, Austria 15 D8
Zwickau, Germany 15 C7
Zwolle, Neths. 14 B4
Żyrardów, Poland 16 B5
Zyryan, Kazakhstan 29 E9